Deviant Behavior

Deviant Behavior

A Text-Reader in the Sociology of Deviance

7th Edition

Edward J. Clarke
Vanguard University

WORTH PUBLISHERS

Publisher: Catherine Woods
Acquisitions Editor: Sarah Berger
Marketing Manager: Amy Shefferd
Cover Designer: Kevin Kall
Associate Managing Editor: Tracey Kuehn
Project Editors: Dana Kasowitz
　　　　　　　 Kat Streever and Wendy Cagle, TSI Graphics
Production Manager: Barbara Anne Seixas
Composition: TSI Graphics
Printing and Binding: RR Donnelley
Cover photograph: Jane Dickson, 23rd Street, Ely Payphone 1

Library of Congress Control Number: 2007938704
ISBN-13: 978-1-4292-0518-4
ISBN-10: 1-4292-0518-0

Worth Publishers
41 Madison Avenue
New York, NY 10010
www.worthpublishers.com

For Crickett

Contents

PART III

Becoming Deviant   255

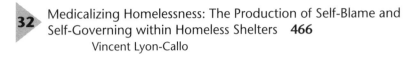

PART **V**

Building Deviant Careers and Identities 521

Preface

Some anthologies dealing with the subject of deviance emphasize the ways in which society responds to deviant behavior. Others, by examining why certain individuals violate the social norm, focus on the motivational element. A few trace the evolution of deviant categories. *Deviant Behavior* has been designed to integrate and balance these concerns in a single volume—to explore, through carefully selected readings, the ramifications of deviance for the individual (the *actor*) and for society.

Part I considers the ways society conceptualizes deviance and produces deviant acts and actors. Deviance is most often thought of as under conformity to normative standards for behavior, but exceeding those standards may also result in a negative social response. Of particular interest is the role that specific individuals—especially those holding social or political power or who serve as social control agents—play in the labeling of actors and acts as deviant. It will become clear to the reader that no individual and no behavior is inherently deviant; it is society's perception of an act as deviant and the subsequent social response to the actor that affixes the label. In other words, deviance—whether referencing under conformity or over conformity—is in the eye of the beholder.

Why does socially prohibited behavior occur—and persist—despite society's efforts to eliminate or discourage it? How can we make sense of deviance? Sociologists approach these questions from a number of different theoretical perspectives. Part II presents readings by major theorists representing the most important of these perspectives. The introductions for each section furnish students with the theoretical framework upon which to build an understanding and an appreciation of these key thinkers. This section contains several empirical pieces that underscore the important relationship that must exist between theory and deviance research. The articles also illustrate how researchers go about their work.

Part III examines how deviance may shape the life experience of individuals within the private domain. For example, families provide an intimate context in which deviance may be transmitted intergenerationally or within sibling structures. Selections depict how an actor may employ a range of strategies to conceal potentially discrediting information about

them in an attempt to avoid stigmatization and the many negative consequences of stigma. Failed attempts to manage deviance within the private
domain can result in some type of institutional control and processing.

Part IV explores the workings of several such people-processing and
people-changing facilities—ranging from the schools to the police—to
examine how such agencies handle clients and how clients, in turn, may
adapt their behavior and their view of self and personal identities to
their surroundings. The selections address important questions regarding the role of formal organizations in the production of deviant careers
and identities: How do organizational process and protocols shape the
likelihood that particular actors and acts will be identified as deviant?
How do interpersonal relationships within social-control agencies influence the rate and range of sanctioning? How are the lives of people
changed as a result of being formally identified as deviant?

For certain types of deviance, institutional controls are far less significant than the traditions and norms of deviant subculture and enterprises. Part V examines the way in which such structures shape the career
of the bookie, the drug dealer, members of deviant corporate structures,
children lacking self control, and others. Important to this discussion is
the process of negotiating identities within the context of deviance.

Part VI analyzes the processes by which deviant categories, actors,
and organizations can be altered or transformed. The first selection
offers contemporary accounts of how selected deviant conceptions and
categories have undergone significant changes. Clearly, if the underlying
content of the prevailing images changes, so, too, must the picture of
deviance change. Thus activities that may have been seen as deviant at
one time may now be perceived as acceptable or even normal by various
audiences. The last two readings describe various personal and institutional barriers that confront those who desire to move from a deviant to
a nondeviant status—in particular, society's reluctance to accept as "normal" anyone who has borne the stigma of deviance. The final selection
outlines specific ways in which deviant organizations, decision makers,
and structures could be controlled, sanctioned, or even rehabilitated. It
focuses on the police.

Overall, then, this book explores the creation and maintenance of
deviant categories; the motivations behind deviant behavior; the identification as deviant of individuals and of particular segments of society,
by formal and informal means; the effects of institutionalization upon
the deviant; and the efforts of deviants to eradicate the label society has
placed upon them. Attention is also given to the ways in which deviant
categories and structures can be altered.

I would like to thank many people for their help in preparing the seventh edition of this book, particularly my editor, Sarah Berger, and project editor, Dana Kusowitz. Decisions about adding and deleting material

from edition to edition are always made with apprehension. It is difficult to presume to make the right choices for both the people you hope will give your book a fresh examination and the people who have been loyal and contented users of previous editions. Suggestions from the following individuals helped make my deliberations considerably easier: Steven Cades, Washington College; Elizabeth Callaghan, Ithaca College; Ryan D. Schroeder, University of Louisville; Jeffery T. Ulmer, Pennsylvania State University; and Georgie Ann Weatherby; Gonzaga University.

I extend a special thanks to Delos Kelly for initiating and sustaining *Deviant Behavior* over many editions. I hope his retirement is as satisfying as his academic career. He has mentored well.

Edward J. Clarke

General Introduction

We all carry in our minds images of deviance and the deviant. To some, deviants are murderers and rapists. Others would include in the list prostitutes, child molesters, wife beaters, and homosexuals. With regard to the motivations behind deviant behavior, some of us would place the blame on the family, while others would emphasize genetic or social factors, especially poverty.

Creating Deviance

Regardless of what kinds of behavior we consider deviant or what factors we believe cause deviance, we must recognize that deviance *and* the deviant emerge out of a continuous process of interaction among people. For deviance to become a public fact, however, several conditions need to be satisfied: (1) some deviant category (e.g., mores and laws) must exist; (2) a person must be viewed as violating the category; and (3) someone must attempt to enforce this violation of the category. If the individuals demanding enforcement are successful in their efforts to label the violator, the social deviant has been created.

The Creation of Deviant Categories

As far as deviant categories are concerned, relatively little attention has been focused on their evolution. Formal and informal codes of conduct are generally accepted as "givens," and investigators concentrate on the examination of *why* the categories are violated and *how* they are enforced. An approach of this kind is inadequate, however, particularly in view of the fact that new categories are continually evolving and old ones are being modified. Obviously,

1

as the definitions or categories of deviance change, the picture of deviance must also be altered. The changing content of the laws governing cocaine provides an example. If there are no penalties for possessing and using cocaine, one cannot be formally charged and processed for doing so.

In studying deviance, then, a central question needs to be raised: How (and why) do *acts* become defined as deviant?[1] Providing answers to this question requires an examination of how deviance is defined, how the definitions are maintained, and how violators of the definitions are processed and treated. This entails a historical and ongoing analysis of those legislative and political processes that affect the evolution, modification, and enforcement of deviant categories. Central focus must be placed on those who possess the power and resources not only to define deviance but also to apply a label of deviance to a violator and to make the label stick. These processes are highlighted in Part I and will be evident in the discussion of the "radical-conflict theory" in Part II.

Reactions to Violators of Deviant Categories

In terms of the *actor*, an equally important question can be asked: How (and why) do violators of various types of deviant categories (mores, laws, and regulations) become labeled as deviant? Answering this question requires an examination of the interaction occurring between an *actor* and an *audience*. A simple paradigm (Figure 1) can illustrate how the deviant is reacted to and thus socially created. This paradigm can be applied to most of the selections in this volume.

The Interactional Paradigm A young man (the social *actor*) is seen selling or snorting cocaine (the *act*, a violation of a deviant category) by a police officer (a social *audience*, an enforcer of the deviant category) and is arrested. The youth's deviation thus becomes a matter of public record, and a deviant career is initiated—a career that may be solidified and perpetuated by legal and institutional processing. Another officer, however, might ignore the offense. In the first case, then, the violator is initially labeled as a "deviant," whereas in the second he is not. Figure 1 indicates that audience response not only is critical, but depends on several factors. The example also helps to underscore the fact that there is nothing inherently deviant about any act or actor—their meanings are derived from the interpretations *others* place on them. Hence the notion is put forth that "deviance lies in the eyes of the beholder." This example can be extended by considering the fourth element of the paradigm: *third parties*, or witnesses. Specifically, a young man may be observed selling or snorting cocaine by a peer, and the peer may choose to ignore the offense. Another peer, however, may not only consider the act illegal or deviant but may decide to do something about it. The peer lacks the power to arrest; he can, however, bring in third parties in an effort to create a shared attitude toward the cocaine user—namely, that he is a "criminal" or

Figure 1 ● Interactional Paradigm

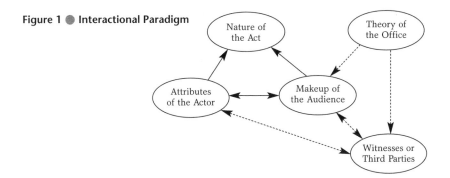

"deviant." The peer may turn to other peers, and they may decide to call the police and have the user arrested. If this happens, the person's "deviance" becomes a public fact.

Thus, the label "deviant" is a status conferred on a person by an observer or observers. Although an understanding of this process requires an examination of the way the four basic elements of the paradigm interact with one another, such an examination is not sufficient. An awareness of the *theory of the office* that a particular agent or audience operates out of is also necessary, especially if the occupant of the office is an agent of social control. The preceding example, as well as the "organizational paradigm" highlighted in Figure 2, can be used to illustrate this requirement. This paradigm represents a refinement of the "interactional paradigm" described in Figure 1. Here we are focusing on the audience, particularly in terms of how an institution expects certain outcomes on the part of its agents. This paradigm will be generally applied throughout this volume.

Figure 2 ● Organizational Paradigm

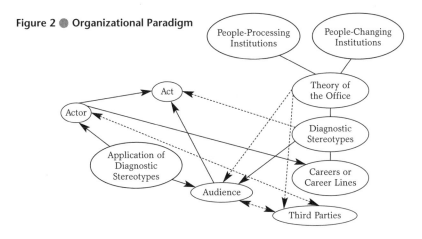

The Organizational Paradigm Although it might be assumed that the police officer in our examples operates on the basis of his or her own initiative, this is frequently far from the truth. The officer, like any institutional or bureaucratic agent concerned with the processing (through the courts) or rehabilitating (in correctional facilities) of clients, is guided and generally constrained by a theory of the office, or "working ideology." The officer, through informal (contacts with other officers) and formal (police academies) socialization experiences, learns how to identify and classify deviants or suspected deviants. These institutional, or "diagnostic," stereotypes (Scheff, 1966) constitute a basic ingredient of a department's official perspective. The officer, for example, learns how to recognize the "typical" case of child molestation, runaway, or rape. These "normal crimes" (Sudnow, 1965), or "social type designations," not only help the officer make sense out of events, they also provide criteria upon which a suspect can be initially identified, classified, and then selected out to play the role of the deviant.

An institution's stereotypes are basic to the *rate production process*—the creation of a body of institutional statistics. If, for example, a police chief feels that homosexual behavior is morally wrong or criminal, not only will this one individual's conception become embedded within the theory of the office, but the officers will be required to zero in on such activity. This response will produce a set of crime statistics exhibiting an unusually high arrest rate for homosexual exchanges. Similarly, if a police chief formally or informally communicates to department personnel that African-Americans, Hispanics, Native Americans, and other minorities constitute the "real" deviants, delinquents, and criminals, such people will be disproportionately selected out to play the role of the deviant—that is, they will become more vulnerable to institutional processing. This, too, will produce a set of statistics reflecting a heavy concentration of these individuals. The statistics can, in turn, serve as justification for heavy and continued surveillance in areas containing such groups. Examples of this phenomenon abound.

If we are to approach an understanding of what causes deviance, and particularly of the ways in which institutional careers arise and are perpetuated, then we need initially to analyze and dissect the existing structure of the institutions of social control. To obtain an understanding of how institutions operate requires, as suggested by Figure 2, sensitization to several basic organizational elements and processes: (1) the institution's theory of the office, (2) the content of the institutional stereotypes embedded within the theory of the office and used to identify clients for typing and processing, (3) the existing careers or career lines (and associated role expectations) into which the identified clients are placed, (4) the socialization of institutional agents and their application of diagnostic stereotypes to clients, and (5) the effects of institutional typing and processing, from the perspectives of both the client and the institution.

Understanding Deviance

In the discussion of the creation of deviance it was argued that some deviant category must exist, a person must be viewed as violating the category, and someone must make a demand for enforcement. Thus far, too, the focus has been upon the evolution and change of deviant categories, as well as on the interactional aspects—how and why violators of categories may be reacted to. Missing from this analysis, however, is a concern for the motivational aspects—the reasons why people may violate deviant categories. This concern has been generally ignored by the labeling or interactionist proponents. Their main interest revolves around examining audience reactions and the impact of those reactions on people. Implicit in such a stand is the idea that the reasons for behavior are relatively unimportant. If, however, we are to approach a more complete understanding of deviance from a dynamic perspective, attention must also be given to motivation. Such a view provides us with an opportunity continually to analyze how behavior and labels interact with each other.

Violations of Deviant Categories

Traditionally, writers have concentrated on trying to explain why people may violate various types of deviant categories. Some have spent their time trying to explain group or structural rates of deviance, and others have concentrated on those processes by which individuals learn culture and traditions. These efforts have produced many schools of thought, each with its own set of assumptions. The "anomie" theorists, for example, argue that blocked opportunity can produce a tendency or strain toward deviation. The "conflict" theorists, by contrast, contend that the powerless may consciously violate the laws formulated by the powerful. Understanding deviance, then, requires that we investigate those reasons why people may violate deviant categories and by their violations bring upon themselves a particular labeling. The selections in Part II offer some representative attempts to explore this question.

Becoming Deviant

With regard to the process of becoming deviant, an initial distinction can be made between *private* and *public* settings. A husband may violate a particular set of expectations by acting strangely. The wife may try to make sense out of such behavior by rationalizing it away or neutralizing it. She may argue to herself and others that her husband has experienced some personal setbacks and that the peculiar behavior will pass. At this stage the wife is trying to develop a counterdefinition of the situation, and she is also refusing to impute a deviant label to her spouse. The husband's behavior may grow increasingly violent, though, to the point where the wife finds it necessary to bring in agents of social control. She may call the police (third parties) or ultimately have her husband committed to a mental institution. If this should happen, not only have the wife's tolerance limits been exceeded but her attempts at various strategies of *accommodation* (e.g., neutralization or rationalization) have failed. The husband may then be typed as, for example, a schizophrenic and processed in accordance with the establishment's expectations of what the schizophrenic career should entail. The patient is expected, thereafter, to live up to his institutional role—to accept the label and act accordingly. The case of McMurphy in *One Flew Over the Cuckoo's Nest* (Kesey, 1962) describes what may happen when a patient protests against his assigned label. Because McMurphy rejects the "sick role," he becomes embroiled in a running battle with Big Nurse, the institution's agent. In our example, a similar situation may evolve with respect to the husband's response: he may repudiate the institutional tag, he may try to ignore it, or he may accept it. His response, like the responses of observers, is frequently difficult to predict.

In private settings, attempts may be made to regulate and control behavior, and these efforts may be successful. However, once third parties or social-control agents (e.g., the police or psychiatrists) are called in, the individual is frequently on his or her way to becoming an institutional deviant— that is, the organizational paradigm becomes operative, not only from the institution's viewpoint but from the actor's perspective. In particular, if a mental institution is involved, the client becomes viewed as a "mental patient"; this label becomes the patient's *master status* (Becker, 1963), and people will then often react to the person on the basis of the label rather than regarding him or her as sane or "normal." The changing of one's status, or the *status degradation ceremony* (Garfinkel, 1956), also affects the views others have of the "deviant" (one's public identity), as well as how the actor views himself or herself (one's personal identity). The change frequently affects the person's self-esteem (how one views self, positively or negatively, relative to others on selected criteria).

▶Institutional and Noninstitutional Careers

An important distinction should be made between *institutional* and *noninstitutional* careers. A noninstitutional career is one that a person pursues primarily as a matter of choice. The individual takes an active role in structuring and presenting a specific image of self to others. The bookie, gambler, con artist, nudist, skid row alcoholic, and homosexual provide examples. Such individuals generally progress through some semblance of a career: once they gain entry or exposure, they begin to learn the existing culture and traditions. The bookie, for instance, may start out as a runner, "learn the ropes," and then move into other phases of the bookmaking operation. Similarly, the skid row alcoholic who wants to become an accepted member of the "bottle-gang culture" will become familiar with the norms prevalent among the skid row inhabitants, particularly norms that relate to the procurement and consumption of alcohol. Violations of the normative code frequently cause a person to be excluded from the group (Rubington, 1973). As with the sanctioning of "deviants" by "nondeviants," the "labeled deviants" have ways of punishing those who deviate from their own code.

Institutional careers, by contrast, involve those in which the individual plays a relatively passive role. Here, the career is initiated and perpetuated by some socializing or social-control institution; this process was briefly noted in the discussion of how one becomes deviant. The careers of the "school misfit," mental patient, delinquent, and criminal are of this type. The major difference between institutional careers and noninstitutional careers concerns the role of the actor, particularly in the matter of choice and in the means of gaining entry. Once the institutional career begins, though, the mental patient, like the skid row alcoholic, is expected to learn and act in accordance with the existing subculture and its traditions.

Institutional and noninstitutional careers are not mutually exclusive. Frequently, a degree of overlap exists between the two. The skid row alcoholic, for example, may be arrested and sent to an alcoholic ward, where his or her behavior becomes subject to institutional or bureaucratic control. Similarly, the prostitute may be arrested and taken to jail. In both instances the activities become a matter of institutional knowledge and record. A secret homosexual, by contrast, may never directly experience the effects of institutional processing.

The Effects of Institutional and Noninstitutional Careers

The distinction between institutional and noninstitutional careers provides a backdrop against which a person's reactions can be assessed. How, for example, is a person likely to respond to institutional typing and processing as a deviant? Will he or she reject or accept the institutional label? Answering these questions requires a consideration of how the "status degradation ceremony" affects an actor's personal and public identity. If the deviant rejects the label, a discrepancy (or *identity crisis*) occurs between one's personal and public identities—that is, between one's view of self as normal and the institution's view of one as a deviant. Obviously, unless some personal gain can be realized, such as the enhancement of one's prestige or status in the eyes of others, most persons will reject a deviant label imputed to them. Maintaining an image of self that is at odds with the institution's image is not without its costs, though, and eventually the individual may come to accept the label and bring his or her behavior into line with institutional expectations. Lemert (1951) argues that *acceptance of the label* is a critical step on the way to secondary or *career* deviance. Not only do some individuals change their view of self—for instance, from that of "normal" to that of "schizophrenic"—but they often change their mode of dress, mannerisms, and circle of acquaintances. Acceptance of the label, it should be noted, is an important precondition to being certified as "sane" or "rehabilitated" by institutions.

Involvement in noninstitutional careers or activities affects both the participants and other members of society. The covert gay or lesbian teacher, for example, engages in sexual activity that some would consider deviant, and a discrepancy may evolve between her personal and public identities. Privately she may view herself as gay and a normal female, but publicly she is viewed and responded to as a heterosexual teacher. As with the institutional deviant, however, an identity crisis may arise. She may decide to "come out" and admit her sexual preference to others. Such a strategy is not without its costs. She may be ostracized by her family, friends, and acquaintances; and, more than likely, she will be either discriminated against on her job or perhaps fired. In view of these possibilities, she may decide to keep her sexual preference hidden and become involved in a gay subculture. Such involvement can provide her with a degree of social support, as well as appropriate rationalizations to legitimize her way of life. Still, she (and other noninstitutional deviants) is aware not only that she is engaging in potentially discrediting behavior but also that she must operate in a society in which many hostile elements remain.

Changing Deviance

Identity problems do not cease when one leaves an institution or decides to "go straight." Public or known ex-deviants, whether of the institutional or noninstitutional variety, continue to be viewed as deviants. What Simmons (1969) calls a "lingering of traces" quite frequently occurs, especially among those who carry an institutionally bestowed label. Institutions, it has been pointed out, are most efficient in assigning deviant labels; they are notoriously inefficient when it comes to removing labels and their associated stigma (Goffman, 1963). Former deviants must continue to bear the brunt of the label—with the result that their behavioral patterns are much less likely to change.

The probability of rehabilitating someone who does not view his or her activity or career as deviant is poor. Many noninstitutional deviants—such as prostitutes, gamblers, and homosexuals—feel little need to "repent"; they believe that the pressure they face and the difficulties they experience result from the intolerance of society. In fact, many of these individuals feel strongly that it is society that should be rehabilitated. On the other hand, some noninstitutional deviants—as well as some institutional deviants, such as mental patients, criminals, and delinquents—may try to transform their "deviant" identity. If they do, they can expect to encounter certain barriers. Job applications, for example, frequently require prospective employees to list any arrests, convictions, or periods of institutionalization—circumstances that can bar entry into many occupations. Such roadblocks can produce feelings of frustration and inferiority. What many ex-deviants soon realize is that even if they change, they will still be effectively discriminated against because of past activities or involvement with stigmatizing institutions. They also learn very quickly that the social and political establishment is virtually unchanging—that the burden of change falls upon *them*.

Summary and Organization of This Volume

This book explores the subject of deviance in a number of ways—by focusing in turn on society, on the individual, and on institutions of control and rehabilitation. Part I describes how deviant categories evolve and how people who violate these categories become defined as social deviants. Part II analyzes why people may elect to violate deviant categories—violations that can initiate the defining or labeling process. Part III deals with the deviant career, particularly as it arises in private, noninstitutional settings. Part IV describes how careers may become initiated and perpetuated by institutions, while Part V examines the rise and furtherance of noninstitutional careers. Finally, Part VI discusses how conceptions, careers, and organizational structures may be altered. Throughout, a major focus is on the impact that involvement in institutional as well as noninstitutional activities and careers has upon actors, audiences, and third parties.

Note

1. For an excellent discussion of questions such as these, see particularly Ronald L. Akers, "Problems in the Sociology of Deviance: Social Definitions and Behavior." *Social Forces*, 46 (June 1968), 455–465.

References

Becker, Howard S. *Outsiders: Studies in the Sociology of Deviance.* New York: Free Press, 1963.

Garfinkel, Harold. "Conditions of Successful Degradation Ceremonies." *American Journal of Sociology*, 61 (March 1956), 420–424.

Goffman, Erving. "The Moral Career of the Mental Patient," *Psychiatry* 22 (1959), 123–142.

——— *Stigma: Notes on the Management of Spoiled Identity.* Englewood Cliffs, N.J.: Prentice Hall, 1963.

Kesey, Ken. *One Flew Over the Cuckoo's Nest.* New York: Viking, 1962.

Lemert, Edwin. *Social Pathology.* New York: McGraw-Hill, 1951.

Rubington, Earl. "Variations in Bottle-Gang Controls." In Earl Rubington and Martin S. Weinberg, eds., *Deviance: The Interactionist Perspective.* New York: Macmillan, 1973.

Scheff, Thomas J. "Typification in the Diagnostic Practices of Rehabilitation Agencies." In Marvin B. Sussman, ed., *Sociology and Rehabilitation.* Washington, D.C.: American Sociological Association, 1966.

Simmons, J. L. *Deviants.* Berkeley: Glendessary, 1969.

Sudnow, David. "Normal Crimes: Sociological Features of the Penal Code," *Social Problems*, 12 (Winter 1965), 255–270.

Creating Deviance

As noted in the general introduction, approaching an understanding of deviance requires an examination of several interrelated factors. An initial concern involves the way in which the subject matter is to be approached, viewed, and subsequently defined. Does the theorist or researcher, for example, conceptualize and define deviance and the deviant in individual terms, or does he or she invoke some type of structural view? Similarly, is there something inherently deviant about certain acts or actors, or do their meanings derive from the interpretations and reactions of others? If the latter, then not only should the student of deviance be aware that a specific image is being advanced (i.e., the notion that deviance and the deviants are social constructs), but he or she must also recognize the need to examine the evolution of deviant categories and the ways in which violators of the categories may be perceived and responded to. As noted earlier, for deviance to become a social fact, a person must be viewed as violating some deviant category and thereafter be labeled as deviant by a social observer.

The first three selections introduce major conceptual and definitional issues within the field of deviance and social control and offer some important analytic tools. The following three selections illustrate how the concepts are utilized. These articles demonstrate the process and the basis for selecting out particular individuals and acts as deviant and how, for example, the medical institution has been co-opted as an important agent of social control. In addition, more systematic attention is given to the basic process involved in the construction of the social deviant: (1) the creation of deviant categories and (2) the reactions to violators of deviant categories.

Conceptions, Entrepreneurs, and Power

The idea that deviant categories can be viewed as social constructs represents a particular image of deviance. Such a view also suggests the possibility of competing conceptions. Jack P. Gibbs, in "Conceptions of Deviant Behavior: The Old and the New," acknowledges these points but stresses that the traditional conceptions continue to dominate. How one comes to "think about" a specific phenomenon influences the definitions that are developed, as well as the theory or explanation that may result. For example, in the area of deviance, do we locate pathological or deviant-producing stimuli within the actor or do we look elsewhere, perhaps to society in general? Gibbs maintains that the former viewpoint is favored in the fields of crime and deviance. Historically, the dominant conception has been one of individual pathology. Gibbs then proceeds to compare what he terms the "older conceptions" (e.g., the idea that deviants or criminals possess some *internal* trait that distinguishes them from nondeviants) with the "new conception" (i.e., the view that the essential characteristic of a deviant or deviant act is *external* to the actor and the act). This new perspective emphasizes the *character of the reaction* that a specific act or actor may elicit. If the responses are of a certain kind, deviance comes into being. Gibbs then offers several criticisms of the new conception. Is, for example, this perspective intended to be a substantive theory of deviant behavior, or is it primarily a definitional/conceptual treatment of it? Even if the perspective is viewed as an explanatory framework, Gibbs maintains that several questions have not been answered adequately. "Why," for example, "is the act in question considered deviant and/or criminal in some societies but not in others?"

Alex Heckert and Druann Maria Heckert go well beyond seeing deviance as simply a negative social fact. Norms can be exceeded as well as violated. The tendency is to see deviance as norm violation and therefore as negative. This inclination is reflected in the meager accumulation of literature focusing on positive deviance over the past 60 years. Important to note is that, although positive deviance is behavior that people judge to be superior, negative evaluations continue to play an important role. For example, social movements and transforming leaders are often originally labeled as negative, and even when the deviance is seen for the most part as positive, derogatory assumptions often follow. In their article "Using an Integrated Typology of Deviance to Analyze Ten Common Norms of the U.S. Middle Class" Heckert and Heckert (2004) offer and assess a scheme identifying both conditions of overconformity and of nonconformity. When normative expectations and societal evaluations are cross-classified, four types of deviance emerge:

negative deviance (negatively evaluated under conformity); rate busting (negatively appraised over conformity); deviance admiration (positive reaction to under conformity); and positive deviance (positively sanctioned over conformity). The authors assess ten "middle-class" norms—loyalty, privacy, prudence, conventionality, responsibility, participation, moderation, honesty, peacefulness, and courtesy—to determine the efficacy of their typology. Each of the potentialities is identified and illustrated for each of the norms.

The preceding articles sensitize one to the fact that the underlying images and conceptions of deviance have changed, and they highlight the manner in which social observers—either individually or collectively—ascribe meaning to the actions of others. Thus, deviance is very much a product of initiative on the part of observers. Logically, then, the reactors and decision makers must become the object of direct study. What, for example, can we say about the content of their conceptions and belief systems? The selection by Howard S. Becker, "Moral Entrepreneurs: The Creation and Enforcement of Deviant Categories," adds some refinements to these issues. Becker also provides an excellent general overview of how deviant categories, particularly rules, evolve. Central to his analysis is the role of *moral entrepreneurs*, whom he categorizes into *rule creators* and *rule enforcers*. Rule creators are individuals who see some "evil" in society and feel that the evil can be corrected only by legislating against it. Frequently their efforts result in the passage of a new law—that is, the creation of a new deviant category. Becker offers several interesting examples that describe this legislative-political phenomenon. He argues that a successful crusade will not only result in "the creation of a new set of rules" but will often give rise to "a new set of enforcement agencies and officials." It becomes the function of these officials to enforce the new rules. Becker concludes his analysis by offering several comments relating to rule enforcers. He contends, for example, that enforcers are concerned primarily with enforcing the law and not its contents; they are also interested in justifying their own position in the organization, as well as in gaining respect from their clients. Many of these same phenomena can be observed in several other selections, especially those that deal with institutional incarceration and deviance.

Conceptions of Deviant Behavior: The Old and the New

Jack P. Gibbs

The ultimate end of substantive theory in any science is the formulation of empirical relations among classes of phenomena, e.g., X varies directly with Y, X is present if and only if Y is present. However, unless such propositions are arrived at by crude induction of sheer intuition, there is a crucial step before the formulation of a relational statement. This step can be described as the way the investigator comes to perceive or "think about" the phenomena under consideration. Another way to put it is the development of a "conception."

There is no clear-cut distinction between, on the one hand, a conception of a class of phenomena and, on the other, formal definitions and substantive theory. Since a conception emphasizes the predominant feature of a phenomenon, it is not entirely divorced from a definition of it; but the former is not identical with the latter. Thus, for example, the notion of exploitation looms large in the Marxian conception of relations among social classes; but exploitation is or may be only one feature of class relations, and it does not serve as a formal definition of them. Further, in certain fields, particularly the social sciences, a conception often not only precedes but also gives rise to operational definitions. As the case in point, if an operational definition of social class relies on the use of "reputational technique," the investigator's conception of social class is in all probability non-Marxian.

What has been said of the distinction between definitions and conceptions holds also for the relation between the latter and substantive theory. A conception may generate a particular theory, but it is not identical with it. For one thing, a conception contains definitional elements and is therefore partially tautological, which means that in itself a conception is never a clear-cut empirical proposition. Apart from its tautological character, a conception is too general to constitute a testable idea. Nonetheless, a conception may generate substantive theory, and it is certainly true that theories reflect conceptions. Durkheim's work is a classic illustration. His theory on suicide clearly reflects his view of society and social life generally.

In a field without consensus as to operational definitions and little in the way of systematic substantive theory, conceptions necessarily occupy a central position. This condition prevails in most of the social sciences. There, what purport to be definitions of classes of phenomena are typically general and inconsistent to the point of lacking empirical applicability (certainly in the operational sense of the world). Moreover, what passes for a substantive theory in the social sciences is more often than not actually a loosely formulated conception. These observations are not intended to deride the social sciences for lack of progress. All fields probably go through a "conceptions" stage; it is only more apparent in some than in others.

Of the social sciences, there is perhaps no better clear-cut illustration of the importance of conceptions than in the field identified as criminology and the study of deviant behavior. As we shall see, the history of the field can be described best in terms of changing conceptions of crime, criminals, deviants, and deviation. But the purpose of this paper is not an historical account of major trends in the field. If it is true that conceptions give rise to formal definitions and substantive theory, then a critical appraisal of conceptions is important in its own right. This is all the more true in the case of criminology and the study of deviant behavior, where conceptions are frequently confused with substantive theories, and the latter so clearly reflect the former.

Older Conceptions

In recent years there has been a significant change in the prevailing conception of deviant behavior and deviants. Prior to what is designated here as the "new perspective," it commonly was assumed that there is something inherent in deviants which distinguishes them from non-deviants.[1] Thus, from Lombroso to Sheldon, criminals were viewed as biologically distinctive in one way or another.[2] The inadequacies of this conception are now obvious. After decades of research, no biological characteristic which distinguishes criminals has been discovered, and this generalization applies even to particular types of criminals (e.g., murderers, bigamists, etc.). Consequently, few theorists now even toy with the notion that all criminals are atavistic, mentally defective, constitutionally inferior. But the rejection of the biological conception of crime stems from more than research findings. Even casual observation and mild logic cast doubt on the idea. Since legislators are not geneticists, it is difficult to see how they can pass laws in such a way as to create "born criminals." Equally important, since most if not all "normal" persons have violated a law at one time or another,[3] the assertion that criminals are so by heredity now appears most questionable.

Although the biological conception generally has been rejected, what is here designated as the analytic conception of criminal acts largely has escaped criticism. Rather than view criminal acts as nothing more or less than behavior contrary to legal norms, the acts are construed as somehow injurious to society. The shift from the biological to the analytical conception is thus from the actors to the characteristics of their acts, with the idea being that some acts are inherently "criminal" or at least that criminal acts share intrinsic characteristics in common.

The analytical conception is certainly more defensible than the biological view, but it is by no means free of criticism. Above all, the "injurious" quality of some deviant acts is by no means conspicuous, as witness Durkheim's observation:

> ... there are many acts which have been and still are regarded as criminal without in themselves being harmful to society. What social danger is there in touching a tabooed object, an impure animal or man, in letting the sacred fire die down, in eating certain meats, in failure to make the traditional sacrifice over the grave of parents, in not exactly pronouncing the ritual formula, in not celebrating holidays, etc.?[4]

Only a radical functionalism would interpret the acts noted by Durkheim as literally injuring society in any reasonable sense of the word. The crucial point is that, far from actually injuring society or sharing some intrinsic feature in common, acts may be criminal or deviant because and only because they are proscribed legally and/or socially. The proscription may be irrational in that members of the society cannot explain it, but it is real nonetheless. Similarly, a law may be "arbitrary" in that it is imposed by a powerful minority and, as a consequence, lacks popular support and is actively opposed. But if the law is consistently enforced (i.e., sanctions are imposed regularly on violators), it is difficult to see how it is not "real."

The fact that laws may appear to be irrational and arbitrary has prompted attempts to define crime independently of legal criteria, i.e., analytically. The first step in this direction was Garofalo's concept of natural crime—acts which violate prevailing sentiments of pity and probity.[5] Garofalo's endeavor accomplished very little. Just as there is probably no act which is contrary to law universally, it is equally true that no act violates sentiments of pity and probity in all societies. In other words, cultural relativity defeats any attempt to compile a list of acts which are crimes universally. Also, it is hard to see why the violation of a rigorously enforced traffic regulation is not a crime even though unrelated to sentiments of pity and probity. If it is not a crime, what is it?

The search for an analytic identification of crime continued in Sellin's proposal to abandon legal criteria altogether in preference for "conduct norms."[6] The rationale for the proposal is simple. Because laws vary and may be "arbitrary" in any one society, a purely legal definition of crime is not suited for scientific study. But Sellin's observations on the arbitrariness of laws apply in much the same way to conduct norms. Just as the content of criminal law varies from one society to the next and from time to time, so does the content of extra-legal norms. Further, the latter may be just as arbitrary as criminal laws. Even in a highly urbanized society such as the United States, there is evidently no rationale or utilitarian reason for all of the norms pertaining to mode of dress. True, there may be much greater conformity to conduct norms than to some laws, but the degree of conformity is hardly an adequate criterion of the "reality" of norms, legal or extra-legal. If any credence whatever can be placed in the Kinsey report, sexual taboos may be violated frequently and yet remain as taboos. As a case in point, even if adultery is now common in the United States, it is significant that the participants typically attempt to conceal their acts. In brief, just as laws may be violated frequently and are "unreal" in that sense, the same applies to some conduct norms; but in neither case do they cease to be norms. They would cease to be norms if and only if one defines deviation in terms of statistical regularities in behavior, but not even Sellin would subscribe to the notion that normative phenomena can or should be defined in statistical terms.

In summary, however capricious and irrational legal and extra-legal norms may appear to be, the inescapable conclusion is that some acts are criminal or deviant for the very simple reason that they are proscribed.

The New Conception

Whereas both the pathological and the analytical conceptions of deviation assume that some intrinsic feature characterizes deviants and/or deviant acts, an emerging perspective in sociology flatly rejects any such assumption. Indeed, as witness the following statements by Kitsuse, Becker, and Erikson, exactly the opposite position is taken.

Kitsuse: Forms of behavior *per se* do not differentiate deviants from non-deviants; it is the responses of the conventional and conforming members of the society who identify and interpret behavior as deviant which sociologically transform persons into deviants.[7]

Erikson: From a sociological standpoint, deviance can be defined as conduct which is generally thought to require the attention of social control agencies—that is, conduct about which "something should be done." Deviance is not a property *inherent in* certain forms of behavior; it is a property *conferred upon* these forms by the audiences which directly or indirectly witness them. Sociologically, then, the critical variable in the study of deviance is the social *audience* rather than individual *person*, since it is the audience which eventually decides whether or not any given action or actions will become a visible case of deviation.[8]

Becker: From this point of view, deviance is *not* a quality of the act a person commits, but rather a consequence of the application by others of rules and sanctions to an "offender." The deviant is one to whom that label has successfully been applied; deviant behavior is behavior that people so label.[9]

The common assertion in the above statements is that acts can be identified as deviant or criminal only by reference to the character of reaction to them by the public or by the official agents of a politically organized society. Put simply, if the reaction is of a certain kind, then and only then is the act deviant. The crucial point is that the essential feature of a defiant or deviant act is *external* to the actor and the act. Further, even if the act or actors share some feature in common other than social reactions to them, the feature neither defines nor completely explains deviation. To take the extreme case, even if Lombroso had been correct in his assertion that criminals are biologically distinctive, the biological factor neither identifies the criminal nor explains criminality. Purely biological variables may explain why some persons commit certain acts, but they do not explain why the acts are crimes. Consequently, since criminal law is spatially and temporally relative, it is impossible to distinguish criminals from noncriminals (assuming that the latter do exist, which is questionable) in terms of biological characteristics. To illustrate, if act X is a crime in society A but not a crime in society B, it follows that, even assuming Lombroso to have been correct, the anatomical features which distinguish the criminal in society A may characterize the noncriminal in society B. In both societies some persons may be genetically predisposed to commit act X, but the act is a crime in one society and not in the other. Accordingly, the generalization that all persons with certain anatomical features are criminals would be, in this instance, false. True, one may assert that the "born criminal" is predisposed to violate the laws of his own society, but this assumes either that "the genes" know what the law is or that the members of the legislature are geneticists (i.e., they deliberately enact laws in such a way that the "born criminal" will violate them). Either assumption taxes credulity.

The new perspective of deviant behavior contradicts not only the biological but also the analytical conception. Whereas the latter seeks to find something intrinsic in deviant or, more specifically, criminal acts, the new conception denies any such characterization. True, the acts share a common denominator—they are identified by the character of reaction to them—but this does not mean that the acts are "injurious" to society or that they are in any way inherently abnormal. The new conception eschews the notion that some acts are deviant or criminal in all societies. For that matter, the reaction which identifies a deviant act may not be the same from one society or social group to the next. In general, then, the new conception of deviant behavior is relativistic in the extreme.

• • •

Notes

1. Throughout this paper crime is treated as a sub-class of deviant behavior. Particular issues may be discussed with reference to crime, but on the whole the observations apply to deviant behavior generally.

2. Although not essential to the argument, it is perhaps significant that the alleged biological differentiae of criminals have been consistently viewed as "pathological" in one sense or another.

3. See Edwin H. Sutherland and Donald R. Cressey, *Principles of Criminology,* 6th ed., Chicago: J.B. Lippincott, 1960, p. 39.

4. Emile Durkheim, *The Division of Labor in Society,* trans. George Simpson, Glencoe, Illinois: The Free Press, 1949, p. 72.

5. Raffaele Garofalo, *Criminology,* Boston: Little, Brown & Co., 1914, Chapter I.

6. Thorsten Sellin, *Culture Conflict and Crime,* New York: Social Science Research Council, Bulletin 14, 1938.

7. John I. Kitsuse, "Societal Reaction to Deviant Behavior: Problems of Theory and Method," *Social Problems,* 9 (Winter, 1962), p. 253.

8. Kai T. Erikson, "Notes on the Sociology of Deviance," *Social Problems,* 9 (Spring, 1962), p. 308.

9. Howard S. Becker, *Outsiders,* New York: The Free Press of Glencoe, 1963, p. 9.

Using an Integrated Typology of Deviance to Analyze Ten Common Norms of the U.S. Middle Class

Alex Heckert
Druann Maria Heckert

According to Sumner (1994) the study of deviance has been a core and vital area of sociological pursuit since the nascent days; specifically, since the 1895 publication of Durkheim's *The Rules of Sociological Method*. Nevertheless, by 1975—under assault from critical ideological stances, including the new criminology (Taylor, Walton, and Young 1973)—the field collapsed, or as Sumner (1994, p. ix) so dramatically proclaimed, "The field now resembles the Somme in 1918." From an opposing ideology and in accord with Moyniham (1993), Hendershott (2002) has argued that deviance has been recalibrated and that much considered deviant in the past (e.g., suicide and drug addiction) is no longer so judged. Along with ceding control to medical professions, she views advocacy groups—more than shared values and culture—as shaping current societal definitions of deviance. Furthermore, although not quite proclaiming that deviance is a moribund substantive area of sociology, Best (2004, p. ix) states that "deviance has come to occupy an insecure, perhaps, even precarious place in sociology." Best (2004) further argues that the field of deviance has been weakened for the following reasons: the critique from the conflict perspective; the feminist emphasis on women's victimization, which countered the kind portrayal of deviants by the labeling perspective; identity politics, which questioned the deviantization of various identities (e.g., disability); the mainstream sociological dismissal of labeling theory as not sustainable by way of quantitative analysis; and the continued separation of criminology from sociology. Essentially, a core sociological substantive tradition has increasingly been questioned and stigmatized.

Best (2004, p. 33) contends that one key problem within the field of deviance is definitional: "If mainstrream sociologists' definition of deviance as rule-breaking had not clearly distinguished between what was and was not deviant, focusing on labeling had not resolved the problem. A sort of definitional creep was developing." He further contends that analytical problems are created when too much is defined as deviant. Conjecturing that, post-1975, criminology started to really ascend as deviance started to descend, Best (2004, p. 72) states, "the list of crimes was shorter and more homogenous than any of the classifications of the various forms of deviance. Whereas sociologists had difficulty agreeing about the boundaries of deviance, crimes were defined by criminal statutes." The clearest issue, then, would appear to be the continuing inability of those in deviance to agree on a definition that could solidify their field. We contend, however, that although criminology has a unifying definition, like deviance, it is not homogenous and covers widely and wildly diverging behaviors. For example, the following are all criminal because they are violations of criminal statutes: serial murder, rape, burglary, underage drinking, jaywalking, and littering. Yet, in terms of complex and nuanced etiology, what does a serial killer have in common with a shoplifter, and what does a person who orchestrates genocide have in common with a person who listened to popular music under the Taliban or an American adolescent who illegally downloads music or runs away from home? Criminologists can study the gamut of human behavior as can those in deviance. Compared with criminologists, then, what sociologists of deviance have lacked is a unifying definition.

We have recently proposed a topology that considers and synthesizes normative and reactivist definitions of deviance (Heckert and Heckert 2002) and sought to ameliorate the definitional problems that have plagued the field. We conclude that deviance is still an integral area of sociology. The typology posits the following categories. Firstly, negative deviance refers to nonconformity or underconformity that is negatively evaluated. Secondly, rate busting considers behavior that is overconformity yet is subject to negative evaluation. Thirdly, deviance admiration describes underconformity or nonconformity that is positively evaluated. Fourthly, positive deviance identifies overconformity that is positively evaluated.

The efficacy of this typology in terms of its application to other issues of deviance is the focus of this article. We utilize this typology to illuminate a normative system; for current and initial purposes, dominant middle-class American norms are highlighted. Tittle and Paternoster (2000) have identified then key norms that permeate middle-class culture in the United States. Those norms include the following: loyalty, privacy, prudence, conventionality, responsibility, participation, moderation, honesty, peacefulness, and courtesy. With this normative system established they were able to delineate the corresponding negative deviance (i.e., underconformity or nonconformity that is negatively evaluated) and to list examples of each. We seek to expand their work by identifying the rate busting, deviance admiration, and positive deviance forms of each of these norms. We also provide nonexhaustive lists of examples for each of these various forms of deviance as well. By providing this formulation we suggest potentially fruitful ways to think about, as well as research, deviance.

A Typology of Deviance Integrating Normative and Reactivist Perspectives

An assortment of definitions have clouded the substantive area of deviance, ranging from an absolutist approach to a statistical one to the more ubiquitous normative and reactivist approaches (Goode 2001). Nevertheless, the predominant bifurcation within the discipline is between the normative and reactivist perspectives (Liska 1981). Normative, or objectivist, definitions, on the one hand, primarily focus on the violation of norms (c.f., Merton 1966); simply and succinctly, Cohen defined deviance as "behavior that violates normative rules" (1966, p. 12). On the other hand, reactivist of subjectivist definitions focus on the dynamics of the reaction of a social audience (c.f., Becker 1963; Erikson 1964; Lemert 1972). As Becker (1963, p. 11) so famously wrote, "Social groups constitute deviance by making rules whose infractions constitute deviance, and by applying those rules to particular people and labeling them as outsiders." Each definition presents a major paradigmatic understanding of deviance. These definitions clearly tend to emphasize behaviors. Most sociologists do, however, extend definitions of deviance to include what Adler and Adler (2000, p. 8) term the "ABCs of deviance: their attitudes, behaviors, or conditions." Although the examples we provide in the current article focus primarily on behaviors, attitudes (or beliefs) and conditions are assuredly essential (since normative expectations and social reactions pertain to both) with regard to deviance and can be fruitfully analyzed using our conceptual framework.

Our typology seeks to integrate the underlying phenomena addressed by each definition (Heckert and Heckert 2002). This typology recognizes the distinction as a false dichotomy and acknowledges the existence of both normative expectations and social reactions. Behavior and conditions can underconform (or nonconform) or overconform to normative expectations, as well as lead to negative or positive reactions. As such, we have cross-classified the significance of both norms and reactions, creating four possible scenarios. As Figure 1 shows, negative deviance, on the one hand, is underconformity or nonconformity that results in negative reactions. On the other hand, rate busting is overconformity that is negatively evaluated. Next, deviance admiration is underconformity or nonconformity that is positively appraised by the collectivity. Finally, positive deviance is overconformity that receives positive reactions. Each type of deviance will be briefly described.

The substantive area of deviance has first and foremost involved the scrutiny of negative deviance. Negative deviance refers to underconformity or nonconformity that is also negatively evaluated; metaphorically, negative deviance is the "Jeffrey Dahmer phenomenon." As Adler and Adler (2000) described this situation, attitudes, behaviors, or conditions can be deviantized. Negative deviants can range from most criminals to the men-

Figure 1 Deviance Typology

Normative Expectations

Social Reactions And Collective Evaluations	Underconformity or Nonconformity	Overconformity
Negative Evaluations	Negative Deviance	Rate busting
Positive Evaluations	Deviance Admiration	Positive Deviance

tally ill to substance abusers to those with unpopular political or religious stances. Essentially, the standard in the field of deviance is the negative reaction to (and sanctioning of) underconformity or nonconformity.

Alternatively, rate busting is negatively appraised overconformity. At the core this cell epitomizes the "geek phenomenon." Various social scientists have noted that norms operate at two levels; the idealized (i.e., that which is believed sublimely better but improbable for most people) and the realistic (i.e., that which is viewed as achievable by typical people) (Homans 1950; Johnson 1978; Heckert 1998). Nevertheless, this overconformity—even if idealized or perhaps because it is idealized—is often subjected to negative evaluations. Rate busting has occurred in various realms of life. For example, Huryn (1986) determined that gifted students are often rejected by their peers; Krebs and Adinolfi (1975) concluded that the attractive are often slighted by members of their same sex; and Heckert (2003) found that blonde women (defined as overconforming to European standards of beauty) are subjected to epic stereotyping, especially related to their intellectual capacity (or assumed lack thereof).

The third cell is deviance admiration, which focuses on underconformity or nonconformity that is favorably assessed. For all intents and purposes, this condition could be labeled the "John Gotti phenomenon." Although the attribute, behavior, or condition is normatively unacceptable to a collectivity, the response of that group is still assenting. Kooistra (1989) concluded that a fair number of criminals, even brutal ones, have been transformed—by the collective imagination—from thugs to icons. In other words, Robin Hood is not relegated to the realm of myth but has bona fide real-life counterparts, ranging from Billy the Kid to D. B. Cooper to Butch Cassidy. As another example, in a society that castigates those individuals who do not meet culturally dominant and created aesthetic images of appearance, there are also many that admire the stigmatized attribute (e.g., people of size and redheads) and individuals with that attribute.

The final category is positive deviance, which describes overconformity that is responded to in a confirmatory fashion. Essentially, this is the "Mother Theresa phenomenon." Similar to negative deviance, positive deviance has been previously defined from various viewpoints, including from a normative perspective (c.f., Wilkins 1965; Winslow 1970), from a labeling point of view (c.f., Freedman and Doob 1968; Hawkins and Tiedeman 1975; Scarpitti and McFarlane 1975; Steffensmeier and Terry 1975), and from the perspective that positive deviance is overconformity that is positively evaluated (Dodge 1985; Heckert and Heckert 2002). Examples of positively appraised overconformity include good neighbors and saints (Sorokin 1950), Congressional Medal of Honor winners (Steffensmeier and Terry 1975), and the physically attractive (c.f., Berscheid and Walster 1964; Bryne 1971; Reis et al. 1982). Exceeding normative expectations, at times, creates a scenario whereby positive reactions and evaluations flow, often producing all kinds of added advantages; thus, the response transcends even the norm at stake.

All in all, this typology recognizes that the traditional distinction between normative expectations and societal reactions involves a false dichotomy and seeks to integrate normative definitions with reactivist definitions. Thus, attitudes, behaviors, and conditions can become conceptualized as negative deviance, rate busting, deviance admiration, and positive deviance. Clearly, as theorists in the field of deviance have long contended, contexts do have to be considered as audiences can differentially react to the same behavior or conditions. In other words, gifted and overachieving students are rate busters to their peers at the same time they are positive deviants to their teachers. Elite tattoo collectors are simultaneously positive deviants to their subculture and negative deviants to the dominant society (Irwin 2003). As well, many individuals who were admired as extraordinary in a later era were castigated in their own era because they dared to not conform to their time's antiquated or oppressive normative code (Coser 1967; Merton 1968; Dinitz, Dynes, and Clarke 1969). Examples include Galileo, Jesus (to Christians), Socrates, and the French Impressionists. Essentially, for divergent reasons, underconformers or nonconformers are often positively evaluated, and overconformers are often negatively evaluated.

This typology allows sociologists to continue to utilize a traditional notion that deviance is relative and that context is critical (Thio 1983). It is important to analyze why underconformity or nonconformity can result in positive evaluations or negative evaluations, depending on the era, place, or social group involved. The same is true for overconformity (Heckert and Heckert 2002). Power and people's self-interest are critical components. In reference to either underconformity or overconformity, negative reactions are likely to emerge when attitudes, behaviors, or conditions threaten the interests of the social group. According to Heckert and Heckert (2002, pp. 468–469):

> Whether or not the negative reactions have an impact (or become "sticky" to use a labeling term) is primarily determined by the relative power of the (potential) deviant(s) and the social audience. The relative power is determined by a number of factors such as the numbers in each group (deviant and reactors), the amount of wealth and income (property) of each group, the relative prestige of each group, the level of organization of each group (from individualized to subcultural to organized), and the relative quality of their discourse or claims (ability to persuade and manipulate symbols). These various sources of power interact in determining the ability of a given social group or audience to apply negative or positive labels to a type of behavior, condition, or particular group of (potential) deviants. Viewed in this light, deviant behavior is, in essence, a test of power relationships and serves as a potential threat to the power of the dominant group(s).

The same is true for overconformity. Other factors are important, as well (Heckert and Heckert 2002). As an example the degree of the norm violation (extreme or minor) is important. The definition of the situation is also vital. High consensus norms (e.g., serial murder) will generally produce more consistent evaluations than will low consensus norms (Thio 2001). These are just some of the explanatory factors; future sociological work should more rigorously investigate these factors.

Norms and Predominant Middle-Class Norms in the United States

Integral components of any cultural system, norms guide expected behavior and are based directly on values held to be important. For example, based on fourteen common definitions of norms, Gibbs (1981, p. 7) asserted that most commonly a norm has been defined as "a belief shared to some extent by members of a social unit as to what conduct *ought to be* in particular situations or circumstances." Gusfield (1963, p. 65) further suggested that these systems produce "regularities of action."

Other sociologists have indicated that norms could be dually conceptualized between the idealized and the more realistic (Johnson 1960; Johnson 1978) or operative norms. In essence, the more idealized are really values (c.f., White 1961; Blake and Davis 1964). Williams (1965) created the seminal and most comprehensive description of the value system of the United States, outlining the following dominant values: achievement and success, individualism, activity and work, efficiency and practicality, science and technology, progress, material comfort, humanitarianism, freedom, democracy, equality, and racism and group superiority. To that list Henslin (1975) added education, religiosity, romantic love, and monogamy. Thus, the American value system has been amply addressed.

Recently, Tittle and Paternoster (2000) have expanded sociological understanding by outlining not the idealized scheme of values but the normative system itself. Their outline is restricted to middle-class values in the United States and includes the following dominant norms: group loyalty, privacy, prudence, conventionality, responsibility, participation, moderation, honesty, peacefulness, and courtesy. Loyalty describes the necessity of the group to survive over individual concerns. Privacy indicates that individuals need to be in command of certain spaces and places. Prudence refers to placing pleasure in perspective and to practicing pleasure with moderation. Conventionality is descriptive of people choosing habits and life scenarios that are similar to those of other people. Responsibility is dependability, especially when others must count on that characteristic. Participation implies personal involvement in both economic and social spheres; alienation constitutes the conforming counterpart. Moderation means an avoidance of the extremes in life. Honesty denotes veracity and candor. Peacefulness illustrates a sedate and calm style. Finally, courtesy revolves around refined social etiquette in human interaction. Overall, one set of consequential norms has been thoroughly delineated.

Table 1   A Classification of U.S. Middle-Class Deviance

Norm	Negative Deviance	Deviance Admiration	Rate Busting	Positive Deviance
Group loyalty	Apostasy	Rebellion	Fanaticism	Altruism
Privacy	Intrusion	Investigation	Seclusion	Circumspection
Prudence	Indiscretion	Exhibitionism	Puritanism	Discretion
Conventionality	Bizarreness	Faddishness	Provincialism	Properness
Responsibility	Irresponsibility	Adventurousness	Priggishness	Hyperresponsibility
Participation	Alienation	Independence	Dependence	Cooperation
Moderation	Hedonism	Roguishness	Asceticism	Temperance
Honesty	Deceitfulness	Tactfulness	Tactlessness	Forthrightness
Peacefulness	Disruption	Revelry	Wimpishness	Pacifism
Courtesy	Uncouthness	Irreverence	Obsequiousness	Gentility

Note: Types of negative deviance taken from Tittle & Paternoster 2000, p. 35.

Applying the Integrated Normative-Reactivist Typology to Middle-Class Norms of the United States

To verify the utility of our integrative typology, we seek to apply this typology to a normative system. In this initial foray, we apply the typology to dominant and current American middle-class norms. Tittle and Paternoster (2000) documented these norms; as well, they highlighted the deviance (or what we will subsequently refer to as, more specifically, negative deviance) forms of each norm. The deviance admiration, rate busting, and positive deviance variety of each norm is specified in Table 1 and will be further discussed in the following sections.

Negative Deviance

To briefly reiterate, negative deviance is underconformity or nonconformity that is negatively evaluated. Tittle and Paternoster (2000) focused on negative deviance and have outlined illuminating examples of each category which are listed in Table 2. Again, these examples are quintessentially representative of the traditional nucleus of the substantive area of the sociological study of deviance.

As an example of the valuable work of Tittle and Paternoster (2000), as the survival of the group is viewed as paramount, apostasy becomes deviantized. Consequently, actions and/or actors such as revolution or revolutionaries are deemed deviant. As privacy is critical, intrusion in the form of theft or rape is deviant. Since prudence is valued, indiscretion in the form of prostitution is negatively stigmatized. Because conventionality forms an important normative idea, bizarreness that can include some mentally ill behavior is deviant. For the reason that responsibility is valued, irresponsibility such as family desertion becomes unacceptable to middle-class Americans. Given that participation is normative, alienation—which can include nonparticipatory lifestyles—becomes snubbed. In view of the fact that moderation is critical to middle-class Americans, hedonism in the guise of chiseling or atheism is negatively appraised. Although Tittle and Paternoster (2000) include asceticism as a type of underconformity to the norm of moderation, utilizing this new model we prefer to conceptualize it as overconformity. Because honesty is appreciated, deceitfulness epitomized by bigamy and price-fixing is deviantized. Seeing that peacefulness is valued, disruption in the form of noisy disorganizing behavior or boisterous reveling is not appreciated in the context of this particular normative system. As courtesy is normalized, uncouthness as exemplified by rudeness or uncleanliness is stigmatized. All in all, Tittle and Paternoster (2000) have provided a comprehensive accounting of various deviantized behaviors within the middle class of the United States. This outline sketches negative deviance, the substance of the long-established and accepted core of the field of deviance.

Table 2   A Classification of U.S. Middle-Class Deviance, Negative Deviance

Norm	Negative Deviance	Examples
Group loyalty	Apostasy	Revolution; betraying national secrets; treason; draft dodging; flag defilement; giving up citizenship; advocating contrary government philosophy
Privacy	Intrusion	Theft; burglary; rape; homicide; voyeurism; forgery; record spying
Prudence	Indiscretion	Prostitution; homosexual behavior; incest; bestiality; adultery; swinging; gambling; substance abuse
Conventionality	Bizarreness	"Mentally ill behavior" (handling excrement, nonsense talking, eating human flesh, fetishes); separatist lifestyles
Responsibility	Irresponsibility	Family desertion; reneging on debts; unprofessional conduct; improper role performance; violations of trust; pollution; fraudulent business
Participation	Alienation	Nonparticipatory lifestyles (being a hermit, street living); perpetual unemployment; receiving public assistance; suicide
Moderation	Hedonism	Chiseling; atheism; alcoholism; total deceit; wasting; ignoring children
Honesty	Deceitfulness	Selfish lying; price-fixing; exploitation of the weak and helpless; bigamy; welfare cheating
Peacefulness	Disruption	Noisy disorganizing behavior; boisterous reveling; quarreling; fighting; contentiousness
Courtesy	Uncouthness	Private behavior in public places (picking nose, burping); rudeness (smoking in prohibited places, breaking in line); uncleanliness

Note: Table from Tittle & Paternoster 2000, p. 35.

Rate Busting

Rate busting refers to the negative reaction not to underconformity but to overconformity and constitutes the "geek phenomenon." In other words, adhering to the idealized level of the norm induces unfavorable evaluations. As Tittle and Paternoster (2000) analyzed a deviant (or negative deviant) form of each norm, we outline a rate busting form of each of the ten norms in Table 3. We also provide a nonexhaustive list of examples for each category of rate busting.

Table 3   A Classification of U.S. Middle-Class Deviance, Rate Busting

Norm	Rate Busting	Examples
Group loyalty	Fanaticism	Various religious cults: Ku Klux Klan (who, of course, engage in acts of negative deviance); Aryan Nation; NRA; religious fanatics; superpatriots; "holier than thou"
Privacy	Seclusion	Hermits; loners; Amish and other reclusive sects; secretive or reclusive behavior; Howard Hughes
Prudence	Puritanism	Negative attitude & behavior toward Amish and other conservative religious sects
Conventionality	Provincialism	Stepford wives; Martha Stewart & her followers; keeping up with the Joneses in following every little rule so as to be accepted; individuals who are negatively evaluated for ritualistically following convention
Responsibility	Priggishness	Negative attitudes regarding people who are self-righteous; jokes and meanness toward Martha Stewart and her followers; some workaholics; straight-A student
Participation	Dependence	Brownnoser; a person trying so hard to be accepted by every group that they lose their individuality; the concepts of codependency and enabling behavior
Moderation	Asceticism	Negative reactions to not drinking; a person so meek that they never take a stand on anything so as not to offend anyone
Honesty	Tactlessness	Being too honest with friends (e.g. about ugly clothing, unattractive haircut); a person so honest they won't tell a "white lie" or who will say something mean to a child because it is honest rather than to protect child's feelings
Peacefulness	Wimpishness	A person who never parties or "lets their hair down"; a person who will never take a stand or stand up to people; "yes man"
Courtesy	Obsequiousness	The person who is overly polite; making fun of Miss Manners and people who are overly courteous

Regarding the norm of group loyalty, overconforming to the group can result in negative evaluations. This category is referred to as fanaticism. As examples, NRA participants and hate group members, accepted subculturally, are too responsive to their groups and are deviantized—by various parts of culture in the first case and by the dominant society in the second case—on this basis (and other important ones as well). Religious cult members are also viewed as too immersed in their groups; their individuality is perceived to be lost to the group. Individuals who are "holier than thou" within dominant religious traditions often estrange members of their own group. "Super patriots" who are too enthusiastic in their display of symbolic representations of nation and who will support government under any circumstance often alienate others. Concerning the norm of privacy, the rate busting equivalent is seclusion. Among those who are negatively reacted to in response to what is deemed their seclusive tendencies are the following: hermit, secretive or reclusive individuals such a Howard Hughes in his later years, and reclusive religious groups, such as the Amish. In reference to the normative orientation respecting prudence, Puritanism refers to those who are overly prudent and negatively stigmatized. For example, very conservative religious sects that seem to eschew what dominant Americans view as necessary pleasures—such as the Amish, Hutterites, Shakers (the very few remaining), and Jehovah's Witnesses—are shunned and/or created into exotic humans and not accepted into the dominant cultural fold. With the situation of conventionality, the rate busting scenario is provincialism. Being overly conventional or mindlessly attempting to conform to the habits of others are often negatively appraised. For example, mass media created the Stepford wives, who are fictionally representative of this category. As a flesh-and-blood counterpart Martha Stewart and her fans have been constant grist for comedians; this stigmatization occurred even prior to her legal troubles. Pertaining to the norm of responsibility, priggishness is the rate busting form. Some workaholics—those motivated by an intense sense of responsibility—have long been subjected to negative treatment by their coworkers, even if praised by their bosses. As well, peers have long taunted overachieving students, who set a high standard in the academic realm.

Concerning participation, dependence is the rate busting counterpart. Among those who overly participate in social and/or economic life are the brownnoser, the codependent and enabling family member of a substance abuser, and the person who wants to be accepted so badly by the group that he or she sacrifices individuality. With regards to moderation, asceticism is overconformity that is negatively appraised. Individuals who drink socially and moderately are conforming; those who do not drink are overconforming and ironically—similarly to pathological drinkers—are negatively evaluated on that basis (even if the stigmatization is not the same type of stigmatization). For example, nondrinkers will often develop explanations (i.e., designated driver) so as to attempt to avoid the almost inevitable questions rooted in disbelief about their choice. In connection with honesty, tactlessness is the overconforming response that will not be positively received. For example, persons so honest that they will never tell a lie, even a socially acceptable lie, are often viewed as tactless. Thus, the following scenario could occur. If a young girl asks an adult if her dress is pretty and the adult replies that it is the ugliest dress ever created, the adult would be veracious and overconforming to honesty. Nevertheless, under middle-class normative conditions, the adult would not be positively received. In respect to peacefulness, the rate busting sort is wimpishness. A meek person who never "lets her or his hair down" or who will never stand up to anybody so as to avoid contentiousness would be looked down upon and labeled with the following appellation: "mousy" or "yes man." Vis-à-vis courtesy, obsequiousness is the rate busting form. A person who is so very courteous in social interaction that every diminutive rule of etiquette is exactly followed is viewed as overconforming and often spurned. Consequently, Miss Manners becomes almost a comically viewed person, rather than the serious person she professes to be as the arbiter of such matters. Eddie Haskell, a fictionalized character from *Leave It To Beaver*, is also viewed similarly.

All in all, for each of the ten norms, a rate busting form of deviance is listed in Table 3. As well, examples readily illuminate each possibility.

Deviance Admiration

To recap, deviance admiration or the "John Gotti phenomenon" occurs in the context of underconformity that is positively evaluated. In other words, people do not view John Gotti as doing right; rather, they accept that he has violated considerably cherished norms and endorse him anyway. Potentially, deviance admiration can surface for each of these norms as shown in Table 4. Each of the examples of negative deviance provided by Tittle and Paternoster (2000), then, could be positively evaluated and therefore potentially could serve as examples of deviance admiration.

Rebellion is the deviance admiration form of group loyalty. Among the most historically revered figures in middle-class American life are the American revolutionaries, including George Washington, Thomas Jefferson, John Hancock, Nathan Hale, and Thomas Paine. They are now emblematic of ultimate patriotism because of their rebellion. Investigation constitutes the deviance admiration of the norm of privacy. For example, revelations on the *Jerry Springer Show* constitute a violation of the norm of privacy; though perhaps not universally admired, the enduring tenure of the show suggests that there are many fans. Exhibitionism composes the deviance admiration type of prudence, whereby pleasure is bounded. Famous strippers and entertainers, such as RuPaul, have fashioned abundant economic lives on this premise. Additionally, participants in extreme sports certainly underconform to norms of prudence and are tremendously acclaimed for this imprudence, especially by the young. Faddishness embodies the deviance admiration form of conventionality. Faddishness describes underconformity to the habits of most others in the context of an appreciation of that behavior. For example, Americans are presently charmed by the Osbournes; other than the love that permeates their family bonds, they are not conventional. As well, tattoos (and body piercing) and individuals—such as Dennis Rodman, Allen Iverson, and virtually any rock star—who acquire these accoutrements of a youthful imaginative aesthetic are often appreciated. Adventurousness makes up the deviance admiration form of responsibility. Many adventurers of unconquered terrains, including expeditionary individuals who made early conquests of the Arctic, Antarctica, Mount Everest, and outer space, have created a permanent place in history for themselves.

Independence represents the deviance admiration counterpart to participation or involving oneself in the social and economic life of a community. Hoboes or other historical figures viewed to be voluntarily not attached to place or community and keenly uninvolved in community geographical boundaries were almost symbolic of freedom—rather than economic hard times—in another era. As well, those individuals who spend time in settlements in Antarctica, especially those who winter over and thus are effectively cut off from the rest of the planet, fall into this category. Roguishness is illustrative of the deviance admiration component of moderation. Assuredly, dominant middle-class culture has often preferred the enchanting and charming rogue to the earnest, but dull, person. Fictionally, Otis on the *Andy Griffth Show* is representative of this phenomenon; amongst the living, so is Bill Clinton. Tactfulness, particularly as resourcefulness (depending on the context), is the deviance admiration characterization of honesty. In other words, middle-class culture does value lying under certain conditions or for certain reasons. For example, the cop who plays loose with the truth to extract a confession from a serial killer would be positively assessed for his or her resourcefulness in underconforming to the norm of honesty, as would an operative who is dishonest in order to capture a terrorist. On the level of social interaction, those who tactfully tell "white lies" or socially accepted lies—for the purpose of protecting the emotional feelings of another—are usually positively reviewed. Revelry serves as the deviance admiration element of peacefulness. Much vacation behavior falls into this category. Among popular vacation ventures and/or venues that are often adored amongst middle-class Americans are the Mardi Gras, spring break on any warm beach, and Times Square on New Year's Eve. Finally, irreverence is the deviance admiration type of courtesy. Mischievous individuals engage in sly imprudence or adopt a mildly mocking stance toward etiquette. The irreverent range from the fictional Dennis the Menace to the real life class clown to virtually any comedian.

Essentially, there is a corresponding deviance admiration form for each of the middle-class norms outlined by Tittle and Paternoster (2000). Various attitudes, behaviors, or conditions (Adler and Adler 2000) exemplify each category.

Table 4   A Classification of U.S. Middle-Class Deviance, Deviance Admiration

Norm	Deviance Admiration	Examples
Group loyalty	Rebellion	James Dean (rebel without a cause); American Revolution; Pentagon papers; admiration for men who went to Canada to avoid draft during Vietnam War
Privacy	Investigation	Investigative journalism; private investigators revelations on *Jerry Springer Show*
Prudence	Exhibitionism	Famous strippers; gay rights movement famous gamblers; flamboyant entertainers (e.g., Liberace, RuPaul, tranvestities, female impersonators); extreme sports; reality television like *The Osbournes* & the *Anna Nicole Smith Show*
Conventionality	Faddishness	*The Osbournes*; tattoos, bizarre subcultures; body piercing; wiccan and similar subcultures
Responsibility	Adventurousness	Extreme sports (e.g., hang gliding, mountain climbing, free diving, etc.); *Jackass the Movie* humor; explorers
Participation	Independence	Romantic loners; mysterious strangers; drifters; hoboes; explorers
Moderation	Roguishness	Charming rogue; the lovable drunk (e.g., Otis on the *Andy Griffith Show*); Bill Clinton
Honesty	Tactfulness	Honest humor on *The Man Show*; telling "tall tales"; the liar who is admired; telling "white lies"; person who lies to achieve greater goal (e.g., national security, confession from serial killer using "good cop, bad cop"strategies, an operative who lies to be able to capture an "enemy" such as terrorist)
Peacefulness	Revelry	Mardi Gras; fraternity partying; loud entertainer at a party; Spring Break phenomenon
Courtesy	Irreverence	Class clown; humor on *The Man Show*; rude humor on shows such as *The Simpsons*, *South Park*, and *Beavis and Butthead*

Positive Deviance

To echo the model, positive deviance denotes overconformity to the norms that is positively evaluated. The "Mother Theresa phenomenon" occurs when positive reactions or labeling follows overconformity to norms. In other words, Mother Theresa overconformed to the norm of altruism; she was almost universally praised as a saintly woman. For each of the norms suggested by Tittle and Paternoster (2000), a corresponding positive deviance category is proffered in Table 5.

Altruism is the positive deviance form of loyalty. In this case, the person is extraordinarily loyal to the group, overconforming to that norm, and that which emerges due to that loyalty is positively viewed. For example, historically, religious and political martyrs have fallen into this category. That is, the person is viewed as having sacrificed greatly for his or her group. Examples would be the Sullivan brothers from Iowa in World War II or Joan of Arc. National holidays commemorate this type of positive deviance. Every soldier is honored on Veteran's Day, and soldiers who have died for their society are venerated on Memorial Day. Religious martyrs include figures such as Stephen (from the Christian faith). As well, assassinated political leaders such as Abraham Lincoln, John F. Kennedy, Martin Luther King Jr., and Robert F. Kennedy are greatly admired.

Circumspection constitutes the positive deviance form of privacy. Individuals who have security clearances and honor that code are admired for their circumspection; as well, so are professionals—such as doctors, nurses, and clergy—who deal with confidential aspects of the lives of people and honor those confidences. Discretion composes the positive deviance aspect of prudence. In other words, someone who eschews unnecessary frivolous and pleasurable activities so as to achieve an important goal is often admired. Olympic athletes are often viewed as having to steadfastly deny themselves various pleasures so as to diligently advance toward their goal. Properness is the positive deviance type of conventionality. At times, admiration is granted toward those who overconform to the expected habits and lifestyles of the middle class. Some admire the Junior Leaguers who engage in exceedingly conventional lifestyles. Hyperresponsibility is the positive deviance form of the norm of responsibility. For example, those who overconform on the norm of responsibility are often positively evaluated. Management values the overachieving worker; parents and teachers affirm the overachieving student; and almost everyone acknowledges the overzealous athlete (e.g., Michael Jordan and Tiger Woods).

Cooperation (doing it for the team) represents the positive deviance profile of participation. At times, individuals are so involved in community life that they will diminish their own egos for the good of community involvement. As an example, when individual talents are de-emphasized so that an athletic team can win, this process occurs. A long-standing joke in the sports world is that Dean Smith was the only person capable of keeping Michael Jordan under twenty points per game; nevertheless, that team's first and foremost philosophy allowed Michael Jordan and his UNC teammates to defeat Georgetown for the national championship. Temperance illustrates the positive deviance of moderation. When their purpose is a more transcendent one, ascetics or others who overconform to moderation

Table 5   A Classification of U.S. Middle-Class Deviance, Positive Deviance

Norm	Positive Deviance	Examples
Group loyalty	Altruism	Kamikaze pilots; martyrs; sharing food or other resources; daring rescues (e.g., at sea, mountains); patriot
Privacy	Circumspection	CIA operatives; FBI/Justice Department agents; loyal company employees (e.g., Oliver North)
Prudence	Discretion	The good friend who practices discretion; a person who denies themselves pleasures to achieve a goal (e.g., Olympians & other athletes)
Conventionality	Properness	Junior League members; Martha Stewart's followers; Boy Scouts, Girl Scouts, and similar groups
Responsibility	Hyperresponsibility	Overachiever; straight-A student (as viewed by parents and teachers); workaholic (as viewed by management); overzealous athlete (e.g., Tiger Woods, Michael Jordan)
Participation	Cooperation	Athletic team where individual talents are deemphasized so the team can win; employees who are positively viewed as team players
Moderation	Temperance	Monks; Nuns; Women's Temperance Movement; Mothers Against Drunk Driving
Honesty	Forthrightness	Honest Abe Lincoln; George Washington cutting down the cherry tree
Peacefulness	Pacifism	Gandhi; Martin Luther King, Jr.; Jimmy Carter
Courtesy	Gentility	Miss Manners; the old-fashioned practitioners of southern hospitality who are admired; the gentleman; the "southern belle"

are positively evaluated. Examples include people who choose religion for their life's calling, including priests, monks, nuns, preachers, and rabbis. Specifically, people—from many faith traditions—admire the Dalai Lama for the sublime and spiritual path of this life.

Forthrightness exemplifies positive deviance for the norm of honesty. Virtually every school child in this country is successfully socialized to esteem the importance of honesty through the story of George Washington and the cherry tree and through the honest individual as epitomized by the iconic and, perhaps, most reverentially viewed president—Abraham Lincoln. Pacifism demonstrates the deviance admiration category of peacefulness. Yearly, the Nobel Prize for Peace serves as a formalized positive reward for individuals in this category. Among individual nearly universally admired in the context of dominant middle-class American values are individuals—such as Gandhi, Martin Luther King Jr., and Jimmy Carter— who practiced peacefulness while working toward social change. Finally, gentility is the positive deviance form of courtesy. Old-world manners (or southern hospitality) are overconforming to norms of courtesy and are often admired.

Certainly, a positive deviance form exists for each of the ten norms assembled by Tittle and Paternoster (2000). Various examples illustrate each of these categories.

Discussion

The integrated normative-reactivist typology has been utilized to highlight a particular normative system, that of the American middle class. Tittle and Paternoster (2000) created a compilation of that system and outlined the negative deviance that corresponds to each of those norms. The integrated normative-reactivist typology allows for the expansion to rate busting, deviance admiration, and positive deviance forms associated with these norms. Clearly, this implementation illuminates the potential efficacy of the integrated typology. Whereas dominant middle-class American norms were chosen for this exercise, future work could utilize this model to shed light on other normative systems.

Deviance is a complex phenomenon. The intricacies of both normative systems embedded within culture and social reactions are both clearly critical. Fascinating processes occur. At times, reactions are consistent: in other words, nonconformity produces negative reactions, and overconformity creates positive responses. At other times, inconsistency is manifest: nonconformity or underconformity leads to positive reactions, and overconformity engenders negative reactions. Yet, each type of deviance—negative deviance, deviance admiration, rate busting, and positive deviance—highlights the multifaceted processes at work within various social contexts. Deviance theorists have long recognized the relativity of deviance. This work certainly supports that point and implies that there are important theoretical processes at work. That relativity, furthermore, is a very vital issue in relation to contextual analysis. Audiences will react in varying manners and behaviors, and/or individuals can and will be defined differentially across cultures, across times, and across subcultures.

Liazos (1975) noted the preoccupation of sociologists within the substantive area of deviance in focusing on "nuts, sluts, and perverts"; furthermore, he viewed such preoccupation as a source of impoverishment within this field. Sorokin (1963, p. 33) identified his life experience as an observer during the twentieth century of "a gigantic explosion of human bestiality and hateful destructiveness of demoralized individual and groups" as the raison d'être for his simultaneously examining both human violence and hatred and sympathy and *agape* (love). Seminally suggesting the importance of expanding beyond the traditional boundaries of the field of deviance, Ben-Yehuda (1990, p. 235) wrote that "theoretical and empirical attention to the full spectrum of the meaning of 'deviance' could open new frontiers and horizons for sociologists of deviance and fertilize research in an unprecedented way."

We propose that new venues of research could accompany the traditional focus on negative deviance. Exploratory examples from each cell other than negative deviance will be suggested.

Firstly, rate busting is a fertile category for potential research. Of particular theoretical concern is discerning why negative reactions occur to overconformity. As Homans (1969) noted in the context of work, strongly negative informal reactions and stigmatization are often experienced by the "rate killer." In line with traditional deviance research, some interesting lines of potential research might develop. How do rate busters at work experience such stigmatization, and how does it impact their identity? What factors produce this overconformity? Additionally, why do some individuals continue to overconform in light of their negative stigmatization? Furthermore, an interesting line of research could develop in terms of the traditional focus of deviance. Regarding alcohol, in the context of dominant society, pathological drinking or alcoholism in nonconformity, moderate drinking constitutes conformity, and nondrinking could be considered overconformity. Nondrinkers are others negatively evaluated for not fitting neatly into a social scenario. Why do individuals choose not to drink? How are individuals evaluated, by different social audiences, for this behavior? How do they react to negative evaluations? Finally, understanding gifted children and why they are negatively stigmatized by their peers would be a fruitful area of research.

Deviance admiration also opens up venues for research. Kooistra (1989) has postulated that sociological analysis of the creation of "heroic criminals" most intensely reflects anomic conditions or structural situations, such as economic difficulties, that disrupt order and allow people to view themselves as "outside the law." During these times of societal difficulty, the law is symbolized as oppressive rather that just. Further sociological research could address whether economic and/or anomic conditions do create an increased number of heroic criminals. Also, the study of "heroic criminals" in oppressed communities or communities marked by consistently stressful anomic conditions would be very illuminating as well. Rogues would also be a scintillating area of research. What are the etiological roots of the rogues? Why and under what conditions are rogues admired? Revelry, in the context of the Mardi Gras and other similar phenomena, is also quite interesting (Redmon 2003). Future research might examine the conditions under which people will underconform at the Mardi Gras but do not do so in the context of their own community. Furthermore, why is this revelry so admired? How does this abandonment of otherwise regularized conformity impact identity?

Finally, the area of positive deviance is ripe with fruitful lines of research topics. Other disciplines are increasingly recognizing the benefit of examining the positive, as well as the negative. As an example, the term positive deviance is widely accepted in child nutrition and, according to Zeitlin, Ghassemi, and Mansour (1990, p. viii), describes children "who grow and develop adequately in low-income families living in impoverished environments, where a majority of children suffer from growth retardation and malnutrition." Importantly, integrated nutritional interventions based on the study of positive deviance have generally been more successful for various outcomes than interventions based on the study of "negative deviance" (i.e., children who are malnourished and fail to thrive) (e.g., Sternin, Sternin, and Marsh 1998; Schroeder et al. 2002; Sripaipan et al. 2002). This research extends beyond nutritional practices to include maternal child rearing practices and the impact of positive parental behaviors on children's psychosocial development (Aruna, Vazir, and Vidyasagar 2001).

Within the field of psychology, Martin E. P. Seligman, a past president of the American Psychological Association, advocates that a disease model is not sufficient in their field and that it is important to focus on developing what is good in humans (Ruark 1999). In organizational and leadership research, there is an increasing focus on "best practices" and researching positive actors and behaviors (including the explicit study of positive deviants and positive deviance) to provide information to improve productivity and promote other positive organizational outcomes (e.g., Cameron, Dutton, and Quinn 2003; Wright 2003). Additionally, resiliency, which refers to children who are able to adapt or even flourish in debilitating social environments, is increasingly being studied (Werner and Smith 1989, 1992; Garmezy 1991a, 1991b). Health researchers, too, have utilized the concept of positive deviance. For example, recent research on AIDS identified factors affecting primary sexual abstinence and condom use among Rwandan youth (Babaloa, Awasum, and Quenum-Renaud 2002) Sociologists could also benefit from such studies, as studying the positive might illuminate the negative and provide useful knowledge for successful interventions. Sociologists are clearly lagging behind these other disciplines in studying positive deviance.

Another potential area of research in positive deviance could focus on adolescents who are positively evaluated for overconformity and do not engage in even minor delinquency or status offending. Etiologically, what are the factors that allow this particular adaptation to emerge? In what social context and by which social audiences are they positively evaluated for their overconformity? Another research agenda of particular interest in the post-9/11 era is that of people who are positively evaluated for succeeding in saving the life of another human being or in attempting to do so. What pertinent etiological factors are involved in this behavior? Could research on altruism produce the practical capability to teach people to be more altruistic?

Conclusion

Long ago Durkheim (1982) pointed out the inevitability or normalcy of deviance; furthermore, Durkheim (1964; 1982) illuminated positive functions of deviance. A variety of social-psychological experiments, such as those by Sherif (1936), Asch (1952), and Schachter (1951), also suggested the fundamental existence of the processes of norms production, conformity, deviance production, and individual and social reactions to (potentially) deviant behaviors, attitudes, and conditions. The importance of power and social context in influencing norms, social reactions, and deviance outcomes cannot be ignored. The behaviors and conditions of more powerful actors are less likely to be deviantized than those of the less powerful. The reactions of powerful actors and social groups, moreover, are more important in determining who and what is successfully labeled deviant. In fact, we have argued that deviant behavior actually serves as a test of power relationships (Heckert and Heckert 2002). When a child lies, for example, she is testing the parent's ability to discern and react to the lie. When the child successfully "gets away" with the lie, a shift in the relative power of the child and parent has occurred.

The central place of norms, social reactions, efforts at social control, and deviance processes, therefore, suggest the importance of an integrated framework for understanding these factors and their interrelationships. Our integrated typology is an initial attempt to eliminate the false dichotomy imposed by previous conceptualizations of deviance.

All in all, human behavior has always been complex, as has been the substantive area of deviance. There are still many important and even uncharted areas of human attitudes, behaviors, and conditions that could be analyzed within the context of the sociology of deviance. Deviance should remain a core area within the discipline of sociology.

Acknowledgments

Both authors would like to thank Dr. Paul C. Heckert, Dr. Diane Manette Heckert, and Sara R. Heckert for their respective sociological imaginations that were demonstrated in the naming of several of these categories. We also would like to thank the insightful comments of anonymous reviewers for helping us to improve this article. An earlier version of this article was presented at the 2002 meeting of the American Society of Criminology, Chicago, Illinois.

References

Adler, Patricia A., and Peter Adler. 2000. *Constructions of Deviance: Social Power, Context, and Interaction.* 3rd ed. Belmont, CA: Wadsworth.

Aruna, M., Shanaz Vazir, and P. Vidyasagar. 2001. "Child Rearing and Positive Deviance in the Development of Preschoolers: A Microanalysis." *Indian Pediatrics* 38:332–339.

Asch, Solomon. 1952. *Social Psychology.* Englewood Cliffs, NJ: Prentice Hall.

Babaloa, Stella, David Awasum, and Brigette Quenum-Renaud. 2002. "The Correlates of Safe Sex Practices among Rwandan Youth: A Positive Deviance Approach." *African Journal of AIDS Research* 1:13–23.

Becker, Howard. 1963. *Outsiders.* New York: The Free Press of Glencoe.

Ben-Yehuda. Nachman. 1990. "Positive and Negative Deviance: More Fuel for a Controversy." *Deviant Behavior* 11:221–243.

Berscheid, Ellen, and Elaine Walster. 1964. "Physical Attractiveness." Pp. 157–215 in *Advances in Experimental Social Psychology.* Vol. 7. New York: Academic Press.

Best, Joel. 2004. *Deviance: Career of a Concept.* Belmont, California: Thomson/ Wadsworth.

Blake, Judith, and Kingsley Davis. 1964. "Norms, Values, and Sanctions." Pp. 456–484 in *Handbook of Modern Sociology,* edited by Robert E. L. Faris. Chicago: Rand McNally.

Byrne, Don. 1971. *The Attraction Paradigm.* New York: Academic Press.

Cameron, K., J. E. Dutton, and R. E. Quinn. 2003. *Positive Organizational Scholarship: Foundations of a New Discipline.* San Francisco: Berrett-Koehler Publishers.

Cohen, Albert K. 1966. *Deviance and Control.* Englewood Cliffs, NJ: The Free Press.

Coser, Lews A. 1967. *Continuities in the Study of Social Conflict.* New York: The Free Press.

Dinitz, Simon, Russell R. Dynes, and Alfred C. Clarke. 1969. *Deviance: Studies in the Process of Stigmatization and Societal Reaction.* New York: Oxford University Press.

Dodge, David L. 1985. "The Over-negativized Conceptualization of Deviance: A Programmatic Exploration." *Deviant Behavior* 6:17–37.

Durkheim, Emile. [1895] 1964. *The Division of Labor in Society.* Trans. J. Solovay and J. Mueller. New York: The Free Press.

———. [1893] 1982. *The Rules of Sociological Method.* Trans. S. Lukes. London: Macmillan.

Erikson, Kai T. 1964. "Notes on the Sociology of Deviance." Pp. 9–20 in *The Other Side,* edited by Howard Becker. New York: The Free Press.

Freedman, Jonathan L., and Anthony N. Doob. 1968. *Deviancy: The Psychology of Being Different.* New York: Academic Press.

Garmezy, N. 1991a. "Resiliency and Vulnerability to Adverse Developmental Outcomes Associated with Poverty." *American Behavioral Scientist* 34:416–43.

———. 1991b. "Resiliency in Children's Adaptation to Negative Life Events and Stressed Environments." *Pediatric Annals* 20:432–466.

Gibbs, Jack P. 1981. *Norms, Deviance and Social Control.* New York: Elsevier.

Goode, Erich. 2001. *Deviant Behavior.* 6th ed. Upper Saddle River, NJ: Prentice-Hall.

Gusfield, Joseph R. 1963. *Symbolic Crusade.* Urbana, IL: University of Illinois Press.

Hawkins, Richard, and Gary Tiedeman. 1975. *The Creation of Deviance.* Columbus, OH: Charles E. Merrill Publishing Company.

Heckert, Alex, and Druann Maria Heckert. 2004. "Using an Integrated Typology of Deviance to Analyze Ten Common Norms of the U.S. Middle Class." *The Sociological Quarterly,* vol. 45, no. 2, Spring 2004, pp. 209–228.

Heckert, Alex, and Druann Maria Heckert. 2002. "A New Typology of Deviance: Integrating Normative and Reactivist Definitions of Deviance." *Deviant Behavior* 23:449–479.

Heckert, Druann. 1998. "Positive Deviance: A Classificatory Model." *Free Inquiry in Creative Sociology* 26:23–30.

———. 2003. "Mixed Blessings: Women and Blonde Hair." *Free Inquiry in Creative Sociology* 31:47–72.

Hendershott, Anne. 2002. *The Politics of Deviance.* San Francisco, CA: Encounter.

Henslin, James M. 1975. *Introducing Sociology: Toward Understanding Life in Society.* New York: Free Press.

Homans, George C. 1950. *The Human Group.* New York: Harcourt, Brace and Company.

———. 1969. "Output Restrictions, Norms, and Social Sanctions." Pp. 4–9 in *Deviant Behavior and Social Process,* edited by William A. Rushing. Chicago: Rand McNally.

Huryn, Jean Scherz. 1986. "Giftedness as Deviance: A Test of Interaction Theories." *Deviant Behavior* 7:175–186.

Irwin, Katherine. 2003. "Saints and Sinners: Elite Tattoo Collectors and Tattooists as Positive and Negative Deviants." *Sociological Spectrum* 23:27–58.

Johnson, Elmer Hubert. 1978. *Crime, Correction, and Society.* Homewood, IL: The Dorsey Press.

Johnson, Harry M. 1960. *Sociology.* New York: Harcourt, Brace and World.

Kooistra, Paul. 1989. *Criminals as Heroes: Structure, Power and Identity.* Bowling Green: Bowling Green State University Popular Press.

Krebs, Dennis, and Allen A. Adinolfi. 1975. "Physical Attractiveness, Social Relations, and Personality Style." *Journal of Personality and Social Psychology* 31:245–253.

Lemert, Edwin M. 1972. *Human Deviance, Social Problems, and Social Control.* Englewood Cliffs, NJ: Prentice-Hall.

Liazos, Alexander. 1975. "The Poverty of the Sociology of Deviance: Nuts, Sluts, and Perverts." Pp. 9–19 in *Examining Deviance Experimentally,* edited by Darrell J. Steffensmeier and Robert M. Terry. Port Washington, NY: Alfred Publishing Company.

Liska, Allen E. 1981. *Perspectives on Deviance.* Englewood Cliffs, NJ: Prentice-Hall.

Merton, Robert K. 1966. "Social Problems and Sociological Theory." Pp. 775–827 in *Contemporary Social Problems,* 2nd ed., edited by Robert K. Merton and Robert Nisbet. New York: Harcourt Brace.

———. 1968. *Social Theory and Social Structure.* New York: The Free Press.

Moynihan, Daniel Patrick. 1993. "Defining Deviance Down: How We've Become Accustomed to Alarming Levels of Crime and Destructive Behavior." *American Scholar* 67:17–30.

Redmon, David. 2003. "Examining Low Self-Control Theory at Mardi Gras: Critiquing the General Theory of Crime within the Framework of Normative Deviance." *Deviant Behavior* 24:373–392.

Reis, Harry T., Ladd Wheeler, Nancy Spiegel, Michael H. Kerns, John Nezlik, and Michael Perry. 1982. "Physical Attractiveness as Social Interaction II: Why Does Appearance Affect Social Experience?" *Journal of Personality and Social Psychology* 43:979–996.

Ruark, Jennifer K. 1999. "Redefining the Good Life: A New Focus in the Social Sciences." *The Chronicle of Higher Education,* February 12, A13–A15.

Scarpitti, Frank R., and Paul T. McFarlalne. 1975. *Deviance: Action, Reaction, Interaction.* Reading, MA: Addison-Wesley Publishing.

Schachter, Stanley. 1951. "Deviance, Rejection, and Communication." *Journal of Abnormal Social Psychology* 46:190–207.

Schroeder, D. G., H. Pachon, K. A. Dearden, T. T. Ha, T. T. Lang, and D. R. Marsh. 2002. "An Integrated Child Nutrition Intervention Improved Growth of Younger, More Malnourished Children in Northern Viet Nam." *Food and Nutrition Bulletin* 23:50–58.

Sherif, Muzifer. 1936. *The Psychology of Social Norms.* New York: Harper.

Sorokin, Pitirim A. 1950. *Altruistic Love.* Boston: The Beacon Press.

———. 1963. *Pitirim A. Sorokin in Review,* edited by Philip J. Allen. Durham, NC: Duke University Press.

Sripaipan, T., D. G. Schroeder, D. R. Marsh, H. Pacho, K. A. Dearden, T. T. Ha, and T. T. Lang. 2002. "Effect of an Integrated Nutrition Program on Child Morbidity Due to Respiratory Infection and Diarrhea in Northern Viet Nam." *Food and Nutrition Bulletin* 23:67–74.

Steffensmeier, Darrell J., and Robert M. Terry. 1975. *Examining Deviance Experimentally.* Port Washington, NY: Alfred Publishing.

Sternin, M., J. Sternin, and D. Marsh. 1998. *Designing a Community-Based Nutrition Program Using the Positive Deviance Approach.* Westport, CT: Save the Children.

Sumner, Colin. 1994. *The Sociology of Deviance: An Obituary.* New York: Continuum.

Taylor, Ian, Paul Walton, and Jock Young. 1973. *The New Criminology.* New York: Harper and Row.

Thio, Alex. 1983. *Deviant Behavior.* 2nd ed. Boston: Houghton Mifflin.

———. *Deviant Behavior.* 6th ed. Boston: Allyn and Bacon.

Tittle, Charles R., and Raymond Paternoster. 2000. *Social Deviance and Crime.* Los Angeles: Roxbury Publishing Company.

Werner, E., and R. Smith. 1989. *Vulnerable But Invincible: A Longitudinal Study of Resilient Children and Youth.* New York: Adams, Bannister, and Cox.

———. 1992. *Overcoming the Odds: High-Risk Children from Birth to Adulthood.* New York: Cornell University Press.

White, Winston. 1961. *Beyond Conformity.* Westport, CT: Greenwood Press.

Wilkins, Leslie. 1965. *Social Deviance.* Englewood Cliffs, NJ: Prentice-Hall.

Williams, Robin M., Jr. 1965. *American Society: A Sociological Interpretation.* 2nd ed. New York: Knopf.

Winslow, Robert W. 1970. *Society in Transition: A Social Approach to Deviance.* New York: The Free Press.

Wright, Thomas A. 2003. "Positive Organizational Behavior: An Idea Whose Time Has Truly Come." *Journal of Organizational Behavior* 24:437–442.

Zeitlin, Marian, Hossien Ghassemi, and Mohamed Mansour. 1990. *Positive Deviance in Child Nutrition.* Tokyo: United Nations University.

3

Moral Entrepreneurs: The Creation and Enforcement of Deviant Categories

Howard S. Becker

Rule Creators

The prototype of the rule creator, but not the only variety as we shall see, is the crusading reformer. He is interested in the content of rules. The existing rules do not satisfy him because there is some evil which profoundly disturbs him. He feels that nothing can be right in the world until rules are made to correct it. He operates with an absolute ethic; what he sees is truly and totally evil with no qualification. Any means is justified to do away with it. The crusader is fervent and righteous, often self-righteous.

It is appropriate to think of reformers as crusaders because they typically believe that their mission is a holy one. The prohibitionist serves as an excellent example, as does the person who wants to suppress vice and sexual delinquency or the person who wants to do away with gambling.

These examples suggest that the moral crusader is a meddling busybody, interested in forcing his own morals on others. But this is a one-sided view. Many moral crusades have strong humanitarian overtones. The crusader is not only interested in seeing to it that other people do what he thinks [is] right. He believes that if they do what is right it will be good for them. Or he may feel that his reform will prevent certain kinds of exploitation of one person by another. Prohibitionists felt that they were not simply forcing their morals on others, but attempting to provide the conditions for a better way of life for people prevented by drink from realizing a truly good life. Abolitionists were not simply trying to prevent slave owners from doing the wrong thing; they were trying to help slaves achieve a better life. Because of the importance of the humanitarian motive, moral crusaders (despite their relatively single-minded devotion to their particular cause) often lend their support to other humanitarian crusades. Joseph Gusfield has pointed out that:

> The American temperance movement during the 19th century was a part of a general effort toward the improvement of the worth of the

> human being through improved morality as well as economic conditions. The mixture of the religious, the equalitarian, and the humanitarian was an outstanding facet of the moral reformism of many movements. Temperance supporters formed a large segment of movements such as sabbatarianism, abolition, woman's rights, agrarianism, and humanitarian attempts to improve the lot of the poor. . . .
>
> In its auxiliary interests the WCTU revealed a great concern for the improvement of the welfare of the lower classes. It was active in campaigns to secure penal reform, to shorten working hours and raise wages for workers, and to abolish child labor and in a number of other humanitarian and equalitarian activities. In the 1880's the WCTU worked to bring about legislation for the protection of working girls against the exploitation by men.[1]

As Gusfield says,[2] "Moral reformism of this type suggests the approach of a dominant class toward those less favorably situated in the economic and social structure." Moral crusaders typically want to help those beneath them to achieve a better status. That those beneath them do not always like the means proposed for their salvation is another matter. But this fact—that moral crusades are typically dominated by those in the upper levels of the social structure—means that they add to the power they derive from the legitimacy of their moral position, the power they derive from their superior position in society.

Naturally, many moral crusades draw support from people whose motives are less pure than those of the crusader. Thus, some industrialists supported Prohibition because they felt it would provide them with a more manageable labor force.[3] Similarly, it is sometimes rumored that Nevada gambling interests support the opposition to attempts to legalize gambling in California because it would cut so heavily into their business, which depends in substantial measure on the population of Southern California.[4]

The moral crusader, however, is more concerned with ends than with means. When it comes to drawing up specific rules (typically in the form of legislation to be proposed to a state legislature or the Federal Congress), he frequently relies on the advice of experts. Lawyers, expert in the drawing of acceptable legislation, often play this role. Government bureaus in whose jurisdiction the problem falls may also have the necessary expertise, as did the Federal Bureau of Narcotics in the case of the marihuana problem.

As psychiatric ideology, however, becomes increasingly acceptable, a new expert has appeared—the psychiatrist. Sutherland, in his discussion of the natural history of sexual psychopath laws, pointed to the psychiatrist's influence.[5] He suggests the following as the conditions under which the sexual psychopath law, which provides that a person "who is diagnosed as a sexual psychopath may be confined for an indefinite period in a state hospital for the insane,"[6] will be passed.

> First, these laws are customarily enacted after a state of fear has been aroused in a community by a few serious sex crimes committed in

quick succession. This is illustrated in Indiana, where a law was passed following three or four sexual attacks in Indianapolis, with murder in two. Heads of families bought guns and watch dogs, and the supply of locks and chains in the hardware stores of the city was completely exhausted. . . .

A second element in the process of developing sexual psychopath laws is the agitated activity of the community in connection with the fear. The attention of the community is focused on sex crimes, and people in the most varied situations envisage dangers and see the need of and possibility for their control. . . .

The third phase in the development of those sexual psychopath laws has been the appointment of a committee. The committee gathers the many conflicting recommendations of persons and groups of persons, attempts to determine "facts," studies procedures in other states, and makes recommendations, which generally include bills for the legislature. Although the general fear usually subsides within a few days, a committee has the formal duty of following through until positive action is taken. Terror which does not result in a committee is much less likely to result in a law.[7]

In the case of sexual psychopath laws, there usually is no government agency charged with dealing in a specialized way with sexual deviations. Therefore, when the need for expert advice in drawing up legislation arises, people frequently turn to the professional group most closely associated with such problems:

In some states, at the committee stage of the development of a sexual psychopath law, psychiatrists have played an important part. The psychiatrists, more than any others, have been the interest group back of the laws. A committee of psychiatrists and neurologists in Chicago wrote the bill which became the sexual psychopath law of Illinois; the bill was sponsored by the Chicago Bar Association and by the state's attorney of Cook County and was enacted with little opposition in the next session of the State Legislature. In Minnesota all the members of the governor's committee except one were psychiatrists. In Wisconsin the Milwaukee Neuropsychiatric Society shared in pressing the Milwaukee Crime Commission for the enactment of a law. In Indiana the attorney-general's committee received from the American Psychiatric Association copies of all the sexual psychopath laws which had been enacted in other states.[8]

The influence of psychiatrists in other realms of criminal law has increased in recent years.

In any case, what is important about this example is not that psychiatrists are becoming increasingly influential, but that the moral crusader, at some point in the development of his crusade, often requires the services of a professional who can draw up the appropriate rules in an appropriate form. The crusader himself is often not concerned with such details. Enough for him that the main point has been won; he leaves its implementation to others.

By leaving the drafting of the specific rule in the hands of others, the crusader opens the door for many unforeseen influences. For those who draft legislation for crusaders have their own interests, which may affect the legislation they prepare. It is likely that the sexual psychopath laws drawn by psychiatrists contain many features never intended by the citizens who spearheaded the drives to "do something about sex crimes," features which do however reflect the professional interests of organized psychiatry.

• • •

Rule Enforcers

The most obvious consequence of a successful crusade is the creation of a new set of rules. With the creation of a new set of rules we often find that a new set of enforcement agencies and officials is established. Sometimes, of course, existing agencies take over the administration of the new rule, but more frequently a new set of rule enforcers is created. The passage of the Harrison Act presaged the creation of the Federal Narcotics Bureau, just as the passage of the Eighteenth Amendment led to the creation of police agencies charged with enforcing the Prohibition Laws.

With the establishment of organizations of rule enforcers, the crusade becomes institutionalized. What started out as a drive to convince the world of the moral necessity of a new rule finally becomes an organization devoted to the enforcement of the rule. Just as radical political movements turn into organized political parties and lusty evangelical sects become staid religious denominations, the final outcome of the moral crusade is a police force. To understand, therefore, how the rules creating a new class of outsiders are applied to particular people we must understand the motives and interests of police, the rule enforcers.

Although some policemen undoubtedly have a kind of crusading interest in stamping out evil, it is probably much more typical for the policeman to have a certain detached and objective view of his job. He is not so much concerned with the content of any particular rule as he is with the fact that it is his job to enforce the rule. When the rules are changed, he punishes what was once acceptable behavior just as he ceases to punish behavior that has been made legitimate by a change in the rules. The enforcer, then, may not be interested in the content of the rule as such, but only in the fact that the existence of the rule provides him with a job, a profession, and a *raison d'être.*

Since the enforcement of certain rules provides justification for his way of life, the enforcer has two interests which condition his enforcement activity: first, he must justify the existence of his position and, second, he must win the respect of those he deals with.

These interests are not peculiar to rule enforcers. Members of all occupations feel the need to justify their work and win the respect of others. Musicians would like to do this but have difficulty finding ways of successfully impressing their worth on customers. Janitors fail to win their tenants' respect, but develop an ideology which stresses the quasi-professional responsibility they have to keep confidential the intimate knowledge of tenants they acquire in the course of their work.[9] Physicians, lawyers, and other professionals, more successful in winning the respect of clients, develop elaborate mechanisms for maintaining a properly respectful relationship.

In justifying the existence of his position, the rule enforcer faces a double problem. On the one hand, he must demonstrate to others that the problem still exists: the rules he is supposed to enforce have some point, because infractions occur. On the other hand, he must show that his attempts at enforcement are effective and worthwhile, that the evil he is supposed to deal with is in fact being dealt with adequately. Therefore, enforcement organizations, particularly when they are seeking funds, typically oscillate between two kinds of claims. First, they say that by reason of their efforts the problem they deal with is approaching solution. But, in the same breath, they say the problem is perhaps worse than ever (though through no fault of their own) and requires renewed and increased effort to keep it under control. Enforcement officials can be more vehement than anyone else in their insistence that the problem they are supposed to deal with is still with us, in fact is more with us than ever before. In making these claims, enforcement officials provide good reason for continuing the existence of the position they occupy.

We may also note that enforcement officials and agencies are inclined to take a pessimistic view of human nature. If they do not actually believe in original sin, they at least like to dwell on the difficulties in getting people to abide by rules, on the characteristics of human nature that lead people toward evil. They are skeptical of attempts to reform rule-breakers.

The skeptical and pessimistic outlook of the rule enforcer, of course, is reinforced by his daily experience. He sees, as he goes about his work, the evidence that the problem is still with us. He sees the people who continually repeat offenses, thus definitely branding themselves in his eyes as outsiders. Yet it is not too great a stretch of the imagination to suppose that one of the underlying reasons for the enforcer's pessimism about human nature and the possibilities of reform is that fact that if human nature were perfectible and people could be permanently reformed, his job would come to an end.

In the same way, a rule enforcer is likely to believe that it is necessary for the people he deals with to respect him. If they do not, it will be very difficult to do his job; his feeling of security in his work will be lost. Therefore, a good deal of enforcement activity is devoted not to the actual enforcement of rules, but to coercing respect from the people the enforcer deals with. This means that one may be labeled as deviant not because he has actually broken a rule, but because he has shown disrespect to the enforcer of the rule.

Westley's study of policemen in a small industrial city furnishes a good example of this phenomenon. In his interview, he asked policemen, "When do you think a policeman is justified in roughing a man up?" He found that "at least 37% of the men believed that it was legitimate to use violence to coerce respect."[10] He gives some illuminating quotations from his interviews:

> Well, there are cases. For example, when you stop a fellow for a routine questioning, say a wise guy, and he starts talking back to you and telling you you are no good and that sort of thing. You know you can take a man in on a disorderly conduct charge, but you can practically never make it stick. So what you do in a case like that is to egg the guy on until he makes a remark where you can justifiably slap him and, then, if he fights back, you can call it resisting arrest.

> Well, a prisoner deserves to be hit when he goes to the point where he tries to put you below him.

> You've gotta get rough when a man's language becomes very bad, when he is trying to make a fool of you in front of everybody else. I think most policemen try to treat people in a nice way, but usually you have to talk pretty rough. That's the only way to set a man down, to make him show a little respect.[11]

What Westley describes is the use of an illegal means of coercing respect from others. Clearly, when a rule enforcer has the option of enforcing a rule or not, the difference in what he does may be caused by the attitude of the offender toward him. If the offender is properly respectful, the enforcer may smooth the situation over. If the offender is disrespectful, then sanctions may be visited on him. Westley has shown that this differential tends to operate in the case of traffic offenses, where the policeman's discretion is perhaps at a maximum.[12] But it probably operates in other areas as well.

Ordinarily, the rule enforcer has a great deal of discretion in many areas, if only because his resources are not sufficient to cope with the volume of rule-breaking he is supposed to deal with. This means that he cannot tackle everything at once and to this extent must temporize with evil. He cannot do the whole job and knows it. He takes his time, on the assumption that the problems he deals with will be around for a long while. He establishes priorities, dealing with things in their turn, handling the most pressing problems immediately and leaving others for later. His attitude toward his work, in short, is professional. He lacks the naive moral fervor characteristic of the rule creator.

If the enforcer is not going to tackle every case he knows of at once, he must have a basis for deciding when to enforce the rule, which persons committing which acts to label as deviant. One criterion for selecting people is the "fix." Some people have sufficient political influence or know-how to be able to ward off attempts at enforcement, if not at the time of apprehension then at a later stage in the process. Very often, this function is professionalized; someone performs the job on a full-time basis, available to anyone who wants to hire him. A professional thief described fixers this way:

> There is in every large city a regular fixer for professional thieves. He has no agents and does not solicit and seldom takes any case except that of a professional thief, just as they seldom go to anyone except him. This centralized and monopolistic system of fixing for professional thieves is found in practically all of the large cities and many of the small ones.[13]

Since it is mainly professional thieves who know about the fixer and his operations, the consequence of this criterion for selecting people to apply the rules to is that amateurs tend to be caught, convicted, and labeled deviant much more frequently than professionals. As the professional thief notes:

> You can tell by the way the case is handled in court when the fix is in. When the copper is not very certain he has the right man, or the testimony of the copper and the complainant does not agree, or the prosecutor goes easy on the defendant, or the judge is arrogant in his decisions, you can always be sure that someone has got the work in. This does not happen in many cases of theft, for there is one case of a professional to twenty-five or thirty amateurs who know nothing about the fix. These amateurs get the hard end of the deal every time. The coppers bawl out about the thieves, no one holds up his testimony, the judge delivers an oration, and all of them get credit for stopping a crime wave. When the professional hears the case immediately preceding his own, he will think, "He should have got ninety years. It's the damn amateurs who cause all the heat in the stores." Or else he thinks, "Isn't it a damn shame for that copper to send that kid away for a pair of hose, and in a few minutes he will agree to a small fine for me for stealing a fur coat?" But if the coppers did not send the amateurs away to strengthen their records of convictions, they could not sandwich in the professionals whom they turn loose.[14]

Enforcers of rules, since they have no stake in the content of particular rules themselves, often develop their own private evaluation of the importance of various kinds of rules and infractions of them. This set of priorities may differ considerably from those held by the general public. For instance, drug users typically believe (and a few policemen have personally confirmed it to me) that police do not consider the use of marihuana to be as important a problem or as dangerous a practice as the use of opiate drugs. Police base this conclusion on the fact that, in their experience, opiate users commit other crimes (such as theft or prostitution) in order to get drugs, while marihuana users do not.

Enforcers then, responding to the pressures of their own work situation, enforce rules and create outsiders in a selective way. Whether a person who commits a deviant act is in fact labeled a deviant depends on many things extraneous to his actual behavior: whether the enforcement official feels that at this time he must make some show of doing his job in order to justify his position, whether the misbehaver shows proper deference to the enforcer, whether the "fix" has been put in, and where the kind of act he has committed stands on the enforcer's list of priorities.

The professional enforcer's lack of fervor and routine approach to dealing with evil may get him into trouble with the rule creator. The rule creator, as we have said, is concerned with the content of the rules that interest him. He sees them as the means by which evil can be stamped out. He does not understand the enforcer's long-range approach to the same problems and cannot see why all the evil that is apparent cannot be stamped out at once.

When the person interested in the content of a rule realizes or has called to his attention the fact that enforcers are dealing selectively with the evil that concerns him, his righteous wrath may be aroused. The professional is denounced for viewing the evil too lightly, for failing to do his duty. The moral entrepreneur, at whose instance the rule was made, arises again to say that the outcome of the last crusade has not been satisfactory or that the gains once made have been whittled away and lost.

Notes

1. Joseph R. Gusfield, "Social Structure and Moral Reform: A Study of the Woman's Christian Temperance Union," *American Journal of Sociology,* LXI (November, 1955), 223.
2. *Ibid.*
3. See Raymond G. McCarthy, editor, *Drinking and Intoxication* (New Haven and New York: Yale Center of Alcohol Studies and The Free Press of Glencoe, 1959), pp. 395–396.
4. This is suggested in Oscar Lewis, *Sagebrush Casinos: The Story of Legal Gambling in Nevada* (New York: Doubleday and Co., 1953), pp. 223–234.
5. Edwin H. Sutherland, "The Diffusion of Sexual Psychopath Laws," *American Journal of Sociology,* LVI (September, 1950), 142–148.
6. *Ibid.,* pp. 142.
7. *Ibid.,* pp. 143–145.
8. *Ibid.,* pp. 145–146.
9. See Ray Gold, "Janitors Versus Tenants: A Status-Income Dilemma," *American Journal of Sociology,* LVII (March, 1952), 486–493.
10. William A. Westley, "Violence and the Police," *American Journal of Sociology,* LIX (July, 1953), 39.
11. *Ibid.*
12. See William A. Westley, "The Police: A Sociological Study of Law, Custom, and Morality" (unpublished Ph.D. dissertation, University of Chicago, Department of Sociology, 1951).
13. Edwin H. Sutherland (editor), *The Professional Thief* (Chicago: University of Chicago Press, 1937), pp. 87–88.
14. *Ibid.,* pp. 91–92.

The Production of Deviant Categories and Actors

Quite clearly, in cases where the moral entrepreneurs and their crusades succeed, society is often confronted with a new deviant category and a corresponding enforcement or social-control apparatus. Becker's general discussion of the dynamics behind the passage of various laws (e.g., the Eighteenth Amendment and sexual psychopath laws) offers illustrations of this.

As a social construction, deviance can be shaped. Groups' ability to guide the construction of deviant categories is closely linked to power structures within society, especially political power. Justin L. Tuggle and Malcolm D. Holmes, in "Blowing Smoke: Status Politics and the Shasta County Smoking Ban," explore the relationship between social status and the creation of deviant categories. Central to their article is the idea that by defining particular acts or activities as deviant, certain groups may be disadvantaged differentially. In the case presented by Tuggle and Holmes, the campaign against smoking targeted the working class, since smoking was a defining characteristic of this group. What emerges from their exploration as being a central concern is the observation that those from higher socioeconomic positions are most likely to be those who prevail in contests concerned with defining deviant categories.

Steven Spitzer, in "The Production of Deviance in Capitalist Society," offers another account of how deviant categories and populations are created. A basic thesis of Spitzer is the argument that most traditional theories of deviance, given their preoccupation with the dramatic and predatory forms of social behavior, have neglected to focus on how deviance and deviant populations are constructed socially. He argues that instead of accepting prevailing definitions as givens, one must become aware of the processes by which deviance is "subjectively constructed" and the way in which deviants are "objectively handled," as well as the "structural bases of behavior and characteristics which come to official attention." Spitzer goes on to provide an insightful account of deviance production and control in capitalist societies. Most insightful, and particularly relevant to Part IV of this book, is his discussion of not only how "problem populations" are produced by the state but how these populations, once constructed, are transformed into deviants and become the objects of official social control. Spitzer cites several factors that influence the rate at which problem populations are transformed into deviants. For example, increasingly large and threatening problem populations are more likely to be controlled through some type of deviance processing.

Spitzer concludes by discussing two rather distinct groups that evolve as a result of social control efforts: the *social junk* and the *social dynamite*. Social junk is relatively costly (e.g., the aged, the mentally ill, the handicapped), yet not especially threatening to the established order. Social dynamite, however, is more threatening as it possesses the potential to call into question such factors as domination and the current mode of production. Spitzer notes further that the social dynamite, given its more youthful, alienated, and politically volatile nature, is more apt to be controlled through a rapid deployment of control resources; this often results in eventual processing through the legal system. The social junk, by contrast, is more likely to be handled by some agency of the welfare state.

Peter Conrad, in "The Discovery of Hyperkinesis: Notes on the Medicalization of Deviant Behavior," provides another historical account of how conceptions of behavior can change. His initial comments are given to the ways in which selected forms of behavior (e.g., alcoholism and drug addiction) become defined as a medical problem or illness and how, thereafter, the medical profession is mandated or licensed to provide the appropriate treatment. Conrad's focus is given to hyperkinesis, particularly its discovery. In his analysis, he describes the various *clinical* (e.g., the effects of amphetamine drugs on children's behavior) and *social* (e.g., the pharmaceutical revolution and associated government action) factors that gave rise to the creation of this new medical diagnostic category. He then moves to a discussion of how deviant behavior on the part of children became conceptualized as a medical problem, as well as why this happened. Conrad concludes with a discussion of some of the important implications that flow from the medicalization of deviant behavior. For example, the medical profession "has not only a monopoly on anything that can be conceptualized as illness," but also the power to define deviant behavior as a medical problem, so that certain procedures can be done that otherwise would not be allowed (e.g., cutting on the body). Moreover, society has a tendency to individualize social problems. Instead of looking to defects of social systems for causes and solutions, we look within the individuals or, instead of analyzing the social situation that affects a perceived difficult child, we prescribe a stimulant medication. Such a treatment strategy, Conrad asserts, deflects our attention away from the real possibility that the family or classroom situation may be the problem. This tendency to characterize problems in individual, clinical, or medical terms, instead of structural-organizational terms, is often the norm.

The selections by Spitzer and Conrad illustrate how, as a result of changing perceptions, behavior may not only become increasingly defined as deviant but may also become criminalized or medicalized. When this occurs, we can speak of the creation of deviant, criminal, or medical categories. And once the categories are in place, we can begin to analyze how others react to the violators of the categories. Many of the selections in Part IV and Part V offer specific illustrations of how actors may be responded to.

Blowing Smoke: Status Politics and the Shasta County Smoking Ban

4

Justin L. Tuggle
Malcolm D. Holmes

Over the past half century, perceptions of tobacco and its users have changed dramatically. In the 1940s and 1950s, cigarette smoking was socially accepted and commonly presumed to lack deleterious effects (see, e.g., Ram 1941). Survey data from the early 1950s showed that a minority believed cigarette smoking caused lung cancer (Viscusi 1992). By the late 1970s, however, estimates from survey data revealed that more than 90% of the population thought that this link existed (Roper Organization 1978). This and other harms associated with tobacco consumption have provided the impetus for an antismoking crusade that aims to normatively redefine smoking as deviant behavior (Markle and Troyer 1979).

There seems to be little question that tobacco is a damaging psychoactive substance characterized by highly adverse chronic health effects (Steinfeld 1991). In this regard, the social control movement probably makes considerable sense in terms of public policy. At the same time, much as ethnicity and religion played a significant role in the prohibition of alcohol (Gusfield 1963), social status may well play a part in this latest crusade.

Historically, attempts to control psychoactive substances have linked their use to categories of relatively powerless people. Marijuana use was associated with Mexican Americans (Bonnie and Whitebread 1970), cocaine with African Americans (Ashley 1975), opiates with Asians (Ben-Yehuda 1990), and alcohol with immigrant Catholics (Gusfield 1963). During the heyday of cigarette smoking, it was thought that

> Tobacco's the one blessing that nature has left for all humans to enjoy.
> It can be consumed by both the "haves" and "have nots" as a common
> leveler, one that brings all humans together from all walks of life re-
> gardless of class, race, or creed. (Ram, 1941, p. 125)

But in contrast to this earlier view, recent evidence has shown that occupational status (Ferrence 1989; Marcus et al. 1989; Covey et al. 1992), education (Ferrence 1989; Viscusi 1992) and family income (Viscusi 1992) are related negatively to current smoking. Further, the relationships of occupation and education to cigarette smoking have become stronger in later age cohorts (Ferrence 1989). Thus we ask, *is the association of tobacco with lower-status persons a factor in the crusade against smoking in public facilities?* Here we examine that question in a case study of a smoking ban implemented in Shasta County, California.

Status Politics and the Creation of Deviance

Deviance is socially constructed. Complex pluralistic societies have multiple, competing symbolic-moral universes that clash and negotiate (Ben-Yehuda 1990). Deviance is relative, and social morality is continually restructured. Moral, power, and stigma contests are ongoing, with competing symbolic-moral universes striving to legitimize particular lifestyles while making others deviant (Schur 1980; Ben-Yehuda 1990).

The ability to define and construct reality is closely connected to the power structure of society (Gusfield 1963). Inevitably, then, the distribution of deviance is associated with the system of stratification. The higher one's social position, the greater one's moral value (Ben-Yehuda 1990). Differences in lifestyles and moral beliefs are corollaries of social stratification (Gusfield 1963; Zurcher and Kirkpatrick 1976; Luker 1984). Accordingly, even though grounded in the system of stratification, status conflicts need not be instrumental; they may also be symbolic. Social stigma may, for instance, attach to behavior thought indicative of a weak will (Goffman 1963). Such moral anomalies occasion status degradation ceremonies, public denunciations expressing indignation not at a behavior per se, but rather against the individual motivational type that produced it (Garfinkle 1956). The denouncers act as public figures, drawing upon communally shared experience and speaking in the name of ultimate values. In this respect, status degradation involves a reciprocal element: Status conflicts and the resultant condemnation of a behavior characteristic of a particular status category symbolically enhances the status of the abstinent through the degradation of the participatory (Garfinkle 1956; Gusfield 1963).

Deviance creation involves political competition in which moral entrepreneurs originate moral crusades aimed at generating reform (Becker 1963; Schur 1980; Ben-Yehuda 1990). The alleged deficiencies of a specific social group are revealed and reviled by those crusading to define their behavior as deviant. As might be expected, successful moral crusades are generally dominated by those in the upper social strata of society (Becker 1963). Research on the anti-abortion (Luker 1984) and antipornography (Zurcher and Kirkpatrick 1976) crusades has shown that activists in these movements are of lower socioeconomic status than their opponents, helping explain the limited success of efforts to redefine abortion and pornography as deviance.

Moral entrepreneurs' goals may be either assimilative or coercive reform (Gusfield 1963). In the former instance, sympathy to the deviants' plight engenders integrative efforts aimed at lifting the repentant to the superior moral plane allegedly held by those of higher social status. The latter strategy emerges when deviants are viewed as intractably denying the moral and status superiority of the reformers' symbolic-moral universe. Thus, whereas assimilative reform may employ educative strategies, coercive reform turns to law and force for affirmation.

Regardless of aim, the moral entrepreneur cannot succeed alone. Success in establishing a moral crusade is dependent on acquiring broader public support. To that end, the moral entrepreneur must mobilize power, create a perceived threat potential for the moral issue in question, generate public awareness of the issue, propose a clear and acceptable solution to the problem, and overcome resistance to the crusade (Becker 1963; Ben-Yehuda 1990).

The Status Politics of Cigarette Smoking

The political dynamics underlying the definition of deviant behaviors may be seen clearly in efforts to end smoking in public facilities. Cigarettes were an insignificant product of the tobacco industry until the end of the 19th century, after which they evolved into its staple (U.S. Department of Health and Human Services 1992). Around the turn of the century, 14 states banned cigarette smoking and all but one other regulated sales to and possession by minors (Nuehring and Markle 1974). Yet by its heyday in the 1940s and 1950s, cigarette smoking was almost universally accepted, even considered socially desirable (Nuehring and Markle 1974; Steinfeld 1991). Per capita cigarette consumption in the United States peaked at approximately 4,300 cigarettes per year in the early 1960s, after which it declined to about 2,800 per year by the early 1990s (U.S. Department of Health and Human Services 1992). The beginning of the marked decline in cigarette consumption corresponded to the publication of the report to the surgeon general on the health risks of smoking (U.S. Department of Health, Education and Welfare 1964). Two decades later, the hazards of passive smoking were being publicized (e.g., U.S. Department of Health and Human Services 1986).

Increasingly, the recognition of the apparent relationship of smoking to health risks has socially demarcated the lifestyles of the smoker and nonsmoker, from widespread acceptance of the habit to polarized symbolic-moral universes. Attitudes about smoking are informed partly by medical issues, but perhaps even more critical are normative considerations (Nuehring and Markle 1974); more people have come to see smoking as socially reprehensible and deviant, and smokers as social misfits (Markle and Troyer 1979). Psychological assessments have attributed an array of negative evaluative characteristics to smokers (Markle and Troyer 1979). Their habit is increasingly thought unclean and intrusive.

Abstinence and bodily purity are the cornerstones of the nonsmoker's purported moral superiority (Feinhandler 1986). At the center of their symbolic-moral universe, then, is the idea that people have a right to breathe clean air in public spaces (Goodin 1989). Smokers, on the other hand, stake their claim to legitimacy in a precept of Anglo-Saxon political culture—the right to do whatever one wants unless it harms others (Berger 1986). Those sympathetic to smoking deny that environmental tobacco smoke poses a significant health hazard to the nonsmoker (Aviado 1986). Yet such arguments have held little sway in the face of counterclaims from authoritative governmental agencies and high status moral entrepreneurs.

The development of the antismoking movement has targeted a lifestyle particularly characteristic of the working classes (Berger 1986). Not only has there been an overall decline in cigarette smoking, but, as mentioned above, the negative relationships of occupation and education to cigarette smoking have become more pronounced in later age cohorts (Ferrence 1989). Moreover, moral entrepreneurs crusading against smoking are representatives of a relatively powerful "knowledge class," comprising people employed in areas such as education and the therapeutic and counseling agencies (Berger 1986).

Early remedial efforts focused on publicizing the perils of cigarette smokers, reflecting a strategy of assimilative reform (Neuhring and Markle 1974; Markle and Troyer 1979). Even many smokers expressed opposition to cigarettes and a generally repentant attitude. Early educative efforts were thus successful in decreasing cigarette consumption, despite resistance from the tobacco industry. Then, recognition of the adverse effects of smoking on nonusers helped precipitate a turn to coercive reform measures during the mid 1970s (Markle and Troyer 1979). Rather than a repentant friend in need of help, a new definition of the smoker as enemy emerged. Legal abolition of smoking in public facilities became one locus of social control efforts, and smoking bans in public spaces have been widely adopted in recent years (Markle and Troyer 1979; Goodin 1989).

The success of the antismoking crusade has been grounded in moral entrepreneurs' proficiency at mobilizing power, a mobilization made possible by highly visible governmental campaigns, the widely publicized health risks of smoking, and the proposal of workable and generally acceptable policies to ameliorate the problem. The success of this moral crusade has been further facilitated by the association of deviant characteristics with those in lower social strata, whose stigmatization reinforces existing relations of power and prestige. Despite the formidable resources and staunch opposition of the tobacco industry, the tide of public opinion and policy continues to move toward an antismoking stance.

Research Problem

The study presented below is an exploratory examination of the link between social status and support for a smoking ban in public facilities. Based on theorizing about status politics, as well as evidence about patterns of cigarette use, it was predicted that supporters of the smoking ban would be of higher status than those who opposed it. Further, it was anticipated that supporters of the ban would be more likely to make negative normative claims denouncing the allegedly deviant qualities of smoking, symbolically enhancing their own status while lowering that of their opponents.

The site of this research was Shasta County, California. The population of Shasta County is 147,036, of whom 66,462 reside in its only city, Redding (U.S. Bureau of the Census 1990). This county became the setting for the implementation of a hotly contested ban on smoking in public buildings.

In 1988, California voters passed Proposition 99, increasing cigarette taxes by 25 cents per pack. The purpose of the tax was to fund smoking prevention and treatment programs. Toward that end, Shasta County created the Shasta County Tobacco Education Program. The director of the program formed a coalition with officials of the Shasta County chapters of the American Cancer Society and American Lung Association to propose a smoking ban in all public buildings. The three groups formed an organization to promote that cause, Smoke-Free Air For Everyone (SAFE). Unlike other bans then in effect in California, the proposed ban included restaurants and bars, because its proponents considered these to be places in which people encountered significant amounts of secondhand smoke. They procured sufficient signatures on a petition to place the measure on the county's general ballot in November 1992.

The referendum passed with a 56% majority in an election that saw an 82% turnout. Subsequently, the Shasta County Hospitality and Business Alliance, an antiban coalition, obtained sufficient signatures to force a special election to annul the smoking ban. The special election was held in April 1993. Although the turnout was much lower (48%), again a sizable majority (58.4%) supported the ban. The ordinance went into effect on July 1, 1993.

Analytic Strategy

Three sources of data were analyzed in our effort to ascertain the moral and status conflicts underlying the Shasta County smoking ban. The first was interviews with five leading moral entrepreneurs and five prominent status quo defenders.[1] These individuals were selected through a snowball

---

[1]Although the term moral entrepreneur is well established in the literature on deviance, there seems to be little attention to or consistency in a corresponding term for the interest group(s) opposing them. Those that have been employed, such as "forces for the status quo" (Markle and Troyer 1979), tend to be awkward. "Status quo defenders" is used here for lack of a simpler or more common term.

sample, with the original respondents identified through interviews with business owners or political advertisements in the local mass media. The selected respondents repeatedly surfaced as the leading figures in their respective coalitions. Semistructured interviews were conducted to determine the reasons underlying their involvement. These data were critical to understanding how the proposed ban was framed by small groups of influential proponents and opponents; it was expected that their concerns would be reflected in the larger public debate about the ban.

A second source of data was letters to the editor of the local paper, the *Record Searchlight*. There were 105 letters published during the periods leading up to the two elections. The editor stated that all letters concerning the ban were published, with none being shortened or otherwise edited. The letters were content-analyzed, with each specific mention of individual rights, health, negative normative evaluations, and purported business effects of the ban being recorded, along with whether the writer was pro- or antiban. The content analysis provides a broader picture of the issues underlying the public debate about the proposed ban. It is particularly noteworthy that most proban writers were nonsmokers and most antiban writers were smokers.[2]

To identify socioeconomic status differences underlying their competing positions on the smoking ban, a measure of each letter writer's personal wealth was obtained. Public documents in the Shasta County Tax Assessor's office provided the number of properties owned by each letter writer and the value of each property. These values were summed to obtain the owner's cumulative property value. There were 57 proban property owners and 31 antiban owners included in the analysis.[3] Whereas the content analysis examined the ideological and symbolic framework of the debate, this comparison permitted an assessment of whether differences in economic status distinguished the pro- and antiban writers, reflecting the negative relationship between socioeconomic status variables and smoking.

▶Findings

Moral Entrepreneur/Status Quo Defender Interviews

The moral entrepreneurs and status quo defenders interviewed represented clearly different interests. The former group included three high-level administrators in the county's chapters of the American Cancer

[2]Most of the pro- and antiban letter writers indicated in their letters whether they smoked. Not surprisingly, among those who revealed their smoking behavior, virtually all ban supporters were nonsmokers, whereas ban opponents were smokers.

[3]Persons who wrote multiple letters were included in the property value analysis only once; there were 10 multiple letter writers, all of whom were proban. Renters were excluded from the analysis; there were 4 renters among the proban writers and 3 among those who were antiban.

Society and American Lung Association. A fourth was an administrator for the Shasta County Tobacco Education Project. The last member of this group was a pulmonary physician affiliated with a local hospital. The latter group included four bar and/or restaurant owners and an attorney who had been hired to represent their interests. Thus the status quo defenders were small business owners who might see their economic interests affected adversely by the ban. Importantly, they were representatives of a less prestigious social stratum than the moral entrepreneurs.

The primary concern of the moral entrepreneurs was health. As one stated,

> I supported the initiative to get the smoking ban on the ballot because of all the health implications that secondhand smoke can create. Smoking and secondhand smoke are the most preventable causes of death in this nation.

Another offered that

> On average, secondhand smoke kills 53,000 Americans each year. And think about those that it kills in other countries! It contains 43 cancer-causing chemical agents that have been verified by the Environmental Protection Agency. It is now listed as a Type A carcinogen, which is in the same category as asbestos.

Every one of the moral entrepreneurs expressed concern about health issues during the interviews. This was not the only point they raised, however. Three of the five made negative normative evaluations of smoking, thereby implicitly degrading the status of smokers. They commented that "smoking is no longer an acceptable action," that "smoke stinks," or that "it is just a dirty and annoying habit." Thus, whereas health was their primary concern, such comments revealed the moral entrepreneurs' negative view of smoking irrespective of any medical issues. Smokers were seen as engaging in unclean and objectionable behavior—stigmatized qualities defining their deviant social status.

The stance of the status quo defenders was also grounded in two arguments. All of them expressed concern about individual rights. As one put it,

> I opposed that smoking ban because I personally smoke and feel that it is an infringement of my rights to tell me where I can and cannot smoke. Smoking is a legal activity, and therefore it is unconstitutional to take that right away from me.

Another argued that

> Many people have died for us to have these rights in foreign wars and those also fought on American soil. Hundreds of thousands of people thought that these rights were worth dying for, and now some small group of people believe that they can just vote away these rights.

Such symbolism implies that smoking is virtually a patriotic calling, a venerable habit for which people have been willing to forfeit their lives in time of war. In the status quo defenders' view, smoking is a constitutionally protected right.

At the same time, each of the status quo defenders was concerned about more practical matters, namely business profits. As one stated, "my income was going to be greatly affected." Another argued,

> If these people owned some of the businesses that they are including in this ban, they would not like it either. By taking away the customers that smoke, they are taking away the mainstay of people from a lot of businesses.

The competing viewpoints of the moral entrepreneurs and status quo defenders revealed the moral issues—health versus individual rights—at the heart of political conflict over the smoking ban. Yet it appears that status issues also fueled the conflict. On the one hand, the moral entrepreneurs denigrated smoking, emphasizing the socially unacceptable qualities of the behavior and symbolically degrading smokers' status. On the other hand, status quo defenders were concerned that their livelihood would be affected by the ban. Interestingly, the occupational status of the two groups differed, with the moral entrepreneurs representing the new knowledge class, and the status quo defenders a lower stratum of small business owners. Those in the latter group may not have been accorded the prestige and trust granted those in the former (Berger 1986). Moreover, the status quo defenders' concern about business was likely seen as self-aggrandizing.

Letters to the Editor

Soon after the moral entrepreneurs went public with their plan to end smoking in public buildings, the general populace became engaged in the debate. Of course the dialogue was carried on in many arenas, most of which left no observable record. A noteworthy exception is letters to the editor, where the competing viewpoints were again exhibited.

As to be expected, the proban writers ($n = 71$) emphasized the issue of health. Sixty nine percent of the proban writers raised this issue, whereas it was mentioned in approximately 18% of the antiban letters ($n = 34$). This substantial difference in the proportion of letters mentioning health from the two camps was statistically significant ($p < .0005$) in the test for differences in proportions (see Blalock 1979, pp. 232–234).[4] Analyzed differently,

---

[4]Significance tests are generally employed to make inferences from samples to populations. In this respect, they are unnecessary with these data because the population of letters is included. That fact notwithstanding, they may also be used to make inferences about causal processes that generate population data (see Blalock 1979, pp. 241–243). The latter use is consistent with our aims and, accordingly, they were reported here. One-tailed tests were reported because all findings were consistent with expectations.

health was mentioned 1.56 times on average (mean) in the proban letters, compared with only .26 times in the antiban letters ($t = 5.39$; $df = 103$; $p < .0005$). That is, proban writers were six times more likely than those who opposed it to mention this concern.

The issue of individual rights also appeared frequently in the letters to the editor, with debate focusing on the right to smoke versus the right not to be subjected to cigarette smoke. Because the issue of individual rights was a cornerstone of the status quo defenders' argument, it is not surprising that this concern was expressed more frequently by the antiban writers. Individual rights were mentioned in approximately 76% of antiban letters, compared with 48% of proban letters. The difference in the proportion of pro- and antiban letters raising this issue was statistically significant ($p < .005$). It was mentioned an average of 1.97 times in the antiban letters and 1.21 times in those supporting the ban ($t = 1.98$; $df = 103$; $p < .025$). Although a substantial difference in the pro- and antiban writers' views again surfaced, it was smaller than observed with respect to health because both sides had concerns about individual rights—that to smoke versus that to clean air.

In addition to concerns about health and individual rights, normative negative evaluations surfaced. For example, one proban writer called smokers "ignorant" and alleged that they used "nicotine-stained lies." On the other side, an antiban writer called ban supporters "clean air freaks." More than 22% of proban letters included such comments, compared with about 15% of those opposing the ban. Although consistent with expectations, this difference is not statistically different. On average, the proban letters contained .38 negative normative evaluations, compared with .15 of the antiban commentaries ($t = 1.94$; $df = 103$; $p < .05$). Thus they appeared two and one half times as often in the proban letters. Letter writers from both sides made negative normative evaluations questioning the character of their opponents, implicitly attacking their social credibility and status. But, like the moral entrepreneurs, proban writers made such claims more frequently.

The pro- and antiban writers were about equally likely to mention possible business effects of the ban (22.5% and 26.4%, respectively), with the issue mentioned an average of .44 times in the letters of both sides. Concerns about business consequences were not as paramount for antiban writers from the general public as for the status quo defenders, who had vested business interests. The antiban writers who mentioned the issue shared the status quo defenders' view that the ban would adversely affect the business of restaurants and bars. The proban writers who mentioned business effects were of the opinion that there would be no impact or that business would actually improve as a result of the ban.

For the public, then, it appears that the primary issues were ethical and moral—the right to health versus the right to smoke. Nonetheless, negative normative evaluations were also employed as a technique of status degradation, especially by those supporting the ban.

Letter Writers' Cumulative Property Value

To better understand the potential status conflicts underlying the opposing viewpoints on the ban, the letter writers' cumulative property values were compared. Here substantial differences in the backgrounds of the pro- and antiban writers appeared. The median cumulative property value for the proban writers was $101,516, compared with $68,766 for the antiban writers.

Table 1 presents a cross-classification of ban support by authors' property value. Here it may be seen clearly that, in general, as property value increased, support for the ban increased. Not only is the positive relationship significant ($p < .05$), Cramer's V (.375) shows that it is fairly strong. A slight nonlinearity appears in the $150,000 to $199,999 property value category, where antiban writers outnumbered proban writers. This irregularity probably occurred because of several bar and restaurant owners in this income range, who feared their business interests would be affected adversely and were among the antiban letter writers.

Comparison of the cumulative property values reveals a difference not discernible from the content of the letters—economic status appears to have been an important determinant of support for the smoking ban. This relationship clearly corresponds to the negative one between socioeconomic status and smoking.

Summary and Discussion

This research has examined the moral and status politics underlying the implementation of a smoking ban in Shasta County, California. Moral entrepreneurs crusading for the ban argued that secondhand smoke damages

Table 1 Frequencies and column percentages for the cross-classification of support for the smoking ban by letter writer's property value ($N = 88$)

	Letter writer's property value in dollars				
Support for ban	1 to 49,999 (%)	50,000 to 99,999 (%)	100,000 to 149,999 (%)	150,000 to 199,999 (%)	200,000 and up (%)
	10	19	13	4	11
Proban	(43.5)	(73.1)	(86.7)	(40.0)	(78.6)
	13	7	2	6	3
Antiban	(56.5)	(26.9)	(13.3)	(60.0)	(21.4)
Total	23	26	15	10	14

Note. $\chi^2 = 12.37$; $df = 3$; $p < .05$; Cramer's $V = .375$.

health, implicitly grounding their argument in the principle that people have a right to a smoke-free environment. Status quo defenders countered that smokers have a constitutional right to indulge wherever and whenever they see fit. Public discourse echoed these themes, as seen in the letters to the editor of the local newspaper. Thus debate about the smoking ban focused especially on health versus smokers' rights; yet evidence of social status differences between the competing symbolic-moral universes also surfaced. Competing symbolic-moral universes are defined not only by different ethical viewpoints on a behavior, but also by differences in social power—disparities inevitably linked to the system of stratification (Ben-Yehuda 1990). Those prevailing in moral and stigma contests typically represent the higher socioeconomic echelons of society.

The moral entrepreneurs who engineered the smoking ban campaign were representatives of the prestigious knowledge class, including among their members officials from the local chapters of respected organizations at the forefront of the national antismoking crusade. In contrast, the small business owners who were at the core of the opposing coalition, of status quo defenders, represented the traditional middle class. Clearly, there was an instrumental quality to the restaurant and bar owners' stance, because they saw the ban as potentially damaging to their business interests. But they were unable to shape the public debate, as demonstrated by the letters to the editor.

An even more distinct difference in social status appears when the cumulative property values of the two letter-writing camps is compared. There was a significant gap between the property values of the pro- and antiban writers, with a fairly strong positive relationship appearing when property value and support for the ban are cross-tabulated. Although the letter writers were probably not representative of the population of Shasta County, insofar as nearly all were property owners, this finding plainly parallels the negative relationships between indicators of socioeconomic status and smoking.

In many respects, the status conflicts involved in the passage of the Shasta County smoking ban were symbolic. The moral entrepreneurs focused attention on the normatively undesirable qualities of cigarette smoking, and their negative normative evaluations of smoking were reflected in public debate about the ban. Those who wrote in support of the ban more frequently offered negative normative evaluations than antiban writers; their comments degraded smoking and, implicitly, smokers. Since the advent of the antismoking crusade in the United States, smoking has come to be seen as socially reprehensible, smokers as social misfits characterized by negative psychological characteristics (Markle and Troyer 1979).

Ultimately, a lifestyle associated with the less educated, less affluent, lower occupational strata was stigmatized as a public health hazard and targeted for coercive reform. Its deviant status was codified in the ordinance banning smoking in public facilities, including restaurants and bars. The ban symbolized the deviant status of cigarette smokers, the prohibition visibly demonstrating the community's condemnation of their behavior. Further, the smoking ban symbolically amplified the purported virtues of the abstinent lifestyle. A political victory such as the passage of a law is a prestige-enhancing symbolic triumph that is perhaps even more rewarding than its end result (Gusfield 1963). The symbolic nature of the ban serendipitously surfaced in another way during one author's unstructured observations in 42 restaurants and 21 bars in the area: Whereas smoking was not observed in a single restaurant, it occurred without sanction in all but one of the bars. Although not deterring smoking in one of its traditional bastions, the ban called attention to its deviant quality and, instrumentally, effectively halted it in areas more commonly frequently by the abstemious.

Although more systematic research is needed, the findings of this exploratory case study offer a better understanding of the dynamics underlying opposition to smoking and further support to theorizing about the role of status politics in the creation of deviant types. Denunciation of smoking in Shasta County involved not only legitimate allegations about public health, but negative normative evaluations of those engaged in the behavior. In the latter regard, the ban constituted a status degradation ceremony, symbolically differentiating the pure and abstinent from the unclean and intrusive. Not coincidentally, the stigmatized were more likely found among society's lower socioeconomic strata, their denouncers among its higher echelons.

Certainly the class and ethnic antipathies underlying attacks on cocaine and opiate users earlier in the century were more manifest than those revealed in the crusade against cigarette smoking. But neither are there manifest status conflicts in the present crusades against abortion (Luker 1984) and pornography (Zurcher and Kirkpatrick 1976); yet the underlying differences of status between opponents in those movements are reflected in their markedly different symbolic-moral universes, as was the case in the present study.

This is not to suggest that smoking should be an approved behavior. The medical evidence seems compelling: Cigarette smoking is harmful to the individual smoker and to those exposed to secondhand smoke. However, the objective harms of the psychoactive substance in question are irrelevant to the validity of our analysis, just as they were to Gusfield's (1963) analysis of the temperance movement's crusade against alcohol use. Moreover, it is not our intention to imply that the proban supporters consciously intended to degrade those of lower social status. No doubt they were motivated primarily by a sincere belief that smoking constitutes a public health hazard. In the end, however, moral indignation and social control flowed down the social hierarchy. Thus we must ask: Would cigarette smoking be defined as deviant if there were a positive correlation between smoking and socioeconomic status?

References

Ashley, Richard. 1975. *Cocaine: Its History, Uses, and Effects.* New York: St. Martin's Press.

Aviado, Domingo M. 1986. "Health Issues Relating to 'Passive' Smoking." Pp. 137–165 in *Smoking and Society: Toward a More Balanced Assessment,* edited by Robert D. Tollison. Lexington, MA: Lexington Books.

Becker, Howard S. 1963. *Outsiders: Studies in the Sociology of Deviance.* New York: Free Press.

Ben-Yehuda, Nachman. 1990. *The Politics and Morality of Deviance: Moral Panics, Drug Abuse, Deviant Science, and Reversed Stigmatization.* Albany, NY: State University of New York Press.

Berger, Peter L. 1986. "A Sociological View of the Antismoking Phenomenon." Pp. 225–240 in *Smoking and Society: Toward a More Balanced Assessment,* edited by Robert D. Tollison. Lexington, MA: Lexington Books.

Blalock, Hubert M. Jr. 1979. *Social Statistics* 2d ed, Rev. New York: McGraw-Hill.

Bonnie, Richard J., and Charles H. Whitebread II. 1970. "The Forbidden Fruit and the Tree of Knowledge: An Inquiry into the Legal History of American Marihuana Prohibition." *Virginia Law Review* 56:971–1203.

Covey, Lirio S., Edith A. Zang, and Ernst L. Wynder. 1992. "Cigarette Smoking and Occupational Status: 1977 to 1990." *American Journal of Public Health* 82:1230–1234.

Feinhandler, Sherwin J. 1986. *The Social Role of Smoking* Pp. 167–187 in *Smoking and Society: Toward a More Balanced Assessment,* edited by Robert D. Tollison. Lexington, MA: Lexington Books.

Ferrence, Roberta G. 1989. *Deadly Fashion: The Rise and Fall of Cigarette Smoking in North America.* New York: Garland.

Garfinkle, Harold. 1956. "Conditions of Successful Degradation Ceremonies." *American Journal of Sociology* 61:402–424.

Goffman, Erving. 1963. *Stigma: Notes on the Management of Spoiled Identity.* Englewood Cliffs, NJ: Prentice-Hall.

Goodin, Robert E. 1989. *No Smoking: The Ethical Issues.* Chicago: University of Chicago Press.

Gusfield, Joseph R. 1963. *Symbolic Crusade: Status Politics and the American Temperance Movement.* Urbana, IL: University of Illinois Press.

Luker, Kristin. 1984. *Abortion and the Politics of Motherhood.* Berkeley, CA: University of California.

Marcus, Alfred C., Donald R. Shopland, Lori A. Crane, and William R. Lynn. 1989. "Prevalence of Cigarette Smoking in United States: Estimates From the 1985 Current Population Survey." *Journal of the National Cancer Institute* 81:409–414.

Markle, Gerald E., and Ronald J. Troyer. 1979. "Smoke Gets in Your Eyes: Cigarette Smoking as Deviant Behavior." *Social Problems* 26:611–625.

Neuhring, Elane, and Gerald E. Markle. 1974. "Nicotine and Norms: The Re-Emergence of a Deviant Behavior." *Social Problems* 21:513–526.

Ram, Sidney P. 1941. How to Get More Fun Out of Smoking. Chicago: Cuneo.

Roper Organization. 1978, May. *A Study of Public Attitudes Toward Cigarette Smoking and the Tobacco Industry in 1978, Volume 1.* New York: Roper.

Schur, Edwin M. 1980. *The Politics of Deviance: Stigma Contests and the Uses of Power.* New York: Random House.

Steinfeld, Jesse. 1991. "Combating Smoking in the United States: Progress Through Science and Social Action." *Journal of the National Cancer Institute* 83:1126–1127.

U.S. Bureau of the Census. 1990. *General Population Characteristics.* Washington, DC: U.S. Government Printing Office.

U.S. Department of Health, Education and Welfare. 1964. *Smoking and Health: Report of the Advisory Committee to the Surgeon General of the Public Health Service.* Washington, DC: U.S. Government Printing Office.

U.S. Department of Health and Human Services. 1986. *The Health Consequences of Involuntary Smoking. A Report of the Surgeon General.* Washington, DC: U.S. Government Printing Office.

U.S. Department of Health and Human Services. 1992. *Smoking and Health in the Americas. A 1992 Report of the Surgeon General, in Collaboration with the Pan American Health Organization.* Washington, DC: U.S. Government Printing Office.

Viscusi, W. Kip. 1992. *Smoking: Making the Risky Decision.* New York: Oxford University Press.

Zurcher, Louis A. Jr., and R. George Kirkpatrick. 1976. *Citizens for Decency: Antipornography Crusades as Status Defense.* Austin, TX: University of Texas Press.

The Production of Deviance in Capitalist Society

Steven Spitzer

• • •

The concept of deviance production offers a starting point for the analysis of both deviance and control. But for such a construct to serve as a critical tool it must be grounded in a historical and structural investigation of society. For Marx, the crucial unit of analysis is the mode of production that dominates a given historical period. If we are to have a Marxian theory of deviance, therefore, deviance production must be understood in relationship to specific forms of socio-economic organization. In our society, productive activity is organized capitalistically, and it is ultimately defined by "the process that transforms on the one hand, the social means of subsistence and of production into capital, on the other hand the immediate producers into wage labourers" (Marx, 1967:714).

There are two features of the capitalist mode of production important for purposes of this discussion. First, as a mode of production it forms the foundation or infrastructure of our society. This means that the starting point of our analysis must be an understanding of the economic organization of capitalist societies and the impact of that organization on all aspects of social life. But the capitalist mode of production is an important starting point in another sense. It contains contradictions which reflect the internal tendencies of capitalism. These contradictions are important because they explain the changing character of the capitalist system and the nature of its impact on social, political, and intellectual activity. The formulation of a Marxist perspective on deviance requires the interpretation of the process through which the contradictions of capitalism are expressed. In particular, the theory must illustrate the relationship between specific contradictions, the problems of capitalist development, and the production of a deviant class.

The superstructure of society emerges from and reflects the ongoing development of economic forces (the infrastructure). In class societies this superstructure preserves the hegemony of the ruling class through a system of class controls. These controls, which are institutionalized in the family, church, private associations, media, schools, and the state, provide a mechanism for coping with the contradictions and achieving the aims of capitalist development.

Among the most important functions served by the superstructure in capitalist societies is the regulation and management of problem populations. Because deviance processing is only one of the methods available for social control, these groups supply raw material for deviance production, but are by no means synonymous with deviant populations. Problem populations tend to share a number of social characteristics, but most important among these is the fact that their behavior, personal qualities, and/or position threaten the *social relations of production* in capitalist societies. In other words, populations become generally eligible for management as deviant when they disturb, hinder, or call into question any of the following:

1. capitalist modes of appropriating the product of human labor (e.g. when the poor "steal" from the rich)
2. the social conditions under which capitalist production takes place (e.g. those who refuse or are unable to perform wage labor)
3. patterns of distribution and consumption in capitalist society (e.g. those who use drugs for escape and transcendence rather than sociability and adjustment)
4. the process of socialization for productive and non-productive roles (e.g. youth who refuse to be schooled or those who deny the validity of "family life")[1]
5. the ideology which supports the functioning of capitalist society (e.g. proponents of alternative forms of social organization)

Although problem populations are defined in terms of the threat and costs that they present to the social relations of production in capitalist societies, these populations are far from isomorphic with a revolutionary class. It is certainly true that some members of the problem population may under specific circumstances possess revolutionary potential. But this potential can only be realized if the problematic group is located in a position of functional indispensability within the capitalist system. Historically, capitalist societies have been quite successful in transforming those who are problematic and indispensable (the protorevolutionary class) into groups who are either problematic and dispensable (candidates for deviance processing), or indispensable but not problematic (supporters of the capitalist order). On the other hand, simply because a group is manageable does not mean that it ceases to be a problem for the capitalist class. Even though dispensable problem populations cannot overturn the capitalist system, they can represent a significant impediment to its maintenance and growth. It is in this sense that they become eligible for management as deviants.

Problem populations are created in two ways—either directly through the expression of fundamental contradictions in the capitalist mode of production or indirectly through disturbances in the system of class rule. An example of the first process is found in Marx's analysis of the "relative surplus-population."

Writing on the "General Law of Capitalist Accumulation" Marx explains how increased social redundance is inherent in the development of the capitalist mode of production:

> With the extension of the scale of production, and the mass of the labourers set in motion, with the greater breadth and fullness of all sources of wealth, there is also an extension of the scale on which greater attraction of labourers by capital is accompanied by their greater repulsion. . . . The labouring population therefore produces, along with the accumulation of capital produced by it, the means by which itself is made relatively superfluous, . . . and it does this to an always increasing extent (Marx, 1967:631).

In its most limited sense the production of a relative surplus-population involves the creation of a class which is economically redundant. But insofar as the conditions of economic existence determine social existence, this process helps explain the emergence of groups who become both threatening and vulnerable at the same time. The marginal status of these populations reduces their stake in the maintenance of the system while their powerlessness and dispensability renders them increasingly susceptible to the mechanisms of official control.

The paradox surrounding the production of the relative surplus-population is that this population is both useful and menacing to the accumulation of capital. Marx describes how the relative surplus-population "forms a disposable industrial army, that belongs to capital quite as absolutely as if the latter had bred it at its own cost," and how this army "creates, for the changing needs of the self-expansion of capital, a mass of human material always ready for exploitation" (Marx, 1967:632).

On the other hand, it is apparent that an excessive increase in what Marx called the "lowest sediment" of the relative surplus-population might seriously impair the growth of capital. The social expenses and threat to social harmony created by a large and economically stagnant surplus-population could jeopardize the preconditions for accumulation by undermining the ideology of equality so essential to the legitimation of production relations in bourgeois democracies, diverting revenues away from capital investment toward control and support operations, and providing a basis for political organization of the dispossessed.[2] To the extent that the relative surplus-population confronts the capitalist class as a threat to the social relations of production, it reflects an important contradiction in modern capitalist societies: a surplus-population is a necessary product of and condition for the accumulation of wealth on a capitalist basis, but it also creates a form of social expense which must be neutralized or controlled if production relations and conditions for increased accumulation are to remain unimpaired.

Problem populations are also generated through contradictions which develop in the system of class rule. The institutions which make up the superstructure of capitalist society originate and are maintained to guarantee the interests of the capitalist class. Yet these institutions necessarily reproduce, rather than resolve, the contradictions of the capitalist order. In a dialectical fashion, arrangements which arise in order to buttress capitalism are transformed into their opposite—structures for the cultivation of internal threats. An instructive example of this process is found in the emergence and transformation of educational institutions in the United States.

The introduction of mass education in the United States can be traced to the developing needs of corporate capitalism (cf. Karier, 1973; Cohen and Lazerson, 1972; Bowles and Gintis, 1972; Spring, 1972). Compulsory education provided a means of training, testing and sorting, and assimilating wage-laborers, as well as withholding certain populations from the labor market. The system was also intended to preserve the values of bourgeois society and operate as an "inexpensive form of police" (Spring, 1973: 31). However, as Gintis (1973) and Bowles (1973) have suggested, the internal contradictions of schooling can lead to effects opposite of those intended. For the poor, early schooling can make explicit the oppressiveness and alienating character of capitalist institutions, while higher education can instill critical abilities which lead students to "bite the hand that feeds them." In both cases educational institutions create troublesome populations (i.e. dropouts and student radicals) and contribute to the very problems they were designed to solve.

After understanding how and why specific groups become generally bothersome in capitalist society, it is necessary to investigate the conditions under which these groups are transformed into proper objects for social control. In other words, we must ask what distinguishes the generally problematic from the specifically deviant. The rate at which problem populations are converted into deviants will reflect the relationship between these populations and the control system. This rate is likely to be influenced by the:

(1) *Extensiveness and Intensity of State Controls.* Deviance processing (as opposed to other control measures) is more likely to occur when problem management is monopolized by the state. As state controls are applied more generally, the proportion of official deviants will increase.

(2) *Size and Level of Threat Presented by the Problem Population.* The larger and more threatening the problem population, the greater the likelihood that this population will have to be controlled through deviance processing rather than other methods. As the threat created by these populations exceeds the capacities of informal restraints, their management requires a broadening of the reaction system and an increasing centralization and coordination of control activities.

(3) *Level of Organization of the Problem Population.* When and if problem populations are able to organize and develop limited amounts of political power, deviance processing becomes increasingly less effective as a tool for social control. The attribution of deviant status is most likely to occur when a group is relatively impotent and atomized.

(4) *Effectiveness of Control Structures Organized through Civil Society.* The greater the effectiveness of the organs of civil society (i.e. the family, church, media, schools, sports) in solving the problems of class control, the less the likelihood that deviance processing (a more explicitly political process) will be employed.

(5) *Availability and Effectiveness of Alternative Types of Official Processing.* In some cases the state will be able effectively to incorporate certain segments of the problem population into specially created "pro-social" roles. In the modern era, for example, conscription and public works projects (Piven and Cloward, 1971) helped neutralize the problems posed by troublesome populations without creating new or expanding old deviant categories.

(6) *Availability and Effectiveness of Parallel Control Structures.* In many instances the state can transfer its costs of deviance production by supporting or at least tolerating the activities of independent control networks which operate in its interests. For example, when the state is denied or is reluctant to assert a monopoly over the use of force, it is frequently willing to encourage vigilante organizations and private police in the suppression of problem populations. Similarly, the state is often benefited by the policies and practices of organized crime, insofar as these activities help pacify, contain, and enforce order among potentially disruptive groups (Schelling, 1967).

(7) *Utility of Problem Populations.* While problem populations are defined in terms of their threat and costs to capitalist relations of production, they are not threatening in every respect. They can be supportive economically (as part of a surplus labor pool or dual labor market), politically (as evidence of the need for state intervention), and ideologically (as scapegoats for rising discontent). In other words, under certain conditions capitalist societies derive benefits from maintaining a number of visible and uncontrolled "troublemakers" in their midst. Such populations are distinguished by the fact that while they remain generally bothersome, the costs that they inflict are most immediately absorbed by other members of the problem population. Policies evolve, not so much to eliminate or actively suppress these groups, but to deflect their threat away from targets which are sacred to the capitalist class. Victimization is permitted and even encouraged, as long as the victims are members of an expendable class.

Two or more or less discrete groupings are established through the operations of official control. These groups are a product of different operating assumptions and administrative orientations toward the deviant population. On the one hand, there is *social junk* which, from the point of view of the dominant class, is a costly yet relatively harmless burden to society. The discreditability of social junk resides in the failure, inability, or refusal of this group to participate in the roles supportive of capitalist society. Social junk is most likely to come to official attention when informal resources have been exhausted or when the magnitude of the problem becomes significant enough to create a basis for "public concern." Since the threat presented by social junk is passive, growing out of its inability to compete and its withdrawal from the prevailing social order, controls are usually designed to regulate and contain rather than eliminate and suppress the problem. Clear-cut examples of social junk in modern capitalist societies might include the officially administered aged, handicapped, mentally ill, and mentally retarded.

In contrast to social junk, there is a category that can be roughly described as *social dynamite*. The essential quality of deviance managed as social dynamite is its potential actively to call into question established relationships, especially relations of production and domination. Generally, therefore, social dynamite tends to be more youthful, alienated, and politically volatile than social junk. The control of social dynamite is usually premised on an assumption that the problem is acute in nature, requiring a rapid and focused expenditure of control resources. This is in contrast to the handling of social junk frequently based on a belief that the problem is chronic and best controlled through broad reactive rather than intensive and selective measures. Correspondingly, social dynamite is normally processed through the legal system with its capacity for active intervention, while social junk is frequently (but not always)[3] administered by the agencies and agents of the therapeutic and welfare state.

Many varieties of deviant populations are alternatively or simultaneously dealt with as either social junk and/or social dynamite. The welfare poor, homosexuals, alcoholics, and "problem children" are among the categories reflecting the equivocal nature of the control process and its dependence on the political, economic, and ideological priorities of deviance production. The changing nature of these priorities and their implications for the future may be best understood by examining some of the tendencies of modern capitalist systems.

• • •

Notes

1. To the extent that a group (e.g. homosexuals) blatantly and systematically challenges the validity of the bourgeois family it is likely to become part of the problem population. The family is essential to capitalist society as a unit for consumption, socialization, and the reproduction of the socially necessary labor force (cf. Frankford and Snitow, 1972; Secombe, 1973; Zaretsky, 1973).

2. O'Connor (1973) discusses this problem in terms of the crisis faced by the capitalist state in maintaining conditions for profitable accumulation and social harmony.

3. It has been estimated, for instance, that one-third of all arrests in America are for the offense of public drunkenness. Most of these apparently involve "sick" and destitute "skid row alcoholics" (Morris and Hawkins, 1969).

References

Baran, Paul, and Paul M. Sweezy. 1966. Monopoly Capital. New York: Monthly Review Press.

Becker, Howard S. 1967. "Whose side are we on?" Social Problems 14(Winter): 239–247.

Becker, Howard, S., and Irving Louis Horowitz. 1972. "Radical politics and sociological research: Observations on methodology and ideology." American Journal of Sociology 78(July): 48–66.

Blauner, Robert. 1969. "Internal colonialism and ghetto revolt." Social Problems 16(Spring): 393–408.

Bowles, Samuel. 1973. "Contradictions in United States higher education." Pp. 165–199 in James H. Weaver (ed.), Modern Political Economy: Radical versus Orthodox Approaches. Boston: Allyn and Bacon.

Bowles, Samuel, and Herbert Gintis. 1972. "I.Q. in the U.S. class structure." Social Policy 3(November/December): 65–96.

Bureau of Prisons. 1972. National Prisoner Statistics. Prisoners in State and Federal Institutions for Adult Felons. Washington, D.C.: Bureau of Prisons.

Cohen, David K., and Marvin Lazerson. 1972. "Education and the corporate order." Socialist Revolution (March/April): 48–72.

Foucault, Michel. 1965. Madness and Civilization. New York: Random House.

Frankford, Evelyn, and Ann Snitow. 1972. "The trap of domesticity: Notes on the family." Socialist Revolution (July/August): 83–94.

Gintis, Herbert. 1973. "Alienation and power." Pp. 431–465 in James H. Weaver (ed.), Modern Political Economy: Radical versus Orthodox Approaches. Boston: Allyn and Bacon.

Gorz, Andre. 1970. "Capitalist relations of production and the socially necessary labor force." Pp. 155–171 in Arthur Lothstein (ed.), All We Are Saying. . . . New York: G. P. Putnam.

Gross, Bertram M. 1970. "Friendly fascism: A model for America." Social Policy (November/December): 44–52.

Helmer, John, and Thomas Vietorisz. 1973. "Drug use, the labor market and class conflict." Paper presented at Annual Meeting of the American Sociological Association.

Karier, Clarence J. 1973. "Business values and the educational state." Pp. 6–29 in Clarence J. Karier, Paul Violas, and Joel Spring (eds.), Roots of Crisis: American Education in the Twentieth Century. Chicago: Rand McNally.

Liazos, Alexander. 1972. "The poverty of the sociology of deviance: Nuts, sluts and preverts." Social Problems 20(Summer): 103–120.

Mandel, Ernest. 1968. Marxist Economic Theory (Volume I). New York: Monthly Review Press.

Marcuse, Herbert. 1964. One-Dimensional Man. Boston: Beacon Press.

Marx, Karl. 1964. Class Struggles in France, 1848–1850. New York: International Publishers; 1967. Capital (Volume I). New York: International Publishers.

Matza, David. 1969. Becoming Deviant. Englewood Cliffs, N.J.: Prentice Hall.

McIntosh, Mary. 1973. "The growth of racketeering." Economy and Society (February): 35–69.

Morris, Norval, and Gordon Hawkins. 1969. The Honest Politician's Guide to Crime Control. Chicago: University of Chicago Press.

Musto, David F. 1973. The American Disease: Origins of Narcotic Control. New Haven: Yale University Press.

National Institute of Mental Health. 1970. Trends in Resident Patients—State and County Mental Hospitals 1950–1968. Biometry Branch, Office of Program Planning and Evaluation. Rockville, Maryland: National Institute of Mental Health.

O'Connor, James. 1973. The Fiscal Crisis of the State. New York: St. Martin's Press.

Piven, Frances, and Richard A. Cloward. 1971. Regulating the Poor: The Functions of Public Welfare. New York: Random House.

Rimlinger, Gaston V. 1961. "Social security, incentives, and controls in the U.S. and U.S.S.R." Comparative Studies in Society and History 4(November): 104–124; 1966. "Welfare policy and economic development: A comparative historical perspective." Journal of Economic History (December): 556–571.

Schelling, Thomas. 1967. "Economics and criminal enterprise." Public Interest (Spring): 61–78.

Secombe, Wally. 1973. "The housewife and her labour under capitalism." New Left Review (January–February): 3–24.

Spring, Joel. 1972. Education and the Rise of the Corporate State. Boston: Beacon Press; 1973. "Education as a form of social control." Pp. 30–39 in Clarence J. Karier, Paul Violas, and Joel Spring (eds.), Roots of Crisis: American Education in the Twentieth Century. Chicago: Rand McNally.

Turk, Austin T. 1969. Criminality and Legal Order. Chicago: Rand McNally.

Zaretsky, Eli. 1973. "Capitalism, the family and personal life: Parts 1 & 2." Socialist Revolution (January–April/May–June): 69–126, 19–70.

The Discovery of Hyperkinesis: Notes on the Medicalization of Deviant Behavior

6

Peter Conrad

Introduction

The increasing medicalization of deviant behavior and the medical institution's role as an agent of social control has gained considerable notice (Freidson, 1970; Pitts, 1968; Kittrie, 1971; Zola, 1972). By medicalization we mean defining behavior as a medical problem or illness and mandating or licensing the medical profession to provide some type of treatment for it. Examples include alcoholism, drug addiction and treating violence as a genetic or brain disorder. This redefinition is not a new function of the medical institution: psychiatry and public health have always been concerned with social behavior and have traditionally functioned as agents of social control (Foucault, 1965; Szasz, 1970; Rosen, 1972). . . .

This paper describes how certain forms of behavior in children have become defined as a medical problem and how medicine has become a major agent for their social control since the discovery of hyperkinesis. By discovery we mean both origin of the diagnosis and treatment for this disorder, and discovery of children who exhibit this behavior. The first section analyzes the discovery of hyperkinesis and why it suddenly became popular in the 1960's. The second section will discuss the medicalization of deviant behavior and its ramifications.

The Medical Diagnosis of Hyperkinesis

Hyperkinesis is a relatively recent phenomenon as a medical diagnostic category. Only in the past two decades has it been available as a recognized diagnostic category and only in the last decade has it received widespread notice and medical popularity. However, the roots of the diagnosis and treatment of this clinical entity are found earlier.

Hyperkinesis is also known as Minimal Brain Dysfunction, Hyperactive Syndrome, Hyperkinetic Disorder of Childhood, and by several other diagnostic categories. Although the symptoms and the presumed etiology vary, in general the behaviors are quite similar and greatly overlap.[1] Typical symptom patterns for diagnosing the disorder include: extreme excess of motor activity (hyperactivity); very short attention span (the child flits from activity to activity); restlessness; fidgetiness; often wildly oscillating mood swings (he's fine one day, a terror the next); clumsiness; aggressive-like behavior; impulsivity; in school he cannot sit still, cannot comply with rules, has low frustration level; frequently there may be sleeping problems and acquisition of speech may be delayed (Stewart et al., 1966, 1970; Wender, 1971). Most of the symptoms for the disorder are deviant behaviors.[2] It is six times as prevalent among boys as among girls. We use the term hyperkinesis to represent all the diagnostic categories of this disorder.

The Discovery of Hyperkinesis

It is useful to divide the analysis into what might be considered *clinical factors* directly related to the diagnosis and treatment of hyperkinesis and *social factors* that set the context for the emergence of the new diagnostic category.

Clinical Factors

Bradley (1937) observed that amphetamine drugs had a spectacular effect in altering the behavior of school children who exhibited behavior disorders or learning disabilities. Fifteen of the thirty children he treated actually became more subdued in their behavior. Bradley termed the effect of this medication paradoxical, since he expected that amphetamines would stimulate children as they stimulated adults. After the medication was discontinued the children's behavior returned to premedication level.

A scattering of reports in the medical literature on the utility of stimulant medications for "childhood behavior disorders" appeared in the next two decades. The next significant contribution was the work of Strauss and his associates (Strauss and Lehtinen, 1947) who found certain behavior (including hyperkinesis behaviors) in postencephalitic children suffering from what they called minimal brain injury (damage). This was the first time these behaviors were attributed to the new organic distinction of minimal brain damage.

This disorder still remained unnamed or else it was called a variety of names (usually just "childhood behavior disorder"). It did not appear as a specific diagnostic category until Laufer et al. (1957) described it as the "hyperkinetic impulse disorder" in 1957. Upon finding "the salient characteristics of the behavior pattern . . . are strikingly similar to those with clear cut organic causation" these researchers described a disorder with no clear-cut history or evidence for organicity (Laufer et al., 1957).

In 1966 a task force sponsored by the U.S. Public Health Service and the National Association for Crippled Children and Adults attempted to clarify the ambiguity and confusion in terminology and symptomology in diagnosing children's behavior and learning disorders. From over three dozen diagnoses, they agreed on the term "minimal brain dysfunction" as an overriding diagnosis that would include hyperkinesis and other disorders (Clements, 1966). Since this time M.B.D. has been the primary formal diagnosis or label.

In the middle 1950's a new drug, Ritalin, was synthesized, that has many qualities of amphetamines without some of their more undesirable side effects. In 1961 this drug was approved by the F.D.A. for use with children. Since this time there has been much research published on the use of Ritalin in the treatment of childhood behavior disorders. This medication became the "treatment of choice" for treating children with hyperkinesis.

Since the early sixties, more research appeared on the etiology, diagnosis and treatment of hyperkinesis (cf. DeLong, 1972; Grinspoon and Singer, 1973; Cole, 1975)—as much as three-quarters concerned with drug treatment of the disorder. There had been increasing publicity of the disorder in the mass media as well. The *Reader's Guide to Periodical Literature* had no articles on hyperkinesis before 1967, one each in 1968 and 1969, and a total of forty for 1970 through 1974 (a mean of eight per year).

Now hyperkinesis has become the most common child psychiatric problem (Gross and Wilson, 1974:142); special pediatric clinics have been established to treat hyperkinetic children, and substantial federal funds have been invested in etiological and treatment research. Outside the medical profession, teachers have developed a working clinical knowledge of hyperkinesis' symptoms and treatment (cf. Robin and Bosco, 1973); articles appear regularly in mass circulation magazines and newspapers so that parents often come to clinics with knowledge of this diagnosis. Hyperkinesis is no longer the relatively esoteric diagnostic category it may have been twenty years ago; it is now a well-known clinical disorder.

Social Factors

The social factors affecting the discovery of hyperkinesis can be divided into two areas: (1) The Pharmaceutical Revolution; (2) Government Action.

(1) The Pharmaceutical Revolution. Since the 1930's the pharmaceutical industry has been synthesizing and manufacturing a large number of psychoactive drugs, contributing to a virtual revolution in drug making and drug taking in America (Silverman and Lee, 1974).

Psychoactive drugs are agents that affect the central nervous system. Benzedrine, Ritalin, and Dexedrine are all synthesized psychoactive stimulants which were indicated for narcolepsy, appetite control (as "diet pills"), mild depression, fatigue, and more recently hyperkinetic children.

Until the early sixties there was little or no promotion and advertisement of any of these medications for use with childhood disorders.[3] Then two major pharmaceutical firms (Smith, Kline and French, manufacturer of Dexedrine, and CIBA, manufacturer of Ritalin) began to advertise in medical journals and through direct mailing and efforts of the "detail men." Most of this advertising of the pharmaceutical treatment of hyperkinesis was directed to the medical sphere; but some of the promotion was targeted for the educational sector also (Hentoff, 1972). This promotion was probably significant in disseminating information concerning the diagnosis and treatment of this newly discovered disorder.[4] Since 1955 the use of psychoactive medications (especially phenothiazines) for the treatment of persons who are mentally ill, along with the concurrent dramatic decline in inpatient populations, has made psychopharmacology an integral part of treatment for mental disorders. It has also undoubtedly increased the confidence in the medical profession for the pharmaceutical approach to mental and behavioral problems.

(2) Government Action. Since the publication of the U.S.P.H.S. report on M.B.D. there have been at least two significant governmental reports on treating school children with stimulant medications for behavior disorders. Both of these came as a response to the national publicity created by the *Washington Post* report (1970) that five to 10 percent of the 62,000 grammar school children in Omaha, Nebraska were being treated with "behavior modification drugs to improve deportment and increase learning potential" (quoted in Grinspon and Singer, 1973). Although the figures were later found to be a little exaggerated, it nevertheless spurred a Congressional investigation (U.S. Government Printing Office, 1970) and a conference sponsored by the Office of Child Development (1971) on the use of stimulant drugs in the treatment of behaviorally disturbed school children.

The Congressional Subcommittee on Privacy chaired by Congressman Cornelius E. Gallagher held hearings on the issue of prescribing drugs for hyperactive school children. In general, the committee showed great concern over the facility in which the medication was prescribed; more specifically that some children at least were receiving drugs from general practitioners whose primary diagnosis was based on teachers' and parents' reports that the child was doing poorly in school. There was also a concern with the absence of follow-up studies on the long-term effects of treatment.

The H.E.W. committee was a rather hastily convened group of professionals (a majority were M.D.'s) many of whom already had commitments to drug treatment for children's behavior problems. They recommended that only M.D.'s make the diagnosis and prescribe treatment, that the pharmaceutical companies promote the treatment of the disorder only through medical channels, that parents should not be coerced to accept any particular treatment and that long-term follow-up research should be done. This report served as blue ribbon approval for treating hyperkinesis with psychoactive medications.

Discussion

We will focus discussion on three issues: How children's deviant behavior became conceptualized as a medical problem; why this occurred when it did; and what are some of the implications of the medicalization of deviant behavior.

How does deviant behavior become conceptualized as a medical problem? We assume that before the discovery of hyperkinesis this type of deviance was seen as disruptive, disobedient, rebellious, anti-social or deviant behavior. Perhaps the label "emotionally disturbed" was sometimes used, when it was in vogue in the early sixties, and the child was usually managed in the context of the family or the school or in extreme cases, the child guidance clinic. How then did this constellation of deviant behaviors become a medical disorder?

The treatment was available long before the disorder treated was clearly conceptualized. It was twenty years after Bradley's discovery of the "paradoxical effect" of stimulants on certain deviant children that Laufer named the disorder and described its characteristic symptoms. Only in the late fifties were both the diagnostic label and the pharmaceutical treatment available. The pharmaceutical revolution in mental health and the increased interest in child psychiatry provided a favorable background for the dissemination of knowledge about this new disorder. The latter probably made the medical profession more likely to consider behavior problems in children as within their clinical jurisdiction.

There were agents outside the medical profession itself that were significant in "promoting" hyperkinesis as a disorder within the medical framework. These agents might be conceptualized in Becker's terms as "moral entrepreneurs," those who crusade for creation and enforcement of the rules (Becker, 1963).[5] In this case the moral entrepreneurs were the pharmaceutical companies and the Association for Children with Learning Disabilities.

The pharmaceutical companies spent considerable time and money promoting stimulant medications for this new disorder. From the middle 1960's on, medical journals and the free "throwaway" magazines contained elaborate advertising for Ritalin and Dexedrine. These ads explained the utility of treating hyperkinesis and urged physicians to diagnose and treat hyperkinetic children. The ads run from one to six pages. For example, a two-page ad in 1971 stated:

> MBD . . . MEDICAL MYTH OR DIAGNOSABLE DISEASE ENTITY
> What medical practitioner has not, at one time or another, been called upon to examine an impulsive, excitable hyperkinetic child? A child with difficulty in concentrating. Easily frustrated. Unusually aggressive. A classroom rebel. In the absence of any organic pathology, the conduct of such children was, until a few short years ago, usually dismissed as . . . spunkiness, or evidence of youthful vitality. But it is now evident that in many of these children the hyperkinetic syndrome exists as a distinct medical entity. This syndrome is readily diagnosed through patient histories, neurologic signs, and psychometric testing—has been classified by an expert panel convened by the United States Department of Health, Education and Welfare as Minimal Brain Dysfunction, MBD.

The pharmaceutical firms also supplied sophisticated packets of "diagnostic and treatment" information on hyperkinesis to physicians, paid for professional conferences on the subject, and supported research in the identification and treatment of the disorder. Clearly these corporations had a vested interest in the labeling and treatment of hyperkinesis; CIBA had $13 million profit from Ritalin alone in 1971, which was 15 percent of the total gross profits (Charles, 1971; Hentoff, 1972).

The other moral entrepreneur, less powerful than the pharmaceutical companies, but nevertheless influential, is the Association for Children with Learning Disabilities. Although their focus is not specifically on hyperkinetic children, they do include it in their conception of Learning Disabilities along with aphasia, reading problems like dyslexia and perceptual motor problems. Founded in the early 1950's by parents and professionals, it has functioned much as the National Association for Mental Health does for mental illness: promoting conferences, sponsoring legislation, providing social support. One of the main functions has been to disseminate information concerning this relatively new area in education, Learning Disabilities. While the organization does have a more educational than medical perspective, most of the literature indicates that for hyperkinesis members have adopted the medical model and the medical approach to the problem. They have sensitized teachers and schools to the conception of hyperkinesis as a medical problem.

The medical model of hyperactive behavior has become very well accepted in our society. Physicians find treatment relatively simple and the results sometimes spectacular. Hyperkinesis minimizes parents' guilt by emphasizing "it's not their fault, it's an organic problem" and allows for nonpunitive management or control of deviance. Medication often makes a child less disruptive in the classroom and sometimes aids a child in learning. Children often like their "magic pills" which make their behavior more socially acceptable and they probably benefit from a reduced stigma also.

The Medicalization of Deviant Behavior

Pitts has commented that "medicalization is one of the most effective means of social control and that it is destined to become the main mode of *formal* social control" (1971:391). Kittrie (1971) has termed it "the coming of the therapeutic state."

Medicalization of mental illness dates at least from the seventeenth century (Foucault, 1965; Szasz, 1970). Even slaves who ran away were once considered to be suffering from the disease *drapedomania* (Chorover, 1973). In recent years alcoholism, violence, and drug addiction as well as hyperactive behavior in children have all become defined as medical problems, both in etiology or explanation of the behavior and the means of social control or treatment.

There are many reaons why this medicalization has occurred. Much scientific research, especially in pharmacology and genetics, has become technologically more sophisticated, and found more subtle correlates with human behavior. Sometimes these findings (as in the case of XYY chromosomes and violence) become etiological explanations for deviance. Pharmacological technology that makes new discoveries affecting behavior (e.g., antabuse, methadone and stimulants) are used as treatment for deviance. In part this application is encouraged by the prestige of the medical profession and its attachment to science. As Freidson notes, the medical profession has first claim to jurisdiction over anything that deals with the functioning of the body and especially anything that can be labeled illness (1970:251). Advances in genetics, pharmacology and "psychosurgery" also may advance medicine's jurisdiction over deviant behavior.

Second, the application of pharmacological technology is related to the humanitarian trend in the conception and control of deviant behavior. Alcoholism is no longer sin or even moral weakness, it is now a disease. Alcoholics are no longer arrested in many places for "public drunkenness," they are now somehow "treated," even if it is only to be dried out. Hyperactive children are now considered to have an illness rather than to be disruptive, disobedient, overactive problem children. They are not as likely to be that "bad boy" of the classroom; they are children with a medical disorder. Clearly there are some real humanitarian benefits to be gained by such a medical conceptualization of deviant behavior. There is less condemnation of the deviants (they have an illness, it is not their fault) and perhaps less social stigma. In some cases, even the medical treatment itself is more humanitarian social control than the criminal justice system.

There is, however, another side to the medicalization of deviant behavior. The four aspects of this side of the issue include (1) the problem of expert control; (2) medical social control; (3) the individualization of social problems; and (4) the "depoliticization" of deviant behavior.

1. *The problem of expert control.* The medical profession is a profession of experts; they have a monopoly on anything that can be conceptualized

as illness. Because of the way the medical profession is organized and the mandate it has from society, decisions related to medical diagnoses and treatment are virtually controlled by medical professionals.

Some conditions that enter the medical domain are not *ipso facto* medical problems, especially deviant behavior, whether alcoholism, hyperactivity or drug addiction. By defining a problem as medical it is removed from the public realm where there can be discussion by ordinary people and put on a plane where only medical people can discuss it. As Reynolds states,

> The increasing acceptance, especially among the more educated segments of our populace, of technical solutions—solutions administered by disinterested politically and morally neutral experts—results in the withdrawal of more and more areas of human experience from the realm of public discussion. For when drunkenness, juvenile delinquency, sub par performance and extreme political beliefs are seen as symptoms of an underlying illness or biological defect the merits and drawbacks of such behavior or beliefs need not be evaluated (1973:200–221).

The public may have their own conceptions of deviant behavior but that of the experts is usually dominant.

2. *Medical social control.* Defining deviant behavior as a medical problem allows certain things to be done that could not otherwise be considered; for example, the body may be cut open or psychoactive medications may be given. This treatment can be a form of social control.

In regard to drug treatment Lennard points out: "Psychoactive drugs, especially those legally prescribed, tend to restrain individuals from behavior and experience that are not complementary to the requirements of the dominant value system" (1971:57). These forms of medical social control presume a prior definition of deviance as a medical problem. Psychosurgery on an individual prone to violent outbursts requires a diagnosis that there was something wrong with his brain or nervous system. Similarly, prescribing drugs to restless, overactive and disruptive school children requires a diagnosis of hyperkinesis. These forms of social control, what Chorover (1973) has called "psychotechnology," are very powerful and often very efficient means of controlling deviance. These relatively new and increasingly popular forms of social control could not be utilized without the medicalization of deviant behavior. As is suggested from the discovery of hyperkinesis, if a mechanism of medical social control seems useful, then the deviant behavior it modifies will develop a medical label or diagnosis. No overt malevolence on the part of the medical profession is implied: rather it is part of a complex process, of which the medical profession is only a part. The larger process might be called the individualization of social problems.

3. *The individualization of social problems.* The medicalization of deviant behavior is part of a larger phenomenon that is prevalent in our society, the individualization of social problems. We tend to look for causes and solu-

tions to complex social problems in the individual rather than in the social system. This view resembles Ryan's (1970) notion of "blaming the victim"; seeing the causes of the problem in individuals rather than in the society where they live. We then seek to change the "victim" rather than the society. The medical perspective of diagnosing an illness in an individual lends itself to the individualization of social problems. Rather than seeing certain deviant behaviors as symptomatic of problems in the social system, the medical perspective focuses on the individual diagnosing and treating the illness, generally ignoring the social situation.

Hyperkinesis serves as a good example. Both the school and the parents are concerned with the child's behavior; the child is very difficult at home and disruptive in school. No punishments or rewards seem consistently to work in modifying the behavior; and both parents and school are at their wits' end. A medical evaluation is suggested. The diagnoses of hyperkinetic behavior leads to prescribing stimulant medications. The child's behavior seems to become more socially acceptable, reducing problems in school and at home.

But there is an alternate perspective. By focusing on the symptoms and defining them as hyperkinesis we ignore the possibility that behavior is not an illness but an adaption to a social situation. It diverts our attention from the family or school and from seriously entertaining the idea that the "problem" could be in the structure of the social system. And by giving medications we are essentially supporting the existing systems and do not allow this behavior to be a factor of change in the system.

4. *The depoliticization of deviant behavior.* Depoliticization of deviant behavior is a result of both the process of medicalization and individualization of social problems. To our western world, probably one of the clearest examples of such a depoliticization of deviant behavior occurred when political dissenters in the Soviet Union were declared mentally ill and confined in mental hospitals (cf. Conrad, 1972). This strategy served to neutralize the meaning of political protest and dissent, rendering it the ravings of mad persons.

The medicalization of deviant behavior depoliticizes deviance in the same manner. By defining the overactive, restless and disruptive child as hyperkinetic we ignore the meaning of behavior in the context of the social system. If we focused our analysis on the school system we might see the child's behavior as symptomatic of some "disorder" in the school or classroom situation, rather than symptomatic of an individual neurological disorder.

Conclusion

I have discussed the social ramifications of the medicalization of deviant behavior, using hyperkinesis as the example. A number of consequences of this medicalization have been outlined, including the depoliticization of deviant behavior, decision-making power of experts, and the role of medicine as an agent of social control. In the last analysis medical social control may be the central issue, as in this role medicine becomes a *de facto* agent of the *status quo*. The medical profession may not have entirely sought this role, but its members have been, in general, disturbingly unconcerned and unquestioning in their acceptance of it. With the increasing medical knowledge and technology it is likely that more deviant behavior will be medicalized and medicine's social control function will expand.

Notes

1. The U.S.P.H.S. report (Clements, 1966) included 38 terms that were used to describe or distinguish the conditions that it labeled Minimal Brain Dysfunction. Although the literature attempts to differentiate M.B.D., hyperkinesis, hyperactive syndrome, and several other diagnostic labels, it is our belief that in practice they are almost interchangeable.

2. For a fuller discussion of the construction of the diagnosis of hyperkinesis, see Conrad (1976), especially Chapter 6.

3. The American Medical Association's change in policy in accepting more pharmaceutical advertising in the late fifties may have been important. Probably the F.D.A. approval of the use of Ritalin for children in 1961 was more significant. Until 1970, Ritalin was advertised for treatment of "functional behavior problems in children." Since then, because of an F.D.A. order, it has only been promoted for treatment of M.B.D.

4. The drug industry spends fully 25 percent of its budget on promotion and advertising. See Coleman et al. (1966) for the role of the detail men and how physicians rely upon them for information.

5. Freidson also notes the medical professional role as moral entrepreneur in this process also:

> The profession does treat the illnesses laymen take to it, but it also seeks to discover illness of which the laymen may not even be aware. One of the greatest ambitions of the physician is to discover and describe a "new" disease or syndrome . . . (1970:252).

References

Becker, Howard S. 1963. *Outsiders: Studies in the Sociology of Deviance.* New York: Free Press.

Bradley, Charles. 1937. "The Behavior of Children Receiving Benzedrine." *American Journal of Psychiatry,* 94 (March): 577–585.

Charles, Alan. 1971. "The Case of Ritalin." *New Republic,* 23 (October): 17–19.

Chorover, Stephen L. 1973. "Big Brother and Psychotechnology." *Psychology Today* (October): 43–54.

Clements, Samuel D. 1966. "Task Force I: Minimal Brain Dysfunction in Children." National Institute of Neurological Diseases and Blindness, Monograph no. 3. Washington, D.C.: U.S. Department of Health, Education and Welfare.

Cole, Sherwood. 1975. "Hyperactive Children: The Use of Stimulant Drugs Evaluated." *American Journal of Orthopsychiatry,* 45 (January): 28–37.

Coleman, James, Elihu Katz, and Herbert Menzel. 1966. *Medical Innovation.* Indianapolis: Bobbs-Merrill.

Conrad, Peter. 1972. "Ideological Deviance: An Analysis of the Soviet Use of Mental Hospitals for Political Dissenters." Unpublished manuscript.

Conrad, Peter 1976. *Identifying Hyperactive Children: A Study in the Medicalization of Deviant Behavior.* Lexington, Mass.: D.C. Heath and Co.

DeLong, Arthur R. 1972. "What Have We Learned from Psychoactive Drugs Research with Hyperactives?" *American Journal of Diseases in Children,* 123 (February): 177–180.

Foucault, Michel. 1965. *Madness and Civilization.* New York: Pantheon.

Freidson, Eliot. 1970. *Profession of Medicine: A Study of the Sociology of Applied Knowledge.* New York: Dodd, Mead.

Grinspoon, Lester and Susan Singer. 1973. "Amphetamines in the Treatment of Hyperactive Children." *Harvard Educational Review,* 43 (November): 515–555.

Gross, Mortimer B. and William E. Wilson. 1974. *Minimal Brain Dysfunction.* New York: Brunner Mazel.

Hentoff, Nat. 1972. "Drug Pushing in the Schools: The Professionals." *The Village Voice,* 22 (May): 21–23.

Kittrie, Nicholas. 1971. *The Right to Be Different.* Baltimore: Johns Hopkins Press.

Laufer, M. W., Denhoff, E., and Solomons, G. 1957. "Hyperkinetic Impulse Disorder in Children's Behavior Problems." *Psychosomatic Medicine,* 19 (January): 38–49.

Lennard, Henry L. and Associates. 1971. *Mystification and Drug Misuse.* New York: Harper and Row.

Office of Child Development. 1971. "Report of the Conference on the Use of Stimulant Drugs in Treatment of Behaviorally Disturbed Children." Washington, D.C.: Office of Child Development, Department of Health, Education and Welfare, January 11–12.

Pitts, Jesse. 1968. "Social Control: The Concept." In David Sills (ed.), *International Encyclopedia of the Social Sciences.* Vol. 14. New York: Macmillan.

Reynolds, Janice M. 1973. "The Medical Institution." In Larry T. Reynolds and James M. Henslin, *American Society: A Critical Analysis.* New York: David McKay.

Robin, Stanley S. and James J. Bosco. 1973. "Ritalin for School Children: The Teacher's Perspective." *Journal of School Health,* 47 (December): 624–628.

Rosen, George. 1972. "The Evolution of Social Medicine." In Howard E. Freeman, Sol Levine, and Leo Reeder, *Handbook of Medical Sociology.* Englewood Cliffs, N.J.: Prentice-Hall.

Ryan, William. 1970. *Blaming the Victim.* New York: Vintage.

Silverman, Milton and Philip R. Lee. 1974. *Pills, Profits and Politics.* Berkeley: University of California Press.

Sroufe, L. Alan and Mark Stewart. 1973. "Treating Problem Children with Stimulant Drugs." *New England Journal of Medicine,* 289 (August 23): 407–421.

Stewart, Mark A. 1970. "Hyperactive Children." *Scientific American,* 222 (April): 794–798.

Stewart, Mark A., A. Ferris, N. P. Pitts, and A. G. Craig. 1966. "The Hyperactive Child Syndrome." *American Journal of Orthopsychiatry* 26 (October): 861–867.

Strauss, A. A. and L. E. Lehtinen. 1947. *Psychopathology and Education of the Brain-Injured Child.* Vol. 1. New York: Grune and Stratton.

Szasz, Thomas S. 1970. *The Manufacture of Madness.* New York: Harper and Row.

U.S. Government Printing Office. 1970. "Federal involvement in the Use of Behavior Modification Drugs on Grammar School Children of the Right to Privacy Inquiry: Hearing Before a Subcommittee of the Committee on Government Operations." Washington, D.C.: 91st Congress, 2nd session (September 29).

Wender, Paul. 1971. *Minimal Brain Dysfunction in Children.* New York: John Wiley and Sons.

Zola, Irving. 1972. "Medicine as an Institution of Social Control." *Sociological Review,* 20 (November): 487–504.

PART **II**

Understanding Deviance: Theories and Perspectives

Part I introduced a specific concern for the ways in which deviant categories arise, as well as the ways in which violators of existing categories may be reacted to. Missing from this introduction was a concern for *why* actors may exhibit behavior in violation of established norms, rules, regulations, and laws—violations that may cause them to be initially labeled as deviants. We believe that to approach a more complete understanding of deviance in terms of social processes, we must not only analyze the creation of deviant categories and the reactions to violators of categories; we must also examine the motivations for deviance. The selections in this part represent some of the major attempts to accomplish this goal.

Explanations of the motivations for deviance have taken various forms. Some observers would place the blame on a defective family structure or arrested personality adjustment; others would emphasize such conditions as poverty or racism; and there are proponents of the thesis that individuals are born deviant. It should be recognized, however, that no single factor can adequately explain why actors commit deviant acts. For example, findings in the area of delinquency research generally conclude that a combination of family, school, and peer variables is the most likely source of motivations for youth crime and deviance.

The actual attempts at understanding or explaining motivations for deviancy can, for our purposes, be roughly grouped into seven categories: (1) functionalist, (2) social conflict, (3) cultural transmission, (4) opportunity, (5) control, (6) interactionist, and (7) integrated approaches. Of the approaches reviewed here, certain divisions should be recognized. Functionalist, control, and opportunity frameworks are basically structural approaches. Structural perspectives seek to understand deviance in society by viewing deviance as a part of the larger social context and asking questions that probe the influence of deviance on social structures and the contribution of social structures to deviance. The cultural transmission and interactionist views are concerned primarily with how, through social-psychological-symbolic processes, actors learn existing cultures and traditions and incorporate them into their self-identity. Conflict theorists focus attention on the struggles and tensions between groups. Special consideration is given to how the powerful influence the creation of deviant categories that result in systematic disadvantage for opposing, less powerful groups. Although each of these approaches explicitly emphasizes certain underlying themes, concepts, or processes, there is frequently an implied or direct overlap among the various models. Such links are demonstrated in integrated approaches combining important elements from various perspectives.

PART II

 # The Functionalist Perspective

SECTION 1

Social scientists who use a functionalist model contend that deviance is an integral part of any social system and that such behavior satisfies some societal need. In terms of sociological analysis, advocates of this model maintain that deviance serves the important function of demarcating and maintaining current boundaries of acceptable behavior. These particular conceptions are embedded in Emile Durkheim's work.

In his statement "The Normal and the Pathological," Durkheim argues that crime not only inheres in all societies but also serves a useful function for the collective conscience, particularly in maintaining the social system. And although forms and definitions of criminal and deviant behavior (i.e., the *collective types* or deviant categories) may vary from society to society, such behaviors do provide members with a basis for punishing violators of the prevailing normative codes. Punishment serves as an important reminder to others that certain behaviors are acceptable while others are not. Thus, achievement of an understanding of deviance and its categories requires an examination of the prevailing definitions of conformity.

In "On the Sociology of Deviance," Kai T. Erikson argues that behavior that may be acceptable within a family setting may not be perceived as such by the larger community. Furthermore, conduct that may be viewed unfavorably by the community may actually go unnoticed in other parts of the culture. In varying situations, then, different standards are used to assess whether or not an actor's behavior exceeds a social unit's "tolerance limits." If it does, the violator may be sanctioned negatively. In a sense, a community or social unit is concerned with the maintenance of its boundaries. Erikson argues that interactions occurring between a potential deviant and a community's official agents play an especially important role in "locating and publicizing the group's outer edges." Such confrontations are not without their individual and structural ramifications, however. Not only may a social actor be selected out, formally processed, and cast into a new status (e.g., that of a criminal), but if the violator is a member of a deviant group, the confrontation and resultant sanctioning may operate in such a way as to actually enhance an actor's esteem in the eyes of his or her peers, as well as to solidify and make more obvious the underlying structure, identity, and character of the group. Erikson goes on to offer some interesting observations. For example, he comments on the fact that even though selected institutions have been created to combat deviance, they, like many deviant groups, often operate in such a way as to encourage, promote, and perpetuate it.

The Normal and the Pathological

Emile Durkheim

Crime is present not only in the majority of societies of one particular species but in all societies of all types. There is no society that is not confronted with the problem of criminality. Its form changes; the acts thus characterized are not the same everywhere; but, everywhere and always, there have been men who have behaved in such a way as to draw upon themselves penal repression. If, in proportion as societies pass from the lower to the higher types, the rate of criminality, i.e., the relation between the yearly number of crimes and the population, tended to decline, it might be believed that crime, while still normal, is tending to lose this character of normality. But we have no reason to believe that such a regression is substantiated. Many facts would seem rather to indicate a movement in the opposite direction. From the beginning of the [nineteenth] century, statistics enable us to follow the course of criminality. It has everywhere increased. In France the increase is nearly 300 per cent. There is, then, no phenomenon that presents more indisputably all the symptoms of normality, since it appears closely connected with the conditions of all collective life. To make of crime a form of social morbidity would be to admit that morbidity is not something accidental, but, on the contrary, that in certain cases it grows out of the fundamental constitution of the living organism; it would result in wiping out all distinction between the physiological and the pathological. No doubt it is possible that crime itself will have abnormal forms, as, for example, when its rate is unusually high. This excess is, indeed, undoubtedly morbid in nature. What is normal, simply, is the existence of criminality, provided that it attains and does not exceed, for each social type, a certain level, which it is perhaps not impossible to fix in conformity with the preceding rules.[1]

Here we are, then, in the presence of a conclusion in appearance quite paradoxical. Let us make no mistake. To classify crime among the phenomena of normal sociology is not to say merely that it is an inevitable, although regrettable phenomenon, due to the incorrigible wickedness of men; it is to affirm that it is a factor in public health, an integral part of all healthy societies. This result is, at first glance, surprising enough to have puzzled even ourselves for a long time. Once this first surprise has been overcome, however, it is not difficult to find reasons explaining this normality and at the same time confirming it.

In the first place crime is normal because a society exempt from it is utterly impossible. Crime, we have shown elsewhere, consists of an act that offends certain very strong collective sentiments. In a society in which criminal acts are no longer committed, the sentiments they offend would have to be found without exception in all individual consciousnesses, and they must be found to exist with the same degree as sentiments contrary to them. Assuming that this condition could actually be realized, crime would not thereby disappear; it would only change its form, for the very cause which would thus dry up the sources of criminality would immediately open up new ones.

Indeed, for the collective sentiments which are protected by the penal law of a people at a specified moment of its history to take possession of the public conscience or for them to acquire a stronger hold where they have an insufficient grip, they must acquire an intensity greater than that which they had hitherto had. The community as a whole must experience them more vividly, for it can acquire from no other source the greater force necessary to control these individuals who formerly were the most refractory. For murderers to disappear, the horror of bloodshed must become greater in those social strata from which murderers are recruited; but, first it must become greater throughout the entire society. Moreover, the very absence of crime would directly contribute to produce this horror; because any sentiment seems much more respectable when it is always and uniformly respected.

One easily overlooks the consideration that these strong states of the common consciousness cannot be thus reinforced without reinforcing at the same time the more feeble states, whose violation previously gave birth to mere infraction of convention—since the weaker ones are only the prolongation, the attenuated form, of the stronger. Thus robbery and simple bad taste injure the same single altruistic sentiment, the respect for that which is another's. However, this same sentiment is less grievously offended by bad taste than by robbery; and since, in addition, the average consciousness has not sufficient intensity to react keenly to the bad taste, it is treated with greater tolerance. That is why the person guilty of bad taste is merely blamed, whereas the thief is punished. But, if this sentiment grows stronger, to the point of silencing in all consciousnesses the inclination which disposes man to steal, he will become more sensitive to the offenses which, until then, touched him but lightly. He will react against them, then, with more energy; they will be the object of greater opprobrium, which will transform certain of them from the simple moral faults that they were and give them the quality of crimes. For example, improper contracts, or contracts improperly executed, which only incur public blame or civil damages, will become offenses in law.

Imagine a society of saints, a perfect cloister of exemplary individuals. Crimes, properly so called, will there be unknown; but faults which appear venial to the layman will create there the same scandal that the ordinary offense does in ordinary consciousnesses. If, then, this society has the power to judge and punish, it will define these acts as criminal and will treat them as such. For the same reason, the perfect and upright man judges his smallest failings with a severity that the majority reserve for acts more truly in the nature of an offense. Formerly, acts of violence against persons were more frequent than they are today, because respect for individual dignity was less strong. As this has increased, these crimes have become more rare; and also, many acts violating this sentiment have been introduced into the penal law which were not included there in primitive times.[2]

In order to exhaust all the hypotheses logically possible, it will perhaps be asked why this unanimity does not extend to all collective sentiments without exception. Why should not even the most feeble sentiment gather enough energy to prevent all dissent? The moral consciousness of the society would be present in its entirety in all the individuals, with a vitality sufficient to prevent all acts offending it—the purely conventional faults as well as the crimes. But a uniformity so universal and absolute is utterly impossible; for the immediate physical milieu in which each one of us is placed, the hereditary antecedents, and the social influences vary from one individual to the next, and consequently diversify consciousnesses. It is impossible for all to be alike, if only because each one has his own organism and that these organisms occupy different areas in space. That is why, even among the lower peoples, where individual originality is very little developed, it nevertheless does exist.

Thus, since there cannot be a society in which the individuals do not differ more or less from the collective type, it is also inevitable that, among these divergences, there are some with a criminal character. What confers this character upon them is not the intrinsic quality of a given act but that definition which the collective conscience lends them. If the collective conscience is stronger, if it has enough authority practically to suppress these divergences, it will also be more sensitive, more exacting; and, reacting against the slightest deviations with the energy it otherwise displays only against more considerable infractions, it will attribute to them the same gravity as formerly to crimes. In other words, it will designate them as criminal.

Crime is, then, necessary; it is bound up with fundamental conditions of all social life, and by that very fact it is useful, because these conditions of which it is part are themselves indispensable to the normal evolution of morality and law.

Indeed, it is no longer possible today to dispute the fact that law and morality vary from one social type to the next, nor that they change within the same type if the conditions of life are modified. But, in order that these transformations may be possible, the collective sentiments at the basis of morality must not be hostile to change, and consequently must have but moderate energy. If they were too strong, they would no longer be plastic. Every pattern is an obstacle to new patterns, to the extent that the first pattern is inflexible. The better a structure is articulated, the more it offers a healthy resistance to all modification; and this is equally true of functional, as of anatomical, organization. If there were no crimes, this condition could not have been fulfilled; for such a hypothesis presupposes that collective sentiments have arrived at a degree of intensity unexampled in history. Nothing is good indefinitely and to an unlimited extent. The authority which the moral conscience enjoys must not be excessive; otherwise no one would dare criticize it, and it would too easily congeal into an immutable form. To make progress, individual originality must be able to express itself. In order that the originality of the idealist whose dreams transcend his century may find expression, it is necessary that the originality of the criminal, who is below the level of his time, shall also be possible. One does not occur without the other.

Nor is this all. Aside from this indirect utility, it happens that crime itself plays a useful role in this evolution. Crime implies not only that the way remains open to necessary changes but that in certain cases it directly prepares these changes. Where crime exists, collective sentiments are sufficiently flexible to take on a new form, and crime sometimes helps to determine the form they will take. How many times, indeed, it is only an anticipation of future morality—a step toward what will be! According to Athenian law, Socrates was a criminal, and his condemnation was no more than just. However, his crime, namely, the independence of his thought, rendered a service not only to humanity but to his country. It served to prepare a new morality and faith which the Athenians needed, since the traditions by which they had lived until then were no longer in harmony with the current conditions of life. Nor is the case of Socrates unique; it is reproduced periodically in history. It would never have been possible to establish the freedom of thought we now enjoy if the regulations prohibiting it had not been violated before being solemnly abrogated. At that time, however, the violation was a crime, since it was an offense against sentiments still very keen in the average conscience. And yet this crime was useful as a prelude to reforms which daily became more necessary. Liberal philosophy had as its precursors the heretics of all kinds who were justly punished by secular authorities during the entire course of the Middle Ages and until the eve of modern times.

From this point of view the fundamental facts of criminality present themselves to us in an entirely new light. Contrary to current ideas, the criminal no longer seems a totally unsociable being, a sort of parasitic element, a strange and unassimilable body, introduced into the midst of society.[3] On the contrary, he plays a definite role in social life. Crime, for its part, must no longer be conceived as an evil that cannot be too much suppressed. There is no occasion for self-congratulation when the crime rate drops noticeably below the average level, for we may be certain that this apparent progress is associated with some social disorder. Thus, the number of assault cases never falls so low as in times of want.[4] With the drop in the crime rate, and as a reaction to it, comes a revision, or the need of a revision in the theory of punishment. If, indeed, crime is a disease, its punishment is its remedy and cannot be otherwise conceived; thus, all the discussions it arouses bear on the point of determining what the punishment must be in order to fulfil this role of remedy. If crime is not pathological at all, the object of punishment cannot be to cure it, and its true function must be sought elsewhere.

Notes

1. From the fact that crime is a phenomenon of normal sociology, it does not follow that the criminal is an individual normally constituted from the biological and psychological points of view. The two questions are independent of each other. This independence will be better understood when we have shown, later on, the difference between psychological and sociological facts.

2. Calumny, insults, slander, fraud, etc.

3. We have ourselves committed the error of speaking thus of the criminal, because of a failure to apply our rule (*Division du travail social,* pp. 395–96).

4. Although crime is a fact of normal sociology, it does not follow that we must not abhor it. Pain itself has nothing desirable about it; the individual dislikes it as society does crime, and yet it is a function of normal physiology. Not only is it necessarily derived from the very constitution of every living organism, but it plays a useful role in life, for which reason it cannot be replaced. It would, then, be a singular distortion of our thought to present it as an apology for crime. We would not even think of protesting against such an interpretation, did we not know to what strange accusations and misunderstandings one exposes oneself when one undertakes to study moral facts objectively and to speak of them in a different language from that of the layman.

8 On the Sociology of Deviance

Kai T. Erikson

Human actors are sorted into various kinds of collectivity, ranging from relatively small units such as the nuclear family to relatively large ones such as a nation or culture. One of the most stubborn difficulties in the study of deviation is that the problem is defined differently at each one of these levels: behavior that is considered unseemly within the context of a single family may be entirely acceptable to the community in general, while behavior that attracts severe censure from the members of the community may go altogether unnoticed elsewhere in the culture. People in society, then, must learn to deal separately with deviance at each one of these levels and to distinguish among them in his own daily activity. A man may disinherit his son for conduct that violates old family traditions or ostracize a neighbor for conduct that violates some local custom, but he is not expected to employ either of these standards when he serves as a juror in a court of law. In each of the three situations he is required to use a different set of criteria to decide whether or not the behavior in question exceeds tolerable limits.

In the next few pages we shall be talking about deviant behavior in social units called "communities," but the use of this term does not mean that the argument applies only at that level of organization. In theory, at least, the argument being made here should fit all kinds of human collectivity—families as well as whole cultures, small groups as well as nations—and the term "community" is only being used in this context because it seems particularly convenient.[1]

The people of a community spend most of their lives in close contact with one another, sharing a common sphere of experience which makes them feel that they belong to a special "kind" and live in a special "place." In the formal language of sociology, this means that communities are boundary maintaining: each has a specific territory in the world as a whole, not only in the sense that it occupies a defined region of geographical space but also in the sense that it takes over a particular niche in what might be called cultural space and develops its own "ethos" or "way" within that compass. Both of these dimensions of group space, the geographical and the cultural, set the community apart as a special place and provide an important point of reference for its members.

When one describes any system as boundary maintaining, one is saying that it controls the fluctuation of its consistent parts so that the whole retains a limited range of activity, a given pattern of constancy and stability, within the larger environment. A human community can be said to maintain boundaries, then, in the sense that its members tend to confine themselves to a particular radius of activity and to regard any conduct which drifts outside that radius as somehow inappropriate or immoral. Thus the group retains a kind of cultural integrity, a voluntary restriction on its own potential for expansion, beyond that which is strictly required for accommodation to the environment. Human behavior can vary over an enormous range, but each community draws a symbolic set of parentheses around a certain segment of that range and limits its own activities within that narrower zone. These parentheses, so to speak, are the community's boundaries.

Now people who live together in communities cannot relate to one another in any coherent way or even acquire a sense of their own stature as group members unless they learn something about the boundaries of the territory they occupy in social space, if only because they need to sense what lies beyond the margins of the group before they can appreciate the special quality of the experience which takes place within it. Yet how do people learn about the boundaries of their community? And how do they convey this information to the generations which replace them?

To begin with, the only material found in a society for marking boundaries is the behavior of its members—or rather, the networks of interaction which like these members together in regular social relations. And the interactions which do the most effective job of locating and publicizing the group's outer edges would seem to be those which take place between deviant persons on the one side and official agents of the community on the other. The deviant is a person whose activities have moved outside the margins of the group, and when the community calls him to account for that vagrancy it is making a statement about the nature and placement of its boundaries. It is declaring how much variability and diversity can be tolerated within the group before it begins to lose its distinctive shape, its unique identity. Now there may be other moments in the life of the group which perform a similar service: wars, for instance, can publicize a group's boundaries by drawing attention to the line separating the group from an adversary, and certain kinds of religious ritual, dance ceremony, and other traditional pageantry can dramatize the difference between "we" and "they" by portraying a symbolic encounter between the two. But on the whole, members of a community inform one another about the placement of their boundaries by participating in the confrontations which occur when persons who venture out to the edges of the group are met by policing agents whose special business it is to guard the cultural integrity of the community. Whether these confrontations take the form of criminal trials, excommunication hearings, courts-martial, or even psychiatric case conferences, they act as boundary-maintaining devices in the sense that they demonstrate to whatever audience is concerned where the line is drawn between behavior that belongs in the special universe of the group and behavior that does not. In general, this kind of information is not easily relayed by the straightforward use of language. Most readers of this paragraph, for instance, have a fairly clear idea of the line separating theft from more legitimate forms of commerce, but few of them have ever seen a published statute describing these differences. More likely than not, our information on the subject has been drawn from publicized instances in which the relevant laws were applied—and for that matter, the law itself is largely a collection of past cases and decisions, a synthesis of the various confrontations which have occurred in the life of the legal order.

It may be important to note in this connection that confrontations between deviant offenders and the agents of control have always attracted a good deal of public attention. In our own past, the trial and punishment of offenders were staged in the market place and afforded the crowd a chance to participate in a direct, active way. Today, of course, we no longer parade deviants in the town square or expose them to the carnival atmosphere of a Tyburn, but it is interesting that the "reform" which brought about this change in penal practice coincided almost exactly with the development of newspapers as a medium of mass information. Perhaps this is no more than an accident of history, but it is nonetheless true that newspapers (and now radio and television) offer much the same kind of entertainment as public hangings or a Sunday visit to the local gaol. A considerable portion of what we call "news" is devoted to reports about deviant behavior and its consequences, and it is no simple matter to explain why these items should be considered newsworthy or why they should command the extraordinary attention they do. Perhaps they appeal to a number of psychological perversities among the mass audience, as commentators have suggested, but at the same time they constitute one of our main sources of information about the normative outlines of society. In a figurative sense, at least, morality and immorality meet at the public scaffold, and it is during this meeting that the line between them is drawn.

Boundaries are never a fixed property of any community. They are always shifting as the people of the group find new ways to define the outer limits of their universe, new ways to position themselves on the larger cultural map. Sometimes changes occur within the structure of the group which require its members to make a new survey of their territory—a change of leadership, a shift of mood. Sometimes changes occur in the surrounding environment, altering the background against which the people of the group have measured their own uniqueness. And always, new generations are moving in to take their turn guarding old institutions and need to be informed about the contours of the world they are inheriting. Thus single encounters between the deviant and his community are only fragments of an ongoing social process. Like an article of common law, boundaries remain a meaningful point of reference only so long as they are repeatedly tested by persons on the fringes of the group and repeatedly defended by persons chosen to represent the group's inner morality. Each time the community moves to censure some act of deviation, then, and convenes a formal ceremony to deal with the responsible offender, it sharpens the authority of the violated norm and restates where the boundaries of the group are located.

For these reasons, deviant behavior is not a simple kind of leakage which occurs when the machinery of society is in poor working order, but may be, in controlled quantities, an important condition for preserving the stability of social life. Deviant forms of behavior, by marking the outer edges of group life, give the inner structure its special character and thus supply the framework within which the people of the group develop an orderly sense of their own cultural identity. Perhaps this is what Aldous Huxley had in mind when he wrote:

> Now tidiness is undeniably good—but a good of which it is easily possible to have too much and at too high a price. . . . The good life can only be lived in a society in which tidiness is preached and practised, but not too fanatically, and where efficiency is always haloed, as it were, by a tolerated margin of mess.[2]

This raises a delicate theoretical issue. If we grant that human groups often derive benefit from deviant behavior, can we then assume that they are organized in such a way as to promote this resource? Can we assume, in other words, that forces operate in the social structure to recruit offenders and to commit them to long periods of service in the deviant ranks? This is not a question which can be answered with our present store of empirical data, but one observation can be made which gives the question an interesting perspective—namely, that deviant forms of conduct often seem to derive nourishment from the very agencies devised to inhibit them. Indeed, the agencies built by society for preventing deviance are often so poorly equipped for the task that we might well ask why this is regarded as their "real" function in the first place.

It is by now a thoroughly familiar argument that many of the institutions designed to discourage deviant behavior actually operate in such a way as to perpetuate it. For one thing, prisons, hospitals, and other similar agencies provide aid and shelter to large numbers of deviant persons, sometimes giving them a certain advantage in the competition for social resources. But beyond this, such institutions gather marginal people into tightly segregated groups, give them an opportunity to teach one another the skills and attitudes of a deviant career, and even provoke them into using these skills by reinforcing their sense of alienation from the rest of society.[3] Nor is this observation a modern one:

> The misery suffered in gaols is not half their evil; they are filled with every sort of corruption that poverty and wickedness can generate; with all the shameless and profligate enormities that can be produced by the impudence of ignominy, the range of want, and the malignity of despair. In a prison the check of the public eye is removed; and the power of the law is spent. There are few fears, there are no blushes. The lewd inflame the more modest; the audacious harden the timid. Everyone fortifies himself as he can against his own remaining sensibility; endeavoring to practise on others the arts that are practised on himself; and to gain the applause of his worst associates by imitating their manners.[4]

These lines, written almost two centuries ago, are a harsh indictment of prisons, but many of the conditions they describe continue to be reported in even the most modern studies of prison life. Looking at the matter from a long-range historical perspective, it is fair to conclude that prisons have done a conspicuously poor job of reforming the convicts placed in their custody; but the very consistency of this failure may have a peculiar logic of its own. Perhaps we find it difficult to change the worst of our penal practices because we *expect* the prison to harden the inmate's commitment to deviant forms of behavior and draw him more deeply into the deviant ranks. On the whole, we are a people who do not really expect deviants to change very much as they are processed through the control agencies we provide for them, and we are often reluctant to devote much of the community's resources to the job of rehabilitation. In this sense, the prison which graduates long rows of accomplished criminals (or, for that matter, the state asylum which stores its most severe cases away in some back ward) may do serious violence to the aims of its founders; but it does very little violence to the expectations of the population it serves.

These expectations, moreover, are found in every corner of society and constitute an important part of the climate in which we deal with deviant forms of behavior.

To begin with, the community's decision to bring deviant sanctions against one of its members is not a simple act of censure. It is an intricate rite of transition, at once moving the individual out of his ordinary place in society and transferring him into a special deviant position.[5] The ceremonies which mark this change of status, generally, have a number of related phases. They supply a formal stage on which the deviant and his community can confront one another (as in the criminal trial); they make an announcement about the nature of his deviancy (a verdict or diagnosis, for example); and they place him in a particular role which is thought to neutralize the harmful effects of his misconduct (like the role of prisoner or patient). These commitment ceremonies tend to be occasions of wide public interest and ordinarily take place in a highly dramatic setting.[6] Perhaps the most obvious example of a commitment ceremony is the criminal trial, with its elaborate formality and exaggerated ritual, but more modest equivalents can be found wherever procedures are set up to judge whether or not someone is legitimately deviant.

Now an important feature of these ceremonies in our own culture is that they are almost irreversible. Most provisional roles conferred by society—those of the student or conscripted soldier, for example—include some kind of terminal ceremony to mark the individual's movement back out of the role once its temporary advantages have been exhausted. But the roles allotted the deviant seldom make allowance for this type of passage. He is ushered into the deviant position by a decisive and often dramatic ceremony, yet is retired from it with scarcely a word of public notice. And as a result, the deviant often returns home with no proper license to resume a normal life in the community. Nothing has happened to cancel out the stigmas imposed upon him by earlier commitment ceremonies; nothing has happened to revoke the verdict or diagnosis pronounced upon him at that time. It should not be surprising, then, that the people of the community are apt to greet the returning deviant with a considerable degree of apprehension and distrust, for in a very real sense they are not at all sure who he is.

A circularity is thus set into motion which has all the earmarks of a "self-fulfilling prophesy," to use Merton's fine phrase. On the one hand, it seems quite obvious that the community's apprehensions help reduce whatever chances the deviant might otherwise have had for a successful return home. Yet at the same time, everyday experience seems to show that these suspicions are wholly reasonable, for it is a well-known and highly publicized fact that many if not most ex-convicts return to crime after leaving prison and that large numbers of mental patients require further treatment after an initial hospitalization. The common feeling that deviant persons never really change, then, may derive from a faulty premise; but the feeling is expressed so frequently and with such conviction that it eventually creates the facts which later "prove" it to be correct. If the returning deviant encounters this circularity often enough, it is quite understandable that he, too, may begin to wonder whether he has fully graduated from the deviant role, and he may respond to the uncertainty by resuming some kind of deviant activity. In many respects, this may be the only way for the individual and his community to agree what kind of person he is.

Moreover this prophesy is found in the official policies of even the most responsible agencies of control. Police departments could not operate with any real effectiveness if they did not regard ex-convicts as a ready pool of suspects to be tapped in the event of trouble, and psychiatric clinics could not do a successful job in the community if they were not always alert to the possibility of former patients suffering relapses. Thus the prophesy gains currency at many levels within the social order, not only in the poorly informed attitudes of the community at large, but in the best informed theories of most control agencies as well.

In one form or another this problem has been recognized in the West for many hundreds of years, and this simple fact has a curious implication. For if our culture has supported a steady flow of deviation throughout long periods of historical change, the rules which apply to any kind of evolutionary thinking would suggest that strong forces must be at work to keep the flow intact—and this because it contributes in some important way to the survival of the culture as a whole. This does not furnish us with sufficient warrant to declare that deviance is "functional" (in any of the many senses of that term), but it should certainly make us wary of the assumption so often made in sociological circles that any well-structured society is somehow designed to prevent deviant behavior from occurring.[7]

It might be then argued that we need new metaphors to carry our thinking about deviance onto a different plane. On the whole, American sociologists have devoted most of their attention to those forces in society which seem to assert a centralizing influence on human behavior, gathering people together into tight clusters called "groups" and bringing them under the jurisdiction of governing principles called "norms" or "standards." The questions which sociologists have traditionally asked of their data, then, are addressed to the uniformities rather than the divergencies of social life: how is it that people learn to think in similar ways, to accept the same group moralities, to move by the same rhythms of behavior, to see life with the same eyes? How is it, in short, that cultures accomplish the incredible alchemy of making unity out of diversity, harmony out of conflict, order out of confusion? Somehow we often act as if the differences between people can be taken for granted, being too natural to require comment, but that the symmetry which human groups manage to achieve must be explained by referring to the molding influence of the social structure.

But variety, too, is a product of the social structure. It is certainly remarkable that members of a culture come to look so much alike; but it is also remarkable that out of all this sameness a people can develop a complex division of labor, move off into diverging career lines, scatter across the surface of the territory they share in common, and create so many differences of temper, ideology, fashion, and mood. Perhaps we can conclude, then, that two separate yet often competing currents are found in any society: those forces which promote a high degree of conformity among the people of the community so that they know what to expect from one another, and those forces which encourage a certain degree of diversity so that people can be deployed across the range of group space to survey its potential, measure its capacity, and, in the case of those we call deviants, patrol its boundaries. In such a scheme, the deviant would appear as a natural product of group differentiation. He is not a bit of debris spun out by faulty social machinery, but a relevant figure in the community's overall division of labor.

Notes

1. In fact, the first statement of the general notion presented here was concerned with the study of small groups. See Robert A. Dentler and Kai T. Erikson, "The Functions of Deviance in Groups," *Social Problems,* VII (Fall 1959), pp. 98–107.

2. Aldous Huxley, *Prisons: The "Carceri" Etchings by Piranesi* (London: The Trianon Press, 1949), p. 13.

3. For a good description of this process in the modern prison, see Gresham Sykes, *The Society of Captives* (Princeton, N.J.: Princeton University Press, 1958). For discussions of similar problems in two different kinds of mental hospital, see Erving Goffman, *Asylums* (New York: Bobbs-Merrill, 1962) and Kai T. Erikson, "Patient Role and Social Uncertainty: A Dilemma of the Mentally Ill," *Psychiatry,* XX (August 1957), pp. 263–274.

4. Written by "a celebrated" but not otherwise identified author (perhaps Henry Fielding) and quoted in John Howard, *The State of the Prisons,* London, 1777 (London: J. M. Dent and Sons, 1929), p. 10.

5. The classic description of this process as it applies to the medical patient is found in Talcott Parsons, *The Social System* (Glencoe, Ill.: The Free Press, 1951).

6. See Harold Garfinkel, "Successful Degradation Ceremonies," *American Journal of Sociology,* LXI (January 1956), pp. 420–424.

7. Albert K. Cohen, for example, speaking for a dominant strain in sociological thinking, takes the question quite for granted: "It would seem that the control of deviant behavior is, by definition, a culture goal." See "The Study of Social Disorganization and Deviant Behavior" in Merton et al., *Sociology Today* (New York: Basic Books, 1959), p. 465.

The Conflict Perspective

A basic premise underlying conflict perspectives is that the life experiences of groups are generally shaped by those who have power over them. From a conflict perspective, then, it is important to understand the different life experiences of groups within the population. In a diverse society such as ours, socializing experiences vary a great deal, and people are often confronted with conflicting definitions of a situation. In some cases, acting in accordance with one's own values may result in being defined as deviant by those others who are successful in attaching the label (those with power). In other cases, populations become eligible for control by those who are able to create deviant categories intended to "manage" certain groups. These ideas are illustrated and elaborated upon in the following three selections.

In "The Conflict of Conduct Norms," Thorsten Sellin argues that actors are members of numerous groups and are, therefore, exposed to many different sets of conduct norms and values. Among those who migrate from one society to another, the sense of cultural conflict may be particularly severe. Migrants frequently find themselves constrained and regulated by a new and unfamiliar set of values. Sellin cites, as an example, the case in which a father kills the seducer of his daughter. In Sicily, killing a seducer is acceptable; in the United States it is considered murder. A lack of consensus with respect to existing norms, then, may not only give rise to cultural conflicts of various types but may also result in the application of deviant labels to those who violate deviant categories.

Jeffrey H. Reiman, in "A Radical Perspective on Crime," offers a contemporary statement on the conflict model. He maintains that laws and the associated criminal justice system operate in such a manner as to support the established social and economic order. Concentrating on the individual wrongdoer, Reiman argues, is a particularly effective way of attaining this end. By blaming the individual, the criminal justice system simultaneously diverts our attention away from the possible evils of the social order and acquits society of any criminality or injustice. Further, Reiman argues that various types of social arrangements actually sustain and benefit from the perpetuation of the ideology of individual failure or blame. Reiman uses portions of Cloward and Ohlin's theory to buttress his case. For example, even though people are encouraged to succeed, many do fail, and especially those from the lower classes. As Reiman puts it: " . . . many are called but few are chosen." Involvement in criminal activities does offer an outlet for those experiencing failure and frustration. Thus, not only is society structured in such a way as to actually produce crime, but those who "reap the benefits of the competition for success" (i.e., those who enjoy a high standard of living) do not have to pay for the costs of this competition. The bill is paid by the poor. In fact, the affluent, Reiman argues, deny that they benefit from an economic system that produces a high degree of suffering and frustration for the poor.

This bias against the poor is manifested in other ways. Reiman speaks specifically of the bonuses associated with such a bias. For example, an image is conveyed that the real threat to a decent society comes from the poor. Another important bonus for the powerful is that the bias generates persistent hostility toward the poor. Reiman then notes some of the indignities that the poor suffer at the hands of the welfare system and its agents. Aid, instead of being viewed as an act of justice, is perceived as an act of charity. Many of these points, we might add, will be elaborated on in Part VI, particularly in our discussion of the need to rehabilitate institutions and social systems.

In their article, "Differential Punishing of African Americans and Whites Who Possess Drugs: A Just Policy or a Continuation of the Past?," Rudolph Alexander, Jr., and Jacquelyn Gyamerah address the issue of race and punishment. Their purpose is to set current charges of racial discrimination in broader historical context that reaches back to slavery and the reconstruction period. They argue that the origins of differential criminal treatment of African Americans can be traced to the need to control slaves. This required different sets of laws that applied to whites and slaves. Laws for slaves were more extensive with far greater limitations, and violations were sanctioned more severely. Alexander and Gyamerah draw our attention to the fact that all groups do not share equal voice in shaping social policy. The article serves as illustration for Reiman's "Radical Conflict Approach" in that (1) populations have been the target for management and (2) management strategies can be employed that differentially impact the target group (such as adding behaviors that are likely a part of the target population to the list of deviance). The "Conflict of Conduct Norms," as presented by Sellin is also illustrated here. Alexander and Gyamerah show how the dominant group is able to shape perceptions, laws, and sanctions related to deviance. Notice that when the dominant group is disadvantaged, laws may, in fact, change to relieve the disadvantage.

9   The Conflict of Conduct Norms

Thorsten Sellin

Culture Conflicts as Conflicts of Cultural Codes

. . . There are social groups on the surface of the earth which possess complexes of conduct norms which, due to differences in the mode of life and the social values evolved by these groups, appear to set them apart from other groups in many or most respects. We may expect conflicts of norms when the rural dweller moves to the city, but we assume that he has absorbed the basic norms of the culture which comprises both town and country. How much greater is not the conflict likely to be when Orient and Occident meet, or when the Corsican mountaineer is transplanted to the lower East Side of New York. Conflicts of cultures are inevitable when the norms of one cultural or subcultural area migrate to or come in contact with those of another.

Conflicts between the norms of divergent cultural codes may arise

1. when these codes clash on the border of contiguous culture areas;
2. when, as may be the case with legal norms, the law of one cultural group is extended to cover the territory of another; or
3. when members of one cultural group migrate to another.[1]

Speck, for instance, notes that "where the bands popularly known as Montagnais have come more and more into contact with Whites, their reputation has fallen lower among the traders who have known them through commercial relationships within that period. The accusation is made that they have become less honest in connection with their debts, less trustworthy with property, less truthful, and more inclined to alcoholism and sexual freedom as contacts with the frontier towns have become easier for them. Richard White reports in 1933 unusual instances of Naskapi breaking into traders' store houses."[2]

Similar illustrations abound in the works of the cultural anthropologists. We need only to recall the effect on the American Indian of the culture conflicts induced by our policy of acculturation by guile and force. In this instance, it was not merely contact with the white man's culture, his religion, his business methods, and his liquor, which weakened the tribal mores. In addition, the Indian became subject to the white man's law and this brought conflicts as well, as has always been the case when legal norms have been imposed upon a group previously ignorant of them. Maunier[3] in discussing the diffusion of French law in Algeria, recently stated: "In introducing the *Code Penal* in our colonies, as we do, we transform into offenses the ancient usages of the inhabitants which their customs permitted or imposed. Thus, among the Khabyles of Algeria, the killing of adulterous wives is ritual murder committed by the father or brother of the wife and not by her husband, as elsewhere. The woman having been sold by her family to her husband's family, the honor of her relatives is soiled by her infidelity. Her father or brother has the right and the duty to kill her in order to cleanse by her blood the honor of her relatives. Murder in revenge is also a duty, from family to family, in case of murder of or even in case of insults to a relative: the vendetta, called the *rekba* in Khabylina, is imposed by the law of honor. But these are crimes in French law! Murder for revenge, being premeditated and planned, is assassination, punishable by death! . . . What happens, then, often when our authorities pursue the criminal, guilty of an offense against public safety as well as against morality: public enemy of the French order, but who has acted in accord with a respected custom? The witnesses of the assassination, who are his relatives, or neighbors, fail to lay charges against the assassin; when they are questioned, they pretend to know nothing; and the pursuit is therefore useless. A French magistrate has been able to speak of the conspiracy of silence among the Algerians; a conspiracy aiming to preserve traditions, always followed and obeyed, against their violation by our power. This is the tragic aspect of the conflict of laws. A recent decree forbids the husband among the Khabyles to profit arbitrarily by the power given him according to this law to repudiate his wife, demanding that her new husband pay an exorbitant price for her—this is the custom of the *lefdi*. Earlier, one who married a repudiated wife paid nothing to the former husband. It appears that the first who tried to avail himself of the new law was killed for violating the old custom. The abolition of the ancient law does not always occur without protest or opposition. That which is a crime was a duty; and the order which we cause to reign is sometimes established to the detriment of 'superstition'; it is the gods and the spirits, it is believed, that would punish any one who fails to revenge his honor."

When Soviet law was extended to Siberia, similar effects were observed. Anossow[4] and Wirschubski[5] both relate that women among the Siberian tribes, who, in obedience to the law, laid aside their veils, were killed by their relatives for violating one of the most sacred norms of their tribes.

We have noted that culture conflicts are the natural outgrowth of processes of social differentiation, which produce an infinity of social

groupings, each with its own definitions of life situations, its own interpretations of social relationships, its own ignorance or misunderstanding of
the social values of other groups. The transformation of a culture from a
homogeneous and well-integrated type to a heterogeneous and disinte-
grated type is therefore accompanied by an increase of conflict situations.
Conversely, the operation of integrating processes will reduce the number
of conflict situations. Such conflicts within a changing culture may be distinguished from those created when different cultural systems come in
contact with one another, regardless of the character or stage of development of these systems. In either case, the conduct of members of a group
involved in the conflict of codes will in some respects be judged abnormal
by the other group.

The Study of Culture Conflicts

In the study of culture conflicts, some scholars have been concerned with
the effect of such conflicts on the conduct of specific persons, an approach
which is naturally preferred by psychologists and psychiatrists and by sociologists who have used the life history technique. These scholars view
the conflict as internal. Wirth[6] states categorically that a culture "conflict
can be said to be a factor in delinquency only if the individual feels it or
acts as if it were present." Culture conflict is mental conflict, but the character of this conflict is viewed differently by the various disciplines which
use this term. Freudian psychiatrists[7] regard it as a struggle between deeply
rooted biological urges which demand expression and the culturally created rules which give rise to inhibitive mechanisms which thwart this expression and drive them below the conscious level of the mind, whence
they rise either by ruse in some socially acceptable disguise, as abnormal
conduct when the inhibiting mechanism breaks down, or as neuroses when
it works too well. The sociologist, on the other hand, thinks of mental conflict as being primarily the clash between antagonistic conduct norms incorporated in personality. "Mental conflict in the person," says Burgess in
discussing the case presented by Shaw in *The Jack-Roller,* "may always be
explained in terms of the conflict of divergent cultures."[8]

If this view is accepted, sociological research on culture conflict and its
relationships to abnormal conduct would have to be strictly limited to a
study of the personality of cultural hybrids. Significant studies could be
conducted only by the life-history case technique applied to persons in
whom the conflict is internalized, appropriate control groups being utilized,
of course. . . .

The absence of mental conflict, in the sociological sense, may, however,
be well studied in terms of culture conflict. An example may make this
clear. A few years ago a Sicilian father in New Jersey killed the sixteen-
year-old seducer of his daughter, expressing surprise at his arrest since he

had merely defended his family honor in a traditional way. In this case a mental conflict in the sociological sense did not exist. The conflict was external and occurred between cultural codes or norms. We may assume that where such conflicts occur violations of norms will arise merely because persons who have absorbed the norms of one cultural group or area migrate to another and that such conflict will continue so long as the acculturation process has not been completed. . . . Only then may the violations be regarded in terms of mental conflict.

If culture conflict may be regarded as sometimes personalized, or mental, and sometimes as occurring entirely in an impersonal way solely as a conflict of group codes, it is obvious that research should not be confined to the investigation of mental conflicts and that contrary to Wirth's categorical statement that it is impossible to demonstrate the existence of a culture conflict "objectively . . . by a comparison between two cultural codes"[9] this procedure has not only a definite function, but may be carried out by researchers employing techniques which are familiar to the sociologist.

The emphasis on the life history technique has grown out of the assumption that "the experiences of one person at the same time reveals the life activities of his group" and that "habit in the individual is an expression of custom in society."[10] This is undoubtedly one valid approach. Through it we may hope to discover generalizations of a scientific nature by studying persons who (1) have drawn their norms of conduct from a variety of groups with conflicting norms, or (2) who possess norms drawn from a group whose code is in conflict with that of the group which judges the conduct. In the former case alone can we speak of mental or internal culture conflict; in the latter, the conflict is external.

If the conduct norms of a group are, with reference to a given life situation, inconsistent, or if two groups possess inconsistent norms, we may assume that the members of these various groups will individually reflect such group attitudes. Paraphrasing Burgess, the experiences of a group will reveal the life activities of its members. While these norms can, no doubt, be best established by a study of a sufficient number of representative group members, they may for some groups at least be fixed with sufficient certainty to serve research purposes by a study of the social institutions, the administration of justice, the novel, the drama, the press, and other expressions of group attitudes. The identification of the groups in question having been made, it might be possible to determine to what extent such conflicts are reflected in the conduct of their members. Comparative studies based on the violation rates of the members of such groups, the trends of such rates, etc., would dominate this approach to the problem.

In conclusion, then, culture conflict may be studied either as mental conflict or as a conflict of cultural codes. The criminologist will naturally tend to concentrate on such conflicts between legal and nonlegal conduct norms. The concept of conflict fails to give him more than a general framework of reference for research. In practice, it has, however, become nearly synonymous with conflicts between the norms of cultural systems or areas. Most researches which have employed it have been done on immigrant or race groups in the United States, perhaps due to the ease with which such groups may be identified, the existence of more statistical data recognizing such groupings, and the conspicuous differences between some immigrant norms and our norms.

Notes

1. This is unfortunately not the whole story, for with the rapid growth of impersonal communication, the written (press, literature) and the spoken word (radio, talkie), knowledge concerning divergent conduct norms no longer grows solely out of direct personal contact with their carriers. And out of such conflicts grow some violations of custom and of law which would not have occurred without them.

2. Speck, Frank G. "Ethical Attributes of the Labrador Indians." *American Anthropologist.* N. S. 35:559–94. October–December 1933. P. 559.

3. Maunier, René. "La diffusion du droit français en Algérie." Harvard Tercentenary Publications, *Independence, Convergence, and Borrowing in Institutions, Thought, and Art.* Cambridge: Harvard University Press. 1937. Pp. 84–85.

4. Anossow, J.J. "Die volkstümlichen Verbrechen im Strafkodex der USSR." *Monatsschrift für Kriminalpsychologie und Strafrechtsreform.* 24:534–37. September 1933.

5. Wirschubski, Gregor. "Der Schutz der Sittlichkeit im Sowjetstrafrecht." *Zeitschrift für die gesamte Strafrechtswissenschaft.* 51:317–28. 1931.

6. Wirth, Louis. "Culture Conflict and Misconduct." *Social Forces.* 9:484–92. June 1931. P. 490. Cf. Allport, Floyd H. "Culture Conflict versus the Individual as Factors in Delinquency." *Ibid.* Pp. 493–97.

7. White, William A. *Crimes and Criminals.* New York: Farrar & Rinehart. 1933. Healy, William. *Mental Conflict and Misconduct.* Boston: Little, Brown & Co. 1917. Alexander, Franz and Healy, William. *Roots of Crime.* New York: Alfred A. Knopf. 1935.

8. Burgess, Ernest W. in Clifford R. Shaw's *The Jack-Roller.* Chicago: University of Chicago Press. 1930. Pp. 184–197, p. 186.

9. Wirth, Louis. *Op. cit.* P. 490. It should be noted that Wirth also states that culture should be studied "on the objective side" and that "the sociologist is not primarily interested in personality but in culture."

10. Burgess, Ernest W. *Op. cit.* P. 186.

Differential Punishing of African Americans and Whites Who Possess Drugs: A Just Policy or a Continuation of the Past?

Rudolph Alexander, Jr.
Jacquelyn Gyamerah

Five African Americans in Minnesota were arrested and charged with possession of a cocaine base, known on the street as crack. The statute that they were charged under provided that possession of 3 or more grams of crack cocaine was a third-degree felony, punishable by up to 20 years of incarceration. In addition, the same statute provided that possession of 10 grams or more of a cocaine powder was a third-degree felony. Less than 10 grams of cocaine powder was a fifth-degree felony, punishable by up to 5 years. In Hennepin County in 1988, 97% of the persons arrested for cocaine base or crack were African Americans, and 80% of the persons arrested for cocaine powder were White. Because of these statistics and differential punishments, the five African Americans contested the constitutionality of the statute. After hearing the presentation of the issues, the Minnesota Supreme Court upheld the challenge and ruled the statute unconstitutional (*State v. Russell*, 1991).

The issue of whether African Americans are punished more severely than are White Americans by the criminal justice system and whether the system is racist has been debated in the literature (Blumstein, 1982; Johnson, 1992, Peterson & Hagan, 1984). On one hand, some criminal justice professionals have called the charge of a racist criminal justice system a myth (Langan, 1985; Wilbanks, 1987) or have stated that the evidence is mixed (Petersilia, 1983; Peterson & Hagan, 1984). However, other professionals have stated that the U.S. criminal justice system indeed is racist (Christianson, 1981/1991; Miller, 1991), and this racism traces itself back to slavery and the reconstruction period and continues today (Johnson & Secret, 1990). The purpose of this article is to recount this history, to discuss within this historical context the Minnesota case and the major federal cases involving charges of racial discrimination in the criminal justice system, and to propose a change in policy regarding possession of crack.

The Origins and Course of Differential Punishing of African Americans

The genesis of differential criminal treatment of African Americans is the slavery period in the United States. Controlling slaves required slave owners to subject slaves to sanctions for behaviors that were not offenses if committed by Whites. Punishable offenses for slaves included leaving the plantation without a pass, being out of their quarters after curfew, and being in a group of more than five slaves without a White man present. Slaves could not own firearms or animals, buy alcohol, give medicine to Whites, work in a drugstore, or work in a printing shop (Sellin, 1976). Moreover, slaves could not address a White person rudely or strike a White person even in self-defense, and these offenses were punishable crimes (Meier & Rudwick, 1976).

Slave-holding legislators did not view their traditional courts for free Whites as adequate for controlling slaves. Punishment for slaves had to be harsher than punishment for Whites because of a need to instill fear and obedience in slaves. As a result, state legislators created special courts to try slaves. These courts were called "Negro courts" and the judges were a combination of county justices and slave owners. For instance, Louisiana tried slaves for noncapital offenses before a court consisting of one justice and four slave holders. Mississippi tried slaves before a court consisting of two justices and five slave holders. Georgia tried slaves before three justices. Punishments decreed in these courts were swift and consisted primarily of whippings (Haunton, 1972/1992). In 1850, Georgia abolished its Negro courts and allowed its regular legal system to handle offenses by slaves, but in the other slave states the Negro courts existed to the end of slavery (Sellin, 1976).

Following slavery and the Civil War, both Presidents Lincoln and Johnson provided considerable latitude to Southern states to address the South's depressed economies, which were no longer going to be based on slave labor. Southern legislators responded with a series of laws, called the Black Codes, designed to reenslave African Americans and reestablish White supremacy (Levesque, 1989/1992; Wilson, 1980). As an example, the vagrancy law was vigorously enforced. Any African American without a permanent address or unemployed could be arrested and fined. If unable to pay the fine, he or she would be bound out to a plantation or leased (Adamson, 1983; Sisk, 1958/1992; Wilson, 1980). As W.E.B. Dubois wrote in 1901, many African Americans in the rural South were peons, "bound by law and custom to economic slavery, from which the only escape is death or the penitentiary" (Dubois, 1970, p. 124).

Wanting to increase the numbers of Africans in prisons in order to control them more effectively, Southern states enacted a series of laws targeting African Americans for differential punishments. As an example, several states increased the penalties for stealing livestock, making such acts grand larceny. Thus, stealing pigs or chickens could be punished by up to 10 years of incarceration (Adamson, 1983). To counter some of these unfair laws, Congress passed the first of a series of civil rights acts and the Fourteenth Amendment. Although the Fourteenth Amendment exists for all Americans, its origin was to address the legal problems of African Americans. As Jacob M. Howard, a member of the Senate Joint Committee on Reconstruction, reportedly wrote, the Fourteenth Amendment "prohibits the hanging of a black man for a crime for which the white man is not to be hanged" (Meltsner, 1973, p. 74).

However, the Fourteenth Amendment failed to provide this protection to African Americans because states continue to punish African Americans more seriously than Whites. The effect of targeting African Americans is seen in their increase in the penal systems. For example, in 1875, North Carolina had 569 African Americans in its penal institutions but only 78 Whites (Sellin, 1976). Similarly, Louisiana had 1,143 persons in its penal institutions in 1901 and 984 were African Americans (Sellin, 1976). In addition, Alabama created its "chain gang" in the 1920s, discarding its lease system. By the end of 1941, Alabama had 25 camps and all 1,717 prisoners in these camps were African Americans (Sellin, 1976). South Carolina's chain gangs in 1926 contained 1,017 African Americans and 298 Whites (Sellin, 1976). These disparate numbers suggest either that African Americans were committing more crimes or states were imposing punishments on African Americans that were not generally imposed on Whites. This latter explanation seems more correct.

For instance, all the persons executed by South Carolina and Virginia for *attempted rape* were African Americans (Bowers, 1984). In one case upholding a death sentence for an African American for attempted rape, the Virginia Supreme Court stressed that prompt convictions and severe penalties were needed in rape or attempted rape cases to decrease the likelihood of lynch law (*Hart v. Commonwealth*, 1921). The court's observation reveals the racial overtones in sexual assault cases, but it does not explain other instances where African Americans were punished more severely than Whites. For example, a few individuals have been executed for armed robbery in this country, and all but one were African Americans (Bowers, 1984).

A few laws were written during slavery that targeted African Americans and survived into the 20th century. For example, Georgia passed an anti-slave insurrection law involving printed materials in 1861, and the penalty was death. The law was broadened in 1871 to include speech and a lesser penalty was included ranging from 5 to 20 years. The law was used in the 1930s in Atlanta, Georgia to try an African American named Angelo Herndon who advocated social equality and self-determination for all African Americans. The prosecutor sought the death penalty for the defendant, but the jury recommended mercy and a sentence of 18 to 20 years at hard labor (Herndon, 1937).

Placed in an overall context of discriminatory responses by the criminal justice system, the issue of differential punishing of African Americans for possessing crack cocaine seems to be a continuation of historical policy. As one article revealed, White individuals use illicit drugs in substantial numbers, but their arrest numbers are substantially lower than for African Americans ("More Whites Use Drugs," 1992). Furthermore, when Whites are arrested and subsequently convicted, they, as the Minnesota case suggests, may face lesser punishment.

The following discussion explores the Minnesota case in more detail and the analytic framework used by courts to decide whether African Americans have been denied their Fourteenth Amendment right to equal protection of the law.

State v. Russell

In 1989 and 1990, the Minnesota legislature grappled with the issue of drug possession and prescribing appropriate penalties. Following legislative testimonies, it decided that possession of 3 or more grams of cocaine base [hereinafter referred to as crack cocaine] was a third-degree felony (Minnesota Statute § 152.023, 1989), and according to its criminal law, a third-degree felony is punishable by up to 20 years. The following year, the Minnesota legislature decreed that possession of 10 or more grams of cocaine powder was a third-degree felony and less than 10 grams of cocaine powder was a fifth-degree felony (Minnesota Statute § 152.025, 1990) and punishable by up to 5 years. Essentially, possession of 3 grams of crack could be punishable by up to 20 years, but an equal amount of cocaine powder was punishable only by up to 5 years.

Five African Americans, charged with possessing three or more grams of crack and facing up to 20 years in the state penitentiary, asked a trial judge to dismiss charges against them. Particularly, the Black defendants contended that there is no substantial difference between crack cocaine and cocaine powder, but the statutes punished them differently and more harshly for crack. Because 97% of the persons arrested for possession of crack in 1988 were African Americans and 80% of those arrested during that same year for cocaine powder were Whites, the statutes had a discriminatory impact and violated the equal protection clauses of both the U.S. and Minnesota Constitutions.

The trial judge, an African American woman, dismissed the charges and certified the following question to the Minnesota Supreme Court for a ruling: Does Minnesota Statute § 152.023, Subdivision 2(1)(1989), as it is applied, violate the equal protection clauses of the Fourteenth Amendment of the United States Constitution and the Minnesota Constitution, Article 1, Section 2? After considering its precedents, a majority of the justices held that the statute in question violated the Minnesota Constitution.

The majority justices arrived at its decision by noting differences in Minnesota's rational basis test and the federal test when challenges are made that a statute violates equal protection of the law. The federal rational basis test requires that (a) the statute serves a legitimate purpose and that (b) it was reasonable for legislators to believe that the statute would serve that purpose. However, Minnesota's rational basis test is substantially higher and requires that

> (1) the distinctions which separate those included within the classification from those excluded must not be manifestly arbitrary or fanciful but must be genuine and substantial, thereby providing a natural and reasonable basis to justify legislation adapted to peculiar conditions and needs; (2) the classification must be genuine and relevant to the purpose of the law; that is there must be an evident connection between the distinctive needs peculiar to the class and the prescribed remedy; and (3) the purpose of the statute must be one that the state can legitimately attempt to achieve. (*State v. Russell*, 1991, p. 888)

Hence, Minnesota's rational basis test is less deferential to the state than the federal test and requires a reasonable connection between the *actual* effects and the statutory aims.

Accordingly, the challenged statute was unconstitutional under Minnesota's rational basis test for three reasons. First, the statute failed to distinguish genuinely and substantially those individuals inside and outside the class. The state's primary justification for prescribing differences in punishment between those persons who possess 3 grams of crack and less than 10 grams of cocaine came from the legislative testimony of one lone prosecutor. According to this prosecutor, these levels indicate whether one is using drugs or selling drugs. That is, a person who possesses 3 or more grams of drugs is a dealer, and a person who possesses 10 or more grams of cocaine powder is also a dealer. However, a report by the Minnesota Department of Public Safety Office of Drug Policy revealed that most prosecutors in Minnesota and other law enforcement officers did not accept the 3 and 10 distinction levels.

The second defect of the statute is that the defenders of it contended that the Minnesota legislature considered crack to be more addictive and dangerous than cocaine powder, and thus the legislature was justified in prescribing harsher penalties for crack possession. However, the majority, viewing this justification similar to the first, stated that the state had failed to establish a genuine and substantial difference between those inside and outside the class. The legislative view that crack is more addictive and dangerous than cocaine powder came from the testimony of a Minneapolis narcotic officer, who was not a trained chemist or scientist. But at the pretrial hearing, a certified chemist testified that crack and cocaine powder react differentially on the central nervous and respiratory systems when crack is smoked and cocaine powder is inhaled. The primary difference is that a smaller amount of crack will produce the same effect as a slightly higher amount of cocaine powder. However, there is no difference in the two drugs' effect if cocaine powder is dissolved in water and injected. Thus, cocaine powder has the same effect as crack if it is injected rather than inhaled.

Third, the state contended that it was justified in prescribing higher penalties for crack because there is more violence associated with crack than with cocaine powder. The majority understood this justification to be the state's contention that crack had a pharmacological effect that leads to violence, but the majority rejected it. The majority, looking at sociological evidence, associated the violence surrounding crack to gang warfare and group dynamics, which do not justify distinguishing statutorily crack and cocaine powder.

The majority also considered the statute to be unconstitutional because the classification between the two drugs did not serve the statutory purpose. Indeed, the state has the right to try to eliminate drug problems by punishing individuals who possess drugs. However, without more substantial evidence, other than the anecdotal testimony, the statute failed to achieve its aims. A person who possesses 3 grams of crack may be a user rather than a dealer, and a person who possesses less than 10 grams of cocaine may be a dealer who intends to convert the drug into more than 3 grams of crack. Thus, the statute is arbitrary and unreasonable. Moreover, the majority considered the statute to be unconstitutional because it assumes that an individual intends to deal drugs, on the basis of the amount possessed, without proof and thus violates due process of law.

▶Federal Decisions Involving Differential Punishing

The U.S. Supreme Court has decided numerous cases that involve racial issues, such as deciding whether African American defendants were deprived of due process of law in the availability of persons for jury duty, and peripherally decided cases involving differential punishing of African Americans. For instance, in 1970, the Court reversed on procedural grounds a death sentence for an African American defendant who had been convicted of rape of a White female. However, in that same case in the court of appeals, the issue of discriminatory practices in rape cases was raised by the defendant's attorneys on the basis of a study by Marvin Wolfgang. Justice Blackmun wrote the majority decision by a three-judge panel and stated that statistical evidence resulting from a study of several states failed to provide convincing evidence of racial discrimination. Particularly, the study showed that the death penalty for rape was primarily given to African Americans who had been convicted of raping White females, but Justice Blackmun noted that the study did not involve the county in which the defendant was convicted (*Maxwell v. Bishop*, 1968).

Arguments continued to be presented to the Court about the racial effects in rape cases, and the Court decided eventually that the death penalty for rape was unconstitutional. In ruling as it did, the Court did not consider the equal protection argument or directly discuss the statistical evidence presented to them. Instead, it focused on the small number of states that retain the death penalty for rape and the seemingly consensus of society that the death penalty for rape was no longer a valid punishment. As a result, the death penalty for rape violated the Cruel and Unusual Punishment Clause of the Eighth Amendment (*Coker v. Georgia,* 1977). Observers speculated, however, that the Court was persuaded by the racial arguments but did not want to state that it had been influenced by the impact of the racial evidence and arguments (*McCleskey v. Kemp,* 1987).

However, the Court had considered several cases involving contentions that official actions were motivated by racial discrimination or had a discriminatory impact and thus violated the Equal Protection Clause of the Fourteenth Amendment. The effect of these decisions was the formulation of a legal framework for deciding cases involving violations of the Equal Protection Clause. In one case, the Court decided whether African American plaintiffs were denied the equal protection of the laws in a zoning case and as a result decided how courts should view officials' decisions that have been alleged to have had a discriminatory effect on African Americans.

The case involved a collaboration between a nonprofit corporation in partnership and a religious order to build low-income housing in Arlington Heights, Illinois, a suburb of Chicago. The area was zoned for detached family homes, and the proposed project required a zoning change to attached multifamily homes. The zoning commission, following heated input by residents, denied the request for a zoning change. The builder, along with several African Americans, filed a lawsuit, contending that the denial of the zoning change had a discriminatory effect on the plaintiffs in that they were more likely to need low-income housing. The U.S. district court ruled for the zoning commission, but the court of appeals reversed the lower court decision. By a 5 to 3 decision, the U.S. Supreme Court reversed the court of appeals and upheld the district court (*Arlington Heights v. Metropolitan Housing Corp.,* 1977).

Central to *Arlington Heights* was how courts should decide cases involving alleged discriminatory effects that result in a racially disproportionate impact. The Court stated that official action will not be held unconstitutional just because it results in a racially disproportionate impact. It is an issue to consider, but alone it does not rise to racial discrimination in violation of the Equal Protection Clause. Although the impact of official action and whether it bears more heavily on one race than another is an important starting point, a racially disparate outcome is not conclusive proof of official discrimination. A plaintiff, to establish a violation of the Equal Protection Clause, must establish proof of racially discriminatory intent or purpose. One evidentiary factor is the historical background of the decision. Another is the sequence of events leading to the challenged decision, such as when the officials did have one policy and suddenly change when learning that an integrated event had been proposed and is about to be presented. Further, minutes, reports, and the testimony of officials may provide evidence of purpose. Although these sources are not conclusive, they are some of the sources that plaintiffs must present to the courts for the determination of discrimination (*Arlington Heights v. Metropolitan Housing Corp.,* 1977).

A second prong in analyzing equal protection lawsuits was gleaned by the Eleventh Circuit Court of Appeals (*Underwood v. Hunter,* 1984) and seconded by the Court in *Hunter v. Underwood* (1985). The case involved an African American and a White plaintiff. Both were convicted of passing worthless checks, a misdemeanor in Alabama, and denied the right to vote because such conviction indicated, according to the Alabama Constitution, flaws in their moral turpitude. Both filed lawsuits against the Alabama registrars, contending that this law had a racist origin and violated the Equal Protection Clause. All parties agreed that the Alabama Constitutional Convention that was called in 1901 had as its primary aim the disenfranchisement of African Americans and poor Whites so as to promote White supremacy. The U.S. district court acknowledged that the 1901 convention had a racist agenda, but the plaintiffs had failed to prove that the Alabama registrars exemplified this same racism in disenfranchising them.

However, the Eleventh Circuit Court of Appeals reversed the U.S. district court. The court of appeals wrote that

> to establish a violation of the Fourteenth Amendment in the face of mixed motives, plaintiffs must prove by a preponderance of the evidence that racial discrimination was a substantial or motivating factor in the adoption of section 182 [Alabama Disenfranchisement Law]. They shall then prevail unless the registrars prove by a preponderance of the evidence that the same decision would have resulted had the impermissible purpose not been considered. (*Underwood v. Hunter,* 1984, p. 617)

Using this test, the court of appeals ruled that the plaintiffs had met this burden and the registrars had not.

The court of appeals observed that before 1901, the Alabama Constitution denied persons who had been convicted of felonious crimes from voting. The conveners of the convention in 1901 were looking for legal reasons to disenfranchise African Americans and poor Whites. They consulted the Alabama justices of the peace, who had responsibility for trying African Americans during and after slavery and learned what crimes African Americans were more likely to be accused of committing and brought to courts. As a result, the 1901 delegates added to the list of disenfranchising offenses those crimes that African Americans were more likely to commit. In addition, they added a catchall phrase, moral turpitude, to embrace behaviors such as living in adultery. Enactment of this statute disenfranchised 10 times as many African Americans as Whites, and the effects of this law were still felt in the 1980s. The Alabama officials tried to defend this law by saying that it disenfranchised Whites and Blacks and, therefore, equal protection of the law was not violated. However, the court of appeals recognized the registrars' impartiality in administering the statute, but their impartiality could not cleanse a purposefully discriminatory law that had current effects.

Later, the Supreme Court examined an equal protection claim by a criminal defendant. The case involved Warren McCleskey, an African American, who was convicted in Atlanta, Georgia, of killing a White police officer and given the death penalty. On the basis of a study by Baldus, he argued that he was denied the equal protection of the law because African American defendants who have killed Whites were more likely to receive death sentences than were White defendants. The Court began its analysis of this equal protection claim by stating that a defendant alleging violation of equal protection shoulders the burden of proving the existence of purposeful discrimination. A corollary of this principle is that a criminal defendant also must prove that the purposeful discrimination had a discriminatory effect on *him or her*. Thus, McCleskey, to prevail in his equal protection argument, must show that the judicial officials in *his* case acted with discriminatory purpose. According to the majority, McCleskey did not and the Baldus study is insufficient. Also, McCleskey contended that the state of Georgia's capital punishment statute violated the Equal Protection Clause and allowed it to remain in force despite its discriminatory application. The Court stated that for McCleskey to prove this aspect, he must prove that the Georgia legislature enacted and maintained the death penalty statute *because* of an anticipatory racially discriminatory effect. However, the Court stated that he had failed to prove this claim, and as a result, his claim of a denial of equal protection must fail (*McCleskey v. Kemp*, 1987).

In sum, federal jurisprudence involving an equal protection claim in the criminal context requires a criminal defendant to prove that state officials acted specifically against him or her. This is a higher burden to overcome than the burden a person involved in a civil action must overcome. Moreover, although studies that show discriminatory racial effects are a starting point in determining a violation of equal protection in a civil matter, they have little effect in a criminal case, and a criminal defendant must show that state officials specifically behaved in a racially discriminatory manner toward him or her.

The federal legal test, applied to *Russell* and considered in federal courts, would result in upholding the constitutionality of Minnesota's statute and its penalties. Simply, African Americans would not be able to prove that Minnesota's legislators enacted the statute specifically for racial reasons. In addition, the federal legal test has been used to uphold differential punishing of persons convicted of the federal Anti-Drug Abuse Act of 1986. This act provides a 100-to-1 ratio, which means that for punishment purposes 100 grams of cocaine powder equal 1 gram of crack (*State v. Russell,* 1991).

Conclusion

Russell and *McCleskey* represent two divergent views on differential punishing of African Americans. The rationale adopted by the Minnesota Supreme Court clearly is the more enlightened approach and promotes social justice. Directly and indirectly targeting African Americans for differential punishing, as this article has discussed, has a long history in the United States and continues today. In the past, state legislatures were blatant in their racial intentions, knowing that African Americans did not have recourse in the courts. Now that African Americans' rights are more recognized, the discrimination is not as blatant and direct and has become more subtle and indirect. Whether blatant or subtle, the effect is the same. All courts, as a result, should look closely at the outcomes and adopt the standard used in Minnesota.

The effect of ensnaring more African Americans in the criminal justice system through drug laws is devastating and represents a major factor in their sharp increase in prisons across the country (Mauer, 1990; Miller, 1992). When vast numbers of middle-class Whites in the 1960s were being threatened with felony convictions for possessing marijuana, the response of policy makers and legislators was to make possession of small amounts a misdemeanor (Peterson & Hagan, 1984). Now, a similar response should be initiated for crack. Mere possession of crack should not be a crime, or if it is a crime, it should not be more than a misdemeanor. In this manner, African Americans will be treated with the same concern as Whites were in shaping social policy regarding marijuana.

References

Adamson, C. R. (1983). Punishment after slavery: southern state penal system, 1965–1980. *Social Problems, 30,* 555–569.

Anti-Drug Abuse Act of 1986, Pub. L. No. 104–316, 19 U.S.C. §2081 (1986).

Arlington Heights v. Metropolitan Housing Corp., 429 U.S. 252 (1977).

Blumstein, A. (1982). On the racial disproportionality of United States prison populations. *Journal of Criminal Law and Criminology, 73,* 1259–1281.

Bowers, W. J. (1984). *Legal homicide: Death as punishment in America, 1964–1982.* Boston: Northeastern University Press.

Christianson, S. (1991). Our Black prisons. In K. C. Haas & G. P. Albert (Eds.), *The dilemmas of corrections* (2nd ed., pp. 62–74). Prospect Heights, IL: Waveland. (Reprinted from *Crime and Delinquency,* 1981, *27,* 364–375).

Coker v. Georgia, 433 U.S. 584 (1977).

Dubois, W. E. B. (1970). The freedman's bureau. In L. J. Austin, L. H. Fenderson, & S. P. Nelson (Eds.), *The Black man and the promise of America* (pp. 112–124). Glenview, IL: Scott, Foresman.

Hart v. Commonwealth, 131 Va 726 (1921).

Haunton, R. H. (1992). Law and order in Savannah, 1850–1860. In P. Finkelman (Ed.), *Race, law, and American history 1700–1990* (pp. 189–212). New York: Garland. (Reprinted from *Georgia Historical Society*, 1972, 56, 1–24).

Herndon, A. (1937). *Let me live.* New York: Random House.

Hunter v. Underwood, 471 U.S. 222 (1985).

Johnson, J. B., & Secret, P. E. (1990). Race and juvenile court decision making revisited. *Criminal Justice Policy Review, 4*, 159–187.

Johnson, W. W. (1992, November). *Racial distribution and punishment: An analysis of state level data in the 1980s.* Paper presented at the annual meeting of the American Society of Criminology, New Orleans, LA.

Langan, P. A. (1985). Racism on trial: New evidence to explain the racial composition of prisons in the United States. *Journal of Criminal Law and Criminology, 76*, 666–683.

Levesque, G. A. (1992). Black political power and criminal justice: Washington county, Texas 1868–1884. In P. Finkelman (Ed.), *Race, law and American history 1700–1990* (pp. 268–279). New York: Garland. (Reprinted from *American Journal of Southern History*, 1989, 55, 391–420).

Mauer, M. (1990). *Young Black men and the criminal justice system: A growing national problem.* Washington, DC: The Sentencing Project.

Maxwell v. Bishop, 398 F. 2d 138 (1968).

McCleskey v. Kemp, 481 U.S. 279 (1987).

Meier, A., & Rudwick, E. (1976). *From plantation to ghetto* (3rd ed). New York: Hill & Wang.

Meltsner, M. (1973). *Cruel and unusual: The supreme court and capital punishment.* New York: Random House.

Miller, J. G. (1991). *Last one over the wall.* Columbus: Ohio State University.

Miller, J. G. (1992). *Hobbling a generation: Young African-American males in D.C.'s criminal justice system.* Alexandria, VA: National Center on Institutions and Alternatives.

Minnesota Statute § 152.023 (1989).

Minnesota Statute § 152.025 (1990).

More Whites use drugs, more Blacks arrested. (1992, November). *Columbus Dispatch,* p. 14A.

Petersilia, J. (1983). *Racial disparities in the criminal justice system.* Washington, DC: National Institute of Corrections.

Peterson, R. D., & Hagan, J. (1984). Changing conceptions of race: Towards an account of anomalous findings of sentencing research. *American Sociological Review, 49*, 56–70.

Sellin, J. T. (1976). *Slavery and the penal system.* New York: Elsevier.

Sisk, G. S. (1992). Crime and justice in the Alabama Black belt, 1875–1917. In Finkelman (Ed.), *Race, law, and American history 1700–1990* (pp. 432–439). New York: Garland. (Reprinted from *Mid-America*, 1958, 40, 106–113).

State v. Russell, 477 N. W. 2d 886 (Minn. 1991).

Underwood v. Hunter, 730 F. 2d 614 (1984).

Wilbanks, W. (1987). *The myth of a racist criminal justice system.* Monterey, CA: Brooks/Cole.

Wilson, W. J. (1980). *The declining significance of race: Black and changing American institutions* (2nd ed). Chicago: University of Chicago Press.

Cultural Transmission/ Social Learning Theory

A central tenet underlying the cultural transmission model is the idea that one learns cultural traditions and values through symbolic communication with others. Two of the more famous representatives of this position are Gresham M. Sykes and David Matza.

In "Techniques of Neutralization: A Theory of Delinquency," Sykes and Matza argue that juveniles do not really reject middle-class values. Rather, because the existing normative structure has a certain flexibility, actors can "bend" the laws to fit their needs. Also basic to this thesis is the idea that when actors contemplate the commission of a delinquent or criminal act, they must come to grips with any immediate or potential threats to their identity. Developing an effective system of "neutralization" or rationalization is one way of accomplishing this. Sykes and Matza assert, moreover, that this attitude of self-justification is operative during and after the commission of an offense as well. The writers make the additional point that we all use rationalizations, whether we are involved in deviant activities or not.

Donald L. McCabe puts the "techniques of neutralization" to the test in an exploration of "The Influence of Situational Ethics on Cheating Among College Students." Situational ethics are guidelines for behavior or rules for behavior that are situationally determined. In short, students know how they should justify their cheating behavior in advance. It should be noticed here that Sykes and Matza argue for a similar temporal order—that rationalizations (typically thought to occur after deviant behavior) "may logically precede the deviant behavior." Of central concern for McCabe is whether techniques of neutralization, as described by Sykes and Matza, are actually used within typical social settings. What becomes clear in McCabe's research is that significant numbers of college students cheat and that these students use the rationalizations of Sykes and Matza to deflect attention onto external contextual factors. While the five techniques of neutralization were not reported equally, each was represented. Students deny responsibility ("it's the only way to keep up"), deny injury ("the grades aren't worth much," "no one gets hurt"), deny the victim (cheating was seen as "justified"), condemn the condemners (professors are more lenient on some), and appeal to higher loyalties (students shouldn't judge their peers).

Techniques of Neutralization: A Theory of Delinquency

Gresham M. Sykes
David Matza

As Morris Cohen once said, one of the most fascinating problems about human behavior is why men violate the laws in which they believe. This is the problem that confronts us when we attempt to explain why delinquency occurs despite a greater or lesser commitment to the usages of conformity. A basic clue is offered by the fact that social rules or norms calling for valued behavior seldom if ever take the form of categorical imperatives. Rather, values or norms appear as *qualified* guides for action, limited in their applicability in terms of time, place, persons, and social circumstances. The moral injunction against killing, for example, does not apply to the enemy during combat in time of war, although a captured enemy comes once again under the prohibition. Similarly, the taking and distributing of scarce goods in a time of acute social need is felt by many to be right, although under other circumstances private property is held inviolable. The normative system of a society, then, is marked by what Williams has termed *flexibility;* it does not consist of a body of rules held to be binding under all conditions.[1]

This flexibility is, in fact, an integral part of the criminal law in that measures for "defenses to crimes" are provided in pleas such as non-age, necessity, insanity, drunkenness, compulsion, self-defense, and so on. The individual can avoid moral culpability for his criminal action—and thus avoid the negative sanctions of society—if he can prove that criminal intent was lacking. *It is our argument that much delinquency is based on what is essentially an unrecognized extension of defenses to crimes, in the form of justifications for deviance that are seen as valid by the delinquent but not by the legal system or society at large.*

These justifications are commonly described as rationalizations. They are viewed as following deviant behavior and as protecting the individual from self-blame and the blame of others after the act. But there is also reason to believe that they precede deviant behavior and make deviant behavior possible. It is this possibility that Sutherland mentioned only in passing and that other writers have failed to exploit from the viewpoint of sociological theory. Disapproval flowing from internalized norms and conforming others in the social environment is neutralized, turned back, or deflected in advance. Social controls that serve to check or inhibit deviant motivational patterns are rendered inoperative, and the individual is freed to engage in delinquency without serious damage to his self-image. In this sense, the delinquent both has his cake and eats it too, for he remains committed to the dominant normative system and yet so qualifies its imperatives that violations are "acceptable" if not "right." Thus the delinquent represents not a radical opposition to law-abiding society but something more like an apologetic failure, often more sinned against than sinning in his own eyes. We call these justifications of deviant behavior techniques of neutralization; and we believe these techniques make up a crucial component of Sutherland's "definitions favorable to the violation of law." It is by learning these techniques that the juvenile becomes delinquent, rather than by learning moral imperatives, values, or attitudes standing in direct contradiction to those of the dominant society. In analyzing these techniques, we have found it convenient to divide them into five major types.

The Denial of Responsibility

Insofar as the delinquent can define himself as lacking responsibility for his deviant actions, the disapproval of self or others is sharply reduced in effectiveness as a restraining influence. As Justice Holmes has said, even a dog distinguishes between being stumbled over and being kicked, and modern society is no less careful to draw a line between injuries that are unintentional, i.e., where responsibility is lacking, and those that are intentional. As a technique of neutralization, however, the denial of responsibility extends much further than the claim that deviant acts are an "accident" or some similar negation of personal accountability. It may also be asserted that delinquent acts are due to forces outside of the individual and beyond his control such as unloving parents, bad companions, or a slum neighborhood. In effect, the delinquent approaches a "billiard ball" conception of himself in which he sees himself as helplessly propelled into new situations. From a psychodynamic viewpoint, this orientation toward one's own actions may represent a profound alienation from self, but it is important to stress the fact that interpretations of responsibility are cultural constructs and not merely idiosyncratic beliefs. The similarity between this mode of justifying illegal behavior assumed by the delinquent and the implications of a "sociological" frame of reference or a "humane" jurisprudence is readily apparent.[2] It is not the validity of this orientation that concerns us here, but its function of deflecting blame attached to violations of social norms and its relative independence of a particular personality structure.[3] By learning to view himself as more acted upon than acting, the delinquent prepares the way for deviance from the dominant normative system without the necessity of a frontal assault on the norms themselves.

The Denial of Injury

A second major technique of neutralization centers on the injury or harm involved in the delinquent act. The criminal law has long made a distinction between crimes which are *mala in se* and *mala prohibita*—that is, between acts that are wrong in themselves and acts that are illegal but not immoral—and the delinquent can make the same kind of distinction in evaluating the wrongfulness of his behavior. For the delinquent, however, wrongfulness may turn on the question of whether or not anyone has clearly been hurt by his deviance, and this matter is open to a variety of interpretations. Vandalism, for example, may be defined by the delinquent simply as "mischief"—after all, it may be claimed, the persons whose property has been destroyed can well afford it. Similarly, auto theft may be viewed as "borrowing," and gang fighting may be seen as a private quarrel, an agreed upon duel between two willing parties, and thus of no concern to the community at large. We are not suggesting that this technique of neutralization, labeled the denial of injury, involves an explicit dialectic. Rather, we are arguing that the delinquent frequently, and in a hazy fashion, feels that his behavior does not really cause any great harm despite the fact that it runs counter to law. Just as the link between the individual and his acts may be broken by the denial of responsibility, so may the link between acts and their consequences be broken by the denial of injury. Since society sometimes agrees with the delinquent, e.g., in matters such as truancy, "pranks," and so on, it merely reaffirms the idea that the delinquent's neutralization of social controls by means of qualifying the norms is an extension of common practice rather than a gesture of complete opposition.

The Denial of the Victim

Even if the delinquent accepts the responsibility for his deviant actions and is willing to admit that his deviant actions involve an injury or hurt, the moral indignation of self and others may be neutralized by an insistence that the injury is not wrong in light of the circumstances. The injury, it may be claimed, is not really an injury; rather, it is a form of rightful retaliation or punishment. By a subtle alchemy the delinquent moves himself into the position of an avenger and the victim is transformed into a wrong-doer. Assaults on homosexuals or suspected homosexuals, attacks on members of minority groups who are said to have gotten "out of place," vandalism as revenge on an unfair teacher or school official, thefts from a "crooked" store owner—all may be hurts inflicted on a transgressor, in the eyes of the delinquent. As Orwell has pointed out, the type of criminal admired by the general public has probably changed over the course of years and Raffles no longer serves as a hero;[4] but Robin Hood, and his latter-day derivatives such as the tough detective seeking justice outside the law, still capture the popular imagination, and the delinquent may view his acts as part of a similar role.

To deny the existence of the victim, then, by transforming him into a person deserving injury is an extreme form of a phenomenon we have mentioned before, namely, the delinquent's recognition of appropriate and inappropriate targets for his delinquent acts. In addition, however, the existence of the victim may be denied for the delinquent, in a somewhat different sense, by the circumstances of the delinquent act itself. Insofar as the victim is physically absent, unknown, or a vague abstraction (as is often the case in delinquent acts committed against property), the awareness of the victim's existence is weakened. Internalized norms and anticipations of the reactions of others must somehow be activated if they are to serve as guides for behavior; and it is possible that a diminished awareness of the victim plays an important part of determining whether or not this process is set in motion.

The Condemnation of the Condemners

A fourth technique of neutralization would appear to involve a condemnation of the condemners or, as McCorkle and Korn have phrased it, a rejection of the rejectors.[5] The delinquent shifts the focus of attention from his own deviant acts to the motives and behavior of those who disapprove of his violations. His condemners, he may claim, are hypocrites, deviants in disguise, or impelled by personal spite. This orientation toward the conforming world may be of particular importance when it hardens into a bitter cynicism directed against those assigned the task of enforcing or expressing the norms of the dominant society. Police, it may be said, are corrupt, stupid, and brutal. Teachers always show favoritism and parents always "take it out" on their children. By a slight extension, the rewards of conformity—such as material success—become a matter of pull or luck, thus decreasing still further the stature of those who stand on the side of the law-abiding. The validity of this jaundiced viewpoint is not so important as its function in turning back or deflecting the negative sanctions attached to violations of the norms. The delinquent, in effect, has changed the subject of the conversation in the dialogue between his own deviant impulses and the reactions of others; and by attacking others, the wrongfulness of his own behavior is more easily repressed or lost to view.

The Appeal to Higher Loyalties

Fifth, and last, internal and external social controls may be neutralized by sacrificing the demands of the larger society for the demands of the smaller social groups to which the delinquent belongs, such as the sibling pair, the gang, or the friendship clique. It is important to note that the delinquent does not necessarily repudiate the imperatives of the dominant normative system, despite his failure to follow them. Rather, the delinquent may see himself as caught up in a dilemma that must be resolved, unfortunately, at the cost of violating the law. One aspect of this situation has been studied by Stouffer and Toby in their research on the conflict between particularistic and universalistic demands, between the claims of friendship and general social obligations, and their results suggest that "it is possible to classify people according to a predisposition to select one or the other horn of a dilemma in role conflict."[6] For our purposes, however, the most important point is that deviation from certain norms may occur not because the norms are rejected but because others' norms, held to be more pressing or involving a higher loyalty, are accorded precedence. Indeed, it is the fact that both sets of norms are believed in that gives meaning to our concepts of dilemma and role conflict.

The conflict between the claims of friendship and the claims of law, or a similar dilemma, has of course long been recognized by the social scientist (and the novelist) as a common human problem. If the juvenile delinquent frequently resolves his dilemma by insisting that he must "always help a buddy" or "never squeal on a friend," even when it throws him into serious difficulties with the dominant social order, his choice remains familiar to the supposedly law-abiding. The delinquent is unusual, perhaps, in the extent to which he is able to see the fact that he acts in behalf of the smaller social groups to which he belongs as a justification for violations of society's norms, but it is a matter of degree rather than of kind.

"I didn't mean it." "I didn't really hurt anybody." "They had it coming to them." "Everybody's picking on me." "I didn't do it for myself." These slogans or their variants, we hypothesize, prepare the juvenile for delinquent acts. These "definitions of the situation" represent tangential or glancing blows at the dominant normative system rather than the creation of an opposing ideology; and they are extensions of patterns of thought prevalent in society rather than something created *de novo*.

Techniques of neutralization may not be powerful enough to fully shield the individual from the force of his own internalized values and the reactions of conforming others, for as we have pointed out, juvenile delinquents often appear to suffer from feelings of guilt and shame when called into account for their deviant behavior. And some delinquents may be so isolated from the world of conformity that techniques of neutralization need not be called into play. Nonetheless, we would argue that techniques of neutralization are critical in lessening the effectiveness of social controls and that they lie behind a large share of delinquent behavior. Empirical research in this area is scattered and fragmentary at the present time, but the work of Redl,[7] Cressey,[8] and others has supplied a body of significant data that has done much to clarify the theoretical issues and enlarge the fund of supporting evidence. Two lines of investigation seem to be critical at this stage. First, there is need for more knowledge concerning the differential distribution of techniques of neutralization, as operative patterns of thought, by age, sex, social class, ethnic group, etc. On a priori grounds it might be assumed that these justifications for deviance will be more readily seized by segments of society for whom a discrepancy between common social ideals and social practice is most apparent. It is also possible, however, that the habit of "bending" the dominant normative system—if not "breaking" it—cuts across our cruder social categories and is to be traced primarily to patterns of social interaction within the familial circle. Second, there is need for a greater understanding of the internal structure of techniques of neutralization, as a system of beliefs and attitudes, and its relationship to various types of delinquent behavior. Certain techniques of neutralization would appear to be better adapted to particular deviant acts than to others, as we have suggested, for example, in the case of offenses against property and the denial of the victim. But the issue remains far from clear and stands in need of more information.

In any case, techniques of neutralization appear to offer a promising line of research in enlarging and systematizing the theoretical grasp of juvenile delinquency. As more information is uncovered concerning techniques of neutralization, their origins, and their consequences, both juvenile delinquency in particular and deviation from normative systems in general may be illuminated.

Notes

1. Cf. Robin Williams, Jr., *American Society,* New York: Knopf, 1951, p. 28.

2. A number of observers have wryly noted that many delinquents seem to show a surprising awareness of sociological and psychological explanations for their behavior and are quick to point out the causal role of their poor environment.

3. It is possible, of course, that certain personality structures can accept some techniques of neutralization more readily than others, but this question remains largely unexplored.

4. George Orwell, *Dickens, Dali, and Others,* New York: Reynal, 1946.

5. Lloyd W. McCorkle and Richard Korn, "Resocialization Within Walls," *The Annals of the American Academy of Political and Social Science,* 293 (May, 1954), pp. 88–98.

6. See Samuel A. Stouffer and Jackson Toby, "Role Conflict and Personality," in *Toward a General Theory of Action,* edited by Talcott Parsons and Edward A. Shils, Cambridge, Mass.: Harvard University Press, 1951, p. 494.

7. See Fritz Redl and David Wineman, *Children Who Hate,* Glencoe, Ill.: The Free Press, 1956.

8. See D. R. Cressey, *Other People's Money,* Glencoe, Ill.: The Free Press, 1953.

12 The Influence of Situational Ethics on Cheating Among College Students

Donald L. McCabe

Introduction

Numerous studies have demonstrated the pervasive nature of cheating among college students (Baird 1980; Haines, Diekhoff, LaBeff, and Clark 1986; Michaels and Miethe 1989; Davis, et al. 1992). This research has examined a variety of factors that help explain cheating behavior, but the strength of the relationships between individual factors and cheating has varied considerably from study to study (Tittle and Rowe 1973; Baird 1980; Eisenberger and Shank 1985; Haines, et al. 1986; Ward 1986; Michaels and Miethe 1989; Perry, Kane, Bernesser, and Spicker 1990; Ward and Beck 1990).

Although the factors examined in these studies (for example, personal work ethic, gender, self-esteem, rational choice, social learning, deterrence) are clearly important, the work of LaBeff, Clark, Haines, and Diekhoff (1990) suggests that the concept of situational ethics may be particularly helpful in understanding student rationalizations for cheating. Extending the arguments of Norris and Dodder (1979), LaBeff et al. conclude

> that students hold qualified guidelines for behavior which are situationally determined. As such, the concept of situational ethics might well describe . . . college cheating [as] rules for behavior may not be considered rigid but depend on the circumstances involved. (1990, p. 191.)

LaBeff et al. believe a utilitarian calculus of "the ends justifies the means" underlies this reasoning process and "what is wrong in most situations might be considered right or acceptable if the end is defined as appropriate" (1990, p. 191). As argued by Edwards (1967), the situation determines what is right or wrong in this decision-making calculus and also dictates the appropriate principles to be used in guiding and judging behavior.

128

Sykes and Matza (1957) hypothesize that such rationalizations, that is, "justifications for deviance that are seen as valid by the delinquent but not by the legal system or society at large" (p. 666), are common. However, they challenge conventional wisdom that such rationalizations typically follow deviant behavior as a means of protecting "the individual from self-blame and the blame of others after the act" (p. 666). They develop convincing arguments that these rationalizations may logically precede the deviant behavior and "[d]isapproval from internalized norms and conforming others in the social environment is neutralized, turned back, or deflated in advance. Social controls that serve to check or inhibit deviant motivational patterns are rendered inoperative, and the individual is freed to engage in delinquency without serious damage to his self image" (pp. 666–667).

Using a sample of 380 undergraduate students at a small southwestern university, LaBeff et al. (1990) attempted to classify techniques employed by students in the neutralization of cheating behavior into the five categories of neutralization proposed by Sykes and Matza (1957): (1) denial of responsibility, (2) condemnation of condemners, (3) appeal to higher loyalties, (4) denial of victim, and (5) denial of injury. Although student responses could easily be classified into three of these techniques, denial of responsibility, appeal to higher loyalties, and condemnation of condemners, LaBeff et al. conclude that "[i]t is unlikely that students will either deny injury or deny the victim since there are no real targets in cheating" (1990, p. 196).

The research described here responds to LaBeff et al. in two ways; first, it answers their call to "test the salience of neutralization . . . in more diverse university environments" (p. 197) and second, it challenges their dismissal of denial of injury and denial of victim as neutralization techniques employed by students in their justification of cheating behavior.

Methodology

The data discussed here were gathered as part of a study of college cheating conducted during the 1990–1991 academic year. A seventy-two item questionnaire concerning cheating behavior was administered to students at thirty-one highly selective colleges across the country. Surveys were mailed to a minimum of five hundred students at each school and a total of 6,096 completed surveys were returned (38.3 percent response rate). Eighty-eight percent of the respondents were seniors, nine percent were juniors, and the remaining three percent could not be classified. Survey administration emphasized voluntary participation and assurances of anonymity to help combat issues of non-response bias and the need to accept responses without the chance to question or contest them.

The final sample included 61.2 percent females (which reflects the inclusion of five all female schools in the sample and a slightly higher return rate among female students) and 95.4 percent U.S. citizens. The sample paralleled the ethnic diversity of the participating schools (85.5 percent Anglo, 7.2 percent Asian, 2.6 percent African American, 2.2 percent Hispanic and 2.5 percent other); their religious diversity (including a large percentage of students who claimed no religious preference, 27.1 percent); and their mix of undergraduate majors (36.0 percent humanities, 28.8 percent social sciences, 26.8 percent natural sciences and engineering, 4.5 percent business, and 3.9 percent other).

Results

Of the 6,096 students participating in this research, over two-thirds (67.4 percent) indicated that they had cheated on a test or major assignment at least once while an undergraduate. This cheating took a variety of different forms, but among the most popular (listed in decreasing order of mention) were: (1) a failure to footnote sources in written work, (2) collaboration on assignments when the instructor specifically asked for individual work, (3) copying from other students on tests and examinations, (4) fabrication of bibliographies, (5) helping someone else cheat on a test, and (6) using unfair methods to learn the content of a test ahead of time. Almost one in five students (19.1 percent) could be classified as active-cheaters (five or more self-reported incidents of cheating). This is double the rate reported by LaBeff et al. (1990), but they asked students to report only cheating incidents that had taken place in the last six months. Students in this research were asked to report all cheating in which they had engaged while an undergraduate—a period of three years for most respondents at the time of this survey.

Students admitting to any cheating activity were asked to rate the importance of several specific factors that might have influenced their decisions to cheat. These data establish the importance of denial of responsibility and condemnation of condemners as neutralization techniques. For example, 52.4 percent of the respondents who admitted to cheating rated the pressure to get good grades as an important influence in their decision to cheat with parental pressures and competition to gain admission into professional schools singled out as the primary grade pressures. Forty-six percent of those who had engaged in cheating cited excessive workloads and an inability to keep up with assignments as important factors in their decisions to cheat.

In addition to rating the importance of such preselected factors, 426 respondents (11.0 percent of the admitted cheaters) offered their own justifications for cheating in response to an open-ended question on motivations for cheating. These responses confirm the importance of denial of responsibility and condemnation of condemners as neutralization techniques. They also support LaBeff et al.'s (1990) claim that appeal to higher loyalties is an important neutralization technique. However, these responses also suggest that LaBeff et al.'s dismissal of denial of injury as a justification for student cheating is arguable.

As shown in Table 1, denial of responsibility was the technique most frequently cited (216 responses, 61.0 percent of the total) in the 354 responses classified into one of Sykes and Matza's five categories of the neutralization. The most common responses in this category were mind block, no understanding of the material, a fear of failing, and unclear explanations of assignments. (Although it is possible that some instances of mind block and a fear of failing included in this summary would be more accurately classified as rationalization, the wording of all responses included here suggests that rationalization preceded the cheating incident. Responses that seem to involve post hoc rationalizations were excluded from this summary). Condemnation of condemners was the second most popular neutralization technique observed (99 responses, 28.0 percent) and included such explanations as pointless assignments, lack of respect for individual professors, unfair tests, parents' expectations, and unfair professors. Twenty-four respondents (6.8 percent) appealed to higher loyalties to explain their behavior. In particular, helping a friend and responding to peer pressures were influences some students could not ignore. Finally, fifteen students (4.2 percent) provided responses that clearly fit into the category of denial of injury. These students dismissed their cheating as harmless since it did not hurt anyone or they felt cheating did not matter

Table 1 Neutralization Strategies; Self-Admitted Cheaters

Strategy	Number	Percent
Denial of responsibility	216	61.0
Mind block	90	25.4
No understanding of material	31	8.8
Other	95	26.8
Condemnation of condemners	99	28.0
Pointless assignment	35	9.9
No respect for professor	28	7.9
Other	36	10.2
Appeal to higher loyalties	24	6.8
Help a friend	10	2.8
Peer pressure	9	2.5
Other	5	1.5
Denial of injury	15	4.2
Cheating is harmless	9	2.5
Does not matter	6	1.7

in some cases (for example, where an assignment counted for a small percentage of the total course grade).

Detailed examination of selected student responses provides additional insight into the neutralization strategies they employ.

The Denial of Responsibility

Denial of responsibility invokes the claim that the act was "due to forces outside of the individual and beyond his control such as unloving parents" (Sykes and Matza 1957, p. 667). For example, many students cite an unreasonable workload and the difficulty of keeping up as ample justification for cheating.

> Here at . . . , you must cheat to stay alive. There's so much work and the quality of materials from which to learn, books, professors, is so bad that there's no other choice.

> It's the only way to keep up.

> I couldn't do the work myself.

The following descriptions of students cheating confirm fear of failure is also an important form of denial of responsibility:

> . . . a take-home exam in a class I was failing.

> . . . was near failing.

Some justified their cheating by citing the behavior of peers:

> Everyone has test files in fraternities, etc. If you don't you're at a great disadvantage.

> When most of the class is cheating on a difficult exam and they will ruin the curve, it influences you to cheat so your grade won't be affected.

All of these responses contain the essence of denial of responsibility: the cheater has deflected blame to others or to a specific situational context.

The Denial of Injury

As noted in Table 1, denial of injury was identified as a neutralization technique employed by some respondents. A key element in denial of injury is whether one feels "anyone has clearly been hurt by (the) deviance." In invoking this defense, a cheater would argue "that his behavior does not really cause any great harm despite the fact that it runs counter to the law" (Sykes and Matza 1957, pp. 667–668). For example, a number of students argued that the assignment or test on which they cheated was so trivial that no one was really hurt by their cheating.

> These grades aren't worth much therefore my copying doesn't mean very much. I am ashamed, but I'd probably do it the same way again.

> If I extend the time on a take home it is because I feel everyone does and the teacher kind of expects it. No one gets hurt.

As suggested earlier, these responses suggest the conclusion of LaBeff et al. that "(i)t is unlikely that students will . . . deny injury" (1990, p. 196) must be re-evaluated.

The Denial of the Victim

LaBeff et al. failed to find any evidence of denial of the victim in their student accounts. Although the student motivations for cheating summarized in Table 1 support this conclusion, at least four students (0.1% of the self-admitted cheaters in this study) provided comments elsewhere on the survey instrument which involved denial of the victim. The common elements in these responses was a victim deserving of the consequences of the cheating behavior and cheating was viewed as "a form of rightful retaliation of punishment" (Sykes and Matza 1957, p. 668).

This feeling was extreme in one case, as suggested by the following student who felt her cheating was justified by the

> realization that this school is a manifestation of the bureaucratic capitalist system that systematically keeps the lower classes down, and that adhering to their rules was simply perpetuating this institution.

This "we" versus "they" mentality was raised by many students, but typically in comments about the policing of academic honesty rather than as justification for one's own cheating behavior. When used to justify cheating, the target was almost always an individual teacher rather than the institution and could be more accurately classified as a strategy of condemnation of condemners rather than denial of the victim.

The Condemnation of Condemners

Sykes and Matza describe the condemnation of condemners as an attempt to shift "the focus of attention from [one's] own deviant acts to the motives and behaviors of those who disapprove of [the] violations. [B]y attacking others, the wrongfulness of [one's] own behavior is more easily repressed or lost to view" (1957, p. 668). The logic of this strategy for student cheaters focused on issues of favoritism and fairness. Students invoking this rationale describe "uncaring, unprofessional instructors with negative attitudes who were negligent in their behavior" (LaBeff et al. 1990, p. 195). For example:

> In one instance, nothing was done by a professor because the student was a hockey player.

> The TAs who graded essays were unduly harsh.

> It is known by students that certain professors are more lenient to certain types, e.g., blondes or hockey players.

> I would guess that 90% of the students here have seen athletes and/or fraternity members cheating on an exam or papers. If you turn in one of these culprits, and I have, the penalty is a five-minute lecture from a coach and/or administrator. All these add up to a 'who cares, they'll never do anything to you anyway' attitude here about cheating.

Concerns about the larger society were an important issue for some students:

> When community frowns upon dishonesty, then people will change.

> If our leaders can commit heinous acts and then lie before Senate committees about their total ignorance and innocence, *then why can't I cheat a little?*

> In today's world you do anything to be above the competition.

In general, students found ready targets on which to blame their behavior and condemnation of the condemners was a popular neutralization strategy.

The Appeal to Higher Loyalties

The appeal to higher loyalties involves neutralizing "internal and external controls . . . by sacrificing the demands of the larger society for the demands of the smaller social groups to which the [offender] belongs. [D]eviation from certain norms may occur not because the norms are rejected but because other norms, held to be more pressing or involving a higher loyalty, are accorded precedence." (Sykes and Matza 1957, p. 669). For example, a difficult conflict for some students is balancing the desire to help a friend against the institution's rules on cheating. The student may not challenge the rules, but rather views the need to help a friend, fellow fraternity/sorority member, or roommate to be a greater obligation which justifies the cheating behavior.

Fraternities and sororities were singled out as a network where such behavior occurs with some frequency. For example, a female student at a small university in New England observed:

> There's a lot of cheating within the Greek system. Of all the cheating I've seen, it's often been men and women in fraternities & sororities who exchange information or cheat.

The appeal to higher loyalties was particularly evident in student reactions concerning the reporting of cheating violations. Although fourteen of the thirty-one schools participating in this research had explicit honor codes that generally require students to report cheating violations they observe, less than one-third (32.3 percent) indicated that they were likely to do so. When asked if they would report a friend, only four percent said they would and most students felt that they should not be expected to do so. Typical student comments included:

> Students should not be sitting in judgment of their own peers.

> The university is not a police state.

For some this decision was very practical.

> A lot of students, 50 percent, wouldn't because they know they will probably cheat at some point themselves.

For others, the decision would depend on the severity of the violation they observed and many would not report what they considered to be minor violations, even those explicitly covered by the school's honor code or policies on academic honesty. Explicit examination or test cheating was one of the few violations where students exhibited any consensus concerning the need to report violations. Yet even in this case many students felt other factors must be considered. For example, a senior at a women's college in the northeast commented:

> It would depend on the circumstances. If someone was hurt, *very likely.* If there was no single victim in the case, if the victim was [the] institution . . . , then *very unlikely.*

Additional evidence of the strength of the appeal to higher loyalties as a neutralization technique is found in the fact that almost one in five respondents (17.8 percent) reported that they had helped someone cheat on an examination or major test. The percentage who have helped others cheat on papers and other assignments is likely much higher. Twenty-six percent of those students who helped someone else cheat on a test reported that they had never cheated on a test themselves, adding support to the argument that peer pressure to help friends is quite strong.

Conclusions

From this research it is clear that college students use a variety of neutralization techniques to rationalize their cheating behavior, deflecting blame to others and/or the situational context, and the framework of Sykes and Matza (1957) seems well supported when student explanations of cheating behavior are analyzed. Unlike prior research (LaBeff et al. 1990), however, the present findings suggest that students employ all of the techniques described by Sykes and Matza, including denial of injury and denial of victim. Although there was very limited evidence of the use of denial of victim, denial of injury was not uncommon. Many students felt that some forms of cheating were victimless crimes, particularly on assignments that accounted for a small percentage of the total course grade. The present research does affirm LaBeff et al.'s finding that denial of responsibility and condemnation of condemners are the neutralization techniques most frequently utilized by college students. Appeal to higher loyalties is particularly evident in neutralizing institutional expectations that students report cheating violations they observe.

The present results clearly extend the findings of LaBeff et al. into a much wider range of contexts as this research ultimately involved 6,096 students at thirty-one geographically dispersed institutions ranging from small liberal arts colleges in the Northeast to nationally prominent research universities in the South and West. Fourteen of the thirty-one institutions have long standing honor-code traditions. The code tradition at five of these schools dates to the late 1800s and all fourteen have codes that survived the student unrest of the 1960s. In such a context, the strength of the appeal to higher loyalties and the denial of responsibility as justifications for cheating is a very persuasive argument that neutralization techniques are salient to today's college student. More importantly, it may suggest fruitful areas of future discourse between faculty, administrators, and students on the question of academic honesty.

References

Baird, John S. 1980. "Current Trends in College Cheating." *Psychology in Schools* 17:512–522.

Davis, Stephen F., Cathy A. Grover, Angela H. Becker, and Loretta N. McGregor. 1992. "Academic Dishonesty: Prevalence, Determinants, Techniques, and Punishments." *Teaching of Psychology.* In press.

Edwards, Paul. 1967. *The Encyclopedia of Philosophy,* no. 3, edited by Paul Edwards, New York: Macmillan Company and Free Press.

Eisenberger, Robert, and Dolores M. Shank. 1985. "Personal Work Ethic and Effort Training Affect Cheating." *Journal of Personality and Social Psychology* 49:520–528.

Haines, Valerie J., George Diekhoff, Emily LaBeff, and Robert Clark. 1986. "College Cheating: Immaturity, Lack of Commitment, and the Neutralizing Attitude." *Research in Higher Education* 25:342–354.

LaBeff, Emily E., Robert E. Clark, Valerie J. Haines and George M. Diekhoff. 1990. "Situational Ethics and College Student Cheating." *Sociological Inquiry* 60:190–198.

Michaels, James W., and Terance Miethe. 1989 "Applying Theories of Deviance to Academic Cheating." *Social Science Quarterly* 70:870–885.

Norris, Terry D., and Richard A. Dodder. 1979. "A Behavioral Continuum Synthesizing Neutralization Theory, Situational Ethics and Juvenile Delinquency." *Adolescence* 55:545–555.

Perry, Anthony R., Kevin M. Kane, Kevin J. Bernesser, and Paul T. Spicker. 1990. "Type A Behavior, Competitive Achievement-Striving, and Cheating Among College Students." *Psychological Reports* 66:459–465.

Sykes, Gresham M., and David Matza. 1957. "Techniques of Neutralization: A Theory of Delinquency." *American Sociological Review* 22:664–670.

Tittle, Charles, and Alan Rowe. 1973. "Moral Appeal, Sanction Threat, and Deviance: An Experimental Test." *Social Problems* 20:488–498.

Ward, David. 1986. "Self-Esteem and Dishonest Behavior Revisited." *Journal of Social Psychology* 123:709–713.

Ward, David, and Wendy L. Beck. 1990. "Gender and Dishonesty." *Journal of Social Psychology* 130:333–339.

Opportunity Theory

Those who subscribe to opportunity theory are concerned primarily with the social conditions that may produce a strain toward deviation. Of particular focus is the way actors posture themselves relative to the existing social structure. Robert K. Merton's article, "Social Structure and Anomie," represents what many consider the classic study, within anomie, or opportunity, theory, of the emergence of deviant behavior.

Basic to Merton's explanation is the contention that any society can be characterized in terms of its structure, particularly its goals and its means. A well-integrated society, he reasons, displays a balance between these elements. In such a society, when people want to obtain societal goals, they will use the appropriate institutionalized means for doing so. American society, according to Merton, does not maintain this sort of balance. It is a society in which emphasis is placed almost exclusively on the achievement of goals—regardless of the methods used to attain them. Those affected the most by the imbalance are the *lower classes*. Most members of the lower classes accept the American dream of attaining success; when they attempt to realize their goals through legitimate means, however, they find themselves blocked, mainly because they do not possess the necessary resources. They may substitute other means—for instance, stealing or robbing. Merton refers to these individuals as "innovators." He argues, further, that when there is a disjunction between goals and means, the result may be cultural chaos, or *anomie*. In this situation, the predictability and regulation of behavior become tenuous.

John M. Hagedorn, in "Homeboys, Dope Fiends, Legits, and New Jacks," offers an empirical account that has some relationship to opportunity theory, particularly those aspects that describe how subcultures may arise. The study also challenges some long-standing beliefs about the nature of gang involvement. The specific research questions addressed are two: (1) What happens as gang members age, and (2) are adult gang members typically the same kinds of people, or do gangs exhibit varying types? Hagedorn draws upon data obtained primarily from interviews with 101 members of some 18 gangs. He notes initially that, although more gang members appear to be working today, their overall involvement in the labor market is quite low. Perhaps most insightful and revealing is the fourfold typology of male adult gang membership that emerges from his data: (1) the *legits*, members who had left the gang; (2) the *homeboys*, members who worked alternatively at conventional jobs and drug sales; (3) the *dope fiends*, members who were addicted and participated in drug sales to maintain their source of drugs; and (4) the *new jacks*, members who pursued the drug game as a career. Hagedorn observes that mobility among the categories did occur. For example, some homeboys became legits, while others adopted the new jack role. Hagedorn continues his analysis by examining how his data compare with some of the major gang theories and studies that have been advanced, several of which are part of the anomie, or opportunity, tradition. He notes, for example, that the new jacks seem to mirror Cloward and Ohlin's conception of the criminal subculture, and most particularly their argument that not only must illegitimate opportunity structures exist but the novice must also learn the necessary skills associated with criminal activity; these contingencies seem to apply to the new jacks. Specifically, the existing cocaine economy and the large market for drugs provide the opportunities whereby the new jacks can, through a process of tutelage (i.e., given the opportunity to perform and learn the skills associated with various roles in the drug profession), become entrenched firmly within the drug world. In a sense, they become career deviants. Hagedorn concludes, in part, that although Cloward and Ohlin's opportunity theory seems to have some explanatory utility, it needs to be recast in light of the societal changes that have occurred over the past four decades.

13 ▶ Social Structure and Anomie

Robert K. Merton

There persists a notable tendency in sociological theory to attribute the malfunctioning of social structure primarily to those of man's imperious biological drives which are not adequately restrained by social control. In this view, the social order is solely a device for "impulse management" and the "social processing" of tensions. These impulses which break through social control, be it noted, are held to be biologically derived. Nonconformity is assumed to be rooted in original nature.[1] Conformity is by implication the result of a utilitarian calculus or unreasoned conditioning. This point of view, whatever its other deficiencies, clearly begs one question. It provides no basis for determining the nonbiological conditions which induce deviations from prescribed patterns of conduct. In this paper, it will be suggested that certain phases of social structure generate the circumstances in which infringement of social codes constitutes a "normal" response.[2]

The conceptual scheme to be outlined is designed to provide a coherent, systematic approach to the study of socio-cultural sources of deviate behavior. Our primary aim lies in discovering how some social structures *exert a definite pressure* upon certain persons in the society to engage in nonconformist rather than conformist conduct. The many ramifications of the scheme cannot all be discussed; the problems mentioned outnumber those explicitly treated.

Among the elements of social and cultural structure, two are important for our purposes. These are analytically separable although they merge imperceptibly in concrete situations. The first consists of culturally defined goals, purposes, and interests. It comprises a frame of aspirational reference. These goals are more or less integrated and involve varying degrees of prestige and sentiment. They constitute a basic, but not the exclusive, component of what Linton aptly has called "designs for group living." Some of these cultural aspirations are related to the original drives of man, but they are not determined by them. The second phase of the social structure defines, regulates, and controls the acceptable modes of achieving these goals. Every social group invariably couples its scale of desired ends with moral or institutional regulation of permissible and required procedures for attaining these ends. These regulatory norms and moral imperatives do not necessarily coincide with technical or efficiency norms. Many procedures which from the standpoint of *particular individuals* would be most efficient in securing desired values, e.g., illicit oil-stock schemes, theft, fraud, are ruled out of the institutional area of permitted conduct. The choice of expedients is limited by the institutional norms.

To say that these two elements, culture goals and institutional norms, operate jointly is not to say that the ranges of alternative behaviors and aims bear some constant relation to one another. The emphasis upon certain goals may vary independently of the degree of emphasis upon institutional means. There may develop a disproportionate, at times, a virtually exclusive, stress upon the value of specific goals, involving relatively slight concern with the institutionally appropriate modes of attaining these goals. The limiting case in this direction is reached when the range of alternative procedures is limited only by technical rather than institutional considerations. Any and all devices which promise attainment of the all important goal would be permitted in this hypothetical polar case.[3] This constitutes one type of cultural malintegration. A second polar type is found in groups where activities originally conceived as instrumental are transmuted into ends in themselves. The original purposes are forgotten, and ritualistic adherence to institutionally prescribed conduct becomes virtually obsessive.[4] Stability is largely ensured while change is flouted. The range of alternative behaviors is severely limited. There develops a tradition-bound, sacred society characterized by neophobia. The occupational psychosis of the bureaucrat may be cited as a case in point. Finally, there are the intermediate types of groups where a balance between culture goals and institutional means is maintained. These are the significantly integrated and relatively stable, though changing, groups.

An effective equilibrium between the two phases of the social structure is maintained as long as satisfactions accrue to individuals who conform to both constraints, viz., satisfactions from the achievement of the goals and satisfactions emerging directly from the institutionally canalized modes of striving to attain these ends. Success, in such equilibrated cases, is twofold. Success is reckoned in terms of the product and in terms of the process, in terms of the outcome and in terms of activities. Continuing satisfactions must derive from sheer *participation* in a competitive order as well as from eclipsing one's competitors if the order itself is to be sustained. The occasional sacrifices involved in institutionalized conduct must be compensated by socialized rewards. The distribution of statuses and roles through competition must be so organized that positive incentives for conformity to roles and adherence to status obligations are provided *for every position* within the distributive order. Aberrant conduct, therefore, may be viewed as a symptom of dissociation between culturally defined aspirations and socially structured means.

Of the types of groups which result from the independent variation of the two phases of the social structure, we shall be primarily concerned with the first, namely, that involving a disproportionate accent on goals. This statement must be recast in a proper perspective. In no group is there an absence of regulatory codes governing conduct, yet groups do vary in the degree to which these folkways, mores, and institutional controls are effectively integrated with the more diffuse goals which are part of the culture matrix. Emotional convictions may cluster about the complex of socially acclaimed ends, meanwhile shifting their support from the culturally defined implementation of these ends. As we shall see, certain aspects of the social structure may generate countermores and antisocial behavior precisely because of differential emphases on goals and regulations. In the extreme case, the latter may be so vitiated by the goal-emphasis that the range of behavior is limited only by considerations of technical expediency. The sole significant question then becomes, which available means is most efficient in netting the socially approved value.[5] The technically most feasible procedure, whether legitimate or not, is preferred to the institutionally prescribed conduct. As this process continues, the integration of the society becomes tenuous and anomie ensues.

Thus, in competitive athletics, when the aim of victory is shorn of its institutional trappings and success in contests becomes construed as "winning the game" rather than "winning through circumscribed modes of activity," a premium is implicitly set upon the use of illegitimate but technically efficient means. The star of the opposing football team is surreptitiously slugged; the wrestler furtively incapacitates his opponent through ingenious but illicit techniques; university alumni covertly subsidize "students" whose talents are largely confined to the athletic field. The emphasis on the goal has so attenuated the satisfactions deriving from sheer participation in the competitive activity that these satisfactions are virtually confined to a successful outcome. Through the same process, tension generated by the desire to win in a poker game is relieved by successfully dealing oneself four aces, or, when the cult of success has become completely dominant, by sagaciously shuffling the cards in a game of solitaire. The faint twinge of uneasiness in the last instance and the surreptitious nature of public delicts indicate clearly that the institutional rules of the game are *known* to those who evade them, but that the emotional supports of these rules are largely vitiated by cultural exaggeration of the success-goal.[6] They are microcosmic images of the social macrocosm.

Of course, this process is not restricted to the realm of sport. The process whereby exaltation of the end generates a *literal demoralization*, i.e., a de-institutionalization, of the means is one which characterizes many[7] groups in which the two phases of the social structure are not highly integrated. The extreme emphasis upon the accumulation of wealth as a symbol of success[8] in our own society militates against the completely effective control of institutionally regulated modes of acquiring of fortune.[9] Fraud, corruption, vice, crime, in short, the entire catalogue of proscribed behavior, becomes increasingly common when the emphasis on the *culturally induced* success-goal becomes divorced from a coordinated institutional emphasis. This observation is of crucial theoretical importance in examining the doctrine that antisocial behavior most frequently derives from biological drives breaking through the restraints imposed by society. The difference is one between a strictly utilitarian interpretation which conceives man's ends as random and an analysis which finds these ends deriving from the basic values of the culture.[10]

Our analysis can scarcely stop at this juncture. We must turn to other aspects of the social structure if we are to deal with the social genesis of the varying rates and types of deviate behavior characteristic of different societies. Thus far, we have sketched three ideal types of social orders constituted by distinctive patterns of relations between culture ends and means. Turning from these types of *culture patterning,* we find five logically possible, alternative modes of adjustment or adaptation *by individuals* within the culture-bearing society or group.[11] These are schematically presented in the following table, where (+) signifies "acceptance," (−) signifies "elimination," and (±) signifies "rejection and substitution of new goals and standards."

		Culture Goals	Institutional Means
I.	Conformity	1	1
II.	Innovation	1	2
III.	Ritualism	2	1
IV.	Retreatism	2	2
V.	Rebellion[12]	6	6

Our discussion of the relation between these alternative responses and other phases of the social structure must be prefaced by the observation that persons may shift from one alternative to another as they engage in different social activities. These categories refer to role adjustments in specific situations, not to personality *in toto*. To treat the development of this process in various spheres of conduct would introduce a complexity unmanageable within the confines of this paper. For this reason, we shall be concerned primarily with economic activity in the broad sense, "the production, exchange, distribution, and consumption of goods and services" in our competitive society, wherein wealth has taken on a highly symbolic cast. Our task is to search out some of the factors which exert pressure upon individuals to engage in certain of these logically possible alternative responses. This choice, as we shall see, is far from random.

In every society, Adaptation I (conformity to both culture goals and means) is the most common and widely diffused. Were this not so, the stability and continuity of the society could not be maintained. The mesh of expectancies which constitutes every social order is sustained by the modal behavior of its members falling within the first category. Conventional role behavior oriented toward the basic values of the group is the rule rather than the exception. It is this fact alone which permits us to speak of a human aggregate as comprising a group or society.

Conversely, Adaptation IV (rejection of goals and means) is the least common. Persons who "adjust" (or maladjust) in this fashion are, strictly speaking, *in* the society but not *of* it. Sociologically, these constitute the true "aliens." Not sharing the common frame of orientation, they can be included within the societal population merely in a fictional sense. In this category are *some* of the activities of psychotics, psychoneurotics, chronic autists, pariahs, outcasts, vagrants, vagabonds, tramps, chronic drunkards, and drug addicts.[13] These have relinquished, in certain spheres of activity, the culturally defined goals, involving complete aim-inhibition in the polar case, and their adjustments are not in accord with institutional norms. This is not to say that in some cases the source of their behavioral adjustments is not in part the very social structure which they have in effect repudiated nor that their very existence within a social area does not constitute a problem for the socialized population.

This mode of "adjustment" occurs, as far as structural sources are concerned, when both the culture goals and institutionalized procedures have been assimilated thoroughly by the individual and imbued with affect and high positive value, but where those institutionalized procedures which promise a measure of successful attainment of the goals are not available to the individual. In such instances, there results a two-fold mental conflict insofar as the moral obligation for adopting institutional means conflicts with the pressure to resort to illegitimate means (which may attain the goal) and inasmuch as the individual is shut off from means which are both legitimate *and* effective. The competitive order is maintained, but the frustrated and handicapped individual who cannot cope with this order drops out. Defeatism, quietism, and resignation are manifested in escape mechanisms which ultimately lead the individual to "escape" from the requirements of the society. It is an expedient which arises from continued failure to attain the goal by legitimate measures and from an inability to adopt the illegitimate route because of internalized prohibitions and institutionalized compulsives, *during which process the supreme value of the success-goal has as yet not been renounced.* The conflict is resolved by eliminating *both* precipitating elements, the goals and means. The escape is complete, the conflict is eliminated, and the individual is associated.

Be it noted that where frustration derives from the inaccessibility of effective institutional means for attaining economic or any other type of highly valued "success," that Adaptations II, III, and V (innovation, ritualism, and rebellion) are also possible. The result will be determined by the particular personality, and thus, the *particular* cultural background, involved. Inadequate socialization will result in the innovation response whereby the conflict and frustration are eliminated by relinquishing the institutional means and retaining the success-aspiration; an extreme assimilation of institutional demands will lead to ritualism wherein the goal is dropped as beyond one's reach but conformity to the mores persists; and rebellion occurs when emancipation from the reigning standards, due to frustration or to marginalist perspectives, leads to the attempt to introduce a "new social order."

Our major concern is with the illegitimacy adjustment. This involves the use of conventionally proscribed but frequently effective means of attaining at least the simulacrum of culturally defined success—wealth, power, and the like. As we have seen, this adjustment occurs when the individual has assimilated the cultural emphasis on success without equally internalizing the morally prescribed norms governing means for its attainment. The question arises, Which phases of our social structure predispose toward this mode of adjustment? We may examine a concrete instance, effectively analyzed by Lohman,[14] which provides a clue to the answer. Lohman has shown that specialized areas of vice in the near north side of Chicago constitute a "normal" response to a situation where the cultural emphasis upon pecuniary success has been absorbed, but where there is little access to conventional and legitimate means for attaining such success. The conventional occupational opportunities of persons in this area are almost completely limited to manual labor. Given our cultural stigmatization of manual labor, and its correlate, the prestige of white collar work, it is clear that the result is a strain toward innovational practices. The limitation of opportunity to unskilled labor and the resultant low income cannot compete *in terms of conventional standards of achievement* with the high income from organized vice.

For our purposes, this situation involves two important features. First, such antisocial behavior is in a sense "called forth" by certain conventional values of the culture *and* by the class structure involving differential access to the approved opportunities for legitimate, prestige-bearing pursuit of the culture goals. The lack of high integration between the means-and-end elements of the cultural pattern and the particular class structure combine to favor a heightened frequency of antisocial conduct in such groups. The second consideration is of equal significance. Recourse to the first of the alternative responses, legitimate effort, is limited by the fact that actual advance toward desired success-symbols through conventional channels is, despite our persisting open-class ideology,[15] relatively rare and difficult for those handicapped by little formal education and few economic resources. The dominant pressure of group standards of success is, therefore, on the gradual attenuation of legitimate, but by and large ineffective, strivings and the increasing use of illegitimate, but more or less effective, expedients of vice and crime. The cultural demands made on persons in this situation are incompatible. On the one hand, they are asked to orient their conduct toward the prospect of accumulating wealth and on the other, they are largely denied effective opportunities to do so institutionally. The consequences of such structural inconsistency are psychopathological personality, and/or antisocial conduct, and/or revolutionary activities. The equilibrium between culturally designated means and ends becomes highly unstable with the progressive emphasis on attaining the prestige-laden ends by any means whatsoever. Within this context, Capone represents the triumph of amoral intelligence over morally prescribed "failure," when the channels of vertical mobility are closed or narrowed[16] *in a society which places a high premium on economic affluence and social ascent for* all *its members.*[17]

This last qualification is of primary importance. It suggests that other phases of the social structure besides the extreme emphasis on pecuniary success must be considered if we are to understand the social sources of antisocial behavior. A high frequency of deviate behavior is not generated simply by "lack of opportunity" or by this exaggerated pecuniary emphasis. A comparatively rigidified class structure, a feudalistic or caste order, may limit such opportunities far beyond the point which obtains in our society today. It is only when a system of cultural values extols, virtually above all else, certain *common* symbols of success *for the population at large* while its social structure rigorously restricts or completely eliminates access to approved modes of acquiring these symbols *for a considerable part of the same population* that antisocial behavior ensues on a considerable scale. In other words, our egalitarian ideology denies by implication the existence of noncompeting groups and individuals in the pursuit of pecuniary success. The same body of success-symbols is held to be desirable for all. These goals are held to *transcend class lines,* not to be bounded by them, yet the actual social organization is such that there exist class differentials in the accessibility of these *common* success-symbols. Frustration and thwarted aspiration lead to the search for avenues of escape from a culturally induced intolerable situation; or unrelieved ambition may eventuate in illicit attempts to acquire the dominant values.[18] The American stress on pecuniary success and ambitiousness for all thus invites exaggerated anxieties, hostilities, neuroses, and antisocial behavior.

This theoretical analysis may go far toward explaining the varying correlations between crime and poverty.[19] Poverty is not an isolated variable. It is one in a complex of interdependent social and cultural variables. When viewed in such a context, it represents quite different states of affairs. Poverty as such, and consequent limitation of opportunity, are not sufficient to induce a conspicuously high rate of criminal behavior. Even the often mentioned "poverty in the midst of plenty" will not necessarily lead to this result. Only insofar as poverty and associated disadvantages in competition for the culture values approved for *all* members of the society are linked with the assimilation of a cultural emphasis on monetary accumulation as a symbol of success is antisocial conduct a "normal" outcome. Thus, poverty is less highly correlated with crime in southeastern Europe than in the United States. The possibilities of vertical mobility in these European areas would seem to be fewer than in this country, so that neither poverty *per se* nor its association with limited opportunity is sufficient to account for the varying correlations. It is only when the full configuration is considered, poverty, limited opportunity, and a commonly shared system of success-symbols, that we can explain the higher association between poverty and crime in our society than in others where rigidified class structure is coupled with *differential class symbols of achievement.*

In societies such as our own, then, the pressure of prestige-bearing success tends to eliminate the effective social constraint over means employed to this end. "The-end-justifies-the-means" doctrine becomes a guiding tenet for action when the cultural structure unduly exalts the end and the social organization unduly limits possible recourse to approved means. Otherwise put, this notion and associated behavior reflect a lack of cultural coordination. In international relations, the effects of this lack of integration are notoriously apparent. An emphasis upon national power is not readily coordinated with an inept organization of legitimate, i.e., internationally defined and accepted, means for attaining this goal. The result is a tendency toward the abrogation of international law, treaties become scraps of paper, "undeclared warfare" serves as a technical evasion, the bombing of civilian populations is rationalized,[20] just as the same societal situation induces the same sway of illegitimacy among individuals.

The social order we have described necessarily produces this "strain toward dissolution." The pressure of such an order is upon outdoing one's competitors. The choice of means within the ambit of institutional control will persist as long as the sentiments supporting a competitive system, i.e., deriving from the possibility of outranking competitors and hence enjoying the favorable response of others, are distributed throughout the entire system of activities and are not confined merely to the final result. A stable social structure demands a balanced distribution of affect among its various segments. When there occurs a shift of emphasis from the satisfactions deriving from competition itself to almost exclusive concern with successful competition, the resultant stress leads to the breakdown of the regulatory structure.[21] With the resulting attenuation of the institutional imperatives, there occurs an approximation of the situation erroneously held by utilitarians to be typical of society generally wherein calculations of advantage and fear of punishment are the sole regulating agencies. In such situations, as Hobbes observed, force and fraud come to constitute the sole virtues in view of their relative efficiency in attaining goals—which were for him, of course, not culturally derived.

It should be apparent that the foregoing discussion is not pitched on a moralistic plane. Whatever the sentiments of the writer or reader concerning the ethical desirability of coordinating the means-and-goals phases of the social structure, one must agree that lack of such coordination leads to anomie. Insofar as one of the most general functions of social organization is to provide a basis for calculability and regularity of behavior, it is increasingly limited in effectiveness as these elements of the structure become dissociated. At the extreme, predictability virtually disappears and what may be properly termed cultural chaos or anomie intervenes.

This statement, being brief, is also incomplete. It has not included an exhaustive treatment of the various structural elements which predispose toward one rather than another of the alternative responses open to individuals; it has neglected, but not denied the relevance of, the factors determining the specific incidence of these responses; it has not enumerated the various concrete responses which are constituted by combinations of specific values of the analytical variables; it has omitted, or included only by implication, any consideration of the social functions performed by illicit responses; it has not tested the full explanatory power of the analytical scheme by examining a large number of group variations in the frequency of deviate and conformist behavior; it has not adequately dealt with rebellious conduct which seeks to refashion the social framework radically; it has not examined the relevance of cultural conflict for an analysis of culture-goal and institutional-means malintegration. It is suggested that these and related problems may be profitably analyzed by this scheme.

Notes

1. E.g., Ernest Jones, *Social Aspects of Psychoanalysis,* 28, London, 1924. If the Freudian notion is a variety of the "original sin" dogma, then the interpretation advanced in this paper may be called the doctrine of "socially derived sin."

2. "Normal" in the sense of a culturally oriented, if not approved, response. This statement does not deny the relevance of biological and personality differences which may be significantly involved in the *incidence* of deviate conduct. Our focus of interest is the social and cultural matrix; hence we abstract from other factors. It is in this sense, I take it, that James S. Plant speaks of the "normal reaction of normal people to abnormal conditions." See his *Personality and the Cultural Pattern,* 248, New York, 1937.

3. Contemporary American culture has been said to tend in this direction. See André Siegfried, *America Comes of Age,* 26–37, New York, 1927. The alleged extreme(?) emphasis on the goals of monetary success and material prosperity leads to dominant concern with technological and social instruments designed to produce the desired result, inasmuch as institutional controls become of secondary importance. In such a situation, innovation flourishes as the *range of means* employed is broadened. In a sense, then, there occurs the paradoxical emergence of "materialists" from an "idealistic" orientation. Cf. Durkheim's analysis of the cultural conditions which predispose toward crime and innovation, both of which are aimed toward efficiency, not moral norms. Durkheim was one of the first to see that "contrairement aux idées courantes le criminel n'apparait plus comme un être radicalement insociable, comme une sorte d'elément parasitaire, de corps étranger et inassimilable, introduit au sein de la société; c'est un agent régulier de la vie sociale." See *Les Règles de la Méthode Sociologique,* 86–89, Paris, 1927.

4. Such ritualism may be associated with a mythology which rationalizes these actions so that they appear to retain their status as means, but the dominant pressure is in the direction of strict ritualistic conformity, irrespective of such rationalizations. In this sense, ritual has proceeded farthest when such rationalizations are not even called forth.

5. In this connection, one may see the relevance of Elton Mayo's paraphrase of the title of Tawney's well-known book. "Actually the problem *is not that of the sickness of an acquisitive society; it is that of the acquisitiveness of a sick society."* *Human Problems of an Industrial Civilization,* 153, New York, 1933. Mayo deals with the process through which wealth comes to be a symbol of social achievement. He sees this as arising from a state of anomie. We are

considering the unintegrated monetary-success goal as an element in producing anomie. A complete analysis would involve both phases of this system of interdependent variables.

6. It is unlikely that interiorized norms are completely eliminated. Whatever residuum persists will induce personality tensions and conflict. The process involves a certain degree of ambivalence. A manifest rejection of the institutional norms is coupled with some latent retention of their emotional correlates. "Guilt feelings," "sense of sin," "pangs of conscience" are obvious manifestations of this unrelieved tension; symbolic adherence to the nominally repudiated values or rationalizations constitute a more subtle variety of tensional release.

7. "Many," and not all, unintegrated groups, for the reason already mentioned. In groups where the primary emphasis shifts to institutional means, i.e., when the range of alternatives is very limited, the outcome is a type of ritualism rather than anomie.

8. Money has several peculiarities which render it particularly apt to become a symbol of prestige divorced from institutional controls. As Simmel emphasized, money is highly abstract and impersonal. However acquired, through fraud or institutionally, it can be used to purchase the same goods and services. The anonymity of metropolitan culture, in conjunction with this peculiarity of money, permits wealth, the sources of which may be unknown to the community in which the plutocrat lives, to serve as a symbol of status.

9. The emphasis upon wealth as a success-symbol is possibly reflected in the use of the term "fortune" to refer to a stock of accumulated wealth. This meaning becomes common in the late sixteenth century (Spenser and Shakespeare). A similar usage of the Latin *fortuna* comes into prominence during the first century B.C. Both these periods were marked by the rise to prestige and power of the "bourgeoisie."

10. See Kingsley Davis, "Mental Hygiene and the Class Structure," *Psychiatry*, 1928, 1:esp. 62–63; Talcott Parsons, *The Structure of Social Action*, 59–60, New York, 1937.

11. This is a level intermediate between the two planes distinguished by Edward Sapir; namely, culture patterns and personal habit systems. See his "Contribution of Psychiatry to an Understanding of Behavior in Society," *Amer. J. Sociol.*, 1937, 42:862–870.

12. This fifth alternative is on a plane clearly different from that of the others. It represents a *transitional* response which seeks to *institutionalize* new procedures oriented toward revamped cultural goals shared by the members of the society. It thus involves efforts to *change* the existing structure rather than to perform accommodative actions *within* this structure, and introduces additional problems with which we are not at the moment concerned.

13. Obviously, this is an elliptical statement. These individuals may maintain some orientation to the values of their particular differentiated groupings within the larger society or, in part, of the conventional society itself. Insofar as they do so, their conduct cannot be classified in the "passive rejection" category (IV). Nels Anderson's description of the behavior and attitudes of the bum, for example, can readily be recast in terms of our analytical scheme. See *The Hobo*, 93–98, *et passim*, Chicago, 1923.

14. Joseph D. Lohman, "The Participant Observer in Community Studies," *Amer. Sociol. Rev.*, 1937, 2:890–898.

15. The shifting historical role of this ideology is a profitable subject for exploration. The "office-boy-to-president" stereotype was once in approximate accord with the facts. Such vertical mobility was probably more common then than now, when the class structure is more rigid. (See the following note.) The ideology largely persists, however, possibly because it still performs a useful function for maintaining the *status quo*. For insofar as it is accepted by the "masses," it constitutes a useful sop for those who might rebel against the entire structure, were this consoling hope removed. This ideology now serves to lessen the probability of Adaptation V. In short, the role of this notion has changed from that of an approximately valid empirical theorem to that of an ideology, in Mannheim's sense.

16. There is a growing body of evidence, though none of it is clearly conclusive, to the effect that our class structure is becoming rigidified and that vertical mobility is declining. Taussig and Joslyn found that American business leaders are being *increasingly* recruited from the upper ranks of our society. The Lynds have also found a "diminished chance to get ahead" for the working classes in Middletown. Manifestly, these objective changes are not alone significant; the individual's subjective evaluation of the situation is a major determinant of the response. The extent to which this change in opportunity for social mobility has been recognized by the least advantaged classes is still conjectural, although the Lynds present some suggestive materials. The writer suggests that a case in point is the increasing frequency of cartoons which observe in a tragi-comic vein that "my old man says everybody can't be President. He says if ya can get three days a week steady on W.P.A. work ya ain't doin' so bad either." See

F. W. Taussig and C. S. Joslyn, *American Business Leaders,* New York, 1932; R. S. and H. M. Lynd, *Middletown in Transition,* 67 ff., chap. 12, New York, 1937.

17. The role of the Negro in this respect is of considerable theoretical interest. Certain elements of the Negro population have assimilated the dominant caste's values of pecuniary success and social advancement, but they also recognize that social ascent is at present restricted to their own caste almost exclusively. The pressures upon the Negro which would otherwise derive from the structural inconsistencies we have noticed are hence not identical with those upon lower class whites. See Kingsley Davis, *op. cit.,* 63; John Dollard, *Caste and Class in a Southern Town,* 66 ff., New Haven, 1936; Donald Young, *American Minority Peoples,* 581, New York, 1932.

18. The psychical coordinates of these processes have been partly established by the experimental evidence concerning *Anspruchsniveaus* and levels of performance. See Kurt Lewin, *Vorsatz, Willie and Bedurfnis,* Berlin, 1926; N. F. Hoppe, "Erfolg und Misserfolg," *Psychol. Forschung,* 1930, 14:1-63; Jerome D. Frank, "Individual Differences in Certain Aspects of the Level of Aspiration," *Amer. J. Psychol.,* 1935, 47:119-128.

19. Standard criminology texts summarize the data in this field. Our scheme of analysis may serve to resolve some of the theoretical contradictions which P. A. Sorokin indicates. For example, "not everywhere nor always do the poor show a greater proportion of crime . . . many poorer countries have had less crime than the richer countries. . . . The [economic] improvement in the second half of the nineteenth century, and the beginning of the twentieth, has not been followed by a decrease of crime." See his *Contemporary Sociological Theories,* 560-561, New York, 1928. The crucial point is, however, that poverty has varying social significance in different social structures, as we shall see. Hence, one would not expect a linear correlation between crime and poverty.

20. See M. W. Royse, *Aerial Bombardment and the International Regulation of War,* New York, 1928.

21. Since our primary concern is with the socio-cultural aspects of this problem, the psychological correlates have been only implicitly considered. See Karen Horney, *The Neurotic Personality of Our Time,* New York, 1937, for a psychological discussion of this process.

Homeboys, Dope Fiends, Legits, and New Jacks

14

John M. Hagedorn

This paper addresses issues that are controversial in both social science and public policy. First, what happens to gang members as they age? Do most gang members graduate from gangbanging to drug sales, as popular stereotypes might suggest? Is drug dealing so lucrative that adult gang members eschew work and become committed to the drug economy? Have changes in economic conditions produced underclass gangs so deviant and so detached from the labor market that the only effective policies are more police and more prisons?

Second, and related to these questions, are male adult gang members basically similar kinds of people, or are gangs made up of different types? Might some gang members be more conventional, and others less so? What are the implications of this "continuum of conventionality" within drug-dealing gangs for public policy? Data from a Milwaukee study on gangs and drug dealing shed some light on these issues.

Gang Members, Drugs, and Work

An underlying question is whether the drug economy provides sufficient incentives to keep gang members away from legal work. If drug sales offer highly profitable opportunities for all who are willing to take the risks, we might expect many adult gang members to be committed firmly to the drug economy. On the other hand, if drug dealing entails many risks and produces few success stories, gang members might be expected to have a more variable relationship to illicit drug sales. In that case we could look at variation within the gang to explain different behaviors.

The research literature contains few empirical studies on the pull of the drug economy away from licit work. On the more general level, Carl Taylor (1990:120) asserts that "when drug distribution becomes the employer, $3.65 or $8.65 can't compare with drug business income." Martin Sanchez

Jankowski (1991:101), in his study of gangs in three cities, found an "entrepreneurial spirit" to be the "driving force in the world view and behavior of gang members." This "entrepreneurial spirit" pushes gang members to make rational decisions to engage in drug sales. Jerome Skolnick (1990) and his students argue that gangs are centrally involved with profitable mid-level drug distribution, although these findings have been challenged by researchers (Klein and Maxson, 1993; Waldorf, 1993).

Others have found that gang involvement in drug sales varies substantially (see Cummings and Monte, 1993; Huff, 1990). Klein et al. (1991) remind us that not all gangs are involved with drug sales, a point that is often overlooked in the discussion of an invariant gang/drug nexus. Among those who sell drugs, actual income varies. Fagan (1991) points out that earnings from drug dealing in two Manhattan neighborhoods ranged from about $1,000 to nearly $5,000 per month. Although most drug sellers had little involvement with the formal economy, 25% of Fagan's dealers also worked in conventional jobs, and most reported both illegal *and* legal income for each month. This finding suggests that incentives from drug sales were not always sufficient to make dealing a full-time job.

Similarly, a Rand Corporation study (MacCoun and Reuter, 1992:485) found that the typical Washington, D.C. small dealer made about $300 per month and the typical big dealer $3,700, with an average of about $1,300. Sullivan (1989) found illicit economic activities in Brooklyn to be a youthful enterprise, quickly outgrown when "real" jobs offered themselves. The seriousness of criminal activity varied with the intactness of networks providing access to legitimate work. Most of Williams's (1989) New York "cocaine kids" matured out of the drug business as they became young adults and their drug-dealing clique broke up. Padilla's (1992:162) "Diamonds" became "disillusioned" with the empty promises of street-level dealing and aspired to legitimate jobs.

These few studies suggest substantial variation in the degree and duration of gang involvement in drug dealing. The drug economy is not an unquestionably profitable opportunity for gang members; rather, its promise appears to be more ambiguous. If that conclusion is valid, research must examine both the actual amounts of money earned by adult gang drug dealers *and* variation within the gang to understand gang involvement in drug dealing. We have a few studies on how much money gang members make from selling drugs, but hardly any contemporary data on different types of gang members.

▶Variation Within the Gang

Some research has portrayed gang members as relatively invariant. Walter Miller (1969) viewed gang delinquents as representative of a lower-class cultural milieu; his six "focal concerns" are persistent and distinctive

features of the entire American "lower class." Similarly, Jankowski
(1991:26–28) said that male gang members were one-dimensional "tough
nuts," defiant individuals with a rational "social Darwinist worldview" who
displayed defiant individualism "more generally" than other people in low-
income communities.

Other research, however, has suggested that gang members vary, particularly on their orientation toward conventionality. Whyte (1943) classified his Cornerville street corner men as either "college boys" or "corner
boys," depending on their aspirations. Cloward and Ohlin (1960:95), applying Merton's (1957) earlier typology, categorized lower-class youths in
four cells of a matrix, depending on their aspirations and "criteria for success." Many of their delinquents repudiated the legitimacy of conventional
society and resorted to innovative solutions to attain success goals. Cloward
and Ohlin took issue with Cohen (1955) and Matza (1964), whose delinquents were internally conflicted but, as a group, imputed legitimacy to the
norms of the larger society.

Some more recent researchers also have found variation in conventionality within gangs. Klein (1971), echoing Thrasher (1927), differentiated between "core" and "fringe" members, a distinction that policy makers often
use today as meaning more or less deviant. In the same view, Taylor
(1990:8–9) saw gang members as "corporates," "scavengers," "emulators,"
"auxiliaries," or "adjuncts," mainly on the basis of their distance from gang
membership. Fagan (1990:206), like Matza and Cohen, found that "conventional values may coexist with deviant behaviors for gang delinquents
and other inner city youth." MacLeod (1987:124) observed surprising variation between ethnic groups. The white "hallway hangers" believed "stag-
nation at the bottom of the occupational structure to be almost inevitable"
and were rebellious delinquents, whereas the African American "brothers"
reacted to similar conditions by aspiring to middle-class status.

Joan Moore is one of the few researchers who have looked carefully at
differentiation within gangs. In her early work (1978), she discovered both
square and deviant career models among East Los Angeles gang members.
In an impressive restudy (1991) she found that most adult gang members
were working conventional jobs, but those who had been active in the gang
in recent years had more difficulty finding employment as job networks collapsed. Many veteran gang members had been addicted to heroin for years,
but by the 1990s few were dealing drugs to support themselves. Moore
found that both male and female Chicano gang members could be categorized as "tecatos," "cholos," or "squares," a typology similar to those suggested for the nongang poor by Anderson (1978, 1990) and Hannerz (1969).

If gang members in fact vary on orientation to conventionality, and if the
drug economy itself offers only an ambiguous lure, jobs and other programs that strengthen "social capital" (Coleman, 1988) might be effective
means of integrating many adult gang members into the community (see
Sampson and Laub, 1993). On the other hand, if adult gang members are

look-alike criminals who are dazzled by the prospect of vast profits in the drug trade, jobs and social programs would have little effect, and our present incarceration strategy may be appropriate.

This paper provides quantitative and qualitative data on the conventional orientations of young adult gang members in Milwaukee. First we report on the licit work and illicit drug-dealing patterns of adult gang members. Then we offer a typology, drawn from Milwaukee data, that demonstrates a "continuum of conventionality" between core members of drug-dealing gangs. In conclusion, we discuss research and public policy consequences of the study.

Research Methods and Sources of Data

The interpretations presented here draw on observation and extensive fieldwork conducted over a number of years, specifically from two funded interview studies, in 1987 and in 1992. During the early 1980s I directed the first gang diversion program in the city and became acquainted with many leaders and other founders of Milwaukee's gangs. I have maintained a privileged relationship with many of these individuals.

In the 1987 study, we interviewed 47 members of 19 Milwaukee male and female gangs (Hagedorn, 1988). These "founders" were the core gang members who were present when their gangs took names. Founders are likely to be representative of hard-core gang members, not of peripheral members or "wannabes." As time has passed, the gang founders' exploits have been passed down, and younger Milwaukee gang members have looked up to them as street "role models." Our research design does not enable us to conclude how fully our sample represents subsequent groups of adult gang members.

As part of our current study, we conducted lengthy audiotaped interviews with 101 founding members of 18 gangs in the city; 90 were male and 11 female. Sixty percent were African American, 37% Latino, and 3% white. Their median age was 26 years, with 75% between 23 and 30. Twenty-three respondents also had been interviewed in the 1987 study; 78 were interviewed here for the first time. Members from two gangs interviewed in the earlier study could not be located. Each respondent was paid $50.

The interview picks up the lives of the founding members since 1987, when we conducted our original study, and asks them to recount their careers in the drug business, to discuss their pursuit of conventional employment, and to reflect on their personal lives. The respondents also were asked to describe the current status of their fellow gang members. In the 1987 study, we collected rosters of all members of each gang whose founders we interviewed. In the current study, we asked each respondent to double check the roster of his or her gang to make sure it was accurate. In both studies, we asked respondents to tell us whether the other members were still alive, had graduated from high school, were currently locked up, or were working. In the 1992 study, we also asked whether each of the founding members was selling or using dope (in our data "dope" means cocaine), had some other hustle, or was on the run, among other questions.

To understand more clearly the variation between and within the gangs, we interviewed nearly the entire rosters of three gangs and about half (64 of 152) of the original founding members from eight male gangs in three different types of neighborhoods. In each of these gangs, we interviewed some who still were involved with both the gang and the dope game and some who no longer were involved. This paper reports on data on all of the 90 males we interviewed and on their accounts of the present circumstances of 236 founders of 14 male gangs.

The interviews in this most recent study were conducted in late 1992 and early 1993.[1] As in the original study, the research follows an inductive and collaborative model (see Moore, 1978), in which gang members cooperate with the academic staff to focus the research design, construct interview schedules, conduct interviews, and interpret the findings.

▶Findings: Drug Dealing and Work

As expected, gang members appear to be working more today than five years ago, but participation in the formal labor market remains quite low (see Table 1).[2]

These low levels of labor market participation apply to more than gang members. A recent Milwaukee study revealed that in 1990, 51% of jobs held by *all* African American males age 20 to 24, slightly younger than our study population, lasted less than six weeks. The average *annual* income in retail trade, where most subjects held jobs, was $2,023; for jobs in service, $1,697; in education, $3,084 (Rose et al., 1992). African American young adults as a whole (and probably nongang Latinos) clearly were not working regularly and were not earning a living wage.

Table 1 1992 Status of Male Gang Founders, 236 Founding Members of 14 Male Groups

Predominant Activity/Status	African American	White	Latino	Total
Work: Part-Time or Full-Time	22.2%	68.8%	27.6%	30.5%
Hustling: Nearly All Selling Cocaine	50.4	15.4	56.3	47.9
Deceased	7.7	6.3	5.7	6.8
Whereabouts Unknown	19.7	9.4	10.3	14.8
Total N = 100%	N = 117	N = 32	N = 87	N = 236

NOTE: Column percentages may not equal 100% because of rounding.

Selling cocaine seems to have filled the employment void. In 1987 only a few gang members dealt drugs, mainly marijuana. Within African American gangs, at least, cocaine dealing was not prevalent. By 1992, however, cocaine had become a major factor in Milwaukee's informal economy, evolving into widespread curbside sales and numerous drug houses (see Hamid, 1992). Of the 236 fellow gang founders, 72% reportedly had sold cocaine at some time in the last five years.[3]

That involvement has not been steady, however. We collected detailed data on the length of involvement in the drug economy and the amount of money made by those we interviewed. We asked our respondents to indicate how they had supported themselves in each month of the past three years, and then asked how much money they made in both legal and illegal employment. For most respondents, selling cocaine was an on-again, off-again proposition. About half (35) of those who had sold cocaine sold in no more than 12 months out of the past 36; only 12% (9) sold in more than 24 of the past 36 months. Latinos sold for slightly longer periods than African Americans, 17.7 months to 13.1 months ($p = .07$).

When gang members did sell dope, they made widely varying amounts of money. About one-third of those who sold reported that they made no more than they would have earned if they worked for minimum wage. Another one-third made the equivalent of $13 to $25 an hour. Only three of the 73 sellers ever made "crazy money," or more than $10,000 per month, at any time during their drug-selling careers. Mean monthly income from drug sales was approximately $2,400, or about $15 per hour for full-time work. By contrast, mean monthly income for legal work was only $677; Latinos made more than African Americans ($797 per month to $604 per month, $p = .08$; table not shown). The *maximum* amount of money earned monthly by any gang member from legal income was $2,400, the *mean* for gang drug sales (see Table 2).[4]

Qualitative data from our interviews support the view that for some respondents, the dope game indeed lives up to its stereotype. One dealer credibly reported income from his three drug houses at about $50,000 per month for several months in 1989. Another told how he felt about making so much money:

> Q: Did you ever make crazy money?
> R#220: Yeah . . . one time my hands had turned green from all that money, I couldn't wash it off, man, I loved it. Oh man, look at this . . . just holding all that money in my hand turned my hands green from just counting all that money. Sometimes I'd sit back and just count it maybe three, four times, for the hell of it.

Even for big dealers, however, that money didn't last. Some "players" were "rolling" for several years, but most took a fall within a year or so. As with Padilla's Diamonds, disappointments with the drug trade seemed to exceed its promise for most gang members. Prison and jail time frequently

Table 2 Mean Monthly Income from Drug Dealing: 1989–1991, 87 African American and Latino Respondents

Average Monthly Income from Drug Sales	African American	Latino[a]	Total
Never sold	15.8%	23.3%	18.4%
Less Than $1,000 Monthly (Equivalent to Less Than $6/Hour)	28.1	30.0	28.7
Between $1,000 and $2,000 Monthly (Equivalent to $7–$12/Hour)	28.1	6.7	20.7
Between $2,000 and $4,000 Monthly (Equivalent to $13–$25/Hour)	25.3	33.3	28.7
More Than $10,000 Monthly	1.8	6.7	3.4
Total N = 100%	N = 57	N = 30	N = 87

[a] Three whites were excluded from the analysis. One white founder never sold, and the other two made less than $2,000 monthly.
NOTE: Column percentages may not equal 100% because of rounding.

interrupted their lives. More than three-quarters of all gang founders on our rosters had spent some time in jail in the past five years, as had two-thirds of our respondents. Even so, our respondents had worked a mean of 14.5 months out of the last 36 in legitimate jobs, had worked 14.5 months selling dope, and had spent the remaining seven months in jail. Twenty-five percent of our respondents had worked legitimate jobs at least 24 of the past 36 months.

Yet an anomaly confronted us as we analyzed our data on work. As might be expected, nine out of 10 of those who were not working at the time of our interview had sold dope in the past three years. We also found, however, that three-quarters of those who *were* working in 1992 had sold dope as well within the previous five years (see Table 3).

Table 3 1992 Work Status by Involvement in Cocaine Sales, 220 Surviving Founding Members of 14 Male Gangs

Sold Dope Last Five Years?	Working Now	Not Working Now[a]	Work Status Unknown	Totals
Have Sold Dope	75.0%	91.2%	40.0%	77.7%
Have Not Sold Dope	16.7	5.3	2.9	8.6
Unknown	8.3	3.5	57.1	13.6
Total N = 100%	N = 72	N = 113	N = 35	N = 220

[a] Includes selling cocaine, being "on the run," being locked up, and being involved in other street hustles.

These findings lend themselves to alternative explanations. It may be that three-quarters of those who were working had sold cocaine in the past, but had stopped and were getting their lives together. A second interpretation is that full-time employment is nothing more than an income supplement or "front" for continuation in the drug game. Some gang founders indeed fit into one or the other of these categories.

A third interpretation evolved as we received reports from our staff and respondents about the current status of their fellow gang members. A few days after an interview with "Roger," one of our staff members would report that "Roger" was no longer working for a temporary agency, as he had reported, but was "back in the dope game." The next week "Roger" might call us from jail. A week or so later, we would learn that he was out on bail, his "lady" had put pressure on him, and he was now working full-time in construction with his brother-in-law. Our offices were flooded with similar reports about dozens of people on our rosters. Working and selling drugs were both part of the difficult, topsy-turvy lives led by our respondents. Elliot Liebow's (1967:219) colorful description of the confused lives on Tally's Corner also fits our data: "Traffic is heavy in all directions."

These vicissitudes became too complicated for us to track, so we "froze" the status of founders on our rosters at the time of the last and most reliable interview. Some of our founders seemed to be committed to the dope business and a few had "gone legit," but most of those we were trying to track appeared to be on an economic merry-go-round, with continual movement in and out of the secondary labor market. Although their average income from drug sales far surpassed their income from legal employment, most Milwaukee male gang members apparently kept trying to find licit work.

To help explain this movement in and out of the formal labor market, we created a typology of adult gang members, using constant comparisons (Strauss, 1987). This categorization has some similarities to earlier typologies, but it differs in that it intends to account for the different orientations of gang members in an era of decreased legitimate economic opportunities and increased drug-related, illicit opportunities.

A Typology of Male Adult Gang Members

We developed four ideal types on a continuum of conventional behaviors and values: (1) those few who had gone *legit,* or had matured out of the gang; (2) *homeboys,* a majority of both African American and Latino adult gang members, who alternately worked conventional jobs and took various roles in drug sales; (3) *dope fiends,* who were addicted to cocaine and participated in the dope business as a way to maintain access to the drug; and (4) *new jacks,* who regarded the dope game as a career.

Some gang members, we found, moved over time between categories, some had characteristics of more than one category, and others straddled the boundaries (see Hannerz, 1969:57). Thus a few homeboys were in the process of becoming legit, many moved into and out of cocaine addiction, and others gave up and adopted a new jack orientation. Some new jacks returned to conventional life; others received long prison terms or became addicted to dope. Our categories are not discrete, but our typology seemed to fit the population of gang members we were researching. Our "member checks" (Lincoln and Guba, 1985:314–316) of the constructs with gang members validated these categories for male gang members.

Legits

Legits were those young men who had walked away from the gang. They were working or may have gone on to school. Legits had not been involved in the dope game at all, or not for at least five years. They did not use cocaine heavily, though some may have done so in the past. Some had moved out of the old neighborhood; others, like our project staff, stayed to help out or "give back" to the community. These are prime examples of Whyte's "college boys" or Cloward and Ohlin's Type I, oriented to economic gain and class mobility. The following quote is an example of a young African American man who "went legit" and is now working and going to college.

> Q: Looking back over the past five years, what major changes took place in your life—things that happened that really made things different for you?
> R#105:   I had got into a relationship with my girl, that's one thing. I just knew I couldn't be out on the streets trying to hustle all the time. That's what changed me, I just got a sense of responsibility.

Today's underclass gangs appear to be fundamentally different from those in Thrasher's or Cloward and Ohlin's time, when most gang members "matured out" of the gang. Of the 236 Milwaukee male founders, only 12 (5.1%) could be categorized as having matured out: that is, they were working full time *and* had not sold cocaine in the past five years. When these data are disaggregated by race, the reality of the situation becomes even clearer. We could verify only two of 117 African Americans and one of 87 Latino male gang founders who were currently working and had not sold dope in the past five years. One-third of the white members fell into this category.[5]

Few African American and Latino gang founders, however, were resigned to a life of crime, jail, and violence. After a period of rebellion and living the fast life, the majority of gang founders, or "homeboys," wanted to settle down and go legit, but the path proved to be very difficult.

Homeboys

"Homeboys" were the majority of all adult gang members. They were not firmly committed to the drug economy, especially after the early thrill of fast money and "easy women" wore off. They had reached an age, the mid-twenties, when criminal offenses normally decline (Gottfredson and Hirschi, 1990). Most of these men were unskilled, lacked education, and had had largely negative experiences in the secondary labor market. Some homeboys were committed more strongly to the streets, others to a more conventional life. Most had used cocaine, some heavily at times, but their use was largely in conjunction with selling from a house or corner with their gang "homies." Most homeboys either were married or had a "steady" lady. They also had strong feelings of loyalty to their fellow gang members.

Here, two different homeboys explain how they had changed, and how hard that change was:

Q: Looking back over the past five years, what major changes took place in your life—things that happened that really made things different for you?

R#211: The things that we went through wasn't worth it, and I had a family, you know, and kids, and I had to think about them first, and the thing with the drug game was, that money was quick, easy, and fast, and it went like that, the more money you make the more popular you was. You know, as I see it now it wasn't worth it because the time that I done in penitentiaries I lost my sanity. To me it feels like I lost a part of my kids, because, you know, I know they still care, and they know I'm daddy, but I just lost out. Somebody else won and I lost.

Q: Is she with somebody else now?

R#211: Yeah. She hung in there about four or five months after I went to jail.

Q: It must have been tough for her to be alone with all those kids.

R#211: Yeah.

Q: What kind of person are you?

R#217: Mad. I'm a mad young man. I'm a poor young man. I'm a good person to my kids and stuff, and given the opportunity to have something nice and stop working for this petty-ass money I would try to change a lot of things. . . .

. . . I feel I'm the type of person that given the opportunity to try to have something legit, I will take it, but I'm not going to go by the slow way, taking no four, five years working at no chicken job and trying to get up to a manager just to start making six, seven dollars. And then get fired when I come in high or drunk or something. Or miss a day or something because I got high smoking weed, drinking beer, and the next day come in and get fired; then I'm back in where I started from. So I'm just a cool person, and if I'm given the opportunity and if I can get a job making nine, ten dollars an hour, I'd let everything go; I'd just sit back and work my job and go home. That kind of money I can live with. But I'm not going to settle for no three, four dollars an hour, know what I'm saying?

Homeboys present a more confused theoretical picture than legits. Cloward and Ohlin's Type III delinquents were rebels, who had a "sense of injustice" or felt "unjust deprivation" at a failed system (1960:117). Their gang delinquency is a collective solution to the failure of institutional arrangements. They reject traditional societal norms; other, success-oriented illegitimate norms replace conventionality.

Others have questioned whether gang members' basic outlook actually rejects conventionality. Matza (1964) viewed delinquents' rationalizations of their conduct as evidence of techniques meant to "neutralize" deeply held conventional beliefs. Cohen (1955:129–137) regarded delinquency as a nonutilitarian "reaction formation" to middle-class standards, though middle-class morality lingers, repressed and unacknowledged. What appears to be gang "pathological" behavior, Cohen points out, is the result of the delinquent's striving to attain core values of "the American way of life." Short and Strodtbeck (1965), testing various gang theories, found that white and African American gang members, and lower- and middle-class youths, had similar conventional values.

Our homeboys are older versions of Cohen's and Matza's delinquents, and are even more similar to Short and Strodtbeck's study subjects. Milwaukee homeboys shared three basic characteristics: (1) They worked regularly at legitimate jobs, although they ventured into the drug economy when they believed it was necessary for survival. (2) They had very conventional aspirations; their core values centered on finding a secure place in the American way of life. (3) They had some surprisingly conventional ethical beliefs about the immorality of drug dealing. To a man, they justified their own involvement in drug sales by very Matza-like techniques of "neutralization."

Homeboys are defined by their in-and-out involvement in the legal and illegal economies. Recall that about half of our male respondents had sold drugs no more than 12 of the past 36 months. More than one-third never served any time in jail. Nearly 60% had worked legitimate jobs at least 12 months of the last 36, with a mean of 14.5 months. Homeboys' work patterns thus differed both from those of legits, who worked solely legal jobs, and new jacks who considered dope dealing a career.

To which goal did homeboys aspire, being big-time dope dealers or holding a legitimate job? Rather than having any expectations of staying in the dope game, homeboys aspired to settling down, getting married, and living at least a watered-down version of the American dream. Like Padilla's (1992:157) Diamonds, they strongly desired to "go legit." Although they may have enjoyed the fast life for a while, it soon went stale. Listen to this homeboy, the one who lost his lady when he went to jail:

Q: Five years from now, what would you want to be doing?
R#211: Five years from now? I want to have a steady job, I want to have been working that job for about five years, and just with a family somewhere.
Q: Do you think that's gonna come true?

R#211: Yeah, that's basically what I'm working on. I mean, this bullshit is over now, I'm twenty-five, I've played games long enough, it don't benefit nobody. If you fuck yourself away, all you gonna be is fucked, I see it now.

Others had more hopeful or wilder dreams, but a more sobering outlook on the future. The other homebody, who said he wouldn't settle for three or four dollars an hour, speaks as follows:

Q: Five years from now, what would you want to be doing?
R#217: Owning my own business. And rich. A billionaire.
Q: What do you realistically expect you'll be doing in five years?
R#217: Probably working at McDonald's. That's the truth.

Homeboys' aspirations were divided between finding a steady full-time job and setting up their own business. Their striving pertained less to being for or against "middle-class status" than to finding a practical, legitimate occupation that could support them (see Short and Strodtbeck, 1965). Many homeboys believed that using skills learned in selling drugs to set up a small business would give them a better chance at a decent life than trying to succeed as an employee.

Most important, homeboys "grew up" and were taking a realistic look at their life chances. This homeboy spoke for most:

Q: Looking back over the past five years, what major changes have taken place in your life—things that made a difference about where you are now?
R#220: I don't know, maybe maturity. . . . Just seeing life in a different perspective . . . realizing that from sixteen to twenty-three, man, just shot past. And just realizing that it did, shucks, you just realizing how quick it zoomed past me. And it really just passed me up without really having any enjoyment of a teenager. And hell, before I know it I'm going to hit thirty or forty, and I ain't going to have nothing to stand on. I don't want that shit. Because I see a lot of brothers out here now, that's forty-three, forty-four and ain't got shit. They's still standing out on the corner trying to make a hustle. Doing this, no family, no stable home and nothing. I don't want that shit. . . . I don't give a fuck about getting rich or nothing, but I want a comfortable life, a decent woman, a family to come home to. I mean, everybody needs somebody to care for. This ain't where it's at.

Finally, homeboys were characterized by their ethical views about selling dope. As a group, they believed dope selling was "unmoral"—wrong, but necessary for survival. Homeboys' values were conventional, but in keeping with Matza's findings, they justified their conduct by neutralizing their violation of norms. Homeboys believed that economic necessity was the overriding reason why they could not live up to their values (see Liebow, 1967:214). They were the epitome of ambivalence, ardently believing that dope selling was both wrong and absolutely necessary. One longtime dealer expressed this contradiction:

Q: Do you consider it wrong or immoral to sell dope?
R#129: Um-hum, very wrong.
Q: Why?
R#129: Why, because it's killing people.
Q: Well how come you do it?
R#129: It's also a money maker.
Q: Well how do you balance those things out? I mean, here you're doing something that you think is wrong, making money. How does that make you feel when you're doing it, or don't you think about it when you're doing it?
R#129: Once you get a (dollar) bill, once you look at, I say this a lot, once you look at those dead white men [*presidents' pictures on currency*], you care about nothing else, you don't care about nothing else. Once you see those famous dead white men. That's it.
Q: Do you ever feel bad about selling drugs, doing something that was wrong?
R#129: How do I feel? Well a lady will come in and sell all the food stamps, all of them. When they're sold, what are the kids gonna eat? They can't eat the dope cause she's gonna go smoke that up, or do whatever with it. And then you feel like "wrong." But then, in the back of your mind, man, you just got a hundred dollars worth of food stamps for thirty dollars worth of dope, and you can sell them at the store for seven dollars on ten, so you got seventy coming. So you get seventy dollars for thirty dollars. It is not wrong to do this. It is not wrong to do this!

Homeboys also refused to sell to pregnant women or to juveniles. Contrary to Jankowski's (1991:102) assertion that in gangs "there is no ethical code that regulates business ventures," Milwaukee homeboys had some strong moral feelings about how they carried out their business:

R#109: I won't sell to no little kids. And, ah, if he gonna get it, he gonna get it from someone else besides me. I won't sell to no pregnant woman. If she gonna kill her baby, I want to sleep not knowing that I had anything to do with it. Ah, for anybody else, hey, it's their life, you choose your life how you want.
Q: But how come—I want to challenge you. You know if kids are coming or a pregnant woman's coming, you know they're going to get it somewhere else, right? Someone else will make their money on it; why not you?
R#109: 'Cause the difference is I'll be able to sleep without a guilty conscience.

Homeboys were young adults living on the edge. On the one hand, like most Americans, they had relatively conservative views on social issues and wanted to settle down with a job, a wife, and children. On the other hand, they were afraid they would never succeed, and that long stays in prison would close doors and lock them out of a conventional life. They did not want to continue to live on the streets, but they feared that hustling might be the only way to survive.[6]

Dope Fiends

Dope fiends are gang members who are addicted to cocaine. Thirty-eight percent of all African American founders were using cocaine at the time of our interview, as were 55% of Latinos and 53% of whites. African Americans used cocaine at lower rates than white gang members, but went to jail twice as often. The main focus in a dope fiend's life is getting the drug. Asked what they regretted most about their life, dope fiends invariably said "drug use," whereas most homeboys said "dropping out of school."

Most Milwaukee gang dope fiends, or daily users of cocaine, smoked it as "rocks." More casual users, or reformed dope fiends, if they used cocaine at all, snorted it or sprinkled it on marijuana (called a "primo") to enhance the high. Injection was rare among African Americans but more common among Latinos. About one-quarter of those we interviewed, however, abstained totally from use of cocaine. A majority of the gang members on our rosters had used cocaine since its use escalated in Milwaukee in the late 1980s.

Of 110 gang founders who were reported to be currently using cocaine, 37% were reported to be using "heavily" (every day, in our data), 44% "moderately" (several times per week), and 19% "lightly" (sporadically). More than 70% of all founders on our rosters who were not locked up were currently using cocaine to some extent. More than one-third of our male respondents considered themselves, at some time in their lives, to be "heavy" cocaine users.

More than one-quarter of our respondents had used cocaine for seven years or more, roughly the total amount of time cocaine has dominated the illegal drug market in Milwaukee. Latinos had used cocaine slightly longer than African Americans, for a mean of 75 months compared with 65. Cocaine use followed a steady pattern in our respondents' lives; most homeboys had used cocaine as part of their day-to-day life, especially while in the dope business.

Dope fiends were quite unlike Cloward and Ohlin's "double failures," gang members who used drugs as part of a "retreatist subculture." Milwaukee dope fiends participated regularly in conventional labor markets. Of the 110 founders who were reported as currently using cocaine, slightly more were working legitimate jobs than were not working. Most dope fiends worked at some time in their homies' dope houses or were fronted an ounce or an "eightball" (3.5 grams) of cocaine to sell. Unlike Anderson's "wineheads," gang dope fiends were not predominantly "has-beens" and did not "lack the ability and motivation to hustle" (Anderson, 1978:96–97). Milwaukee cocaine users, like heroin users (Johnson et al., 1985; Moore, 1978; Preble and Casey, 1969), played an active role in the drug-selling business.

Rather than spending their income from drug dealing on family, clothes, or women, dope fiends smoked up their profits. Eventually many stole dope belonging to the boss or "dopeman" and got into trouble. At times their dope use made them so erratic that they were no longer trusted and were forced to leave the neighborhood. Often, however, the gang members who were selling took them back and fronted them cocaine to sell to put them back on their feet. Many had experienced problems in violating the cardinal rule, "Don't get high on your own supply," as in this typical story:

> R#131: . . . if you ain't the type that's a user, yeah, you'll make fabulous money but if you was the type that sells it and uses it and do it at the same time, you know, you get restless. Sometimes you get used to taking your own drugs. . . . I'll just use the profits and just do it . . . and then the next day if I get something again, I'd just take the money to pay up and keep the profits. . . . You sell a couple of hundred and you do a hundred. That's how I was doing it.

Cocaine use was a regular part of the lives of most Milwaukee gang members engaged in the drug economy. More than half of our respondents had never attended a treatment program; more than half of those who had been in treatment went through court-ordered programs. Few of our respondents stopped use by going to a treatment program. Even heavy cocaine use was an "on-again, off-again" situation in which most gang members alternately quit by themselves and started use again (Waldorf et al., 1991).

Alcohol use among dope fiends and homeboys (particularly 40-ounce bottles of Olde English 800 ale) appears to be even more of a problem than cocaine use. Like homeboys, however, most dope fiends aspired to have a family, to hold a steady job, and to find some peace. The wild life of the dope game had played itself out; the main problem was how to quit using.[7]

New Jacks

Whereas homeboys had a tentative relationship with conventional labor markets and held some strong moral beliefs, new jacks had chosen the dope game as a career. They were often loners, strong individualists like Jankowski's (1991) gang members, who cared little about group norms. Frequently they posed as the embodiment of media stereotypes. About one-quarter of our interview respondents could be described as new jacks: they had done nothing in the last 36 months except hustle or spend time in jail.

In some ways, new jacks mirror the criminal subculture described by Cloward and Ohlin. If a criminal subculture is to develop, Cloward and Ohlin argued, opportunities to learn a criminal career must be present, and close ties to conventional markets or customers must exist. This situation distinguishes the criminal from the violent and the retreatist subcultures. The emergence of the cocaine economy and a large market for illegal drugs provided precisely such an opportunity structure for this generation of gang members. New jacks are those who took advantage of the opportunities, and who, at least for the present, have committed themselves to a career in the dope game.

> Q: Do you consider it wrong or immoral to sell dope?
> R#203: I think it's right because can't no motherfucker live your life but you.
> Q: Why?
> R#203: Why? I'll put it this way . . . I love selling dope. I know there's other niggers out here love the money just like I do. And ain't no motherfucker gonna stop a nigger from selling dope . . . I'd sell to my own mother if she had the money.

New jacks, like other gang cocaine dealers, lived up to media stereotypes of the "drug dealer" role and often were emulated by impressionable youths. Some new jacks were homeboys from Milwaukee's original neighborhood gangs, who had given up their conventional dreams; others were members of gangs that were formed solely for drug dealing (see Klein and Maxson, 1993). A founder of one new jack gang described the scene as his gang set up shop in Milwaukee. Note the strong mimicking of media stereotypes:

> R#126: . . . it was crime and drug problems before we even came into the scene. It was just controlled by somebody else. We just came on with a whole new attitude, outlook, at the whole situation. It's like, have you ever seen the movie *New Jack City*, about the kid in New York? You see, they was already there. We just came out with a better idea, you know what I'm saying?

New jacks rejected the homeboys' moral outlook. Many were raised by families with long traditions of hustling or a generation of gang affiliations, and had few hopes of a conventional future. They are the voice of the desperate ghetto dweller, those who live in Carl Taylor's (1990:36) "third culture" made up of "underclass and urban gang members who exhibit signs of moral erosion and anarchy" or propagators of Bourgois's (1990:631) "culture of terror." New jacks fit the media stereotype of all gang members, even though they represent fewer than 25% of Milwaukee's adult gang members.

Discussion: Gangs, the Underclass, and Public Policy

Our study was conducted in one aging postindustrial city, with a population of 600,000. How much can be generalized from our findings can be determined only by researchers in other cities, looking at our categories and determining whether they are useful. Cloward and Ohlin's opportunity theory is a workable general theoretical framework, but more case studies are needed in order to recast their theory to reflect three decades of economic and social changes. We present our typology to encourage others to observe variation within and between gangs, and to assist in the creation of new taxonomies and new theory.

Our paper raises several empirical questions for researchers: Are the behavior patterns of the founding gang members in our sample representative of adult gang members in other cities? In larger cities, are most gang members now new jacks who have long given up the hope of a conventional life, or are most still homeboys? Are there "homeboy" gangs and "new jack" gangs, following the "street gang/drug gang" notion of Klein and Maxson (1993)? If so, what distinguishes one from the other? Does gang members' orientation to conventionality vary by ethnicity or by region? How does it change over time? Can this typology help account for variation in rates of violence between gang members? Can female gang members be typed in the same way as males?

Our data also support the life course perspective of Sampson and Laub (1993:255), who ask whether present criminal justice policies "are producing unintended criminogenic effects." Milwaukee gang members are like the persistent, serious offenders in the Gluecks' data (Glueck and Glueck, 1950). The key to their future lies in building social capital that comes from steady employment and a supportive relationship, without the constant threat of incarceration (Sampson and Laub, 1993:162–168). Homeboys largely had a wife or a steady lady, were unhappily enduring "the silent, subtle humiliations" of the secondary labor market (Bourgois, 1990:629), and lived in dread of prison. Incarceration for drug charges undercut their efforts to find steady work and led them almost inevitably back to the drug economy.

Long and mandatory prison terms for use and intent to sell cocaine lump those who are committed to the drug economy with those who are using or are selling in order to survive. Our prisons are filled disproportionately with minority drug offenders (Blumstein, 1993) like our homeboys, who in essence are being punished for the "crime" of not accepting poverty or of being addicted to cocaine. Our data suggest that jobs, more accessible drug treatment, alternative sentences, or even decriminalization of nonviolent drug offenses would be better approaches than the iron fist of the war on drugs (see Hagedorn, 1991; Reinarman and Levine, 1990; Spergel and Curry, 1990).

Finally, our typology raises ethical questions for researchers. Wilson (1987:8) called the underclass "collectively different" from the poor of the past, and many studies focus on underclass deviance. Our study found that some underclass gang members had embraced the drug economy and had forsaken conventionality, but we also found that the *majority* of adult gang members are still struggling to hold onto a conventional orientation to life.

Hannerz (1969:36) commented more than two decades ago that dichotomizing community residents into "respectables" and "disrespectables" "seems often to emerge from social science writing about poor black people or the lower classes in general." Social science that emphasizes differences within poor communities, without noting commonalities, is one-sided and often distorts and demonizes underclass life.

Our data emphasize that there is no Great Wall separating the underclass from the rest of the central-city poor and working class. Social research should not build one either. Researchers who describe violent and criminal gang actions without also addressing gang members' orientation to conventionality do a disservice to the public, to policy makers, and to social science.

Notes

1. This study was funded by NIDA Grant R01 DA 07218. The funding agency bears no responsibility for data or interpretations presented here.

2. Rosters of gangs in 1992 were refined and new gangs were added; thus it was difficult to make comparisons with 1987 rosters. In 1987, with $N = 225$, 20% of white male gang members, 10% of Latinos, and 27% of African Americans were working.

3. Selling cocaine is not only a gang-related phenomenon. Half of those who were reported as no longer involved with the gang also had sold cocaine within the last five years.

4. We asked respondents to report on the number of months they worked legitimate jobs, worked selling dope, and were in prison. We then asked them to tell us the average amount of money they made in those months working or selling dope. Hourly estimates are based on the monthly average divided by 160 hours. Most respondents reported that they worked selling dope "24/7," meaning full time.

5. About 15% of the founders whereabouts were not known by our informants, but "unknown" status was no guarantee that the missing member had gone legit. One founder of an African American gang was reported to us in a pretest as having "dropped from sight," but later we learned that he had been a victim of one of serial killer Jeffrey Dahmer's grisly murders. Others, with whom our respondents no longer have contact, may be heavy cocaine users who left the gang and the neighborhood because they were no longer trustworthy.

6. Homeboys varied as well. Some were entrepreneurs or players; typically they were the "dopemen" who started a "dopehouse" where other gang members could work. Others worked only sporadically in dopehouses as a supplement to legitimate work or during unemployment. Finally, some, often cocaine users, worked most of the time at the dopehouse and only sporadically at legitimate jobs. Although homeboys also varied over time in their aspirations to conventionality, as a group they believed that the lack of jobs and the prison time were testing their commitment to conventional values. We found no significant differences between Latino and African American homeboys.

7. It is too early to tell how many persons will succeed at freeing themselves from cocaine use. Ansley Hamid (1992) found that by the 1990s, most New York crack users were in their thirties and poor; their heavy drug involvement had ruined their chances for conventional careers.

References

Anderson, Elijah
  1978 A Place on the Corner. Chicago: University of Chicago Press.
  1990 Streetwise: Race, Class, and Change in an Urban Community. Chicago: University of Chicago Press.
Blumstein, Alfred
  1993 Making rationality relevant. Criminology 31:1–16.
Bourgois, Phillippe
  1990 In search of Horatio Alger: culture and ideology in the crack economy. Contemporary Drug Problems 16:619–649.
Cloward, Richard and Lloyd Ohlin
  1960 Delinquency and Opportunity. Glencoe, Ill.: Free Press.
Cohen, Albert
  1955 Delinquent Boys, Glencoe, Ill.: Free Press.

Coleman, James S.
    1988 Social capital in the creation of human capital. American Journal of Sociology 94:S95–S120.
Cummings, Scott and Daniel J. Monte
    1993 Gangs. Albany: State University of New York Press.
Fagan, Jeffrey
    1990 Social processes of delinquency and drug use among urban gangs. In C. Ronald Huff (ed.), Gangs in America. Newbury Park: Sage.
    1991 Drug selling and licit income in distressed neighborhoods: The economic lives of street-level drug users and dealers. In Adele V. Harrell and George E. Peterson (eds.), Drugs, Crime, and Social Isolation. Washington: Urban Institute Press.
Glueck, Sheldon and Eleanor Glueck
    1950 Unraveling Juvenile Delinquency. New York: Commonwealth Fund.
Gottfredson, Michael and Travis Hirschi
    1990 A General Theory of Crime. Stanford: Stanford University Press.
Hagedorn, John M.
    1988 People and Folks: Gangs, Crime, and the Underclass in a Rustbelt City. Chicago: Lakeview.
    1991 Gangs, neighborhoods, and public policy. Social Problems 38:529–542.
Hamid, Ansley
    1992 The developmental cycle of a drug epidemic: the cocaine smoking epidemic of 1981–1991. Journal of Psychoactive Drugs 24:337–348.
Hannerz, Ulf
    1969 Soulside: Inquiries into Ghetto Culture and Community. New York: Columbia University Press.
Huff, C. Ronald
    1990 Gangs in America. Newbury Park: Sage.
Jankowski, Martin Sanchez
    1991 Islands in the Street: Gangs and American Urban Society. Berkeley: University of California Press.
Johnson, Bruce D., Terry Williams, Kojo Dei, and Harry Sanahria
    1985 Taking Care of Business: The Economics of Crime by Heroin Abusers. Lexington, Mass.: Heath.
Klein, Malcolm W.
    1971 Street Gangs and Street Workers. Englewood Cliffs, N.J.: Prentice Hall.
    1992 The new street gang . . . or is it? Contemporary Sociology 21:80–82.
Klein, Malcolm W. and Cheryl L. Maxson
    1993 Gangs and cocaine trafficking. In Craig Uchida and Doris Mackenzie (eds.), Drugs and the Criminal Justice System. Newbury Park: Sage.
Klein, Malcolm W., Cheryl L. Maxson, and Lea C. Cunningham
    1991 Crack, street gangs, and violence. Criminology 29:623–650.
Liebow, Elliot
    1967 Tally's Corner. Boston: Little, Brown.
Lincoln, Yvonna S. and Egon G. Guba
    1985 Naturalistic Inquiry. Beverly Hills: Sage.
MacCoun, Robert and Peter Reuter
    1992 Are the wages of sin $30 an hour? Economic aspects of street-level drug dealing. Crime and Delinquency 38:477–491.
MacLeod, Jay
    1987 Ain't No Makin' It: Leveled Aspirations in a Low-Income Neighborhood. Boulder: Westview.
Matza, David
    1964 Delinquency and Drift. New York: Wiley.
Merton, Robert K.
    1957 Social Theory and Social Structure. 1968. New York: Free Press.

Miller, Walter B.
1969 Lower class culture as a generating milieu of gang delinquency. Journal of Social Issues 14:5–19.

Moore, Joan W.
1978 Homeboys: Gangs, Drugs, and Prison in the Barrios of Los Angeles. Philadelphia: Temple University Press.
1991 Going Down to the Barrio: Homeboys and Homegirls in Change. Philadelphia: Temple University Press.

Padilla, Felix
1992 The Gang as an American Enterprise. New Brunswick: Rutgers University Press.

Preble, Edward and John H. Casey
1969 Taking care of business: The heroin user's life on the street. International Journal of the Addictions 4:1–24.

Reinarman, Craig and Harry G. Levine
1990 Crack in context: politics and media in the making of a drug scare. Contemporary Drug Problems 16:535–577.

Rose, Harold M., Ronald S. Edari, Lois M. Quinn, and John Pawasrat
1992 The Labor Market Experience of Young African American Men from Low-Income Families in Wisconsin. Milwaukee: University of Wisconsin–Milwaukee Employment and Training Institute.

Sampson, Robert J. and John H. Laub
1993 Crime in the Making: Pathways and Turning Points through Life. Cambridge: Harvard University Press.

Short, James F. and Fred L. Strodtbeck
1965 Group Process and Gang Delinquency. Chicago: University of Chicago Press.

Skolnick, Jerome H.
1990 The social structure of street drug dealing. American Journal of Police 9:1–41.

Spergel, Irving A. and G. David Curry
1990 Strategies and perceived agency effectiveness in dealing with the youth gang problem. In C. Ronald Huff (ed.), Gangs in America. Beverly Hills: Sage.

Strauss, Anselm L.
1987 Qualitative Analysis for Social Scientists. Cambridge: Cambridge University Press.

Sullivan, Mercer L.
1989 Getting Paid: Youth Crime and Work in the Inner City. Ithaca: Cornell University Press.

Taylor, Carl
1990 Dangerous Society. East Lansing: Michigan State University Press.

Thrasher, Frederick
1927 The Gang. 1963. Chicago: University of Chicago Press.

Waldorf, Dan
1993 Final Report of the Crack Sales, Gangs, and Violence Study: NIDA Grant 5#R01DA06486. Alameda: Institute for Scientific Analysis.

Waldorf, Dan, Craig Reinarman, and Sheigla Murphy
1991 Cocaine Changes: The Experience of Using and Quitting. Philadelphia: Temple University Press.

Whyte, William Foote
1943 Street Corner Society. Chicago: University of Chicago Press.

Williams, Terry
1989 The Cocaine Kids. Reading, Mass.: Addison-Wesley.

Wilson, William Julius
1987 The Truly Disadvantaged. Chicago: University of Chicago.

Control Theory

A central feature of control theory is the view that various levels and types of societal commitment, when coupled with other factors, are often important precursors to the commission of deviant acts. Travis Hirschi offers a well-known statement of this position.

In "A Control Theory of Delinquency," he notes that control theorists assume that delinquency will result when an actor's bond to society is weakened or broken. He then proceeds to discuss and analyze the various elements that comprise the bond of society, particularly as they relate to the question of motivation. For example, the "commitment" element refers to the idea that most people invest a great deal of time and energy in conventional lines of activity (e.g., educational and occupational pursuits). When deviant behavior is contemplated, the risks of such deviation must be considered. The guiding assumption is that involvement in deviance or crime would jeopardize one's investments. Hirschi concludes with a section on "belief," another major element of the bond to society. The underlying premise is that society is characterized by a common value system. If this is correct—and if, further, one retains some type of allegiance to established values—then a basic question presents itself: "Why does a man violate the rules in which he believes?" Hirschi, in his attempt to answer this question, rejects the view that an actor must rationalize or neutralize his or her behavior. Hirschi prefers, instead, the notion that the weakness of one's beliefs can be used to explain motivation. When a person's belief in the validity of norms is weakened, the probability of delinquency and deviance increases.

Barbara Castello, Bradley Anderson, and Michael Stein test hypotheses that derive from control theory. Their interest is in patterns of heavy episodic drinking among 938 9th, 10th, and 11th grade students. The authors integrate Hirschi's (1969) conceptualization of the "social bond" (including attachment, commitment, involvement, and belief) with a more recent version developed by Gottfredson and Hirschi (1990) which emphasizes the importance of self-control. Hirschi's early version emphasized the social forces that restrain individuals from participating in deviant acts—a natural consequence of human nature. Gottfredson and Hirschi (1990) focus less on social control, preferring "self-control"—"internalized control produced through socialization." As the authors note, there is much research supporting social control through social bonds. Each of the elements of the social bond (with the exception of involvement) has received substantial empirical support. Further, virtually all tests of self control theory have found "self-control to be related to criminal or analogous behavior." However, there has been no application of these theories to heavy episodic drinking, a growing contemporary social problem. Their analysis provides additional support for the theories showing that attachment to parents, belief in law, commitment to school and self control are all strongly related to adolescent heavy episodic drinking.

15 A Control Theory of Delinquency

Travis Hirschi

Control theories assume that delinquent acts result when an individual's bond to society is weak or broken. Since these theories embrace two highly complex concepts, the *bond* of the individual to *society,* it is not surprising that they have at one time or another formed the basis of explanations of most forms of aberrant or unusual behavior. It is also not surprising that control theories have described the elements of the bond to society in many ways, and that they have focused on a variety of units as the point of control. . . .

Elements of the Bond

Attachment

In explaining conforming behavior, sociologists justly emphasize sensitivity to the opinion of others.[1] Unfortunately, . . . they tend to suggest that man *is* sensitive to the opinion of others and thus exclude sensitivity from their explanations of deviant behavior. In explaining deviant behavior, psychologists, in contrast, emphasize insensitivity to the opinion of others.[2] Unfortunately, they too tend to ignore variation, and, in addition, they tend to tie sensitivity inextricably to other variables, to make it part of a syndrome or "type," and thus seriously to reduce its value as an explanatory concept. The psychopath is characterized only in part by "deficient attachment to or affection for others, a failure to respond to the ordinary motivations founded in respect or regard for one's fellow";[3] he is also characterized by such things as "excessive aggressiveness," "lack of superego control," and "an infantile level of response."[4] Unfortunately, too, the behavior that psychopathy is used to explain often becomes part of the *definition* of psychopathy. As a result, in Barbara Wootton's words: "[The psychopath] is . . . *par excellence,* and without shame or qualification, the model of the circular process by which mental abnormality is inferred from anti-social behavior while anti-social behavior is explained by mental abnormality."[5]

The problems of diagnosis, tautology, and name-calling are avoided if the dimensions of psychopathy are treated as causally and therefore problematically interrelated, rather than as logically and therefore necessarily bound to each other. In fact, it can be argued that all of the characteristics attributed to the psychopath follow from, are effects of, his lack of attachment to others. To say that to lack attachment to others is to be free from moral restraints is to use lack of attachment to explain the guiltlessness of the psychopath, the fact that he apparently has no conscience or superego. In this view, lack of attachment to others is not merely a symptom of psychopathy, it *is* psychopathy; lack of conscience is just another way of saying the same thing; and the violation of norms is (or may be) a consequence.

For that matter, given that man is an animal, "impulsivity" and "aggressiveness" can also be seen as natural consequences of freedom from moral restraints. However, since the view of man as endowed with natural propensities and capacities like other animals is peculiarly unpalatable to sociologists, we need not fall back on such a view to explain the amoral man's aggressiveness.[6] The process of becoming alienated from others often involves or is based on active interpersonal conflict. Such conflict could easily supply a reservoir of *socially derived* hostility sufficient to account for the aggressiveness of those whose attachments to others have been weakened.

Durkheim said it many years ago: "We are moral beings to the extent that we are social beings."[7] This may be interpreted to mean that we are moral beings to the extent that we have "internalized the norms" of society. But what does it mean to say that a person has internalized the norms of society? The norms of society are by definition shared by the members of society. To violate a norm is, therefore, to act contrary to the wishes and expectations of other people. If a person does not care about the wishes and expectations of other people—that is, if he is insensitive to the opinion of others—then he is to that extent not bound by the norms. He is free to deviate.

The essence of internalization of norms, conscience, or superego thus lies in the attachment of the individual to others.[8] This view has several advantages over the concept of internalization. For one, explanations of deviant behavior based on attachment do not beg the question, since the extent to which a person is attached to others can be measured independently of his deviant behavior. Furthermore, change or variation in behavior is explainable in a way that it is not when notions of internalization or superego are used. For example, the divorced man is more likely after divorce to commit a number of deviant acts, such as suicide or forgery. If we explain these acts by reference to the superego (or internal control), we are forced to say that the man "lost his conscience" when he got a divorce; and, of course, if he remarries, we have to conclude that he gets his conscience back.

This dimension of the bond to conventional society is encountered in most social control-oriented research and theory. F. Ivan Nye's "internal control" and "indirect control" refer to the same element, although we avoid the problem of explaining changes over time by locating the "conscience" in the bond to others rather than making it part of the personality.[9] Attachment to others is just one aspect of Albert J. Reiss's "personal controls"; we avoid his problems of tautological empirical *observations* by making the relationship between attachment and delinquency problematic rather than definitional.[10] Finally, Scott Briar and Irving Piliavin's "commitment" or "stake in conformity" subsumes attachment, as their discussion illustrates, although the terms they use are more closely associated with the next element to be discussed.[11]

Commitment

"Of all passions, that which inclineth men least to break the laws, is fear. Nay, excepting some generous natures, it is the only thing, when there is the appearance of profit or pleasure by breaking the laws, that makes men keep them."[12] Few would deny that men on occasion obey the rules simply from fear of the consequences. This rational component in conformity we label commitment. What does it mean to say that a person is committed to conformity? In Howard S. Becker's formulation it means the following:

> First, the individual is in a position in which his decision with regard to some particular line of action has consequences for other interests and activities not necessarily [directly] related to it. Second, he has placed himself in that position by his own prior actions. A third element is present though so obvious as not to be apparent; the committed person must be aware [of these other interests] and must recognize that his decision in this case will have ramifications beyond it.[13]

The idea, then, is that the person invests time, energy, himself, in a certain line of activity—say, getting an education, building up a business, acquiring a reputation for virtue. When or whenever he considers deviant behavior, he must consider the costs of this deviant behavior, the risk he runs of losing the investment he has made in conventional behavior.

If attachment to others is the sociological counterpart of the superego or conscience, commitment is the counterpart of the ego or common sense. To the person committed to conventional lines of action, risking one to ten years in prison for a ten-dollar holdup is stupidity, because to the committed person the costs and risks obviously exceed ten dollars in value. (To the psychoanalyst, such an act exhibits failure to be governed by the "reality-principle.") In the sociological control theory, it can be and is generally assumed that the decision to commit a criminal act may well be rationally determined—that the actor's decision was not irrational given the risks and costs he faces. Of course, as Becker points out, if the actor is capable of in some sense calculating the costs of a line of action, he is also capable of calculational errors: ignorance and error return, in the control theory, as possible explanations of deviant behavior.

The concept of commitment assumes that the organization of society is such that the interest of most persons would be endangered if they were to engage in criminal acts. Most people, simply by the process of living in an organized society, acquire goods, reputations, prospects that they do not want to risk losing. These accumulations are society's insurance that they will abide by the rules. Many hypotheses about the antecedents of delinquent behavior are based on this premise. For example, Arthur L. Stinchcombe's hypothesis that "high school rebellion . . . occurs when future status is not clearly related to present performance"[14] suggests that one is committed to conformity not only by what one has but also by what one hoped to obtain. Thus "ambition" and/or "aspiration" play an important role in producing conformity. The person becomes committed to a conventional line of action, and he is therefore committed to conformity.

Most lines of action in a society are of course conventional. The clearest examples are educational and occupational careers. Actions thought to jeopardize one's chances in these areas are presumably avoided. Interestingly enough, even nonconventional commitments may operate to produce conventional conformity. We are told, at least, that boys aspiring to careers in the rackets or professional thievery are judged by their "honesty" and "reliability"—traits traditionally in demand among seekers of office boys.[15]

Involvement

Many persons undoubtedly owe a life of virtue to a lack of opportunity to do otherwise. Time and energy are inherently limited: "Not that I would not, if I could, be both handsome and fat and well dressed, and a great athlete, and make a million a year, be a wit, a bon vivant, and a lady killer, as well as a philosopher, a philanthropist, a statesman, warrior, and African explorer, as well as a 'tone-poet' and saint. But the thing is simply impossible."[16] The things that William James here says he would like to be or do are all, I suppose, within the realm of conventionality, but if he were to include illicit actions he would still have to eliminate some of them as simply impossible.

Involvement or engrossment in conventional activities is thus often part of a control theory. The assumption, widely shared, is that a person may be simply too busy doing conventional things to find time to engage in deviant behavior. The person involved in conventional activities is tied to appointments, deadlines, working hours, plans, and the like, so the opportunity to commit deviant acts rarely arises. To the extent that he is engrossed in conventional activities, he cannot even think about deviant acts, let alone act out his inclinations.[17]

This line of reasoning is responsible for the stress placed on recreational facilities in many programs to reduce delinquency, for much of the concern with the high school dropout, and for the idea that boys should be drafted into the army to keep them out of trouble. So obvious and persuasive is the idea that involvement in conventional activities is a major deterrent to delinquency that it was accepted even by Sutherland: "In the general area of juvenile delinquency it is probable that the most significant difference between juveniles who engage in delinquency and those who do not is that the latter are provided abundant opportunities of a conventional type for satisfying their recreational interests, while the former lack those opportunities or facilities."[18]

The view that "idle hands are the devil's workshop" has received more sophisticated treatment in recent sociological writings on delinquency. David Matza and Gresham M. Sykes, for example, suggest that delinquents have the values of a leisure class, the same values ascribed by Veblen to *the* leisure class: a search for kicks, disdain of work, a desire for the big score, and acceptance of aggressive toughness as proof of masculinity.[19] Matza and Sykes explain delinquency by reference to this system of values, but they note that adolescents at all class levels are "to some extent" members of a leisure class, that they "move in a limbo between earlier parental domination and future integration with the social structure through the bonds of work and marriage."[20] In the end, then, the leisure of the adolescent produces a set of values, which, in turn, leads to delinquency.

Belief

Unlike the cultural deviance theory, the control theory assumes the existence of a common value system within the society or group whose norms are being violated. If the deviant is committed to a value system different from that of conventional society, there is, within the context of the theory, nothing to explain. The question is, "Why does a man violate the rules in which he believes?" It is not, "Why do men differ in their beliefs about what constitutes good and desirable conduct?" The person is assumed to have been socialized (perhaps imperfectly) into the group whose rules he is violating; deviance is not a question of one group imposing its rules on the members of another group. In other words, we not only assume the deviant *has* believed the rules, we assume he believes the rules even as he violates them.

How can a person believe it is wrong to steal at the same time he is stealing? In the strain theory, this is not a difficult problem. (In fact, . . . the strain theory was devised specifically to deal with this question.) The motivation to deviance adduced by the strain theorist is so strong that we can well understand the deviant act even assuming the deviator believes strongly that it is wrong.[21] However, given the control theory's assumptions about motivation, if both the deviant and the nondeviant believe the deviant act is wrong, how do we account for the fact that one commits it and the other does not?

Control theories have taken two approaches to this problem. In one approach, beliefs are treated as mere words that mean little or nothing if the other forms of control are missing. "Semantic dementia," the dissociation between rational faculties and emotional control which is said to be characteristic of the psychopath, illustrates this way of handling the problem.[22] In short, beliefs, at least insofar as they are expressed in words, drop out of the picture; since they do not differentiate between deviants and nondeviants, they are in the same class as "language" or any other characteristic common to all members of the group. Since they represent no real obstacle to the commission of delinquent acts, nothing need be said about how they are handled by those committing such acts. The control theories that do not mention beliefs (or values), and many do not, may be assumed to take this approach to the problem.

The second approach argues that the deviant rationalizes his behavior so that he can at once violate the rule and maintain his belief in it. Donald R. Cressey had advanced this argument with respect to embezzlement,[23] and Sykes and Matza have advanced it with respect to delinquency.[24] In both Cressey's and Sykes and Matza's treatments, these rationalizations (Cressey calls them "verbalizations," Sykes and Matza term them "techniques of neutralization") occur prior to the commission of the deviant act. If the neutralization is successful, the person is free to commit the act(s) in question. Both in Cressey and in Sykes and Matza, the strain that prompts the effort at neutralization also provides the motive force that results in the subsequent deviant act. Their theories are thus, in this sense, strain theories. Neutralization is difficult to handle within the context of a theory that adheres closely to control theory assumptions, because in the control theory there is no special motivational force to account for the neutralization. This difficulty is especially noticeable in Matza's later treatment of this topic, where the motivational component, the "will to delinquency," appears *after* the moral vacuum has been created by the techniques of neutralization.[25] The question thus becomes: Why neutralize?

In attempting to solve a strain-theory problem with control-theory tools, the control theorist is thus led into a trap. He cannot answer the crucial question. The concept of neutralization assumes the existence of moral obstacles to the commission of deviant acts. In order plausibly to account for a deviant act, it is necessary to generate motivation to deviance that is at least equivalent in force to the resistance provided by these moral obstacles. However, if the moral obstacles are removed, neutralization and special motivation are no longer required. We therefore follow the implicit logic of control theory and remove these moral obstacles by hypothesis. Many persons do not have an attitude of respect toward the rules of society; many persons feel no moral obligation to conform regardless of personal advantage. Insofar as the values and beliefs of these persons are consistent with their feelings, and there should be a tendency toward consistency, neutralization is unnecessary; it has already occurred.

Does this merely push the question back a step and at the same time produce conflict with the assumption of a common value system? I think not.

In the first place, we do not assume, as does Cressey, that neutralization occurs in order to make a specific criminal act possible.[26] We do not assume, as do Sykes and Matza, that neutralization occurs to make many delinquent acts possible. We do not assume, in other words, that the person constructs a system of rationalizations in order to justify commission of acts he *wants* to commit. We assume, in contrast, that the beliefs that free a man to commit deviant acts are *unmotivated* in the sense that he does not construct or adopt them in order to facilitate the attainment of illicit ends. In the second place, we do not assume, as does Matza, that "delinquents concur in the conventional assessment of delinquency."[27] We assume, in contrast, that there is *variation* in the extent to which people believe they should obey the rules of society, and, furthermore, that the less a person believes he should obey the rules, the more likely he is to violate them.[28]

In chronological order, then, a person's beliefs in the moral validity of norms are, for no teleological reason, weakened. The probability that he will commit delinquent acts is therefore increased. When and if he commits a delinquent act, we may justifiably use the weakness of his beliefs in explaining it, but no special motivation is required to explain either the weakness of his beliefs or, perhaps, his delinquent act.

The keystone of this argument is of course the assumption that there is variation in belief in the moral validity of social rules. This assumption is amenable to direct empirical test and can thus survive at least until its first confrontation with data. For the present, we must return to the idea of a common value system with which this section was begun.

The idea of a common (or perhaps better, a single) value system is consistent with the fact, or presumption, of variation in the strength of moral beliefs. We have not suggested that delinquency is based on beliefs counter to conventional morality; we have not suggested that delinquents do not believe delinquent acts are wrong. They may well believe these acts are wrong, but the meaning and efficacy of such beliefs are contingent on other beliefs and, indeed, on the strength of other ties to the conventional order.[29]

Notes

1. Books have been written on the increasing importance of interpersonal sensitivity in modern life. According to this view, controls from within have become less important than controls from without in *producing* conformity. Whether or not this observation is true as a description of historical trends, it is true that interpersonal sensitivity has become more important in *explaining* conformity. Although logically it should also have become more important in explaining nonconformity, the opposite has been the case, once again showing that Cohen's observation that an explanation of conformity should be an explanation of deviance cannot be translated as "an explanation of conformity has to be an explanation of deviance." For the view that interpersonal sensitivity currently plays a greater role than formerly in producing conformity, see William J. Goode, "Norm Commitment and Conformity to Role-Status Obligations," *American Journal of Sociology,* LXVI (1960), 246–258. And, of course, also see David Riesman, Nathan Glazer, and Rouel Denney, *The Lonely Crowd* (Garden City, New York: Doubleday, 1950), especially Part I.

2. The literature on psychopathy is voluminous. See William McCord and Joan McCord, *The Psychopath* (Princeton: D. Van Nostrand, 1964).

3. John M. Martin and Joseph P. Fitzpatrick, *Delinquent Behavior* (New York: Random House, 1964), p. 130.

4. *Ibid.* For additional properties of the psychopath, see McCord and McCord, *The Psychopath,* pp. 1–2.

5. Barbara Wootton, *Social Science and Social Pathology* (New York: Macmillan, 1959), p. 250.

6. "The logical untenability [of the position that there are forces in man 'resistant to socialization'] was ably demonstrated by Parsons over 30 years ago, and it is widely recognized that the position is empirically unsound because it assumes [!] some universal biological drive system distinctly separate from socialization and social context—a basic and intransigent human nature" (Judith Blake and Kingsley Davis, "Norms, Values, and Sanctions," *Handbook of Modern Sociology,* ed. Robert E. L. Faris [Chicago: Rand McNally, 1964], p. 471).

7. Emile Durkheim, *Moral Education,* trans. Everett K. Wilson and Herman Schnurer (New York: The Free Press, 1961), p. 64.

8. Although attachment alone does not exhaust the meaning of internalization, attachments and beliefs combined would appear to leave only a small residue of "internal control" not susceptible in principle to direct measurement.

9. F. Ivan Nye, *Family Relationships and Delinquent Behavior* (New York: Wiley, 1958), pp. 5–7.

10. Albert J. Reiss, Jr., "Delinquency as the Failure of Personal and Social Controls," *American Sociological Review,* XVI (1951), 196–207. For example, "Our observations show . . . that delinquent recidivists are less often persons with mature ego ideals or non-delinquent social roles" (p. 204).

11. Scott Briar and Irving Piliavin, "Delinquency, Situational Inducements, and Commitment to Conformity," *Social Problems,* XIII (1965), 41–42. The concept "stake in conformity" was introduced by Jackson Toby in his "Social Disorganization and Stake in Conformity: Complementary Factors in the Predatory Behavior of Hoodlums," *Journal of Criminal Law, Criminology and Police Science,* XLVIII (1957), 12–17. See also his "Hoodlum or Business Man: An American Dilemma," *The Jews,* ed. Marshall Sklare (New York: The Free Press, 1958), pp. 542–550. Throughout the text, I occasionally use "stake in conformity" in speaking in general of the strength of the bond to conventional society. So used, the concept is somewhat broader than is true for either Toby or Briar and Piliavin, where the concept is roughly equivalent to what is here called "commitment."

12. Thomas Hobbes, *Leviathan* (Oxford: Basil Blackwell, 1957), p. 195.

13. Howard S. Becker, "Notes on the Concept of Commitment," *American Journal of Sociology,* LXVI (1960), 35–36.

14. Arthur L. Stinchcombe, *Rebellion in a High School* (Chicago: Quadrangle, 1964), p. 5.

15. Richard A. Cloward and Lloyd E. Ohlin, *Delinquency and Opportunity* (New York: The Free Press, 1960), p. 147, quoting Edwin H. Sutherland, ed., *The Professional Thief* (Chicago: University of Chicago Press, 1937), pp. 211–213.

16. William James, *Psychology* (Cleveland: World Publishing Co., 1948), p. 186.

17. Few activities appear to be so engrossing that they rule out contemplation of alternative lines of behavior, at least if estimates of the amount of time men spend plotting sexual deviations have any validity.

18. *The Sutherland Papers,* ed. Albert K. Cohen et al. (Bloomington: Indiana University Press, 1956), p. 37.

19. David Matza and Gresham M. Sykes, "Juvenile Delinquency and Subterranean Values," *American Sociological Review,* XXVI (1961), 712–719.

20. *Ibid.,* p. 718.

21. The starving man stealing the loaf of bread is the image evoked by most strain theories. In this image, the starving man's belief in the wrongness of his act is clearly not something that must be explained away. It can be assumed to be present without causing embarrassment to the explanation.

22. McCord and McCord, *The Psychopath,* pp. 12–15.

23. Donald R. Cressey, *Other People's Money* (New York: The Free Press, 1953).

24. Gresham M. Sykes and David Matza, "Techniques of Neutralization: A Theory of Delinquency," *American Sociological Review,* XXII (1957), 664–670.

25. David Matza, *Delinquency and Drift* (New York: Wiley, 1964), pp. 181–191.

26. In asserting that Cressey's assumption is invalid with respect to delinquency, I do not wish to suggest that it is invalid for the question of embezzlement, where the problem faced by the deviator is fairly specific and he can reasonably be assumed to be an upstanding citizen. (Although even here the fact that the embezzler's nonsharable financial problem often

results from some sort of hanky-panky suggests that "verbalizations" may be less necessary than might otherwise be assumed.)

27. *Delinquency and Drift,* p. 43.

28. This assumption is not, I think, contradicted by the evidence presented by Matza against the existence of a delinquent subculture. In comparing the attitudes and actions of delinquents with the picture painted by delinquent subculture theorists, Matza emphasizes—and perhaps exaggerates—the extent to which delinquents are tied to the conventional order. In implicitly comparing delinquents with a supermoral man, I emphasize—and perhaps exaggerate—the extent to which they are not tied to the conventional order.

29. The position taken here is therefore somewhere between the "semantic dementia" and the "neutralization" positions. Assuming variation, the delinquent is, at the extremes, freer than the neutralization argument assumes. Although the possibility of wide discrepancy between what the delinquent professes and what he practices still exists, it is presumably much rarer than is suggested by studies of articulate "psychopaths."

Heavy Episodic Drinking Among Adolescents: A Test of Hypotheses Derived from Control Theory

Barbara J. Costello
Bradley J. Anderson
Michael D. Stein

Introduction

Heavy episodic drinking among young people is increasingly perceived as an important social problem, and it has received considerable scholarly attention in recent years. The NIAAA created a Task Force on College Drinking in 1998, and in the past several years the journals *Psychology of Addictive Behaviors and the Journal of Studies on Alcohol* have devoted special issues to heavy episodic drinking. Research has revealed a number of important correlates of heavy episodic drinking, including developmental factors such as the transition to college, individual factors such as impulsivity and fraternity/sorority membership, and environmental factors such as perceived drinking norms and availability of alcohol (NIAAA, 2002). Despite the increasing focus on heavy episodic drinking among both scholars and the popular media, there has been little attention given to this issue in the sociological and criminological literature. Likewise, much research that has been conducted on heavy episodic drinking has not incorporated sociological or criminological perspectives or research findings. The primary purpose of this paper is to assess the extent to which a popular theory of crime and deviance, control theory, can explain heavy episodic drinking in a sample of high school students. We also explore the implications of our findings for further research on heavy episodic drinking incorporating the control theory perspective.

Social control theory (Hirschi, 1969) focuses on social forces restraining individuals from committing criminal or deviant acts, such as heavy drinking. The theory assumes that such behavior is a natural consequence of human nature, viewing deviance as a means to achieve desires with little effort. Thus, social control theory views deviance as nonproblematic, and instead aims to explain conformity. According to Hirschi (1969), most people conform most of the time due to their bond to society; which consists of four elements. An individual's emotional *attachment* to others, such as parents, deters deviation because individuals are concerned about the loss of respect that would likely result if their deviation were discovered. *Commitment* to long-term goals, such as educational or occupational pursuits, reduces the likelihood of deviation because it might jeopardize the individual's ability to achieve these goals. *Involvement* in conventional activities reduces the likelihood of deviance because time is limited—busy people have less time to get involved in deviant or illegal activity. Finally, *belief* in the moral validity of the law provides an additional restraint from deviance—to the extent that individuals believe that the law should be obeyed, they will be less likely to deviate from it. The four elements of the social bond are analytically separable, but Hirschi argued that they are empirically related—those with a strong bond in one area are likely to have strong bonds in other respects as well. In short, those who are more socially integrated are less likely to deviate from social norms.

A more recent version of control theory focuses less on social control and more on internalized control produced through early childhood socialization. Gottfredson and Hirschi's (1990) self-control theory starts with the same assumption as social control theory, or that people are naturally inclined to commit criminal acts and acts "analogous" to crime, such as heavy drinking, unprotected sex, and reckless driving. Gottfredson and Hirschi argue that these behaviors have important characteristics in common—they tend to provide immediate gratification and often have long-term negative consequences, require little skill or planning, and tend to be exciting or thrilling. Corresponding to these characteristics of criminal and analogous acts, Gottfredson and Hirschi argue that those with low self-control tend to pursue short-term gratification, to fail to consider the consequences of behavior, to be self-interested, and to prefer physical, risky, or thrilling activities to more intellectual or sedate ones. Thus, they argue that crime and analogous behaviors are the result of individuals pursuing immediate, self-interested goals when an easy opportunity to do so arises.

Gottfredson and Hirschi (1990) thus view deviant behavior as essentially unsocialized behavior, and argue that self-control is an acquired characteristic that is produced through early childhood socialization. Parents must consistently and appropriately supervise and punish children for disruptive or dangerous behavior. If they fail to do so, children will not develop self-control, and self-control is a characteristic that is unlikely to be learned later in life. Thus, Gottfredson and Hirschi highlight the stability of self-control over the life course, and emphasize the extent to which criminal and analogous behaviors also tend to remain stable over time.

Social and self-control theories make similar empirical predictions, albeit for slightly different reasons. For example, the two theories both point to the importance of family-related variables in reducing deviant behaviors. Social control theory explicitly predicts that current social bonds reduce delinquency due to the individual's desire to maintain those bonds (Hirschi, 1969). Self-control theory points to the importance of adequate early socialization in producing conformity, essentially arguing that social control in early childhood produces self-control later in life (Gottfredson & Hirschi, 1990). Because self-control theory sees stable adult relationships as one outcome of high levels of self-control, it predicts that those with stronger bonds to family and others should be less likely to engage in deviance, essentially viewing current social bonds as an indicator of one's level of self-control. Similarly, both theories predict that measures of commitment to school will be negatively associated with deviance. For social control theory, commitment provides a "stake in conformity" that individuals are unwilling to risk losing. For self-control theory, commitment can again be viewed as an indicator of one's underlying level of self-control— those who work hard at school do so largely because they have higher levels of self-control. Thus, while the causal mechanisms differ between the two theories, their empirical predictions are sufficiently similar to allow us to test the theories simultaneously.

Control theory's major predictions have received substantial empirical support. Attachment to parents, commitment to educational and occupational pursuits, and belief in the validity of the law are robust correlates of delinquent behavior (Costello & Vowell, 1999; Hirschi, 1969; Wadsworth, 2000). Hirschi's (1969) predictions regarding involvement in conventional activities have been less well supported, likely because so many delinquent activities require very little time to complete (Hirschi, 1969). Self-control theory (Gottfredson & Hirschi, 1990) has also garnered substantial empirical support, with virtually all tests of the theory finding self-control to be negatively related to criminal or analogous behavior (Pratt & Cullen, 2000).

Studies examining control theory's ability to explain substance use have also been largely supportive of the theory. For example, Krohn and Massey (1980) found that social control theory explained 29% of the variation in alcohol/marijuana use among their sample of adolescents, and other studies of adolescent substance use find similarly supportive results (Lopez, Redondo, & Martin, 1989; Murray, 1986.) Keane, Maxim, and Teevan (1993) found that measures of low self-control were associated with drinking and driving for both males and females. However, most criminological research conceptualizes delinquency or deviance as a set of illegal or socially undesirable behaviors, and uses composite indexes of a variety of behaviors such as property offenses, violent crimes, and substance use. While this approach is consistent with control theory's focus on the commonalities between various types of deviant behavior, it limits our ability to draw conclusions about the theory's ability to explain drinking specifically.

This approach has also likely minimized the impact of criminological research on more specialized areas of research in psychology and other social sciences, including heavy episodic drinking research. The recent special issues of journals noted previously cite very few criminological or sociological studies, and there have been no studies to date on the ability of the most influential theories of crime to explain heavy episodic drinking. We believe that this lack of disciplinary integration has had negative consequences on the state of knowledge about heavy episodic drinking, in that criminological theories can provide a framework for better understanding the known correlates of heavy episodic drinking and can suggest new avenues for research that can inform both the heavy episodic drinking literature and the field of criminology.

For example, studies on the individual correlates of heavy episodic drinking sometimes include family-related variables such as parental norms related to alcohol or level of parental supervision (Beck & Treiman, 1996; Fitzgerald & Arndt, 2002; Lo, 1995; Perkins, 2002; Wechsler, Dowdall, Davenport, & Castillo, 1995). Such studies generally find that parents have only modest impact on their children's drinking (Perkins, 2002), and family-related factors are not a focus of most research on heavy episodic drinking among college students. However, social control theory suggests that the extent to which children, even adult children, are attached to their parents should influence the extent to which children feel the "psychological presence" of their parents and consider parents' likely reactions to their behavior (Hirschi, 1969). Thus, social control theory suggests that attachment to parents is an important additional consideration in studies of parental influence.

Self-control theory also provides an alternative framework for organizing some of the known correlates of heavy episodic drinking. For example, this perspective suggests an alternative to the view that heavy episodic drinking leads to negative consequences such as poor academic performance, problems with interpersonal relationships, or other forms of deviant behavior (D'Amico, McCarthy, Applebaum, Metrik, Frissell, & Brown, 2001; Jones, Oeltmann, Wilson, Brener, & Hill, 2001). Because self-control theory emphasizes the versatility of individuals' deviant behavior, it suggests that heavy episodic drinking and other correlated behaviors are both consequences of an underlying tendency toward reckless, self-interested, and shortsighted actions. Although self-control theory would not argue that heavy episodic drinking *cannot* be causally related to academic performance, it would argue that those students who drink heavily would be likely to show lower academic performance than their peers even if they were prevented from drinking. Similarly, self-control theory's generality helps us understand the correlation between heavy episodic drinking and smoking or other forms of substance use (Jones et al., 2001; Johnson, Boles, Vaughan, & Keller, 2000). This generality also helps account for findings showing that a number of different personality measures, such as impulsivity and sociability, are related to heavy episodic drinking (Baer, 2002).

For these and other reasons discussed below, we believe that the control theory perspective has much to offer studies of heavy episodic drinking. To empirically assess this claim, we hypothesize that measures of control theory constructs will be significantly related to heavy episodic drinking among our adolescent sample. From social control theory, we hypothesize that attachment to parents, belief in the law, and commitment to conventional goals will be positively related to each other, and negatively associated with heavy episodic drinking net of the effects of demographic characteristics, religiosity, and peers' delinquency.[1] From self-control theory, we hypothesize that self-control will be positively related to each of the social control measures noted above, and that self-control will be negatively related to heavy episodic drinking net of the effects of the other variables in the model.

Methods

The data for this study were collected as part of an effort to replicate Hirschi's (1969) original test of social control theory. A self-administered questionnaire was completed by a convenience sample of 1,136 9th through 11th grade students in four schools in Fayetteville, Arkansas in 1997.

The control theory measures are summated-rating indexes (see Appendix for all questionnaire items,). Measures of background characteristics included gender, race, family's welfare status, and family structure. A measure of religiosity was included as a statistical control, given that prior research has shown it to be related to problem drinking and heavy episodic drinking (Donovan, Jessor, & Costa, 1999; Wechsler et al., 1995). Friends' delinquency was also included as a control variable because prior research on both heavy episodic drinking and delinquency shows a robust relationship between individuals' behavior and that of their friends (Bahr, Marcos, & Maughan, 1995; Costello & Vowell, 1999; Donovan et al., 1999; Perkins, 2002).

Heavy episodic drinking was measured with the question, "During the past 30 days, on how many days did you have 5 or more drinks of alcohol in a row, that is, within a couple of hours?" Gender specific measures of heavy episodic drinking were not available. The original response format included 5 ordered categories giving a range of days. We estimated the number of heavy episodic drinking days as the midpoint of the original

---

[1]We do not test the social control theory prediction that involvement in conventional activities is associated with delinquency, due to the lack of empirical support for this prediction in previous research.

category interval: "0 days" = 0, "1 to 3 days" = 2, "4 to 6" days = 5, "7 to 10 days" = 8.5, and "more than 10 days" = 20. To assess the degree to which our results might be sensitive to the somewhat arbitrary assignment of 20 to the 44 students who reported heavy episodic drinking on "more than 10 days," we replicated the analysis setting the last category equal to 10,15, 25, and 30 drinking days. The results were substantively and statistically consistent with those we report.

Only 996 (87.4%) of the students answered the question on heavy episodic drinking, which was included near the end of the questionnaire. From previous research we know that students who fail to complete questionnaires tend to have more academic problems and are more likely to commit delinquent acts than completers. However, it is not our purpose to provide an accurate estimate of the prevalence of heavy episodic drinking among Arkansas youth, and the data include a sufficient number of cases to test our hypotheses after listwise deletion of missing cases. Our results are based on the 938 students for whom complete data are available.

As is typical of count variables, frequency of heavy episodic drinking was not approximately normally distributed; almost 2/3 (66.4%) reported zero heavy episodic drinking days in the past month. Therefore, we used negative-binomial regression to analyze the data. We standardized all continuous predictor variables prior to analysis. Following Long (1997), effects are expressed as the percentage change in the number of heavy episodic drinking days for a one-unit change in the predictor variable.

Results

The sample was 46.5% male and 89.7% White, with 56.7% living with both biological parents. Approximately 3.9% were living in families currently receiving welfare benefits, and an additional 12.7% had received welfare benefits in the past. The average age of students in the sample was 15.7 years old, with about 38.5% in the 9th grade, 32.2% in the 10th grade, 29.3% in the 11th grade.

Those who answered the question on binge drinking (completers) did not differ significantly from non-completers with respect to age ($t = .93$, $p = .350$) but females (92.7%) were more likely ($\chi^2 = 27.18$, $p = .000$) to complete the question than males (82.4%) and whites (89.1%) were more likely ($\chi^2 = 14.72$, $p = .000$) to complete the question than minorities (77.7%). Children living in families that had ever received welfare (82.5%) were slightly though significantly ($\chi^2 = 1.34$, $p = .007$) less likely to complete the question than those in families that had never received welfare benefits (89.4%), and those living in family with both biological parents present (89.9%) were slightly and significandy ($\chi^2 = 7.73$, $p = .005$) more

Table 1   Zero-order association between measures of control theory constructs (Spearman rank-order correlations)[a]

	Attachment to Parents	Commit.	Belief
Commitment	.405		
Belief	.419	.481	
Self-Control	.402	.618	.694

[a]All relationships significant at $p < .000$.

likely to complete the question than those in families with other structures (84.4%).

Overall, 33.6% of the sample reported at least one episode of heavy drinking in the month prior to survey administration. This is similar to the prevalence of heavy episodic drinking reported in a similar sample, in that D'Amico et al. (2001) report that 35% of their high school sample were "persistent binge drinkers" (2001: 341). National data show a heavy episodic drinking prevalence in 2000 of 26.2% among 10th graders in a 2-week time frame (U.S. Department of Health and Human Services, 2000). The similarity between the prevalence of heavy episodic drinking in our sample and these other studies lends confidence to the validity of our measure.

Because we expect the control theory measures to be significantly related to each other, we first performed a correlation analysis on these measures (see Table 1). As predicted, the social control and self-control measures are all significantly related, with particularly strong relationships between self-control and commitment, and self-control and belief. Factor loadings from exploratory factor analysis of the 35 items underlying the self-control and social-control indexes (estimated by iterative principal factoring, promax rotation, and 4-factor solution) supports the control theory prediction that these measures are empirically distinct despite the strong relationships between them. All items common to a specific index loaded at .38 or higher on the same factor (all but four items had loadings on the expected factor of .45 or higher) and only two items had loadings on other factors that exceeded the observed loading on the expected factor. These results do suggest caution, however, in interpreting the results of multivariate analyses including all of these independent variables.

The unadjusted (bivariate) effects on heavy episodic drinking are presented in the first two columns of Table 2. The results show that students more likely to report heavy episodic drinking are older, male, from families that receive welfare benefits, are not living in intact families, are attending religious services less frequently, and are more likely to have delinquent friends than those who have not drunk heavily in the month

Table 2 Unadjusted (Bivariate) and Adjusted (Multivariate) Estimated Effects for Negative Binomial Research Models

	UNADJUSTED EFFECTS		ADJUSTED EFFECTS	
	B	100*(exp(b)−1)[b]	B	100*(exp(b)−1)[b]
Age[a]	.206**	22.9%	.246**	27.8%
Sex (Male)	.317*	37.3%	−.160	−14.8%
Race (White)	−.320	−27.4%	.041	4.2%
Welfare (Yes)	.497*	39.2%	.092	8.8%
Religious Attend.[a]	−.186*	−17.0%	−.083**	−7.9%
Fam. Struct. (Intact)	−.608**	−45.6%	−.383*	−31.8%
Friends' Delinq.[a]	.628***	87.4%	.451**	57.0%
Attach. to Parents[a]	−.301**	−26.0%	−.250*	−22.1%
Commitment[a]	−.703***	−50.5%	−.217*	−19.5%
Belief[a]	−.744***	−52.5%	−.526***	−40.9%
Self-Control[a]	−.724**	−51.5%	−.279*	−24.3%

*p < .05; ** p < .01

[a] Effects for continuous predictor variables are semi-standardized. Continuous predictor variables were standardized prior to analysis.

[b] Effects expressed as the expected percentage change in number of heavy episodic drinking days for a unit change in the predictor variable.

prior to the survey. Race was not significantly related to heavy episodic drinking. As hypothesized, all of the control theory measures were related to heavy episodic drinking, so that those with higher levels of attachment to parents, commitment to goals, belief in the law, and self-control were less likely to report drinking.

The results of the multivariate analysis are presented in the third and fourth columns of Table 2. In terms of demographic correlates, age is still positively related to heavy episodic drinking, but controlling for the effects of other variables in the model reduced the effects of sex and welfare status to nonsignificance. The control theory variables are all significantly and negatively related to the number of heavy drinking days, providing support for our major hypothesis. For example, for each standard deviation increase in commitment to long-term goals, the expected number of heavy drinking days decreases by 19.5%, and for each standard deviation increase in belief in the validity of the law, the expected number of heavy drinking days decreases by about 41%. Friends' delinquency persists as a major predictor of heavy episodic drinking, with a one standard deviation increase in the number of delinquent friends associated with a 57% increase in the number of heavy episodic drinking days.

Discussion

The results support our hypothesis that control theories can help explain heavy episodic drinking. Measures of control theory have statistically significant and substantively important effects on heavy episodic drinking among this sample of 9th through 11th grade students, suggesting that future studies of heavy episodic drinking could benefit by including such measures.

While the current study had relatively modest goals, specifically to determine whether control theory can explain some of the variation in heavy episodic drinking, we believe that the implications of our study are more far reaching. For example, self-control theory predicts stability in crime and analogous acts over time, consistent with research showing that rates of heavy episodic drinking in high school are strongly correlated with heavy episodic drinking in college (Lo, 1995; Wechsler et at., 1995). In general, this suggests that at least some of the underlying causes of heavy episodic drinking come into play before students enter college. Our results point to some of these possible causes, including the quality of relationships with parents, and assuming that self-control is learned in early childhood, parental childrearing practices. Thus, control theory offers one set of potential causes of heavy episodic drinking that have been under investigated in the literature. We therefore agree with Beck and Treiman's (1996) recommendation that the alcohol literature consider a wider range of parent variables as possible causes of alcohol misuse among young people.

Control theory's general focus on social integration as a deterrent to a variety of deviant behaviors also points to some new avenues of research on heavy episodic drinking. Although the current research is cross-sectional and thus cannot determine causal direction, control theory suggests that a number of variables often viewed as consequences of heavy episodic drinking might be usefully viewed as causes or merely correlates of it. For example, a low level commitment to academic goals may be viewed as a cause of heavy episodic drinking from the perspective of social control theory, suggesting that any efforts to reduce drinking to improve students' performance would be targeting the effect rather than the cause. Similarly, social control theory would argue that problems with relationships, rather than being consequences of drinking, are an indicator of a low level of attachment and a cause of heavy drinking (Hirschi, 1969). Self-control theory predicts a spurious correlation between relationship problems and heavy drinking—both are seen as consequences of low self-control (Gottfredson & Hirschi, 1990). Future research on heavy episodic drinking designed to test some of these hypotheses could contribute to the drinking literature as well as to the more general body of crime and delinquency literature.

The idea that social integration deters deviant behavior also suggests a different view of the correlation between individuals' and friends' deviance. Criminological learning theories (Akers, 1973; Sutherland, 1947) hold that friends' deviance is causally related to the individual's deviance due to processes of value transmission, so that members of deviant groups see deviant behavior as acceptable and are thus more likely to engage in it. This perspective is similar to normative explanations of college student drinking that argue that perceived group norms, or the actual behavior of peers, encourage students to drink to excess (Beck & Treiman, 1996; Perkins, 2002). It is also consistent with claims that students who are more socially integrated are more likely to drink heavily (Perkins, 2002). However, the argument that higher social integration leads to higher levels of deviant behavior is contrary to control theory, which explicitly argues that social integration is associated with lower levels of deviance.

Control theory assumes that acts that have negative consequences for oneself and especially for others are universally disapproved. Although the extent to which one believes in the norms of society can vary, this varies largely as a result of individuals' level of integration in other respects. Hirschi (1969:16) quotes Durkheim, "The more weakened the groups to which [the individual] belongs, the less he depends on them, the more he consequently depends only on himself and recognizes no other rules of conduct than what are founded on his private interests" (as cited in Durkheim, 1951:209). Thus, control theory predicts that what we might refer to as "deviant groups" tend to be only loosely knit, with members relatively low in concern for each other's welfare. This prediction suggests that in addition to using measures of social integration like fraternity membership or number of friends (see Perkins 2002 for a review), a more complete measure would also take into consideration the esteem with which these friends and associates are regarded. The conflicting views on the effect of social integration held by control theory and normative explanations of heavy episodic drinking provide the opportunity for a critical test between the two perspectives, and thus could contribute to the longstanding debate about these issues in the criminological literature.

Additional hypotheses can be derived from control theory's explanation for the correlation between peer deviance and individual deviance. Control theory explains this correlation in two ways—self-selection or opportunity. As some studies of heavy episodic drinking have noted (Baer, 2002; Bahr et al., 1995; Beck & Treiman, 1996), it is possible that students who drink heavily tend to seek out friends who also drink heavily, implying that the correlation between friends' and individuals' behavior is spurious. An alternative is that friends do have a causal effect on heavy episodic drinking, but only because they increase opportunity (Longshore & Turner, 1998; Osgood, Wilson, O'Malley, Bachman, & Johnston, 1996). Having friends who drink increases the availability of alcohol or provides the individual with temptations to drink that may not exist for the individual with few or no friends who drink. Control theory thus points out that a causal effect of peers on the individual's deviant behavior may simply be the result of a greater number of invitations to engage in deviant behavior (Costello, 1997).

Finally, our findings suggest that it would be of value to assess the relative merits of control theories and existing theories of heavy episodic drinking or deviant behavior. For example, there are some important similarities and differences between control theory and Jessor and Jessor's (1977) problem behavior theory. Both incorporate consideration of attachment to others, but problem behavior theory draws on elements of strain theories of delinquency (Merton, 1957) that are explicitly rejected by control theories. Both theories also account for versatility in offending, but control theory emphasizes stability over time and problem behavior theory takes a more developmental approach. It may also prove useful to assess the extent to which well-accepted predictors of heavy episodic drinking, such as alcohol expectancies, are themselves associated with lower levels of self-control or social control. Such approaches would go a long way toward greater cross-disciplinary integration in the study of heavy episodic drinking as well as other deviant or criminal acts, and could lead to new approaches to the prevention of heavy episodic drinking.

Clearly, we cannot resolve all of these issues with a single cross-sectional study of heavy episodic drinking. However, our results do suggest that social integration, broadly conceptualized, can reduce the likelihood of heavy episodic drinking, and thus that control theory holds promise as a new direction of heavy episodic drinking research.

References

Akers, R. L. (1973). *Deviant behavior: A social learning approach.* Belmont, CA: Wadsworth.

Baer, J. S. (2002). Student factors: Understanding individual variation in college drinking, *Journal of Studies on Alcohol,* Supplement No. 14, 40–53.

Bahr, S. J., Marcos, A. C, & Maughan, S. L. (1995). Family, educational and peer influences on the alcohol use of female and male adolescents, *Journal of Studies on Alcohol, 56,* 457–469.

Beck, K. H., & Treiman, K. A. (1996). The relationship of social context of drinking, perceived social norms, and parental influence to various drinking patterns of adolescents. *Addictive Behaviors, 21,* 5, 633–644.

Costello, B. J. (1997). On the logical adequacy of cultural deviance theories. *Theoretical Criminology, 1,* 403–428.

Costello, B. J., & Vowell, P. R. (1999). Testing control theory and differential association: A reanalysis of the Richmond youth project data. *Criminology, 57,* 815–842.

D'Amico, E. J., McCarthy, D. M., Applebaum, M., Metrik, J., Frissell, K. C., & Brown, S. A. (2001). Progression into and out of binge drinking among high school students. *Psychology of Addictive Behaviors, 15,* 341–349.

Donovan, J. E., Jessor, R., & Costa, E M. (1999). Adolescent problem drinking: Stability of psychosocial and behavioral correlates across a generation. *Journal of Studies on Alcohol, 60,* 352–361.

Durkheim, E. (1951). *Suicide.* New York: The Free Press.

Fitzgerald, J. L., & Arndt, S. (2002). Reference group influence on adolescent alcohol use. *Journal of Alcohol and Drug Education, 47,* 42–56.

Gottfredson, M. R., & Hirschi, T. (1990). *A general theory of crime.* Stanford, CA: Stanford University Press.

Hirschi, T. (1960). *Causes of delinquency.* Berkeley, CA: University of California Press.

Jessor, R., & Jessor, S. L. (1977). *Problem behavior and psychosocial development: A longitudinal study of youth.* New York: Acadetnic Press.

Johtison, P. B., Boles, S. M., Vaughan, R., & Keller, H. D. (2000). The co-occurrence of smoking and binge drinking in adolescence. *Addictive behaviors, 25,* 779–783.

Jones, S. E., Oeltmann, J., Wilson, T. W, Brener, N. D., & Hill, C.V. (2001). Binge drinking among undergraduate college students in the United States: Implications for other substance use. *Journal of American College Health, 30,* 33–47.

Keane, C, Maxim, P. S., & Teevan, J. J. (1993). Drinking and driving, self-control, and gender: Testing a general theory of crime. *Journal of Research in Crime and Delinquency, 30,* 30–46.

Krohn, M. D., & Massey, J. L. (1980). Social control and delinquent behavior: An examination of the elements of the social bond. *Sociological Quarterly, 21,* 529–543.

Lo, C. C. (1995). Gender differences in collegiate alcohol use. *Journal of Drug Issues, 25,* 817–837.

Long, J. S. (1997). *Regression models for categorical and limited dependent variables.* Thousand Oaks, CA: Sage.

Longshore, D. L., & Turner, S. (1998). Self-control and criminal opportunity: Cross-sectional test of the general theory of crime. *Criminal Justice and Behavior, 25,* 81–98.

Lopez, J. M. O., Redondo, L. M., & Martin, A. L. (1989). Influence of family and peer group on the use of drugs by adolescents. *International Journal of the Addictions, 24,* 1065–1082.

Merton, R. K. (1957). *Social theory and social structure.* New York: Free Press.

Murray, G. F. (1986). Marijuana use and social control: A sociological perspective on deviance. *International Journal of the Addictions, 21,* 657–669.

National Institute on Alcohol Abuse and Alcoholism, Task Force on College Drinking (2002). *High-risk drinking in college: What we know and what we need to learn.* Retrieved from www.collegedrinkingprevention.gov.

Osgood, D. W., Wilson, J. K., O'Malley, P. M., Bachman, J. G., & Johnston, L. D. (1996). Routine activities and individual deviant behavior. *American Sociological Review, 61,* 635–655.

Perkins, H. W. (2002). Social norms and the prevention of alcohol misuse in collegiate contexts. *Journal of Studies on Alcohol, 14*(Suppl.), 164–172.

Pratt, T. C., & Cullen, F. T. (2000). The empirical status of Gottfredson and Hirschi's general theory of crime: A meta-analysis. *Criminology, 38,* 931–964.

Sutherland, E. H. (1947). *Principles of Criminology,* 4th ed. Philadelphia: Lippincott.

United States Department of Health and Human Services (2000). Monitoring the future survey released: Moderating trend among teen drug use continues. HHS News, Dec. 14, 2000.

Wadsworth, T. (2000). Labor markets, delinquency, and social control theory: An empirical assessment of the mediating process. *Social Forces, 78,* 1041–1066.

Wechsler, H., DowdaU, G. W., Davenport, A., & Castillo, S. (1995). Correlates of college student binge drinking. *American Journal of Public Health, 85,* 921–927.

Correspondence concerning this article should be addressed to Barbara J. Costello, Department of Sociology and Anthropology, University of Rhode Island, Kingston, RI 02822, Phone 401-874-2877; Fax 401-874-2588. E-mail: Costello@uri.edu.

Appendix

Questionnaire items and reliability of indexes

Unless otherwise noted, all measures were scored with a 5-point Likert response framework, and appropriate items were reverse scored so that a higher scale score equals a higher level of the variable measured.

Attachment to Parents (alpha = .81)
I share my thoughts and feelings with my mother.
I would like to be the kind of person my mother is.
I would like to be the kind of person my father is.
I talk over future plans with my parents.
My mother seems to understand me.
My parents know where I am when I am away from home.
My parents always know who I am dating.

Commitment (alpha = .72)
On average, how many hours per week do you spend studying or doing homework?

How important is getting good grades to you? (4-point scale ranging from completely unimportant to very important.)

What kind of grades do you get?

How much education do you plan to get? (5-point scale ranging from "some high school" to "college graduation")

Do you care what teachers think of you? (3-point scale ranging from "I care a lot" to "I don't care much")

I usually finish my homework.

Belief (alpha = .81)

Only fools tell the truth all the time.

To get ahead, you have to do some things that are not right.

It's okay to get around the law if you can get away with it.

Rules were made to be broken.

It's okay to take something from big business because they won't miss it.

I have lots of respect for the police.

There is no good reason for one person to hit another.

Most things people call delinquency don't really hurt anyone.

Fools and suckers deserve what they get.

Self-Control (alpha = .72)

I am usually pretty cautious.

Sometimes, I take a risk just for the fun of it.

Hitchhiking is too dangerous for me.

I don't devote much thought and effort to preparing for the future.

I have had dates with more than one person in the same week.

I live for today and let tomorrow take care of itself.

An easy life is a happy life.

I try to save as much money as 1 can.

I lose my temper easily.

I try to get things I want even when I know that it's causing problems for other people.

I try hard in school.

I see no need for hard work.

Whatever I do I try hard.

Control Variables

Age in years

Sex (1 if male)

Race (1 if white, 0 otherwise)

Family Structure, composite of two questions asking, "Who currently acts as a father [mother] for you? Coded 1 if biological mother and father both lived at bome, 0 otherwise.

Friends' Delinquency, response to the question "Have any of your friends been picked up by the police?" Ranges from 0 to 4 or more friends.

Welfare Status (1 if family had ever received welfare, 0 otherwise)

Religious Attendance, response to the question, "On average, how often do you attend religious services?" Response categories ranged from "never or almost never" to "once a week or more," on a 5-point scale.

The Interactionist, Societal Reactions, or Labeling Perspective

Individuals who subscribe to the interactionist, or labeling, school examine those social and psychological, or interactional, processes that take place among actors, audiences, and third parties, particularly in terms of their impact on the personal and social-public identity of the actor. The production of a range of deviant careers and identities is also given focus. The main concern, then, is definitional processes and products, and their effects.

Howard S. Becker has explored the concept of *career*, the major orienting focus of this volume, in some depth. He also introduces some important analytical distinctions. In "Career Deviance," he argues that public labeling is generally the most crucial step in building a long-term deviant career. Not only does being branded a deviant affect one's continued social participation, but it frequently produces notable changes in the actor's self-image. The most drastic change, however, seems to occur with respect to the actor's public identity—that is, how others view him or her. Suddenly, in the eyes of others he or she has become a different person; this new status can be effectively referred to as a *master status*. In offering an important distinction between master and subordinate statuses, Becker argues that master statuses assume a certain priority and appear to override most other status considerations.

The status of a deviant is one such status. In relating to a deviant, people will frequently respond to the label and not to the individual. Treatment of an actor in this fashion—as if he or she is generally deviant and not specifically deviant—can serve as a self-fulfilling prophecy whereby attempts are made to mold the actor into the image others have of him or her. Deliberate attempts may be made, for example, to exclude the deviant from any meaningful social intercourse. The actor may respond negatively to such treatment, and, over time, exclusion and its associated reactions can actually give rise to more deviance. The treatment situation, Becker claims, is especially likely to produce such a result.

The statement by Frank Tannenbaum, "Definition and the Dramatization of Evil," represents one of the earliest attempts at describing how individuals may be singled out for special treatment by the community. His basic thesis is that two opposing definitions of the situation may arise. For example, what may be viewed as play or fun by the young actor may be seen as a form of evil or delinquency by community members. Gradually there may occur a shift "from definition of the specific acts as evil to a definition of the individual as evil." This defining process is not without its effects. To the community, the individual has become a bad or evil person. To the individual, a sense of injustice emerges; this forces him to realize that he is different from other boys in the neighborhood, school, street, and community. Tannenbaum suggests further that such a person may not only change his personal identity—that is, come to view himself as a young criminal or delinquent—but may become part of a group or subculture that shares his activities. Primarily as a result of the self-fulfilling prophecy, then, he may begin to act in accordance with the expectations associated with his label. He may, moreover, move into a pattern of career deviance or crime.

17 Career Deviance

Howard S. Becker

One of the most crucial steps in the process of building a stable pattern of deviant behavior is likely to be the experience of being caught and publicly labeled as a deviant. Whether a person takes this step or not depends not so much on what he does as on what other people do, on whether or not they enforce the rule he has violated. . . . First of all, even though no one else discovers the nonconformity or enforces the rules against it, the individual who has committed the impropriety may himself act as an enforcer. He may brand himself as deviant because of what he has done and punish himself in one way or another for his behavior. This is not always or necessarily the case, but may occur. Second, there may be cases like those described by psychoanalysts in which the individual really wants to get caught and perpetrates his deviant act in such a way that it is almost sure he will be.

In any case, being caught and branded as deviant has important consequences for one's further social participation and self-image. The most important consequence is a drastic change in the individual's public identity. Committing the improper act and being publicly caught at it place him in a new status. He has been revealed as a different kind of person from the kind he was supposed to be. He is labeled a "fairy," "dope fiend," "nut," or "lunatic," and treated accordingly.

In analyzing the consequences of assuming a deviant identity let us make use of Hughes' distinction between master and auxiliary status traits.[1] Hughes notes that most statuses have one key trait which serves to distinguish those who belong from those who do not. Thus the doctor, whatever else he may be, is a person who has a certificate stating that he has fulfilled certain requirements and is licensed to practice medicine; this is the master trait. As Hughes points out, in our society a doctor is also informally expected to have a number of auxiliary traits: most people expect him to be upper middle class, white, male, and Protestant. When he is not there is a sense that he has in some way failed to fill the bill. Similarly, though skin color is the master status trait determining who is Negro and who is white, Negroes are informally expected to have certain status traits and not to have others; people are surprised and find it anomalous if a Negro turns out to be a doctor or a college professor. People often have the master status trait but lack some of the auxiliary, informally expected characteristics; for example, one may be a doctor but be female or Negro.

Hughes deals with this phenomenon in regard to statuses that are well thought of, desired and desirable (noting that one may have the formal qualifications for entry into a status but be denied full entry because of lack of the proper auxiliary traits), but the same process occurs in the case of deviant statuses. Possession of one deviant trait may have a generalized symbolic value, so that people automatically assume that its bearer possesses other undesirable traits allegedly associated with it.

To be labeled a criminal one need only commit a single criminal offense, and this is all the term formally refers to. Yet the word carries a number of connotations specifying auxiliary traits characteristic of anyone bearing the label. A man who has been convicted of housebreaking and thereby labeled criminal is presumed to be a person likely to break into other houses; the police, in rounding up known offenders for investigation after a crime has been committed, operate on this premise. Further, he is considered likely to commit other kinds of crimes as well, because he has shown himself to be a person without "respect for the law." Thus, apprehension for one deviant act exposes a person to the likelihood that he will be regarded as deviant or undesirable in other respects.

There is one other element in Hughes' analysis we can borrow with profit: the distinction between master and subordinate statuses.[2] Some statuses, in our society as in others, override all other statuses and have a certain priority. Race is one of these. Membership in the Negro race, as socially defined, will override most other status considerations in most other situations; the fact that one is a physician or middle-class or female will not protect one from being treated as a Negro first and any of these other things second. The status of deviant (depending on this kind of deviance) is this kind of master status. One receives the status as a result of breaking a rule, and the identification proves to be more important than most others. One will be identified as a deviant first, before other identifications are made. The question is raised: "What kind of person would break such an important rule?" And the answer is given: "One who is different from the rest of us, who cannot or will not act as a moral human being and therefore might break other important rules." The deviant identification becomes the controlling one.

Treating a person as though he were generally rather than specifically deviant produces a self-fulfilling prophecy. It sets in motion several mechanisms which conspire to shape the person in the image people have of him.[3] In the first place, one tends to be cut off, after being identified as deviant, from participation in more conventional groups, even though the specific consequences of the particular deviant activity might never of themselves have caused the isolation had there not also been the public knowledge and reaction to it. For example, being a homosexual may not affect one's ability to do office work, but to be known as a homosexual in an office may make it impossible to continue working there. Similarly, though the effects of opiate drugs may not impair one's working ability, to be known as an addict will probably lead to losing one's job. In such cases, the individual finds it difficult to conform to other rules which he had no intention or desire to break, and perforce finds himself deviant in these areas as well. The homosexual who is deprived of a "respectable" job by the discovery of his deviance may drift into unconventional, marginal occupations where it does not make so much difference. The drug addict finds himself forced into other illegitimate kinds of activity, such as robbery and theft, by the refusal of respectable employers to have him around.

When the deviant is caught, he is treated in accordance with the popular diagnosis of why he is that way, and the treatment itself may likewise produce increasing deviance. The drug addict, popularly considered to be a weak-willed individual who cannot forego the indecent pleasures afforded him by opiates, is treated repressively. He is forbidden to use drugs. Since he cannot get drugs legally, he must get them illegally. This forces the market underground and pushes the price of drugs up far beyond the current legitimate market price into a bracket that few can afford on an ordinary salary. Hence the treatment of the addict's deviance places him in a position where it will probably be necessary to resort to deceit and crime in order to support his habit.[4] The behavior is a consequence of the public reaction to the deviance rather than a consequence of the inherent qualities of the deviant act.

Notes

1. Everett C. Hughes, "Dilemmas and Contradictions of Status," *American Journal of Sociology,* L (March, 1945), 353–359.
2. *Ibid.*
3. See Marsh Ray, "The Cycle of Abstinence and Relapse Among Heroin Addicts," *Social Problems,* 9 (Fall, 1961), 132–140.
4. See *Drug Addiction: Crime or Disease?* Interim and Final Reports of the Joint Committee of the American Bar Association and the American Medical Association on Narcotic Drugs (Bloomington, Indiana: Indiana University Press, 1961).

Definition and the Dramatization of Evil

Frank Tannenbaum

In the conflict between the young delinquent and the community there develop two opposing definitions of the situation. In the beginning the definition of the situation by the young delinquent may be in the form of play, adventure, excitement, interest, mischief, fun. Breaking windows, annoying people, running around porches, climbing over roofs, stealing from pushcarts, playing truant—all are items of play, adventure, excitement. To the community, however, these activities may and often do take on the form of a nuisance, evil, delinquency, with the demand for control, admonition, chastisement, punishment, police court, truant school. This conflict over the situation is one that arises out of a divergence of values. As the problem develops, the situation gradually becomes redefined. The attitude of the community hardens definitely into a demand for suppression. There is a gradual shift from the definition of the specific acts as evil to a definition of the individual as evil, so that all his acts come to be looked upon with suspicion. In the process of identification his companions, hang-outs, play, speech, income, all his conduct, the personality itself, become subject to scrutiny and question. From the community's point of view, the individual who used to do bad and mischievous things has now become a bad and unredeemable human being. From the individual's point of view there has taken place a similar change. He has gone slowly from a sense of grievance and injustice, of being unduly mistreated and punished, to a recognition that the definition of him as a human being is different from that of other boys in his neighborhood, his school, street, community. This recognition on his part becomes a process of self-identification and integration with the group which shares his activities. It becomes, in part, a process of rationalization; in part, a simple response to a specialized type of stimulus. The young delinquent becomes bad because he is defined as bad and because he is not believed if he is good. There is a persistent demand for consistency in character. The community cannot deal with people whom it cannot define. Reputation is this sort of public definition. Once it is established, then unconsciously all agencies combine to maintain this definition even when they apparently and consciously attempt to deny their own implicit judgment.

Early in his career, then, the incipient professional criminal develops an attitude of antagonism to the regulated orderly life that he is required to lead. This attitude is hardened and crystallized by opposition. The conflict becomes a clash of wills. And experience too often has proved that threats, punishments, beatings, commitments to institutions, abuse and defamation of one sort or another, are of no avail. Punishment breaks down against the child's stubbornness. What has happened is that the child has been defined as an "incorrigible" both by his contacts and by himself, and an attempt at a direct breaking down of will generally fails.

The child meets the situation in the only way he can, by defiance and escape—physical escape if possible, or emotional escape by derision, anger, contempt, hatred, disgust, tantrums, destructiveness, and physical violence. The response of the child is just as intelligent and intelligible as that of the schools, of the authorities. They have taken a simple problem, the lack of fitness of an institution to a particular child's needs, and have made a moral issue out of it with values outside the child's ken. It takes on the form of war between two wills, and the longer the war lasts, the more certainly does the child become incorrigible. The child will not yield because he cannot yield—his nature requires other channels for pleasant growth; the school system or society will not yield because it does not see the issues involved as between the incompatibility of an institution and a child's needs, sometimes physical needs, and will instead attempt to twist the child's nature to the institution with that consequent distortion of the child which makes an unsocial career inevitable. The verbalization of the conflict in terms of evil, delinquency, incorrigibility, badness, arrest, force, punishment, stupidity, lack of intelligence, truancy, criminality, gives the innocent divergence of the child from the straight road a meaning that it did not have in the beginning and makes its continuance in these same terms by so much the more inevitable.

The only important fact, when the issue arises of the boy's inability to acquire the specific habits which organized institutions attempt to impose upon him, is that this conflict becomes the occasion for him to acquire another series of habits, interests, and attitudes as a substitute. These habits become as effective in motivating and guiding conduct as would have been those which the orderly routine social institutions attempted to impose had they been acquired.

This conflict gives the gang its hold, because the gang provides escape, security, pleasure, and peace. The gang also gives room for the motor activity which plays a large role in a child's life. The attempt to break up the gang by force merely strengthens it. The arrest of the children has consequences undreamed-of, for several reasons.

First, only some of the children are caught though all may be equally guilty. There is a great deal more delinquency practiced and committed by the young groups than comes to the attention of the police. The boy arrested, therefore, is singled out in specialized treatment. This boy, no more guilty than the other members of his group, discovers a world of which he knew little. His arrest suddenly precipitates a series of institutions, attitudes, and experiences which the other children do not share. For this boy there suddenly appear the police, the patrol wagon, the police station, the other delinquents and criminals found in the police lock-ups, the court with all its agencies such as bailiffs, clerks, bondsmen, lawyers, probation officers. There are bars, cells, handcuffs, criminals. He is questioned, examined, tested, investigated. His history is gone into, his family is brought into court. Witnesses make their appearance. The boy, no different from the rest of his gang, suddenly becomes the center of a major drama in which all sorts of unexpected characters play important roles. And what is it all about? about the accustomed things his gang has done and has been doing for a long time. In this entirely new world he is made conscious of himself as a different human being than he was before his arrest. He becomes classified as a thief, perhaps, and the entire world about him has suddenly become a different place for him and will remain different for the rest of his life. . . .

The first dramatization of the "evil" which separates the child out of his group for specialized treatment plays a greater role in making the criminal than perhaps any other experience. It cannot be too often emphasized that for the child the whole situation has become different. He now lives in a different world. He has been tagged. A new and hitherto non-existent environment has been precipitated out for him.

The process of making the criminal, therefore, is a process of tagging, defining, identifying, segregating, describing, emphasizing, making conscious and self-conscious; it becomes a way of stimulating, suggesting, emphasizing, and evoking the very traits that are complained of. If the theory of relation of response to stimulus has any meaning, the entire process of dealing with the young delinquent is mischievous in so far as it identifies him to himself or to the environment as a delinquent person.

The person becomes the thing he is described as being. Nor does it seem to matter whether the valuation is made by those who would punish or by those who would reform. In either case the emphasis is upon the conduct that is disapproved of. The parents or the policeman, the older brother or the court, the probation officer or the juvenile institution, in so far as they rest upon the thing complained of, rest upon a false ground. Their very enthusiasm defeats their aim. The harder they work to reform the evil, the greater the evil grows under their hands. The persistent suggestion, with whatever good intentions, works mischief, because it leads to bringing out the bad behavior that it would suppress. The way out is through a refusal to dramatize the evil. The less said about it the better. The more said about something else, still better.

> The hard-drinker who keeps thinking of not drinking is doing what he can to initiate the acts which lead to drinking. He is starting with the stimulus to his habit. To succeed he must find some positive interest or line of action which will inhibit the drinking series and which by instituting another course of action will bring him to his desired end.[1]

The dramatization of the evil therefore tends to precipitate the conflict situation which was first created through some innocent maladjustment. The child's isolation forces him into companionship with other children similarly defined, and the gang becomes his means of escape, his security. The life of the gang gives it special mores, and the attack by the community upon these mores merely overemphasizes the conflict already in existence, and makes it the source of a new series of experiences that lead directly to a criminal career.

In dealing with the delinquent, the criminal, therefore, the important thing to remember is that we are dealing with a human being who is responding normally to the demands, stimuli, approval, expectancy, of the group with whom he is associated. We are dealing not with an individual but with a group.

> In a study of 6,000 instances of stealing, with reference to the number of boys involved, it was found that in 90.4 per cent of the cases two or more boys were known to have been involved in the act and were consequently brought to court. Only 9.6 per cent of all the cases were acts of single individuals. Since this study was based upon the number of boys brought to court, and since in many cases not all of the boys involved were caught and brought to court, it is certain that the percentage of group stealing is therefore even greater than 90.4 per cent. It cannot be doubted that delinquency, particularly stealing, almost invariably involves two or more persons.[2]

That group may be a small gang, a gang of children just growing up, a gang of young "toughs" of nineteen or twenty, or a gang of older criminals of thirty. If we are not dealing with a gang we may be dealing with a family. And if we are not dealing with either of these especially we may be dealing with a community. In practice all these factors—the family, the gang, and the community—may be important in the development and the maintenance of that attitude towards the world which makes a criminal career a normal, an accepted and approved way of life.

Direct attack upon the individual in these circumstances is a dubious undertaking. By the time the individual has become a criminal his habits have been so shaped that we have a fairly integrated character whose whole career is in tune with the peculiar bit of the environment for which he has developed the behavior and habits that cause him to be apprehended. In theory isolation from that group ought to provide occasion for change in the individual's habit structure. It might, if the individual were transplanted to a group whose values and activities had the approval of the wider community, and in which the newcomer might hope to gain full acceptance eventually. But until now isolation has meant the grouping in close confinement of persons whose strongest common bond has been their socially disapproved delinquent conduct. Thus the attack cannot be made without reference to group life.

The attack must be on the whole group; for only by changing its attitudes and ideals, interests and habits, can the stimuli which it exerts upon the individual be changed. Punishment as retribution has failed to reform, that is, to change character. If the individual can be made aware of a different set of values for which he may receive approval, then we may be on the road to a change in his character. But such a change of values involves a change in stimuli, which means that the criminal's social world must be changed before he can be changed.

The point of view here developed rejects all assumptions that would impute crime to the individual in the sense that a personal shortcoming of the offender is the cause of the unsocial behavior. The assumption that crime is caused by any sort of inferiority, physiological or psychological, is here completely and unequivocally repudiated.

This of course does not mean that morphological or psychological techniques do not have value in dealing with the individual. It merely means that they have no greater value in the study of criminology than they would have in the study of any profession. If a poor IQ is a bad beginning for a career in medicine, it is also a poor beginning for a career in crime. If the psychiatrist can testify that a psychopath will make an irritable doctor he can prove the same for the criminal. But he can prove no more. The criminal differs from the rest of his fellows only in the sense that he has learned to respond to the stimuli of a very small and specialized group; but that group must exist or the criminal could not exist. In that he is like the mass of men, living a certain kind of life with the kind of companions that make that life possible.

This explanation of criminal behavior is meant to apply to those who more or less consistently pursue the criminal career. It does not necessarily presume to describe the accidental criminal or the man who commits a crime of passion. Here perhaps the theories that would seek the cause of crime in the individual may have greater application than in attempting to deal with those who follow a life of crime. But even in the accidental criminal there is a strong presumption that the accident is the outcome of a habit situation. Any habit tends to have a background of social conditioning.

> A man with the habit of giving way to anger may show his habit by a murderous attack upon some one who has offended. His act is nonetheless due to habit because it occurs only once in his life. The essence of

habit is an acquired predisposition to *ways* or modes of response, not to particular acts except as, under special conditions, these express a way of behaving. Habit means special sensitiveness or accessibility to certain classes of stimuli, standing predilections and aversions, rather than bare recurrence of specific acts. It means will.[3]

In other words, perhaps the accidental criminal also is to be explained in terms such as we use in discussing the professional criminal.

Notes

1. John Dewey, *Human Nature and Conduct,* p. 35. New York, 1922.
2. Clifford R. Shaw and Earl D. Myers, "The Juvenile Delinquent," *The Illinois Crime Survey,* pp. 662–663. Chicago, 1929.
3. Dewey, op. cit., p. 42.

An Integrated Approach

As we suggested earlier, explanations often implicitly overlap or directly share common themes, concepts, or processes. For Merton, identifying these overlaps and underlying similarities should be of central concern to sociology. The following article contributes to the sociology of deviance by integrating three different perspectives. Jeffery T. Ulmer, in "Commitment, Deviance, and Social Control," addresses a current debate in the sociology of deviance by arguing that the "opposing positions share a common sociological goal—the explanation of continuity and change in lines of action." On one side of the debate are perspectives suggesting that individuals may be socialized into traditions favorable to deviance. These perspectives include differential association and social learning approaches which emphasize personal relationships and definitions of self that may lead to commitment to deviant behaviors and identities. Others argue that deviance is the expression of the lack of commitment to conventional traditions.

Ulmer is concerned with going beyond the debate to provide tools to address questions related to the different positions. Suggesting that the notion of commitment is central to the projects of differential association, social learning, and social control perspectives, Ulmer argues that a threefold framework of commitment (including structural, personal, and moral commitment) and their sources should be used. This and other attempts to integrate theories represent important steps toward a more complete understanding of deviance in society.

Moving to an integrated theoretical perspective requires that the overlapping common themes are tested in multiple contexts. The following article tests hypotheses deriving from two different theoretical frames—sub-cultural and drift—using an international youth study. Both of these approaches suggest that rapid social change and deteriorating social fabric increases juvenile delinquency. Using elements from each of these theories reveals a path of influence toward deviant behavior. In their article "Juvenile Delinquency Under Conditions of Rapid Social Change" Klaus Boehnke and Dagmar Bergs-Winkels (2002) examine the importance of social structural conditions that may give rise to prodelinquent attitudes and behavior while providing an opportunity infrastructure for deviance. The rapid social, economic, and political changes and the accompanying surge in crime and delinquency rates occurring in Europe provide the context for evaluation. The hope is a better understanding of the relationship between social change and delinquent drift. Boehnke and Bergs-Winkel assume, as does Merton, that certain youth possess resources (derived through family and public life) that better meet the requirements for social success. The authors' research emphasizes the complexity of social structural stressors (societal level of analysis) and interactive patterns (individual level analysis) among significant others. For example social change (conceptualized as a stressful event) may act on parents and youth directly by influencing personal choices and indirectly through shaping parent–child interactions. As the authors note however, social change does not always function as a stressor. In certain cases negative social changes were related to a sense of greater justice, more parental caring and less drift into delinquency.

Commitment, Deviance, and Social Control

Jeffery T. Ulmer

The dialectics of structural constraint and agency, continuity and change, and self and social organization are fundamental sociological issues (Giddens 1984; Westby 1991; Shalin 1986; Mead 1934). The concept of commitment occupies a central conceptual space where these issues intersect (Katz 1994; Strauss 1993). I apply a commitment framework, created by Michael Johnson (1991), to deviance and conformity as types of situational action embedded in the contexts of corporal and phantom communities (Athens 1998). Developed in Johnson's (1991) research on personal relationships, this framework identifies three conceptually distinct types of commitment (structural, personal, and moral), each with its own particular sources. Each type depicts selves choosing between lines of action, sometimes in the face of internal or external constraints, and thus negotiating continuity and change in lines of action and biography.

The study of deviance and social control has been a core area of sociological concern since the work of Marx, Durkheim, and Weber. An important debate currently exists between prominent control theorists and proponents of differential association and social learning approaches. The latter emphasize socialization favorable to deviance, as well as personal relationships between deviant peers and definition of self in terms of deviant identities (Akers 1996; 1998; Heimer and Matsueda 1994; Warr 1993). On the other hand, Kornhauser (1978), Hirschi (1996), and Gottfredson (1999) sharply criticize what they derisively call "cultural deviance" theories as contrary to human nature and the nature of social organization. They argue instead that commitment to deviance is a contradiction in terms (Hirschi 1996), that "crime represents the antithesis of culture and that it necessarily spoils rather than enhances interpersonal relations" (Gottfredson 1999, p. 284).

The conceptualization of commitment I apply here transcends this debate by illustrating that these opposing positions share a common sociological goal—the explanation of continuity and change in lines of action. I argue that commitment is central to the projects of both differential association/social learning and social control perspectives. However, despite Howard Becker's (1960) call for a more systematic conceptualization of commitment, most scholars of deviance—as well as scholars working in other substantive areas—use the term in a simplistic, undifferentiated manner (see reviews by Johnson 1991; Bernard 1987; Ulmer 1994).

In an earlier article (Ulmer 1994) I applied Johnson's (1991) threefold commitment framework to labeling theory, arguing that structural, moral, and personal commitment contingencies were the mechanisms by which sanctions may entrench people further into deviance careers. This article goes beyond that to make two contributions. First, if commitment is an important concept for deviance and social control, then it is critical to inquire into the possibility of different types of commitment and determine whether distinct sources produce them. This article presents a theoretical framework with which to investigate such questions for the field of deviance. I argue that any time deviance scholars investigate commitment, we should rely on the threefold framework.

Second, Makkai and Braithwaite (1991, p. 213) argue that future work needs to "explore new strategies of theoretical integration that transcend the existing criminological frameworks" (see also Matsueda 1988; 1992; Agnew 1995; Tittle 1989). The threefold commitment framework is a useful tool for such integration, as well as new insights, because it accomplishes three tasks that Merton (1997, p. 520) identified as essential for sociology: (1) conceptual clarification, (2) synthesis and integration of different theories by identifying underlying complementarities, and (3) "explicit identification of theoretical problems and the emergence of consequential concepts that [have] remained implicit in prior formulations."

Some of this framework's types and sources of commitment are explicitly recognized in differential association, opportunity, labeling, or social control theories. Others are merely implied, and some are unique to the commitment framework itself. Furthermore, none of the major deviance theories, by themselves, encompass or incorporate all of the types and sources of continuity in deviance or conventionality recognized by the threefold commitment framework, nor do other efforts at theoretical integration encompass such breadth (e.g., Braithwaite 1989; Tittle 1995).

▶ A Threefold Commitment Typology

Several general conceptualizations and typologies of commitment have been developed (Becker 1960; Kanter 1972; Etzioni 1964; Stryker 1980; Burke and Reitzes 1991). The concept has proved particularly useful in research on close relationships (Johnson 1973; 1991), social movements (Walsh and Warland 1983; McAdam 1989; Hirsch 1990; Klandermans 1997), and organizations and work (Selznick 1969; Etzioni 1964; Faulkner 1974; Kanter 1977; Clarke 1991).

Michael Johnson developed the threefold commitment typology as a framework for explaining continuity in personal relationships. He has written extensively about the framework, its advantages compared to other commitment conceptualizations, and its potential for application beyond the topic of close relationships (Johnson 1973; 1976; 1982; 1991). I have also applied it to the relationship between labeling contingencies and entrenched commitment to deviant activity (Ulmer 1994). The framework extends and refines Becker's (1960; 1964) and Strauss's (1969) treatments of commitment (see also Gerson 1976). Becker (1960; 1964) described adjustment (change in lines of action in order to adapt to problematic situations or life course transitions) and commitment (continuity in lines of action produced by temporally prior lines of action by self and others) as twin, mutually reinforcing social processes in that, for example, the situational adjustments of the present can become the commitments of the future. Strauss (1969) later expanded on Becker's treatment of commitment by emphasizing the self and identity in commitment processes (see also Burke and Reitzes 1991) and by distinguishing between the development of commitments and the experience or awareness of them at problematic life course "turning points" (see also Bolton 1961). As in Becker's and Strauss's work, Johnson's threefold framework focuses on people making decisions and acting within situational opportunities and constraints, that are in turn shaped by larger scale structural arrangements.

Table 1 summarizes the three commitment types and their sources. Each type is defined in terms of a dialectic of constraint and desired choice.[1] The framework further distinguishes between external and internal constraints. Each commitment type is also defined by a distinct experience and definition of the situation.

Johnson (1991) defines the three types primarily in terms of phenomenological experiences. While I certainly do not disagree with Johnson's original formulation, I note that each commitment type also corresponds to a distinct kind of situational definition. To define the three types of commitment in terms of distinct situational definitions is to say that they represent three distinct sets of causes of continuity in action. I am using the term "cause" in the same sense as Blumer (1969; 1990; see also Maines and Morrione 1990, p. xx; Athens 1993) and Strauss (1993). That is, causes of action lie in how actors (both individual and collective ones) interpret and define their situations.[2]

Structural commitment is characterized by external constraints of two kinds: (1) the external constraints that structure and influence choices between lines of action and (2) the external constraints that restrict the termination of a given line of action. Structural commitment is defined by the situational definition that one "has to" pursue a line of action; it has four sources: (1) the availability and attractiveness of alternative lines of action, (2) irretrievable investments in lines of action, (3) difficulty of processes necessary to terminate a line of action, and (4) social reaction to

---

Table 1   Three Types of Commitment and Their Sources

Structural commitment (external constraint)

1. Alternative lines of action

   a. availability of alternatives

   b. relative attractiveness of available alternatives

2. Irretrievable investments

3. Difficulty of terminating lines of action once they are started

4. Social reactions to terminating lines of action once they are started

Personal commitment (internal choice)

1. Attitudes toward lines of action

2. Attitudes toward others with whom one participates in lines of action

3. Definitions of self in terms of identities mobilized by lines of action

Moral commitment (internal constraint)

1. Sense of moral obligation to others with whom one participates in lines of action

2. Internalization of action-specific norms that discourage termination of specific lines of action once they are started

3. Internalization of general norms of consistency in lines of action

---

termination of a line of action. Structural commitment is focused on the level at which larger scale structural arrangements shape situations within which individuals make decisions, act, and interact. This is the meso-level that symbolic interactionists emphasize as crucial to sociological analysis (Maines 1982; Blumer 1990; Couch 1995; Hall 1997); McCarthy and Hagan (1992) call this level a fundamental but underemphasized one in contemporary studies of deviance.

Personal commitment is defined by choice driven by internal desire to continue a line of action. In other words, personal commitment refers to individuals continuing a line of action because they define it as desirable, something they *want* to do. As shown in Table 1, personal commitment flows from three sources: (1) positive attitudes toward lines of action, (2) positive attitudes toward others with whom one engages in a line of action, and (3) self-definitions in terms of identities mobilized by lines of action.

Sociologists have long recognized internal as well as external constraints as important influences on decisions and action (Durkheim [1897]1951) and as potential factors producing continuity in deviance or conventionality (Lemert 1951; Lofland 1969; Reckless 1973). Moral commitment involves this kind of internal constraint.[3] It is characterized by the situational definition that one "ought to" continue a line of action regardless of whether one wants to or has to. Moral commitment has three sources: (1) perceived moral obligations to others with whom one participates in a line of action, (2) internalization of action-specific norms discouraging termination of a line of action once one has already gotten involved in it, and (3) internalization of general cultural values that encourage consistency in lines of action.

Contexts of Commitment: Corporal and Phantom Communities

Commitment processes are embedded in two dialectically related communities, one external, one internal. "Corporal communities" refer to the external, corporal social environment (Athens 1998, p. 677). These communities are the arena in which larger-scale social organization and structure enter group life and shape situational action (Blumer 1990; Giddens 1984). Examples include neighborhoods, workplaces, organizations, networks, and race or ethnic communities. Especially important are corporal communities' power relations and dominance orders, because these most immediately shape situational contexts (Hall 1997; Athens 1998). Situational contexts set parameters for decisions, actions, and interactions. Action and interaction, in turn, react back on situations and corporal communities (Giddens 1984).

Modifying Mead's (1934) conception of the self, Athens (1994, p. 526; see also 1997; 1998) depicts the self as a ongoing soliloquy with phantom others: "The phantom other is both a single and multiple entity because the individual phantom companions, when taken together, comprise a *phantom community*, which provides people with a multi but unified voice and sounding board for making sense of their varied social experiences." "Through soliloquizing, [actors] interpret the situations that confront them daily in their corporal communities, and, on the basis of their interpretations, assemble their actions" (Athens 1998, p. 676).

Commitment processes are embedded in and occur through actors engaging, confronting, and participating in corporal and phantom communities. The corporal community presents and shapes situations in which actors make choices as well as the available lines of action to which actors can become committed or to which they can commit themselves. The situational definitions and sources of all three types of commitment engage the corporal community and represent lines along which that community enters individual decisions and actions—corporal communities present the objects and events that actors define and the potential actions from which they choose (Blumer 1990, p. 152). Structural commitment focuses especially on the definitions of situations and decisions as actors confront their corporal communities in the situations, rules and resources, and social reactions they present. Actors form the distinctive definitions of situations that characterize structural, personal, and moral commitment through soliloquies with their phantom communities. Each source of each commitment type works through—and actors assess each source through—dialogue with their phantom communities.

Continuity in both deviant and conventional behavior represents two sides of the same coin (see also Athens 1985). That is, both involve generic social processes of structural, personal, or moral commitment to lines of action. Some lines of action are defined as deviant and some are defined as conventional within particular structures of power relations, cultures, subcultures, or historical periods, but the commitment processes are the same. Also, the threefold commitment framework does not imply any particular overarching societal consensus on deviance definitions and norms, as some other treatments of commitment and social control do (Kornhauser 1978; Hirschi 1969; 1996, p. 255). Rather, the framework recognizes that deviance definitions are inextricably intertwined with politics and power (Quinney 1970; Hagan 1992) as well as cultural and media processes (Altheide 1997). Further, it is congruent with "Chicago School" symbolic interactionism's assumption that collectivities of all kinds are as likely—perhaps more likely— to be characterized by normative conflicts as by normative consensus (Maines, Bridger, and Ulmer, 1996; Park 1926; 1938).

Johnson's commitment framework is not limited in scope to one gender. For example, Johnson (1982; 1991) has forcefully argued that the framework is crucial to understanding why women exit or stay in unsatisfying marriages or partnerships, including abusive ones. Rachel Einwohner (1999) has recently applied the framework in research on both male and female targets of social protest, and their commitment to engaging in the protested-against activities. Likewise, my use of the framework here applies to deviance careers of both males and females. In fact, the sources of each type of commitment are highly likely to condition gender variation in the amount and qualitative nature of deviance.

Commitment to Deviance

Opportunity, differential association/social learning (along with neutralizations and accounts), and labeling theories provide a set of concepts and propositions that are compatible with one another and are recognized by many as central to any theoretical discussion of continuity in deviant behavior. Each of these theories implies processes and contingencies by which actors develop, maintain, and change sources of structural, personal, and moral commitment to deviance. More importantly, the commitment framework specifies potential factors that these theories either merely imply or fail to recognize.

Structural Commitment

Larger scale structures and culture shape situations, and actors make decisions, act, and interact within those situations (Blumer 1962; Maines 1982; Hall 1997). In crime and deviance, this situational level of analysis is undertheorized and underresearched (McCarthy and Hagan 1992; Matsueda

1992; Matsueda and Heimer 1997). This level is exactly what structural commitment is all about.

Structural commitment has four sources. First, actors are structurally committed to lines of action to the extent that alternatives are either unavailable or to the extent that available alternatives are unacceptable. Actors' assessments of the *availability and attractiveness of alternatives* implies the process by which actors face and interpret opportunity structures. The causal mechanism linking opportunity structures (Cloward and Ohlin 1960; Steffensmeier 1983) and action is actors' definitions of alternatives according to their availability and attractiveness. Thus, opportunity structures do not determine action but set constraints within which actors make choices on the basis of their definitions of situations (Blumer 1969; Maines 1977).

This first source of structural commitment thus constitutes a crucial link between the individual and larger scale social structural arrangements. Broader structural contexts within which actors' lives are embedded condition the situational alternatives they confront. For example, Shover's (1996) study of persistent property offenders and Baron and Hartnagel's (1997) study of street youth both depict actors who actively choose between the situated conventional and criminal alternatives they see as being realistically available and attractive. Excellent ethnographies of the heavily gender-stratified worlds of crack dealing (Maher and Daly 1996) and street robbery (Miller 1998) provide further examples. The female crack dealers described by Maher and Daly (1996) and street robbers described by Miller (1998) skillfully find gender-specific niches within these male-dominated criminal activities, in the face of severely restricted conventional *and* criminal alternatives.

Further, this source of structural commitment is not static. People's choices and adjustments to present problematic situations, social positions, or roles can restrict the availability and/or attractiveness of their future alternatives, a process Becker (1960) called "unfitting." A person's adjustment to deviant roles through learning skills, attitudes, and motives favorable to given forms of deviance may restrict his/her opportunity to enact conventional roles in the future, or may render such conventional roles unattractive.[4]

A second source of structural commitment involves the extent to which actors perceive that they have *irretrievable investments* in a line of action. Action consumes resources, which are perceived as investments when made in anticipation of future returns that are not yet realized and the expenditures are not seen as returnable (Johnson 1991; Glaser and Strauss 1971). Pursuing deviant learning and performance opportunities can potentially foster structural commitment through irretrievable investments. The learning necessary for successful performance of deviant activities and the cultivation of relationships with networks of deviant others may entail the investment of considerable personal resources such as time, energy, or money (Steffensmeier 1986). To the extent that one later defines such investments as irretrievable, this may lead to an experience of structural commitment to deviant lines of action (e.g., "I can't back out now, I'm committed"). For example, one may spend a great deal of time and energy learning the necessary skills for manufacturing, smuggling, or marketing illegal drugs in pursuit of a lucrative career in upper-level drug trafficking (Adler and Adler 1983). Since many such skills are not readily transferable to more conventional lines of action, the investments made in learning them may become a source of structural commitment to obtaining income through such drug trafficking activities.

The third source of structural commitment involves the *difficulty of termination procedures*. The difficulty of terminating different lines of action varies greatly. For example, casual involvement in shoplifting is relatively simple to quit, compared to ceasing involvement in an organized crime network, which could require a set of complex, costly, and potentially hazardous actions. Variations in the degree of difficulty in terminating a line of action therefore present structural constraints of varying strength, depending on the organizational characteristics of deviant activities and networks (Best and Luckenbill 1994; Steffensmeier 1983).

The strength of ties (Granovetter 1973), the emotional intensity of relationships with deviant others (which is also related to a source of personal commitment to deviance, as discussed below), the complexity of deviant networks, and one's centrality to those networks potentially influence the level of difficulty of terminating involvement in those networks (Adler and Adler 1983). Extensive participation in deviant activities, networks, and relationships may make later termination very difficult indeed (Best and Luckenbill 1994). For example, complex, organized criminal activities that require special skills or integration into supportive networks may require complex and costly processes for termination, or at least termination procedures that are structured and governed by certain informal norms (e.g., on termination of membership in outlaw biker gangs, see Ulmer 1994; Abadinsky 1994; Wolf 1991). As another example, anecdotal accounts describe how some street gangs will allow members to quit, but they must be "beaten out." The member can quit but must submit to a beating at the hands of other gang members first. On the other hand, for some forms of deviance, this source of structural commitment would be irrelevant. Some deviant activities (e.g., casual petty theft, surfing the Internet for pornography) may require little integration into supporting networks, few strong ties to deviant others, and few or no structured procedures for termination. For such forms of deviance, termination procedures would be relatively simple. Thus, the key empirical question posed by this source of structural commitment is, how difficult, in a practical sense, is it to exit a given line of deviant behavior?

The final source of structural commitment involves *contingencies of social reaction* that involve potential concrete rewards or penalties. Obviously, this source may often be interrelated with difficulty of termination procedures, but it is conceptually distinct. With the source involving difficulty of termination procedures, individuals may be allowed to quit the activity or relationship as long as they "jump through the hoops" that others may expect (by analogy, a person is allowed to end a marriage, but must go through a number of complex and costly social and legal procedures first [Johnson 1991]). This final source of structural commitment, however, involves social reactions from others that actually *hamper or prevent* quitting (by analogy, an oppressive boss may threaten to sabotage an employee's future job prospects if the employee quits).

If social reactions in the conventional world can foster continuity in conventional lines of action, might social reactions from deviant others foster continuity in deviance? Evidence indicates that this can sometimes be the case. For example, when female offenders are involved in criminal activity in the service of male partners, the fear of violent reaction from those male partners is a very real, salient barrier to the women's quitting. Also, involvement in some types of crime (e.g., organized, lucrative crime in the underworld) entails immersion in networks of interdependence and exchange (Steffensmeier 1983; 1986; Best and Luckenbill 1994). Ceasing involvement in such networks can entail penalties or retaliation, since quitting can threaten either the material interests or the "cover" of associates.[5]

In sum, the concept of structural commitment would first direct researchers to the processes by which actors become aware of and interpret deviant opportunity structures in terms of availability and attractiveness and to key decision processes between deviant and conventional lines of action. Second, research could investigate how actors interpret investments of resources in the onset of deviant careers and how expectations of future returns on these resources affect the continuation, frequency, and termination of offending. Third, studies could also explore variations in the difficulty of concrete procedures required to terminate deviant activities, how these might vary according to different forms of deviance social organization (Best and Luckenbill 1994), and how actors' awareness and definitions of these procedures fosters continuity in deviant activities, networks of relationships, and subcultures. Research could explore potential similarities and differences in structural commitment contingencies between "street crime" and white-collar crime or between "underworld" and "upperworld" crime (to use Steffensmeier's [1983] terminology). Finally, research could focus on ways in which social reactions from either deviant networks or labeling from conventional authorities produce or exacerbate sources of structural commitment to deviant careers and how these contingencies might vary according to gender, age, race, class, resources, the actor's position in deviant networks (if any), and other factors (see Ulmer 1994; Heimer and Staffen 1995; Stebbins, 1971).

Personal Commitment

Socialization favorable to deviance involves learning definitions, attitudes, behaviors, skills, and vocabularies of motive favorable to given forms of deviance (Sutherland 1947; Akers et al. 1979; Sykes and Matza 1957), as well as forming relationships with deviant others (Warr 1993) and self-definitions in terms of deviant identities (Glaser 1956; Matsueda 1992). Three sources of personal commitment encompass these process of deviant socialization as they produce continuity in deviant lines of action based on individuals' personal desires or "tastes" (Steffensmeier 1986, p. 231) for that activity. For example, Heimer and Matsueda (1994, p. 368) propose that "the likelihood of delinquency should be increased by delinquent views of the self from the standpoint of others, attitudes favorable to delinquency, perceptions that others would approve of delinquency, friendships with delinquent peers, and histories of delinquent habit." All of these factors involve sources of personal commitment.

First, personal commitment flows from one's attitudes toward specific lines of action. Personal commitment to deviance can result from the development of favorable attitudes toward given lines of deviant activity. This source of personal commitment to deviance focuses on the subjective rewards of the deviant activity itself, which of course sometimes necessitate learning to perceive the activity and its consequences as rewarding (Becker 1960). For example, a skilled burglar may continue to steal because he/she feels it is lucrative, may enjoy the thrills and risks entailed, and may develop the "larceny sense" that is crucial to continued participation in serious and lucrative property crime (Steffensmeier 1986). Katz's (1988) discussion of the "thrills and seductions" of certain kinds of deviant activity provides another example of this source of personal commitment (though a limited one, see McCarthy 1995). Adler and Adler (1983) show that one significant obstacle to the termination of careers in upper-level drug smuggling was participants' enjoyment of the lifestyle and rewards. Plus, neutralizations and accounts (Sykes and Matza 1957; Benson 1985) may foster this source of personal commitment by providing a vocabulary of motive and rhetoric of justification for continuing a given type of deviant activity.

The second source of personal commitment is positive attitudes toward others with whom one acts in a given line of action. Involvement in relationships with deviant others and deviant networks can be another source of personal commitment to deviance in that such relationships may foster the development of favorable attitudes toward deviant others (Schur 1969, p. 316). Contrary to depictions of "cold and brittle" relationships between deviants (Hirschi 1969; Gottfredson and Hirschi 1990), considerable support exists for the notion of close relationships between individuals involved in a variety of forms of deviance. These relationships and attitudes can certainly be a factor that keeps such individuals participating in deviance. For example, recovering alcoholics often say that one key difficulty in quitting drinking is that everything and *everyone* they enjoy is connected to alcohol (Denzin 1987). To list just a few among many other examples, Giordano et al.'s (1986) findings regarding delinquent peer groups and Adler and Adler's (1983) research on upper-level drug traffickers have shown how friendship bonds in deviant networks can foster continuity in deviant activities. Further, Kandel and Davies (1991) found that gang members' friendships with and positive sentiments toward fellow members were key factors in keeping them involved in crime and delinquency. Studies by Warr (1996), Warr and Stafford (1991), and Zhang and Messner (1995) also illustrate a variety of ways in which delinquent peer friendships sustain and channel careers in juvenile delinquency. Finally, deviant role modeling (Akers 1998) is a process by which actors emulate the deviant behavior of role models toward whom they have positive attitudes.

The third source of personal commitment involves the definition of self in terms of identities mobilized by lines of action—a dimension of commitment also noted by Burke and Reitzes (1991). The importance of identity and self-definition in producing continuity in deviance has been recognized for decades (Lemert 1951; Becker 1963; Lofland 1969). The development of deviant self-definitions can occur through differential identification (Glaser 1956), implicating personal commitment through the definition of self in terms of identities mobilized by deviant lines of action. Adler and Adler's (1983, p. 611) work on upper-level drug traffickers implies how personal commitment to deviance can come from the definition of self in terms of criminal activities: "Dealers and smugglers identified with . . . the occupation of drug trafficking. Their self-images were tied to that role and could not be easily disengaged." More recently, Ross Matsueda (1992) has emphasized the important part that identities and reflected appraisals of self can play in producing and sustaining deviant behavior.

The concept of personal commitment can help future researchers conceptually to distinguish and organize sources of continuity in crime derived from attitudes and self-definitions learned through association with deviant definitions, deviant others, and participation in deviant activities. Too often, we gloss over these factors or lump them all together as deviant socialization or differential association, without careful analytical distinctions (but see Akers 1998). While existing research implies ways in which sources of personal commitment to crime are developed, there is less research on how actors experience such commitments in situational decisions. For example, how do problematic situations and turning points mobilize attitudes and self-definitions favorable to continued involvement in deviance? How do actors' awareness and experience of these sources translate into continuity in crime through concrete decisions? Future research into such questions would greatly improve our understanding of personal, interpretive sources of continuity and change in deviant activity (Matsueda 1988, pp. 351–353).

Moral Commitment

Moral commitment derives from three sources. First, it flows from actors' normative values governing the termination of specific lines of action in specific contexts. This source does not refer to individuals' attitudes or beliefs about the moral rightness or wrongness of a given line of action per se (a source of personal commitment). Rather, moral commitment refers to moral beliefs that discourage terminating a given line of action after becoming involved in it (Johnson 1991). For example, one may stay in an unhappy marriage because he/she believes that divorce is immoral. The second source of moral commitment has to do with the extent to which actors define themselves as incurring moral obligations to specific others with whom they are involved in lines of action. The final source of moral commitment involves the extent to which one generally values consistency in one's own action. For example, sayings such as "stick to your guns," or "quitters never win" embody such general consistency values in contemporary U.S. culture (Johnson 1991, p. 121).

Moral commitment to deviance—as well as personal commitment— might develop through deviant socialization as well. The possibility of moral commitment to crime is undertheorized and underresearched. But involvement in some kinds of organized deviant networks can entail learning action-specific norms, such as those emphasizing dependability, trustworthiness, loyalty, and a sense of moral obligation to other members (Best and Luckenbill 1994). These norms and obligations sometimes foster consistency in relations between members of deviant networks and can discourage unexpected termination of involvement in violation of those norms and obligations (Luckenbill and Best 1981). For example, such personal codes of conduct and informal rules of obligations are especially important in coordinating and safeguarding activities among networks of relatively skilled, successful thieves and fences (Steffensmeier 1983; 1986; Klockars 1974). Furthermore, a reputation for dependability, for recognizing obligations to associates by keeping one's mouth shut when one gets in trouble, and an ability to keep one's word are all prized attributes in the realm of organized, lucrative, underworld crime (Steffensmeier 1983). Steffensmeier's subject in *The Fence* (1986, p. 58) captures the importance of this kind of dependability and trustworthiness, which can be seen as involving moral commitment to deviance through action-specific norms and perceived obligations to others:

> Thieves have to have confidence in each other. That's where heart comes in, too. . . . That's when you're going to have to depend on a person. Not have a guy that's going to get all shitty and run out, and he gets away and you get popped. That's part of being trustworthy, too. Being dependable. You got to know the man's on your back all the time. . . . Another thing, if the good thief is caught and has to do time, you will not hear a peep out of him. As long as the cops didn't set him up, fuck him over, you'd hear no peep out of him.

A sense of moral obligation to specific deviant others, as well as general consistency values, might also be used as a neutralization of conventional moral codes to self and as an account to agents of social control, such as "appeals to higher loyalties" or "a defense of necessity" (Sykes and Matza 1957; Klockars 1974). These neutralizations and accounts can then foster continuity in deviance by justifying continued involvement. Thus, the concept of moral commitment suggests that entrenchment in deviant networks and internalization of their normative codes (if any) may produce continuity in deviant lines of action. Moral commitment to deviance might develop to the extent that differential association processes produce a sense of moral obligation to other members of interdependent deviant networks and foster learning and applying norms emphasizing consistency in deviant action.

The term "moral commitment to crime" might seem like an oxymoron, and some would see it as a conceptual impossibility (e.g., Kornhauser 1978; Gottfredson and Hirschi 1990). I suspect this is why the study of deviance has paid comparatively little explicit attention to what this framework identifies as sources of moral commitment to crime. Such lack of attention leaves several interesting questions about deviance unanswered. For example, how might informal rules of obligation and action-specific norms vary in degree and importance in relation to social organizational differences in deviant networks and subcultures (Best and Luckenbill 1994; Steffensmeier 1983)? How might such informal rules and norms be learned and interpreted by participants in such networks and subcultures, and how much importance do members attach to them as constraints? If participants internalize a deviant group's rules and norms that foster moral commitment to crime, can these be neutralized by the same kinds of techniques that are used to neutralize conventional moral beliefs (Jacobs 1992)? How do specific situations and contexts mobilize sources of moral commitment in actors' awareness, and how do these moral commitments figure into concrete decisions to produce continuity in deviant lines of action?

Moral commitment would also have particular relevance for certain kinds of female crime. Women's criminal activity is often embedded in relationships with men in that such women often serve as accomplices to male partners or even directly "work for" male partners (e.g., selling drugs, prostitution, theft, see Steffensmeier 1983; Steffensmeier and Allan 1995). A sense of obligation to these male partners might be an important source of moral commitment to deviance for such women.

Commitment to Conformity

The importance of commitment in conventional social control is well established (Reckless 1973; Hirschi 1969; Bernard 1987). Thus, I argue that the threefold framework provides a more analytically precise conceptualization of commitment than that found in the social control literature. At the same time, the framework specifies how deviance theories that many

treat as competitors (e.g., Hirschi 1996; Gottfredson 1999) are compli-
mentary.

A tension has traditionally existed between social control theory and differential association, opportunity, and labeling theories. In fact, Hirschi
(1969) and Kornhauser (1978) argued for the outright rejection of other theories in favor of social control theory. More recently, Sampson and Laub
(1993) have recognized the importance of opportunity structures and associations with deviant peers, but argued that their age-graded social control
theory yields the most explanatory power (but see Warr 1998). In spite of
surface differences, however, all these theories implicitly share a common
underlying goal: the explanation of continuity (and discontinuity) in lines
of action. Debates about whether one or another of these theories is "better" are unnecessary and unproductive, *since both represent two sides of a
generic social process.* Only a handful of deviance scholars have explicitly
recognized this point (e.g., Athens 1985; Matsueda and Heimer 1997),[6]
while others deny the possibility of commitment to deviance (Goffman
1967; Kornhauser 1978; Gottfredson and Hirschi 1990; Hirschi 1996). The
commitment framework therefore integrates insights from control, opportunity, differential association, and labeling theories in order to explain
continuity in deviant and conventional activity.

This integration, however, hinges on revising Hirschi's (1969) and Kornhauser's (1978) social control theory assumption of the constancy of deviant motivation, replacing it with both differential association theory's
assumption that the motivations for different types of crime are learned,
and opportunity theory's assumption that the opportunity to learn them is
differentially distributed throughout society (see also Athens 1985). Further, the development and strength of stakes in conformity are themselves
conditioned by the relative availability and attractiveness of conventional
and deviant alternatives and by actors' choices on the basis of these
alternatives.

Such integration would also call for revising Hirschi's (1969; Gottfredson and Hirschi 1990) argument that commitment to deviance is a non-
sensical concept, recognizing instead (as Athens [1985] and Matsueda and
Heimer [1997] do) that commitment to deviant lines of action and relationships with deviant others is an empirical possibility. In this view, deviant and conventional careers are twin, intertwined aspects of the same
generic process—the development and experience of commitments that
produce continuity in lines of action. Plus, the threefold commitment
framework does not imply an overarching normative consensus in society,
as do Hirschi (1969) and Kornhauser (1978) (for treatments of social control that do not rely on an assumption of societal normative consensus, see
Heimer and Matsueda 1994; Matsueda and Heimer 1997). Instead, this
framework simply describes different types of commitment to lines of action of any kind. Some lines of action are defined as deviant at particular

times and places by particular groups, with particular interests and power (Quinney 1970; Schur 1980).

The threefold commitment framework could make several specific contributions to explaining continuity in conventional action and would provide social control researchers with more refined tools for investigating commitment to conformity. First, the framework would be a valuable tool for developmental and life course research in deviance (Thornberry 1995; Agnew 1997; Sampson and Laub 1997). For example, Agnew (1997) and Sampson and Laub (1997) argue that variation in (and disruption of) commitments to conventional activity and conventional adult roles account for variation in the onset, persistence, and termination of criminal careers throughout the life course. The commitment framework could help specify exactly what kinds of commitments to conventional activity (and their sources) are developed or disrupted over the life course, and allow more refined studies of the development and experience of these commitments at key life-course turning points in which decisions are made. In addition, Sampson and Laub (1997, p. 138) call for deviance concepts and theories that are processual rather than static. The processual nature of the threefold commitment framework and its interactionist assumptions would seem to make it (like labeling theory, see Sampson and Laub 1997, p. 138) an especially attractive conceptual tool for research on deviance and the life course, since it is sensitive to intraindividual differences in the types of commitment and their sources over time.

Sampson and Laub's (1993; Laub, Nagin, and Sampson 1998) age-graded social control theory is loaded with implications for the utility of the threefold commitment framework in explaining continuity in both deviant and conventional lines of action. Their work argues that both stability and change in deviant career trajectories throughout life are systematically produced by social bonds to conventional adult institutions of informal social control, particularly bonds to work and family. Arguably, their analysis could just as easily be framed as a study of structural, personal, and perhaps even moral commitments to deviant versus conventional activities, as well as continuity and change in those commitments over the life course. While their interpretations emphasize the ways in which their data support their age-graded social control theory, their findings also show that factors such as associations with deviant peers and contact with the criminal justice system produce continuity in deviant careers (see also Warr 1998). Within the threefold commitment framework, such findings are not surprising, and in fact they illustrate twin sides of a generic set of commitment processes to deviant and conventional lines of action and transitions between them throughout the life course. Regarding the effects of formal criminal justice sanctions on later criminal behavior, for example, the sources of each type of commitment specify intervening mechanisms by which labeling effects produce future stability or entrenchment in deviant behavior (see also Ulmer 1994).[7] In fact, interrelated chains of commitment processes may produce what Sampson and Laub (1997, p. 144) describe as cumulative disadvantages over time in terms of conventional adult social bonds and conventional controls. Structural, personal, and/or moral commitment processes may be the mechanisms behind the long-term labeling consequences and effects of conventional social bonds, including cumulative disadvantages, found in Sampson and Laub's body of life course research. The types of commitment and their sources may therefore be intervening mechanisms between labeling processes, the disruption of conventional adult social bonds, and entrenched deviant careers.

In addition, Warr's (1998) study of life course transitions and crime finds that marriage contributes to desistance from crime by producing a shift away from relations with deviant peers in favor of spouse and children. Warr (1998, p. 209) states that this finding "offers preliminary evidence for *a general mechanism* of desistance that may explain the links between life-course transitions and crime" (my emphasis added). The commitment processes described here, especially the potential interplay of structural and personal commitment, specify this general mechanism in life course transitions from deviant peer relations to conventional ties. Further, as implied above, the commitment framework would also suggest the opposite possibility—that negative life events (e.g., divorce, arrest, job loss, etc.) can disrupt conventional commitment processes and foster deviant ones. Again, the sources of the different types of commitment—especially structural and personal commitment sources—may be *intervening factors* in the relationship between life-course events and conventional or deviant behavior and therefore worthy of further study.

The threefold commitment framework would also extend Matsueda and Heimer's (1997; Heimer and Matsueda 1994; Matsueda 1992) theory of differential social control. They rely heavily on Becker's (1960), Stryker's (1980), and Burke and Reitzes's (1991) conceptualizations of commitment, which are extended and refined by the threefold framework (Johnson 1991; Ulmer 1994). Matsueda and Heimer (1997, p. 174) identify two general mechanisms that produce continuity in either deviant or conventional behavior over the life course: (1) the "endogenous" or "subjective" process "in which actors consider aspects of the life course in carrying out meaningful, self-conscious behavior" and (2) the "exogenous social structuring that may or may not condition the consciousness of actors." Clearly, the sources of personal and moral commitment specify the former processes in greater detail, while structural commitment sources specify the latter processes. Plus, the concept of structural commitment specifies sources of what Heimer and Matsueda (1994, p. 369) call "differential organizational control," that is, social organizational arrangements within which processes of differential social control are embedded. The four structural commitment sources would each be important social organizational factors that produce more or less conventional control. Finally, the threefold commitment framework answers Heimer and Matsueda's (1994, p. 384) call for a greater conceptual focus on individual motivations in problematic situations, and how these situations are lodged in "contexts of structural locations, commitment to social roles, and institutional arrangements." Such a focus, after all, is at the heart of the threefold commitment framework.

Conclusion

Since commitment is central to the study of deviance and social control, it makes sense to conceptualize it in all its variation, complexity, and implications. In addition to the more specific research directions involving the source of commitment discussed above, the threefold commitment framework as a whole has broader implications for deviance research. First, class, race, ethnicity, and gender are key social statuses correlated with the distribution of resources, power, and life chances and are likely to be associated with different contingencies of structural, personal, and moral commitment to deviance and conformity. To take just one example, the contingencies of structural commitment to deviance and conformity would likely be very different for a seventeen-year-old black male from a poor family in an inner city neighborhood compared to an affluent thirty-five-year-old white woman in a small town. These two individuals would also likely be enmeshed in different personal relationships and socialization processes; they would transact different identities and hold different self-definitions, and these would be all differentially favorable to different kinds of deviance or conformity. The framework directs attention to the ways in which larger scale patterns of social structure (e.g., race, class, and gender stratification, the social organization of aging, and the life course) operate in people's lives by shaping situational alternatives and constraints within which actors make decisions, act, and interact. The commitment framework may be especially relevant for examining aspects of certain kinds of careers in crime and deviance among women. Many women often stay involved in crime (Steffensmeier and Allan 1995; Maher and Daly 1996) or some types of deviance (e.g., Thio 1988) through either: (1) restricted and unattractive alternatives (invoking the first source of structural commitment from Table 1) or (2) enmeshment in relationships with men involved in crime (invoking, at the very least, the third source of structural commitment, the second source of personal commitment, and/or the first source of moral commitment).

Second, future research could investigate ways in which types of commitment and their sources might mutually interrelate and interact. For example, Hagan's (1991) finding that the effects of adolescent participation in "partying" or "delinquent" subcultures were class-specific implies that the effect of personal commitment to deviant activity is contingent on class-based structural commitment contingencies now and later in the life course, such as the availability and attractiveness of alternatives. Hagedorn's (1994) typology of adult gang members' careers also suggests the interactive nature of sources of structural, personal, and perhaps moral commitment to crime and conventionality.[8]

Furthermore, Matsueda and Anderson (1998) note the need for theories of crime and deviance to incorporate theories of peer relations and friendship networks. Johnson (1991) developed the threefold commitment framework through research on personal relationship dynamics. Its concepts of personal commitment, and the conditioning influences of structural commitment, have a great deal to offer in understanding peer selection processes, friendship networks, and their reciprocal relation to deviance and conventional social control.

Third, one exciting research direction would involve the commitment framework's potential use in analyzing the social organization of deviant activity. Commitments are the "glue" of conventional organizations (Gerson 1976; Clarke 1991). The threefold commitment framework suggests that organized groups centered around deviant activity may be held together by the glue of structural, personal, or moral commitment to deviant activities and relationships. Just as the framework challenges Gottfredson and Hirschi's (1990) notion that relationships between deviant peers are cold and brittle, the framework likewise questions their notion that organized deviant or criminal activity is an illusion. In both cases, the commitment framework recognizes deviant peer relations and organized deviant activities as lines of action for which structural, personal, or moral commitments may potentially be developed. In fact, it is probable that moral commitment to deviance is *most* likely to be found in the context of organized deviant groups.

Variations in the types and strength of commitments between members of deviant groups to each other, to the group, and to its activities are likely a measure of the degree of deviant groups' organizational complexity, and vice versa. The commitment framework could be used to study the structure and relationships of organized deviant groups and how these affect the careers of the individuals within them. For example, commitment types and sources would likely vary a great deal in relevance, importance, and consequences along Best and Luckenbill's (1994) continuum of the organizational complexity of deviant activity. The strength and consequences of different types of commitment would likely vary between groups that differ in organizational sophistication, from small delinquent groups to large-scale "formal organizations" that persist in time and space. On one hand, organizationally sophisticated groups like La Cosa Nostra in the United States, or the Japanese Yakusa are likely held together by complex webs of personal, structural, and moral commitments. On the other hand, Warr (1996, pp. 13, 26) found that preexisting friendship ties and peer pressure (a possible combination of personal commitment and structural commitment) fostered continuity in delinquent activities and groups, but also shaped the social organization (however primitive) of small, transitory delinquent groups and roles within those groups. Thus, preexisting personal and structural commitments affected the social organization of even small, short-lived delinquent groups, which in turn affected delinquent career contingencies such as length of participation and specialization.

Other Applications

The threefold commitment framework is relevant not just to personal relationships (as Johnson's work shows) or to deviance and social control (as I have argued here), but to a wide variety of substantive areas of sociological inquiry. I close by briefly suggesting some of the framework's potential contributions to the topics of social movements and the sociology of organizations as further examples.

The threefold commitment framework would be potentially useful for analyzing continuity in participation in social movement activities. For example, factors that may discourage termination of participation include fear of negative social reaction from one's network of movement associates (a source of structural commitment), a sense of moral obligation to movement associates or to social movement goals (moral commitment), or the definition of self in terms of identities invoked by movement participation (personal commitment) (McAdam 1986; 1989; Walsh and Warland 1983). Furthermore, Einwohner (1999) examines how the three types of commitment and their sources help to explain variation in the willingness or ability of *targets* of protest (in this case hunters versus circus patrons, two targets of animal rights protesters) to change behavior against which others have grievances. In other words, the commitments of targeted actors or audiences to the activities that are the object of protest vary not only in strength, but also in type. Since protest "success" is often measured as getting targets to stop or change what they are doing, it follows that the chances for protest success in part depend on such targets' structural, personal, or moral commitments to the protested activity (Einwohner 1999).

Commitments are the "glue" of conventional as well as deviant organizations (Gerson 1976; Clarke 1991). I suggest that variations in the types, degrees, and objects of organizational members' commitment strongly influence organizational structuration, culture, and politics. For example, members' structural, personal, and moral commitments to organizations and relational networks within them will likely influence the manner in which organizations mobilize and coordinate joint actions in pursuit of formal goals. Also, complex and conflicting webs of personal, structural, and moral commitments between organizational actors probably shape and are shaped by organizational negotiations, politics, and conflicts (Clarke 1991; Couch 1986; Couch and Weiland 1986; Hall and McGinty 1997).

Commitment stands at the intersection of at least three of sociology's core dialectics: continuity and change, agency and constraint, and self and society. It is hard to think of a substantive area of sociology in which commitment is not relevant. It also makes sense to push the concept further, so that it can sensitize researchers to the differences in situational definitions, experiences, and processes of development that we have typically lumped under the general heading of commitment. That is what the Johnson commitment framework does, and I think our empirical inquiries into any area of group life will be the richer for using it.

Notes

1. This framework's interactionist conception of a dialectical relationship between choice and constraint, or agency and structure, is compatible with Giddens's (1984) theory of structuration and notion of "duality of structure." As Hall (1997) describes, both interactionism and structuration theory view structure (whether at the micro-, meso-, or macrolevels) as both constraining and enabling. Furthermore, both theories hold that actors' situational decisions and actions are shaped and channeled by external structures, but also always reproduce, modify, and even sometimes radically change those structures.

2. This interpretive conception of causal processes is certainly congruent with, but more basic than, the idea of vocabularies of motive and the derivative concepts of accounts (Scott and Lyman 1968) and disclaimers and neutralizations (Hewitt and Stokes 1975; Sykes and Matza 1957). Such vocabularies of motive are, of course, definitions of situations themselves, and actors use them rhetorically to explain their conduct to themselves and others (Mills 1940). In particular, actors use such vocabularies of motive to excuse or justify deviant conduct to self and others retrospectively (accounts) or prospectively (disclaimers, neutralizations).

The situational definitions characteristic of the three types of commitment can certainly be articulated as general vocabularies of motive, as well as accounts and neutralizations. In addition, each of the sources of structural, personal, and moral commitment could provide actors with potential accounts, disclaimers, or neutralizations for deviant activity, or even for articulating the reasons for conformity to deviant audiences (Jacobs 1992). A full exploration of how actors might draw on the situational definitions characteristic of each type of commitment as vocabularies of motive is beyond the scope of this article, but would be an excellent and novel line of empirical inquiry.

3. Moral commitment "is not to be confused with moral aspects of social reaction, a source of structural commitment, which has its locus outside the individual" (Johnson 1991, p. 121).

4. As an extreme example, a career as a professional "hitter" requires complicated opportunity structures and learning elaborate skills, attitudes, and neutralizations favorable to murder for profit (Levi 1989), yet a career in murder-for-hire hardly opens up conventional job opportunities.

5. "Made members" of La Cosa Nostra cannot terminate their involvement without risk of severe and violent reactions from other members of their La Cosa Nostra families (Abadinsky 1994). As another example, members of outlaw biker clubs who fail to participate in club functions, such as meetings, road runs, or fights, face violent punishments from club leaders (Ulmer 1994).

6. For example, in his critique of Goffman's (1967) idea of violent crimes as "character contests," Athens (1985) argues that people may have commitments to (or "stakes in") deviant as well as conventional social worlds. The threefold framework extends this idea, enabling investigations into what *kinds* of commitment, and what distinct sources produce them.

7. For example, criminal justice sanctions may, under certain circumstances, reduce the availability and attractiveness of conventional alternatives and increase the availability and attractiveness of deviant alternatives. This source of structural commitment, in turn, can set in motion chains of processes that foster the development of other structural and personal commitment sources, such as irretrievable investments in further pursuit of deviant activities, relationships with deviant peers, further socialization processes that foster positive attitudes toward deviant lines of action, and engulfment in deviant identities (Stebbins 1971; Ulmer 1994).

8. Hagedorn (1994) distinguishes between "legits," "homeboys," "dope fiends," and "new jacks." In terms of the threefold commitment framework, legits exited gang life by developing personal and structural commitment to conventionality through conventional work and family. Homeboys had little personal commitment to gang life but faced few available and attractive conventional alternatives. Dope fiends "unfitted" themselves for conventional work

and relationships through continued drug use and immersion in the practical constraints of heroin or cocaine addiction. Finally, new jacks were structurally embedded in gang activities and had significant personal commitment to gang life and money.

References

Abadinsky, Howard. 1994. *Organized Crime.* Chicago: Nelson-Hall.

Adler, Patricia, and Peter Adler. 1983. "Relations Between Dealers: The Social Organization of Illicit Drug Transactions." *Sociology and Social Research* 67:260–278.

Agnew, Robert. 1995. "Determinism, Indeterminism, and Crime: An Empirical Exploration." *Criminology* 33:83–110.

——. 1997. "Stability and Change in Crime over the Life Course: A Strain Theory Explanation." Pp. 101–131 in *Developmental Theories of Crime and Delinquency,* edited by Thornberry.

Akers, Ronald. 1996. "Is Differential Association/Social Learning Cultural Deviance Theory?" *Criminology* 34:229–248.

——. 1998, *Social Learning and Social Structure: A General Theory of Crime and Deviance.* Boston: Northeastern University Press.

Akers, Ronald, Marvin Krohn, Lonn Lanza-Kaduce, and Maria Radosevich. 1979. "Social Learning and Deviant Behavior: A Specific Test of a General Theory." *American Sociological Review* 44:635–655.

Altheide, David. 1997. "Crime, Media, and the Production of Fear." *The Sociological Quarterly* 38:645–666.

Athens, Lonnie. 1985. "Character Contests and Violent Criminal Conduct: A Critique." *The Sociological Quarterly* 26:419–432.

——. 1993. "Blumer's Advanced Course on Social Psychology." *Studies in Symbolic Interaction* 18:245–261.

——. 1994. "The Self as a Soliloquy." *The Sociological Quarterly* 35:521–532.

——. 1997. *Violent Criminal Acts and Actors Revisited.* Urbana: University of Illinois Press.

——. 1998. "Dominance, Ghettos, and Violent Crime." *The Sociological Quarterly* 39:673–691.

Baron, Stephen, and Timothy Hartnagel. 1997. "Attributions, Affect, and Crime: Street Youths' Reactions to Unemployment." *Criminology* 35:409–434.

Becker, Howard. 1960. "Notes on the Concept of Commitment," *American Journal of Sociology* 66:32–40.

——. 1963. *Outsiders.* New York: Macmillan.

——. 1964. "Personal Change in Adult Life." *Sociometry* 27(1):40–53.

Benson, Michael. 1985. "Denying the Guilty Mind: Accounting for Involvement in White Collar Crime." *Criminology* 23:583–607.

Bernard, Thomas. 1987. "Structure and Control: Reconsidering Hirschi's Concept of Commitment." *Justice Quarterly* 4:409–424.

Best, Joel, and David Luckenbill. 1994. *Organizing Deviance.* Englewood Cliffs, NJ: Prentice-Hall.

Blumer, Herbert. 1962. "Society as Symbolic Interaction," in *Human Behavior and Social Processes,* edited by A. Rose. Boston: Houghton-Mifflin.

——. 1969. *Symbolic Interactionism.* Englewood Cliffs, NJ: Prentice-Hall.

——. 1990. *Industrialization as an Agent of Social Change.* New York: Aldine de Gruyter.

Bolton, Charles. 1961. "Mate Selection as the Development of a Relationship." *Marriage and Family Living* 23:234–240.

Braithwaite, John. 1989. *Crime, Shame, and Reintegration.* Cambridge: Cambridge University Press.

Burke, Peter, and Donald Reitzes, 1991. "An Identity Theory Approach to Commitment." *Social Psychology Quarterly* 54:239-251.

Clarke, Adele. 1991. "Social Worlds/Arenas Theory as Organizational Theory." Pp. 119-158 in *Social Organization and Social Process: Essays in Honor of Anselm Strauss,* edited by David Maines. New York: Aldine de Gruyter.

Cloward, Richard, and Lloyd Ohlin. 1960. *Delinquency and Opportunity.* Glencoe, IL: Free Press.

Couch, Carl. 1986. "Structural Conditions of Intergroup Negotiations." *Studies in Symbolic Interaction.* Supplement 2:353-364.

———. 1995. "Let Us Rekindle the Passion by Constructing a Robust Science of the Social." *The Sociological Quarterly* 36:1-14.

Couch, Carl, and Marion Weiland. 1986. "A Study of the Representative-Constituent Relationship," in *Studies in Symbolic Interaction: The Iowa School,* Supplement 2:375-392.

Denzin, Norman. 1987. *The Alcoholic Self.* Newbury Park, CA: Sage.

Durkheim, Emile. [1897] 1951. *Suicide.* Glencoe, IL: The Free Press.

Einwohner, Rachel. 1999. "Practices, Opportunity, and Protest Effectiveness: Illustrations from Four Animal Rights Campaigns." *Social Problems* 46:169-188.

Etzioni, Amitai. 1964. *Modern Organizations.* Englewood Cliffs, NJ: Prentice-Hall.

Faulkner, Robert. 1974. "Coming of Age in Organizations: A Comparative Study of Career Contingencies and Adult Socialization." *Sociology of Work and Occupations* 1:131-173.

Gerson, Elihu M. 1976. "On 'Quality of Life.'" *American Sociological Review* 41:793-806.

Giddens, Anthony. 1984. *The Constitution of Society.* Berkeley: University of California Press.

Giordano, Peggy, Stephen Cernovich, and M.D. Pugh. 1986. "Friendships and Delinquency." *American Journal of Sociology* 91:1170-1202.

Glaser, Barney, and Anselm Strauss. 1971. *Status Passage.* Chicago: Aldine de Gruyter.

Glaser, Daniel. 1956. "Criminality Theories and Behavioral Images." *American Journal of Sociology* 61:440-441.

Goffman, Erving. 1967. *Interaction Ritual.* New York: Doubleday.

Gottfredson, Michael. 1999. Review of *Social Learning and Social Structure,* by Ronald Akers. *American Journal of Sociology* 105:283-284.

Gottfredson, Michael, and Travis Hirschi. 1990. *A General Theory of Crime.* Stanford, CA: Stanford University Press.

Granovetter, Mark. 1973. "The Strength of Weak Ties." *American Journal of Sociology* 78:1360-1380.

Hagan, John. 1991. "Destiny and Drift: Subcultural Preferences, Status Attainments, and the Risks and Rewards of Youth." *American Sociological Review* 56:567-581.

———. 1992. "The Poverty of a Classless Criminology." *Criminology* 30:1-20.

Hagedorn, John. 1994. "Homeboys, Dope Fiends, Legits, and New Jacks." *Criminology* 32:197-220.

Hall, Peter. 1997. "Meta-Power, Social Organization, and the Shaping of Social Action." *Symbolic Interaction* 20:397-418.

Hall, Peter, and Peter McGinty. 1997. "Policy as the Transformation of Intentions: Producing Program from Statute." *The Sociological Quarterly* 38:439-468.

Heimer, Carol, and Lisa Staffen. 1995. "Interdependence and Reintegrative Social Control." *American Sociological Review* 60:635-654.

Heimer, Karen, and Ross Matsueda. 1994. "Role Taking, Role Commitment, and Delinquency: A Theory of Differential Social Control." *American Sociological Review* 59(3):365-390.

Hewitt, John, and Randall Stokes. 1975. "Disclaimers." *American Sociological Review* 40:1–11.

Hirsch, Eric. 1990. "Sacrifice for the Cause: Group Processes, Recruitment, and Commitment in a Student Social Movement." *American Sociological Review* 55:243–254.

Hirschi, Travis. 1969. *Causes of Delinquency.* Berkeley, CA: Free Press.

———. 1996. "Theory without Ideas: Reply to Akers." *Criminology* 34(2):249–256.

Jacobs, Bruce. 1992. "Undercover Drug Use and Evasion Tactics: Excuses and Neutralizations." *Symbolic Interaction* 15:435–454.

Johnson, Michael. 1973. "Commitment: A Conceptual Structure and Empirical Application." *The Sociological Quarterly* 14:395–406.

———. 1976. "The Role of Commitment in Social Problems Theory." Paper presented at the annual meetings of the Society for the Study of Social Problems, New York, NY.

———. 1982. "Social and Cognitive Features of the Dissolution of Commitment to Relationships." Pp. 51–73 in *Personal Relationships 4: Dissolving Personal Relationships,* edited by Steven Duck. New York: Academic Press.

———. 1991. "Commitment to Personal Relationships." Pp. 117–143 in *Advance in Personal Relationships,* Vol. 3, edited by William Jones and Dan Perlman. London: Jessica Kingsley Publishers.

Kandel, Denise, and Mark Davies. 1991. "Friendship Networks, Intimacy, and Illicit Drug Use in Young Adulthood: A Comparison of Two Theories." *Criminology* 29:441–470.

Kanter, Rosabeth Moss. 1972. *Commitment and Community.* Cambridge, MA: Harvard University Press.

———. 1977. *Men and Women of the Corporation.* New York: Basic Books.

Katz, Jack. 1988. *Seductions of Crime: Moral and Sensual Attractions of Doing Evil.* New York: Basic Books.

———. 1994. "Jazz in Social Interaction: Personal Creativity, Collective Constraint, and Motivational Explanation in the Social Thought of Howard S. Becker." *Symbolic Interaction* 17:253–280.

Klandermans, Bert. 1997. *The Social Psychology of Protest.* Cambridge, MA: Blackwell.

Klockars, Carl. 1974. *The Professional Fence.* New York: Free Press.

Kornhauser, Ruth. 1978. *Social Sources of Delinquency.* Chicago: University of Chicago Press.

Laub, John, Daniel Nagin, and Robert Sampson. 1998. "Trajectories of Change in Criminal Offending: Good Marriages and the Desistance Process." *American Sociological Review* 63:225–238.

Lemert, Edwin. 1951. *Social Pathology.* New York: McGraw-Hill.

Levi, Ken. 1989. "Neutralizations in a Very Deviant Career: The Case of Professional Hit-Men." Pp. 447–458 in *Deviant Behavior,* edited by Delos Kelly. New York: St. Martin's Press.

Lofland, John. 1969. *Deviance and Identity.* Englewood Cliffs, NJ: Prentice-Hall.

Luckenbill, David F., and Joel Best. 1981. "Careers in Deviance and Respectability: The Analogy's Limitations." *Social Problems* 29:197–206.

Maher, Lisa, and Kathleen Daly. 1996. "Women in the Street Level Drug Economy: Continuity or Change." *Criminology* 34:465–492.

Maines, David R. 1977. "Social Organization and Social Structure in Symbolic Interactionist Thought." *Annual Review of Sociology* 3:235–259.

———. 1982. "In Search of Mesostructure: Studies in the Negotiated Order." *Urban Life* 11:267–279.

Maines, David R., and Thomas Morrione. 1990. "On the Breadth and Relevance of Blumer's Perspective." Pp. xi–xxiv in *Industrialization as an Agent of Social Change,* by Herbert Blumer. New York: Aldine.

Maines, David R., Jeffrey Bridger, and Jeffrey Ulmer. 1996. "Mythic Facts and Park's Pragmatism: On Predecessor Selection and Theorizing in Human Ecology." *The Sociological Quarterly* 37:521–549.

Makkai, Toni, and John Braithwaite. 1991. "Criminological Theories and Regulatory Compliance." *Criminology* 29:191–220.

Matsueda, Ross. 1982. "Testing Control Theory and Differential Association: A Causal Modeling Approach." *American Sociological Review* 47:489–504.

——. 1988. "The Current State of Differential Association Theory." *Crime and Delinquency* 34:277–306.

——. 1992. "Reflected Appraisals, Parental Labeling, and Delinquency: Specifying a Symbolic Interactionist Theory." *American Journal of Sociology* 97:1577–1611.

Matsueda, Ross, and Karen Heimer. 1997. "Developmental Theories of Crime." Pp. 174–186 in *Advances in Criminological Theory*, edited by Terence Thornberry. New Brunswick, NJ: Transaction.

Matsueda, Ross, and Kathleen Anderson. 1998. "The Dynamics of Delinquent Peers and Delinquent Behavior." *Criminology* 36:269–308.

McAdam, Douglas. 1986. "Recruitment to High-Risk Activism: The Case of Freedom Summer." *American Journal of Sociology* 94:64–90.

——. 1989. "The Biographical Consequences of Activism." *American Sociological Review* 54:744–760.

McCarthy, Bill. 1995. "Not Just 'for the Thrill of It': An Instrumentalist Elaboration of Katz's Explanation of Sneaky Thrill Property Crimes." *Criminology* 33:519–538.

McCarthy, Bill, and John Hagan. 1992. "Mean Streets: The Theoretical Significance of Situational Delinquency among Homeless Youths." *American Journal of Sociology* 98:597–627.

Mead, George Herbert. 1934. *Mind, Self, and Society*. Chicago: University of Chicago Press.

Merton, Robert. 1997. "On the Evolving Synthesis of Differential Association and Anomie Theory: A Perspective from the Sociology of Science." *Criminology* 35:517–525.

Miller, Jody. 1998. "Up It Up: Gender and the Accomplishment of Street Robbery." *Criminology* 36:37–66.

Mills, C. Wright. 1940. "Situated Actions and Vocabularies of Motive." *American Sociological Review* 5:904–913.

Park, Robert. 1926. "The Urban Community as a Spatial and Moral Order." Pp. 3–18 in *The Urban Community*, edited by Ernest Burgess. Chicago: University of Chicago Press.

——. 1938. "Reflections on Communication and Culture." *American Journal of Sociology* 44:187–205.

Quinney, Richard. 1970. *The Social Reality of Crime*. Boston: Little, Brown.

Reckless, Walter. 1973. *The Crime Problem*, 5th ed. Englewood Cliffs, NJ: Prentice-Hall.

Sampson, Robert, and John Laub. 1993. *Crime in the Making: Pathways and Turning Points through Life*. Cambridge, MA: Harvard University Press.

——. 1997. "A Life-Course Theory of Cumulative Disadvantage and the Stability of Delinquency." Pp. 133–161 in *Developmental Theories of Crime and Delinquency*, edited by Terence Thornberry. New Brunswick, NJ: Transaction.

Schur, Edwin. 1969. "Reactions to Deviance: A Critical Assessment." *American Journal of Sociology* 75:309–322.

——. 1980. *The Politics of Deviance: Stigma Contests and the Uses of Power*. Englewood Cliffs, NJ: Prentice-Hall.

Scott, Marvin, and Stanford Lyman. 1968. "Accounts." *American Sociological Review* 33:46–62.

Selznick, Philip. 1969. *TVA and the Grass Roots.* Los Angeles: University of California Press.

Shalin, Dmitri. 1986. "Pragmatism and Social Interactionism." *American Sociological Review* 51:9–27.

Shover, Neal. 1996. *Great Pretenders: Pursuits and Careers of Persistent Thieves.* Boulder, CO: Westview Press.

Stebbins, Robert A. 1971. *Commitment to Deviance.* Westport, CT: Greenwood.

Steffensmeier, Darrell. 1983. "Organization Properties and Sex-Segregation in the Underworld: Building a Sociological Theory of Sex Differences in Crime." *Social Forces* 6:1010–1032.

———. 1986. *The Fence: In the Shadow of Two Worlds.* Totowa, NJ: Rowman and Littlefield.

Steffensmeier, Darrell, and Emilie Allan. 1995. "Gender, Age, and Crime." Pp. 67–94 in *Criminology,* edited by Joseph Sheley. Belmont, CA: Sage.

Strauss, Anselm. 1969. *Mirrors and Masks.* San Francisco: Sociology Press.

———. 1993. *Continual Permutations of Action.* New York: Aldine de Gruyter.

Stryker, Sheldon. 1980. *Symbolic Interaction: A Social Structural Version.* Menlo Park, CA: Benjamin/Cummings.

Sutherland, Edwin. 1947. *Principles of Criminology.* Philadelphia: Lippincott.

Sykes, Gresham, and David Matza. 1957. "Techniques of Neutralization: A Theory of Delinquency." *American Sociological Review* 22:664–670.

Thio, Alex. 1988. *Deviant Behavior.* New York: Harper and Row.

Thornberry, Terence. 1995. *Developmental Theories of Crime and Delinquency.* New Brunswick, NJ: Transaction.

Tittle, Charles. 1989. "Prospects for Synthetic Theory." Pp. 161–178 in *Theoretical Integration in the Study of Deviance and Crime,* edited by Steven Messner, Marvin Krohn, and Allen Liska. Albany, NY: State University of New York Press.

———. 1995. *Control Balance: Toward a General Theory of Deviance.* Boulder, CO: Westview Press.

Ulmer, Jeffery T. 1994. "Revisiting Stebbins: Labeling and Commitment to Deviance." *The Sociological Quarterly* 35:135–157.

Wallerstein, Immanuel. 1997. "Social Science and the Quest for a Just Society." *American Journal of Sociology* 102:1241–1257.

Walsh, Edward, and Rex Warland. 1983. "Social Movement Involvement in the Wake of a Nuclear Accident: Activists and Free Riders in the Three Mile Island Area." *American Sociological Review* 48:764–781.

Warr, Mark. 1993. "Age, Peers, and Delinquency." *Criminology* 31:17–40.

———. 1996. "Organization and Instigation in Delinquent Groups." *Criminology* 34:11–37.

———. 1998. "Life-Course Transitions and Desistance from Crime." *Criminology* 36:183–216.

Warr, Mark, and Mark Stafford. 1991. "The Influence of Delinquent Peers: What They Think or What They Do?" *Criminology* 29:851–866.

Westby, David. 1991. *The Growth of Sociological Theory: Human Nature, Knowledge, and Social Change.* Englewood Cliffs, NJ: Prentice-Hall.

Wolf, Daniel. 1991. *The Rebels: A Brotherhood of Outlaw Bikers.* Toronto: University of Toronto Press.

Zhang, Lening, and Steven Messner. 1995. "Family Deviance and Delinquency in China." *Criminology* 33:359–388.

20 ▶ Juvenile Delinquency Under Conditions of Rapid Social Change

Klaus Boehnke
Dagmar Bergs-Winkels

▶Introduction

The last decade has seen vast political and economic changes in many parts of the world. Starting with the fall of the Berlin Wall, Europe has undergone transformation processes unprecedented at least in the second half of the twentieth century (Crockett and Silbereisen, 2000). Following the collapse of the "Soviet Empire," Eastern Europe experienced the total breakdown of its state planned economic system. A new political order was established "overnight." Europe had to adapt to the new situation with little warning. With the change to a market-oriented economy, Eastern European countries encountered significant reductions in real gross national product (Encyclopaedia Britannica, 1993). Several countries broke apart (Soviet Union, Czechoslovakia) or were united (Germany). The pace of modernization rapidly accelerated, resulting in intensified feelings of public insecurity. This situation often seems to be overlooked in North America, as that continent is probably the only one that does not experience social change at the pace at which other parts of the world currently undergo it.

The unanticipated accompaniments of the enumerated abrupt changes included surging crime and delinquency rates. The upturn in crime and delinquency is often assumed to have been caused by the political and economic transformations. Empirical evidence that supports this causal hypothesis is, however, scarce. The assumption that political and economic transformations are responsible for changes in crime and delinquency rates is a difficult causal process to test, a problem often discussed in earlier work (e.g., Campbell and Converse, 1972; Krohn and Wellford, 1977). First, we must define what "rapid social change" is. Second, we have to specify the unanticipated social problems, such as crime and delinquency, to consider. Third, we have to answer the questions *why* rapid social change might cause unanticipated social problems such as youth crime and *how* this process materializes.

Furthermore, the assumption that "change causes problems" does not differentiate between societies and individuals. Is it that societies experiencing a measurably accelerated pace of social change are the societies that have to cope with an increased amount of unanticipated disruptive behaviors? Or is it that individuals who have to cope with rapid social change engage in socially disruptive behavior to an increased extent? And, if the latter is the case, is it so in any society or only in certain societies?

No natural congruence exists between society-level explanations and individual-level explanations—in spite of the fact that common sense understandings seem to imply this. Keeping the danger of an ecological fallacy in mind, research aiming to increase the understanding of interrelations of rapid social change and juvenile delinquency, the youth problem we address, must incorporate different levels of analysis. This paper jointly undertakes societal, individual, and cross-cultural comparisons in analyzing the association between social change and juvenile delinquency.

Broad Explanations of Juvenile Delinquency

Two broad approaches to the explanation of crime and delinquency focus on subcultural and subterranean processes in society. The first approach dates to the work of Sellin (1938) and assumes the existence of oppositional groups in society. Generational conflicts between adults and adolescents can be looked at in this way (Eisenstadt, 1956; Mead, 1970), with status offenses called juvenile delinquency, such as underage smoking, drinking, and driving, being regarded as youthful claims to adult symbols. Sometimes the symbolic provocations can become more broadly offensive and dangerous. Wearing Nazi symbols, for example, and/or carving the swastika into a school bench, can be seen as such symbolic behavior, behavior that youth engage in to antagonize others, knowing that such behavior is unacceptable to adults and the broader cultural mainstream of society.

The second general approach can be traced to the work of Sutherland (1949). This approach presumes that adolescents act out subterranean values or impulses that are an accepted part of a culture, but nonetheless tend to be obscured and to a greater or lesser extent controlled in the mainstream of society. Such theories tend to see violence, in-group favoritism, deceiving customers and competitors, and the like, as typical activities in Western market-oriented culture (see Matza, 1964). In a well-functioning society subterranean forces are counterbalanced by principles of justice, loyalty, conformity, and the like. In less stable settings, however, there is a danger that the *subterranean traditions* of a culture can gain influence and even supremacy (Matza and Sykes, 1961). An example of the surfacing of subterranean forces involves the spraying of Nazi graffiti. This behavior can be seen as the acting out of a subterranean tradition of ethnocentrism that exists in most cultures. Average adults in a society might rarely do it, because constraints that bar the acting out of such ethnocentric subterranean traditions are much stronger for them than they are for adolescents.

Rapid Social Change and Juvenile Delinquency

The common sense notion that rapid social change increases juvenile delinquency encompasses a mixture of assumptions drawn from the above approaches. On the one hand, youth are often seen as distinctly different from, and opposed to, the main adult culture. At the same time, reduced social control is frequently seen as the cause of both problems, especially in the media. Both of these assumptions are plausible.

One motivation for adolescent oppositional behavior in times of rapid social change may involve feelings of injustice. Youth who feel that the forces of change are overwhelming them may have strong feelings of injustice that lead them to engage in hostile counterculture acts of delinquency. Meanwhile, the subterranean tradition suggests that rapid social change—leading to weakened social control—gives more leeway to the acting out of subterranean values. Research within the counterculture approach would therefore focus on the extent to which youth feel unjustly treated in a given society at a given time in history, while research within the subterranean approach would more likely focus on whether parents actually exercise reduced control in times of rapid social change. In principle, the influence of rapid social change on juvenile delinquency can be envisaged within the subterranean tradition as well as in the counterculture approach.

We have already mentioned that—although both conceptual approaches are North American in their origin—empirical North American research into effects of social change on juvenile delinquency is scarce. Two multiedition monographs on *Juvenile Delinquency* (Kratcoski and Kratcoski, 1990; Trojanowicz and Morash, 1992) do not address the topic at all. A fairly recent edited volume in the field, *The Sociology of Juvenile Delinquency* (Berger, 1991), also deals with the question only tangentially. Even the topic of more general effects of social change is not really a hot topic of sociology in North America. The above cited monograph, *The Human Meaning of Social Change* by Campbell and Converse (1972), is a fairly rare instance where the topic is touched. This may have its reasons in the fact that there has been little sociopolitical and structural change in the United States in the second half of the twentieth century. It is, thus, no surprise that the most prominent exceptions from the rule—social change being of little interest to North American sociology—stem from or deal with events from the first half of the twentieth century. They deal with effects of migration, in *The Polish Peasant in Europe and America* (Thomas and Znaniecki, 1918), or with effects of the great depression, in *Children of the Great Depression* (Clausen, 1995; Elder, 1974).

Glen Elder's work can be seen as paradigmatic for North American studies on effects of political and macroeconomic changes on individual behavior. He favors a family stress model of deviant behavior among adolescents. He shows that social change in the form of unprecedented economic hardship puts the family under stress, undermines the quality of parental relations, makes parents less nurturant in the education of and communication with their children who then react by increased deviance. More recently Elder and Conger (2000; Conger and Elder, 1994) have analyzed effects of the Iowa farm crisis in the 1980s and have found additional evidence for their supposition. We will later incorporate the conceptual thinking of Elder and Conger into the interpretation of our results.

Before we go into a more detailed formulation of our conceptual model we have to define, however, what we mean by rapid social change. More so than Elder and Conger, we treat social change as a macro*structural* phenomenon. It can be described in terms of rapid changes in the political and legal system of a society, as occurred during the change from a one-party rule to a multiparty system in Eastern Europe. Rapid social change can also be described in macro*economic* terms, as was the case in Eastern Europe, with an abrupt, often problematic shift from a planned to a market economy. In this study we put less emphasis on changes of the more immediate context (like family income changes, individual unemployment, etc.) than have been focused on in much work inspired by Elder's thinking (Trommsdorff, 2000).

In summary, two hypotheses—rooted in the two contrasting theoretical paradigms portrayed above—have been advanced to explain why rapid social change can cause increased juvenile delinquency. The first hypothesis is that such change leads to feelings of injustice among youth and that this in turn produces delinquency. The second hypothesis is that the stress of rapid social change induces decreased parental control and/or undermines the delinquency-reducing effects of parental control and nurturance, a situation favoring increased adolescent delinquency and maladjustment. The latter supposition can easily be incorporated into Conger and Elder's family stress model (Conger *et al.*, 2000).

Justice, Parental Educational Orientations, and Adolescent Lifestyles

Juvenile delinquency can take many forms, including vandalism, political deviance, substance use, etc. Here we concentrate on deviant behavior among young people in school (see Stinchcombe, 1964). It is important to suggest why rapid social change might influence these forms of delinquency. These behaviors may be reactions to rapid changes in schooling.

In Eastern Europe, schools were central institutions of ideological education. Before the political turn-about, teachers were important transmitters of the ideologically cherished values. The revolutionary changes not only invalidated values that had been advocated just weeks before, but teachers in particular were in danger of losing their credibility more or less overnight. Delinquency was a predictable result. As subcultural theory suggests, there were more targets to oppose, and as the subterranean approach anticipates, the level of control declined.

More can be said about the youthful context of these behaviors. Adolescents usually do not act alone but in groups (Coleman, 1961). Just sensing reduced control in a social institution and increased opportunities to oppose adults is not enough to transform ordinary adolescents into delinquents. What is needed in addition is a juvenile lifestyle that rewards delinquency. Borrowing from Matza (1964), Hagan (1991) calls this lifestyle "delinquent drift." Delinquent drift is a lifestyle that involves a compelling openness to legal and illegal forms of excitement. These activities are further encouraged by the context of the group. Following Hagan (1991,1994) we assume that rapid social change increases youth's tendencies to engage in prodelinquent peer activities that serve as subcultural environments that reward deviance taking—in our case—the form of deviant school behavior.

▲ Theory of Rapid Social Change as a Precursor of Deviant School Behavior

We can summarize our expectations graphically (see Fig. 1). We assume that neither rapid social change per se nor a reduced sense of justice and decreased parental control/nurturance as such make deviant school behavior more probable. Rather, a reduced sense of justice and decreased parental control and nurturance enhance adolescent tendencies to engage in prodelinquent peer activities, that is, in delinquent drift. Delinquent drift is then seen as the precursor of deviant school behavior.

Figure 1   The interrelation of rapid social change and deviant school behavior: A conceptual model.

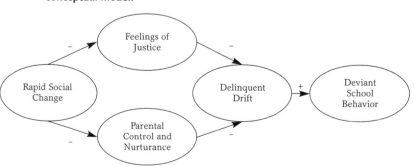

Methodologial Considerations

Indicators of Rapid Social Change

As noted above, we assume that rapid social change can be described in objective macrosociological terms. We see it as a time-bound economic and politicoideological process. Periods of rapid social change are characterized by economic "disturbances" and politicoideological "unrest." They are processes and *not* just single events (e.g., the fall of the Berlin Wall). The events are simply visible markers of an increasing rapidness of change. On the other hand, rapid change cannot last forever. No society can survive a prolonged state of rapid change. Social constructionist discourse (see Gergen and Gergen, 1981) notwithstanding, a measure of rapid social change requires at least three components, namely an economic indicator, a politicoideological indicator, and time.

Time is of special importance. Societal change does not necessarily become immediately relevant for individuals. People can cope with feelings of insecurity for a certain amount of time. "Pathological" consequences of societal irregularities become evident only after a sufficient "incubation time." Similarly, macroeconomic variation is unlikely to lead to immediate reactions among individuals, but instead influences personal lives after a sufficient time lag.

The present study draws on data collected in East and West Germany, Poland, Russia, Bulgaria, Slovakia, Hungary, Czechia, and Greece. We studied 42 independent samples of seventh graders in these countries in the years 1992–95. One indicator of social change is the politicoideological status of the respective country. Has the *politicoideological system* changed: Greece and West Germany have not, while the others have. The implicit assumption here is that youth living under changing conditions will experience more acute feelings of public injustice and a substantial reduction in parental control and nurturance.

A second politicoideological indicator is whether a state has changed its *legal borders* since 1989 or not: East and West Germany, Russia, Slovakia, and Czechia have, the others have not. Again the implicit assumption is that the conditions of change pose greater threats to subjective feelings of justice and to parental control/nurturance.

The "time" indicator is simply the *number of years* that have passed since 1989. Studies from Germany show that the change process itself varies in its characteristics from year to year (Merkens, 1996), so "historic" time in itself is an important change indicator. Here, the conceptual rationale is that the longer an "insecure" situation lasts, the more it will generate "pathological" consequences, such as reduced feelings of justice and lower parental nurturance.

The economic indicator we use is the annual *change in per capita gross national product* in the period from 3 years before to 2 years before the survey.

This means that we measure the lagged impact of economic changes in a way that makes the historic year 1989 (3 years before our first surveys) the point of reference. We assume that seventh graders will not be affected by macroeconomic changes at the very time these changes commence. There will especially be a time lag in effects of macroeconomic changes on younger adolescents. As Walper and Gerhard (1999) show, macroeconomic changes do influence parental nurturance; however, the process is prolonged, and takes considerable time.

Levels of Analysis

Explanatory models like the one presented in Fig. 1 can serve two purposes in sociology. They can either make assumptions about societies per se or about individuals as parts of societies. In reference to societies per se, our model proposes that rapid change will result in lower *average* parental control and nurturance and higher average feelings of public injustice among adolescents, leading to higher average levels of delinquent drift, resulting in higher general levels of deviant school behavior. In reference to individuals as parts of societies, our model proposes that adolescents who experience less parental control and nurturance and an increased feeling of being treated unjustly in public—due to rapid social change—engage in more prodelinquent peer activities, which in turn foster deviant school behavior. In the latter case additional attention has to be given to whether the process assumed in the model is valid in *all* countries included in the study, or only under particular societal circumstances. Conceptually our model claims validity on the societal level *and* on the individual level, while the validity of the model in every country included in our study is open to empirical examinations.

Leung and Bond (1989) suggest a unified analytic strategy to testing models at the societal and individual levels. They insist that a relationship valid on the societal as well as on the individual level must emerge (a) in the structural relations of societal *means* of indicators, (b) in the structural relations of individual measures across all countries, and (c) in individual data from each society included in the study. For example, assume we are interested in testing the assumption that punitive parenting increases adolescent aggressiveness. To corroborate the validity of this assumption on the societal level, we have to show that countries with higher average punitiveness among parents are the countries in which a higher average aggressiveness of youth is found. Second, we have to show that—regardless of societal context—individual adolescents who are more aggressive tend to have experienced substantially more punitive parenting. Third, we have to show that independent of the country-specific level of punitiveness or of aggressiveness, the relation of high aggressiveness with high parental punitiveness can be found in all societies included in a study.

We will take these three steps in testing our model of precursors of juvenile delinquency under conditions of rapid social change with the use of a structural equations approach. LISREL analyses based on aggregate data are conducted first. Here, means of the 42 samples are the unit of analysis. Second, measures of the 7282 individuals are the unit of analysis. Third, the grand sample of individuals is subdivided into the eight national subsamples, and the model is probed in a simultaneous multisample analysis of individual measures. Before reporting the results of our analyses, we first describe the samples for our study and the measurement instruments applied.

Samples

The data originate from an international youth study of societal transformation processes in Eastern Europe. The study was conducted between 1990 and 1998. In order to capture the ongoing transformation process, surveying had to start as early after 1989 as possible. To facilitate this, the study built on existing cross-national research infrastructure of the former Academy of Pedagogical Sciences of the German Democratic Republic and of the Free University of [West] Berlin. The time-pressures implied by the research goal required some compromises in systematic sampling strategies and instrumentation.

Samples chosen for the present study incorporate data from 7282 seventh graders. We include data from annual surveys in the years 1992-95. The number of students studied in 42 samples from eight different countries are shown in Table 1.[1] Overall, we have 1936 students from "Western" samples (West Germany and Greece) and 5346 students from "Eastern" samples (all other Central and Eastern European countries). Data collection took place in schools. National subsamples were convenience samples of school classes. The cooperating scientists chose sampling points on the basis of accessibility. There were, however, general rules for sample selection. Whenever seventh graders could go to different types of schools in a country, all major school types were to be included. Schools from a variety of socioeconomic backgrounds were to be sampled. Samples may not be entirely representative of the respective countries, but they likely reflect the youth in the urban centers of the societies included well.

Instruments

The selection of items for the analyses reported in the present paper was a multistage process. There are numerous reasons why in cross-national studies—even more so if they incorporate 42 samples from eight countries—instruments are and cannot ever be fully identical across location and time. This paper is not the place to discuss such problems in-depth: However, taking these problems into consideration, we decided to include only items in

Table 1 Sample Characteristics

City/country	1992	1993	1994	1995
Ioannina (Greece)	201	162	161	
Moscow (Russia)	152	150	109	
East Berlin (East Germany)	174	299	286	259
West Berlin (West Germany)	187	231	210	243
Prague (Czechia)	126	128	136	137
Frankfurt/Oder (East Germany)	210	218	221	211
Slubice (Poland)	162	155	121	164
Warsaw (Poland)	197	146	119	194
Bratislava (Slovakia)		151	173	207
Sofia (Bulgaria)		164	155	79
Budapest (Hungary)		116	64	
Korfu (Greece)		157	132	
Chemnitz(East Germany)				163
Siegen (West Germany)				252
Annual subsamples (*n*)	1409	2077	1887	1909

our analyses that were used in all countries. Furthermore, only those items were incorporated into our scales that showed item-total correlations of a minimum of $r_{it} > 0.10$ in their pertinent a-priori-specified scales in the aggregate data, and in the separate samples of individuals in each of the eight countries. The 0.10 threshold value was proposed for cross-cultural studies by Scott *et al.* (1991). At the aggregate data level this resulted in our using 42 sample means of items as data. Items that did not meet the 0.10 criterion were excluded from further analyses. The same type of analysis was performed for individual data within each culture. Again items that did not satisfy the 0.10 criterion for item-total correlations were rejected. If nonequivalent results emerged from analyses on the two data aggregation levels, analyses were repeated. This time items that only had to be rejected on the grounds of analyses conducted for one level of data were also excluded in the analyses for the other level of data aggregation.

As noted above, one-item indicators were used to measure rapid social change. To capture economic change we tabulated per capita gross national products in U.S. dollars for (a) the third year before the year of measurement (*x* – 3) and (b) the second year before the year of measurement (*x* – 2) from the respective *Books of the Year of Encyclopaedia Britannica* (1990–94). The score of (b) – (a) then went into our analyses as a predictor variable that captures *change in per capita gross national product.* Changes in the political situation were indicated in a binary form (no change in politicoideological system = 0, change in politicoideological system since 1989 = 1). Second, we formed an indicator that bore the information whether a country had changed its legal borders since 1989, where 0 stood for no change and 1 stood for change. Furthermore the *year of measurement* was incorporated into our analyses as a variable.[2]

To measure the subjective feeling of justice in public we used an item that originates from earlier work of the Akademie der Pädagogischen Wissenschaften der DDR (1989). The item read "Do you think you are treated with fairness in public?" Answering options ranged from 0 (no, never) to 3 (yes, always).

Parental control and nurturance was measured with a two-step procedure. The so-called parental bonding instrument developed by Parker *et al.* (1979) was drawn from the questionnaire responses. This scale involves four subscales each on paternal and maternal nurturance, permissiveness, punitiveness, and restrictive (over-)protection. Items like the following are included: "My mother/father could make me feel better when I was upset" (nurturance), ". . . let me decide things for myself" (permissiveness), ". . . often hit me" (punitiveness), and ". . . did not want me to grow up" (restrictive protection). Responses were on a scale ranging from 0 (completely false) to 3 (completely true). In analyses of comparable adolescent data from seven countries, Boehnke (1996) has shown that these eight scales form a bipolar dimension. Nurturance and permissiveness of both mother and father load positively on this dimension, whereas punitiveness and restrictive protection load negatively. In line with those findings we used the eight scale scores as eight quasi-items for a second-order scale. The punitiveness and restrictive protection scores were reversed for reliability analyses and scale score calculations, so that high scores on the second-order scale stand for something that Boehnke (1996) calls *"caring lenience,"* a nurturant form of parental control and discipline techniques.

The mediator variable, *delinquent drift,* initially was measured by several items in the 42 samples, but since no cross-nationally valid scale could be established, we decided to use only one item that had the highest face-validity vis-à-vis the theoretical considerations of Hagan (1991): "If you meet other youth in your spare time, do you hang around looking for action and trouble?" This item was answered on a rating scale ranging from 0 (never) to 3 (very often).

Our dependent variable, *deviant school behavior,* was measured using seven items asking about harassing teachers, damaging things, beating up weaker persons, spreading stories about classmates, fighting with others, challenging other people, and insulting teachers. The items were answered on a rating scale ranging from 0 = "never" to 3 = "often."

Consistencies of the scales on caring lenience and deviant school behavior were checked for all levels of analysis. For the caring lenience scale alphas varied between 0.81 (individual data from Bulgaria) and 0.46 (individual data from Slovakia) with a median alpha of 0.65.[3]

For the scale on deviant school behavior alphas varied between 0.94 (aggregate data) and 0.80 (individual data from Germany) with a median alpha of 0.87, reflecting the high reliability of this scale.

An inspection of the means of "feelings of justice," "caring lenience," "delinquent drift," and "deviant school behavior" showed that for feelings of justice and parental caring lenience empirical means were above the scales' middle scores (1.5).Variation within cultures was quite low for both indicators, ranging from 0.31 to 0.79 for a 4-point scale. Considerable mean differences were found for delinquent drift. Means ranged from 0.89 (Czechia) to 2.14 (Greece) on a scale ranging from 0 to 3. This variable at the same time was somewhat skewed and hyperkurtotic in several samples. For deviant school behavior means ranged from 0.75 (Bulgaria) to 1.40 (Greece). Skewness and kurtosis were within acceptable bounds in all sub-samples.

For changes in GNP, data are not in themselves very informative. Across time a U-shaped distribution emerged with a slight average increase in the beginning, declines (sometimes sharp) for measurement points 2 and 3, and an average increase at measurement point 4. Greece was the only country that showed increases in all 4 years of measurement, while Russia showed the highest average decrease of per capita GNP over the years (–$2177).

Results

Our data analyses were conducted in several steps. First, the theoretical model (Fig. 1), was tested for the societal level, using the 42 sample means of all included variables. Then the theoretical model was tested at the individual level both in the grand sample and in the eight country subsamples, using individual measures. LISREL 8.14 (Jöreskog and Sörbom, 1993) was used to conduct these analyses.[4] In a subsequent step the theoretical model was empirically modified in society-level and individual-level analyses.

Before reporting the results of the various LISREL analyses, we first discuss our general approach. One of the great advantages of structural equation modeling (SEM) over ordinary multiple regression analysis is that SEM can incorporate models of measurement error using multiple indicators of latent variables. However, this is not possible when, as in our aggregate analyses, the sample size is as small as 42: The number of free parameters to be estimated by LISREL would become larger than the number of sample means included in the analyses. In individual-level analyses and in analyses of individual data within countries the inclusion of measurement models into structural equations would certainly have been possible; but in order to keep analyses on the different aggregation levels equivalent, we decided to conduct all analyses as classic path analyses with scale scores, using LISREL to estimate the models. Measurement equivalence of deviant school behavior and of parental caring lenience across countries was, however, tested in additional multisample confirmatory factor analyses. These analyses showed strong measurement equivalence across countries for de-

viant school behavior as a one-factor construct. For parental caring lenience the same was true, once correlated errors were allowed for the same
parental styles of mothers and fathers, i.e., of mothers' and fathers' nurturance, permissiveness, punitiveness, and restrictiveness.

Our first analytic step was a test of our conceptual model. Results are
presented in Fig. 2. The figure reports significant path coefficients[5] of a
minimum size of 0.10 for the analysis of the aggregate data (left coefficient)
and the grand sample of individuals (right coefficient). Country-specific
coefficients are omitted here. The four indicators of social change were
specified to be correlated.

It is obvious from Fig. 2 that the conceptual model shows empirical validity only for the aggregate level of data analysis—at best. The low overall
fit between theoretical model and empirical data becomes even more evident if one takes a closer look at the goodness-of-fit indices for the three
analyses undertaken. For the aggregate data, indices are $\chi^2 = 25.541$, $p =
0.007$, df $= 11$, GFI $= 0.885$, RMSEA $= 0.189$. For the individual grand
sample analysis, indices are $\chi^2 = 693.324$, $p < 0.001$, df $= 11$, GFI $= 0.977$,
RMSEA $= 0.092$. For the multisample within-country analysis, indices are
$\chi^2 = 606.758$, $p = 0.001$, df $= 84$, GFI $= 0.964$, RMSEA $= 0.082$. These indices do not require outright rejection of our conceptual model, but they
call for substantial model modification.

In our second analytic step, we introduced the model modifications encouraged by our initial results. On all data levels, paths were successively
set free for which a significant improvement of the fit was suggested by
LISREL. Also, in this course of analysis, paths were fixed that no longer

Figure 2 The interrelation of rapid social change and deviant school behavior empirical
test of the conceptual model.

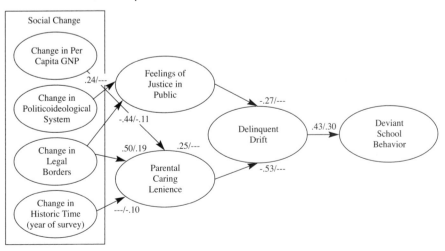

achieved significance after a new path had been set free.[6] Eventually the model documented in Fig. 3 emerged. The figure reports significant paths[7] above 0.10 for society-level and grand sample individual-level data. Table II gives an account of significant within-country paths from the multisample analysis. Fit coefficients for the modified models were $\chi^2 = 0.614$, $p = 0.736$, df = 2, GFI = 0.996. RMSEA = 0.000 (for the aggregate data). $\chi^2 = 0.761$, $p = 0.684$, df = 2, GFI = 1.000, RMSEA = 0.000 (for the individual grand sample), and $\chi^2 = 54.627$, $p = 0.002$, df = 28, GFI = 1.000, RMSEA = 0.034 (for the multisample within-country analysis).

The figure of the empirically modified model(s) shows a very important difference between societal-level and individual-level findings. On the individual level, delinquent drift was the best predictor of deviant school behavior in all countries, as anticipated in the conceptual model. On the societal level no relationship between these two variables was found. Individual adolescents who engaged in prodelinquent activities with their peers were quite likely to also engage in deviant school behavior. The country-specific betacoefficients varied between 0.15 and 0.37, the individual grand sample beta was at 0.28. An individual adolescent's delinquent drift, however, *could not* usually be predicted by the climate this adolescent experienced in his or her family and in the general public. The path from parental nurturance was significant in the German sample only, whereas the path from feelings of justice was significant only in the Polish sample.

The single valid predictor of the extent to which an individual adolescent lived a prodelinquent lifestyle is his/her country of residence. The difference in delinquent drift between countries that have not experienced a

Figure 3   The interrelation of rapid social change and deviant school behavior empirically modified model.

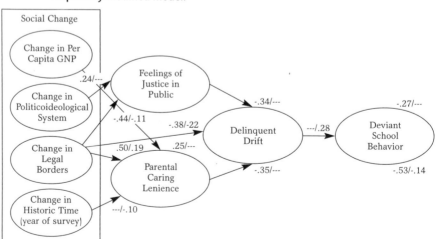

Table II   Significant Paths in Individual Level Analyses per Country

Path from	To	Greece	Russia	Germany	Poland	Czechia	Slovakia	Bulgaria	Hungary
Year of measurement	Feelings of justice	-0.18							
Year of measurement	Parental control and nurturance		-0.14	-0.10				-0.24	
Year of measurement	Delinquent drift		0.29						
Year of measurement	Delinquent school behavior	0.14							
Feelings of justice	Parental control and nurturance[a]	0.10							
Feelings of justice	Delinquent drift				-0.14				
Feelings of justice	Delinquent school behavior				-0.08				
Parental control and nurturance	Delinquent drift			-0.16					
Parental control and nurturance	Delinquent school behavior			-0.11	-0.11	-0.16	-0.20		
Delinquent drift	Delinquent school behavior	0.15	0.33	0.37	0.23	0.23	0.16	0.16	0.17

[a]In the Greek sample this relationship was specified as a correlation, not as a path.

border change since 1989 (Poland, Bulgaria, Hungary, Greece) and those that have (Germany, Czechia, Slovakia, Russia) was significant ($\gamma = -0.22$). In our conceptualization of social change this means that delinquent drift was higher in countries that experienced *less* change. A nurturant style of parental control did not serve as a protection factor against individual adolescents' prodelinquent leisure style. Neither did the individual adolescent's feeling of being treated justly in public. How nurturant parents were perceived and how just adolescents felt treated in public also depended to a considerable extent on the culture they lived in. Parental caring lenience was *higher* in cultures that experienced a border change ($\gamma = 0.19$), i.e., it was higher in countries that experienced *more* social change. Justice vis-à-vis youth, on the other hand, was lower in these countries ($\gamma = -0.11$). Finally, historic time also played a role: Parental caring lenience tended to be lower in the later years of our study ($\gamma = -0.10$, within countries paths were significant in Russia, Germany, and Bulgaria).

In spite of the fact that parental caring lenience did not prove to be a protective factor against delinquent drift in the individual-level analyses, it nevertheless had some reducing influence on the degree to which an individual adolescent engaged in deviant school behavior: In the individual grand sample and in four of the eight countries, adolescents whose parents were reported as caringly lenient also reported less involvement in deviant behavior at school.

One unexpected finding is that there was a negative relation between GNP change and feelings of justice among adolescents. If there was a *positive* change in per capita GNP in the years before the survey, feelings of justice were lower than in samples where a negative change occurred.

The negative path from caring lenience to deviant school behavior was the only link between individual-level and societal-level analyses. Samples that reported a higher average degree of parental caring lenience were also the samples that reported lower average amounts of deviant school behavior. All other paths among endogenous variables emerged differently on the societal and individual levels in our test of a model for predicting deviant school behavior in times of rapid social change. In the aggregate data, a high adolescent feeling of justice in public and a pronounced caringly lenient parental style did indeed covary negatively with delinquent drift. This means that samples reporting more parental caring lenience and more perceived public justice among adolescents were the samples that also reported less delinquent drift. Perceived public justice and—as noted above—parental caring lenience were also higher in samples that reported lower average involvement in deviant school behavior.

The sharpest difference between aggregate- and individual-level analyses pertained to the relationship of delinquent drift and deviant school behavior. In the aggregate data it was by no means the case that deviance in school behavior was higher in samples that reported higher delinquent drift. The significant path from delinquent drift mean scores to deviant school behavior mean scores that had emerged in the strict model test (Fig. 2) was almost entirely a result of the covariation of *both* deviant behavior means and delinquent drift means with average parental caring lenience and average feelings of public justice. This was not considered in our conceptual model.

Effects of social change indicators in the aggregate data analyses were similar to those in the individual-level analyses. Feelings of justice in public were high in samples from countries that experienced a change in the politicoideological system ($\gamma = 0.24$), but not a border change (i.e., Poland, Bulgaria). Average parental caring lenience was higher in countries that experienced a border change ($\gamma = 0.50$, especially Germany), whereas delinquent drift was lower in these countries ($\gamma = -0.22$). Changes in per capita GNP was related to parental caring lenience on the aggregate level of data: Samples that experienced a downward change had lower average caring lenience means ($\gamma = 0.25$).

Discussion

The discussion will first summarize the most important findings, juxtaposing societal-level and individual-level results. Implications of our findings for further research will then be considered.

It goes without saying that all our data are correlational. Significant path coefficients between indicators of social change and so-called endogenous variables do not in itself mean that social change *causes* differences in adolescents' feelings of public justice, the style of control and nurturance their parents exercise, and/or the degree to which youngsters engage in prodelinquent peer activities. However, the amount of variance of deviant school behavior explained by social change variables is worth highlighting. It amounts to 20.0% (total, i.e., direct and indirect effects) for the aggregate data, and to 1.9% for the individual data (grand sample). In contrast to this, the endogenous variables (feeling of justice in public, parental caring lenience, and delinquent drift) explain 26.1% and 10.0% of the variance, respectively for the aggregate and the individual data. This finding shows that—to a noteworthy degree—deviant school behavior is a cultural phenomenon. Even in the large multiculture sample of individuals, one sixth of the explainable variance of this form of adolescent maladjustment is accounted for by the cultural context in which the adolescent lives. In the aggregate data this proportion goes up to almost 45%. Obviously, a culture does not per se *suffer* from frequent incidents of deviant school behavior, *because* adolescents tend to engage in prodelinquent peer activities, but deviance in the school increases in a societal climate that intensifies adolescents' feelings of being treated unjustly, that approves of punitive and restrictive parenting, and that does not thwart prodelinquent peer activities.

The role that rapid social change plays in the genesis of delinquency remains somewhat unclear, but a direct influence can be ruled out. Only one of all possible direct paths from a social change indicator to deviant school behavior emerged as significant, namely the path from year of measurement in Greece ($p = 0.10$). In all other cases the relationship was indirect, as hypothesized in our model.

Contrary to our assumptions, however, social change—as conceptualized in our study—did not always function in the way of a stressor. The "more" or "more negative" change condition sometimes covaried with more justice, more parental caring, and/or less delinquent drift. We refrain from interpreting single results here, but emphasize that more in-depth analyses of the meaning of social change are necessary (see Shanahan and Hood, 2000). Rapid social change is not per se a risk factor, but can also offer chances for improved adolescent adjustment.

From a preventative point of view, mode of parenting seems to be very important for curbing school-related delinquency. More or less irrespective of culture a nurturant, autonomy-oriented style of parental control is a safeguard against deviant school behavior, not an overcontrolling, punitive, restrictive parental style. The question though, *how* parental caring lenience keeps school vandalism and related behavior low, cannot fully be answered in the present study. In contrast with our conceptual model, the caring lenience experience by an individual adolescent does *not* keep delinquent drift low across the cultures included in this study. Neither do high levels of delinquent drift in a society predict high amounts of deviance in school. Both on the aggregate level and on the individual level the diminishing impact of caring lenience on deviant school behavior is more direct than indirect. One might see this as evidence for the classical frustration-aggression hypothesis (Dollard *et al.*, 1939). Adolescents who experience a caringly lenient parental style are presumably the ones who suffer less frustration and therefore engage in less aggressive behavior, but such an interpretation is largely speculation for the time being. On the other hand, the fact that direct effects from parental caring lenience on deviant school behavior were found on the individual level, but not mediated effects through delinquent drift, may also suggest that the appropriate mediators remained unmeasured. It may, however, also mean that parental caring lenience is indeed a direct predictor of (low) adolescent deviance. This interpretation would be plausible within the family stress model referenced above (Conger *et al.*, 2000). In this case low parental caring lenience would be a consequence of a disturbed intrafamilial communication, which is seen by Elder and Conger (2000) or by Clausen (1995) as the gateway through which social change finds its way into the lives of children and adolescents. Our finding that social change influences parenting style, which in turn has a direct influence on adolescent maladjustment, indeed replicates findings from Conger and Elder's Iowa farm study. There, Simons *et al.* (1994) were able to show that economic hardship actually predicted harsh parenting, the opposite of caring lenience, to a significant degree. Eight percent of fathers' harsh parenting was directly predictable on the grounds of economic hardship (2.5% for mothers). Analyzing data from the same study, Conger *et al.* (2000: 210) were able to show that almost 25% of the variation of adolescent adjustment was explainable on the grounds of "Nurturant/Involved Parenting."

The cultural climate vis-à-vis juvenile delinquent drift also is a very important factor in curbing deviance in schools: On the individual level "country" (in our case whether a country experienced a border change since 1989) is the only valid predictor of an adolescent's tendency to engage in prodelinquent peer activities. In further research it is necessary to look for additional individual-level predictors of delinquent drift. In earlier work, the first author (Boehnke *et al.*, 1998a,b) has shown the impact of two other possible precursors of a prodelinquent leisure style, namely a lack of self-esteem due to school failure and a pronounced feeling of anomia (cf. Claßen 1997). Further research is also needed with regard to the country or culture effect. *What* in its cultural climate makes a country prone to high levels of adolescent delinquent drift? To answer this question, society level analyses are necessary that have delinquent drift as a dependent variable and as many descriptors of a culture as possible as predictors. Such data can originate from archives as well as from expert interviews. Our study shows how important it is to disentangle society-level and individual-level evidence while at the same time it links well to change studies in the realm of Elder's work on "Families in Troubled Times" (Conger and Elder, 1994).

Acknowledgments

The study reported in this paper was partially funded through grants of the German Research Council (DFG) to the first author (Bo 929/3-1.2.3,4,5) and by the Free University of Berlin. The authors are thankful to Prof. John Hagan, currently fellow of the Russell Sage Foundation in New York, for his invaluable editorial help with the paper and to the anonymous reviewers of an earlier version for their most challenging and constructive comments. E. Adamska, P. Butz, G. Claßen, J. Dvoracek, J. Gesicki, A. E. Gotovos, R. Gurova, E. Hajduk, G. Hefler, S. Köntös, E. Narkiewicz-Niedbalec, Z. Obdrzalek, R. Orzelek-Bujak, M. Panasenko, I. Steiner, A. Stompe, R. Taulova, G. Wenzke, and A. Wessel cooperated in the organization of the study. Hans Merkens, Freie Universität Berlin, is principal investigator of the study. We thank all these colleagues for their work investment. Without them this study would never have taken place.

Notes

1. The order of the samples has "historic" reasons: Sample numbers were distributed on a "first-come-first-serve" basis.

2. The selection of these indicators meant that on the individual level of data analysis, all adolescents from one country surveyed in the same year, had identical scores with no interindividual variation.

3. Consistencies of the eight scales from the parental bonding instrument never were below 0.75, so the somewhat lower consistencies incurred here reflect a slight inhomogeneity of the construct "caring lenience," not imprecise measurement of parenting style.

4. All analyses were conducted with the maximum likelihood estimator. Unweighted least square analyses were conducted additionally as a safeguard against possible effects of nonnormal skewness and kurtosis of the delinquent drift variable, but results did not differ.

5. $p \leq 0.05$ for aggregate data ($N = 42$), $p \leq 0.001$ for the individual grand sample.

6. In the separate analyses by country two of the four social change indicators had to be omitted: Indicators of change in the politico-ideological system and the legal borders are, of course, constants. The German sample is an exception here, because for East Germans both the politico-ideological system and borders changed, whereas for West German participants only the legal borders changed. For reason of comparability, both indicators were, however, left aside in Germany as they had to in the other countries.

7. Same probability levels as before.

References

Akademie der Pädagogischen Wissenschaften der DDR. 1989. "Berufslaufbahnen, Lebenspläne und Wertorientierungen [Vocational and professional careers, life plans, and value orientations]." Research Report of the Department of Educational Sociology.

Berger, Ronald J. (ed.) 1991. The Sociology of Juvenile Delinquency. Chicago: Nelson-Hall.

Boehnke, Klaus. 1996. Is Intelligence Negligible? The Relationship of Family Climate and School Behavior in a Cross-Cultural Perspective. Münster: Waxmann.

Boehnke, Klaus, John Hagan, and Hans Merkens. 1998a. "Right-wing extremism among German adolescents: Risk factors and protective factors." Applied Psychology—An International Review 47:109-126.

Boehnke, Klaus, Gerd Hefler, Hans Merkens, and John Hagan. 1998b. "Jugendlicher Rechtsextremismus: Zur Bedeutung von Schulerfolg und elterlicher Kontrolle" [Juvenile rightwing extremism: On the meaning of academic success and parental control]. Zeitschrift für Pädagigische Psychologie 12:236-249.

Campbell, Angus, and Philip E. Converse. 1972. The Human Meaning of Social Change. New York: Russell Sage.

Claßen, Gabriele. 1997. Zur Genese von abweichendem Verhalten: Die Bedeutung familiärer Erziehungsstile und Wertorientierungen für die Herausbildung eines anomischen Lebensgefühls bei deutschen und polnischen Jugendlichen [The Genesis of Deviant Behavior: On the Role of Parental Style and Value Orientations for the Development of Anomia Among German and Polish Adolescents]. Hamburg: Kovac.

Clausen, John A. 1995. American Lives: Looking Back at the Children of the Great Depression. Berkeley: University of California Press.

Coleman, James. 1961. The Adolescent Society. The Social Life of the Teenager and its Impact on Education. New York: Free Press.

Conger, Rand D., and Glen H. Elder. 1994. Families in Troubled Times: Adapting to Change in Rural America. New York: A. de Gruyter.

Conger, Katherine J., Martha A. Rueter, and Rand D. Conger. 2000. "The role of economic pressure in the lives of parents and their adolescents: The family stress model." In Lisa J. Crockett and Rainer K. Silbereisen (eds.), Negotiating Adolescence in Times of Social Change: 201–223. Cambridge: Cambridge University Press.

Crockett, Lisa J., and Rainer K. Silbereisen (eds.). 2000. Negotiating Adolescence in Times of Social Change. Cambridge: Cambridge University Press.

Dollard, John, Leonard W. Doob, Neal E. Miller, Orval H. Mowrer, and Robert R. Sears. 1939. Frustration and Aggression. New Haven: Yale University Press.

Eisenstadt, Shmuel N. 1956. From Generation to Generation: Age Groups and Social Structure. London: Routledge & Kegan Paul.

Elder, Glen H. 1974. Children of the Great Depression: Social Change in Life Experience. Chicago: University of Chicago Press.

Elder, Glen H., and Rand D. Conger. 2000. Children of the Land: Adversity and Success in Rural America. Chicago: University of Chicago Press.

Encyclopaedia Britannica. 1990 Book of the Year. 1989. Chicago: Encyclopaedia Britannica. 1991 Book of the Year. 1990. Chicago: Encyclopaedia Britannica. 1992 Book of the Year. 1991. Chicago: Encyclopaedia Britannica. 1993 Book of the Year. 1992. Chicago: Encyclopaedia Britannica. 1994 Book of the Year. 1993. Chicago: Encyclopaedia Britannica.

Gergen, Kenneth J., and Margret M. Gergen. 1981. Social Psychology. New York: Harcourt. Brace. Jovanovich.

Hagan, John. 1991. "Destiny and drift: Subcultural preferences, status attainment and the risks and rewards of youth." American Sociological Review. 56:567-582. 1994. Crime and Disrepute. Newbury Park: Pine Forge Press.

Jöreskog, Karl, and Dag Sörbom. 1993. LISREL 8: Structural Equation Modeling With the SIMPLIS Command Language. Chicago: Scientific Software International.

Kratcoski, Peter C., and Lucille D. Kratcoski. 1990. Juvenile Delinquency. Englewood Cliffs, NJ: Prentice-Hall.

Krohn, Marvin D., and Charles F. Wellford. 1977. "A static and dynamic analysis of crime and the primary dimensions of nations." International Journal of Criminology and Penology 5:1–16.

Leung, Kwok, and Michael H. Bond. 1989. "On the empirical identification of dimensions of cross-cultural comparisons." Journal of Cross-Cultural Psychology 20:133-151.

Matza, David. 1964. Delinquency and Drift. New York: Wiley.

Matza, David, and Gresham Sykes. 1961. "Juvenile delinquency and subterranean values." American Sociological Review 26:712-730.

Mead, Margaret. 1970. Culture and Commitment: A Study of the Generation Gap. Garden City. NY: Natural History Press.

Merkens, Hans. 1996. Jugend in pädagogischer Perspektive: Ergebnisse empirischer Studien [Youth in a Pedagogical Perspective: Results of Empirical Studies]. Battmannsweiler: Schneider Hohengehren.

Parker, G., H. Tupling, and L. B. Brown. 1979. "A parental bonding instrument." British Journal of Medical Psychology 52:1–10.

Scott, William A., Ruth Scott, Klaus Boehnke, S.-W. Cheng, Kwok Leung, and M. Sasaki. 1991. "Children's personality as a function of family relations within and between cultures." Journal of Cross-Cultural Psychology 22:182–208.

Sellin, Thorsten. 1938. Culture Conflict and Crime. New York: Social Science Research Council.

Shanahan, Michael J., and Kathryn E. Hood. 2000. "Adolescents in changing social structures: Bounded agency in life course perspective." In Lisa J. Crockett and Rainer K. Silbereisen (eds), Negotiating Adolescence in Times of Social Change: 123–134. Cambridge: Cambridge University Press.

Simons, Ronald L., Les B. Whitbeck, Janet N. Melby, and Chyi-In Wu. 1994. "Economic pressure and harsh parenting." In Rand D. Conger and Glen H. Elder (eds.), Families in Troubled Times: Adapting to Change in Rural America: 207–222. New York: A. de Gruyter.

Stinchcombe, Arthur. 1964. Rebellion in a High School. Chicago: Quadrangle Books.

Sutherland, Edwin. 1949. White Collar Crime. New York: Dryden.

Thomas, William I., and Florian Znaniecki. 1981. The Polish Peasant in Europe and America. Chicago: University of Chicago Press.

Trojanowicz, Robert C., and Merry Morash. 1992. Juvenile Delinquency: Concepts and Control. Englewood Cliffs, NJ: Prentice-Hall.

Trommsdorff, Gisela. 2000. "Effects of social change on individual development: The role of social and personal factors and the timing of events." In Lisa J. Crockett and Rainer K. Silbereisen (eds.), Negotiating Adolescence in Times of Social Change: 58–68. Cambridge: Cambridge University Press.

Walper, Sabine, and Anna K. Gerhard. 1999. "Konflikte der Eltern, Trennung und neue Partnerschaft: Einflüsse auf die Individuation von Kindern und Jugendlichen" [Conflict among parents, Separation, and new partnership: Consequences for the individuation of children and adolescents]. In Sabine Walper and Beate Schwarz (eds.). Was wird aus den Kindern?: 143-170. Munich: Juventa.

PART III

> # Becoming Deviant

PART III

> ## Private Domains, Information Control, and Accommodation

SECTION 1

In Part I, we made some general statements about the way deviant categories arise and the way violators of these categories may be reacted to. In Part II, we explored some of the major theories and perspectives that serve to explain why actors may commit deviant acts. In this part of the book, we will deal more systematically with reactions that may bring about early stages of deviant careers—careers which may ultimately become subject to institutional control and regulation (Part IV).

In the General Introduction, a distinction was made between the initiation of the labeling ceremony in a private domain and initiation in the public domain. We also noted how those engaged in deviant pursuits attempt to manage their behavior and attitudes in such a way as to avoid detection by socially significant "straights," especially formal agents of social control. This avoidance clearly indicates both the existence of some potentially stigmatizing or discreditable feature of their biography and the knowledge that detection is frequently associated with a range of personal and social costs. As an example, the drug pusher runs the risk of being sanctioned by the courts. It is conceivable, of course, that the pusher may never experience any direct contact with the social-control apparatus. In such a case he or she would remain what we have termed a noninstitutional deviant. Still, the pusher is aware of the potentially damaging nature of his or her activities and realizes that if authorities became aware of those activities, that knowledge could be used to initiate some type of institutional career.

In the analysis of strategies for information control and management, it is useful, therefore, to think in terms of actor *and* audience response. The pusher, in an effort to protect his or her self-image and identity cluster, as well as to reduce the odds of being officially designated as a deviant, may employ certain strategies (e.g., denying to self and others that he or she is a pusher). Similarly, those who must deal with actual or potential deviance often invoke various types of coping or accommodative strategies. A wife, for example, may try to accommodate herself to her husband's increasingly violent behavior. If she is successful, the deviance will remain primarily a matter of private knowledge, regulation, and management—although the wife herself may consider her husband to be deviant. If, on the other hand, the wife's accommodative strategies (e.g., attempts at neutralization or rationalization) fail, she may find it necessary to bring in third parties (e.g., social-control agents such as the police) to regulate her husband's behavior. Not only have the wife's "tolerance limits" been exceeded in this case, but behavior that had been managed in the private setting now becomes subject to institutional control. And the husband may be typed, processed, and responded to as an involuntary mental patient.

The selections that follow explore some of the ways in which strategies for management and accommodation operate in private settings. The lead article introduces an important analytical distinction concerning public and personal identity, while the remaining pieces illustrate how audiences may not only help in the production of deviant behavior or beginning deviant careers, but also how audiences may respond to deviance on the part of significant or generalized others. These pieces also provide excellent illustrations of the usefulness of many of the basic concepts and processes introduced in Parts I and II. For example, McCabe specifically tests the techniques of neutralization presented by Sykes and Matza (selection 12 in this book). Although some attention is placed on an actor's behavior, it should be emphasized that the primary focus in this part is given to audience response to perceived or actual deviance on the part of others.

Erving Goffman, in "Information Control and Personal Identity: The Discredited and the Discreditable," draws an important distinction between the *discredited* and the *discreditable*. He notes that when there is a discrepancy between an actor's actual social identity and his or her virtual one, it is possible that this information, if it is stigmatizing, will become known to us before we interact with the actor. A stigmatizing feature or, as Goffman prefers, a "spoiled identity," can affect how we actually relate to the stigmatized. We may, for example, recognize a discrediting feature or make no notice of it. The actor is, however, often viewed as a discredited person. When the "known differentness" or stigmatizing feature of an actor's biography is not known, he or she must be viewed, conceptually, as potentially discreditable. This situation, Goffman argues, presents the actor with a dilemma. Does one tell or not tell? Does one lie or not lie? Or, does one release the potentially discrediting and stigmatizing information to selected individuals in specific settings or domains? Goffman reasons that the release of stigmatizing information can produce certain effects. For example, the release of information can help to confirm or round out the image one may have of an actor. At this point, Goffman introduces a useful distinction among *prestige symbols, stigma symbols*, and *disidentifiers*. A prestige symbol (e.g., a wedding band or a badge) often draws attention to a positive aspect of one's identity, while a stigma symbol (e.g., a conviction for rape or child molestation) causes focus on a discrediting or debasing feature of identity. A disidentifier (e.g., an advanced education of a street person) can be a sign that may disrupt or cast doubt on the validity of an actor's virtual identity. Goffman cautions that not only do signs vary in their reliability, but they can be used as a source of information about the identity of others. He cites, as an example, how anyone who associates with a known criminal or person wanted for arrest can be contaminated.

The contamination of others discussed above can be thought of as the transference of "stigma"—a concept of growing interest. One challenge currently being addressed is in defining the concept. Bruce Link and Jo Phelan address many issues related to defining stigma in their article "Conceptualizing Stigma" (2001). Link and Phelan note the broad variation in current definitions and suggest that the variety of definitions has emerged in part as a result of researchers' application of the concept. Examinations of stigma across various circumstances may lead to somewhat unusual conceptualizations of the concept. A second likely source of the varied definitions of stigma is the multidisciplinary interest in the concept including contributions from anthropologists, psychologists, political scientists, sociologists and others. To move beyond these problems, the authors suggest that stigma should be conceptualized as the "co–occurrence of its components—labeling, stereotyping, separation, status loss, and discrimination"—and that stigmatization necessarily requires the exercise of power. Each of the component parts of stigma and the dependence of stigma on power is discussed. Link and Phelan address several implications of their conceptualization of stigma "for how one might reason about several persistent questions" related to stigma such as the application, definition, and personal experience including life chances.

Antisocial behaviors carry the potential for stigmatization. Understanding the link between social experiences and antisocial behavior may help in our examination of processes related to becoming deviant. Primary groups such as the family constitute very socialization contexts. Behavioral and interactive patterns are learned within the family. Just as parents and the dynamics within the family shape personal outcomes, siblings play important roles in the developmental processes and outcomes of younger brothers and sisters. In their article "The Consequences of Antisocial Behavior in Older Male Siblings for Younger Brothers and Sisters" (2005), Jim Synder and Bert Lew Burraston-Bank examine the contribution of childhood and adolescent sibling relationships to the development of antisocial behaviors. The children of concern in this study are the younger siblings of young men who participated in the Oregon Youth Study. "These young men had high rates of antisocial behavior and other adjustment problems and associated with a variety of deviant male peers." Their findings point toward a sequential influence of older siblings on younger brothers and sisters moving from early childhood into adolescence. Two social processes seem to be operating. The first process involves exposure to, and imitation of, older sibling's coercive tactics. The second process involves the younger siblings' participation in deviant activities with their older brother.

The advent of the Internet has stimulated much sociological research. Chat rooms and chat room cultures have been of particular interest. For example, how is it that norms emerge and particular behaviors are selected as deviant? Further, how are these deviations from the norm managed within "virtual communities"? Audience response is at the center of Rhonda D. Evans' article "Examining the Informal Sanctioning of Deviance in a Chat Room Culture." Of interest to her are the following questions: (1) How are behaviors judged to be deviant? (2) What are the probable origins of deviance in the chat room setting? and (3) What are the likely consequences—how is deviance sanctioned?

Considering informal sanctioning reveals many important elements central to the study of deviance in society. What becomes apparent is that mechanisms that function to identify and manage deviance at the formal, societal level are built into and operate within informal settings as well. The first mechanism is to directly confront the deviance. Virtual communities have developed unique mechanisms because of the limitations of the technology and those resulting from propinquity. The second mechanism allows members of the virtual community to limit access to communal activities. Here again, unique mechanisms have been built in (e.g., members can simply ignore the violating individual). Penetrating the barriers of acceptable behaviors defines the boundaries of group norms, as well as reinforcing the norms through collective response.

Information Control and Personal Identity: The Discredited and the Discreditable

21

Erving Goffman

When there is a discrepancy between an individual's actual social identity and his virtual one, it is possible for this fact to be known to us before we normals contact him, or to be quite evident when he presents himself before us. He is a discredited person, and it is mainly he I have been dealing with until now. As suggested, we are likely to give no open recognition to what is discrediting of him, and while this work of careful disattention is being done, the situation can become tense, uncertain, and ambiguous for all participants, especially the stigmatized one.

The cooperation of a stigmatized person with normals in acting as if his known differentness were irrelevant and not attended to is one main possibility in the life of such a person. However, when his differentness is not immediately apparent, and is not known beforehand (or at least known by him to be known to the others), when in fact his is a discreditable, not a discredited, person, then the second main possibility in his life is to be found. The issue is not that of managing tension generated during social contacts, but rather that of managing information about his failing. To display or not to display; to tell or not to tell; to let on or not to let on; to lie or not to lie; and in each case, to whom, how, when, and where. For example, while the mental patient is in the hospital, and when he is with adult members of his own family, he is faced with being treated tactfully as if he were sane when there is known to be some doubt, even though he may not have any; or he is treated as insane, when he knows this is not just. But for the ex-mental patient the problem can be quite different; it is not that he must face prejudice against himself, but rather that he must face unwitting acceptance of himself by individuals who are prejudiced against persons of the kind he can be revealed to be. Wherever he goes his behavior will falsely confirm for the other that they are in the company of what in effect they demand but may discover they haven't obtained, namely, a mentally untainted person like themselves. By intention or in effect the ex-mental patient conceals information about his real social identity, receiving and accepting treatment based on false suppositions concerning himself. It is this second general issue, the management of undisclosed discrediting information about self, that I am focusing on in these notes, in brief, "passing." The concealment of creditable facts—reverse passing—of course occurs, but is not relevant here.[1]

The information of most relevance in the study of stigma has certain properties. It is information about an individual. It is about his more or less abiding characteristics, as opposed to the moods, feelings, or intents that he might have at a particular moment.[2] The information as well as the sign through which it is conveyed, is reflexive and embodied; that is, it is conveyed by the very person it is about, and conveyed through bodily expression in the immediate presence of those who receive the expression. Information possessing all of these properties I will here call "social." Some signs that convey social information may be frequently and steadily available, and routinely sought and received; these signs may be called "symbols."

The social information conveyed by any particular symbol may merely confirm what other signs tell us about the individual, filling out our image of him in a redundant and unproblematic way. Some lapel buttons, attesting to social club membership, are examples, as are male wedding rings in some contexts. However, the social information conveyed by a symbol can establish a special claim to prestige, honor, or desirable class position—a claim that might not otherwise be presented or, if otherwise presented, then not automatically granted. Such a sign is popularly called a "status symbol," although the term "prestige symbol" might be more accurate, the former term being more suitably employed when a well-organized social position of some kind is the referent. Prestige symbols can be contrasted to *stigma symbols,* namely, signs which are essentially effective in drawing attention to a debasing identity discrepancy, breaking up what would otherwise be a coherent overall picture, with a consequent reduction in our valuation of the individual. The shaved head of female collaborators in World War II is an example, as is an habitual solecism through which someone affecting middle class manner and dress repeatedly employs a word incorrectly or repeatedly mispronounces it.

In addition to prestige symbols and stigma symbols, one further possibility is to be found, namely, a sign that tends—in fact or hope—to break up an otherwise coherent picture but in this case in a positive direction desired by the actor, not so much establishing a new claim as throwing severe doubt on the validity of the virtual one. I shall refer here to disidentifiers. One example is the "good English" of an educated northern Negro visiting the South[3]; another is the turban and mustache affected by some urban lower class Negroes.[4] A study of illiterates provides another illustration:

> Therefore, when goal orientation is pronounced or imperative and there exists a high probability that definition as illiterate is a bar to the

achievement of the goal, the illiterate is likely to try to "pass" as literate. . . . The popularity in the group studied of windowpane lenses with heavy horn frames ("bop glasses") may be viewed as an attempt to emulate the stereotype of the businessman-teacher-young intellectual and especially the high status jazz musician.[5]

A New York specialist in the arts of vagrancy provides still another illustration:

> After seven-thirty in the evening, in order to read a book in Grand Central or Penn Station, a person either has to wear horn-rimmed glasses or look exceptionally prosperous. Anyone else is apt to come under surveillance. On the other hand, newspaper readers never seem to attract attention and even the seediest vagrant can sit in Grand Central all night without being molested if he continues to read a paper.[6]

Note that in this discussion of prestige symbols, stigma symbols, and disidentifiers, signs have been considered which routinely convey social information. These symbols must be distinguished from fugitive signs that have not been institutionalized as information carriers. When such signs make claims to prestige, one can call them points; when they discredit tacit claims, one can call them slips.

Some signs carrying social information, being present, first of all, for other reasons, have only an overlay of informational function. There are stigma symbols that provide examples: the wrist markings which disclose that an individual has attempted suicide; the arm pock marks of drug addicts; the handcuffed wrists of convicts in transit;[7] or black eyes when worn in public by females, as a writer on prostitution suggests:

> Outside [the prison where she now is] I'd be in the soup with it. Well, you know how it is: the law sees a chick with a shiner figures she's up to something. Bull figures maybe in the life. Next thing trails her around. Then maybe bang! busted.[8]

Other signs are designed by man solely for the purpose of conveying social information, as in the case of insignia of military rank. It should be added that the significance of the underlay of a sign can become reduced over time, becoming, at the extreme, merely vestigial, even while the informational function of the activity remains constant or increases in importance. Further, a sign that appears to be present for non-informational reasons may sometimes be manufactured with malice aforethought solely because of its informing function, as when dueling scars were carefully planned and inflicted.

Signs conveying social information vary according to whether or not they are congenital, and, if not, whether, once employed, they become a permanent part of the person. (Skin color is congenital; a brand mark or maiming is permanent but not congenital; a convict's head-shave is neither congenital nor permanent.) More important, impermanent signs solely employed to convey social information may or may not be employed against the will of the informant; when they are, they tend to be stigma symbols.[9] Later it will be necessary to consider stigma symbols that are voluntarily employed.

It is possible for signs which mean one thing to one group to mean something else to another group, the same category being designated but differently characterized. For example, the shoulder patches that prison officials require escape-prone prisoners to wear[10] can come to mean one thing to guards, in general negative, while being a mark of pride for the wearer relative to his fellow prisoners. The uniform of an officer may be a matter of pride to some, to be worn on every possible occasion; for other officers, weekends may represent a time when they can exercise their choice and wear mufti, passing as civilians. Similarly, while the obligation to wear the school cap in town may be seen as a privilege by some boys, as will the obligation to wear a uniform on leave by "other ranks," still there will be wearers who feel that the social information conveyed thereby is a means of ensuring control and discipline over them when they are off duty and off the premises.[11] So, too, during the eighteen hundreds in California, the absence of a pigtail (queue) on a Chinese man signified for Occidentals a degree of acculturation, but to fellow-Chinese a question would be raised as to respectability—specifically, whether or not the individual had served a term in prison where cutting off of the queue was obligatory; loss of queue was for a time, then, very strongly resisted.[12]

Signs carrying social information vary of course as to reliability. Distended capillaries on the cheek and nose, sometimes called "venous stigmata" with more aptness than meant, can be and are taken as indicating alcoholic excess. However, teetotalers can exhibit the same symbol for other physiological reasons, thereby giving rise to suspicions about themselves which aren't justified, but with which they must deal nonetheless.

A final point about social information must be raised; it has to do with the informing character of the "with" relationship in our society. To be "with" someone is to arrive at a social occasion in his company, walk with him down a street, be a member of his party in a restaurant, and so forth. The issue is that in certain circumstances the social identity of those an individual is with can be used as a source of information concerning his own social identity, the assumption being that he is what the others are. The extreme, perhaps, is the situation in criminal circles: a person wanted for arrest can legally contaminate anyone he is seen with, subjecting them to arrest on suspicion. (A person for whom there is a warrant is therefore said "to have smallpox," and his criminal disease is said to be "catching.")[13] In any case, an analysis of how people manage the information they convey about themselves will have to consider how they deal with the contingencies of being seen "with" particular others.

Notes

1. For one instance of reverse passing, see "H.E.R. Cules" and "Ghost-Writer and Failure," in P. Toynbee, ed., *Underdogs* (London: Weidenfeld, and Nicolson, 1961), Chap. 2, pp. 30–39. There are many other examples. I knew a physician who was careful to refrain from using external symbols of her status, such as car-license tags, her only evidence of profession being an identification carried in her wallet. When faced with a public accident in which medical service was already being rendered the victim, or in which the victim was past helping, she would, upon examining the victim at a distance from the circle around him, quietly go her way without announcing her competence. In these situations she was what might be called a female impersonator.

2. The difference between mood information and other kinds of information is treated in G. Stone, "Appearance and the Self," in A. Rose, *Human Behavior and Social Processes* (Boston: Houghton Mifflin, 1962), pp. 86–118. See also E. Goffman, *The Presentation of Self in Everyday Life* (New York: Doubleday & Co., Anchor Books, 1959), pp. 24–25.

3. G. J. Fleming, "My Most Humiliating Jim Crow Experience," *Negro Digest* (June 1954), 67–68.

4. B. Wolfe, "Ecstatic in Blackface," *Modern Review,* III (1950), 204.

5. Freeman and Kasenbaum, *op. cit.,* p. 372.

6. E. Love, *Subways Are for Sleeping* (New York: Harcourt, Brace & World, 1957), p. 28.

7. A. Heckstall-Smith, *Eighteen Months* (London: Allan Wingate, 1954), p. 43.

8. T. Rubin, *In the Life* (New York: The Macmillan Company, 1961), p. 69.

9. In his *American Notes,* written on the basis of his 1842 trip, Dickens records in his chapter on slavery some pages of quotations from local newspapers regarding lost and found slaves. The identifications contained in these advertisements provide a full range of identifying signs. First, there are relatively stable features of the body that in context can incidentally provide partial or full positive identification: age, sex, and scarrings (these resulting from shot and knife wounds, from accidents, and from lashings). Self-admitted name is also provided, though usually, of course, only the first name. Finally, stigma symbols are often cited, notably branded initials and cropped ears. These symbols communicate the social identity of slave but, unlike iron bands around the neck or leg, also communicate something more narrow than that, namely, ownership by a particular master. Authorities then had two concerns about an apprehended Negro: whether or not he was a runaway slave, and, if he was, to whom did he belong.

10. See G. Dendrickson and F. Thomas, *The Truth About Dartmoor* (London: Victor Gollancz, 1954), p. 55, and F. Norman, *Bang to Rights* (London: Secker and Warburg, 1958), p. 125. The use of this type of symbol is well presented in E. Kogon, *The Theory and Practice of Hell* (New York: Berkley Publishing Corp., n.d.), pp. 41–42, where he specifies the markings used in concentration camps to identify differentially political prisoners, second offenders, criminals, Jehovah's Witnesses, "shiftless elements," Gypsies, Jews, "race defilers," foreign nationals (according to nation), feeble-minded, and so forth. Slaves on the Roman slave market also were often labeled as to nationality; see M. Gordon, "The Nationality of Slaves Under the Early Roman Empire," in M. I. Finley, ed., *Slavery in Classical Antiquity* (Cambridge: Heffer, 1960), p. 171.

11. T. H. Pear, *Personality, Appearance and Speech* (London: George Allen and Unwin, 1957), p. 58.

12. A. McLeod, *Pigtails and Gold Dust* (Caldwel, Idaho: Caxton Printers, 1947), p. 28. At times religious-historical significance was also attached to wearing this queue; see *ibid.,* p. 204.

13. See D. Maurer, *The Big Con* (New York: Pocket Books, 1949), p. 298.

22 Conceptualizing Stigma

Bruce G. Link
Jo C. Phelan

Introduction

Erving Goffman's (1963) book *Stigma: Notes on the Management of Spoiled Identity* inspired a profusion of research on the nature, sources, and consequences of stigma. Both PsychInfo and Medline show dramatic increases in the number of articles mentioning the word stigma in their titles or abstracts from 1980 (PsychInfo 14, Medline 19) to 1990 (PsychInfo 81, Medline 48) to 1999 (PsychInfo 161, Medline 1 14).

Research since Goffman's seminal essay has been incredibly productive, leading to elaborations, conceptual refinements, and repeated demonstrations of the negative impact of stigma on the lives of the stigmatized. The stigma concept is applied to literally scores of circumstances ranging from urinary incontinence (Sheldon & Caldwell 1994) to exotic dancing (Lewis 1998) to leprosy (Opala & Boillot 1996), cancer (Fife & Wright 2000), and mental illness (Angermeyer & Matschinger 1994, Corrigan & Penn 1999, Phelan et a1 2000). It is used to explain some of the social vagaries of being unemployed (Walsgrove 1987), to show how welfare stigma can lead to the perpetuation of welfare use (Page 1984), and to provide an understanding of situations faced by wheelchair users (Cahill & Eggleston 1995), stepparents (Coleman et al 1996), debtors (Davis 1998), and mothers who are lesbian (Causey & Duran-Aydintug 1997).

A substantial portion of the productive research on stigma has been contributed by social psychologists who have used the insights of the social cognitive approach to understand how people construct categories and link these categories to stereotyped beliefs. This line of research represents a major advance in the understanding of stigma processes, and sociologists would do well to attend to it thoroughly (for a comprehensive review, see Crocker et al 1998). Given these advances in the social psychology of stigma and given the accumulated scientific impact of research on stigma more generally, we propose a return to the stigma concept from a distinctly sociological perspective. We engage our sociological perspective by attending to several core criticisms of the stigma concept and its application. The first of these criticisms is directed toward the clarity of the concept and follows from the observation that stigma is defined in different ways by different investigators. The second is a set of criticisms regarding the way in which the stigma concept has been applied by some researchers. We use these criticisms both as a stimulus to return to the stigma concept and as a critical analytic lens in constructing a revised conceptualization. We follow our explication of the stigma concept with a more detailed discussion of each of its component parts. We end by applying our conceptualization to several core issues in the stigma literature with an eye to assessing whether our conceptualization is helpful in understanding those issues. In doing so, we attend more to the nature and consequences of stigma than to its sources. (For a review of some ideas about the origins of stigma see Crocker & Lutsky 1986.)

▶Variations in the Definition of Stigma

One of the curious features of literature concerning stigma is the variability that exists in the definition of the concept (Stafford & Scott 1986). In many circumstances investigators provide no explicit definition and seem to refer to something like the dictionary definition ("a mark of disgrace") or to some related aspect like stereotyping or rejection (e.g., a social distance scale). When stigma is explicitly defined, many authors quote Goffman's definition of stigma as an "attribute that is deeply discrediting" and that reduces the bearer "from a whole and usual person to a tainted, discounted one" (Goffman 1963, p. 3).

Since Goffman, alternative or elaborated definitions have varied considerably. For example, Stafford & Scott (1986, p. 80) propose that stigma "is a characteristic of persons that is contrary to a norm of a social unit" where a "norm" is defined as a "shared belief that a person ought to behave in a certain way at a certain time" (p. 81). Crocker et al (1998, p. 505) indicate that "stigmatized individuals possess (or are believed to possess) some attribute, or characteristic, that conveys a social identity that is devalued in a particular social context." An especially influential definition is that of Jones et al (1984), who use Goffman's (1963, p. 4) observation that stigma can be seen as a relationship between an "attribute and a stereotype" to produce a definition of stigma as a "mark" (attribute) that links a person to undesirable characteristics (stereotypes). In our own reviews of stigma and mental illness (e.g., Link & Phelan 1999), we have added the component of discrimination to the Jones et al (1984) definition.

Of the many reasons that definitions of stigma vary, two seem particularly prominent. First, as indicated above, the stigma concept has been applied to an enormous array of circumstances. Each one of these is unique, and each one is likely to lead investigators to conceptualize stigma in a somewhat different way. Second, research on stigma is clearly multidisciplinary, including contributions by psychologists, sociologists, anthropologists, political scientists, and social geographers. Although there is a great deal of overlap in interests across these disciplines, there are nevertheless some differences in emphasis. Even within disciplines, people approach the stigma concept from different theoretical orientations that produce somewhat different visions of what should be included in the concept. Thus, different frames of reference have led to different conceptualizations.

Because of the complexity of the stigma phenomenon, it seems wise to continue to allow variation in definition so long as investigators are clear as to what is meant by stigma when the term is used. Having said this, we shall also attempt to move matters ahead by specifying a conceptualization of stigma that includes many of the concerns that people working in this area of research share. Before proceeding, however, it is important to note that the use of the stigma concept has been challenged by some social scientists who have focused on the perspective of persons who are stigmatized (Schneider 1988, Fine & Asch 1988, Sayce 1998; Kleinman et al 1995). Understanding these challenges is important for the further development of research on stigma, particularly from a sociological perspective.

Challenges to the Stigma Concept

There are two main challenges to the stigma concept. The first is that many social scientists who do not belong to stigmatized groups, and who study stigma, do so from the vantage point of theories that are uninformed by the lived experience of the people they study (Kleinman et al 1995, Schneider 1988). For example, in writing about the experience of disability, Schneider (1988) asserts that "most ablebodied experts" give priority "to their scientific theories and research techniques rather than to the words and perceptions of the people they study." The result is a misunderstanding of the experience of the people who are stigmatized and the perpetuation of unsubstantiated assumptions. Writing about disability, Fine & Asch (1988) identify five assumptions: (a) that disability is located solely in biology, (b) that the problems of the disabled are due to disability-produced impairment, (c) that the disabled person is a "victim," (d) that disability is central to the disabled person's self-concept, self-definition, social comparisons, and reference groups, and (e) that having a disability is synonymous with needing help and social support.

The second challenge is that research on stigma has had a decidedly individualistic focus. For example, according to Oliver (1992), the central thrust of stigma research has been focused on the perceptions of individuals and the consequences of such perceptions for micro-level interactions. According to Oliver (1992), research examining the sources and consequences of pervasive, socially shaped exclusion from social and economic life are far less common. Interestingly, this criticism is echoed by at least one renowned student of stereotyping, prejudice, and discrimination. In her review of these topics, Susan Fiske (1998) concludes that (at least within social psychology) the literature on discrimination is far less extensive than that on stereotyping and that more attention needs to be addressed to structural issues. In another vein, even though Goffman (1963, p. 3) initially advised that we really needed "a language of relationships, not attributes," subsequent practice has often transformed stigmas or marks into attributes of persons (Fine & Asch 1988). The stigma or mark is seen as something *in the person* rather than a designation or tag that others affix to the person. In this respect the term stigma directs our attention differently than a term like "discrimination." In contrast to "stigma," "discrimination" focuses the attention of research on the producers of rejection and exclusion—those who do the discriminating—rather than on the people who are the recipients of these behaviors (Sayce 1998). Thus, the terms we use could lead to "different understandings of where responsibility lies for the 'problem' and as a consequence to different prescriptions for action" (Sayce 1998).

Researchers on stigma could respond to these challenges by disputing their validity or pointing to exceptions in the now voluminous literature on stigma. We find these critiques to provide a useful stimulus for a reassessment of the conceptualization of stigma and related concepts. One way in which some of the issues raised by the critiques can be addressed is to propose that stigma be described with reference to the relationships between a set of interrelated concepts.

Defining Stigma in the Relationship of Interrelated Components

An important precedent to locating the meaning of stigma in the relation between concepts is available in Goffman's observation that stigma can be seen as the relationship between an "attribute and a stereotype." We expand the nexus of relationships somewhat with the intent of capturing a fuller set of meanings for the term by doing so. We state our conceptualization as concisely as we can and then elaborate the components it contains.

In our conceptualization, stigma exists when the following interrelated components converge. In the first component, people distinguish and label human differences. In the second, dominant cultural beliefs link labeled persons to undesirable characteristics—to negative stereotypes. In the third, labeled persons are placed in distinct categories so as to accomplish some degree of separation of "us" from "them." In the fourth, labeled persons experience status loss and discrimination that lead to unequal outcomes.

Finally, stigmatization is entirely contingent on access to social, economic, and political power that allows the identification of differentness, the construction of stereotypes, the separation of labeled persons into distinct categories, and the full execution of disapproval, rejection, exclusion, and discrimination. Thus, we apply the term stigma when elements of labeling, stereotyping, separation, status loss, and discrimination co-occur in a power situation that allows the components of stigma to unfold. With this brief explication of the stigma concept as background, we turn to a more detailed examination of each component we identified.

Component 1—On Distinguishing and Labeling Differences

The vast majority of human differences are ignored and are therefore socially irrelevant. Some of these—such as the color of one's car, the last three digits of one's social security number, or whether one has hairy ears—are routinely (but not always) overlooked. Many others such as one's food preferences or eye color are relevant in relatively few situations and are therefore typically inconsequential in the large scheme of things. But other differences, such as one's skin color, IQ, sexual preferences, or gender are highly salient in the United States at this time. The point is that there is a social selection of human differences when it comes to identifying differences that will matter socially.

The full weight of this observation is often overlooked because once differences are identified and labeled, they are typically taken for granted as being just the way things are—there are black people and white people, blind people and sighted people, people who are handicapped and people who are not. The taken-for-granted nature of these categorizations is one of the reasons that designations like these carry such weight. There are, however, some observations we can make that bring to light just how social this social selection of human differences is.

First, substantial oversimplification is required to create groups. One example is the assignment of individuals to categories of "black" or "white" when there is enormous variability within the resulting categories and no clear demarcation between categories on almost any criterion one can think of, even attributes like skin color, parentage, or facial characteristics that are believed to define the categories (Fullilove 1998). The same can be said for other categorizations like gay or straight, blind or sighted, handicapped or not.

Second, the central role of the social selection of human differences is revealed by noting that the attributes deemed salient differ dramatically according to time and place. For example, in the late nineteenth century, human physical characteristics such as small foreheads and large faces were particularly salient—these characteristics were thought to be ape-like—and were believed to reveal the criminal nature of the people possessing them (Gould 1981). And, of course, cultures vary extensively in characteristics deemed socially significant. For example, ancient Mayan culture gave unusual significance to being cross-eyed and sought to create this desirable characteristic in children through devices that encouraged babies to focus on objects in ways that forced their eyes to cross. Sociological studies of social construction and medicalization are also good examples (Conrad 1992). Hyperactivity is much more salient now, as an indicator of a disorder, than it used to be, and the medical term ADHD (attention deficit hyperactivity disorder) is part of common parlance.

Because human differences are socially selected for salience, we have chosen to use the word "label" rather than "attribute," "condition" or "mark." Each of these latter terms locates the thing that is being referred to in the stigmatized person and risks obscuring that its identification and election for social significance is the product of social processes. In contrast, a label is something that is affixed. Moreover in the absence of qualifications, terms like "attribute," "condition," or "mark" imply that the designation has validity. In contrast the word "label" leaves the validity of the designation an open question—an option that has great utility as, for example, when one wishes to discuss the stigma some women experienced as a consequence of being labeled witches.

With regard to this aspect of the stigma process, the critical sociological issue is to determine how culturally created categories arise and how they are sustained. Why is it that some human differences are singled out and deemed salient by human groups while others are ignored? What are the social, economic, and cultural forces that maintain the focus on a particular human difference?

Component 2—On Associating Human Differences with Negative Attributes

The second component of stigma occurs when labeled differences are linked to stereotypes. This aspect of stigma was highlighted in Goffman's (1963) work and has been central to the conceptualization of stigma ever since. It is the aspect of stigma that has been most salient in the psychological literature about stigma, perhaps because it poses critical questions of a psychological nature about the thought processes that facilitate connections between labels and stereotypes. Consistent with this emphasis in psychology is the centrality of this dimension in psychologists' definitions of stigma. For example, Crocker and colleagues (1998) define stigma, as noted above, as an "attribute or characteristic that conveys a social identity that is devalued in a particular context."

In our terms, this aspect of stigma involves a label and a stereotype, with the label linking a person to a set of undesirable characteristics that form the stereotype. An example of this component is evident in a vignette experiment conducted by Link et al (1987). The study experimentally manipulated labeling, tagging a random half of the vignettes "former mental patients" and the other half "former back-pain patients." It also included a measure of the extent to which respondents believed that mental patients *in general* were "dangerous." When the vignette described a former back-pain patient, beliefs about the dangerousness of people with mental illness played no part in rejecting responses toward the vignette subject. When the vignette described a former mental patient, however, these beliefs were potent predictors of rejecting responses: Respondents who believed mental patients were dangerous reacted negatively to the person described as a former mental patient in the vignette. Apparently, for many people, the "mental patient" label linked the described person to stereotyped beliefs about the dangerousness of people with mental illness, which in turn led them to desire for social distance from the person.

As indicated above, this connection between labels and stereotypes has been a major aspect of the psychological study of stigma in recent years, following the social cognitive approach (Fiske 1998). This intriguing and very fruitful body of research seeks to elucidate the cognitive processes underlying the use of categories and the linking of those categories to stereotypes (Crocker et al 1998). We focus briefly on some selected aspects of this extensive body of research.

According to this literature, categories and stereotypes are often "automatic" and facilitate "cognitive efficiency." The automatic nature is revealed in experiments that indicate that categories and stereotypes are used in making split-second judgments and thus appear to be operating preconsciously. For example, Gaertner & McLaughlin (1983) conducted an experiment in which one group of white subjects was primed by the word "whites" and another by the word "blacks," and then both groups were tested as to the speed with which they were able to identify whether two strings of letters were both words. Both high- and low-prejudiced subjects responded more rapidly to positive words like "smart," "ambitious," and "clean" when primed by the word "whites" than when primed by the word "blacks." In addition to operating in a preconscious, automatic way, some studies suggest that category use preserves cognitive resources. Thus, for example, if subjects are provided with labels like doctor, artist, skinhead, or real estate agent when asked to form an impression of a vignette, they are better able to simultaneously perform another task like turning off a beeping computer than are subjects who are not provided these labels (Macrae et al 1994). Thus, from a psychological standpoint, culturally given categories are present even at a preconscious level and provide people with a means of making shorthand decisions that free them to attend to other matters. At the same time, other research in social psychology reveals considerable latitude in the cognitive processes that transpire such that very different outcomes may occur depending on the nature of the cognitions people employ and the contexts in which people are embedded (Crocker et al 1998).

Component 3—On Separating "Us" from "Them"

A third feature of the stigma process occurs when social labels connote a separation of "us" from "them" (Morone 1997, Devine et al 1999). United States history and politics offer many examples as established old-order Americans defined African-American slaves, American Indians, and successive waves of immigrants as outgroups—the "them" who were very different from "us." Few groups were entirely spared. For example, Morone (1997) provides quotes from Benjamin Franklin's observations of the impact of Dutch immigrants ("them") on the English colonists ("us"). "Already the English begin to quit particular neighborhoods, surrounded by the Dutch, being made uneasy by the disagreeableness of dissonant manners . . . Besides, the Dutch under-live, and are thereby enabled to under-work and under-sell the English who are thereby extremely incommoded and consequently disgusted" (Franklin 1752). And of course, while the groups representing "us" and "them" have changed, this separation is still prominent today. "They" are a menace to "us" because they are immoral, lazy, and predatory (Morone 1997). Thus, other components of the stigma process—the linking of labels to undesirable attributes—become the rationale for believing that negatively labeled persons are fundamentally different from those who don't share the label–different types of people. At the same time, when labeled persons are believed to be distinctly different, stereotyping can be smoothly accomplished because there is little harm in attributing all manner of bad characteristics to "them." In the extreme, the stigmatized person is thought to be so different from "us" as to be not really human. And again, in the extreme, all manner of horrific treatment of "them" becomes possible.

Evidence of efforts to separate us from them are sometimes directly available in the very nature of the labels conferred. Incumbents are thought to "be" the thing they are labeled (Estroff 1989). For example, some people speak of persons as being "epileptics" or "schizophrenics" rather than describing them as having epilepsy or schizophrenia. This practice is revealing regarding this component of stigma because it is different for other diseases. A person *has* cancer, heart disease, or the flu—such a person is one of "us," a person who just happens to be beset by a serious illness. But a person *is* a "schizophrenic."

Component 4—Status Loss and Discrimination

In this component of the stigma process, the labeled person experiences status loss and discrimination. Most definitions of stigma do not include this component, but as we shall see, the term stigma cannot hold the meaning we commonly assign to it when this aspect is left out. In our reasoning, when people are labeled, set apart, and linked to undesirable characteristics, a rationale is constructed for devaluing, rejecting, and excluding them.

Thus, people are stigmatized when the fact that they are labeled, set apart, and linked to undesirable characteristics leads them to experience status loss and discrimination.

Consistent with this, stigmatized groups are disadvantaged when it comes to a general profile of life chances like income, education, psychological well-being, housing status, medical treatment, and health (e.g. Druss et al 2000, Link 1987). While some groups escape the experience of some disadvantaged outcomes sometimes (e.g., African Americans regarding self-esteem—see Crocker 1999), when one considers the profile of all possible outcomes, the general principle clearly holds for most stigmatized groups. How does this happen?

Status Loss

An almost immediate consequence of successful negative labeling and stereotyping is a general downward placement of a person in a status hierarchy. The person is connected to undesirable characteristics that reduce his or her status in the eyes of the stigmatizer. The fact that human beings create hierarchies is, of course, evident in organizational charts, who sits where in meetings, who defers to whom in conversational turn-taking, and so on. One strand of sociological research on social hierarchies, the so-called expectation-states tradition, is particularly relevant to the study of stigma and status loss (Cohen 1982, Driskell & Mullen 1990). Based on finding a reliable tendency of even unacquainted individuals to form fairly stable status hierarchies when placed in group situations, researchers set out to understand the processes that produced this state of affairs. What they have found is relevant to research on stigma in many ways, two of which we shall emphasize here. First, this research shows that external statuses, like race and gender, shape status hierarchies within small groups of unacquainted persons even though the external status has no bearing on proficiency at a task the group is asked to perform. Men and whites are more likely than women and blacks to attain positions of power and prestige— they talk more frequently, have their ideas more readily accepted by others, and are more likely to be voted group leader (Mullen et al 1989). These findings are important to research on stigma because they show how having a status that is devalued in the wider society can lead to very concrete forms of inequality in the context of social interactions within small groups. Second, although inequalities in status-related outcomes definitely occur in the groups, they do not result from forms of discrimination that would be readily apparent to a casual observer. Instead group members use external statuses (like race and gender) to create performance expectations that then lead to a labyrinth of details that involve taking the floor, keeping the floor, referring to the contributions of others, head nodding, interrupting, and the like. This is important to research on stigma because it shows that substantial differences in outcome can occur even when it is difficult for participants to specify a single event that produced the unequal outcome.

Discrimination

INDIVIDUAL DISCRIMINATION   The standard way of conceptualizing the connection between labeling, stereotyping, and discrimination in the stigma literature follows a relatively simplistic formulation. In this approach, the importance of attitudes and beliefs are thought to lie in whether person A's labeling and stereotyping of person B leads person A to engage in some obvious forms of overt discrimination directed at person B, such as rejecting a job application, refusing to rent an apartment, and so on. There is no doubt that this rather straightforward process occurs with considerable regularity, although some social psychologists with interests in stigma have recently bemoaned the fact that documenting discriminatory behavior has not been their strong suit (Fiske 1998). Connecting attitudes to behaviors is, therefore, conceptualized as something the area of research on stigma and stereotyping needs (Fiske 1998). In this regard Ajzen & Fishbein's (1980) "theory of reasoned action" has been successfully applied to the prediction of many behaviors and might also be useful in predicting discriminatory behaviors. The approach they propose is effective because it asks us to narrow our focus to a very specific behavior and to be attentive to the intricacies of the beliefs and attitudes toward performing the specific act in question. But the area of stigma research needs to expand its conception of the processes through which labeling and stereotyping lead to social inequalities in life circumstances. By itself the standard model that asks "what-makes-person-A-discriminate-against-person-B "is inadequate for explaining the full consequences of stigma processes. In fact, getting tangled up in the narrow intricacies of explaining a specific act from knowledge of a specific set of attitudes and beliefs could cloud rather than illuminate our understanding of why stigmatized groups experience so many disadvantages.

STRUCTURAL DISCRIMINATION   The concept of institutional racism sensitizes us to the fact that all manner of disadvantage can result outside of a model in which one person does something bad to another. Institutional racism refers to accumulated institutional practices that work to the disadvantage of racial minority groups even in the absence of individual prejudice or discrimination (Hamilton & Carmichael 1967). For example, employers (more often white) rely on the personal recommendations of colleagues or acquaintances (more often white and more likely to know and recommend white job candidates) for hiring decisions. The same kind of structural discrimination is, of course, present for other stigmatized groups. For example, disabled persons may be limited in their ability to work not so much because of their inherent limitations but because they are exposed to what Hahn (1983) calls "a disabling environment" created by the barriers to participation that reside in architecture we humans have constructed (Fine & Asch 1988). Consider some possible examples of structural discrimination for a mental illness like schizophrenia. Suppose that because the illness is stigmatized, less funding is dedicated to research about it than for other illnesses and less money is allocated to adequate care and management. Moreover, consider that, because of historical processes influenced by stigma, treatment facilities tend to be either isolated in settings away from other people (Rothman 1971) or confined to some of the most disadvantaged neighborhoods in urban settings in communities that do not have enough clout to exclude this stigmatized group from their midst (Dear & Lewis 1986). At the same time, the most successful and accomplished mental health personnel tend to accrue more status and money by treating less serious illnesses in private offices in affluent areas, leaving the care of people with schizophrenia to a generally less accomplished group (Link 1983). To the extent that the stigma of schizophrenia has created such a situation, a person who develops this disorder will be the recipient of structural discrimination whether or not anyone happens to treat him or her in a discriminatory way because of some stereotype about schizophrenia. Stigma has affected the structure around the person, leading the person to be exposed to a host of untoward circumstances.

STATUS LOSS AS A SOURCE OF DISCRIMINATION   In keeping with observations about the role of stigma in the loss of status, it is important to note that lower placement in a status hierarchy can begin to have effects of its own on a person's life chances. It is not necessary to revisit the labeling and stereotyping that initially led to the lower status, because the lower status itself becomes the basis of discrimination. For example, low status might make a person less attractive to socialize with, to involve in community activities, or to include in a business venture that requires partners who have political influence with local politicians. In this way, a lower position in the status hierarchy can have a cascade of negative effects on all manner of opportunities. Because the discrimination that occurs is one step removed from the labeling and stereotyping, it is easy to miss the more distal effects of these factors in any accounting of the effects of these stigma components.

SOCIAL PSYCHOLOGICAL PROCESSES OPERATING THROUGH THE STIGMATIZED PERSON   Once the cultural stereotype is in place, it can affect labeled persons in important ways that do not involve obvious forms of discriminatory behavior on the part of people in the immediate presence of the stigmatized person. For example, according to a modified labeling theory about the effects of stigma on people with mental illnesses (Link 1982, Link et al 1989), people develop conceptions of mental illness early in life as part of socialization into our culture (Angermeyer & Matschinger 1996, Scheff 1966, Wahl 1995). Once in place, people's conceptions become a lay theory about what it means to have a mental illness (Angermeyer & Matschinger 1994, Furnham & Bower 1992). People form expectations as to whether most people will reject an individual with mental illness as a friend, employee, neighbor, or intimate partner and whether most people will devalue a person with mental illness as less trustworthy, intelligent, and competent. These beliefs have an especially poignant relevance for a person who develops a serious mental illness, because the possibility of devaluation and discrimination becomes personally relevant. If one believes that others will devalue and reject people with mental illnesses, one must now fear that this rejection applies personally. The person may wonder, "Will others look down on me, reject me, simply because I have been identified as having a mental illness?" Then to the extent that it becomes a part of a person's world view, that perception can have serious negative consequences. Expecting and fearing rejection, people who have been hospitalized for mental illnesses may act less confidently and more defensively, or they may simply avoid a potentially threatening contact altogether. The result may be strained and uncomfortable social interactions with potential stigmatizers (Farina et al 1968), more constricted social networks (Link et al 1989), a compromised quality of life (Rosenfield 1997), low self-esteem (Wright et al 2000), depressive symptoms (Link et al 1997), unemployment and income loss (Link 1982, 1987). While this theory has been most thoroughly examined with respect to mental illnesses, the process is probably much more general. In keeping with this possibility, Pinel (1999) has recently called the expectation of stereotyping "stigma consciousness" and has proposed its application to other stigmatized statuses.

A related but slightly different approach to understanding the effect of stereotypes is Steele & Aronson's (1995) concept of "stereotype threat." According to this idea, people know about the stereotypes that might be applied to them—African Americans know they are tagged with attributes of violence and intellectual inferiority, gay men know they are seen as flamboyant and promiscuous, and people with mental illnesses know that they are believed to be unpredictable and dangerous. The insight that Steele & Aronson provide is that the stereotype becomes a threat or challenge either because one might be evaluated in accordance with the stereotype or because one might confirm the stereotype through one's behavior. In keeping with this idea, Steele & Aronson have shown that, controlling for initial differences on SAT scores, African-American students perform worse than white students on a test when study participants are led to believe that the test measures intellectual ability. In contrast, when the same test is not labeled as being diagnostic of ability, African Americans score as well as whites. This research tells us that the existence of a stereotype and the administration of a test of "ability" can lead to an invalid assessment of the academic potential of African-American students and thereby to discrimination against such students on the basis of a seemingly "objective" test.

Note that in both the modified labeling theory and theory about stereotype threat, no one in the immediate context of the person needs to have engaged in obvious forms of discrimination. Rather, the discrimination lies anterior to the immediate situation and rests instead in the formation and sustenance of stereotypes and lay theories. Still the consequences are sometimes severe and undoubtedly contribute greatly to differences in the life chances of people in stigmatized groups.

INTERCHANGEABLE MECHANISMS   The problem of stigma has been described as a predicament or a dilemma by Goffman and others (Ainlay et al 1986, Crocker et al 1998). One reason for this is brought to light by the sociological observation that mechanisms like the ones we have described are both interchangeable and mutually reinforcing in achieving ends that discriminate against stigmatized groups (Lieberson 1985). If powerful groups are motivated to discriminate against a stigmatized "them," there are many ways in which such discrimination can be achieved. If stigmatized persons cannot be persuaded to voluntarily accept their lower status and inferior rewards, direct discrimination can be used to accomplish the same outcome. If direct discrimination becomes ideologically difficult, sophisticated forms of structural discrimination—such as tests that induce stereotype threat—can achieve some of the same ends. The mechanisms are mutually reinforcing as well. To the extent that stigmatized groups accept the dominant view of their lower status, they are less likely to challenge structural forms of discrimination that block opportunities they desire. Further, direct discrimination reinforces the belief among stigmatized groups that they will be treated in accordance with stereotypes and therefore reinforces processes like those explicated in the context of modified labeling theory and the stereotype-threat concept. From this vantage point, stigma is a predicament in the following sense—as long as dominant groups sustain their view of stigmatized persons, decreasing the use of one mechanism through which disadvantage can be accomplished simultaneously creates the impetus to increase the use of another. This latter observation brings us to the final aspect of our stigma concept—its dependence on power differences.

The Dependence of Stigma on Power

Stigma is entirely dependent on social, economic, and political power—it takes power to stigmatize. In some instances the role of power is obvious. However, the role of power in stigma is frequently overlooked because in many instances power differences are so taken for granted as to seem unproblematic. When people think of mental illness, obesity, deafness, and having one leg instead of two, there is a tendency to focus on the attributes associated with these conditions rather than on power differences between people who have them and people who do not. But power, even in these circumstances, is essential to the social production of stigma.

In order to reason about the role of power in stigma, first consider instances in which it is clear that social power is important. To begin, take the example provided earlier in which eighteenth century English colonists tagged the Dutch with attributes of disagreeableness and low-living. Along the same lines, people of Irish background were stereotyped as "temperamental, dangerous, quarrelsome, idle and reckless" by old-order Americans in the nineteenth century. The Irish at the time were likened to apes and were portrayed as such in cartoons of the day (Feagin & Feagin 1996). In the light of current circumstances, it is clear that English colonists of the eighteenth century and the old-order Americans of the nineteenth century were able to stigmatize the Dutch and Irish because of their positions of power over these groups at the time. And, of course, it was the power of the Nazis that allowed their thorough and devastating stigmatization of Jewish people.

But how can we think of the role of power in circumstances like mental illness, obesity, deafness, and one leggedness? One way is to recognize that stigmatized groups often engage in the same kinds of stigma-related processes in their thinking about individuals who are not in their stigmatized group. Consider for example patients in a treatment program for people with serious mental illness. Patients in such a setting are likely to identify and label human differences in staff members. For instance, they might tag some clinicians with the label "pill pusher" and apply stereotypes connected with the labels they create such as that pill pushers are cold, paternalistic, and arrogant. Finally they might treat the people they identify as pill pushers differently in accordance with the conclusions they have drawn about them by avoiding or minimizing communication with them, exchanging derogatory comments and jokes about them, and so on. Thus although the patients might engage in every component of stigma we identified, the staff would not end up being a stigmatized group. The patients simply do not possess the social, cultural, economic, and political power to imbue their cognitions about staff with serious discriminatory consequences.

Consider further that scenarios similar to the one just described exist for all sorts of other circumstances in which relatively powerless groups create labels and stereotypes about more powerful groups and treat members of the more powerful group in accordance with those stereotypes. Such a realization clarifies why the definition of stigma must involve reference to power differences. Without such a reference, stigma becomes a very different and much broader concept that might be applied to lawyers, politicians, Wall Street investors, and white people. Stigma is dependent on power.

Because of the importance of power in stigmatization, it is critical to ask the following set of questions: Do the people who might stigmatize have the power to ensure that the human difference they recognize and label is broadly identified in the culture? Do the people who might confer stigma have the power to ensure that the culture recognizes and deeply accepts the stereotypes they connect to the labeled differences? Do the people who might stigmatize have the power to separate "us" from "them" and to have the designation stick? And do those who might confer stigma control access to major life domains like educational institutions, jobs, housing, and health care in order to put really consequential teeth into the distinctions they draw? To the extent that we can answer yes to these questions, we can expect stigma to result. To the extent that we answer no, some of the cognitive components of stigma might be in place, but what we generally mean by stigma would not exist.

Implications of the Stigma Concept

The stigma concept we have articulated has implications for how one might reason about several persistent questions including: (a) the definition of stigma, (b) stigma as a matter of degree, (c) the origins of stigma, (d) the image of the stigmatized person as a passive victim versus an active challenger, (e) the consequences of stigma, (f) stigma as a persistent dilemma, (g) what we should do to change stigma processes, and (h) the importance of stigma in understanding the distribution of life chances.

The Definition of Stigma

Our explication of the stigma concept is revealing with regard to why so many definitions of stigma are extant in the literature—there are several components, each one of which has been described as stigma. We chose to define stigma in the convergence of interrelated components. Thus, stigma exists when elements of labeling, stereotyping, separation, status loss, and discrimination occur together in a power situation that allows them. This is a definition that we derived, not one that exists in some independent existential way. As such, its value rests in its utility. One reason it is helpful is that the term stigma is in very wide use, and some degree of clarity will help us communicate about the concept. Second, there are words that aptly describe each of the components like label (or mark or status), stereotyping, exclusion, status loss, and discrimination so that the use of the word stigma to describe any particular aspect is not necessary. Third, the definition coheres with the current usage of the term as it is applied to groups that are commonly referred to as stigmatized groups. Recall that if we only used the cognitive components of labeling and stereotyping to define stigma, groups like lawyers, politicians, and white people would have to be considered stigmatized groups. Our incorporation of power, status loss and discrimination allows the formal definition we derived to cohere with current understandings of what a stigmatized group is. Fourth, we believe that the definition helps us envision and thereby more fully understand several important issues in the stigma literature as described below.

Stigma as a Matter of Degree

Our conceptualization leads to the conclusion that stigma exists as a matter of degree. The labeling of human differences can be more or less prominent. A label can connect a person to many stereotypes, to just a few or to none at all. Moreover, the strength of the connection between labels and undesirable attributes can be relatively strong or relatively weak. The degree of separation into groups of "us" and "them" can be more or less complete, and finally the extent of status loss and discrimination can vary. This means that some groups are more stigmatized than others and that some of the components we have described can be used analytically to think about why differences in the extent of stigma experienced vary from group to group.

The Origins of Stigma

Our paper has been focused on the nature and consequences of stigma rather than its sources. Nevertheless our conceptualization provides some ideas about how to think about the origins of stigma. As we indicated at the outset of this paper, a great deal of attention in the literature on stigma has been directed toward the cognitive processing of stigma-relevant information. As crucial as the knowledge gained from this literature is, it is not a sufficient basis for understanding the origins of stigma. As we have pointed out, groups both with and without power label and form stereotypes about the other group—members of each group engage in the kinds of cognitive processes that are studied in the now voluminous social psychological literature. But what matters is whose cognitions prevail—whose cognitions carry sufficient clout in social, cultural, economic, and political spheres to lead to important consequences for the group that has been labeled as different. Here is where the sociological study of stigma is badly needed—for while cognitive processes may be necessary causes for the production of stigma, they are not sufficient causes. We need to further understand the social processes that allow one group's views to dominate so as to produce real and important consequences for the other group.

Passive Victim Versus Active Challenger

One of the most troublesome issues in the study of stigma emerges when social scientists seek to articulate the real constraints that stigma creates in people's lives, and in doing so they end up portraying members of the stigmatized group as helpless victims (Fine & Asch 1988). Ironically, this produces more lines in the list of undesirable attributes that form the stereotype about the stigmatized group—they are additionally "passive," "helpless," or "acquiescent." Because of this, there are from time to time articles that remind us that people artfully dodge or constructively challenge stigmatizing processes (e.g. Reissman 2000). These are very important reminders, and the message they deliver needs to be incorporated into our understanding of stigma. At the same time, the simple fact that these forms of resistance exist suggests there *is* something out there to avoid and that there *are* powerful constraining forces at work. How can we reason about these contrasting images and portray constraint and resistance in research about stigma? Here, our emphasis on the importance of power differences in stigma and our observation that stigma is a matter of degree are helpful. Specifically, these allow us to see issues of constraint and resistance in the context of a power struggle. We can see that people in stigmatized groups actively use available resources to resist the stigmatizing tendencies of the more powerful group and that, to the extent that they do, it is inappropriate to portray them as passive recipients of stigma. At the same time, to the extent that power differences exist, resistance cannot fully overcome constraint. The amount of stigma that people experience will be profoundly shaped by the relative power of the stigmatized and the stigmatizer.

The Outcomes of Stigma

Our conceptualization of stigma demands the assessment of multiple outcomes, not just one or two. We cannot assess the extent of stigmatization when we assess just one outcome, whether that single outcome be self-esteem, housing status, or access to medical care. From one vantage point, this is an odd stricture to impose on the study of stigma. If we adopt a narrow conceptualization of stigma, for example as a label linked to a stereotype, we might expect specificity in the outcomes. We might identify the elements of the stereotype and then, based on what the stereotype entails, predict which outcomes might be affected. If the stereotype is math incompetence, then we might expect the person to be excluded from endeavors where math competence is required. As important as this kind of theorizing might be for understanding some aspects of stigma, it will cloud our vision of the full consequences if it is the only approach we employ.

Among the reasons our conceptualization of stigma calls for the scrutiny of many outcomes are three we consider here. First, stigma involves status loss—downward placement in the status hierarchy. To the extent that this occurs, we can expect members of stigmatized groups to accrue all manner of untoward outcomes associated with lower placement in a status hierarchy, ranging from the selection of sexual partners to longevity. Second, structural discrimination can produce negative outcomes that have little to do with the stereotyped beliefs that initially motivated the structural discrimination. For example, the Not In My Back Yard (NIMBY) phenomenon resulted in treatment facilities for people with mental illness being located in relatively poor and powerless areas of the city that were also crime ridden and dangerous (Dear & Lewis 1986). As a consequence, people with mental illness are much more likely to be victimized than other people. Third, people's efforts to cope with stigma may have untoward consequences that are seemingly unrelated to the stereotype (James et al 1984, Smart & Wegner 1999). For example, social epidemiologist Sherman James puts forward the concept of what he calls "John Henryism"—the tendency for some African Americans to work extremely hard and with great pressure to disprove the stereotype of laziness and inability. According to James et al (1984), under some conditions this coping effort bears costs in the form of hypertension. In short, a comprehensive exploration of the stigma concept makes it clear that stigma can involve many outcomes and that any full assessment must look to a broad range of such outcomes.

Stigma as a Persistent Predicament

As previously mentioned, the literature makes reference to stigma as a predicament or dilemma. Our conceptualization draws attention to one way in which stigma is a persistent predicament—why the negative consequences of stigma are so difficult to eradicate. When powerful groups forcefully label and extensively stereotype a less powerful group, the range of mechanisms for achieving discriminatory outcomes is both flexible and extensive. We mentioned three generic types of mechanisms—individual discrimination, structural discrimination, and discrimination that operates through the stigmatized person's beliefs and behaviors. But lying below these broad-band designations are a whole multitude of specific mechanisms—there are many ways to achieve structural discrimination, many ways to directly discriminate, and many ways in which stigmatized persons can be encouraged to believe that they should not enjoy full and equal participation in social and economic life. Moreover, if the mechanisms that are currently in place are blocked or become embarrassing to use, new ones can always be created. This is the main reason that stigma is such a persistent predicament. When people in a stigmatized group take action to avoid a negative consequence, they frequently do so by counteracting (e.g. confronting or avoiding) the specific mechanism that leads to the undesirable outcome they seek to escape. But when the range of possible mechanisms is broad, the benefit is only temporary because the mechanism that has been blocked or avoided can be easily replaced by another.

A second and related reason that stigma is a persistent predicament is that there are a multitude of associated outcomes. One can exert great effort to avoid one stigma-related outcome, like discrimination in medical insurance or injury to self-esteem, but doing so can carry costs. For instance, the coping effort can be stressful, as in the case of John Henryism and hypertension levels among African Americans (James et al 1984). In that example, the effort to eliminate one bad outcome ironically produces strain that leads to another. Also, focusing particular attention on one outcome means that less attention is available to deal with other aspects of life. As a result, while benefits may accrue in one domain, concomitant harms may result in others. It is the existence of multiple stigma mechanisms and multiple stigma outcomes that helps explain why stigma is a persistent predicament—why, on average, members of stigmatized groups are disadvantaged in a broad range of life domains (e.g. employment, social relationships, housing, and psychological well-being).

We end our discussion of stigma as a persistent predicament with a point of clarification. First, to say that stigma is a persistent predicament is not to say that every individual in a group suffers the same outcome.

Individual differences in personal, social, and economic resources also shape the life circumstances of persons in stigmatized groups, thereby producing substantial variation within stigmatized groups in any outcome one might consider. Thus, no one is fully trapped in a uniform disadvantaged position. All of the other characteristics of persons influence an outcome in the same way they influence outcomes for persons who are not members of the stigmatized group in question. The persistent predicament refers to a general pattern of disadvantage that is connected to stigma processes of labeling, stereotyping, status loss, and discrimination.

Changing Stigma

If stigma is a persistent predicament, how can it be changed? One approach is to focus on a particular behavior in a particular group. For example, one might target hiring practices with the aim of increasing the employment chances for a stigmatized group such as people with mental illnesses. One could then try to change employers' beliefs about and attitudes toward hiring persons with such illnesses. This approach is very appealing because it breaks down the morass of interconnecting stigma-facets into a more tractable problem. If one were to develop an intervention, one could target the intervention to the specific beliefs, attitudes, and behaviors of employers, thereby increasing the likelihood of an apparently successful outcome for the intervention research study. But what is appealing about this approach is also what makes it such an inadequate response to the broader problem of stigma. The intense focus on one specific behavior in one specific group leaves the broader context untouched and as a consequence even the very positive outcomes of an unusually successful program will erode with time. This will occur for reasons we have stated: There exists a flexible package of mutually reinforcing mechanisms linking the attitudes and beliefs of dominant groups to an array of untoward outcomes for stigmatized persons.

Our conceptualization leads us to focus on two principles in considering how to really change stigma. The first is that any approach must be multifaceted and multilevel. It needs to be multifaceted to address the many mechanisms that can lead to disadvantaged outcomes, and it needs to be multilevel to address issues of both individual and structural discrimination. But second, and most important, an approach to change must ultimately address the fundamental cause of stigma—it must either change the deeply held attitudes and beliefs of powerful groups that lead to labeling, stereotyping, setting apart, devaluing, and discriminating, or it must change circumstances so as to limit the power of such groups to make their cognitions the dominant ones. In the absence of fundamental changes, interventions targeted at only one mechanism at a time will ultimately fail, because their effectiveness will be undermined by contextual factors that are left untouched by such a narrowly conceived intervention. Thus, in considering a multifaceted multilevel response to stigma, one should choose interventions that either produce fundamental changes in attitudes and beliefs or change the power relations that underlie the ability of dominant groups to act on their attitudes and beliefs.

Understanding the Influence of Stigma Processes on the Distribution of Life Chances

A core concern of sociology is to understand the distribution of life chances, whether those refer to careers, earnings, social ties, housing, criminal involvement, health, or life itself. We believe that stigma processes have a dramatic and probably a highly underestimated impact on such life chances. Most research proceeds by examining the stigma associated with one circumstance at a time (e.g. AIDS, obesity, mental illness, minority racial status, female gender, homosexuality, etc), and most also assesses only one outcome at a time (e.g. earnings, self-esteem, housing, social interactions, etc.). When this occurs, researchers often find some level of effect for a particular stigmatized group on a particular outcome. However, it is also usually true that many factors other than the stigma processes in question influence the outcome, leaving stigma as just one factor among many. This can lead to the conclusion that stigma matters but that its effect is relatively modest compared to other factors. This accounting is misguided for two reasons. First, in seeking to understand the impact of stigma for a particular circumstance, one must keep in mind that it can affect many life chances, not just one. Thus, a full accounting must consider the overall effect on a multitude of outcomes. Second, there are a host of stigmatizing circumstances that need to be considered in studying a particular outcome. A full assessment of the impact of stigma on such an outcome must recognize that many stigmatizing circumstances contribute to that outcome and not just the one selected for the particular study in question. When viewed broadly, stigma processes likely play a major role in life chances and deserve scrutiny not just by investigators who happen to be interested in stigma but by a variety of social scientists who are interested in the distribution of life chances more generally.

Conclusion

Almost forty years after the publication of Goffman's book on stigma, we revisited the concept in light of research that has been undertaken in the interim. Attending to criticisms of the concept and its application by researchers from Goffman to the present, we constructed a revised conceptualization of the term. In our definition, stigma exists when elements of labeling, stereotyping, separating, status loss, and discrimination co-occur in a power situation that allows these processes to unfold. After developing this definition and explicating its component parts, we found it useful in providing a substantially different perspective on several crucial issues in the literature on stigma. Moreover, our conceptualization suggests that stigma is likely to be a key determinant of many of the life chances that sociologists study, from psychological well-being to employment, housing, and life itself. A propitious avenue for future research would involve the incorporation of stigma concepts and measures in community-based survey research that seeks to understand the social determinants of a broad array of life chances. Such an undertaking would greatly advance research on stigma because it would assess the linkage between stigma and outcomes that clearly matter in people's lives, thereby overcoming the criticism we alluded to earlier regarding the overemphasis on microlevel interactions in stigma research. At the same time, the incorporation of stigma concepts and measures in research focused on life chances would provide investigators in many areas of sociological research with additional possibilities for understanding the social distributions of the particular outcomes that are the focus of their attention. Most importantly, however, such an endeavor would tell us much more than we already know about the conditions under which stigma is related to untoward outcomes in real life situations. Knowledge of this sort should form the basis for the kinds of multifaceted multilevel interventions that represent our best hope for producing real change in stigma-related processes.

Acknowledgments

We thank Patrick Corrigan, Bruce Dohrenwend, David Penn, and Elmer Struening for valuable comments on an earlier version of this paper.

References

Ainlay S. C., Becker G, Colman L. M. 1986. *The Dilemma of Difference: A Multidisciplinary View of Stigma.* New York: Plenum.

Ajzen I., Fishbein M. 1980. *Understanding Attitudes and Predicting Social Behavior.* Englewood Cliffs, NJ: Prentice Hall.

Angermeyer M., Matschinger H. 1994. Lay beliefs about schizophrenic disorder: the results of a population study in Germany. *Acta Psychiatr. Scand.* 89:39–45.

Angermeyer M. C., Matschinger H. 1996. The effect of violent attacks by schizophrenia persons on the attitude of the public towards the mentally ill. *Soc. Sci. Med.* 43:1721–28.

Cahill S., Eggleston R. 1995. Reconsidering the stigma of physical disability. *Sociol. Q.* 36:681–98.

Causey K. A., Duran-Aydintug C. 1997. Tendency to stigmatize lesbian mothers in custody cases. *J. Divorce Remarriage* 28: 171–82.

Cohen E. G. 1982. Expectations states and interracial interaction in school settings. *Annu. Rev. Sociol.* 8:209–235.

Coleman M., Ganong L., Cable S. 1996. Perceptions of stepparents: an examination of the incomplete institutionalization and social stigma hypotheses. *J. Divorce Remarriage* 26:25–48

Conrad P. 1992. *Deviance and Medicalization: From Badness to Sickness.* Philadelphia: Temple Univ. Press.

Conigan P. W., Penn D. l. 1999. Lessons from social psychology on discrediting psychiatric stigma. *Am. Psychol.* 54:765–76.

Crocker J., Lutskey N. 1986. Stigma and the dynamics of social cognition. In *The Dilemma of Difference*, ed. S. C. Ainlay, G. Becker, L. M. Coleman. New York: Plenum.

Crocker J. 1999. Social stigma and self-esteem: situational construction of self-worth. *J. Exp. Soc. Psychol.* 35:89–107.

Crocker J., Major B., Steele C. 1998. Social stigma. *In The Handbook of Social Psychology*, ed. D. T. Gilbert, S. T. Fiske, 2:504–53. Boston, MA: McGraw-Hill.

Davis K. R. 1998. Bankruptcy: a moral dilemma for women debtors. *Law Psychol. Rev.* 22:235–49.

Dear M. L., Lewis G. 1986. Anatomy of a decision: recent land use zoning appeals and their effect on group home locations in Ontario. *Can. J. Commun. Mental Health* 5:5–17.

Devine P. G., Plant E. A., Harrison K. 1999. The problem of us versus them and aids stigma. *Am. Behav. Sci.* 42:1212–28.

Driskell J. E., Mullen B. 1990. Status, expectations, and behavior: a meta-analytic review and test of the theory. *Personality Soc. Psychol. Bull.* 16:541–53.

Druss B. G., Bradford D. W., Rosenheck R. A., Radford M. J., Krumholz H. M. 2000. Mental disorders and the use of cardiovascular procedures after myocardial infarction. *J. Am. Med. Assoc.* 283:506–11.

Estroff S. E. 1989. Self, identity and subjective experiences of schizophrenia: in search of the subject. *Schizophrenia Bull.* 15:189–96

Farina A., Allen J. G., Saul B. 1968. The role of the stigmatized in affecting social relationships. *J. Personality* 36: 169–82.

Feagin J. R., Feagin C. B. 1996. *Racial and Ethnic Relations*. Upper Saddle River, NJ: Prentice Hall.

Fife B. L., Wright E. R. 2000. The demensionality of stigma: a comparison of its impact on the self of persons with HIV/AIDS and cancer. *J. Health Soc. Behav.* 41:50–67.

Fine M., Asch A. 1988. Disability beyond stigma: social interaction, discrimination, and activism. *J. Soc. Issues* 44:3–22.

Fiske S. T. 1998. Stereotyping, prejudice, and discrimination. In *The Handbook of Social Psychology*, ed. D. T. Gilbert, S. T. Fiske, 2:357–411. Boston, MA: McGraw Hill.

Franklin B. 1752. Letter to James Parker. In *The Importance of Gaining and Preserving the Friendship of the Indians to the British Interest Considered*, ed. A Kennedy. London: E. Cave.

Fullilove M. T. 1998. Abandoning race as a variable in public health research: an idea whose time has come. *Am. J.Pub. Health* 88:1297–98.

Furnham A., Bower P. 1992. A comparison of academic and lay theories of schizophrenia. *Br. J. Psychiatr.* 161:201–10.

Gaertner S. L., McLaughlin J. P. 1983. Racial stereotypes: associations and ascriptions of positive and negative characteristics. *Soc. Psychol. Q.* 46:23–30.

Goffman E. 1963. *Stigma: Notes on the Management of Spoiled Identity*. Englewood Cliffs, NJ: Prentice Hall.

Gould S. J. 1981. *The Mismeasure of Man*. New York: Norton.

Hahn H. 1983. Paternalism and public policy. *Society* XX:36–46.

Hamilton C., Carmichael S. 1967. *Black Power*. New York: Random House.

James S. A., LaCroix A. Z., Kleinbaum D. G., Strogatz D. S. 1984. John Henryism and blood pressure differences among black men: II. The role of occupational stressors. *J. Behav. Med.* 7:259–75.

Jones E., Farina A., Hastorf A., Markus H., Miller D. T., Scott R. 1984. *Social Stigma: The Psychology of Marked Relationships*. New York: Freeman.

Kleinman A., Wang W-Z, Li S-C, Cheng X. M., Dai X-Y, Li K-T, Kleinman J. 1995. The social course of epilepsy: chronic illness as social experience in interior China. *Soc. Sci. Med.* 40: 13 19–30.

Lewis J. 1998. Learning to strip; the socialization experiences of exotic dancers. *Can. J. Hum. Sexuality* 7:5 1–66.

Lieberson S. 1985. *Making It Count: The Improvement of Social Research and Theory.* Berkeley: Univ. Calif. Press.

Link B. 1982. Mental patient status, work, and income: an examination of the effects of a psychiatric label. *Am. Sociol. Rev.* 47:202–15.

Link B. 1987. Understanding labeling effects in the area of mental disorders: an assessment of the effects of expectations of rejection. *Am. Sociol. Rev.* 52:96–112.

Link B. G. 1983. Reward system of psychotherapy: implications for inequities in service delivery. *J. Health Soc. Behav.* 24:61–69.

Link B.G., Cullen F. T., Frank J., Wozniak J. 1987. The social rejection of ex-mental patients: understanding why labels matter. *Am. J.Sociol.* 92:1461–1500.

Link B. G., Cullen F. T., Struening E., Shrout P., Dohrenwend B. P. 1989. A modified labeling theory approach in the area of mental disorders: an empirical assessment. *Am. Sociol. Rev.* 54: 100–23.

Link B. G., Phelan J. C. 1999. Labeling and stigma. In *The Handbook of the Sociology of Mental Health,* ed. C. S. Aneshensel, J. C. Phelan. New York: Plenum.

Link B. G., Struening E. L., Rahav M., Phelan J. C., Nuttbrock L. 1997. On stigma and its consequences: evidence from a longitudinal study of men with dual diagnoses of mental illness and substance abuse. *J. Health Soc. Behav.* 38:177–90.

Macrae C. N., Milne A. B., Bodenhausen G. V. 1994. Stereotypes as energy saving devices: a peek inside the cognitive toolbox. *J. Personality Soc. Psychol.* 66:37–47.

Morone J. A. 1997. Enemies of the people: the moral dimension to public health. *J. Health Polit., Policy Law* 22:993–1020.

Mullen B., Salas E., Driskell J. E. 1989. Salience, motivation, and artifact as contributions to the relation between participation rate and leadership. *J. Exp. Soc. Psychol.* 25:545–59.

Oliver M. 1992. *The Politics of Disablement.* Basingstoke: Macmillan.

Opala J., Boillot F. 1996. Leprosy among the limba: illness and healing in the context of world view. *Soc. Sci. Med.* 42:3–19.

Page R. M. 1984. *Stigma.* London: Routledge & Keegan Paul.

Phelan J. C., Link B. G., Stueve A., Pescosolido B. 2000. Public conceptions of mental illness in 1950 and 1996: What is mental illness and is it to be feared. *J. Health Soc. Behav.* 41:188–207.

Pinel E. C. 1999. Stigma consciousness: the psychological legacy of social stereotypes. *J. Personality Soc. Psychol.* 76: 114–128.

Reissman C. K. 2000. Stigma and everyday resistance: childless women in South India. *Gender Soc.* 14: 111–35.

Rosenfield S. 1997. Labeling mental illness: the effects of received services and perceived stigma on life satisfaction. *Am. Sociol. Rev.* 62:660–72.

Rothman D. 1971. *The Discovery of the Asylum.* Boston: Little Brown & Company.

Sayce L. 1998. Stigma, discrimination and social exclusion: what's in a word *J. Mental Health* 7:331–43.

Scheff T. J. 1966. *Being Mentally Ill: A Sociological Theory.* Chicago, IL: Aldine de Gruyter.

Schneider J. W. 1988. Disability as moral experience: epilepsy and self in routine relationships. *J.Soc. Issues* 44:63–78.

Sheldon K., Caldwell L. 1994. Urinary incontinence in women: implications for therapeutic recreation. *Ther. Recreation J.* 28:203–12.

Smart L., Wegner D. M. 1999. Covering up what can't be seen: concealable stigma and mental control. *J. Personality Soc. Psychol.* 77:474–86.

Stafford M. C., Scott R. R. 1986. Stigma deviance and social control: some conceptual issues. In *The Dilemma of Difference,* ed. S.C. Ainlay, G. Becker, L.M. Coleman. New York: Plenum.

Steele C. M., Aronson J. 1995. Stereotype vulnerability and the intellectual test performance of African Americans. *J. Personality Soc. Psychol.* 69:797–811.

Wahl O. F. 1995. *Media Madness: Public Images of Mental Illness.* New Brunswick NJ: Rutgers Univ. Press.

Walsgrove D. 1987. Policing yourself: social closure and the internalization of stigma. In *The Manufacture of Disadvantage,* ed. G Lee, R Loveridge. Philadelphia: Open Univ. Press.

Wright E. R., Gonfrein W. P., Owens T. J. 2000. Deinstitutionalization, social rejection, and the self-esteem of former mental patients. *J. Health Soc. Behav.* 41:68–90.

The Consequences of Antisocial Behavior in Older Male Siblings for Younger Brothers and Sisters

23

Jim Snyder
Lew Bank
Bert Burraston

Research on siblings provides a number of unique opportunities to ascertain the linkage of developmental processes and outcomes (Scarr & Grajek, 1982). First, the relative similarity of siblings' developmental trajectories is a phenomenon that requires explanation (Kellam & Rebok, 1992). Second, the study of siblings permits the analysis of total family effects on individual child development, including both shared genetic and shared and unshared environmental influences (Hetherington, Henderson, & Reiss, 1999; Rowe, Rodgers, & Meseck-Bushey, 1992). Third, the simultaneous operation of multiple intrafamilial as well as extrafamilial environmental influences can be assessed; relationships with siblings as well as with parents and peers serve as powerful vehicles for socialization (Bank, Burraston, & Snyder, 2004; Slomkowski, Rende, Conger, Simons, & Conger, 2001). The goal of this report is to describe the social processes by which sibling relationships during childhood and adolescence contribute to the development of antisocial behavior.

Bank, Patterson, and Reid (1996) and Slomkowski et al. (2001) have described two social processes by which siblings may contribute to the risk for antisocial behavior. The first process entails training in coercion resulting from children's exposure to and imitation of siblings' coercive interactions with parents and from direct practice in coercive behavior during sibling conflict. The second process involves siblings' collusion and coparticipation in deviant activities during adolescence. Bank, Slomkowski, and their colleagues suggest that these developmentally sequential social processes are compatible and operate in a complementary fashion to increase risk. Coercive sibling interaction provides basic training in aggression. Once these coercive tactics are acquired, siblings who are similarly aggressive coparticipate in and mutually reinforce a wider variety of deviant activities that facilitate increasingly serious and diverse forms of antisocial behavior.

Previous research indicates that boys' coercive interaction and conflict with siblings during childhood incrementally increase the risk for poor peer relationships, antisocial behavior, arrests during adolescence and adulthood, and aggression toward adult partners (Bank et al., 1996). Research also suggests that the contribution of sibling conflict to antisocial development may be unique and complements risk resulting from parent–child conflict (Bank et al., 2004). Pike, McGuire, Hetherington, Reiss, and Plomin (1996) reported that sibling negativity is reliably associated with concurrent antisocial behavior during adolescence and primarily reflects shared environmental influences. Sibling relationships of children with diagnosed oppositional defiance and conduct disorders are characterized by four to five times as much aversive social exchange and lower levels of positive social exchange relative to the sibling relationships of children with other psychiatric disorders (Slomkowski, Cohen, & Brook, 1997).

Extensive sibling conflict also involves victimization, especially of younger by older siblings. Intersibling aggression is very common and includes very serious forms such as punching, hitting with an object, and threats to use and actual use of weapons (Roscoe, Goodwin, & Kennedy, 1987; Strauss, Gelles, & Steinmetz, 1980). Victimization, in turn, increases the risk for a variety of later problems, including violence, drug use, and early high-risk sexual behavior (Gully, Dengerink, Pepping, & Berstrom, 1981; Widom & Kuhns, 1996; Widom, Weiler, & Cottler, 1999).

Research indicates the collusion and coparticipation of siblings in deviant activities also increase risk for antisocial behavior. Collusion refers to mutually reinforced talk about deviant activities, including aggression, stealing, and alcohol and drug use. Collusion has been observed during the interaction of siblings (Bullock & Dishion, 2002) and may be associated with subsequent risk for deviant behavior (Shortt, Capaldi, Dishion, Bank, & Owen, 2003). Siblings spend a good deal of time together in late childhood and early adolescence, and parental supervision of siblings' time together decreases with age (Larson & Richards, 1991). Given an older sibling who is relatively antisocial, uses drugs, and associates with a deviant peer group, younger siblings are likely to be systematically exposed to antisocial talk and its reinforcement and to be invited to coparticipate in deviant behavior and criminal activities (Reiss & Farrington, 1991), especially if parental monitoring is limited.

Siblings also share peer networks. Involvement with and exposure to an older sibling's deviant peers may exacerbate a younger sibling's early initiation and progression into antisocial behavior and drug use and may increase a younger sibling's risk for victimization by those peers. In support of this notion, Rowe and Gulley (1992) found that siblings' sharing of mutual friends was a strong predictor of same-sex younger siblings' delinquency and drug use, after controlling for older siblings' delinquency and drug use. The synergistic effects of sharing friends and high levels of older sibling deviancy added to the prediction after accounting for main effects.

Exposure to older siblings' deviant peers may provide early experience with sophisticated forms of deviant talk and activities beyond those available in younger siblings' same-aged peer group, even if that group is highly deviant.

The manner in which these social processes operate in same- versus opposite-gender sibling relationships is less clear. Correlation coefficients for same-gender sibling similarity in antisocial behavior, drug use, and other disruptive behavior problems (i.e., among brothers and among sisters) are comparable in magnitude (Slomkowski et al., 2001) even though males relative to females show more behavior problems (Goodman & Kohlsdorf, 1994), have higher rates of arrests (Giordano & Cernkovich, 1997), and are more frequently diagnosed with disruptive behavior disorders (Zoccolillo, 1993). In contrast, intraclass correlations indexing the concordance for disruptive behavior problems in opposite-gender siblings are typically less than those of same-gender sibling pairs and occasionally not different from zero.

The social processes that increase risk may be different according to the gender combination of the sibling pair. Slomkowski et al. (2001), for example, found that younger siblings who were more involved with older delinquent siblings were at increased risk for delinquency during adolescence, but this held only for male–male, not female–female, sibling pairs. The social processes by which risk for antisocial behavior is transmitted in male–female sibling pairs is typically not addressed because of the low resemblance of opposite-gender sibling pairs. However, the reduced resemblance in specific antisocial outcomes in opposite-gender sibling pairs does not necessarily indicate an absence of sibling influence. Behavioral influence may not be isomorphic. For example, the antisocial behavior of an older male sibling may be associated with victimization–trauma or with precocious sexual activity rather than (or in addition to) the antisocial behavior of his younger female sibling.

In summary, extant research indicates that siblings may play important and potentially unique roles in the development of antisocial behavior, drug use, and other problems. Attempts to replicate and elaborate previous findings would be optimized by several tactics: collection of data from samples of siblings who represent the full range of antisocial behavior; the use of a longitudinal design that adequately represents multiple sibling processes as they are sequenced in development; and assaying the role of sibling influence in models that include other family and peer social processes.

The focal children in this study are the younger sisters and brothers of young men who participated in the Oregon Youth Study (OYS; Capaldi & Patterson, 1987; Patterson, Reid, & Dishion, 1992). As adolescents, these young men had high levels of antisocial behavior and other adjustment problems and associated with a variety of deviant male peers. To test the scope and isomorphism of sibling influence, an array of adolescent adjustment outcomes for younger siblings of the OYS males were assessed, including drug use, arrests, antisocial behavior, precocious sexual activity, association with same-aged deviant peers, and trauma–victimization. A series of models were tested that reflect the multiple mechanisms by which older siblings may contribute to the adjustment of younger siblings and that examine sibling mechanisms in the context of parent influence. These models were applied to both older brother–younger brother and older brother–younger sister dyads.

We tested four hypotheses:

1. The negative adolescent adjustment of younger sisters and brothers is associated with coercion training during interaction with their older brothers during preadolescence and with involvement in and exposure to the deviant activities and deviant peer associates of their older brothers during adolescence.
2. Involvement with older male siblings' deviant activities and peers is more strongly associated with trauma and victimization in younger female siblings and with antisocial behavior and arrests in younger male siblings.
3. The relationship of ineffective parenting and sibling coercion training to adjustment problems in adolescence is mediated through younger brothers' and sisters' exposure to and involvement in the deviant activities of their older brothers and their older brothers' peers.
4. The relationship of younger siblings' involvement with the deviant activities and deviant peer associates of their older brothers to younger siblings' adjustment in adolescence is maintained when controlling for concurrent parenting practices for the younger siblings.

Method

Participants

The OYS (Capaldi & Patterson, 1987; Patterson et al., 1992) sample consists of 206 boys and their families. The current study is an extension of the longitudinal OYS to include 155 younger sisters and brothers. Of the 206 OYS families, 105 had at least one younger sibling living in the same household at the first assessment wave when the OYS (older) brothers were 10 years old. From these 105 families, 82 younger sisters (from 68 families) and 73 younger brothers (from 57 families) provided data. For all analyses in this report, only one younger sibling, who was closest in age to the OYS boy and regardless of gender, per family was included. At Wave 11 (10 years later), the mean age for the younger sisters was 16.4 years and for the younger brothers 16.1 years. The research protocol was approved by the institutional review board. Signed, informed consent was obtained from participating parents and older and younger siblings before involvement in the research at appropriate points in this longitudinal project.

At Wave 1, approximately 33% of the families consisted of two biological parents, 33% consisted of one biological parent with a stepparent (almost all stepfathers), and 33% consisted of single biological parents (90% mothers). Juvenile court records indicate the high-risk nature of the sample. By age 18, 53% of the OYS boys had been arrested at least once, and 33% had multiple arrests. The families were predominately lower income, lower or working class, and White. In the first year of the study, 20% of the families had no employed parent and 33% received welfare. The families were highly mobile: 50% moved in the first 2 years of the study. The average family income in the fifth year of the study (1988–1989) was $20,000 per year.

Procedures

We used a multiagent, multimethod approach to data gathering. The agents included the younger siblings and their OYS older brothers, parents, teachers, interviewers, and observers. The methods included face-to-face and telephone interviews, questionnaires, home observations, laboratory interaction tasks, staff ratings, and official records. Parents and OYS older brothers were interviewed separately at Waves 1, 3, and 5, and younger siblings and parents were interviewed at Wave 11. Staff completed rating scales concerning parent and child behavior after each assessment contact. Parents, teachers, OYS brothers, and younger siblings completed questionnaires.

Instruments and Constructs

Patterson and Bank (1986, 1989) provide a detailed description of the general approach to construct building used in this study. Ideally, each construct was defined by multiple methods and agents. The process of building constructs involved a series of steps. The first step entailed theoretical definition of the construct, which was used to create a priori scales. Scales with alphas of less than .60 were excluded from further analysis. Individual items that generated item–total correlations less than .20 were dropped from scales, as were items with zero or near-zero variance. Scales were tested for convergent validity by exploratory factor analysis. Scales with factor loadings of less than .30 were excluded. Technical reports that provide the details of each construct (see Table 1 for a summary) are available from the Oregon Social Learning Center.

Predictor constructs measured during Waves 1 and 3 include sibling conflict and ineffective parenting. During Waves 1 and 3, OYS older brothers were in the fourth and sixth grades and were an average age of 9.5 and 11.5 years, respectively, and younger sibling were an average age of 6.3 and 8.3 years. Association with deviant peers was measured at Wave 5 for the OYS older brothers when they were 13.5 years of age. Parenting data that specifically targeted the younger siblings and the younger siblings' reports of time spent with their OYS older brother and his peers were collected at Wave 11 when the OYS older brothers averaged 19.5 years of age and their younger siblings 16.3 years of age. The criterion construct is a higher order poor adjustment factor composed of the younger siblings' scores for antisocial behavior, arrests, substance use, deviant peer association, early sexual activity, and exposure to trauma, all measured at Wave 11 when the younger siblings averaged 16.3 years of age. Each construct is now described in more detail. Bank et al. (2004) provide additional information about the sibling conflict and ineffective parenting constructs.

SIBLING CONFLICT   The sibling conflict construct measures overt (e.g., hitting and fighting) and covert (e.g., stealing and cheating) coercive exchanges between the siblings. It is defined by four measures: two observational measures, the rate per minute of conflict bouts between the OYS older brother and his siblings, and observers' global ratings of how well the siblings got along during interaction; the two other indicators were parents' and OYS older brothers' reports of sibling conflict (see Table 1).

INEFFECTIVE PARENTING   Ineffective parenting is a higher order construct that draws from three parenting construct indicators: poor problem solving, poor supervision, and parent conflict bouts. Problem solving was assessed in the laboratory; two family problems, one selected by the OYS older brother and the other by the parents, were discussed for 10 minutes each (Patterson & Capaldi, 1990). Problem-solving interaction was videotaped and then scored using the Solving Problems in Family Interactions coding system (Forgatch, Fetrow, & Lathrop, 1985). Two elements make up the parent supervision construct: (a) parental rules and expectations concerning the type and amount of information they require from their child and (b) how much time the child is with the parents and the number of hours the child is unsupervised by an adult. Parents' and OYS older brothers' reports and staff ratings were used to define these elements. The parent conflict construct was defined as rate per minute of conflict observed in the home, designated as conflict between the parents or between a parent and one child without any involvement of siblings.

OLDER BROTHER DEVIANT PEER ASSOCIATION   Association with deviant peers by the OYS older brother at age 13.5 years is a higher order construct defined by four first-order constructs described by Patterson, Dishion, and Yoerger (2000). The first construct is derived from the Peer Interaction Task (PIT; Dishion, Spraklen, Andrews, & Patterson, 1996). The PIT entails coding the content of the discourse of the older brother and his close friend. Indicators from the PIT included the duration of rule-breaking talk, the proportion of rule-breaking to total talk, the proportion reinforcement of rule-breaking talk to total reinforcement, interviewer's rating of the friend's encouragement of antisocial behavior, and observer ratings of the friend's antisocial behavior during the PIT task.

Table 1   Measurements of Constructs

Construct/indicators	Sample items	α
Sibling conflict (Waves 1 and 3)		.69
Rate per minute of observed conflict bouts		
Observer ratings		
Parent Ratings		
OYS brother's rating		
Ineffective parenting (Waves 1 and 3)		.59
Problem solving (observer ratings		
Outcomes	"Clear definition of problem"	
Solutions	"Number of solutions"	
Child participation	"Parent encouraged child"	
Supervision of older brother (Waves 1 and 3)		
Parent report scale	"Number of hours child unsupervised"	
Child report scale	"Clear parental rules"	
Observer ratings		
Rates per minute of conflict (Waves 1 and 3		
Parent–child	Observed rate of conflict bouts	
Parent–parent	Observed rate of conflict bouts	
Older brother's deviant peer association (Wave 5)	See text	
Observed PIT (older brother–friend)		
Deviant talk	Observed duration	
Deviant talk	Observed % of all talk	
Reinforcement	Observed % of friend's positive responses for deviant talk	
Interviewer rating	Peer involved with deviant friends	
Observer ratings	Showed aggression, threats	
Brother's association with deviant peers		
Child interview	Friends stolen something less than $5	
Teacher report form	Hangs with kids who get in trouble	
Child Behavior Checklist	Hangs with kids who get in trouble	
Antisocial behavior of peers		
Child Behavior Checklist	Friends are a bad influence	
Child interview	How many friends damage things	
Coder ratings of peer	Indicated friends were antisocial	
Amount of time spent with peers		
Parents' report	Son prefers to be with friends	
Parent telephone interview	Involved in unsupervised activity	
Child self report	Spend free time with friends	
Hanging out with older brother (Wave 11)		.68
Younger sibling report of coparticipation w/older brother	Substance use, illegal acts, activities with deviant peers	
Younger sibling poor adjustment (Wave 11)		
Early sexual activity (self-report)	Kissing, genitals–breast touch	.67
Arrests	Official records	
Antisocial behavior		.79
Elliott Behavior Checklist-parent		
Child Behavior Checklist		
Parent interview		
Elliott Behavior Checklist—child		
Telephone interview—child		
Child interview rating		
Deviant peer association		See text
Child Behavior Checklist		
Child interview		
Child report describing best friends		
Substance use		See text
Child Behavior Checklist	"Uses drugs or alcohol"	
Parent interview		
Child interview	Frequency and pattern of use of tobacco, alcohol, marijuana, other	
Traumatic stress		.78
Child interview	Exposure to assault, MVA,	
Child interview	Frequency of trauma memory	
Child interview	Reaction: numb, jumpy	
Parental discipline of younger sibling (Wave 11)		.63
Parent report	Consistent, effective	
Child report	Fair, how discipline	
Interviewer rating		

Note: OYS = Oregon Youth Study; PIT = Peer Interaction Task; MVA = motor vehicle accident.

The second construct is composed of teacher and parent reports about the OYS boys' association with peers who get into trouble. The third construct, the antisocial behavior of the OYS older brother's peers, is defined by parent and child reports of friends who have a bad influence and by coder ratings of association with antisocial friends. The fourth construct, amount of time the OYS older brother spends with peers, is derived from parent and child reports and child telephone interviews about the extent of unsupervised time with peers.

HANGING OUT WITH OLDER BROTHER   This composite is designed to measure the deviant behavior of the younger sibling that was performed in the company of the older brother. It is derived from the younger sibling's report on the Sibling Interaction Scale (Bank et al., 1996) and contains five indicators of coparticipation in deviant activities with an older sibling, including substance use, illegal acts, arrests, time spent with the OYS older brother and his peers, and threats by older brother's peers.

YOUNGER SIBLING POOR ADJUSTMENT   This construct is a higher order factor composed of early sexual activity, arrests, antisocial behavior, deviant peer association, substance use, and traumatic stress. The early sexual activity variable assesses younger siblings' self-reported engagement in kissing and petting as reported during a structured interview. Younger siblings' arrests were obtained from police records of arrests from each county in which the child had lived.

The younger sibling antisocial behavior composite measured both overt (e.g., hitting, threats, disorderly conduct, and gang involvement) and clandestine (e.g., stealing, lying, cheating, and trafficking in stolen goods) behaviors occurring in and out of the home from the perspectives of parents, children, and the child's interviewer. Parents' reports were based on the Elliott Behavior Checklist (Elliott, Ageton, Huizinga, Knowles, & Canter, 1983), the Child Behavior Checklist (Achenbach, 1993), and an interview.

Information from the child was based on the Elliott Behavior Checklist (Elliott et al., 1983), a telephone interview, and a face-to-face interview with the child. The interviewer rating data are derived from the Interviewer Impressions Checklist.

The younger sibling deviant peer association composite assesses deviant behavior of the younger siblings' peer associates, including drug use, stealing, fighting, and vandalism, from the perspective of parents and children. Parent report is based on the Child Behavior Checklist (Achenbach, 1993). The child's report is based on the child interview and the Describing Friends scale. Correlation between the parent and child report is .46 ($p < $ .001).

The younger sibling substance use composite measured the frequency and pattern of substance use based on parent and child report. The parent report is based on one item from the Child Behavior Checklist (Achenbach,

1993) and one item from the parent interview (both reflecting general substance use). Younger siblings' self-reports focus on the frequency and patterns of use of tobacco, alcohol, marijuana, and illicit drugs, assessed during a child interview. Correlation between the parent and child report is .47 ($p < .001$).

Younger sibling traumatic stress gauges the occurrence of specific traumatic events and the impact of the event on the respondent. The indicator is based on three items from the younger sibling's interview. Exposure to traumatic events inquires about the sibling's own or a close friend's experience of the following events over the previous year: robbed or mugged; assaulted or raped; in a motor vehicle accident; unexpected death of a loved one; injury or property damage; forced to evacuate home; a shocking or terrifying experience; and change in job, residence, or relationships. The second component, memories of the trauma, inquires about the frequency of memories and sudden reminders of the event, intrusive thoughts, nightmares about the event, and avoidance of situational reminders of the event. The final component, reaction to traumatic stress, inquires about the frequency over the previous month of feeling numb, reduced enjoyment of people and activities that were formerly pleasurable, feeling jumpy or easily startled, being unusually forgetful or having trouble concentrating, and having trouble sleeping.

PARENTAL DISCIPLINE OF YOUNGER SIBLINGS This composite variable was designed to assess discipline applied to the younger siblings at the time of the Wave 11 assessments when these younger siblings were an average of 16.3 years old. Multiple items concerning discipline were derived from three sources: parent report, sibling report, and interviewer ratings. Items for the various sources were similar and focused on parent consistency, effectiveness, fairness, strictness, and agreement on discipline.

Results

Analysis Strategy

The hypotheses were tested in two steps. The first step entailed fitting measurement models to the data to assess the relation of the observed measures to their underlying constructs, with the constructs allowed to intercorrelate freely. This step establishes the confirmatory assessment of construct validity (Anderson & Gerbing, 1988). The second step ascertained the fit of a series of nested structural models that directly tested Hypotheses 1 to 4. It should be noted that previous confirmatory factor analyses (Bank et al., 2004) have already established that the two key constructs operationally defining early family processes at Waves 1 and 3, sibling conflict and ineffective parenting, each provide unique information (i.e., represent two separate rather than one common factor). As in most longitudinal studies, there were missing data and using listwise deletion would have reduced sample size considerably. We used SPSS to determine the missing value patterns for structural equation modeling. For calculating the measurement and structural equation models, we used AMOS to compute full-information maximum likelihood estimates in the presence of missing data (Arbuckle, 1996).

Measurement Model and Construct Intercorrelations

One critical aspect of the measurement model involves specification of the construct for younger siblings' adjustment at age 16. All of the indicators for the younger sibling poor adjustment construct loaded significantly. As expected, deviant peer association (standardized coefficient [SC] = .92, critical ratio [CR] = 10.95), antisocial behavior (SC = .84, fixed for scaling), and substance use (SC = .72, CR = 8.47) most powerfully defined the construct, whereas arrests (SC = .42, CR = 4.19), early sexual activity (SC = .55, CR = 5.07), and traumatic stress (SC = .52, CR = 5.38) loaded significantly but somewhat less powerfully.

Three indicators of younger sibling poor adjustment were significantly related to the age difference between the older and younger sibling; younger siblings who were closer in age to their older brothers were at greater risk: early sexual activity SC = −.36, CR = −3.64; traumatic stress SC = −.22, CR = −2.57; substance use SC = −.19, CR = −2.68. Younger sisters were also more likely to have experienced traumatic stress (SC = .19, CR = 2.27) than were younger brothers.

Table 2 provides the correlations among the predictors and younger sibling poor adjustment. Sibling conflict and older brother (OB) deviant peer association were both at least marginally correlated with all of the major constructs (excluding younger sibling gender and age difference) in the model. Ineffective parenting was highly related to concurrent sibling conflict and OB deviant peer association 2 to 4 years later but not reliably related to younger sibling poor adjustment in adolescence about 8 years later. OB deviant peers was significantly correlated with younger sibling poor adjustment about 6 years later.

Tests of Hypothesized Models

Table 3 provides the standardized path coefficients, critical ratios, and goodness-of-fit indexes for a series of models that represent iterative refinements of the fit of the data to relationships posited in Hypotheses 1 through 4. The five models shown in Table 3 are nested, and each adequately fits the data. In Model 1 all of the paths from the prospective predictor variables to younger sibling poor adjustment were estimated. As hypothesized, ineffective parenting has a significant effect on OB deviant peer association (SC = .49, CR = 5.22). Contrary to our hypothesis, sibling

Table 2 Construct Intercorrelations From the Measurement Model

Variable	1	2	3	4	5	6	7	8	9
1. Sibling conflict	—								
2. Ineffective parenting	.40 (3.76)	—							
3. OB deviant peers	.27 (2.59)	.48 (4.32)	—						
4. Hanging out w/ OB	.29 (2.79)	.12 (1.15)	.27 (2.56)	—					
5. Sibling Conflict × Hanging out w/ OB	.02 (0.17)	.11 (1.09)	.12 (1.21)	.31 (2.94)	—				
6. Younger sibling gender	-.09 (-0.87)	.07 (0.71)	-.06 (-0.58)	-.10 (-0.98)	.13 (1.32)	—			
7. Sibling age difference	.05 (0.54)	.18 (1.78)	.14 (1.39)	-.27 (-2.58)	-.05 (-0.46)	-.03 (-0.34)	—		
8. Parent discipline at Wave 11	-.19 (-1.81)	-.07 (-0.68)	-.08 (-0.81)	-.38 (-3.41)	-.18 (-1.65)	.07 (0.65)	.22 (2.04)	—	
9. Younger sibling poor adjustment	.22 (2.02)	.14 (1.31)	.35 (3.04)	.54 (4.28)	.30 (2.69)	-.20 (-1.90)	-.11 (-1.04)	-.36 (-2.95)	—

Note: Measurement model fit: $\chi^2(49) = 51.68$, $p = .40$, normed fit index = .96, comparative fit index = 1.00. Critical ratios for the correlations are shown in parentheses. OB = older brother.

Table 3 Path Models for the Relation of Sibling Conflict, Ineffective Parenting, and Older Brother Deviant Peers to Younger Siblings' Poor Adjustment

Variable	OB deviant peers	YS poor adjustment	χ^2 (df)	NFI	CFI	$\Delta\chi^2$
Model 1			40.6 (37)	0.97	1	—
Sibling conflict	0.05 (0.50)	0.18 (1.70)				
Ineffective parenting	0.49 (5.22)	0.00 (−0.01)				
OB deviant peers		0.22 (1.95)				
YS gender		−0.24 (−2.42)				
Sibling age difference		−0.14 (−1.43)				
Model 2			40.6 (38)	0.97	1	0
Sibling conflict	0.05 (0.50)	0.18 (1.80)				
Ineffective parenting	0.49 (5.22)					
OB deviant peers		0.22 (2.20)				
YS gender		−0.24 (−2.42)				
Sibling age difference		−0.14 (−1.44)				
Model 3			43.69 (39)	0.97	1	3.09
Sibling conflict	0.05 (0.49)					
Ineffective parenting	0.49 (5.22)					
OB deviant peers		0.27 (2.73)				
YS gender		−0.25 (−2.56)				
Sibling age difference		−0.13 (−1.36)				
Model 4			43.35 (38)	0.97	1	2.75
Sibling conflict	0.05 (0.49)					
Ineffective parenting	0.49 (5.22)	0.07 (0.59)				
OB deviant peers		0.24 (2.06)				
YS gender		−0.25 (−2.58)				
Sibling age difference		−0.15 (−1.48)				
Model 5			43.31 (38)	0.97	1	2.71
Sibling conflict	0.05 (0.50)	0.20 (1.84)				
Ineffective parenting	0.49 (5.21)	0.11 (0.98)				
OB deviant peers						
YS gender		−0.21 (−2.15)				
Sibling age difference		−0.16 (−1.58)				

Note: Critical ratios are shown in parentheses. OB = older brother; YS = younger sibling; NFI = normed fit index; CFI = comparative fit index.

conflict did not predict OB deviant peer association (SC = .05, CR = 0.50). Ineffective parenting accounted for most of the 26% of the explained variance in OB deviant peer association. As anticipated, OB deviant peer association (SC = .22, CR =1.95) had the strongest effect (relative to ineffective parenting and sibling conflict) on younger sibling poor adjustment, followed by sibling conflict (SC = .18, CR = 1.70). In the context of OB deviant peer association and sibling conflict, ineffective parenting had no direct effect on younger sibling poor adjustment (SC = .00, CR = 0.01). This lack of effect does not indicate a mediator effect as the correlation of ineffective parenting and younger sibling poor adjustment was also not significant in the measurement model. Younger sisters were less likely to experience adjustment problems than younger brothers (SC = −.24, CR = −2.42). Younger sibling poor adjustment did not significantly vary with the age difference between the younger sibling and OB (SC = −.14, CR = −1.43). OB deviant peer association, sibling conflict, and gender together explained 18% of the variance in younger sibling poor adjustment.

A series of models were used to further estimate the relative influence of the prospective predictors under various conditions. Model 2 set the nonsignificant path from ineffective parenting to younger sibling poor adjustment to 0. The paths from OB deviant peer association and sibling conflict did not change, nor did the fit of the model to the data. The path from ineffective parenting to poor adjustment was not necessary to fit the model to the data, and Model 2 was more parsimonious than Model 1. In Model 3, the path from sibling conflict to poor adjustment was also set to 0. The chi-square statistic indicated an acceptable fit, but there was a marginally significant decrement in the fit of Model 3 relative to Model 2 ($\Delta\chi^2 = 3.09$, $\Delta df = 1$, $p < .08$), suggesting the importance of the sibling conflict to poor adjustment path. Model 4 set the path from sibling conflict to younger sibling poor adjustment to 0 and again freely estimated the path from ineffective parenting to poor adjustment; this path remained nonsignificant (SC = 07, CR = 0.59). Model 5 set the path from OB deviant peer association to poor adjustment to 0. The path from sibling conflict (SC = .20, CR = 1.84) to poor adjustment was marginally significant, but the path from ineffective parenting (SC = .11, CR = 0.98) to poor adjustment remained nonsignificant. The change in the chi-square fit statistic between Models 1 and 5 is marginally significant, indicating that Model 1 fits the data better than Model 5 ($\Delta\chi^2 = 2.71$, $\Delta df = 1$, $p < .10$) and suggesting the importance of the OB deviant peer association to poor adjustment path.

In summary, younger siblings who evidenced poor adjustment in adolescence (mean age = 16 years) were more likely to have engaged in frequent conflict (at ages 6–8 years) with their older brothers and to have older brothers who associated with deviant peers when the younger siblings were children (mean age = 10 years). Conflictual sibling relationships and exposure to older siblings with deviant peers each significantly increased younger siblings' risk for antisocial behavior, drug use, arrest, early sexual activity, and traumatic experiences some 6 to 10 years later. This increased risk was apparent even after controlling for ineffective parental discipline, problem solving, and monitoring during the younger siblings' childhood. Ineffective parenting when younger siblings were 6 to 8 years of age did not have a direct impact on the younger siblings' adjustment in adolescence but rather increased risk for poor adjustment as a result of failures to manage early sibling conflict and older brothers' association with deviant peers.

The predictors in the previous models clearly have a prospective relationship to younger siblings' adolescent adjustment. A more complex model to predict younger sibling poor adjustment was tested, adding a measured variable indicating the degree to which younger siblings are hanging out with older brothers (hanging out; measured concurrently with poor adjustment at Wave 11) and a Sibling Conflict (measured at Waves 1 and 3) × Hanging Out (measured at wave 11) interaction term. We hypothesized that hanging out with an older deviant sibling in adolescence (Wave 11) and its accompanying opportunities for coparticipation in deviant activities would mediate the relationship between the OB deviant peer association (Wave 5) and younger sibling poor adjustment. The Sibling Conflict × Hanging Out interaction term examines whether siblings' early involvement in conflict and coercion and their later coparticipation and mutual encouragement of deviant activities increase the risk for poor adjustment in a synergistic as well as additive manner.

The correlations among the three latent variables, OB deviant peer association, hanging out, and poor adjustment (see Table 2), were all statistically significant ($p < .05$). These correlations are derived from a measurement model and thus represent correlations between latent constructs. Because these correlations are disattenuated, the magnitudes of the coefficients are enhanced compared with zero-order correlations. Younger sisters relative to younger brothers were slightly less likely to demonstrate poor adjustment ($r = -.20$) but more likely to report traumatic experiences ($r = .19$).

This more complex model is shown in Figure 1. The results support the hypothesis that hanging out may partially mediate the relation between the OB deviant peer association (Wave 5) and poor adjustment (Wave 11). The path from OB deviant peer association to younger siblings' hanging out was significant (SC = .27, CR = 2.65) as was the path from hanging out to poor adjustment (SC = .44, CR = 4.53). OB deviant peer association has both a direct effect (SC = .21, CR = 2.26) and an indirect effect on younger sibling poor adjustment through hanging out. As expected, the greater the age difference between the siblings, the less likely they were to hang out together (SC = −.30, CR = −3.48). The Sibling Conflict × Hanging Out interaction term also reliably predicted younger sibling poor adjustment (SC = .19, CR = 2.14). The fit of this more complex model to the data was quite good, $\chi^2(58) = 65.07$, $p = .244$, normed fit index (NFI) .947, comparative fit index (CFI) = .994. The model accounts for 38% of the variance in younger siblings' poor adjustment in adolescence.

One additional model was fit to the data, adding paths from effective parent discipline as a measured variable to younger siblings' hanging out and to younger sibling poor adjustment, all of which were measured concurrently at Wave 11. The rationale for this model was to assess whether hanging out continued to contribute to concurrent poor adjustment with the inclusion of concurrent parent discipline focused on the younger sibling. The paths from effective parent discipline to poor adjustment (SC = −.28, CR = −3.00) and to hanging out (SC = −.27, CR = −2.99) were

Figure 1   The contribution of sibling social relational processes during childhood and adolescence to younger siblings' adolescent adjustment.

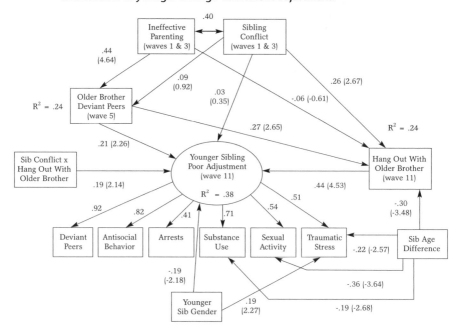

both reliable, but all of the other paths shown in Figure 1 retained their predictive value and statistical reliability. The fit of this more complex model to the data was modest, $\chi^2(67) = 88.65$, $p = .040$, NFI = .930, CFI = .981.

Older siblings' influence on younger siblings' adolescent adjustment continues to unfold over development. Younger siblings who were involved in frequent coercive interaction with their older brothers and who were exposed to older brothers' peer associates before adolescence were more likely to hang out and to coparticipate in deviant activities with their older brothers in adolescence. Early sibling conflict appears to facilitate a later sibling compatibility, association, and mutual involvement in deviant activities. Later high levels of sibling association and mutual involvement in deviant actions, in turn, promote a range of adjustment problems in younger siblings. These early and later sibling effects are sufficiently powerful to be maintained despite parents' efforts to manage younger siblings' behavior problems during adolescence. The closer the siblings are in age, the more powerful are the effects on younger siblings, especially regarding substance use, sexual activity, and exposure to traumatic experiences. In terms of traumatic experience, in particular, younger sisters and younger brothers are affected in different ways by their older brothers.

Discussion

There was general support for the hypothesized sibling influence model. Early sibling conflict, exposure to the deviant activities and associates of an older brother during childhood, and younger siblings' association and coparticipation in deviant activities with their older brothers during adolescence reliably increased younger sisters' and brothers' risk for a variety of serious behavior problems in adolescence. These findings are consistent with previous research (Bank et al., 1996; Rowe & Gulley, 1992; Slomkowski et al., 1997, 2001) that documents the powerful socialization role of siblings. The data in this report provide the first test and confirmation of the dual-sibling social process model offered by Bank, Slomkowski, and their colleagues. The data suggest that sibling influence unfolds in an iterative fashion from early childhood through adolescence and entails a developmental sequencing of different social processes, from conflict and disagreement in early childhood to exposure to and coparticipation in deviant activities in later childhood and adolescence. The sequential influences of early sibling conflict, older brothers' association with deviant peers, and siblings' coparticipation in deviant activities on younger siblings' adolescent adjustment entail indirect linkages between earlier and later sibling experiences and combine in a cumulative and synergistic fashion to increase risk.

The substantial and unique power of sibling influence can also be inferred from the inclusion of a multicomponent, multimethod measure of parenting during childhood and the inclusion of a concurrent measure of parental discipline in adolescence. The observed substantial and multiple influences of older brothers on their younger siblings maintained their reliability and magnitude in the context of such parenting influences. The co-occurring parent and sibling influence apparent in this analysis is consistent with previous analyses with this sample that focused on the adjustment of the older OYS boys (Bank et al., 2004).

The power of sibling influence is also apparent in the wide range of developmental outcomes used to define younger siblings' adolescent adjustment, including arrests, drug use, antisocial behavior, deviant peer association, early sexual activity, and traumatic stress. The impact of siblings on a range of externalizing outcomes reported in previous research (e.g., K. J. Conger, Conger, & Scaramella, 1997; R. D. Conger & Reuter, 1996; Rowe & Gulley, 1992; Slomkowski et al., 2001) is clearly replicated in these data.

The current research also suggests that sibling influence on antisocial development is contextually sensitive. Influence appears to be stronger for siblings who are closer in age, perhaps by affecting how much time older and younger siblings spend with one another and how much they coparticipate in deviant activities. Influence also depends on the gender composition of the sibling dyad. Younger sisters relative to younger brothers, for example, were more likely to report traumatic experiences even though they demonstrated lower levels of overall poor adjustment. Girls with an antisocial older brother may be exposed to and have significant contact with his antisocial peers and, consequently, may be at increased risk for physical or sexual victimization (Capaldi & Clark, 1998). Because of their relatively lower levels of strength and aggressiveness, younger sisters more than younger brothers may be perceived as more vulnerable targets by an older brother and his peers (Schrepferman, Snyder, & Bank, 2003).

The current data provide a glimpse into the processes by which older brothers affect their younger brothers' and sisters' adolescent adjustment. Early sibling conflict, especially when accompanied by ineffective parenting, may shape the use of coercive and aggressive interpersonal tactics (Snyder & Stoolmiller, 2002). As they move into later childhood and adolescence, siblings may engage in mutual discourse about deviant activities, modeling of deviant acts, and actual collusion and coparticipation in drug use and other antisocial activities (Bullock & Dishion, 2002). Although these processes probably entail reciprocal sibling influence if the siblings are closer in age, older siblings may exert more influence because they are generally likely to have been exposed to and to have engaged in a greater variety of antisocial activities.

However, younger siblings' hanging out with their older brother brings another potentially pathogenic social process into play: exposure to and involvement with the deviant peers of the older brother (Larson & Richards, 1991). Although antisocial younger siblings may have established their own (deviant) affiliations with same-aged peers, hanging out with an antisocial older brother and his deviant associates is likely to accelerate the deviancy training process beyond that occurring in the younger sibling's sameage peer group. Exposure to an older brother's deviant peers not only provides the opportunity for participation in an even wider variety of antisocial activities but may do so without the protection of familial or blood loyalty and identification. Direct involvement with an older brother's deviant peers may particularly increase the risk for younger sisters' trauma, victimization, and involvement in precocious sexual activity.

The seemingly powerful and developmentally persistent influence of siblings on risk for antisocial behavior suggests that the sibling relationship may provide a useful venue for preventive interventions, complementing more standard parent, peer, and school intervention contexts. The data in this report suggest that preventive efforts should focus on the sibling relationship relatively early in development, before the at-risk older sibling becomes heavily involved with deviant peers. Such early sibling intervention may be implemented as an additional, systematic component of parent training (Johnston & Freeman, 1998) or delivered in its own right with or without accompanying parenting intervention (Bank, Snyder, & Prescott, 2002; Kramer, 2004). In fact, sibling intervention provides a "two for one" modality of service delivery, serving as a simultaneous clinical intervention for an older sibling with significant conduct problems and as a preventive intervention for the at-risk younger sibling. Although sibling relationship enhancement may be beneficial when applied to low-risk adolescent sibling dyads, the current data suggest that sibling interventions targeting high-risk sibling dyads during adolescence may face the same obstacles and potential iatrogenic effects encountered in peer interventions for antisocial adolescents (Dishion, McCord, & Poulin, 1999).

Some methodological characteristics of this study increase the confidence that can be placed in the findings. Its design is largely, although not exclusively, prospective, locating constructs in development in a manner consistent with theory. Multimethod and multisource measurement of many of the constructs reduces measurement error and mitigates shared source variance as a competing explanation for the observed relationships among the major constructs. The children in the sample represent a full range of adjustment so that the size of the relationships among constructs is likely to be reasonably well estimated.

However, the study also has several methodological characteristics that attenuate the clarity with which the results can be interpreted and the degree to which the findings may be generalized. Measures of early sibling conflict were not specific to the focal older brother and younger sibling but rather reflected the often multiple sibling relationships that occurred in the families in the OYS sample. Measures of ineffective parenting likely better represent the parenting experienced by the OYS boys who served as older brothers in this report than the parenting experienced by the focal younger siblings in this study. The OYS sample is atypical in several regards. The children in the sample were at considerable risk for antisocial behavior. The children and families evidenced limited variation and range in terms of socioeconomic status and ethnicity and were derived from a specific geographic location. Thus, generalization of the findings to the larger population remains tentative. Only older brother-younger sister and older brother-younger brother combinations were represented in the current report, and different sibling influences may occur when the older sibling is female rather than male. Finally, the use of a correlational longitudinal design necessarily makes inferences about causality tentative. Not all theoretically relevant constructs (e.g., peer influences for younger siblings, parental monitoring) were measured and included in the model. Stronger inferences await experimental manipulation of sibling and family relationship in randomized prevention or clinical trials. However, this as well as other empirical reports concerning the role of sibling relationships as a risk factor in the development of antisocial behavior clearly suggest that such trials are reasonable and may be efficacious.

References

Achenbach, T. M. (1993). *Manual for the Child Behavior Checklist/4–18 and 1991 profile.* Burlington: University of Vermont, Department of Psychiatry.

Anderson, J. C., & Gerbing, D. W. (1988). Structural equation modeling in practice: A review and recommended two-step approach. *Psychological Bulletin, 103,* 411–423.

Arbuckle, J. L. (1996). Full information estimation in the presence of incomplete data. In G. A. Marcoulides & R. E. Schumacker (Eds.), *Advanced structural equation modeling: Issues and techniques* (pp. 243–277). Mahwah, NJ: Erlbaum.

Bank, L., Burraston, B., & Snyder, J. (2004). Sibling conflict and ineffective parenting as predictors of adolescent boys' antisocial behavior and peer difficulties: Additive and interactional effects. *Journal of Research on Adolescence, 14,* 99–125.

Bank, L., Patterson, G. R., & Reid, J. B. (1996). Negative sibling interaction patterns as predictors of later adjustment problems in young male adolescents. In G. H. Brody (Ed.), *Sibling relationships: Their causes and consequences* (pp. 197–229). Norwood, NJ: Ablex.

Bank, L., Snyder, J., & Prescott, A. (2002). *Sibling relationship intervention in the prevention and treatment of antisocial behavior: Rationale, description and advantages.* Unpublished manuscript.

Bullock, B. M., & Dishion, T. J. (2002). Sibling collusion and problem behavior in early adolescence: Toward a process model for family mutuality. *Journal of Abnormal Child Psychology, 30,* 143–153.

Capaldi, D. M., & Clark, S. (1998). Prospective family predictors of aggression toward female partners for at-risk young men. *Developmental Psychology, 34,* 1175–1188.

Capaldi, D. M., & Patterson, G. R. (1987). *Psychometric properties of fourteen latent constructs from the Oregon Youth Study.* New York: Springer-Verlag.

Conger, K. J., Conger, R. D., & Scaramella, L. V. (1997). Parents, siblings, psychological control and adolescent adjustment. *Journal of Adolescent Research, 12,* 113–138.

Conger, R. D., & Reuter, M. A. (1996). Siblings, parents, and peers: A longitudinal study of social influence in adolescent risk for alcohol use and abuse. In G. H. Brody (Ed.), *Sibling relationships: Their causes and consequences* (pp. 1–30). Norwood, NJ: Ablex.

Dishion, T. J., McCord, J., & Poulin, F. (1999). When interventions harm: Peer groups and problem behavior. *American Psychologist, 54,* 755–764.

Dishion, T. J., Spraklen, K. M., Andrews, D. W., & Patterson, G. R. (1996). Deviancy training in male adolescent friendships. *Behavior Therapy, 27,* 373–390.

Elliott, D. S., Ageton, S. S., Huizinga, D., Knowles, B., & Canter, R. J. (1983). The prevalence and incidence of delinquent behavior: 1976–1980. In *National estimates of delinquent behavior by sex, race, social class, and other selected variables* (National Youth Survey Report No. 26). Boulder, CO: Behavioral Research Institute.

Forgatch, M. S., Fetrow, B., & Lathrop, M. (1985). *Solving problems in family interaction: A training manual.* Eugene, OR: Oregon Social Learning Center.

Giordano, P. C., & Cernkovich, S. A. (1997). Gender and antisocial behavior. In D. M. Stoff, J. Breiling, & J. D. Maser (Eds.), *Handbook of antisocial behavior* (pp. 496–510). New York: Wiley.

Goodman, S. H., & Kohlsdorf, B. (1994). The developmental psychopathology of conduct problems. In D. C. Fowles, P. Sutker, & S. H. Goodman (Eds.), *Experimental personality and psychopathology research* (pp. 121–161). New York: Springer.

Gully, K. J., Dengerink, H. A., Pepping, M., & Berstrom, D. (1981). Research note: Sibling contribution to violent behavior. *Journal of Marriage and the Family, 43,* 333–337.

Hetherington, E. M., Henderson, S. H., & Reiss, D. (1999). Adolescent siblings in stepfamilies: Family functioning and adolescent adjustment. *Monographs of the Society for Research in Child Development, 64*(4, Serial No. 259).

Johnston, C., & Freeman, W. (1998). Parent training interventions for sibling conflict. In C. E. Schaefer & J. Briesmeister (Eds.), *Handbook of parenting: Parents as cotherapists for children's behavior problems* (2nd ed., pp. 153–176). New York: Wiley.

Kellam, S. G., & Rebok, G. W. (1992). Building developmental and etiological theory through epidemiologically based prevention trials. In J. McCord & R. Tremblay (Eds.), *Preventing antisocial behavior: Interventions from birth through adolescence* (pp. 162–195). New York: Guilford Press.

Kramer, L. (2004). Experimental interventions in sibling relations. In R. D. Conger, F. O. Lorenz, & K. A. S. Wickrama (Eds.), *Continuity and change in family relations: Theory methods and empirical findings* (pp. 345–380). Mahwah, NJ: Erlbaum.

Larson, R., & Richards, M. H. (1991). Daily companionship in late childhood and early adolescence: Changing developmental contexts. *Child Development, 62,* 284–300.

Patterson, G. R., & Bank, L. (1986). Bootstrapping your way in the nomological thicket. *Behavioral Assessment, 8,* 49–73.

Patterson, G. R., & Bank, L. (1989). Some amplifying mechanisms for pathologic processes in families. In M. R. Gunnar & E. Thelen (Eds.), *Systems and development: The Minnesota Symposia on Child Psychology* (Vol. 22, pp. 167–209). Hillsdale, NJ: Erlbaum.

Patterson, G. R., & Capaldi, D. M. (1990). A mediational model for boys' depressed mood. In J. E. Rolf, A. Masten, D. Cicchetti, K. Nuechterlein, & S. Weintraub (Eds.), *Risk and protective factors in the development of psychopathology* (pp. 141–163). Cambridge, UK: Cambridge University Press.

Patterson, G. R., Dishion, T. J., & Yoerger, K. (2000). Adolescent growth in new forms of problem behavior: Macro- and micro-peer dynamics. *Prevention Science, 1,* 3–13.

Patterson, G. R., Reid, J. B., & Dishion, T. J. (1992). *A social interactional approach: Vol. 4: Antisocial boys.* Eugene, OR: Castalia.

Pike, A., McGuire, S., Hetherington, E. M., Reiss, D., & Plomin, R. (1996). Family environment and adolescent depressive symptoms and antisocial behavior: A multivariate genetic analysis. *Developmental Psychology, 32,* 590–603.

Reiss, A. J., & Farrington, D. P. (1991). Advanced knowledge about co-offending: Results from a prospective longitudinal survey of London males. *Journal of Criminal Law and Criminology, 82,* 360–395.

Roscoe, B., Goodwin, M. P., & Kennedy, D. (1987). Sibling violence and agonistic interactions experienced by early adolescents. *Journal of Family Violence, 2,* 121–137.

Rowe, D. C., & Gulley, B. L. (1992). Sibling effects on substance use and delinquency. *Criminology, 30,* 217–233.

Rowe, D. C., Rodgers, J. L., & Meseck-Bushey, S. (1992). Sibling delinquency and the family environment: Shared and unshared influences. *Child Development, 63,* 59–67.

Scarr, S., & Grajek, S. (1982). Similarities and differences among siblings. In M. E. Lamb & B. Sutton-Smith (Eds.), *Sibling relationships: Their nature and significance across the lifespan* (pp. 357–382). Hillsdale, NJ: Erlbaum.

Schrepferman, L., Snyder, J., & Bank, L. (2003). *The validity of retrospective reports of childhood experiences: Factors affecting the accuracy of recall of sibling relationships.* Manuscript submitted for publication.

Shortt, J. W., Capaldi, D. M., Dishion, T. J., Bank, L., & Owen, L. D. (2003). The role of adolescent peers, romantic partners, and siblings in the emergence of the adult antisocial lifestyle. *Journal of Family Psychology, 17,* 521–533.

Slomkowski, C., Cohen, P., & Brook, J. (1997). The sibling relationships of adolescents with antisocial and comorbid mental disorders: An epidemiological investigation. *Criminal Behavior and Mental Health, 7,* 353–368.

Slomkowski, C., Rende, R., Conger, K. J., Simons, R. L., & Conger, R. D. (2001). Sisters, brothers, and delinquency: Evaluating social influence during early and middle adolescence. *Child Development, 72,* 271–283.

Snyder, J., & Stoolmiller, M. (2002). Reinforcement and coercion mechanisms in the development of antisocial behavior: The family. In J. B. Reid, J. R. Patterson, & J. Snyder (Eds.), *Antisocial behavior in children and adolescents: A developmental analysis and model for intervention* (pp. 65–100.) Washington, DC: American Psychological Association.

Strauss, M. A., Gelles, R. J., & Steinmetz, S. K. (1980). *Behind closed doors: Violence in the American family.* Garden City, NJ: Anchor Books.

Widom, C. S., & Kuhns, J. B. (1996). Childhood victimization and subsequent risk for promiscuity, prostitution, and teenage pregnancy: A prospective study. *American Journal of Public Health, 86,* 1607–1612.

Widom, C. S., Weiler, B. L., & Cottler, L. B. (1999). Childhood victimization and drug abuse: A comparison of prospective and retrospective findings. *Journal of Consulting and Clinical Psychology, 67,* 867–880.

Zoccolillo, M. (1993). Gender and the development of conduct disorder. *Development and Psychopathology, 5,* 63–78.

24 ▶ Examining the Informal Sanctioning of Deviance in a Chat Room Culture

Rhonda D. Evans

Introduction

With the advent of computer technology, and more specifically the Internet, as a mode of communication and a virtual place in which to engage in social interaction, a plethora of social science research studies have erupted. Multiple issues concerning cyberspace communication have been explored. Some scholars have focused attention of the issues of identity formation within cyberspace communications (Zizek 1998; Bromberg 1996; Turkle 1996, 1997; Poster 1995). Other researchers have focused on the possibility of forming transcultural global communities via the Internet (Levalley 1997) as well as the possibility of promoting egalitarian transnational global communities (Ribeiro 1997). Feminist scholars have explored the possibility of transforming gender relations through cyberspace and the impediments to such transformation (Cushing 1996; Morse 1997; Plant 1996; Wise 1997). An abundance of research has been conducted on sexual and intimate relationships formed through cyberspace communications (Cooper and Sportolari 1997; Lieblum 1997; Mills 1998; Schnarch 1997; and Zizek 1996). However, the study of deviant behavior on the Internet has been largely confined to the examination of chat communities as a social space for engaging in forms of sexual deviance (Durkin and Bryant 1995, 1999; Lamb 1998) and the opportunity for promoting such behavior through the distribution of pornographic materials (Barak and Safir 1997).

This study explores the nature of everyday deviance at the micro level, within the context of a Married Life (ML) chat room culture. It focuses on the normative structure of the ML chat culture through examination of the process of informal social sanctioning of behavior that is defined as deviant within the culture. It also examines this particular culture in order to identify the mechanisms of sanctioning deviance within cybercultures in general. Several main questions are addressed. First, how are particular behaviors judged to be deviant in chat cultures? Second, what are the probable causes of deviance within the culture? And third, what are the likely consequences of the deviant behavior for the individual that has transgressed the norms and the cultural system of which the person is a part? Also, the relevance of contemporary sociological theories of deviance for explaining these processes is explored.

Methodology

The data for this study were collected via participant observation within the ML chat room over the course of several months. This researcher initially participated as a guest within the culture and later became a member. It is necessary, due to the nature of chat rooms, to participate as a full member in order to truly understand the normative system of the culture and the defining and sanctioning processes of deviance within the culture. Observations and interactions took place at various times of the day. The nature of cyberspace communication creates difficulties in the study of deviance, due to the lack of human bodies and, more specifically, body language. It is only through understanding written communications that take the form of visible gestures and symbols within the culture that the norms of the culture become apparent.

The Nature of the Married Life Chat Room

The particular chat room where observations and participation were conducted for the purpose of this study is part of the larger social system of Virtual Places (VP). VP is a software program that offers various chat rooms in which to interact through typed messages. However, it also offers graphic images and gestures that serve as symbols of communication within the chat cultures as well as avatars, which serve as visual representations of the individual chatter. Because communications and interactions within VP are limited to typed messages, various forms of emotional symbolic expression have developed to take the place of the invisible body. For example, the symbol :) represents a smile and :(a frown. While such symbols can take various forms, it is important to note that chatters have developed symbols with which to express their emotional reactions to behaviors, and these symbols can function as sanctioning mechanisms within the culture.

The language used within the cultures relies heavily on abbreviations to cut back on the amount of time it takes to communicate typed messages. The following are common abbreviations that are used within the Married Life chat room: lol = laughing out loud; lmao = laughing my ass off; wb = welcome back; ty = thank you; yw = you're welcome; sis = sister; Reg = regular member of the VP culture in general and within the context of the current culture of Married Life in particular; and Mug = a person that chats as a guest. It is necessary to be familiar with these abbreviations in order to understand the interaction between chatters within the culture. Also, capitalization of typed messages can serve as either an expression of anger or excitement or as an indicator that an individual is screaming.

Much of the communication between chatters takes the form of gestures that are generic typed messages. This research[1] identified four main types of gestures within the chat room culture that are differentiated by their prospective functions. The first type will be termed "solidarity gestures" because they serve the function of promoting cohesiveness within the chat culture. The following are examples of solidarity gestures:

> Married Life . . . sometimes you wanna go where everybody knows your name.
>
> Hubby said if I come to VP one more time he leavin!!!! Man I am Gonna Miss Him!!!
>
> ML REGS . . . Thank you for being a friend . . . 1999
>
> A Salute to the REGS
>
> True friendship is seen through the heart, not the eyes.

These gestures serve the purpose of declaring a commitment to the ML culture and comembers and also offer an indication as to the purpose of the culture. The married life culture exists for the purpose of allowing individuals with the common characteristic of being married to interact and make friends. As many of the members have suggested it is the perfect place to visit with friends for people that lead busy lives. Over and over again they comment that they do not have to leave their homes in order to interact with other adults and make good friends from all over the world. These solidarity gestures serve to promote the cohesiveness of the group members. They also make the relationships seem more "real" in the context of cyberspace.

The second type of gestures function as markers of status and therefore are termed "symbolic status gestures." These take the form of gestures for individual members that promote the status of the individual member. The Regulars have access to their fellow reg's gestures. These gestures are played when a member arrives in the room to mark their entrance and serve as symbols of their status within the culture room. Persons that are not of a high status within the culture do not have personal gestures. The written message that is played by members of the culture is visible to all, letting others know that this person is of a higher and more accepted status within the culture. However, the visual dimension of the gesture is only available to those that have access to the gesture, thus excluding lesser members from partaking in the privilege of sharing the total experience of the symbol. The visual

---

[1]Virtual Places installed voice chat shortly after this research was conducted.

dimension usually takes the form of graphic images of the person's avatar with music playing. It is similar to a clip from a movie. The following are some of the status gestures of individual members within the Married Life culture:

~Jill is here . . . Ready to put some spice in your LIFE~~

Big Mom . . . Protector of the Innocent, washer of the dirty shorts

Jake has arrived . . . Who's First!?

Dallaste is here . . . Watch him work his magic!!!

~~Stephanie is here time to grab your boots the shit's getting deep~~

~~~Sand Man . . . He's an . . . All Nite Man~~~ Sand Man . . . He's gonna keep u up all nite . . . such a smoothie

~~~Love is . . . What Letty is all about~~~

Trisha is here and she is so Yummy for your Tummy!!!!

Little is HERE to THRILL YOUR SOUL . . . so LET the GOOD TIMES ROLL!!!!

~~~Sexy is now OFFDUTY . . . and READY to PLAY~~~

Jim's Here For Some R & R

~~~Just being here with Slide is . . . HOT

Jim might be CHEAP but he's not EASY

The third type of gestures are used largely for the purpose of facilitating interaction of various kinds within the culture, thus they are termed "facilitative gestures." These gestures most commonly take the form of music, sexually flirtatious comments, or humorous comments. The most common form of facilitating gesture is sexually flirtatious in nature. These gestures also function as a socializing mechanism for new members of the culture in that they allow new members to quickly become familiar with the type of interactions that are prescribed within the culture. All regs are expected to engage in this type of interaction with their fellow regs. The following are just a few examples of such gestures:

I don't cyber, but DAMN I love to tease

Give White Rose

smooch I wuv you

The fourth, and most important type of gesture for the purposes of the current study are "sanctioning gestures." These are gestures that are used to sanction deviant behavior within the chat culture. However, many of these are also indicative of the low status of mugs within the culture. The following are examples of such gestures:

Mugg Toss!!! . . . (CRASH!!!!!)

I don't cyber mugs!!!!!!!!!

I drink from mugs, I don't talk to them

Lord be with our guest, and prepare them for the butt whoopin they're about to receive!!

What do you mean you're a GUEST? I never fuckin invited ya

MUG stands for Mother Fuckin Uninvited Guest

Hello mug suicide hotline . . . yes sir, put your face right up to the barrel and PULL THE TRIGGER! /// MUG KILL

CALL THE COPS, I'VE BEEN MUGGED!!!!

Damn Mugs! Why must you needlessly complicate everything?

VP REGS PISS ON MUGS!!!!!!!!!

Mug hunting season is declared OPEN!!

Excuse me? Do you see the word guest by your name and not mine? Know your place

Forgive them Father, for they are mugs and know not how to download

Horny Mug ALERT!!!!

Attention K-Mart shoppers, an asshole just entered the room!

Just because I wear a sexy AV [avatar] doesn't mean I want to cyber every loser in the room

We have Attitude in MARRIED LIFE . . . So Bite US!!!!

<<<<Go check your ATTITUDE at the door!!!>>>>

I can go from 0 to bitch in 1.2 secs., Don't Push Me!!!

Will the owner of the GREAT BIG BUTT, please move it out of my face!

As is evident in the above gestures the most common form of sanctioning is in reaction to mugs. This demonstrates that to be a mug is considered deviant in and of itself. The social context of Virtual Places does not distinguish between VP users and Java users. Java users are forced to sign on as guests in VP, but they chat in the same rooms as the Virtual Places users. These two groups of users are distinguished by whether or not they have access to the VP software and therefore the status symbols that are valued within the culture, such as avatars and gestures. Because the environment does not have different rooms for mugs and regs to chat it creates a conflict between the two groups.

The structure of the cyberspace can be likened to the geographical characteristics of inner city areas that were studied by the Chicago theorists in the first half of the 20th century (Park et al. 1925 and Shaw and McKay 1931). Many of the elements of social disorganization that were conducive to increasing crime rates are an inherent part of cyberspace of which the ML culture is a part. Like the zone of transition (Faris and Dunham 1999) in Chicago, cyberspace is set up in such a way that heterogeneity and transiency are central features, as is anonymity. The VP community is set up so that people can quickly move in and out of chat rooms, and the community is available to anyone with access to a computer. Because the individual has the option of changing their identity once they have been sanctioned for deviant behavior and reentering the community incognito, the structure of cyberspace offers anonymity to the people using it, which creates an increased willingness to engage in deviant behavior. These combined features of the social structure, in which ML culture is embedded, result in an increase in the frequency of occurrences of deviant acts and the need to sanction these behaviors in order to maintain the boundaries and normative structure of the culture. These characteristics of cyberspace in general and VP and ML in particular combine to influence the nature of deviant behavior and the form of sanctioning that arises in response to deviant acts within the married life culture.

Sanctioning Mechanisms of Chat Room Cultures

As in all cultures, an act can be judged to be deviant by examining the negative responses to the act and the sanctioning that follows. Conversely, identification of what is deviant within a culture also serves to define the normative boundaries of that particular culture. There are two general types of sanctioning mechanisms within the context of the ML culture and VP more generally. The first and most obvious is the use of gestures or typed text as written symbols of sanctioning. The second is the use of the ignore button which puts a person that is engaging in rude or inappropriate behavior on ignore. One also can choose to ignore an individual's avatar. More often than not, the ignore sanction is used only as a last resort when someone is behaving in a manner that is disruptive to the communication of the other chat members. When this happens all of the other members will place the person on ignore. This results in the person being excluded from communication and interaction within the culture.

Social Positioning, Roles, and Normative Expectations

While all of the participants in the culture share the common social position of "chatter" within chat rooms, there is a hierarchy of social status within the Married Life culture. Observations revealed that a large part of the sanctioning that occurs within the Married Life culture serves as a socializing mechanism designed to teach new and potential members both the values and norms of the society as well as new members' proper position within the culture. This demonstrates that individuals occupying certain social positions are expected to behave in certain ways within the culture. This form of sanctioning is most acutely demonstrated in the course of interaction between mugs and regs. Mugs are considered lower class members of the culture, because they lack certain attributes. First, they have not downloaded the VP software and therefore show up as a visual image of a coffee cup in the chat room environment. They also lack access to gestures, which are a key component to extensive participation in the culture, through witty generic remarks, that are often sexual in content. Regs are those members that have been a part of the culture for an extensive period of time, have access to the valued avatars and gestures and are most thoroughly skilled in the valued attributes within the culture, being humorous and flirtatious.

Occupying the status of mug within the culture does not preclude interaction with other members. However, this researcher's observations of incidents of sanctioning within the culture indicate that there are certain expectations concerning how a mug should behave. The first expectation is that you will not challenge the authority of regs. The second expectation is that mugs will follow the conversation set up by the regs and refrain from expressing their disagreement with the regs' choice of social interaction. If mugs deviate from these prescribed behaviors they are likely to be sanctioned with gestures that express anti-mug sentiments by all of the regs in the room. Also, to the extent that the culture is largely based on flirtatious behavior, this largely takes place between regs. When mugs flirt with regs it is considered disrespectful and sanctioning follows. Thus, they are sanctioned for engaging in the same behaviors that regs engage in due to their social status. A mug identity is in essence a negative ascriptive characteristic. However, it is not completely ascribed; part of the negative evaluation of mugs is due to the nature of their participation in the culture. Because many of the individuals that chat as mugs often consider themselves transitory within the culture, they are much more likely to engage in explicit solicitation of sexual interaction, which is a proscribed behavior within the culture. It is typically believed that they are there to seek out cyber sex, not to participate in the culture. This negative stereotype results in a need for mugs to prove their commitment to the culture in order to be accepted. Once this is done they are then accepted as honorary members of the culture and regs will try to encourage them to download the VP software in order to enjoy the full privileges of membership. By doing so the mug expresses his or her commitment to the values within the culture.

The Nature of Deviance in the Married Life Culture

Much of the deviance within this culture seems to result from improper socialization, due to the nature of cyberspace. Because there aren't firm boundaries within cyberspace people can move with ease from one chat room to another. Thus, many people that enter the cultural milieu are not familiar with the cultural practices and norms or the positions of the members within the culture. In such a context, communication with gestures serves as a mechanism for quick socialization, but the heterogeneity and quick turnover of the population within the culture creates a sort of social disorganization within.

In the case of men overtly asking for sex in the ML chat room, there appears to be a complex of intertwining reasons. First these men are typically not aware of the normative expectations of the particular culture as is evident in the reactions of some men to these sanctions. For example, it is common for them to respond that they thought all chat rooms were for the purpose of sex talk. Some will apologize and choose to join the ML culture because they like the interaction that takes place within it. Others will exit the room once they have been sanctioned as outsiders and search for cybersex in some other room. This suggests that the nature of the broader VP environment indeed motivates some individuals to engage in sexual behaviors that might be considered deviant in the more inclusive culture of ML. The overarching belief that chat rooms are for the purpose of sex chat or cybersex leads people to discount the normative system of the particular chat room. Such individuals can be assumed to be abiding by the normative structure of VP and therefore the norms of ML are not relevant to them. They are outsiders that are being sanctioned according to the normative structure of the more inclusive married life culture.

Although far less frequent, another form of deviance observed within the culture appears to take the form of occupying conflicting roles. For example, some individuals are more committed to their role as a religious member of their church in their real lives than they are to their role in the ML culture. To the extent that the ML culture promotes overt sexually flirtatious behavior, these members react negatively to such behavior. In turn the more committed members of the culture will sanction the negative reactions because this type of interaction is highly valued as a form of fun within the culture. If the person doesn't apologize and refrain from making comments regarding the nature of the behavior within the chat room, they will be sanctioned with comments suggesting that they are in the wrong chat room and that they should try a religious one. This same process of sanctioning occurs when men come into the room and overtly suggest engaging in sexual relations with others. They are told to go to a sex chat room.

The most disruptive form of deviance seems to stem from bad or negative experiences within the ML cultural milieu. This type of deviance is far less frequent than the other types previously mentioned. This usually takes the form of an individual entering the chat room with the sole purpose of being disruptive because they have previously been rejected or sanctioned for not acting appropriately in the culture. They will type messages that are crude and aimed at challenging the norms of the culture or play nonsense gestures over and over, so as to impede the communication and interaction of the cultural members. The sanctioning of such incidents depends highly on the length of duration of the deviant behavior. Typically the individual will first be sanctioned with gestures, then if that doesn't work the entire group will resort to putting the individual on ignore. When individual members of the group put an individual on ignore, the person's typed communication no longer shows up on the screen. Essentially, the offending individual has been excluded from the conversation and interaction within the culture.

A form of deviance that is more likely to be displayed by members of the culture than by outsiders is that of improper avatar etiquette. The married life culture has a range of avatars that are considered appropriate for the room. This can range from those that have no sexually explicit symbolic value to those that are provocative. However, avatars that are considered vulgar are unacceptable within the culture. If an individual wears an avatar that is considered inappropriate to the culture the person will be sanctioned through comments that may or may not take on a humorous nature. For example, a male member of the culture came in with an avatar that was completely nude and the other members expressed their disapproval with comments like "OMG!!" (oh my God!!) and requested that he put clothing back on. The person did as he was asked and joked about the incident as a form of reaffirming his commitment to the culture.

Another incident in which avatar etiquette was violated was when one of the women that participates in the culture put up an avatar with her real picture. The picture was of her dancing in a strip club with no top on. She was proud of this avatar and said, "look everyone this is me!" The room responded in silence and pretended that they didn't see her statement. Meanwhile numerous private instant messages were popping up on my screen from both male and female fellow chatters with derogatory comments expressing their disapproval of her behavior. From that time on she was ostracized from the group and limited in her social interactions. She eventually quit coming to ML.

Although infrequent, a form of deviance considered serious by members of the culture is what they refer to as "stalking." This refers to any unwanted advances that occur or harassment of one member by another. Typically this takes the form of one individual interpreting his or her relationship with another individual as more intimate or serious than it is. Generally, the member that is being stalked will discuss it with other members when the person accused of stalking is not present. It is generally known among the central members of the culture that a person is engaging in stalking behavior, and members will avoid any private conversations with that person. Members also avoid engaging in flirtatious communication within the chat room with this person. He or she is thus excluded from any type of intimate relationships with others in the ML culture because he or she has been labeled a "stalker." Once this has occurred the person is limited in the types of interaction that he or she can engage in with other members. Stalking is sanctioned rather harshly because the nature of the behavior is threatening to the anonymity of the member the individual is stalking and there is a potential for the stalker to interfere with the other member's real life, and his or her marriage. The stalker has been defined as breaking the informal rule of not getting too close to other members.

While relationships with other members are highly valued within the culture, it is understood that there is a boundary that relationships will not cross. Because all of the members are identified as married people, the flirtatious behavior is regarded as harmless and fun, and is expected to stay at that level. This is not to say that some members may not engage in serious relationships with one another that spill over into their personal lives, but such behavior is not overtly condoned within the culture.

Members are sometimes sanctioned for the failure to meet proscribed expectations of humorous and flirtatious behavior in the context of the culture. This is seen when people come into the room and talk about heavy topics such as financial problems or marital problems. Although members of the culture may listen briefly to such accounts, if the individual continues to talk about such incidents they will be sanctioned. This can take the form of being ignored, having other members change the topic, or receiving direct verbal sanctions that tell the person that he or she is ruining the fun in the room.

Observation suggests that individual instances of deviance are most likely to be committed by those persons that do not share or value the norms of the culture (mugs), those who participate less often in the culture, and those that occupy a position of lesser status within the culture. Most of the deviant acts that occur are committed by persons that are not actual members of the culture (mugs) or by those individuals that are in the process of being socialized within the culture. Although less frequent, deviance also can occur when a person occupies conflicting social roles or has a commitment to another culture that he or she values more highly than their participation in the ML culture.

The examination of sanctioning suggests that a functional analysis is fitting to the study of deviance within the Married Life Chat Culture. The sanctioning of mugs as outsiders in particular serves to strengthen the moral fabric of the culture and creates group cohesion as does the sanctioning of individuals that openly solicit sex within the chat room (Coser 1956). The sanctioning of such behavior reaffirms the commitment of the group members to both the value they place on the interaction offered by access to the VP software and their commitment to the norm that defines the boundaries of interaction and innocent flirtation. To the extent that members talk about sex, it is in a light and humorous manner between fellow members and all members understand that humor is the purpose of such interaction. Also the instances in which group members are sanctioned for engaging in serious conversations reaffirm the commitment of the group to a norm of humorous and fun interaction. Deviance within this culture appears to serve the function of boundary maintenance as articulated by Kai Erikson (1999) and Joseph Gusfield (1963). In essence, deviance serves the purpose of identifying the normative boundaries of the culture for its members.

Consequences of Deviant Behavior for the Individual Deviant

For those persons that are not a part of the culture, to be labeled deviant has no negative consequences, other than possibly the realization that they will have to search for another chat room. Some of the obvious consequences of being labeled deviant within the context of the ML chat culture for members is that it restricts interactions with other members of the culture and therefore limits the positive value of engaging in the culture. While the psychological consequences of deviant behavior for the individual cannot be ascertained in the course of the current analysis, it can be assumed that the consequences will be more negative for those who identify most strongly with the norms of the culture and value the positive social interactions they receive by being members of the culture (Gusfield 1963). However, the context of cyberspace also makes it possible for individuals that have been ostracized from the culture to change their identity and reemerge as an unidentified member. However, for individuals that valued the friendships they made and invested much time in creating an identity within the culture, this would not be a desirable option.

Consequences of Deviance for the Married Life Culture

As functionalist theorists have asserted, deviant incidents serve both positive and negative functions for the functioning of the cultural system. Within the context of the Married Life Culture, the sanctioning of deviance in general and that of mugs in particular serves the function of creating cohesiveness among the group members. When mugs are sanctioned for who they are, the value of being a member of VP and the status and prestige that come with such membership is reaffirmed. When individuals are sanctioned for soliciting cybersex in ML, this affirms the commitment to the norm that such behavior is inappropriate. When members are sanctioned for engaging in conversation that is too serious this reaffirms the commitment of the members to the value of having fun within the culture. All these instances of deviance function to reaffirm the group's values.

However, there are also negative social consequences for the functioning of the social system that stem from deviance. The most obvious negative consequence is that it impedes the proper functioning of the system. When people engage in behaviors that are disruptive to the culture it impedes the interaction and communication of other members within the culture. Time is wasted on responding to and sanctioning deviance that could be otherwise spent engaging in positive social interaction within the culture. Also, deviant occurrences impede the socialization process of the person committing the deviant act.

Conclusion

This paper demonstrates that the nature of deviance can be studied within the context of cyberspace and offers insight into the forms sanctioning will take within the context of cyberspace chat cultures. The observations suggest that incidents of deviance occur within the context of chat rooms for various reasons, ranging from improper socialization to rejection of the cultural norms. It is argued that the structure of cyberspace contributes to the frequency and the nature of deviance within chat rooms by creating a perpetual state of social disorganization within chat rooms. Future research should examine other cultures to see if the same factors influence the nature of deviance. Researchers also should examine the possible effects that sanctioning may have on the individual on a psychological level through interviews with people that engage in deviant behavior and have been sanctioned within a chat room culture. Another important avenue for research is to explore the extent to which the identity and self-esteem of individuals within chat room cultures are dependent upon their participation in such cultures. In essence, researchers need to ask if this culture is influential in the participant's life and to their identity, and if so how this affects the nature of deviance. While one would assume that the nature of cyberspace would make participation in such cultures somehow less than real, observation suggests that for some of the members in the ML culture participation was extensive, often occupying a central place in their lives.

References

Barak, Azy and Marilyn P. Safir. 1997. "Sex and the Internet: An Israeli Perspective." *Journal of Sex Education & Therapy* 22(1):67–73.

Bromberg, Heather. 1996. "Are MUDs Communities? Identity, Belonging and Consciousness in Virtual Worlds." Pp. 143–152 in *Cultures of Internet: Virtual Spaces, Real Histories, and Living Bodies,* edited by Rob Shields. London, England: Sage.

Coser, Lewis A. 1956. *The Functions of Social Conflict.* New York: Free Press.

Cushing, Pamala J. 1996. "Gendered Conversational Rituals on the Internet: An Effective Voice Is Based on More than Simply What One Is Saying." *Anthropologica* 38(1):47–80.

Durkin, Keith F. and Clifton D. Bryant. 1995. "Log on to Sex: Some Notes on the Carnal Computer and Erotic Cyberspace as an Emerging Research Frontier." *Deviant Behavior* 16(3):179–200.

Durkin, Keith F. and Clifton D. Bryant. 1999. "Propagandizing Pederasty: A Thematic Analysis of the On-Line Exculpatory Accounts of Unrepentant Pedophiles." *Deviant Behavior* 20(2):103–127.

Erikson, Kai T. 1999. "On the Sociology of Deviance." Pp. 22–30 in *Theories of Deviance,* edited by Stuart H. Traub and Craig B. Little. Itasca, IL: F. E. Peacock.

Faris, Robert E. L. and H. Warren Dunham. 1999. "Natural Areas of the City." Pp. 74–82 in *Theories of Deviance,* edited by Stuart H. Traub and Craig B. Little. Itasca, IL: F. E. Peacock.

Gusfield, Joseph R. 1963. *Symbolic Crusade: Status Politics and the American Temperance Movement.* Urbana, IL: University of Illinois Press.

Lamb, Michael. 1998. "Cybersex: Research Notes on the Characteristics of the Visitors to Online Chat Rooms." *Deviant Behavior* 19(2):121–135.

Levalley, Janet. 1997. "Doing it in Cyberspace: Cultural Sensitivity in Applied Anthropology." *Anthropology of Consciousness* 8(4): 113–132.

Lieblum, Sandra Risa. 1997. "Sex and the Net: Clinical Implications." *Journal of Sex Education & Therapy* 22(1):21–27.

Mills, Russell. 1998. "Cyber: Sexual Chat on the Internet." *Journal of Popular Culture* 32(3):31–46.

Morse, Margaret. 1997. "Virtually Female: Body and Code." Pp. 23–35 in *Processed Lives: Gender and Technology in Everyday Life,* edited by Jennifer Terry and Melodie Calvert. London, England: Routledge.

Park, Robert E., Ernest W. Burgess, and Roderick D. McKenzie. 1925. The City. Chicago, IL: University of Chicago Press.

Plant, Sadie. 1996. "On the Matrix: Cyberfeminist Simulations." Pp. 170–183 in *Cultures of Internet: Virtual Spaces, Real Histories, and Living Bodies,* edited by Rob Shields. London, England: Sage.

Poster, Mark. 1995. "Postmodern Virtualities." *Body and Society* 1(3–4): 79–95.

Ribeiro, Gustavo Lins. 1997. "Transnational Virtual Community? Exploring Implications for Culture, Power and Language." *Organization* 4(4):496–505.

Schnarch, David. 1997. "Sex, Intimacy, and the Internet." *Journal of Sex Education & Therapy* 22(1):15–20.

Shaw, Clifford R. and Henry D. McKay. 1931. "Formal Characteristics of Delinquency Areas." Pp. 60–108 in National Commission of Law Observance and Enforcement Report on the Causes of Crime, Vol II. United States Government Printing Office.

Turkle, Sherry. 1996. "Parallel Lives: Working on Identity in Virtual Space." Pp. 156–175 in *Constructing the Self in a Mediated World,* edited by Debra Grodin and Thomas R. Lindlof. Thousand Oaks, CA: Sage.

Turkle, Sherry. 1997. "Multiple Subjectivity and Virtual Community at the End of the Freudian Century." *Sociological Inquiry* 67(1):72–84.

Wise, Patricia. 1997. "Always Already Virtual: Feminist Politics in Cyberspace." Pp. 179–196 in *Virtual Politics: Identity and Community in Cyberspace,* edited by David Holmes. London, England: Sage.

Zizek, Slavoj. 1996. "Sex in the Age of Virtual Reality." *Science as Culture* 4(25):506–525.

Zizek, Slavoj. 1998. "Cyberspace, or, How to Transverse the Fantasy in the Age of the Retreat of the Big Other." *Public Culture* 10(3):483–513.

PART **IV**

> # The Production of Institutional Careers and Identities

Part III described how deviant behavior may initially be managed in a private setting. The material that was presented demonstrated how such behavior may become subject to regulation by a social-control agent or agency. When such regulation occurs, the actor's behavior is screened by the institution and its staff, and a label may be placed on him or her. The individual then becomes an institutional deviant, expected thereafter to conform to the institution's definition of the label. Some people will accept this labeling. In this event, the person's public identity (how others view him or her) meshes with personal identity (how the person views himself or herself), so that we can speak of the secondary, or career, deviant. Other deviants, however, will reject the label and attempt to structure and present to others a nondeviant image of self. The selections in this part explore such possibilities as these; they also illustrate clearly how institutional careers are initiated, perpetuated, and transformed. Throughout the following discussion of the various articles, the "organizational paradigm," which was presented in the general introduction, is applied.

PART IV

> ## Organizational Structures, Ideologies, Social-Control Agents, and Recruitment: The Institutional Backdrop

SECTION 1

It is difficult to understand the processes behind the production of deviance and deviants unless we first analyze the institution out of which a specific social-control agent operates. It is particularly important to know how the prevailing theory of the office, existing

323

deviant categories, and diagnostic stereotypes are applied to clients. The first selection, "Bureaucratic Slots and Client Processing," from Delos H. Kelly's book *Creating School Failure, Youth Crime, and Deviance*, not only elaborates on these ideas but presents an in-depth analysis of how the "organizational paradigm" can be applied to the study of social deviance. Kelly initially stresses the importance of analyzing how social institutions are structured. Here, by drawing particularly upon the works of Cicourel and Kitsuse, and Hargreaves, he describes the origin of a range of school career lines (e.g., ability groups and track systems). He notes, for example, in terms of actor selection and placement, that students who give teachers a hard time or are perceived as troublemakers often land in the low, basic, or non-college-prep tracks. After describing selected organizational structures and components, he moves to a general discussion of how clients are identified, selected, sorted, and processed by bureaucrats. Critical to an understanding of this process is the *content* of an agency's existing theory of the office and associated working ideology. Not only is the theory of the office embedded within an agency's organizational fabric (see Part I), but it becomes, through socializing experiences in formal and informal settings, inculcated within relevant actors, audiences, and third parties.

Kelly uses certain aspects of the structure and process of schooling to underscore the importance of locating, describing, and characterizing the content of an agency's theory of the office. If, as argued, society and its educational institutions are predicated firmly on an ideology that *presumes differential ability*, then we can expect to obtain outcomes commensurate with that view. Hence, some students will be destined to fail while others will be programmed for success. Ability groups, track systems, and other means for stratifying students offer graphic representations of how a society's educational philosophy becomes translated into bureaucratic entities. Actually predicting who will succeed or fail requires an analysis of how existing student stratification systems articulate with student attributes. For example, is the person of color more likely, independent of demonstrated academic success and competence, to be relegated to a low or basic track? If this happens (and there is increasing evidence that it does), then what can we say about the educational decision maker? Is he or she, either advertently or inadvertently, acting in a discriminatory or bigoted fashion? After addressing questions such as these, Kelly provides additional observations on what he terms the *bureaucratic matching game*, the decision-making process whereby a bureaucrat or decision maker assesses a client's attributes or traits and then renders an assignment decision. Kelly concludes by offering an overview of how client processing can destroy an actor's personal and public identity, as well as produce an erosion of self-image. He also comments on how institutions create, use, and misuse records.

Ideologies that orient social systems, and individuals within them, exist at many levels. Ideas that support the privatization of public services, for example, have resulted in the privatization of correctional facilities and a subsequent "correctional industry." While privatization of prisons promised greater efficiency, according to the driving ideology, there are also several important issues to consider. David Shichor, in "The Corporate Context of Private Prisons," addresses the privatization of correctional institutions. Shichor's concerns revolve around the "corporate nature of the private providers," a context that may easily result in exploitation and various forms of corporate deviance.

As explained by Shichor, free competition in the pursuit of profit is at the core of the privatization movement and is also at the heart of potential problems. In fact, when a profit motive is added to the correctional system, the "customer" is at greatest risk. Corporations can use their political power to encourage a "tough on crime" policy that, in effect, insures a more durable clientele. If profits fail to meet expectations, costs, in particular any remunerations for "clients," are easily altered. The primary concern here is that in a privatized system of corrections, it is possible to increase the costs to the government through contracts in a number of ways, while reducing the "quality of care" that is characteristic of for-profit firms.

Social-control agents, both formal (e.g., the police) and semi-formal (e.g., the school administrator), must become familiar with and act according to the agency's theory of the office. This socialization takes place within formal and informal domains. We have police academies and we have on-the-job training. We have teacher education programs and we have teacher lounges. Regardless of the specific institution or interactional context considered, however, a novice must "learn the ropes." And what he or she is taught in a formal setting (e.g., the police academy) may not mesh with what is expected in an informal context (e.g., the streets). The official mandate or theory of the office might be "to protect and serve all" or "to provide equal access for all to educational opportunities." An important question arises: How is an agency's theory of the office or official perspective translated into action? Are all citizens actually accorded equal protection under the law? Are all students provided equal access to educational opportunities? We need to examine how the theory of the office actually becomes translated into action. Is there a direct correspondence between an agency's official perspective and its actual working ideology? Answering these questions requires an ongoing examination of how social-control agents go about processing clients. In a very real sense, we need to get inside the minds of the bureaucrats and examine their decision-making processes. For example, what can we say about the content and range of diagnostic stereotypes that are used to identify, select, sort, process, sanction, and treat clients? Is one hiding under the cloak of bureaucratic competence?

Christine Horne addresses the implications of intragroup relationships for the production of deviant careers and identities in her article, "The Enforcement of Norms: Group Cohesion and Meta Norms." Horne suggests that understanding the relationships between potential sanctioners and nondeviant group members is essential to predicting the likelihood that sanctions will be applied. In other words, social control agents (potential sanctioners) are connected to other group members in a network of social relationships. As a result of the relationship qualities that exist between potential sanctioners and others, some individuals may influence sanctioners' behavior. It should be remembered that those who sanction also assume certain risks such as retaliation. Horne finds that group cohesion increases the rewards given to those who punish. These increased rewards for sanctioners may in turn affect the frequency of sanctioning. Several implications were discussed. First, the application of sanctions (initiation into institutional careers) is shaped, at least to some extent, by the quality of relationships within the group (cohesion increases the size of incentive to sanction). Second, the application of sanctions (based on diagnostic stereotypes) may be shaped by the relationship networks of sanctioners and deviant actors.

25

Bureaucratic Slots
and Client Processing

Delos H. Kelly

I have illustrated how actors may become progressively defined by a range of others as societal misfits. Understanding this process, I have argued, requires a preliminary consideration of how, over time, individual traits, features, and biographies articulate with organizational components and processes to produce selected organizational products (e.g., the academic failure, troublemaker, or school dropout). Even more basic than this, I have argued that one must initially describe, as well as dissect, an institution's underlying organizational structure; this need was documented most graphically by Cicourel and Kitsuse's (1963) research on the origin of school career lines. They, it may be recalled, were able to locate three distinct career lines (i.e., the academic, clinical, and delinquent). These career lines not only composed an integral element of the school's organizational structure but they also provided the molds for student placement. Another significant finding of the Cicourel-Kitsuse (1963) study that should be made note of, once again, is the fact that the career lines could be characterized by a set of deviant and non-deviant labels. Teachers, for example, referred to those who gave them trouble or who were late as delinquents or pre-delinquents. The significance of this observation becomes especially meaningful when we find these same labels being invoked in the student selection and assignment processes. Thus, students who were late, did not work, or gave the teachers difficulty were more apt to be relegated to the delinquent career line. Thereafter, they became subject to the values associated with their low or deviant school status. The research by Hargreaves (1967) was used to buttress this observation, as well as claim.

Like the Cicourel-Kitsuse (1963) evidence, Hargreaves' (1967) observations point to the need for dissecting and understanding organizational structures. At Lumley, not only were student and teacher attitudes, reactions, and behaviors stream-specific, but the streaming system itself operated in such a fashion as to cut off effectively interaction between the lowest and highest streams; this organizational impediment to communication was also linked to subcultural differentiation. Hence, Lumley came to be characterized by two basic subcultures (i.e., the academic and the delinquescent), each possessing a set of dominant values. Low-stream students, it may be remembered, received positive sanctions by teachers and peers when they acted in accordance with the reigning values. The content of some of these values was such that misbehavior, even petty delinquency, was encouraged and supported by group members.

In effect, then, approaching a feeling for the structural roots or origins of school crime requires a basic and initial examination and documentation of the school's underlying organizational structure. Not only must the career lines and their labels be noted, but the corresponding value systems must also be mapped out; these comprise the basic structures to which individuals become molded.

Once the basic structural features of the educational system have been fixed, one can begin to examine student identifying, selecting, sorting, and processing. In this respect, I have argued that teachers-educators play a critical role in the initiation of a range of deviant careers; they are what I have termed "initiators of status degradation ceremonies." Several works were offered to support the fact that many teachers do invoke non-academic criteria (e.g., class, color, stigma symbols) in deciding which students will occupy the deviant, delinquent, or non-academic career lines. The importance of these observations, however, is found in the fact that once a pupil is assigned to a low school status or deviant career line, then that student must become subject to and be influenced by the prevailing value system, the general content of which is frequently non-academic in nature. It is in this way that a deviant, delinquent, and, perhaps ultimately, a criminal career is launched. The impact of the school experience and associated deviant labels is frequently more critical and wide-ranging than this. The efforts by Cicourel and Kitsuse (1963), and Polk (1975) were used to underscore this point.

As Cicourel and Kitsuse (1963) acknowledge, the school actually serves as a clearinghouse, and in this capacity it both sends and receives information about its students. Selected bits of biographical or stigmatizing material, however, seem especially vulnerable to dissemination and particularly that which evolves out of what I have termed "the success-fail philosophy" that permeates our society and its basic institutions. Thus, to fail academically, most assuredly, foretells of failure in other domains. In this regard, Polk (1975) noted that students who had been formally tagged as an academic failure by the school (i.e., a socializing institution) *and* who also had been adjudicated as a delinquent by the court (i.e., a social control institution) were more likely to possess an adult criminal record. Specific labels, or combinations of labels, thus assume a certain priority in our society, most notably those associated with the educational and social control apparatus. In fact, such labels have common meanings and are used interchangeably by institutions.

The Organizational Paradigm and Institutional Processing

. . . Most interactions or status degradation ceremonies become eminently more meaningful when examined within an institutional context. Once we understand, for example, how the school is structured (i.e., the type and range of career lines), then the exchanges between teachers and pupils, or between students, make more sense. Similarly, after one becomes familiar with and understands how a law enforcement agency is structured in terms of its available career lines, then citizen-agent encounters take on added meaning and significance. Thus, the institutional fabric provides the backdrop against which interactions must be evaluated.

Elsewhere, in my studies of deviance (Kelly, 1979) and crime (Kelly, 1980), I have developed an analytical tool that can be used to gain an understanding of how organizations, in general, are structured and function. I have termed this the *organizational paradigm;* this basic paradigm or tool can be applied to the study of school crime.

What must be recognized initially is that the educational system has been given the major task of socializing or educating our youth. In this capacity, the educational decision makers must, as the major differentiators of academic talent, decide which students possess ability and which do not; this task, however, is not especially difficult, nor is it, necessarily, left to chance, primarily because the educators operate on the basis of a theory of the office which is, as I have stressed, predicated fundamentally upon the presumption of differential ability—a working ideology that guarantees the continued production of winners and losers. Not only have educators, parents, students, and others been effectively socialized into this dominant, all-pervading educational philosophy but, and upon closer examination, it becomes obvious that the success-fail philosophy can be characterized by a range of school labels (i.e., diagnostic stereotypes) and associated career lines. The career lines, however, become the most objective, bureaucratic representation of this ideology; they can, as Cicourel and Kitsuse (1963) demonstrated, be located and described. Moreover, the career lines or organizational entities constitute the molds into which students, once identified and tagged by the authorized school personnel, are placed. The paradigm illuminates this process very nicely.

The Organizational Paradigm and Client Processing: A Brief Overview

Conceptually, the major audience in the case of the school is usually the counselor; this institutional representative or agent has, during the course of formal and informal socializing experiences and influences, been indoctrinated with the school's theory of the office and associated elements (i.e., the diagnostic stereotypes and career lines). . . . The diagnostic stereotypes, once mastered, serve as the criteria by which actors (i.e., students) are selected out and placed into the existing career lines. . . . If, for example, and to sketch a brief scenario, an actor (i.e., student) violates a school rule, regulation, or expectation (i.e., this is the act in terms of the paradigm), and is observed doing so by the primary audience (i.e., the counselor), this violation may, and depending upon the content of the audience's diagnostic stereotypes (e.g., the counselor may, and probably does, feel that problem or difficult students belong in the non-academic career lines), be enough to result in placement in a deviant or delinquent career line. In this event, not only has the status degradation ceremony been initiated, but the student may, by virtue of his or her implication in a deviant status, be on the road to the development of a delinquent career and identity. Quite obviously, a single act of defiance, deviance, or misconduct may not constitute sufficient grounds for such treatment.

The probability, however, increases with repeated violations, and particularly so if the acts are observed by others (i.e., third parties or witnesses in terms of my paradigm); this, it may be recalled, is one of the major messages offered by the works of Tannenbaum (1938), Becker (1963), and Lemert (1951). Stated somewhat more directly, if others report acts of misbehavior to the counselor, then a conception of an individual may evolve to the effect that he or she is truly an academic misfit and should be processed and treated accordingly. Thus, third parties or witnesses are often important in structuring a degree of *consensus* about an actor (e.g., that he or she is evil, a troublemaker, a gang member, an academic failure, and the like).

As I indicated previously, the organizational paradigm can be used to refine Polk's (1975) "status flow chart." . . . Specifically, the paradigm can be applied in such a way as to *flesh out* the underlying organizational structure. For example, and in looking at the school—the domain Polk (1975) considers critical in the generation of delinquent careers and identities, his conceptualization of the role and significance of academic performance could be easily recast into a discussion of career lines. Thus, and similar to Cicourel and Kitsuse (1963), we can speak of deviant and non-deviant career lines, as well as the dominant value systems that, according to Hargreaves' (1967) research, characterize a school's career lines. Also evident in Polk's (1975) analysis of status flows is the idea that certain students, by virtue of their status origins (e.g., low social class or minority status), are more apt to land in a low school status or deviant career line; this notion, too, can be handled very easily by the paradigm, particularly if we incorporate a concern for the role that the educational decision maker (i.e., the school's primary audience) plays. In effect, and as the evidence by Schafer and Olexa (1971), Pink and Sweeney (1978), Kelly (1976), Kelly and Grove (1981), and others indicates clearly, decision makers often apply non-academic criteria (i.e., class and race) in the selection and assignment processes, and, accordingly, students who fit the diagnostic stereotypes are selected out to play the role of the deviant, delinquent, or academic misfit. Polk's (1975) treatment of the interconnections between the educational system (i.e., a major socializing institution) and other social control institutions (i.e., police units, courts, and training schools) can also benefit from this type of refinement.

Not only do social control institutions become attuned to and act on the basis of a selected range of institutional labels (i.e., diagnostic stereotypes) but they, like the educational system, can also be described in terms of their underlying organizational structure. Thus, each agency can be analyzed relative to its prevailing theory of the office, diagnostic stereotypes, career lines, staff socializing procedures (both the formal and informal aspects), client selection and assignment routines (i.e., the application of diagnostic stereotypes to actors), and the like.

The police, by way of illustration, are expected to maintain peace and enforce the law. In this capacity, they are generally guided and constrained by what I would term a "good guy-bad guy" philosophy or, perhaps more generally, a "we-they" working ideology. Rookies, as do any other novices (Scheff, 1966), become socialized into this ideology, and they soon learn how to recognize the good guys from the bad guys; this is accomplished through familiarity with and application of a department's diagnostic stereotypes to clients or suspected clients. Officers, for example, develop conceptions of the "typical" features of the burglar, how the act of burglary is apt to be committed, where the event is likely to occur, and the range of possible victims. Similarly, the officer is taught how to spot, classify, and handle suspected cases of rape, homicide, spouse abuse, child molestation, and the like; these typical cases, or "normal crimes" in Sudnow's (1965) usage, are extremely important in the initiation of a *public* deviant identity and career, primarily because the initial classification of an actor (e.g., police labeling as a drunk driver or suspected rapist) has a direct bearing upon how that individual will be processed. Stated somewhat differently, the law enforcement apparatus contains a set of career lines commensurate with the diagnostic stereotypes or normal crimes; therefore, if a person is tagged as a child molester, murderer, or rapist, then he or she will be treated as such throughout the system. Not only this but what is often lost sight of is the fact that the suspected or adjudicated criminal, delinquent, or deviant is expected to act in accordance with the new public identity, status and associated roles. In effect, then, clients are examined with an eye toward seeing if they match the organization's selection criteria or standards.

Diagnostic Stereotypes and Client Processing: The Matching Game

One of the best illustrations of this matching process is found in Wiseman's (1970) research on skid row alcoholics, particularly her description of the judicial screening process. By using various combinations of physical appearance, past performance, and social position, she was able to produce a paradigm of expected social types and matching sentences. . . .

Of significance is the observation that there was an excellent fit between the derived social types and actual sentencing. Derelicts, for example, who looked rough, as well as men who were repeaters, were more apt to serve time and receive the longest sentences. Similarly, derelicts who appeared rough were "the least likely of any social type to escape jail" (Wiseman, 1970:93).

Even though the judge must, according to my paradigm, be conceptualized as occupying the position as major audience in the court, it must be recognized that, in the determination of a sentence, he or she often relies heavily on the inputs from others. In Pacific City, two court helpers—"the Rapper" and "the Knocker"—assumed a major role in the sentencing process. Specifically, the Rapper, an ex-alcoholic himself, not only claimed intimate knowledge of the skid row alcoholics and their life style, but he acted as the major advisor to the judge. Thus, and as each case passed before the judge, the Rapper would offer a recommended case disposition and the judge then passed sentence (Wiseman, 1970:94). The Knocker, operating in his capacity as record keeper, also supplied information to the judge. In fact, and according to Wiseman (1970:95–96), it was often difficult to distinguish the Knocker's role (i.e., supplier of information to the judge) from the Rapper's (i.e., recommender of sentence to the judge). A major conclusion Wiseman (1970:97) offers is that:

> Far from freeing the judge to make idiosyncratic personalized decisions, the result of the drunk court system is to *standardize drunks on the basis of social types* and then with the *assistance of court aides objectify them in such a way as to fit the predetermined types.* Thus the decision of the patrolman in typification of the Skid Row Drinker is not only accepted in the court without question—it is reinforced and embellished. [Italics mine]

Thus, and as I have argued, the initial typification or labeling of an actor contains certain consequences for subsequent processing and treatment. In the case of the public drunk, the police type this person in a specified way (e.g., as a derelict, young repeater, or out-of-towner) and this designation then determines how the individual will be handled. Emerson's (1969) research on the court processing of juveniles also illustrates very nicely how clients are identified and processed in accordance with existing organizational categories or career lines and associated diagnostic stereotypes.

Emerson (1969:83) makes a beginning statement to the effect that juveniles appearing before the court have created problems for some institution:

> . . . youths brought before the juvenile court generally represent "trouble" for some caretaking or control institution. In this sense every delinquent is "trouble" for someone. It may be added here that every delinquency complaint represents a plea that the court "do something"

to remedy or alleviate that "trouble." Hence, one fundamental set of problems and demands confronting the juvenile court arises from the pressures and expectations of those initiating court action that "something be done." In this sense the court must work out practical solutions to cases that satisfy, or at least take some cognizance of, the concerns of complainants.

Diagnostic Stereotypes and Client Processing: The Destruction of Identity

Not all cases, however, represent "trouble" in the eyes of the court. Rather, cases are subjected to two rather distinct phases of organizational screening or sorting. During phase one, troubled cases are separated from the untroubled or, more specifically, attempts are made to distinguish between cases requiring special handling as opposed to those that can be released. Assessing a juvenile's moral character triggers the subsequent, second phase of screening. At this juncture, the court specifies how the case is to be processed. If a decision is reached that no trouble exists, then the assumption is the delinquent's moral character is *normal*. If, by contrast, trouble is found to exist, then one's moral character is viewed as being *problematic* in nature; this latter decision brings about additional scrutiny by court personnel. Emerson (1969:90–91) maintains that, during the decision-making process, court staff endeavor to fit the juvenile into one of three kinds of moral character:

> . . . First, a youth may be *normal*, i.e., basically like most children, acting for basically normal and conventional reasons, despite some delinquent behavior. Second, a youth may be regarded as a *hard-core* or *criminal-like* delinquent, maliciously or hostilely motivated, consciously pursuing illegal ends. Third, a youth may be *disturbed*, driven to acting in senseless and irrational ways by obscure motives or inner compulsions. [Italics his]

Emerson (1969:91) goes on to say that the existing categories of moral character not only "provide institutionally relevant means for 'explaining' or 'accounting for' the patterns of behavior that led to the identification of 'trouble'" but placement in a category "both suggests and justifies particular court actions to deal with it." To determine that a person is "disturbed" explains or accounts for one's "bizarre" behavior. Such a finding would indicate a need for psychiatric treatment. It would also justify such care or institutionalization. Categories of moral character are thus associated with rather specific courses of action. In Emerson's (1969:91) words:

> . . . The three classes of moral character recognized by the court—normal, criminal, and disturbed—correspond to the following general reactions which the court may try to implement: (a) routine handling of

the case: generally probation and the relatively minor obligations and checks accompanying it; (b) incarceration in reform school or some other institution of that nature; and (c) special care and treatment, especially in a psychiatric setting.

Even though the court looks for trouble and then assesses moral character, this does not mean that a decision relative to character will be linked to a specific outcome or disposition. Rather, and as Emerson (1969:96–97) points out, an initial decision often represents nothing more than a recommendation, primarily because the court must deal with several practical considerations (e.g., those of placement and treatment). As an illustration, he cites the case of the "disturbed" delinquent. Specifically, the decision makers may decide that such an individual needs hospitalization, yet the youth may never be institutionalized. To obtain the desired recommendation (i.e., institutionalization), psychiatrists must validate the "disturbed" or "sick" diagnosis, and the court must convince the mental hospital to accept the case. If these contingencies are not met, the youth's case will be disposed of differently.

> . . . Contingencies surrounding the actual "solution" of a case may lead to different case outcomes despite common assessments of moral character. For example, the juvenile court may come to classify a boy as a dangerous, criminally motivated person, in which case some penal sanction such as commitment to reform school would seem indicated. But the decision actually to invoke this sanction is influenced by factors such as the boy's home situation and the availability of alternatives to reform school. Thus a boy who is a state ward is more likely to be committed to reform school than a boy judged just as criminally inclined but from a stable home. Commitment follows for the first case because there is no other place to put the public ward. [Emerson, 1969:97]

The Destruction of Identity: The Role of Witnesses

Once a youth has been initially typed (e.g., by a police officer) relative to moral character, efforts must be made, thereafter, to convince others (e.g., the probation officer), and even the actor, of the correctness of the decision. As Emerson (1969:101) stresses:

> Moral character is not passively established. It is the product of interaction and communicative work involving the delinquent, his family, enforcers, complainants generally, and the court itself. *Specific versions of moral character must be successfully presented if they are to be adopted by others* (Garfinkel, 1956). Officials, who play the dominant role in this process, both directly communicate their opinions of the moral character of the youth involved and more indirectly make selective reports of incidents and information pertinent to the court's evaluation of this

character. In general, *the version of moral character finally established is negotiated from among these presented "facts," opinions, and reports.* [Italics mine]

In effect, then, competing versions of moral character are presented to the court, and the judge, acting in his or her capacity as the major audience or decision maker, must decide ultimately which version of moral character will prevail; this, according to Emerson (1969:102), often leads to contests over moral character:

> Character-related presentations are inextricably linked to issues of disposition. For moral character is established in the process of negotiating a disposition of a case among the various expectations and demands of the parties involved. In this process, the court determines an outcome not by balancing the relative merits and demerits of possible disposition alternatives, but by attempting to establish a correspondence between a youth's moral character and a particular alternative. As a result, issues of disposition lead to contests over moral character, and parties to these contests, who seek to influence the outcome of a particular case, have to marshal and present evidence to establish a version of moral character appropriate to their desired outcome.

Not only is the court concerned with establishing a linkage between a juvenile's moral character and a particular disposition but the success of this process depends heavily upon inputs from other third parties or witnesses. In this respect, the probation officer frequently plays a central role in the construction of one's moral character. Similar to the Knocker and the Rapper in Wiseman's research, he or she attempts to convey a specific image of character to the judge; this is especially evident in the following case reported in Emerson's (1969:102–103) research:

> Rodney Knight, a 16-year-old Negro boy, was accused of stealing a handbag from a woman in a subway station. The police told of the arrest, and complained that the boy had given them "difficulties," particularly by using false names, address, and age. The probation officer recommended that Knight be held in county jail under $1,000 bail until the hearing. The judge reacted: "My only problem is the county jail. I can understand the $1,000 bail for this crime—it's serious enough to warrant it. But I'm curious about the recommendation of county jail." Probation officer replied that the boy had a previous record for use without authority at the municipal court. In addition he had been "uncooperative-information limited" with the police. Judge: "Let me put it this way: Is this something that in your opinion could not be handled at the YCA [Detention Center]?" Probation Officer (hesitating): "It's a problem of either the one or the other. (pause) I think that possibly the YCA is more of a picnic grounds." Judge: "Are you making this recommendation because of uncooperativeness, or because of some knowledge you have of his previous conduct?" Probation officer replied that he knew nothing about the boy's prior life and conduct. But another

probation officer reported that the municipal court had told him that Knight had not done well while on probation there. The arresting policeman again told of how much trouble the boy had given them. The judge finally agreed to county jail, but with considerable reluctance.

In the preceding case, the probation officer obviously tries to convince the judge that the youth's moral character is criminal in nature. The judge initially balks at this suggestion; however, additional witnesses (i.e., the second probation officer and policeman) are brought into the picture, and they testify in such a manner as to corroborate or validate the probation officer's image of Knight. Thus consensus is reached (i.e., that the youth is criminal) and the judge uses this information as a basis for sentencing to jail. At this point, a beginning delinquent career becomes solidified, at least in terms of the individual's public identity.

What the research by Emerson (1969) and others (e.g., Wiseman, 1970) indicates very clearly is that organizational personnel are interested in matching clients with the existing organizational categories or career lines. And if the efforts in this direction are successful, then the actor does, at least in the eyes of the institution, become effectively molded to the category or line he or she has been cast into. Emerson's (1969) observations also provide additional substance to my claim that there is often a high degree of correspondence between one social control agency's diagnostic stereotypes and another's; this is probably most apparent in Emerson's discussion of how the first probation officer used statements by the policeman—the actual initiator of the status degradation ceremony—and another probation officer to convince the judge that the court was dealing with a young criminal. What should be noted, however, is the fact that processes and associated outcomes such as these are not only routine and recurring features of the court but they become eminently more meaningful once we realize that the underlying organizational structure of the judicial system guarantees this kind of handling. Stated very simply, the court does not deal in individuals per se. It deals in social types, categories, and labels. Thus, and similar to the statements and research by Wiseman, court personnel, and especially the probation officer, are concerned primarily with the "typicalness" of their cases. Can, for example, a delinquent act be classified and processed in accordance with any of the court's existing categories of "typical delinquencies?" This is the basic question.

Organizational Slots and Processing: Further Observations on Becoming a Client

Organizational constructs (e.g., categories of typical academic types or delinquencies), once mastered, provide for the smooth and efficient processing of clients; this was pointed out by Scheff (1966). In effect, once a staff member has been effectively inculcated with the current diagnostic stereotypes, he or she becomes more proficient in the screening and processing of prospective clients (i.e., in the application of diagnostic stereotypes). Unfortunately, and as also suggested by Scheff's (1966) comments, the perceptions of many staff members seem to be locked in at the stereotypic level. Hence, the individual merits or demerits of a case are often lost sight of or else ignored. Of major concern to the staff member or social control agent is whether or not there are enough typical features of an event or case to allow for classification in terms of reigning categories. Emerson (1969), in drawing upon the work by Sudnow, stresses the important role that "typical delinquencies" play in the structuring of a successful degradation ceremony.

> Court personnel regularly deal with a recurring sequence of delinquent acts. In this activity, they come to make certain characterizations about routinely encountered delinquencies and delinquents. *A given delinquent act is understood in terms of these characterizations; that is, its organizationally relevant meaning derives from its membership in a known class of "typical delinquencies."* Typical delinquencies are constructs of the typical features of regularly encountered delinquent acts, embodying the court staff's previous experience with and common-sense knowledge of the situations and setting of delinquent acts. . . . [Emerson, 1969:106–107] [Italics mine]

To illustrate the substantive nature of typical delinquencies, Emerson (1969:107) offers some comments made by probation officers:

> *Boy shoplifters:* "Usually it's very mild type of boy. There are not many seriously delinquent boys." Generally no previous record. Often from "well-to-do families" and taking goods "for kicks." "Usually they're pretty nice children. They give you no trouble." Seldom in court again. "Usually they're not thieves at heart. They're in the store and they succumb to a beautiful display or something that looks good to them."

Typical delinquencies, according to Emerson (1969:107), actually "indicate *the kind of actor* typically involved." Similar to Sudnow's usage, typical delinquencies (1) "identify typical actors in terms of such *social characteristics* as age, sex, class, and residence," (2) "provide explanations or 'reasons' for the particular delinquent act, including but not limited to the actor's *immediate motives;*" and (3) "identify the kind of typical actor in terms of *moral character*" (Emerson, 1969:107–108) [italics his].

Throughout court processing or, for that matter, any status degradation ceremony, an actor's public identity is under attack. And if the assault is successful, an individual becomes viewed, at least in the eyes of others, as a new or different person; this, it may be recalled, is one of the basic messages contained in the works by Werthman (1967), Tannenbaum (1938), Garfinkel (1956), Becker (1963), Hughes (1945), and Lemert (1951). I argued subsequently, however, that prior to making any statements or conducting any analysis relative to status denunciation ceremonies or institutional handling, one must see the underlying organizational structure. The research by especially Wiseman and Emerson illustrates the need for doing so. Evidence of this type also indicates that potential clients are processed in accordance with the existing organizational categories or career lines. Not only this, but fitting a candidate to a particular career line often involves various stages of screening. For example, Emerson's juveniles were subjected to two distinct stages of screening. Another excellent illustration of this process is contained in McCleary's (1978) research with parolees, particularly his discussion of those stages involved in becoming a client. . . .

McCleary (1978:124–127) points out that parole officers work with a set of social types. Thus when a prisoner's dossier is received, the officer must decide how to classify the individual; this is an important decision, primarily because, and as illustrated by the efforts of Wiseman and Emerson, each decision and corresponding type or organizational category is associated with a specific line of action. In terms of actual typing, the officer must decide initially whether the prisoner should be typed as a criminal or non-criminal. If the decision is to the effect that the person is a non-criminal, the decision-making process moves to stage four where the individual will be labeled subsequently as a client or paper man. If, by contrast, the parole officer decides that the parolee is a criminal, then another decision must be made: Is the parolee controllable? This is determined during the site visit. For example, if selected environmental factors exist (e.g., a good job or stable family) as potential controls, then, and similar to the non-criminal's processing, the prisoner will be designated as a client or paper man. Some parolees, however, are not only viewed as criminals and uncontrollable but they are perceived as dangerous; these men are kept under surveillance and returned to prison at the first sign of trouble. A parolee who is judged as sincere becomes transformed into a client; this person interacts frequently with the officer and if problems develop, attempts will be made to "save" the client. The paper man category or type comprises those who have been judged as insincere, yet controllable, and those who have not been judged; these men remain on the books, however, they experience very little interaction with the parole officer. Most see the officer a couple of times a year. Clients and dangerous men usually see the officer once a week. In fact, McCleary (1978) characterizes the interaction between the officer and the paper man as being one of "mutual disinterested toleration."

Institutional Records: Their Creation, Use, and Misuse

Even though it may be assumed that parole records accurately describe a parolee's behavior relative to the classification criteria, this is often not the case. Rather, McCleary (1978:129) maintains that "parole records are more likely to reflect the needs and problems of the POs [parole officers];" this produces a bureaucratic dysfunction, one that can be related directly to the discretionary license allowed the officer, particularly in the creation or production of parole records. In McCleary's (1978:129) words:

> . . . [the] bureaucratic dysfunction can be attributed to the great discretion allowed POs in the gathering and reporting of information. In most cases, the PO himself decides what portion of the information he has gathered will actually go into the official record. By exercising editorial discretion in this area, the PO can suppress information that might make his job more difficult or complex and can include information that might facilitate work goals or objectives. This is how POs "use" their records.

Although rarely acknowledged, the parole officer, like any other bureaucrat, must come to grips with several bureaucratic demands—considerations that have a significant impact upon the production of records. In fact, and according to McCleary (1978:129), the parole officer's work environment consists of two distinct halves: PO-parolee interaction and PO-bureaucracy interaction. McCleary (1978:129–130) points out that successful parole officers must not only control their clients but they must satisfy the bureaucracy's explicit and implicit demands. A feature common to both halves, however, is record-keeping and successful POs know how to "use" their records. Record-keeping is not necessarily a simple or straightforward task, primarily because the officers must weigh the costs or benefits that may ensue from "using" their records. McCleary's (1978:130) major argument is that, other things being equal,

> . . . a PO will not report any of the minor crimes, incidents, or violations he observes in his caseload. When a PO does report an incident, he is creating records that will accomplish some end, the benefits of which are expected to outweigh the practical costs of reporting the incident. The implication of this argument is that parole records do not accurately reflect the behavior of parolees, but rather, reflect the many problems that arise in the PO's work environment. Three general problems . . . lead to the three most common "uses" of records: (1) records created to threaten parolees, (2) records created to get rid of troublesome parolees, and (3) records created to protect the PO and his superiors.

Not only is the creation of a record associated with potential costs but organizational incentives exist for underreporting. McCleary (1978:131–136) lists and describes several practical considerations a parole officer must deal with. For example, the complete or full reporting of each event may cut into the parole officer's "free" time (e.g., many of them moonlight) or place the officer in jeopardy (e.g., a lengthy hearing may result). Full reporting may also create a great deal of "busy work" for the officer, as well as restrict his or her options (e.g., most feel that their job is to counsel and not catch clients).

The significance of the preceding observations can be found in the fact that not only do bureaucratic factors affect the production of records but they must also impact significantly on client processing. Teachers, I might add, are not immune from these influences; they, too, must come to grips with demands of their profession, as well as the bureaucracy they are immersed in.

References

Becker, H. S. (1963) *Outsiders: Studies in the Sociology of Deviance*. New York: Free Press.

Cicourel, A. V. and J. I. Kitsuse (1963) *The Educational Decision Makers*. New York: Free Press.

Emerson, R. M. (1969) *Judging Delinquents*. Chicago: Aldine.

Garfinkel, H. (1956) "Conditions of successful degradation ceremonies." *The American Journal of Sociology* 61:420–424.

Hargreaves, D. (1967) *Social Relations in a Secondary School*. New York: Humanities Press.

Hughes, E. C. (1945) "Dilemmas and contradictions of status." *The American Journal of Sociology* 50:353–359.

Kelly, D. H. (1976) "The role of teachers' nominations in the perpetuation of deviant adolescent careers." *Education* 96:209–217.

Kelly, D. H., Ed. (1979) *Deviant Behavior*. New York: St. Martin's.

Kelly, D. H., Ed. (1980) *Criminal Behavior*. New York: St. Martin's.

Kelly, D. H. and W. D. Grove (1981) "Teachers' nominations and the production of academic 'misfits'." *Education* 101:246–263.

Lemert, E. M. (1951) *Social Pathology*. New York: McGraw-Hill.

McCleary, R. (1978) *Dangerous Men*. Beverly Hills: Sage.

Pink, W. T. and M. E. Sweeney (1978) "Teacher nomination, deviant career lines and the management of stigma in the junior high school." *Urban Education* 13:361–380.

Polk, K. (1975) "Schools and the delinquency experience." *Criminal Justice and Behavior* 2:315–338.

Schafer, W. E. and C. Olexa (1971) *Tracking and Opportunity*. Scranton: Chandler.

Scheff, T. J. (1966) "Typification in the diagnostic practices of rehabilitation agencies." In M. B. Sussman, Ed., *Sociology and Rehabilitation*. Washington, D.C.: American Sociological Association.

Sudnow, D. (1965) "Normal crimes: sociological features of the penal code in a public defender office." *Social Problems* 12:255–276.

Tannenbaum, F. (1938) *Crime and Community*. New York: Ginn and Company.

Werthman, C. (1967) "The function of social definitions in the development of delinquent careers." In the President's Commission on Law Enforcement and Administration of Justice, *Task Force Report: Juvenile Delinquency and Youth Crime*. Washington, D.C.: U.S. Government Printing Office.

Wiseman, J. P. (1970) *Stations of the Lost*. Chicago: University of Chicago Press.

The Corporate Context of Private Prisons

26

David Shichor

Introduction

Since the 1970s there has been a growing interest in Western countries in the privatization of public services. This interest increased considerably during the 1980s when conservative social philosophy and political climate proved favorable to the curtailment of the functions of government and the financing and management of social programs became a major issue. This development was also felt in the field of corrections. Such a trend is not a new phenomenon in the United States and Western Europe. During the 19th century there was extensive private involvement in U.S. corrections (see, for instance, Adamson, 1983; Ayers, 1984; Sellin, 1976; Rothman, 1980; Walker, 1988; McAfee and Shichor, 1990; Cody and Bennett, 1987) and on the continent (e.g., O'Brien, 1982; Babington, 1971). However, for various reasons privatization in corrections had declined in the first part of the 20th century.

The revival of the interest in privatization of corrections contains some distinctive features: (a) It includes the privatization of the management of entire prisons. This was only seldom advocated in the past and is different from the privatization of prison industries and various services (medical treatment, laundry, etc.) which has been in practice for some time. (b) Modern correctional privatization is being done by firms which have been formed specifically for this purpose (e.g. Corrections Corporation of America, Buckingham) or are specialized subsidiaries of large corporations (e.g., RCA, Westinghouse, General Electric Wackenhut). Usually the stocks of these corporations are publicly traded. This development also has some historical precedents, since during the 19th century there were numerous prisons in the U.S. that were leased out in their entirety to commercial companies (Sellin, 1976; Ayers, 1984; Carleton, 1971; Cody and Bennett, 1987; Walker, 1988).

The involvement of corporations in the privatization of prisons was undoubtedly propelled by the immense amount of money spent on corrections

341

342 ◀▶ Part IV: The Production of Institutional Careers and Identities

in Western Societies, especially in the United States. There exists today, according to Lilly (1991) an international "correctional industry" which remains to be studied. The present paper reviews some of the major issues involved in the private management of entire correctional facilities with a special emphasis on the corporate context of this trend and the possible ramifications of it for corrections.

Privatization of Correctional Facilities: Theoretical Premises

The current interest in the privatization of entire prisons for profit stems from several interrelated sources: First, the Reagan and Thatcher administrations favored private involvement in the management of social and public services which until recently were considered to be the exclusive domain of the public sector.[1] This trend was influenced by libertarian arguments and reflected a basic distrust of the state and of "big" government and a conviction that the private sector would be more efficient than government agencies in providing public services. Second, the unprecedented growth in prison population during the 1980s, due to the "get tough" criminal justice policies that emphasize retribution, deterrence, and incapacitation, rather than rehabilitation. Third, the public inability and reluctance to pay the increased cost of corrections involved with the overcrowding of prisons. In this trend it was very tempting to launch an attempt to divest the state of the "expensive crime-control functions by allowing private enterprise to process deviant populations for profit" (Cohen, 1985:63). Fourth, the slow bureaucratic process of siting and building of new government-run correctional facilities. Fifth, the generally accepted perception that existing public prisons are mismanaged and prison conditions are so bad that no change can worsen the prevailing situation.

As mentioned, there is an increasing trend toward using private providers for the provision of various public services. Many consider the private sector to be more efficient because it is driven by the profit motive, thus it has an incentive to do better, it is more flexible and less encumbered by restrictions than the public sector. Therefore, it is suggested that the private sector will provide public services cheaper and better than public agencies do, and it will be more flexible to add services or to answer new demands (e.g., Savas, 1982).

On the ideological level, the privatization trend is greatly influenced by the neoclassical economic theory promoted by the "public choice" approach. It claims that "the competitive marketplace produces goods and services efficiently, whereas monopolies, whether public or private, tend toward both inefficiency and unresponsiveness" (De Hoog, 1984:4). Basic to this argument are the principles of classical economy focusing on the free enterprise system, free competition, and profit maximization. According to the classical approach, "'profit-and-loss' incentives are superior to bureaucratic, or 'budget-based', incentives in the delivery of public services; the quest for profit makes private operators efficient" (Weiss, 1989:31). Profit seeking, following the classical-liberal model, should take place through free competition, which will lead to maximum productivity. The best way to achieve this is by reducing state intervention into the economic marketplace. This principle is the cornerstone of the laissez-faire socioeconomic theory.

The Reagan administration followed this philosophy by easing regulations and by abolishing government regulatory agencies or severely diminishing their activities and effectiveness (e.g. Calavita, 1983). Critics of these policies claim that regulations provide protection against the avarice of the marketplace and that deregulation played down the importance of protecting the public (Tolchin and Tolchin, 1983). To a large degree it brought back the "caveat emptor" philosophy as a driving force of American economy. In several deregulated industries the free competition is eroding because of mergers and bankruptcies (see Dempsey, 1991). In the case of private correctional institutions, one of the major questions is to what degree the free competition model applies?

Theoretically, economic competition is considered to work for the general social good. It is assumed that customers shop around and choose needed merchandise or services according to their best judgment and interest. However, in corrections there are some problems in applying this economic model. First, in corrections and in other human service organizations for profit into which government agencies place clients, the customers (the government agencies which pay for the services) are not identical with the people who are the direct recipients of the services. Client relationship assumes a long-term, mutually dependent interaction between the provider of a service and the recipient of it, while a customer relationship is based on economic exchange of money for goods and services (Parsons, 1970). Besides that, there is another client relationship (dependence) between the service recipients and the government agency which is paying for the services. Thus, in the case of prisons, immates have a more complex web of relationships in which they are dependent on the government agency, the official representative of the entity which has the legal authority to punish and the "hired hand" company which executes the punishment. In this web of relationships, recipients of services do not have the same direct control over services as the customers have; they cannot pick and choose, "take it or leave it." It is problematic to establish the nature of relations in this triad: who is responsible for what, who handles complaints, who evaluates the services and on what basis, who makes final decisions regarding institutional conditions, who is monitoring and "judging" inmate behavior?

Another question in this vein is: Whose interest should be the determining one regarding the nature, the quality, and the cost of the services? Garsombke and Garsombke (1987) make the distinction between "customers" who pay for the services and "users" who receive the services and show the complexities of this relationship in public services provided by private for-profit corporations. The needs and wants of these two groups do not always coincide. In the case of private prisons, this problem is even more pointed because the "users" are usually politically, economically and socially powerless, stigmatized, and unwanted people. In this conjunction, Jayewardene and Talbot (1983:184) state that: "One of the main problems that must be faced in a situation where services are rendered by one party to a second party with payment made by a third party is the fraud that the system can generate." For instance, doctors often submit bills to Medicare, or other government programs, for services that they did not provide for patients on these programs (e.g., Pontell et al., 1982). Private correctional companies may be tempted to overcharge the government for services not rendered, or rendered through unqualified personnel.[2] In this case, there is an organizational blurring of the "cui bono"—who benefits[3]—principle, since the primary beneficiaries are the owners and managers of the organization ("business concerns") rather than the clients ("service organizations") or the public-at-large ("commonwealth organizations") as is the case, at least in theory, in public prisons (Blau and Scott, 1962).

Second, as implied, inmates are not free to seek out the "best" services, products and deals for themselves, and they cannot change facilities if they are not satisfied with the one into which they are placed (e.g., Palumbo, 1986). According to Hasenfeld and English (1974:468), in human service organizations clients ". . . potentially have little or no control over their fate in the organization. This is particularly the case whenever the client is involuntarily committed to the organization." Thus, the free-market model of private corrections seems to be overstated. If any "shopping around" would occur it would be done by the customer (government) rather than by the users (inmates). If that would occur, it is likely that the major concern would be cost, rather than quality of services, since in the case of businesses "the ultimate profit is the bottom line. There are no exceptions, for business does nothing unless it can see some benefit for itself or its investors" (Carroll and Easton, 1987:20).

Third is the issue of the profit motive. The major motivation of private corporations, according to the classical model, is the maximization of profit (e.g. Garsombke and Garsombke, 1987). Although there are claims that corporations seek a "satisfactory" level of profits rather than "maximization" of profits (e.g., Stone, 1975) the definition of what is satisfactory remains in the hands of the management of corporations vis à vis the shareholders. Since organizations are formally rational, the congruence between their procedures and their substantive goals is closer than that of most other social groups (Sutton and Wild, 1978). This means that profit-making can be rigorously and systematically pursued by private corporations.

The introduction of the principle of profit-making to corrections is controversial. Advocates of privatization point out that nothing is wrong with having this motive in corrections. They argue that in the application of punishment the motivation of those who apply is not relevant; the important thing is that the criminal procedure will follow due process requirements, and that the sentence will be meted out "for the right reasons" (Logan, 1987:38). Second, it is maintained that profit motives already exist in the punishment process because prison officials and employees earn their livelihood from the penal system. Following this argument, the profit motive in corrections is universal; thus objecting to the "profit motive" in the private sector alone is discriminatory and prejudicial (Logan, 1990). However, some critics categorically object to the idea that profit should be pursued through the deliberate imposition of suffering on other people. It can also be argued that to work for a salary as a prison employee is not exactly the same profit motive as that of the management of a corporation (Rutherford, 1990) that has to produce a profit for its stockholders and can increase personal benefits by increasing the income and/or decreasing costs. Ryan and Ward (1989:61) claim in this regard that ". . . to equate these wage earners with those who wish to exploit the penal system for corporate gain is quite simply wrong. . . ." They continue their statement using Marxist concepts to counter the above pro-privatization argument by pointing out that: "it fails to make the obvious distinction between those who sell their labor and those who own and control capital." As implied earlier, the privatization of prisons is a part of the conservative agenda. It is ideologically justified by libertarian principles according to which the state should be ultimately dispensed with or there should be "a 'minimal' state in which political coercion is strictly confined to the task of protecting property and enforcing contracts" (Hoffman, 1988). In this kind of state private organizations are supposed to fulfill most of the government functions including punishment. Paradoxically, Feeley (1991:5) in his historical analysis of the privatization of prisons demonstrated that ". . . the reliance on private contractors facilitated the expansion of the capacity of the criminal justice system. . . ." Thus, instead of reducing the state's coercive power, privatization of prisons helped to expand it.

Issues of Organizational Deviance

There are other issues, beyond the moral principle, which are of concern. The centrality of the free competition in the privatization movement was mentioned earlier. Some critics point out that often the pursuit of profit seeking and free competition are conflicting (Conklin, 1977). As known, the profit motive in corporate America became so prevalent that it was often used to justify questionable business practices, especially through the embracement of the "caveat emptor" doctrine (Hamilton, 1931; Shichor, 1989). While, as mentioned, some scholars question the "maximum profit seeking" nature of corporations (e.g., Stone, 1975), it seems that their "paramount objectives" remain maximum profit and financial success (Clinard, 1990).

A corporation can increase its profit and market share by limiting free competition (Conklin, 1977; Vaughan, 1980). Sutherland (1956:90) pointed out that "big business does not like competition, and it makes careful arrangements to reduce it and even eliminate it." Indeed, large corporations tend to engage in various strategies to limit competition in order to reduce uncertainty that can obstruct their goal attainment (Thompson, 1967). In several major industries (e.g., car manufacturing, defense, oil), a handful of large corporations dominate the market (Mills, 1956). Certain kinds of accommodations and market sharing among these companies are likely to develop (Moore, 1962). Thus a symbiosis among corporations rather than a genuine competition becomes a reality (Blau and Scott, 1962). This often leads to unlawful practices such as antitrust violations and price fixing (Geis, 1967). An oligopolic trend among private firms contracting in corrections was found by Camp and Camp (1985), who reported that a few companies account for a large portion of private contracting.

In an emerging field of enterprise, such as the private management of correctional facilities, the oligopolic trend issue is even more critical, because a few dominant corporations can have a strong influence in setting standards for the evolving marketplace, a fact which may have far-reaching consequences.[4]

The pursuance of profit has other ramifications as well. Corporations, by setting performance standards often tied to income goals, can "indirectly initiate deviant actions by establishing particular norms, rewards, and punishments for people occupying lower-level positions" (Ermann and Lundman, 1982:7). Executives frequently realize that the violation of laws, regulations, or norms are the shortest way for higher profits, and such violations can be mandated through policy directives to lower echelon workers and mid-level managers (Meyer, 1972). The corporate culture often generates a crimogenic atmosphere which in a private correctional institution may influence lower echelon employees (guards) who are usually underpaid, have few opportunities to advance, and lack job security. Those who want to keep their jobs and advance in the corporation may feel a pressure to follow deviant practices to further organizational goals (e.g., cut corners to increase profits, write reports that are favorable for the prison, etc.) or not to report violations of procedures or inmates' rights. Clinard (1983) found that financially oriented top executives, as opposed to the professionally oriented ones, were primarily concerned with short-term profits and were more inclined to resort to deviance. Because most corporations have shareholders seeking short-term profits and there is a trend in American business to place financial experts in top management positions, there is considerable possibility of the emergence of an organizational climate in the private correctional industry which may be conducive to follow certain deviant practices.

Legal Issues

A central question of privatization is to what degree will a balance be maintained between the corporate economic concerns on the one hand, and accountability for the correctional services rendered and for the maintenance of human rights of the clientele on the other (Bozeman, 1988). Several students of privatization have raised this issue, pointing out, among other things, that

> the public and private sectors have distinctive characters and that these distinctions are premised on legal principles, not economic or social science theories . . . the public sector is being profoundly altered, and ultimately harmed by the deliberate blurring of these public and private characteristics (Moe, 1988:674).

One of the major problems with the diminishing public and private distinction is that the government delegates some of its powers and functions to a party whose legitimacy is not always clear (Moe, 1988).

Another important issue having legal ramifications is involved in economic strategies for revamping corporations to make them more profitable. During the 1980s there was an unprecedented trend for corporate takeovers (friendly and hostile), "reorganizations" resulting in the "spinning off" of companies and divisions from a corporation which was losing money or making less profit than anticipated. It is a major question how the government's reliance on private prison management would fare in this kind of situation. What are the legal guarantees to the government if a correctional corporation is bought out or sold out by its parent company? What happens if a corporation is taken over by a foreign company, a situation which occurs quite frequently? Is it acceptable that a foreign corporation will handle American prisoners and will make profit on it?

Furthermore, what would happen if a private prison corporation would declare bankruptcy? What would be the legal obligations of the government vis à vis the creditors of the prison corporation (American Bar Association, 1986)? How would it affect the legal and other obligations of the private corporations themselves toward the government, and how would it affect the government agencies? How will it be ensured that the prison will continue to operate? Holley (1988) deals with the legal complexities of this problem, but the potential operational complexities are even greater, e.g., who will step in to continue the operations of a facility.

The problematic nature of this issue should be seen in light of the complexities[5] of corporate bankruptcies which can be used as business strategies, such as the alteration of bargaining positions, renegotiation of debts and contracts, stalling for time, and shifting the financial risk to other parties (Delaney, 1990) not to mention the increasing number of fraudulent bankruptcies. Many corporations become dependent on financial institutions which control their capital flow (Glasberg, 1981). Most businesses raise their money for the start up from these institutions. They also need financial institutions in the case of expansion, mergers, takeovers, or in other occasions when they get into a difficult economic situation. Banks, because of their lending power often are able to gain a seat on the recipients' board of directors. Also they are usually the major holders of bonds which are longer-term loans. In the case of bankruptcy of a company, bondholders' claims have a precedence over stockholders' claims (Glasberg, 1989). Thus other corporate entities, which do not have any experience in prison management and do not have a direct contract with the government, may become involved in the running of a private facility. This underlines the potentially strong influence and interest of financial institutions in the privatization of prisons even though they do not get involved in the hands on management of the facility.

As an example, we can mention the E.F. Hutton brokerage company which intended to move into the private prison business during the early 1980s. Later, this firm was found to be involved in illegally using its clients' money without interest through check kiting and it had to pay two million dollars in fines. Shortly after, Hutton merged with Shearson and Lehman, which owns American Express. These possibilities underline the problem of stability and continuity of private enterprise in the correctional business, a field in which it is not likely that many corporations will be available to step in and take over companies that get into financial or legal troubles.

Robbins (1986; 1989), a student of the legal aspects of correctional privatization, shows that privatization will not reduce government liability for the handling of prisoners. For instance, under 42 U.S.C. Sec. 1983, the government will be liable for any civil rights violations against inmates in a private prison (Thomas and Hanson, 1989; Pellicciotti, 1987). A major problem will be the inability to use the sovereign-immunity defense in a civil rights violation lawsuit (Robbins, 1989). Several writers mention that this problem should be dealt with by making certain that the private corporation carries a high liability insurance contract (e.g., Thomas, 1987; Robbins, 1989). In third party suits against the government ("deep pocket"), when privately operated correctional institutions are sued for civil rights violations, government agencies will have less control to avoid such cases than they had before when the prisons were run by public agencies.

Monitoring Correctional Corporations and Evaluating Performance

The previous deliberation leads to the issue of the monitoring and regulation of the private prison "industry." This is important because "corporations have become powerful, autonomous institutions, largely independent of external influence of control" (Mizruchi, 1982:15).

Several scholars have pointed out that often the cost of monitoring is not calculated into the economic analysis of prison privatization (e.g., Gentry,

1986). To maintain meaningful supervision over private corporations delivering human services, especially in corrections, a rigorous monitoring mechanism has to be established. The extra expenses involved with monitoring will influence the cost effectiveness of private prisons. However, McDonald (1990) estimates the monitoring cost only to be about one percent of the total contract. Oversight must be especially rigorous, since as seen, the usual control mechanism of the free marketplace, exercised by customers and clients, may have only a limited role in the prison business. A clearly written and detailed contract is a key element in the success of correctional privatization (e.g., Woolley, 1985; Mullen, 1985; McAfee, 1987). Effective monitoring mechanisms are needed to determine whether the contractor meets the standards laid down in the contract (Keating, 1990).

A related issue is that it is hard to evaluate correctional performance. If we accept that the prison, which is a total institution (Goffman, 1961) based on coercive compliance (Etzioni, 1961), has only one major task (e.g., incapacitation—locking people away to protect society), then probably measuring effectiveness is manageable. But currently, even with the decline of the ideal of rehabilitation, we expect the attainment of multiple goals by the prison (Cressey, 1965) which makes evaluation much more complex. Also, since for-profit private correctional institutions run by corporations are relatively new, there is very little collected data available that could serve as evaluative benchmarks. Similarly, there may be some reluctance from the management and staff to fully cooperate with the researchers (Durham, 1988), although Roberts and Powers (1985) claim that the evaluation of private prisons is not much different from that of other prisons. Nevertheless, there is a lack of adequate evaluation of the performance of private prisons (Durham, 1989).

Close monitoring may raise similar problems as the regulation of private industry does. Regulations, as mentioned, are vigorously objected to by the proponents of laissez-faire economy who claim that it distorts the meaning of a free marketplace. While contract monitoring and legal regulations are not the same, some of their problems are similar. One concern is the "revolving door" syndrome. There are privatized correctional institutions (prisons, detention camps, facilities for parole violators) in which State officials monitor the operations, but at the same time a job is waiting for them at the corporation that runs the facility upon their retirement.[6]

The experience of government agencies with private contractors indicates that even when contracts are clearly written, there are problems with securing adherence to them. Critics of privatization of human services or, as some refer to them, "soft services . . . performed for or on people" (Nelson 1980:431) point out that standards set for regulations are being reduced by the (for profit) propriety lobby.[7]

Private corporations contracting with government agencies often know from the beginning that there is a good chance that they will not be able to deliver the promised product or services for the price indicated in their bid. They bank on the dependency of the government agency on their services that is going to make it hard to terminate a contract (e.g., Keating, 1990). Thus, not only is the way the contract is written important, but also that there will be alternative private prison companies available. Ring (1987:25) underscores this problem in the following:

> Cost will increase, according to opponents, because private operators will engage in low-balling: intentionally underestimating costs in their initial bids in the hope that the government will become dependent upon their services over time. Once this occurs, the contractor will raise his fees or allow conditions to deteriorate, gambling that the government will accept the charges rather than risk losing his services.

Contract violations by companies dealing with the government is a common occurrence; various types of violations in the defense industry are well documented (e.g., Goodwin, 1985; Glazer and Glazer, 1989). For example, Northrop Corporation in 1990 pleaded guilty to 34 criminal fraud charges and was fined 17 million dollars; 141 other charges were dropped in a plea bargain agreement. One of the main charges was the falsification of tests on the components for nuclear-armed cruise missiles (Weinstein, 1990). It can be assumed that if in the field of national defense, a major concern of government, there are serious corporate violations, then in the provision of human services, which have a politically powerless and socially neglected clientele, the likelihood of corporate violations will be greater. Thus, the rational nature of organizations, which is harnessed to achieve profits, opens ample opportunities for corporate violations, especially in the case of human services provided for undesired populations. The legal enforcement of the contract and the provision of proof that there was an intent to deceive the government is also a complex drawn-out process requiring time and allocation of resources (e.g., Goodwin, 1985).

Another contention by critics is that many companies prefer contracts which detail only the most essential services that will be provided; anything beyond that will become an "extra" service, charged for separately, or the contract will have to be renegotiated for a higher price.

The corporation's risk of being penalized for contract violations is minimized by factors such as (1) reduced competition, since only a few companies are active in a limited market; (2) the lack of state ability to take over the facilities; (3) lack of adequate monitoring;[8] (4) the lack of deterrent effect, since penalties assessed against corporations are usually fines that are far below the gains derived from illegal activities or from regulation violations (e.g., Fisse, 1985; Stone, 1975); (5) the shielding of top decision-makers from individual criminal liability: since the decision-making in corporations is diffused, there is an opportunity to abdicate personal responsibility (Clinard and Yeager, 1980; Kramer, 1982); (6) corporations have access to expert legal services[9] and, if there is a court case, they often have more resources to outlast government prosecutors, as the well-known Pinto case demonstrated (Cullen et al., 1987).

This discussion indicates that it is feasible that under certain conditions private corporations contracted to serve government's functions may have an incentive to carry out their state's function imperfectly since their major concern is to serve their own interest (Gentry, 1986).

Political Influence

Another relevant issue concerns the political influence of corporations moving into the prison business. Large corporate interests often organize in political action committees (PACs) through which they can make substantial contributions to political candidates. Those contributions are given, even so that it is often denied, with the intent to influence legislation favorable to the PACs' interests. It is feasible that corporations involved in corrections for profit will form their own PACs and organize other lobbying efforts. The development of PACs in the U.S. during the 1970s and 1980s has demonstrated the growing political and social influence of corporations in America. A major aim of this political involvement has been the neutralization of "government regulation of business practices and to obtain government assistance for business activities" (Ryan et al., 1987:105). PACs are well organized and are using the most modern management skills to raise money and the latest computer methods to evaluate political candidates' standings on issues of interest to them (Fraser/Associates, 1980). Political activity of corporations that operate prisons may be very rigorous since it is suggested that those companies which are more dependent on the government for the sale of their products or services display more intense political activity than corporations which depend less on government contracts (Jacobs et al., 1991).

Conceivably, private correction PACs will seek to influence issues that are of importance to the industry. At the same time, they also may collaborate with other PACs to form a political force in contributing to "candidates whose ideology is perceived as compatible with free enterprise values and business positions on public policy issues" (Ryan et al., 1987:119). As Kamerman and Kahn (1989) note, privatization is basically a political act aimed at diminishing the social role of government.

These features of corporate political activity should be seen in light of the fact that there are no comparable PACs or lobbying organizations dedicated for the sole purpose of representing the inmates. The ACLU and other civil rights organizations which often take up the interests of inmates are not geared to put all their efforts and resources into this one issue. Prisoners constitute a "throw away" population which is ignored by most "decent" people. While there is lately more emphasis on the formal legal rights of prisoners (Alpert, 1980), they are not able to command a widespread public concern for their interests. Basically, "prisoners are declasse, they are the outcasts of society, exercising virtually no suasion upon public policy" (Geis, 1987:78). They cannot even vote, and there should be a continuous concern that privatization may have a negative impact on their rights (Sullivan, 1989).

Regarding the public's concern with the handling of convicts, Donahue (1988:21) comments that:

> One might legitimately wonder whether a public that has refused to put up the resources to bring public prisons up to minimal standards will resist the temptation to turn a blind eye on the conditions of confinement in bargain-rate private prisons.

Thus, there may not be a balance between the corporate private prison lobby's influence and organizations that are likely to be concerned with prisoners' rights.

Management Issues

The privatization trend is based on the belief that innovations and flexibility to attack problems will come only from private initiatives (Greenwood, 1981; McConville, 1987). There is a great emphasis on the importance of effective management. In this regard, DiIulio (1988:75) states:

> Most claims that private corrections firms can outperform public corrections agencies rest on two assumptions. The first is that there are significant differences between public and private management, that business firms are necessarily more "efficient," "effective," and "innovative" than government agencies, and that these advantages of private management are universal: they obtain whether the task is picking up garbage or locking up prisoners. The second assumption is that the public sector's administrative experience in corrections has been an unmitigated disaster: prisons and jails have been, and continue to be, horrible places that are horribly run.

Several works underline the crucial role of executive leadership in correctional institutions (e.g., Street et al., 1966; Morris, 1974; Jacobs, 1977; DiIulio, 1988, 1990). This role includes the setting of specific goals and policies for the institution, the maintenance of communication with the outside community, and the definition of roles and responsibilities inside the organization.

One of the interesting features of corporations which manage private prisons is that, among the managers they employ, former administrators of state departments of corrections and prisons are prominent. Some of these managers had legal and disciplinary problems during their tenure in public institutions (Becker and Stanley, 1985; McShane and Williams, 1989). The question is how these administrators, some of whom did not show much creativity and efficiency in the public sector, will be able to run a new, more effective private correctional institution. They will have to perform under different circumstances than before. In the private corporate sector "profit, not morality, is the ultimate test of effectiveness" (Clinard and Yeager, 1980:273). Their performance, corporate status, and monetary compensation will be determined mainly on the basis of the economic balance sheet of the corporation.

Research on corporations indicates that managers can be pressured by profit standards set too high to resort to questionable, sometimes even illegal practices to attain these goals (Clinard and Yeager, 1980). Similarly, corporate crime literature suggests that executives have a special responsibility for setting the tone of corporate cultures including the readiness to violate rules (Braithwaite, 1989).

DiIulio (1988) points out that the quality of life in prisons and jails depends mainly on the quality of management. Thus the issue of management of private prisons is an area which has to be a major concern for policy makers and for everyone who has a genuine interest in corrections.

There are some additional factors that raise concern regarding corporate managers of private institutions. Managers in corporations seem to have a very wide range of discretion; in effect, they have more actual power than the legal owners, the shareholders have (e.g., Ermann and Lundman, 1982). Therefore, they may be freer to resort to unethical or deviant practices to manage the institution. As Clinard (1983) has shown, corporate managers with financial backgrounds more readily "cut corners" to achieve performance goals than technologically oriented managers. Also, corporations tend to "shield" their top managers from personal liability by delegation of responsibility to various departments and middle-range managers (e.g., Braithwaite, 1989; Conklin, 1977; Vaughan, 1980) who are judged by how close they come to their set target of profits (Gross, 1980). The risk of penalty for corporate executives who violate rules is relatively minor (Clinard and Yeager, 1980), a fact which may mitigate the preventive effect of deterrence which otherwise may well be strong with corporate crime because of its national nature (Braithwaite and Geis, 1982).

Labor Related Issues

One of the controversies regarding the privatization of prisons is related to the labor force in these institutions. Several issues recur: (a) the quality of the work force; (b) labor relations; (c) the authority of the officers in a private prison.

Corrections is a labor intensive industry; between 60–80 percent of the correctional cost is labor related (Donahue, 1988; McDonald, 1990). As seen, private corporations claim that they can deliver the same or better correctional services at a lower cost than the government does. This implies that they will be able to reduce their labor cost, which can be achieved in several ways: (1) cutting salaries or the pay scale of employees, (2) providing less or no fringe benefits and pension funds, (3) economizing on the screening procedures, (4) hiring fewer employees, (5) providing less training, (6) combination of any of the above.

Paying lower salaries to correctional employees, whose income is not considered to be very lucrative to begin with, may result in the reduction of the quality of lower echelon employees in private prisons. Private prison guards usually come from the unskilled labor force, many of them working only part-time (Weiss, 1989). Referring to private security guards as one likely pool for private prison employees, Donahue (1988) indicates that public employees are more likely to be high school graduates, full-time workers, and to be in the prime working age than the pool of private security employees. A lower-paid labor force usually means a lower-quality labor force. Schuman (1989) found an unusually high staff turnover in privately run correctional facilities. Many staff members eventually applied for the better paid and more secure public sector positions. High turnover rate may influence the quality of services because of lack of stability in the institutions. A similar situation occurs in the private police organizations. Often individuals who, for various reasons, are not hired as law enforcement agents get jobs as private police officers. Generally, private security companies have a high turnover rate. Relying on information from the 1970s, Lipson (1975) concludes that private security firms did not have minimum standards for physical or mental fitness or for educational or literacy levels. Similarly, the job training of the officers was minimal. South (1988) indicates similar trends in the British private security industry. He points to low wages, low standards, little training, and high turnover in this industry. He also found that private security companies try to cut corners in their contract in order to be able to make profit.

Dissatisfaction with low pay and difficult working conditions may lead to many employee strikes in private prisons if and when employees unionize (although private correctional companies make every effort not to employ unionized workers and not to let their workforce unionize). There also may be employee refusal to work with certain kinds of inmates (e.g., AIDS patients). As Novey (1985:8) points out: "Being in the private sector, employees will have the legal right to organize a union and conduct slow downs with potential strikes as an end result." If this problem arises government authorities may have to intervene by manning the facility until the strike is over or the correctional corporation is able to hire strike breakers, who probably will be less qualified than the striking workers, and because of the emergency situation will not have even the minimal training that the permanent officers had. If the correctional officers in private prisons will not be able to unionize, which is clearly an aim of the corporations, the question will be raised whether the government should work with companies that make their profits because their workers do not have civil service and union protections. Some critics of privatization of prisons refer to these practices as a form of union-busting (e.g., Geis, 1987). On the other hand, avid supporters of privatization go out of their way to attack public workers' unions by accusing them of involvement in various kinds of corruption (see Logan, 1990). Any problems emanating from the labor disputes, such as labor violence or mishandling of inmates by inexperienced personnel, still will be the government's liability.

Punishment is a public function supposedly executed by government authorities. The question is how much authority can be delegated to the staff in a private facility who are hired to fulfill the public function of executing punishment. The interaction between correctional staff and inmates in a private facility often affects the extent and nature of punishment. A disciplinary write up by a private correctional officer may cause the loss of "good time" or may have other punishment consequences.

One of the questions in this regard is whether a private corporation should be involved in the adjudication of disciplinary charges. The issue is that the maintenance of discipline is an integral part of management of a correctional facility. Punishment of inmates is a part of this task. Even if the final judgment of a disciplinary case were determined by an officer of the State Department of Corrections, the disciplinary write-up would be done by private employees and the investigation might be seriously influenced by them (Press, 1990). Besides, to fulfill the disciplinary function itself will cost money for the Department of Corrections, an expense which will have to be calculated into the cost of private corrections. Disciplinary practices have a direct influence on the duration of the stay of a prisoner in the facility and may have other direct punitive implications, such as spending time in segregation cells and losing various privileges. This means that the government function of punishment is contracted away (Elvin, 1985) and introduces a private discretionary element into the system.

Direct or indirect influence by corporate staff on the length of stay of inmates has economic implications as well; it may result in more expanded periods of incarceration, thus it can contribute to the occupancy level of the facility, which is a major corporate concern when per-diem payment is involved. In the current situation when an overabundance of convicts is the case, this does not seem to be a problem; presently the replacement of released inmates is secured (Logan, 1990). However, when far-reaching, long-term policies are contemplated, such factors have to be taken into consideration. There are also indications that the "flow" of new inmates is slowing down (Hurst, 1991).

Economic Issues

The major argument for privatization is economic. It is said to save money. So far, available assessments of the economic results of privatization of correctional management tends to be favorable. Most reports indicate real or potential savings by private correctional facilities (e.g., Sellers, 1989; Logan and Rausch, 1985; Camp and Camp, 1985; Logan and McGriff, 1989; Mc-Donald, 1990); others report no substantial difference in cost between private and public institutions (e.g., Urban Institute, 1989; Levinson, 1985). McDonald (1990) in a detailed analysis of the various problems entailed in trying to entangle the most correct ways of cost comparison did not come to a clear conclusion in establishing whether private corrections is cheaper than public corrections, although he lent some support to the claims of the proponents of privatization.

Several hidden and not so hidden problems exist concerning the cost of private corrections. One of the controversial issues is the "marginal cost" of institutionalization (McDonald, 1989). Almost all private corporations that manage correctional facilities are paid on a per-diem per capita basis. While at a certain capacity level a private prison can cost less per inmate, increasing population may decrease the expenses in a public institution vis à vis a private facility "because so many of the costs of imprisonment are relatively fixed, the cost of adding additional prisoners is actually much less than the average cost per prisoner in a facility" (McDonald, 1989:20). In this respect, publicly managed institutions can be more flexible in handling a growing inmate population without increasing substantially the cost, while in private prisons each new prisoner will add to the budget an equal amount. On the other hand, this feature of public facilities may contribute to the increased number of prison sentences and to prison overcrowding.

There are additional issues that may have economic implications. One of them concerns the possible dependence of government agencies on private corporations after the initial contract is in effect. It is likely that competition will be limited in the prison industry, since the only customers are government agencies and, therefore, only a few companies will compete for contracts. The latest private facility census conducted by Thomas and Foard (1991) found 14 private companies operating 44 facilities. Two companies, CCA (14) and Wackenhut (8) operate 22 (50 percent) of the facilities, handling 56.6 percent (7,559) of the total number of inmates (13,348) in private facilities. This can result in a situation in which criminal justice agencies will be at the mercy of a few corporations, which may try and succeed to raise prices, lower standards, and violate some contract clauses. In addition, when the current contract expires and a new one is negotiated, the bargaining position of the government may become weaker because of its growing reliance on private corporations, the lack of competition, the lack of alternative public facilities, and the lack of available management and staff personnel. Thus the option of reopening government institutions or reorganizing private facilities by government agencies would not be an easy one to take. Also, to change private contractors may be problematic because the changeover from one company to another having different policies, management styles, staffing practices, etc., may cause disruptions and disturbances.

It is reasonable to assume that private corporations, by using their political influence and public relation abilities, will be able to push legislation for longer prison sentences, thus making sure that their "occupancy rate" will be at the maximum. In that way, they also may impact penal policies in favor of extension of incarceration and away from alternatives to imprisonment (Anderson et al., 1985).[10] Government agencies usually have to guarantee a certain level of occupation rate, below which the per diem rate goes up in order to reimburse the contractors for their investments and for their income loss. Thus, there is a built in incentive to continue a high level of incarceration rate (State of California, 1985). Therefore, if government becomes dependent on private corporations for incarceration, it will either be compelled to keep people imprisoned who otherwise would be released, or will have to agree to price adjustments. Common sense would suggest that government agencies will keep the prison population at a certain level rather than pay the same sum of money for the incarceration of fewer inmates.

Borna (1986) mentions the hidden cost of the interest payments and tax breaks which would come out of taxpayers' money and would go to private developers or finance corporations and their investors involved in the construction of private prisons. Private corporations also use consultants for various services (e.g., drawing up the lease agreements). Consulting costs are included in the lease payments. In addition, facility and equipment depreciations will be reimbursed. The government also reimburses corporations for changes in variable interest rates if they are used for the construction or other financing of a facility.

Another issue connected with the hidden cost of private corrections is that private corporations would still rely on certain public services, especially in the case of emergencies such as prison riots, public health problems, employee strikes, and bankruptcy (Bowditch and Everett, 1987). The cost of these services cannot be estimated currently because of the lack of benchmark data.

Conclusions

This paper has reviewed some of the major issues concerning the privatization of management of correctional facilities with special attention to the corporate nature of the private providers. In this analysis certain problems are general to corrections but exacerbated by the corporate involvement; others are unique to the corporate context of private corrections.

The corporate involvement in correctional privatization amplifies the political influence of the private sector upon correctional public policy-making. Through political lobbying, PACs, and campaign contributions, corporations are likely to continue and even to accelerate incapacitation oriented policies by which more people spend longer periods of time in correctional institutions. Conversely, this trend will diminish the emphasis on alternative programs that emphasize rehabilitation and will result in the pursuance of the "Hilton Inn mentality," i.e., trying to maintain high occupancy rates for profit purposes.

There is also a concern that by using their political influence, corporations will be able to "cream the crop," meaning that they will be able either to deal with inmates classified as lower security risks—which allows the institution to hire fewer custody personnel and operate without major disturbances avoiding adverse public reaction, or to manage institutions with specified clientele (e.g., drug addicts), since higher profits can be made when "specific" or "professional" services are provided. In this situation, the most violent inmates and career criminals would have to be handled by the public institutions while the private corporations could demonstrate a better performance record, working with less hard core offenders, on top of their higher profits.

The issue of profit-making in human services in general and in corrections in particular is a controversial one. Is it proper to make profits by causing deliberate suffering to others? Profit-making will be rationally and systematically pursued by a corporation which will have to show profits to its investors. Some of the profit-making rigor may lead to unethical or even illegal practices. Even so that contracts will be carefully written, they will be closely scrutinized by the legal departments of the corporations to minimize corporate risks. Rigorous monitoring of compliance with the contract will cost extra money for the government; these costs are often not calculated fully into the budget. Since only a limited number of corporations will offer complete facility management services, the government may have a difficult time replacing companies which do not abide by the contracts and/or will not perform according to the expectations. Meanwhile, government agencies may lose their organizational structure and resources to take over management. This can be a major problem with the increased number of corporate bankruptcies, mergers, takeovers, and "spin-offs."

There may be problems with waging legal cases against private corporations since they can afford high quality legal defense and their resources for long-term litigations may be greater than those of local governments. Also the risk of penalties for corporate wrong-doings is minimized since usually the corporations are punished rather than the corporate decision makers. In general, punishments are monetary and not substantial. Because of the uniqueness of the "correctional marketplace," adverse publicity, which is suggested as an option for corporate punishment (e.g., Fisse, 1985), will be minimized as a deterrent.

The fact that corporations often violate legal or at least moral and ethical codes is underscored by the extensive scholarly literature on corporate ethics (e.g., Donaldson, 1982; Bradshaw and Vogel, 1981; Anderson, 1989). Thus it is recognized that large corporations often do not act according to the highest moral standards or the law. This can be particularly disturbing in the case of human services provided to groups that are politically powerless and do not attract much public interest and support. Robbins (1989: 542) expresses this concern by stating: "privatization is not a panacea; the private sector is more interested in doing well than in doing good."

The credibility of corporations became particularly shaky during the 1980s and early 1990s during the savings and loans crisis, with the bankruptcy of large insurance companies and with the revelation of constant overcharging of government agencies, cost overruns on government contracts and corruption of inspectors. And as Sagarin and Maghan (1985:E4) pointed out concerning E.F. Hutton's intent to enter into the private prison business: "It is only an added irony that E.F. Hutton itself became involved in one of the largest white collar frauds in American history. Is this the company to which we are going to turn over the prisons?"

Involvement of corporations in the private management of correctional facilities is often held out as a panacea, or at least a major step forward and a way out of the shameful conditions that generally mark the operation of correctional facilities today. This opinion is buttressed by some scholarly works with conservative leanings that in the current political context are appealing. But, as this paper implies, in many instances the privatization of corrections may further aggravate an already malignant condition. It seems that a revamping and upgrading of the public prisons could be an alternative venue in corrections which would eliminate at least the problem of private "greed" from the administration of punishment. One core problem of corrections seems to be that the government does not fulfill sufficiently its "duty to govern" (DiIulio, 1990).

Keeping governmental inefficiency and negligence in the management of correctional institutions in mind, Wecht's concern should be taken seriously: "While state prison authorities may be inept or worse, they lack the incentives to raise prices and reduce quality which characterize a for-profit firm" (Wecht, 1987:829). This situation may become more a reality after the initial "honeymoon" period—in which the private corporation will make efforts to live up to all standards and to perform exceptionally—will be over (Wecht, 1987).

Notes

1. For British sources, see Papadakis and Taylor-Gosby (1987), Riddel (1989), Ryan and Ward (1989), etc. In Britain the government policies toward privatized institutions are not very clear. While ideologically the conservative government supports privatization of corrections in 1989 the plan to establish private jails was abandoned (Cowdry, 1989). On the other hand, the Home Office Secretary Kenneth Baker announced on the 5th of December, 1991, that half of Britain's prisons are to be privatized (Daily Mail, 1991). Also there is an interest in privately managed prisons in Australia and the Correctional Corporation of America has opened a facility with Australian partners in Queensland.

2. In their study of placements of juveniles in public and private institutions, Shichor and Bartollas (1990) found that a number of private institutions that were supposedly providing psychological treatment for juveniles (and charging the county accordingly) did not have the fully qualified staff, and/or did not have the professionals on the premises for the required number of hours per day.

3. Blau and Scott (1962:43) suggest using this principle in organizational analysis. According to this scheme, four types of organizations can be distinguished: (1) "mutual benefit associations," where the prime beneficiary is the membership, (2) "business concerns," where the owners are the prime beneficiary; (3) "service organizations," where the client group is the prime beneficiary; and (4) "commonwealth organizations," where the prime beneficiary is the public-at-large.

4. The tendency for reduced competition in the privatization of public services other than correction is mentioned by Starr (1987).

5. Some of the problems that government may face in the case of bankruptcy of a private company with which it has contracts are analyzed by Flener (1989).

6. In one case known to the author, the wife of the official responsible for the monitoring was working for the private facility supervised by him while he was getting ready to retire and to assume a position at the same facility. Thus, there has to be more sensitivity to "conflict of interest". This case is only one example and should only be seen as an illustration of an issue.

7. In January 1991 Wackenhut Corrections Corporation, the private contractor of Monroe County jail in Florida broke its contract and returned control of the jail to the Sheriff. The company asked for $2.6 million extra for the four-year contract because it planned to staff the jail with six guards per shift; however, state standards require 11 guards per shift. The corporation claimed that it was unaware of this requirement. The county commissioners accepted Wackenhut's proposal for a settlement that included a $300,000 payment to the company to settle its claims over the staffing issue, utility bills and transportation costs. The county also agreed to pay $206,000 for equipment at the jail that the corporation purchased (Keating, 1991).

8. This may include the purposeful corruption of government inspectors by corporations (Coleman, 1989), and the lack of resources to upgrade monitoring by the inability to train inspectors that would gain high levels of expertise (e.g. Lynxwiler et al., 1984).

9. Mann (1985) in his book "Defending White-Collar Crime" describes the strategies and complexities of legal counsel that may go into white collar and corporate law cases and the expertise of these highly paid lawyers.

10. So far, available accounts on private facilities do not indicate such practices (e.g., Brakel, 1988).

References

Adamson, Christopher R., "Punishment after Slavery: Southern State Penal Systems, 1865–1890," *Social Problems,* 1983 (30), 555–569.

Alpert, Geoffrey P., (ed.), *Legal Rights of Prisoners* (Beverly Hills, CA: Sage, 1980).

American Bar Association, *Section of Criminal Justice,* Report to the House of Delegates (Chicago: American Bar Association Division for Communications and Public Affairs, 1986).

Anderson, Jr., Jerry W., *Corporate Social Responsibility* (Westport, CT: Quorum Books, 1989).

Anderson, Patrick, Charles R. Davoli and Laura J. Moriarity, "Private Corrections: Feast or Fiasco?", *The Prison Journal,* 1985 (452), 32–41.

Ayers, Edward L., *Vengeance and Justice: Crime and Punishment in the 19th-Century American South* (New York: Oxford University Press, 1984).

Babington, Anthony, *The English Bastille: A History of Newgate Gaol and Prison Conditions in Britain, 1188–1902* (London: MacDonald, 1971).

Becker, Craig and Amy Dru Stanley, "The Downside of Private Prisons," *The Nation* (June 15, 1985): 728–730.

Blau, Peter M. and W. Richard Scott. *Formal Organizations* (San Francisco: Chandler, 1962).

Borna, Shaheen. "Free Enterprise Goes to Prison," *The British Journal of Criminology* 1986 (26), 321–334.

Bowditch, Christine and Ronald S. Everett, "Private Prisons: Problems within the Solution," *Justice Quarterly* 1987 (3), 441–453.

Bozeman, Barry, "Exploring the Limits of Public and Private Sectors: Sector Bound-aries as Maginot Line," *Public Administration Review*, 1988 (March–April): 672–674.

Bradshaw, Thorton and David Vogel (eds.), *Corporations and Their Critics* (New York: McGraw-Hill, 1981).

Braithwaite, John, "Criminological Theory and Organizational Crime," *Justice Quar-terly*, 1989(6), 333–358.

Braithwaite, John and Gilbert Geis, "On Theory and Action for Corporate Crime Control," *Crime and Delinquency*, 1982 (28), 292–314.

Brakel, Samuel J., "Prison Management, Private Enterprise Style: The Inmate's Evaluation." *The New England Journal on Criminal and Civil Confinement*, 1988 (14): 175–244.

Calavita, Kitty, "The Demise of the Occupational Safety and Health Administration: A Case Study in Symbolic Action," *Social Problems*, 1983 (30), 437–448.

Camp, Camille and George Camp, "Correctional Privatization in Perspective," *The Prison Journal*, 1985 (45(2)): 14–31.

Carleton, Mark T., *Politics and Punishment* (Baton Rouge, LA: Louisiana University Press, 1971).

Carroll, Barry J., and Thomas A. Easton, "Motivating the Private Sector: What Role for Public Policy," in Barry J. Carroll, Ralph W. Conant, and Thomas A. Easton (eds.), *Private Means—Public Ends: Private Business in Social Service Delivery* (New York: Praeger, 1987).

Clinard, Marshall B., *Corporate Corruption: The Abuse of Power* (New York, NY: Praeger, 1990).

Clinard, Marshall B., *Corporate Ethics and Crime* (Beverly Hills, CA: Sage, 1983).

Clinard, Marshall B. and Peter C. Yeager, *Corporate Crime* (New York: The Free Press, 1980).

Cody, W. J. Michael and Andy D. Bennett, "The Privatization of Correctional Insti-tutions: The Tennessee Experience," *Vanderbilt Law Review*, 1987 (40): 829–849.

Cohen, Stanley, *Visions of Social Control* (Cambridge [Eng]: Polity Press, 1985).

Coleman, James W., *The Criminal Elite: The Sociology of White Collar Crime* (New York: St. Martin's Press, 1989).

Conklin, John E., "Illegal But Not Criminal": *Business Crime in America* (Englewood-Cliffs, NJ: Prentice-Hall, 1977).

Cowdry, Quentin, "Tories to Abandon Private Jails Plan," *Times of London*, 1989 (No-vember 24).

Cressey, Donald R., "Prison Organizations," In James G. March (ed.), *Handbook of Organizations* (Chicago: Rand McNally, 1965).

Cullen, Francis T., William J. Maakestad and Gray Cavender, *Corporate Crime Under Attack: The Ford Pinto Case and Beyond* (Cincinnati: Anderson, 1987).

Daily Mail, "Speeding to Private Jails: Baker Aims to Contract Out Half the Prisons," 1991, December 5.

De Hoog, Ruth Hoogland, *Contracting Out for Human Services* (Albany: State Uni-versity of New York Press, 1984).

Delaney, Kevin J., "Power, Intercorporate Networks, and 'Strategic Bankruptcy'," *Law and Society Review*, 1990 (23): 643–666.

Dempsey, Paul S., "Perspective on Airline Deregulation. Successful Reform? Horrid Results," *Los Angeles Times*, 1991 (April 8).

DiIulio, Jr., John J., "What Is Wrong With Private Prisons," *The Public Interest*, 1988 (92): 66–83.

DiIulio, Jr., John J., "A Critical Perspective on the Private Management of Prisons and Jails," in Douglas C. McDonald (ed.), *Private Prisons and the Public Interest* (New Brunswick, NJ: Rutgers University Press, 1990).

Donahue, John D., *Prisons for Profit: Public Justice, Private Interests* (Washington, DC: Economic Policy Institute, 1988).

Donaldson, Thomas, *Corporations and Morality* (Englewood Cliffs, NJ: Prentice Hall, 1982).

Durham, III, Alexis M., "Evaluating Privatized Correctional Institutions: Obstacles to Effective Assessment," *Federal Probation,* 1988 (52(2)): 65–71.

Durham, III, Alexis M., "Origins of Interest in the Privatization of Punishment: The Nineteenth and Twentieth Century American Experience," *Criminology,* 1989 (27): 107–139.

Elvin, John, "A Civil Liberties View of Private Prisons," *The Prison Journal,* 1985 (45(2)): 48–52.

Ermann, M. David and Richard J. Lundman, *Corporate Deviance* (New York: Holt. Rinehart and Winston, 1982).

Etzioni, Amitai, *A Comparative Analysis of Complex Organizations* (New York: Free Press, 1961).

Feeley, Malcolm M., "The Privatization of Prisons in Historical Perspective," *Criminal Justice Research Bulletin,* 1991 (6(2)): 1–10.

Fisse, Brent, "New Penal Sanctions Against Corporations," Paper Presented at the Annual Meeting of the Pacific Sociological Association, 1981.

Fisse, Brent, "Sanctions Against Corporations: The Limitations of Fines and the Enterprise of Creating Alternatives," in Brent Fisse and Peter A. French (eds.), *Corrigible Corporations and Unruly Law* (San Antonio, TX: Trinity University Press, 1985).

Flener, Mark H., "Legal Considerations in Privatization and the Role of Legal Counsel," in Lawrence K. Finley (ed.), *Public Sector Privatization* (Westport, CT: Quorum, 1989).

Fraser/Associates, *Political Action for Business: The PAC Handbook* (Cambridge, MA: Ballinger, 1980).

Garsombke, Diane J. and Thomas W. Garsombke, "Strategic Marketing of Social Services," in Barry J. Carroll, Ralph W. Conant and Thomas A. Easton (eds.), *Private Means—Public Ends: Private Business in Social Service Delivery* (New York: Praeger, 1987).

Geis, Gilbert, "The Heavy Electrical Equipment Antitrust Cases of 1961," in Marshall B. Clinard and Richard Quinney (eds.), *Criminal Behavior Systems* (New York: Holt, Rinehart and Winston, 1967).

Geis, Gilbert, "The Privatization of Prisons: Panacea or Placebo?", in Barry J. Carroll, Ralph W. Conant and Thomas A. Easton (eds.), *Private Means—Public Ends: Private Business in Social Service Delivery* (New York: Praeger, 1987).

Gentry, James T., "The Panopticon Revisited: The Problem of Monitoring Private Prisons," *Yale Law Journal,* 1986 (96): 353–375.

Glasberg, Davita Silfen, "Corporate Power and Control: The Case of Leasco Corporation Versus Chemical Bank" *Social Problems,* 1982 (29): 104–116.

Glasberg, Davita S., *The Power of Collective Purse Strings: The Effect of Bank Hegemony on Corporations and the State* (Berkeley, CA: University of California Press, 1989).

Glazer, Myron P. and Penina Migdal Glazer, *The Whistleblowers: Exposing Corruption in Government and Industry* (New York: Basic Books, 1989).

Goffman, Erving, *Asylums* (Garden City, NY: Doubleday, Anchor Books, 1961).

Goodwin, Jacob, *Brotherhood of Arms* (New York: Times Books, 1985).

Greenwood, Peter, *Private Enterprise Prisons? Why Not? The Job Would Be Done and at Less Cost* (Santa Monica, CA: The Rand Corporation, 1981).

Gross, Edward, "Organization Structure and Organizational Crime," in Gilbert Geis and Ezra Stotland (eds.), *White-Collar Crime: Theory and Research* (Beverly Hills, CA: Sage, 1980).

Hamilton, Walton H., "The Ancient Maxim Caveat Emptor," *Yale Law Review,* 1931 (40): 1133–1187.

Hasenfeld, Yeheskel and Richard A. English (eds.), *Human Service Organizations* (Ann Arbor: The University of Michigan Press, 1974).

Hoffman, John, *State, Power and Democracy* (Sussex: Delinquency Books, 1988).

Holley, Cathy E., "Privatization of Corrections: Is the State out on a Limb When the Company Goes Bankrupt?," *Vanderbilt Law Review,* 1988 (41): 317–339.

Hurst, John, "$1.5 Billion Savings Seen as Prison Admissions Drop," *Los Angeles Times,* 1991 (October 8), p. A3.

Jacobs, David, Michael Useem and Mayer N. Zald, "Firms, Industries and Politics," *Research in Political Sociology,* 1991 (5):141–165.

Jacobs, James B., *Stateville* (Chicago: University of Chicago Press, 1977).

Jayewardene, C. H. S. and C. K. Talbot, "Entrusting Corrections to the Private Sector," *International Journal of Offender Therapy and Comparative Criminology,* 1983 (26): 177–187.

Kamerman, Sheila B. and Alfred J. Kahn, "Conclusion: Continuing the Discussion and Taking a Stand," in Sheila B. Kamerman and Alfred J. Kahn (eds.), *Privatization and the Welfare State* (Princeton, NJ: Princeton University Press, 1989).

Keating, Dan, "Monroe County Sheriff Gets Back Control of Jail from Wackenhut," *The Miami Herald,* 1991, January 30, 4B.

Keating, Jr., J. Michael, "Public on Private: Monitoring the Performance of Privately Operated Prisons and Jails," in Douglas C. McDonald (ed.), *Private Prisons and the Public Interest* (New Brunswick, NJ: Rutgers University Press, 1990).

Kramer, Ronald C., "Corporate Crime: An Organizational Perspective," in Peter Wickman and Timothy Dailey (eds.), *White Collar Crime and Economic Crime* (Lexington, MA: D.C. Heath, 1982).

Levinson, Robert B., "Okeechobee: An Evaluation of Privatization in Corrections," *The Prison Journal,* 1985 (45(2)): 75–94.

Lilly, J. Robert, "Power, Profit, and Penality: A Beginning." Paper Presented at the Annual Meeting of the American Society of Criminology (San Francisco, November, 1991).

Lipson, Milton, *On Guard: The Business of Private Security* (New York: Quadrangle, 1975).

Logan, Charles H., "The Propriety of Proprietary Prisons," *Federal Probation,* 1987 (51(3)): 35–40.

Logan, Charles H., *Private Prisons: Cons and Pros* (New York: Oxford University Press, 1990).

Logan, Charles H. and Bill W. McGrift, *Comparing Cost of Public and Private Prisons: A Case Study. National Institute of Justice Research in Action* (Washington, DC: Department of Justice, 1989).

Logan, Charles H. and Sharla P. Rausch, "Punish and Profit: The Emergence of Private Enterprise Prisons," *Justice Quarterly,* 1985 (2): 303–318.

Lynxwiler, John, Neal Shover and Donald Clelland, "Determinants of Sanction Severity in a Regulatory Bureaucracy," in Ellen Hochstedler (ed.), *Corporations as Criminals* (Beverly Hills, CA: Sage, 1984).

McAfee, Ward M., "Tennessee's Private Prison Act of 1986: An Historical Perspective with Special Attention to California's Experience," *Vanderbilt Law Review,* 1987 (40): 851–865.

McAfee, Ward M. and David Shichor, "A Historical-Sociological Analysis of California's Private Prison Experience in the 1850s: Some Modern Implications," *Criminal Justice History,* 1990 (11): 89–103.

McConville, Sean, "Aid from Industry? Private Corrections and Prison Crowding," in Stephen D. Gottfredson and Sean McConville (eds.), *America's Correctional Crisis* (Westport, CT: Greenwood Press, 1987).

McDonald, Douglas C., "The Cost of Corrections: In Search of the Bottom Line," *Research in Corrections,* 1989 (2): 1–25.

McDonald, Douglas C., "The Cost of Operating Public and Private Correctional Facilities," in Douglas C. McDonald (ed.), *Private Prisons and the Public Interest* (New Brunswick, NJ: Rutgers University Press, 1990).

McKanna, Clare V., "1851–1880: The Origins of San Quentin," *California History,* 1987 (March): 49–54.

McShane, Marilyn D. and Frank P. William, III, "Running on Empty: Creativity and the Correctional Agenda," *Crime and Delinquency,* 1989 (35): 562–576.

Mann, Kenneth, *Defending White-Collar Crime* (New Haven: Yale University Press, 1985).

Meyer, Jr., John C., "An Action-Orientation Approach to the Study of Occupational Crime," *Australian and New Zealand Journal of Criminology,* 1972 (5): 35–48.

Mills, C. Wright, *The Power Elite* (New York: Oxford University Press, 1956).

Mizruchi, Mark S., *The American Corporate Network* (Beverly Hills, CA: Sage, 1982).

Moe, Ronald C., "'Law' versus 'Performance' as Objective Standard," *Public Administration Review,* 1988 (March–April): 674–675.

Moore, Wilbert E., *The Conduct of the Corporation* (New York: Vintage Books, 1962).

Morris, Norval, *The Future of Imprisonment* (Chicago: University of Chicago Press, 1974).

Mullen, Joan, "Corrections and the Private Sector," *The Prison Journal,* 1985 (45(2)):1–13.

Nelson, B. J., "Purchase of Service," in G. J. Washnis (ed.), *Productivity Improvement Handbook for State and Local Government* (New York: John Wiley, 1980).

Novey, Donald L., "Privatization in Prisons: A Potential Forest Fire Across the USA," *Correctional Peacekeeper,* 1985 (3):8.

O'Brien, Patricia., *The Promise of Punishment: Prisons in Nineteenth-Century France* (Princeton NJ: Princeton University Press, 1982).

Palumbo, Dennis J., "Privatization and Corrections Policy," *Policy Studies Review,* 1986 (5): 598–605.

Papadakis, Elim and Peter Taylor-Gosby, *The Private Provision of Public Welfare* (New York: St. Martin's Press, 1987).

Parsons, Talcott, "How Are Clients Integrated into Service Organizations?," in William R. Rosengreen and Mark Lefton (eds.), *Organizations and Clients: Essays in the Sociology of Service* (Columbus, OH: Charles E. Merrill, 1970).

Pellicciotti, Joseph M., "42 U.S.C. Sec. 1983 Correctional Officials Liability: A Look to the New Century," *Journal of Contemporary Criminal Justice,* 1987 (3): 1–9.

Pontell, Henry N., Paul D. Jesilow and Gilbert Geis, "Policing Physicians: Practitioner Fraud and Abuse in a Government Medical Program," *Social Problems,* 1982 (30): 117–125.

Press, Aric, "The Good, the Bad, and the Ugly: Private Prisons in the 1980s," in Douglas McDonald (ed.), *Private Prisons and the Public Interest* (New Brunswick, NJ: Rutgers University Press, 1990).

Riddell, Peter, *The Thatcher Decade* (Oxford: Basil Blackwell, 1989).

Ring, Charles, *Contracting for the Operation of Private Prisons* (College Park, MD: The American Correctional Association, 1987).

Robbins, Ira P., "Privatization of Corrections: Defining the Issues," *Federal Probation,* 1986 (50) (September): 24–30.

Robbins, Ira P., "The Legal Dimensions of Private Incarceration," *The American University Law Review,* 1989 (3): 531–854.

Roberts, Albert R. and Gerald T. Powers, "The Privatization of Corrections: Methodological Issues and Dilemmas Involved in Evaluative Research," *The Prison Journal,* 1985 (45(2)): 95–107.

Rothman, David J., *Conscience and Convenience: The Asylum and Its Alternatives in Progressive America* (Boston: Little, Brown, 1980).

Rutherford, Andrew, "Prison Privatization in Britain," in Douglas C. McDonald (ed.), *Private Prisons and the Public Interest* (New Brunswick, NJ: Rutgers University Press, 1990).

Ryan, Mick and Tony Ward, "Privatization and Penal Politics," in Roger Matthews (ed.), *Privatizing Criminal Justice* (London: Sage, 1989).

Ryan, Mike H., Carl L. Swanson and Rogene A. Buchholz, *Corporate Strategy, Public Policy and the Fortune 500: How America's Major Corporations Influence Government* (Oxford: Basil Blackwell, 1987).

Sagarin, Edward and Jess Maghen, "Should States Opt for Private Prisons? No," *The Hartford (CT) Journal,* 1986 (January 12): E1–E4.

Savas, E. S., *Privatizing the Public Sector* (Chatham, NJ: Chatham House, 1982).

Schuman, Alan M., "The Cost of Correctional Services: Exploring a Poorly Chartered Terrain," *Research in Corrections,* 1989 (2): 27–33.

Sellers, Martin P., "Private and Public Prisons: A Comparison of Costs, Programs and Facilities," *International Journal of Offender Therapy and Comparative Criminology,* 1989 (33): 241–256.

Sellin, J. Thorsten, *Slavery and the Penal System* (New York: Elsevier, 1976).

Shichor, David, "On Corporate Deviance and Corporate Victimization: A Review and Some Elaborations," *International Review of Victimology,* 1989 (1): 67–88.

Shichor, David and Clemens Bartollas, "Private and Public Placements: Is There a Difference?," *Crime and Delinquency,* 1990 (36): 296–299.

South, Nigel, *Policing for Profit* (London: Sage, 1988).

Starr, Paul, "The Limits of Privatization," *Proceedings of the Academy of Political Science,* 1987 (3/3): 124–137.

State of California, *Financial Management Handbook for Private Return-to-Custody Facilities* (Sacramento: Department of Corrections, 1985).

Stone, Christopher D., *Where the Law Ends* (New York: Harper and Row, 1975).

Street, David, Robert D. Vinter and Charles Perrow, *Organization for Treatment* (New York: The Free Press, 1966).

Sullivan, Harold J., "Privatization of Corrections and the Constitutional Rights of Prisoners," *Federal Probation,* 1989 (53(2)): 36–42.

Sutherland, Edwin H., "Crime of Corporations," in Albert Cohen, Alfred Lindesmith and Karl Schuessler (eds.), *The Sutherland Papers* (Bloomington: Indiana University Press, 1956).

Sutton, Adam and Ron Wild, "Corporate Crime and Social Structure," in Paul R. Wilson and John Braithwaite (eds.), *Two Faces of Deviance: Crimes of the Powerless and the Powerful* (Brisbane, Queensland, Australia: University of Queensland Press, 1978).

Thomas, Charles W. and Suzanne L. Foard, *Private Correctional Facility Census. Gainesville, FL: Private Corrections Project, Center for Studies in Criminology and Law* (University of Florida, 1991).

Thomas, Charles W. and Linda S. Calvert Hanson, "The Implications of 42 U.S.C. § 1983 for the Privatization of Prisons," *Florida State University Law Review,* 1989 (16): 933–962.

Thomas, John C., "Privatization of Prisons: A New Breed of Liability," *Journal of Security Administration,* 1987 (10): 27–34.

Thompson, James D., *Organizations in Action* (New York: McGraw-Hill, 1967).

Tolchin, Susan J. and Martin Tolchin, *Dismantling America: The Rush to Deregulate* (Boston: Houghton Mifflin Company, 1983).

United States Committee on Education and Labor, *Private Police Systems* (Washington, DC: U.S. Government Printing Office, 1939).

Urban Institute, *Comparison of Privately and Publicly Operated Corrections Facilities in Kentucky and Massachusetts* (Washington, DC: The Urban Institute, 1989).

Vaughan, Diane, "Crime Between Organizations: Implications for Victimology," in Gilbert Geis and Ezra Stotland (eds.), *White Collar Crime: Theory and Research* (Beverly Hills, CA: Sage, 1980).

Walker, Donald R., *Penology for Profit: A History of the Texas Prison System 1867–1912* (College Station, TX: Texas A&M University Press, 1988).

Wecht, David N., "Breaking the Code of Deference: Judicial Review of Private Prisons," *The Yale Law Journal,* 1987 (96): 815–837.

Weinstein, Henry, "Northrop, Guilty in Fraud Case, Is Fined $17 Million," *Los Angeles Times,* 1990 (February 28).

Weiss, Robert P., "Private Prisons and the State," in Roger Matthews (ed.), *Privatizing Criminal Justice* (London: Sage, 1989).

Woolley, Mary R., "Prisons for Profit: Policy Considerations for Government Officials," *Dickinson Law Review,* 1985 (90): 307–331.

The Enforcement of Norms: Group Cohesion and Meta-Norms

Christine Horne

Many scholars argue that group cohesion contributes to social order—that norms are more effective in tight-knit communities (see, for example, Hechter 1987; Hechter and Kanazawa 1993). One explanation for this correlation suggests that it can be attributed to higher rates of sanctioning in solidary groups.[1] Criminologists, for example, emphasize the role of community integration in controlling deviant behavior. They argue that when a community disintegrates, it "ceases to function effectively as a means of social control. . . . Resistance . . . to delinquent and criminal behavior is low, and such behavior is tolerated" (Shaw 1929:204-205). Studies show that in cohesive communities, people express greater willingness to impose sanctions against those who engage in deviant behavior (Sampson, Raudenbush, and Earls 1997:918). At least some research, then, suggests that one reason for higher levels of order in cohesive groups is that deviance is more likely to be punished in such groups (see, for example, Homans 1961).

This conclusion has been challenged, however. Scholars argue that in many situations, individuals are unwilling to impose sanctions because the costs are greater than the benefits (Coleman 1990). In fact, evidence indicates that people are highly aware of the dangers of sanctioning and are discouraged by them (Flache 1996; Flache and Macy 1996; Molm 1997). Sanctioning may create the risk that the deviant will retaliate. It also requires resources that could be used more profitably in other personally beneficial exchanges.[2] Group cohesion may increase, rather than reduce, these sanctioning costs, in part because a negative reaction from someone on whom the individual is dependent may be much more unpleasant than reactions from those with whom that person has little meaningful interaction. People therefore may be less willing to run the risk of punishing fellow members of a cohesive group. Thus we have good reason to think that cohesion increases the costs of sanctioning, which in turn, decrease sanctioning frequency.

If cohesion indeed increases these costs, why do we observe sanctioning in cohesive communities? Are there mechanisms that might compensate for the greater costs experienced by sanctioners in such groups? In this paper, I draw on insights from instrumental actor approaches to develop an argument suggesting one mechanism through which group cohesion may increase the frequency of sanctioning—a process that has the potential to counteract, at least partially, the fear of retaliation that may exist in cohesive communities. I argue that in explaining social control processes, one must recognize that potential sanctioners are connected to a network of people who influence their behavior. The strength of these ties to third parties affects the level of support that sanctioners receive, in turn influencing the likelihood that they will be willing to bear the costs of imposing punishments. In other words, cohesion encourages sanctioning not directly, but by increasing the rewards given to those who punish deviance. That is, it increases the strength of meta-norms favoring sanctioning, which then affect sanctioning decisions.

Theoretical Argument

Scope Conditions

The research described here is part of a larger project that relies on an instrumental actor approach to explain the emergence and enforcement of social norms, and uses experimental methods to evaluate the resulting hypotheses (Horne 2000, 2001a, 2001b, 2001c). The conditions of the present study are consistent with the framework of this research program.

REPEATED INTERACTIONS The argument applies to situations in which individuals are able to exchange with a finite number of others over time. Actors engage in repeated interactions and have a limited supply of valued exchange partners.

SANCTIONING The theory applies under conditions in which sanctioning (a term used throughout this paper as synonymous with *punishing*)[3] is a public good: costly to the sanctioner, but creating benefits for all group members (Oliver 1980:1361; Yamagishi 1995).[4] That is, any group member may be affected negatively by antisocial behavior, whereas everyone benefits when deviance is punished. Sanctioning enforces social norms; it is not simply an attempt at vengeance (as it might be if the benefits were purely personal).

HOMOGENEITY The theory applies to groups in which members are equal in resources and network ties. In other words, the structure of interaction is such that any group member is equally likely to interact with any other. Power is balanced (Emerson 1972; for discussions of average power and power imbalance, see Lawler 1986; Molm 1997).The group contains no structurally created cliques.

INSIDER SANCTIONERS   The argument focuses on situations in which sanctions are imposed by group members rather than by outsiders such as the state or members of other groups.[5] Here the emphasis is on the factors affecting how individuals react to fellow group members who sanction, not on their responses to sanctioning by a specialized agent or nongroup members.

FUNGIBILITY OF SANCTIONING BENEFITS   The argument applies when changes in the collective good produced as a result of sanctioning enhance the ability of group members to engage in productive exchange, thereby improving their personal welfare.

INFORMATION   Finally, the argument assumes that actors have information about others' sanctioning decisions. They know when group members sanction deviance, and they are aware of the benefits that accrue when antisocial behavior is punished.

Theoretical Background

Cohesion is defined as the extent to which group members are dependent on each other (Emerson 1972; Molm and Cook 1995). In turn, dependence refers to the value that individuals place on their relationships and the goods they can obtain through those relationships (Emerson 1962, 1972; Molm and Cook 1995).[6] The higher the average level of dependence, the more cohesive the group.

Much research focuses on the effects of variation in dependence structures on behavior (see, for example, Cook and Emerson 1978; Markovsky, Willer, and Patton 1988; Molm 1997; Willer and Anderson 1981). In this work it is recognized that individuals use rewards to influence others, seeking to increase the benefits that accrue from an exchange relationship. In addition to rewarding, however, individuals may exercise coercive power (Bacharach and Lawler 1981; Blalock and Wilken 1979; Molm 1997; Willer and Anderson 1981), and they perceive the use of this power very differently than the use of rewards. Scholars explore these differences, making predictions about how dependence affects the likelihood that individuals will reward and/or sanction exchange partners. Results suggest that the use of rewards and punishments ought to be distinguished conceptually because they are neither perceived nor treated as identical by actors (Blalock 1987; Molm 1997; Oliver 1980). Sanctions impose a cost; rewards confer a benefit (Molm 1997:68). This difference is likely to affect an actor's willingness to use them, and is essential to the argument developed below.

SANCTIONING AND META-NORMS   Why is any individual willing to bear the costs of sanctioning, particularly when that person alone experiences those costs while all group members share in the benefits?[7] (For discussions of this second-order social dilemma, see Axelrod 1986; Coleman 1990; Heckathorn 1989; Yamagishi 1986, 1988, 1995; Yamagishi and Takahashi 1994.) One answer is that potential sanctioners may take into account not only the direct personal benefit of sanctioning and the possibility of retaliation by the deviant, but also the reactions of interested third parties (Coleman 1990). In other words, if a meta-norm exists within the group that encourages individuals to sanction deviant behavior, they will be more likely to do so (Axelrod 1986; for a discussion of the related topic of remedial norms, see Ellickson 1991). Such a meta-norm emerges insofar as group members reward those who punish deviance. In turn, when people who sanction receive larger rewards from others, the incentive to sanction increases. Thus when meta-norms favoring sanctioning are stronger, norms are more likely to be enforced.

But this answer gives rise to further questions. Why do such meta-norms emerge? In other words, why do people reward those who punish deviance? Even if they benefit from others' sanctioning decisions and therefore are interested in those decisions, why are they willing to bear the costs of rewarding? Does group cohesion enhance the ability to overcome this third-order social dilemma? Addressing these questions is essential if we wish to understand the emergence of meta-norms, the role of group cohesion in that process, and ultimately the enforcement of norms.

The Argument

In this paper I suggest a possible mechanism linking group cohesion to meta-norms.[8] I begin by assuming that actors reward others in order to affect future reciprocal rewards, including both the size and the likelihood of returns from others (Molm 1997; for a discussion of cooperative behavior in iterated interactions, see Axelrod 1984). Thus individuals give rewards with the hope of improving their personal welfare. This assumption helps to explain how people make decisions about responding to sanctioners. I identify two specific considerations that affect these choices.

MAINTAINING RELATIONSHIPS   I argue that people reward sanctioners in order to maintain relationships with them (Horne 2000). Just as actors give to group members in general in order to increase the likelihood of reciprocal rewards, so too do they give to sanctioners. Insofar as individuals value their relationship with someone who punishes deviance and does not want to risk losing it, they will give support to that person. In the short term, of course, such behavior may result in a loss. It might appear more sensible to give to those who have not experienced the costs of responding to deviance—those who have retained all their resources and therefore have something with which to reciprocate immediately—rather than to give to a sanctioner, whose resources may be depleted. Why then do actors not neglect the punisher in favor of rewarding other group members who have more resources for exchange?

I propose that individuals reward a person who sanctions because they do not want to risk losing the relationship. If they fail to reward, and if some other group member does so, then the sanctioner is likely to defect to this more loyal acquaintance in the future. If individuals treat all exchange partners who are temporarily short of resources in this way, eventually they will run out of people with whom to interact. In a sense, then, individuals compete with other group members for relationships. To ensure the survival of a relationship, they must continue to supply rewards.

The motivation to maintain ties is stronger when those relationships are valued, in other words, when the group is cohesive. In such communities, by definition, people are dependent on others for attaining desired ends. They value their interactions with each other and the goods they can receive from those interactions. In these groups, therefore, people give rewards,[9] even at a short term loss, in order to increase the likelihood of ongoing returns and to reduce the risk of losing a profitable relationship.[10] In cohesive groups, then, individuals give more rewards to their exchange partners, including those who sanction, than in less cohesive groups.

By contrast, in weaker communities people place little value on their interactions and therefore are not motivated to maintain them. When a fellow group member incurs the costs associated with sanctioning, the individual has little reason to reward that person because the relationship is unlikely to be profitable and is not worth the investment. As a result, rewards given to those who sanction deviance will be small, just as reward levels in general are low. Thus group cohesion affects the size of rewards given to exchange partners, including those who impose sanctions.

> *Hypothesis 1:* Group cohesion has a positive direct effect on the size of rewards given to sanctioners.

INCREASING PROFITS FROM EXCHANGE This argument, however, implies that reward levels *in general* increase in cohesive groups. Individuals give greater rewards to sanctioners, but they give larger rewards to all their other exchange partners as well. That is, there is no additional incentive for sanctioning as opposed to not sanctioning. Thus the question arises: In cohesive groups, do the rewards given to those who sanction increase *relative* to the rewards given to those who choose not to sanction? I argue that group cohesion indeed affects the difference between the size of rewards given to sanctioners and to those who fail to punish deviance.

Exchange is more profitable in cohesive groups than in weaker communities. Yet even in highly cohesive groups, if people have few resources, not much exchange can occur and profits remain low. Individuals therefore prefer other group members to be well-off because they desire the benefits that come from exchanging with people who have resources.[11] Sanctioning contributes to those resources.[12] In other words, individuals are not only concerned about the direct personal benefit (their share of the collective good) resulting from another's decision to sanction. They also care about the indirect benefit they receive from exchanging with people who, as a result of a sanctioning decision, have more resources for exchange.

Accordingly, people prefer that others behave so as to contribute to the group good. To encourage behaviors, such as sanctioning, that add to collective resources, people will give larger rewards to those who sanction than to those who do not. This difference will be larger in cohesive than in noncohesive groups because the benefits of exchange are greater in such groups.[13] In other words, in cohesive communities, the direct benefits of sanctioning (a share of the group good) are magnified through exchange with well-off others to produce larger personal payoffs. This means that the greater payoffs that flow from another's sanctioning decision are more likely to compensate for the costs of giving extra rewards to that person.[14] Thus group cohesion increases the difference between the size of rewards given to those who punish deviance and those who choose not to do so.

> *Hypothesis 2:* Group cohesion has a positive direct effect on the difference between rewards given to sanctioners and to nonsanctioners.

This argument predicts that cohesion will exert a positive effect on *reward differences*—the size of the incentive to sanction. It does not imply, however, a corresponding increase in the *proportion* of resources devoted to enforcing meta-norms relative to other exchanges. In cohesive groups, as I argued above, individuals have a greater interest in the benefits that sanctioning produces because those benefits can be multiplied through exchange. Yet there is also an increase in the profitability of exchange with group members relative to interaction with sanctioners (who have incurred costs and therefore have few resources to give in return). Therefore individuals may give larger rewards to those who sanction than to those who have the opportunity but fail to do so, and may still not invest a greater proportion of their available resources in enforcement. In other words, people in cohesive groups may spend a smaller proportion of their resources on enforcing meta-norms. Even so, they will still provide a greater incentive for group members to punish rather than not because they wish to encourage the production of the benefit that sanctioning, in conjunction with exchange, allows.

THE EFFECT OF REWARDS ON SANCTIONING In turn, the larger incentives found in cohesive communities affect sanctioning frequency. If individuals expect to receive larger rewards when they sanction, they will be more highly motivated to impose punishments. By contrast, if they expect that others will fail to respond, they will be less likely to sanction. Group cohesion leads to greater rewards for punishing than for not punishing. This difference then produces higher levels of sanctioning.

> *Hypothesis 3:* Group cohesion has a positive indirect effect on the frequency of sanctioning through its effect on rewarding.

Methods

I tested the three hypotheses using experimental methods. The experiment involved two conditions: high group cohesion and low group cohesion. I conducted 20 experimental groups in each condition, for a total of 40 groups.[15]

In both conditions, participants were vulnerable to the antisocial behavior (theft) of a deviant (computer-simulated) actor, had the opportunity to make decisions about sanctioning the deviant, and were able to make choices about rewarding sanctioners and other group members. Thus the experiment manipulated group cohesion and allowed for the measurement of reward amounts and sanctioning frequency in each condition.

Subjects and Procedures

Subjects were recruited from undergraduate classes by offering them the opportunity to earn money. I contacted them individually by telephone to schedule their participation and told them to come to the experimental laboratory in the Sociology Department at Louisiana State University. There they were randomly assigned to an experimental condition.

Subjects participated in the experiment in groups of four. Upon arrival, each individual was escorted into a separate room. At no time were subjects allowed to see each other; their only interaction occurred over the computer network.

Once all participants had arrived and were in their places, they read instructions on their computer screen and engaged in some practice trials to ensure their understanding. During the instructions and practice rounds, they were able to ask questions of the experimenter by speaking over an intercom.

The experiment consisted of five practice trials and 25 actual trials. Subjects were not told the number of rounds beforehand. At the end of the experiment they were debriefed individually and were paid on the basis of the number of points they had accumulated. Then they were escorted from the laboratory one at a time so that they had no contact with each other even after the experiment was completed.

Overview of the Experiment

BEGINNING EACH TRIAL On every trial, subjects were given a personal income of 30 points each, which was displayed in the "personal income" window on their computer screen. They knew that others received the same number of points.

DEVIANT BEHAVIOR Next, a computer-simulated actor stole 10 points from one subject chosen randomly by the computer. These points were subtracted from the victim's income. On each trial any one subject, or no subject, might be the victim of a theft.[16] In the instructions, subjects were told that the thief was another student like themselves who had volunteered to participate in the experiment. They also were told that the thief made money by stealing, but they received no information about the thief's payoff structure.[17]

The thief was not a group member with whom subjects could exchange rewards. Although theoretically the deviant could be either a member of the group or an outsider, the experiment tested the theory in a situation in which the thief was not a member of the group. As a practical matter, allowing exchange between the deviant and other group members would have added another level of complexity to the experiment, making the results more difficult to analyze. In addition, if the framework was to be convincing, all participants would have needed opportunities to steal (as well as to sanction and reward). I chose to begin more simply by allowing subjects to make two kinds of decisions (sanctioning and rewarding), rather than three (stealing, sanctioning, and rewarding).

In addition, in the present study, I focus on the effects of variation in the strengths of the relationships between sanctioners and other group members. Therefore I did not allow for the exchange of rewards between the thief and the subjects. Eliminating reward exchanges between deviants and others allowed me to control for the effects of cohesion on potential retaliation,[18] and instead to examine the effects of varying the levels of dependence among potential sanctioners and third parties.

SANCTIONING DECISION After the theft, the victim had the opportunity to respond.[19] Subjects were told that they could decide to punish the thief or to do nothing. It would cost them 10 points to punish the thief. As a consequence of imposing a punishment, points would be taken away from the thief, and everyone in the group would receive three points. These options were listed on the computer screen.[20] After the victim made his or her sanctioning decision, information about the choice was displayed on all subjects' screens. If a sanction was imposed, three points were added to the total in each subject's personal income window.

Sanctioning thus produced a benefit for all four subjects in the group (the victim as well as the three others). The idea here is that everyone benefited from an individual's sanctioning effort. Although the victim lost points by sanctioning (three points benefit minus 10 points cost), the group as a whole benefited (12 points benefit minus 10 points cost).[21] If the victim decided to do nothing, no one received any points. This operationalization is consistent with the theoretical conceptualization, and with the scope conditions which require sanctioning to be a collective good.

The only direct benefit of sanctioning was the addition of three points to each subject's income; the frequency of theft did not decline.[22] I operationalized benefits in this way for two reasons. First, as a practical matter, if theft declined in response to sanctioning (as much existing literature suggests would happen), subjects soon might be left with no deviant behavior to which to react. To avoid this occurrence, I controlled the amount of deviance, thereby ensuring opportunities for sanctioning decisions. I then operationalized the benefits of sanctioning as benefit points. Second, by controlling the rate of theft, I was able to focus on the effects of group cohesion on sanctioning and rewarding without the confounding effect of change in rates of deviance, the original triggering behavior.

One might argue that this approach made sanctioning simply another form of contributing to the group good. Therefore one could imagine a simpler experiment in which subjects simply made an outright donation to the group, and others were allowed to react to their decision. The problem with this approach is that sanctioning may differ in important ways from other kinds of contributions. For example, punishment imposes a harm on another individual. It thus creates the possibility of retaliation, which positive contributions do not. In addition, notions about appropriate responses to deviance may be affected by ideas about justice, retribution, and so forth, which are not necessarily relevant for other types of public goods. To allow for these possibilities, it is important to frame subjects' choices in terms of sanctioning rather than donating.

I accomplished this framing by telling participants in the instructions that they had the opportunity to punish the thief, and that a decision to punish would cause points to be taken away from the thief. Discussions with subjects during pretesting and debriefing suggest that they indeed viewed the sanctioning choice as pertaining to punishment, not simply contributing to a collective good. Some said that they did not want to punish the thief because they did not want the thief to retaliate by stealing even more from them, but that they did want others to punish. Other participants said that they sanctioned the thief because they hoped that, if they did so, the thief would steal from other people rather from them. Still others said essentially that they punished because they felt that it was the right thing to do, or because "he stole!" They seemed to have the sense that those who did something wrong should suffer consequences.

These comments imply a perception among the subjects that a decision to sanction would produce a negative effect for the thief. Future work should explicitly articulate the differences between public goods in general and those which take the form of sanctioning, and should examine them empirically. For the time being, however, I simply allow for the possibility of such differences, and frame subjects' choices as a matter of sanctioning.

REWARDING DECISION   After the victim made his or her sanctioning decision, everyone was told what that person had decided. Then all subjects were able to exchange points. Everyone, including the victim, could give any number of points from their income box to any person, including themselves. They could reward the individual who had made the sanctioning decision, they could keep points for themselves, and/or they could give points to nonvictims. Decisions to give points to others were made simultaneously.

The choice about giving to a sanctioner was made in conjunction with choices about giving to other participants and about keeping points. Exchanges were reciprocal, not negotiated. Participants proceeded at their own pace; no time limits were imposed. They could use their knowledge of the victim's sanctioning decision, as well as their experience from earlier trials, in making their choices. Thus the decision to give points to a sanctioner represented both a response to a sanctioning decision and a part of a mutually rewarding interaction that might continue over many rounds.

After all subjects had made their rewarding decisions, each individual's screen showed them how many points they had given to each other participant, and how many points they had received from each. Points they had given away were subtracted from their personal income display; points they had received from others were added. Participants were not told others' exchange outcomes—only their own.

ENDING EACH TRIAL   After all exchanges in a particular trial were completed, subjects' personal incomes were transferred into their "savings windows." Points in savings accumulated during the experiment and could not be used in any future trials. The transfer of points into savings marked the end of a round. A new trial then began, and subjects again were given an income of 30 points. The number of points in each participant's savings at the end of the experiment determined each of their earnings.

The experiment exposed subjects to deviant behavior, gave them opportunities to punish that behavior, and allowed them to react to others' sanctioning decisions and to engage in ongoing exchange with them. This design allows for analysis of the effects of varying levels of group cohesion on both rewarding and sanctioning decisions.

Operationalization of Variables

I operationalized *group cohesion* by varying the value of points that subjects received from others relative to the points that they kept for themselves. The higher the value of the points received from others, the more valuable the relationships and the more cohesive the community.

In the instructions, subjects were given information on these values. In the high-cohesion condition, points from others were worth three times as much as the individual's own points. In other words, if subject W gave subject Z 10 points, Z actually received 30 points. Exchange was very profitable in this condition. By contrast, in the low-cohesion condition, points received from others were worth the same amount as points the individual kept for themself. If W gave Z 10 points, Z only received 10 points. As a result, there was little benefit to exchanging. Subjects could do just as well alone as if they interacted. They were not dependent on others. Group cohesion therefore was low.

I measured *sanctioning frequency* by counting the number of times sanctions were imposed over all 25 trials in an experimental group, and dividing that total by the number of sanctioning opportunities (the number of times the thief stole).

The hypotheses make predictions about the effect of cohesion on rewards for sanctioning and on reward differences. I measured *rewards for sanctioning* by calculating the mean number of points given to a victim on the trial in which he or she chose to sanction. Rewards for victims who did not sanction were measured by determining the mean number of points given to a victim on the trial in which that person chose not to sanction. I then calculated the *difference* in the mean rewards given to victims who sanctioned and to victims who did not sanction.

In addition, I measured the rewards to nonvictims by determining the mean number of points given to subjects who were not victims of a theft. Finally, I calculated the proportion of rewards used for meta-norm enforcement as the mean number of points given to sanctioners divided by the mean number of points given to any group member.

When I describe the mean rewards given to a subject, I am referring to the amount of the reward *before* it is altered by the exchange ratio, not the amount the person actually receives. Accordingly, in the low-cohesion condition, a mean reward of 5 indicates that the mean amount given by subjects to the sanctioner is five points. To determine the amount the subject actually received, one would have to multiply that number by 3 (the number of subjects potentially giving rewards) and multiply the product by 1 (the exchange ratio in the low-cohesion condition). In the high-cohesion condition, one would multiply the number by 3 (the number of subjects) and then multiply that product by 3 (the exchange ratio in the high-cohesion condition).

Results

The experiment produced a data set that included sanctioning and rewarding decisions for every subject on each round of the experiment. These data were pooled across subjects and trials, thus producing a group-level data set that contained the mean sanctioning frequency and rewards given in each experimental group. I used this group-level data set for all analyses.[23] Analysis of variance was employed to examine the effects of cohesion on rewarding. OLS regression was used to look at the indirect effects of cohesion on sanctioning.

I first report the results for analyses examining the effects of the independent variables on size of rewards. A comparison of mean reward levels across strong and weak groups suggests that they vary as predicted (Hypothesis 1). The mean reward given to sanctioners is 9.52 in the high-cohesion condition and 2.92 in the low-cohesion condition (see Table 1). These figures reflect the rewards given, not the rewards received. That is, Table 1 reports amounts before they are multiplied by the exchange ratio. In the weak groups, sanctioners received an average of 2.92 (2.92 × 1) points from each other person; in the strong groups, they received an average of 28.6 (9.52 × 3) points from each subject. The premultiplier reward sizes make it clear not only that sanctioners *receive* more points in high-cohesion conditions, but also (as predicted) that subjects *give* more points to sanctioners in those conditions.

Statistical analyses confirm that the mean rewards *given* to those who sanction are higher in more cohesive groups. The effect of cohesion on rewards given to sanctioners is statistically significant at the .0001 level ($F(1,39) = 93.9$, $p < .0001$). Hypothesis 1 is supported.

One interesting implication of the argument predicting this finding is that it may be less costly for individuals to sanction in more cohesive groups, even if the amount that subjects receive when they sanction is no more than they receive when they do not. Assume that each potential sanctioner has 30 points that they can use to punish or to reward. Also assume that whether they reward or sanction, they receive 90 points from others. In such a situation it makes no difference whether they use all 30 points in exchange, or whether they use 10 points to sanction and 20 to reward. In either case they end up with 90 − 30 = 60 points. (And if they sanction, they receive an additional three-point benefit.) Sanctioning therefore may be virtually costless in cohesive groups with resources. Of course, subjects could decide neither to sanction nor to reward, and to save their points for themselves, but this strategy is unlikely to be productive in the long run because people will be reluctant to continue rewarding those who never give to them. If rewards from others are the same whether one sanctions or exchanges, and if sanctioning results in an additional (even if small) benefit, then it makes sense for individuals to punish deviance.

Table 1 Mean Rewards and Sanctions in Each Condidion

	Low Group Cohesion			High Group Cohesion		
	Mean	SD	N	Mean	SD	N
Rewards to Sanctioners	2.92	(1.25)	20	9.52	(2.78)	20
Rewards to Nonsanctioners	1.18	(.927)	18	5.77	(3.31)	19
Rewards to Nonvictims	1.27	(.971)	20	5.55	(1.80)	20
Reward Differences	1.80	(.820)	18	3.43	(3.16)	19
Sanctions	.609	(.189)	20	.748	(.187)	20

On the other hand, if a sanctioner receives only five points from others regardless of his or her choice, then sanctioning is costly. The five points in reward (even with an additional three-point benefit) does not compensate for the 10 points in cost. The optimal decision here would be to not sanction. This argument implies that even without a preference for sanctioning over nonsanctioning, individuals may be more likely to impose punishments in cohesive groups simply because of the overall size of rewards.

In fact, however, subjects prefer that others sanction. Victims who choose to punish receive larger rewards than those who do not. Also, as predicted, the difference in this amount is larger in cohesive than in noncohesive groups (Hypothesis 2). The mean difference in the size of rewards *given* is 1.80 in weak groups and 3.43 in strong groups (see Table 1).[24] Analysis reveals that the variation in this difference is statistically significant at the .05 level ($F(1, 36) = 4.71, p < .05$). The results support the prediction that group cohesion has a positive effect on the preference that others sanction rather than not. In other words, in cohesive groups, meta-norms favoring sanctioning are stronger than in less cohesive groups.

This result, however, does not mean that group members used a larger proportion of their resources to enforce meta-norms. In fact, although the size of the incentive to sanction increased in cohesive groups, the proportion of resources actually spent in producing this incentive declined. In the low-cohesion condition, the proportion of resources used to sanction relative to those used in general exchange is .593 (sd = .178), while in the high-cohesion condition it is .467 (sd = .0708).This difference is statistically significant at the .005 level ($F(1,39) = 8.73, p < .005$). Thus cohesion reduces the proportion of resources used to enforce meta-norms, but simultaneously increases the difference between the rewards given to victims who choose to sanction and those who do not. In cohesive groups, then, meta-norms are stronger in the sense that they provide a greater incentive for victims to sanction.

Rewards given to nonvictims are approximately the same as those given to victims who do not punish (see Table 1). This finding suggests two points. First, people reward sanctioners because they impose punishments, not merely out of pity that they were victimized. Second, they do not punish failure to sanction. Rather, they give additional rewards to those who do sanction and withhold those extra rewards from those who do not. This finding is consistent with the argument that individuals may be reluctant to sanction for fear of retaliation. They need not hesitate to reward, however. Consequently group cohesion increases the likelihood that individuals will reward those who contribute to the public good. It does not necessarily increase the probability that they will punish those who fail to do so.

What about sanctioning frequency? Hypothesis 3 predicts that group cohesion will have a positive effect on sanctioning frequency through its effect on reward levels. In the low-cohesion condition, the mean reward given to sanctioners is 2.92. Sanctioners receive $2.92 \times 3 \times 1 = 8.76$. This amount, plus the three points of benefit resulting from sanctioning, is greater than the 10-point cost. Further, the difference between rewards given to those who sanctioned and those who did not is 1.80. Accordingly the difference in rewards received by victims who sanctioned and those who did not is $1.80 \times 3 \times 1 = 5.40$. This amount plus three points of benefit equals 8.40, only slightly less than the 10-point cost. Therefore even in the weak groups, we might not be surprised to see some sanctioning.

In the high-cohesion condition, the rewards for punishing are greater. The mean reward given to sanctioners is 9.52. Thus a sanctioner receives $9.52 \times 3 \times 3 = 85.7$ points from others in addition to the three-point sanctioning benefit. The difference between rewards given to those who sanction and those who do not is 3.43. Therefore, the difference in the amount received by sanctioners is $3.43 \times 3 \times 3 = 30.9$. This amount is larger than in the low-cohesion condition, and certainly ought to be enough to motivate sanctioning.

The results are consistent with these expectations. The mean sanctioning frequency is .748 in the strong-group condition and .609 in the weak-group condition (see Table 1). This difference is statistically significant at the .05 level (see Table 2). When the differences between rewards given to those who sanction and those who do not are included in the regression equation, their effect on sanctioning is statistically significant at the .05 level, and the effect of cohesion becomes statistically insignifiant.[25] These results are consistent with the argument that group cohesion has a positive indirect effect on sanctioning through its effect on rewarding.

Of course, this kind of statistical support is weak when compared with experimentally controlled results because it simply provides evidence of a correlation. Ideally one would conduct another study in which rewards were controlled experimentally, and their effects on sanctioning determined. The immediate project, however, is designed to focus on the effects of cohesion on rewarding; it provides some initial support for the indirect effects of cohesion on sanctioning through rewarding.[26]

Table 2   OLS Regression of Sanctioning on Group Cohesion and Reward Differences

	Model 1[a]		Model 2[b]	
	Coefficient	SE	Coefficient	SE
Intercept	.609****	(.0420)	.536****	(.0427)
Group Cohesion	.139*	(.0593)	.0834	(.0563)
Reward Differences			.0294*	(.0119)
R^2	.13		.26	

Notes: In three of the experimental groups, the difference between the rewards given to victims who sanctioned and those who did not cannot be calculated because subjects always chose to sanction.
[a]$N = 40$
[b]$N = 37$
*$p < .05$; ****$p < .0001$ (two-tailed tests)

Discussion and Conclusion

In the present research I identify one mechanism through which group cohesion strengthens social control. Cohesion increases the rewards given to those who punish deviance. In particular, it increases the difference between the size of rewards given to those who punish deviance and to those who do not. This increase in rewards, in turn, encourages sanctioning.

Yet although cohesion increases the strength of meta-norms—the size of the incentive to sanction—it does not increase the proportion of resources allocated to enforcement efforts. Scholars argue that increases in group cohesion may reduce social control efforts by increasing people's interest in exchange relative to the exercise of control (Flache and Macy 1996). This argument would suggest that people are reluctant to enforce meta-norms insofar as by doing so, they lose the rewards available through bilateral exchange. The finding that cohesion reduces the proportion of resources allocated to enforcing meta-norms appears to be consistent with this argument. This reduction, however, has no effect on sanctioning frequency and therefore does not appear to interfere with social control efforts. Thus, although cohesion reduces the proportion of resources used to encourage sanctioning, it also (as predicted here) increases the size of the incentive to do so.

What about other possible negative effects of cohesion? Scholars argue that increased cohesion may contribute to potential sanctioners' fears of retaliation. The present findings do not contradict this argument. Potential sanctioners probably will be less inclined to sanction a deviant on whom they are dependent; this study suggests one way in which that fear may be counteracted. Although increasing cohesion may contribute to the costs of sanctioning (a loss of rewards from the deviant), it also increases the rewards (responses from and opportunities to exchange with other group members). The rewarding process described here presumably occurs along with potential sanctioners' evaluations of the likelihood of retaliation. To see these processes unfold simultaneously, future work should allow variation both in the relationship between the victim and deviant and the relationships among the victim and other group members. Further experiments should test the theory in situations in which the deviant is a member of the group and can interact with other group members. In the study described here, the theory is tested when the deviant is an outsider; it ought to be applicable to both kinds of situations.[27] Support for the theoretical argument will be strengthened by further empirical work in settings in which group members are allowed to engage in deviant behavior.

In addition to being tested under other conditions, the argument also ought to be developed and its scope enlarged. The theory should be expanded, for example, to examine the effects of altering the strengths of relationships among deviants and between multiple deviants and sanctioners. Potential sanctioners contemplating punishing one deviant may be influenced by the reactions of other deviant individuals with whom they interact. Also, the support that deviants receive from other antisocial friends may offset the threat of sanctions. Therefore even if punishment occurs, it may be ineffective under conditions in which deviants have alternative sources of rewards.[28]

Finally, the argument developed here (which explicitly addresses a second- and third-order dilemma) may be applied to examine the provision of public goods other than sanctioning (a first- and second-order dilemma). Further study would clarify the extent to which sanctioning operates like any other public good, and the ways in which it differs. For example, contributing positively to the group may be less costly than contributing through imposing sanctions because it does not incur the same risk of retaliation. In addition, the rates of cooperative behavior, relative to sanctioning, may affect whether it is more efficient to use punishments or rewards as incentives (Oliver 1980). The processes that affect responses to cooperative behavior should be compared with those which occur in reaction to the sanctioning of antisocial deviance.

The present research supports the argument that group cohesion increases the rewards given for sanctioning. It suggests one mechanism through which cohesion affects meta-norms and, in turn, the punishment of deviance. Extensions of this work will further explain norm enforcement processes.

Notes

1. According to another view, rates of sanctioning remain the same, but have a greater impact on deviants who are more dependent on the group (Homans 1961).

2. In more cohesive groups, individuals might prefer to "build personal relationships that are privately satisfying" rather than use "social ties to enforce group obligations" (Macy, Kitts, and Flache 1997:3).

3. The term *sanctioning* typically is used to refer to both negative and positive reactions to others' behavior. This approach makes sense when punishment and reward are conceptually similar. In the present paper, however, they are viewed as different in important ways—particularly in the reactions they invoke in the recipients. Therefore, for clarity, I use *sanctioning* to refer to negative sanctioning or punishing, and *rewarding* to refer to positive responses.

4. For examples of work on social dilemmas and public goods, see Foddy et al. (1999); Marwell and Ames (1979); Orbell and Dawes (1981); and Yamagishi (1995).

5. For an example of work focusing on group members' reactions to sanctions imposed by external agents, see Heckathorn (1990).

6. The traditional exchange theory formulation defines dependence in terms of value and alternatives (Emerson 1962,1972; Molm 1997). Here I focus only on value. The content of what is valued is left unspecified; whatever it is that people need from each other, the more value they place on it, the more dependent they are.

7. Some scholars suggest that sanctioning often is costless (Pettit 1993). Most, however, assume that it is costly, and attempt to explain its occurrence in light of this assumption.

8. Coleman (1990) proposes another solution to the third-order social dilemma. He argues that although people may be reluctant to respond negatively to others' sanctioning decisions, they are more willing to give positive responses because rewarding is inherently less costly than punishing. It is easy, for example, to smile or give a nod of approval. Consequently if an individual sanctions appropriately, group members are likely to give rewards to that person. The problem with this argument is that it is not necessarily easier to give rewards than punishments. Therefore, just as the reduction in deviant behavior produced by sanctioning may not be enough to offset the costs of punishing deviants, it also may not be sufficient to motivate rewarding.

9. Many studies show that exchange is more likely in cohesive groups (see, for example, Bacharach and Lawler 1981; Michaels and Wiggins 1976).

10. This calculation may be affected by individuals' discount rates. If they discount the future too much, they will have little desire to give costly short term rewards in order to increase the likelihood of long run benefits. Here I make no assumptions about discount rates. Rather, I argue that however actors weight the future, the value of future rewards will be higher in cohesive than in noncohesive groups, and therefore more likely to affect behavior.

11. See Cook and Emerson (1978) for a description of positive exchange networks—those in which exchange in one relation affects exchange in another. As Heckathorn (1990) puts it, there is a "spill-over" effect: "a reward received by one individual benefits other group members" because of "interdependence within the group" (p. 367). Here the sanctioning benefit received by one person affects his or her ability to exchange with others.

12. See the discussion of scope conditions.

13. If we consider the size of the sanctioning benefit alone, we would not expect cohesion to increase rewarding. We have reason to expect such an effect only if the benefit is magnified by community members' interdependence.

14. Although a share of the group benefit alone may not be sufficient to motivate rewards, in cohesive communities that benefit is enhanced through exchange. The enhanced benefit creates a greater incentive to reward sanctioners.

15. Subjects were assigned to same-sex groups. In each condition, 10 sessions were conducted with all male subjects and 10 with all female subjects. Gender was not a factor of theoretical interest in the present experiment; I included it as a block variable for control purposes. Statistical analyses revealed no effect, however. Therefore, in the present paper I combine men and women in the analyses, and present the results without controls for gender.

16. Thefts occurred in every seven out of eight trials; the particular trials were chosen randomly by the computer.

17. This information is not relevant theoretically and would have created more detail for subjects to absorb and process. I did not want participants to be bogged down in calculating payoffs for the thief; therefore I purposely did not provide information about those payoffs, and told them that they would not see the instructions given to the thief.

18. In the present study, from the subject's point of view, the thief could retaliate only by stealing again from the person who imposed the sanction. Because the thief and sanctioner were not engaged in ongoing exchange, the thief could not reduce rewards.

19. The person who had the opportunity to sanction—in this case, the victim—was identified clearly. That is, only one person was able to respond to an instance of deviant behavior. This was done in order to avoid problems with diffusion of responsibility; that issue has been the subject of much research but is not the focus here.

20. In the instructions the options were described as follows:
Option 1: Punish the thief. If you choose this option, points will be taken away from the thief. It will cost you 10 points to punish the thief. As a result of punishing the thief, you, X, Y, and Z will each receive 3 points.
Option 2: Not punish the thief. If you choose this option nothing will happen to the thief. It will cost you nothing and no one will receive any points.

21. Neither cost nor benefit varied across conditions. Conceptually, cost may include elements such as effort, time, money, or retaliation by the deviant. The effects of such variations are not the focus of the present study, however.

22. Subjects seemed unaware of the frequency of the thefts, possibly in part because they were focused on strategies that would make them money. It also may be that no particular subject was victimized very often, and thefts occurred randomly. Therefore, for any one subject, determining the rate of theft or a change in the rate of theft was not a straightforward process.

23. Although sanctioning and rewarding are not predicted to vary across time, before pooling the data I looked to see whether they did so. Subjects' decisions, however, remained relatively constant. I found no statistically significant differences across time blocks.

24. Again, one can calculate the difference in points actually received by the victim. In the low-cohesion condition, the mean difference in the number of points received from each subject is 1.80 (1.80 × 1). In strong groups, the mean difference is 10.3 (3.43 × 3).

25. Not surprisingly, the proportion of resources used specifically to encourage sanctioning, relative to those used to engage in general exchange, has no such effect.

26. Another possible approach would be to determine whether rewards given at time 1 affect sanctioning at time 2. The difficulty here is that the theory does not specify a means of deciding the relevant time periods. Should the most recent reward be considered? The mean

rewards over a recent period? Cumulative total rewards? Evaluations of the prospective rewards? Future work may develop the theory further in order to make such specifications.

27. This does not mean that deviants will necessarily be punished to an equal extent in these different circumstances. My argument does not address the effects of varying the relationship between the deviant and the potential sanctioner. One might well expect these factors to affect sanctioning. Whether or not such effects occur, however, the mechanisms described here linking cohesion to rewarding and in turn to sanctioning, ought still to operate.

28. See Macy et al. (1997) for an argument that "cohesive friendship networks" may " effectively insulate particpants from social control" (p. 4).

REFERENCES

Axelrod, Robert. 1984. *The Evolution of Cooperation.* New York: Basic Books.
———. 1986. "An Evolutionary Approach to Norms." *American Political Science Review* 80:1095–1111.
Bacharach, Samuel B. and Edward J. Lawler. 1981. *Bargaining: Power, Tactics, and Outcomes.* San Francisco: Jossey-Bass.
Blalock, Hubert J., Jr. 1987. "A Power Analysis of Conflict Processes." Pp. 1–40 in *Advances in Group Processes*, vol. 4, edited by Edward J. Lawler and Barry Markovsky. Greenwich, CT: JAI.
Blalock, Hubert J. and Paul H. Wilkin. 1979. *Intergroup Processes: A Micro-Macro Perspective.* New York: Free Press.
Coleman, James. 1990. *Foundations of Social Theory.* Cambridge, MA: Harvard University Press.
Cook, Karen and Richard M. Emerson. 1978. "Power, Equity and Commitment in Exchange Networks." *American Sociological Review* 43:721–39.
Ellickson, Robert C. 1991. *Order Without Law: How Neighbors Settle Disputes.* Cambridge, MA: Harvard University Press.
Emerson, Richard M. 1962. "Power-Dependence Relations." American Sociological Review 27:31–41.
———.1972. "Exchange Theory, Part II: Exchange Relations and Networks." Pp. 58–87 in *Sociological Theories in Progress*, vol. 2, edited by Joseph Berger, Morris Zelditch Jr., and Bo Anderson. Boston, MA: Houghton Mifflin.
Flache, Andreas. 1996. *The Double Edge of Networks.* Amsterdam: Thesis Publishers.
Flache, Andreas and Michael Macy. 1996. "The Weakness of Strong Ties: Collective Action Failure in a Highly Cohesive Group." *Journal of Mathematical Sociology* 21(1):3–28.
Foddy, Margaret, Michael Smithson, Sherry Schneider, and Michael Hogg, eds. 1999. *Resolving Social Dilemmas: Dynamic, Structural, and Intergroup Aspects.* Philadelphia: Psychology Press.
Hechter, Michael. 1987. *Principles of Group Solidarity.* Berkeley: University of California Press.
Hechter, Michael and Satoshi Kanazawa. 1993. "Group Solidarity and Social Order in Japan." *Journal of Theoretical Politics* 5:455–93.
Heckathorn, Douglas D. 1989. "Collective Action and the Second Order Free Rider Problem." *Rationality and Society* 1:78–100.
———. 1990. "Collective Sanctions and Compliance Norms: A Formal Theory of Group-Mediated Social Control." *American Sociological Review* 55:366–84.
———. 1993. "Collective Action and Group Heterogeneity: Voluntary Provision Versus Collective Incentives." *American Sociological Review* 58:329–50.
Homans, George C. 1961. *Social Behavior: Its Elementary Forms.* New York: Harcourt Brace Jovanovich.
Horne, Christine. 2000. "Community and the State: The Relationship Between Normative and Legal Controls." *European Sociological Review* 16(3):225–43.

———. 2001a. "The Contribution of Norms to Social Welfare: Grounds for Hope or Pessimism?" *Legal Theory* 7:159–77.

———. 2001b. "Sociological Perspectives on the Emergence of Norms." Pp. 3–34 in *Social Norms*, edited by Michael Hechter and Karl- Dieter Opp. New York: Russell Sage.

———. 2001c. "Sex and Sanctioning: Evaluating Two Theories of Norm Emergence." Pp. 305–24 in *Social Norms*, edited by Michael Hechter and Karl-Dieter Opp. New York: Russell Sage.

Lawler, Edward J. 1986. "Bilateral Deterrence and Conflict Spiral: A Theoretical Analysis." Pp. 107–30 in *Advances in Group Processes*, vol. 3, edited by Edward J. Lawler. Greenwich, CT: JAI.

Macy, Michael W., James A. Kitts, and Andreas Flache. 1997. "The Weakness of Strong Ties II: Collective Action Failure in a Self-Organizing Social Network." Presented to the Mathematical Sociology Section at the Annual Meeting of the American Sociological Association, August 11, Toronto.

Markovsky, Barry, David Willer, and Travis Patton. 1988. "Power Relations in Exchange Networks." *American Sociological Review* 53:220–36.

Marwell, Gerald and Ruth E. Ames. 1979. "Experiments on the Provision of Public Goods, I: Resources, Interest, Group Size, and the Free-Rider Problem." *American Journal of Sociology* 84:1335–60.

Michaels, James W. and James A. Wiggins. 1976. "Effects of Mutual Dependency and Dependency Asymmetry on Social Exchange." *Sociometry* 39:368–376.

Molm, Linda. 1997. *Coercive Power in Social Exchange*. Cambridge, UK: Cambridge University Press.

Molm, Linda and Karen S. Cook. 1995. "Social Exchange and Exchange Networks." Pp. 209–35 in *Sociological Perspectives on Social Psychology*, edited by Karen S. Cook, Gary Alan Fine, and James S. House. Boston: Allyn and Bacon.

Oliver, Pamela. 1980. "Rewards and Punishments as Selective Incentives for Collective Action: Theoretical Investigations." *American Journal of Sociology* 85:1356–75.

Orbell, John and Robyn M. Dawes 1981. "Social Dilemmas." Pp. 37–65 in *Progress in Applied Social Psychology*, vol. 1, edited by G. Stephenson and J.H. Davis. Chichester: Wiley.

Pettit, Philip. 1993. *The Common Mind: An Essay on Psychology, Society and Politics*. New York: Oxford University Press.

Sampson, Robert J., Stephen W. Raudenbush, and Felton Earls. 1997. "Neighborhoods and Violent Crime: A Multilevel Study of Collective Efficacy." *Science* 277:918–24.

Shaw, Clifford R. 1929. *Delinquency Areas*. Chicago: University of Chicago Press

Willer, David and Bo Anderson, eds. 1981. *Networks, Exchange and Coercion: The Elementary Theory and Its Applications*. New York: Elsevier.

Yamagishi, Toshio. 1986. "The Provision of a Sanctioning System as a Public Good." *Journal of Personality and Social Psychology* 51:110–16.

———. 1988. "Seriousness of Social Dilemmas and the Provision of a Sanctioning System." *Social Psychology Quarterly* 51:32–42.

———. 1995. "Social Dilemmas." Pp. 311–35 in *Sociological Perspectives on Social Psychology*, edited by Karen S. Cook, Gary Alan Fine, and James S. House. Boston, MA: Allyn and Bacon.

Yamagishi, Toshio and Nobuyuki Takahashi. 1994. "Evolution of Norms Without Meta-Norms." Pp. 311–26 in *Social Dilemmas and Cooperation*, edited by W. Albers Schulz and U. Mueller. New York: Springer-Verlag.

Quite clearly, social control agents must become familiar with an agency's theory of the office, its working ideology, associated diagnostic stereotypes, and the like. Once we have located and described an institution's underlying formal and informal organizational structures, components, and decision making processes, much more attention and research must be focused on the decision makers themselves, one of the messages of Horne's research discussed in the preceding selection. We can ask: Are the decision makers rendering decisions on the basis of organizational and/or individual stereotypes? Stated differently, are selected bureaucrats applying a range of gender, racial, and class stereotypes in the identifying, processing, and sanctioning of clients? Evidence suggests that some agents may very well be doing this.

In "The Epistemological Challenge of the Early Attack on 'Rate Construction,'" Troy Duster addresses the issue of "how we know what we know" about crime and deviance. Duster provides a brief history of the alternative approaches to the study of deviance (e.g., using official data versus field studies). Previous approaches to the study of deviance are compared to the new approach, which asks "What are the social processes that explain why some get classified and others don't—even though both are engaged in the same or similar behavior?" Duster's answers are unsettling, to some extent, because they point to systematic selection processes that emerge from organizational operating strategies. These issues are echoed and further expanded upon in the following work by Albert J. Meehan.

Meehan, in "The Organizational Career of Gang Statistics: The Politics of Policing Gangs" reminds us that "all statistics have an organizational career." Meehan recognizes that gangs are real—not simply the creation of the police. However, what is clear is that the record keeping practices and the statistics that they create contribute, in a significant way, to the perception and interpretation of gangs and gang activities. Further, record keeping practices of police are shaped to meet the requirements of political and organizational leaders, as well as the community that they serve. In the end, the gang problem, and the problem of deviance more generally, must be understood in the overall context of community, organizational, and political exigencies—the expressions of the theory of the office.

Meehan's work helps to demonstrate, once again, the way in which the theory of the office generates organizational procedures, processes, and protocol by directing attention to how these organizational elements shape the construction of reality. The article also focuses on the interdependent relationships that exist among police records, the statistics that are generated by the records, and the subsequent legitimation of any social-control activity that may result. We argue that the theory of the office lies at that core of these relationships. It is the theory of the office that shapes the bureaucratic slots generated for categorizing deviance and establishes a set of exigencies/responsibilities. One can also notice in the article the importance of accountability and how such accountability is satisfied by social-control agents. Satisfying accountability creates a statistical reality that supports the social-control activities or the expansion of them.

Corporate wrongdoing, when compared to street crime, presents unique problems for agents of social control in identifying, processing, and sanctioning. Corporate wrongs are often "morally ambiguous in terms of crime, criminal, and victim." In addition, corporate crime often lacks drama and clear resolution. Gray Cavender and Aogán Mulcahy view the media as potential significant actors in the process of social control. Cavender and Mulcahy examine the relationship between news reports of corporate deviance and issues of salience and regulations of corporate misdeeds. The authors create a conceptual model of the standard crime news frame which includes four features: attributions of responsibility, individualization of responsibility, condemnation of the violation of moral boundaries, and resolution (implying that the system works). Noting that the standard crime news frame best fits street crime, they show that, when the standard frame is used, the negative coverage may induce corporate change. They apply the model to two cases of newspaper coverage of alleged corporate misdeeds: the investigation into General Motors pickups' vulnerability to fire in side impact crashes, and NBC's *Dateline* program in which a GM truck was rigged to catch fire in a simulation. The analysis suggests that the presentation of corporate wrongdoing in the media is shaped by the standard crime news frame of corporate deviance and may increase the newsworthiness of corporate wrongs. News frames, however, may also contribute to the low salience of corporate deviance and the relevance of the media as agents of social control since they "facilitate, through denials, scapegoats, and resignations, efforts to wipe the slate clean so that the organization can continue with its good name intact." In the end, while the media are potential actors in the process of social control, "the media shamed a corporation that staged a fake truck fire as severely as they shamed a corporation whose real truck fires may have caused people's deaths."

The Epistemological Challenge of the Early Attack on "Rate Construction"

28

Troy Duster

The philosopher Alisdair McIntyre calls it an "epistemological crisis" when something that we acknowledge has just happened forces us to question the very foundation of what we otherwise have accepted as a truism. In its crispest form, that would be: "If what I am seeing is true, then other things that I thought were true are no longer certain. How can I now have confidence in my capacity—or confidence in the tools I have been using to assess what I thought I knew?"

At mid-century, in the period when the Society for the Study of Social Problems was just coming off the starting blocks, there were two major competing sociological approaches to the study of deviance, law, and the criminal justice system in the United States. The first was centered at Columbia and could be described, grossly, as that dominated by Merton and functionalist theory. Drawing from both Durkheim and Parsons, Merton and his students and colleagues approached the study of deviance by exploring (a) the theoretical relationship between "the deviant world" and "the normal world" through (b) an empirical strategy relying on statistical aggregates of deviant and criminal behavior as reflected in local police records and the Uniform Crime Reports of the FBI. While there was an occasional foray into field site investigations, the overwhelming tendency of this approach assumed that the data from official statistics sufficiently reflected the phenomenal world that theorizing from these databases warranted little (theoretically consequential) concern.

Chicago was the alternative and competitive approach, with a long tradition of field site investigations of particular forms of "deviance"—from "the gang" to "the hobo" to the prostitute, gambler, and other vice sets and settings. The Chicago tradition assumed the stance of "the natural world" of common-sense actors. Their practitioners *literally* went to those places in the society that any competent actor would presume to be the site of deviance. Folklore has it that one of the most celebrated sociologists of the era got "caught with his pants down" in an up-close ethnography of prostitution—

and that both the *Chicago Tribune* and the University of Chicago joined in the demand that his head roll. This tale is not so much a digression, but rather one of the more colorful remembrances of the extent of Chicago's commitment to the study of deviance in its natural setting. Yet, as Martin Nicolas would point out years later, Chicago was not doing fieldwork on white-collar crimes such as the Great Electrical Conspiracy. In short "Chicago" most generally accepted the domain assumptions about the taxonomies of the deviant world, even when challenging and correcting the accuracy of the most popular representations.

While there were significant differences between Chicago and the Columbia rendering of deviance, in very important ways, both adopted a "taken-for-granted" empirical world.

As the Sixties dawned, a third set of key players would quickly shift the focus to challenge the epistemological foundations of the whole playing field, and not just of theory and research on deviance. Egon Bittner, Aaron Cicourel, and Joseph Gusfield would ride around in police cars and see just how and when police used discretion in their arrest procedures. David Sudnow would go to the Public Defender's office and record the way in which the Public Defender and the Prosecuting Attorney worked in concert to secure guilty pleas from "certain suspects," but let others bargain "harder" when their legal representation took a private turn. Erving Goffman would even venture into mental hospital wards and break the path for the next generation that would study intake decisions for mental institutions.

When Kitsuse and Cicourel tried to publish their now classic article on the use and misuse of official statistics in the *American Sociological Review, Social Forces,* and the *American Journal of Sociology,* they ran headfirst into a brick wall with patterns and predictable grooves. Reviewers from both traditions (noted above) wrote critiques that explicitly acknowledged, "if this were true, we would have to go back to the drawing board and reorient research and theory." (Kitsuse would later write about how the "social reaction" approach to deviance required that the investigator go out into the field and study the social responses to deviance in its natural setting. So, while this approach affirmed the "natural setting" methodology of the Chicago School, it asked the investigator to look at the social patterns in the discretions and strategies of sorting and naming and classifying.) After those many tries in which they could not get the article published, Cicourel and Kitsuse told the story to Howie Becker. Just at that time, Becker had become the editor of *Social Problems.* He published it. Indeed, the new journal began to publish a series of articles that would later dominate the literature and push the other schools to the back burner. It was *Social Problems* that opened the door that led the other journals to incorporate a much richer theoretical dialogue. The Sixties later exploded with a host of competing paradigms—from Marxist theory to ethnomethodology—each with its own challenge of how to approach control and deviance. The border did not end with the sub-field of deviance. For example, in medical sociology, Irving Zola would observe and analyze how medical doctors read and interpreted the symptoms of Jewish, Italian, and Irish patients—how their presenting symptoms for the same medical condition were dramatically different. The implications for medical diagnosis and practice are deeply consequential, and Zola's work is frequently incorporated in medical training.

In some ways, the methodology of this new breed of work seemed parallel to the earlier field research traditions. However, in fundamental ways, the domain assumptions were strikingly different. Chicago was mainly trying to find out and explain what "the deviants were really like" in their natural setting. The new approach, appearing in the first decade of *Social Problems,* was to raise a different order of question: "What are the social processes that explain why some get classified and others don't—*even though both are engaged in the same or similar behavior?*" When Cicourel and Bittner were riding around in police cars observing and recording how official statistics are compiled, they were asserting that the point at which rate construction occurs is the preferred site for an investigation of those "taken for granted" statistics that had been the structural underpinning database for theorizing about deviance and crime. It would not be much of a leap to conclude that, if the site of rate construction was the preferred focal point for inquiry and theorizing about these data, then surely it would have bearing and impact on all manners of rate construction, from epidemiological work in public health to coroner's collective accounts of the causes of death.

On a personal note, I should say why this was so appealing to me as a fledgling would-be sociologist trying to make sense of the remarkably divergent police behavior that I had both witnessed and experienced. I grew up for the first 17 years on the streets near the South Side of Chicago, in an overwhelmingly black community. For example, my high school, with nearly 2,400 students, had only one student who was not black. He was the son of Chinese immigrants who owned a restaurant in the area. Then, I traveled about twenty miles north (and 10,000 light years away) to Northwestern University as an undergraduate, which, at that time, was 98 percent white. In short, from the spring of my last year in high school to the fall of my first semester of college, I went from the nearly all-black scene I just described to a college in which I was one of seven blacks on a campus of more than 7,000 whites. I did not have to earn a doctorate to discern the strikingly different police behavior in the two settings. I had not changed any of my behavior. Set and setting had changed—and so would the nature of my contact with the police.

This was long before the drug war—long before systematic racial profiling and before incarceration rates had reached our current obscene levels, with an eight to one ratio of race differences we are now witnessing across the nation. But even back in those years, the only way one could believe that real behavioral differences were reflected in those official statistics was if one never had to deal with rate construction at the site in which actors make decisions about what to sort and classify. If sociology was a behavioral science, I reasoned, it was the behavior that should be the focal point, not the already-collected statistics where the behavior was assumed to be reflected in the numbers. Many of my peers and most of the profession did not see it that way. Or at least, even if they acknowledged "a problem," for the purposes of getting on with publishing, one must act as if it is not true. No crisis of epistemology for them.

But as the Ramparts police scandal surfaces in Los Angeles, some of my colleagues in sociology come by my office, scratching their heads and struggling to make sense of it. They have to "exceptionalize it" as "bad apples" because to accept the systematic focus on young people of color as patterned practice (with occasional planting of drugs and other contraband—with false testimony in courts), would be to force a whole new way of thinking about the use of official statistics. No matter that similar police scandals have surfaced in New Orleans, Philadelphia, Chicago, Newark, and New York City in the last two decades. In the tradition of McIntyre's "epistemological crisis," if they are to believe that happens routinely, they would have to "go back to the drawing boards." An audience of members of the Society for the Study of Social Problems knows that this field went back to that drawing board forty years ago. The rich tradition of theory and research that it spawned and fostered has enhanced our understandings of many forms of behavior.

The Organizational Career of Gang Statistics: The Politics of Policing Gangs

Albert J. Meehan

How social problems are constructed by those claims makers with the power to do so is a critical sociological issue (Spector and Kitsuse 1977; Best 1995). The emergence of gangs as a social problem is arguably as much a product of the various interactional and recordkeeping practices of the police that have developed in response to the problem as it is to "labeling" in a broader sense. The daily work practices of persons working in organizations are responsive not only to public and media pressure but also to internal recordkeeping procedures and the various legal and political bodies to which they are accountable (Emerson 1991; Bowditch 1993; Margolin 1992; Meehan 1986). This means that interactional and recordkeeping practices, in essential ways, create and reproduce reality (Garfinkel 1967; Collins 1981, 1987; Rawls 1987; Fine 1991) and make an important contribution to the construction of social problems. Consequently, an understanding of these interactional and recordkeeping practices is indispensable to the study of social problems (Maynard 1988).

In the late 1970s I conducted research in a large urban East Coast police department (Bigcity) during a time when a special gang program was developed by the incumbent mayor (in an election year) to rid the city's neighborhoods of gangs. During the 1990s I collected data on the emerging response to gangs from a Midwestern police department (Plantville). Then, as now, such programs make use of the police and their recordkeeping practices in the construction of a "reality" that legitimates the political agendas of those in a position to influence matters in a police department. All statistics have an organizational career. The significance of recordwork in creating the statistics with which gangs and other social problems are measured and organizational effectiveness assessed is the subject of this article.

Throughout the twentieth century, Americans have had a recurring concern with "gangs" of young people inhabiting their streets and committing disorderly and illegal behaviors. Efforts to prevent the formation of gangs and to control their behaviors have preoccupied law enforcement and social work personnel, researchers and lawmakers alike. Indeed, in the past ten years, interest in the gang issue has intensified and shows little sign of abatement. Legislators and criminal justice officials continue to develop laws, such as the Federal Gang Violence Act (U.S. Senate 1997), and implement model strategies for Urban Street Gang Enforcement (U.S.BJA 1997). Concurrently, efforts by social scientists to integrate community-wide approaches to gang problems within the current law enforcement suppression strategy are reflected in, for example, the National Youth Gang Suppression and Intervention Program (Spergel 1994; 1995). Despite such efforts, however, the prevalent view is that, if anything, gangs have become more widespread (Klein 1995; Curry, Ball, and Decker 1996), their behaviors more violent and lethal (Fagan 1996), and their criminal behavior more highly organized (Padilla 1992; Skolnick, Bluthenthal, and Correl 1993; Taylor 1990; Sanchez-Jankowski 1991), although these last two trends are much debated (Klein 1995; Short 1997).

There is an important question, however, as to whether the increase in "gang" statistics reflects an actual increase in serious or "real" gang activity or a complex social construction. Police officers frequently express opinions that accord with a social constructionist view:

Author: Does your community have a gang problem?
Officer: When you take two officers from patrol division and put them together with two undercover detectives from special investigations for intelligence purposes to form a gang unit, I *guarantee* you that they will find gangs in the city; there will be a gang problem. This is an issue for the mayor not a real problem for the police. (Plantville PD field notes, March 15, 1998)[1]

For the officer in this exchange, "gangs" in his city are a *political* problem not a crime problem; one that the police socially construct in response to political pressure, as the officer puts it "not a real problem for the police." The officer's view accords with that of Richard C. McCorkle and Terence D. Miethe (1998) who argue that a socially constructed "fear" of "gangs" (or moral panic) has been used strategically by politicians and criminal justice officials to increase budgets and gain support for legislation that increases the powers of the police. Given the national focus of personnel and resources on gangs, combined with a response that is primarily punitive, the question of the degree to which gang problems are an artifact of political interests and their effect on police practices is an important one.

This article focuses on the relationships between police records, the statistics they generate, and the local exigencies of police work during the critical period when gangs were becoming recognized as a widespread national problem. At one point during a two-year field study in Bigcity, in 1979, youth gangs were identified as a significant problem and a special "gang" car program was instituted for dealing with it. These cars were special units specifically designated to handle "gang problems." The institution of the gang car facilitated the categorization of problems as "gang" relevant as well as heightening the visibility of a gang problem for the public. Using data from citizens' calls for service, the police response, and corresponding records generated by the police, I argue that the category "gang" became a resource for citizens and police personnel (e.g., police operators, dispatchers, and responding officers) to categorize a variety of problems with young people—usually not gangs—as "gang" problems.

The daily work practices of persons working in organizations are accountable to a variety of different internal organizational and external (e.g., political, legal, and normative) expectations (Emerson 1991; Margolin 1992). The details of those practices are organized to satisfy the demands of that accountability in ways that affect how records are constructed and maintained and the view of reality it produces (Mills 1940; Garfinkel 1967). This means not only that interactional practices reproduce and create reality in essential ways, but that this micro production always occurs within a context of accountability that shapes it in essential ways (Gill and Maynard 1995; Manning 1997; Meehan 1986). In practical organizational terms, this means that if those with political power (e.g., strong mayors) view gangs as a problem, then the police will legitimate this view and, in doing so, create its statistical reality. In this way, political interests can make use of the police and their recordkeeping practices in the construction of a "reality" that legitimates the political agendas of those in a position to influence matters in a police department. The significance of police record- keeping and its responsiveness to political contexts of accountability is generally overlooked in contemporary discussions of America's street gang problems (for an exception to this point, see Klein 1995).

The definition of what constitutes a "gang" is generally assumed to determine what will be measured as gang activity. If definitions vary—and there is considerable debate and discussion about the definition of a gang (Klein 1995; Huff 1996; Short 1997)—most researchers believe that the activities measured and classified as gang activities would necessarily vary as well. For example, Cheryl Maxson and Malcolm Klein (1996) have demonstrated that police adoption of a member versus motive conception of gang-related homicide affects the rate of reported gang-related homicides in a jurisdiction. Confounding this issue is the widespread diffusion of gang culture that has spawned behaviors by small, highly transitory groups that "pass" as gang behavior in suburban communities and smaller cities (Short 1996).

More important than the official definitions, however, are the working practices used by the police in recording their activities as gang related. The application of definitions in practice is not necessarily affected by official or even informal definitions of gangs. If a practice develops in a particular department, that certain sorts of incidents can most efficiently be labeled as gang incidents, or, if there is a unit designated to take care of gangs, or if citizens for some reason begin to refer to certain problems as related to gangs, then those activities are more likely to be recorded as gang activities and consequently produce gang statistics in that department, regardless of the existence of an official definition of gangs.[2]

Crime statistics have often been created and manipulated by political pressure to accomplish a variety of ends (McCorkle and Miethe 1998, pp. 54–56; Chambliss 1994; Zatz 1987; Seidman and Couzens 1974). In Bigcity, the "problem" with youth gangs was identified during an election year and consequently had political implications. In such a context, the claimed presence of gangs allowed the Bigcity police organization to enhance and reinforce the mayor's claim that he was doing something "for the neighborhoods" by bringing the youth gangs under control. Such external political pressures constitute an important context of accountability for the police, and the police as an organization tend to manage such pressures through the manipulation of their records (Seidman and Couzens 1973; Manning 1997; Meehan 1993).[3]

This article illustrates how this management of political and organizational accountability is achieved at the local interactional level across the various layers of the police response. The context of accountability has a political and organizational dimension but the police practices that satisfy the demands of accountability and create the statistical reality that supports organizational and political accountability are *interactional*. An analysis of the documentary reality (Smith 1974; Wheeler 1969) created by the organization through local interactional practices is particularly relevant to understanding how the police "solve" a problem, in this case creating, maintaining, and controlling the appearance of the street gang problem. I am not suggesting that there are no street gangs in Bigcity. In "Corktown," the district I studied, officers thought there were one, maybe two identifiable street gangs, but they felt that most of the so-called "gang calls" they were assigned to handle were unrelated to "real" gang activity. By "real," the police refer to activities that *they* believed to be gang activities, as opposed to the way the police organization expected them to report gang activities. Both are social constructions, but at different levels. When asked what a "real" gang was, officers utilized a classic "social science" definition: an organized group of young people (typically teenagers) with a leadership structure, who wore common identifiable clothing and who committed serious and/or violent crime. Yet officers and dispatchers routinely and unproblematically interchanged "gang" and "group" when referring to young people. The issue here is not whether there are real gang problems but rather to analyze how an increased awareness of a public problem places particular kinds of constraints upon the police as an organization to show itself as accountable and as solving that problem. In doing so, we can see how groups of ordinary young people were constituted as gangs at various points in the course of citizen complaints and police responses to incidents during a time when gangs have been publicly designated as a problem.

I refer to the various stages at which such constitutive formulations of activities into "gang" activities occur as the organizational career of a statistic. This career involves:

1. Citizens' formulation of a problem to the police operator in a call for service and how such formulations are understood by operators as constituting a gang/group problem and subsequently encoded into an organizationally relevant and actionable category;
2. Dispatchers' formulation of the problem to the patrol officers assigned to respond to a call;
3. Patrol officers' understanding of the dispatchers' formulation of the problem to which they are responding;
4. Patrol officers' location and assessment of the "problem";
5. Patrol officers' response to the "problem";
6. The various records produced by patrol officers regarding their response and the gang statistics that result from those records.

Methods and Data

Whereas other researchers have used surveys and vignette scenarios (Decker and Kempf-Leonard 1991) or a combination of media reports, statistics, and legislative responses (McCorkle and Miethe 1998) to document the social construction of gang problems, I focus on the various stages and practices through which activities are transformed officially into gang activities by the police and the context of accountability within the police organization. This allows the formulation of an organizational "career" for statistics. Examining the organizational career of statistics necessarily involves utilizing a multimethod approach, and I draw upon several types of data.

The first data set consists of a sample of telephone calls to the Bigcity 911 emergency number that were categorized as gang calls by the police operators and dispatchers and subsequently assigned to the gang car in Bigcity's Corktown police district. The organizational career of most police patrol work begins with the citizen's call for service (Reiss 1971; Skogan 1975; Lundman 1980; Maxfield, Lewis and Szoc 1980; Manning 1988; 1992). Consequently, the citizens' calls to the police analyzed below can be treated as constituting the first step in the organizational career of most statistics. The calls were identified by obtaining gang car patrol logs ($N = 34$) from the Corktown police district for a twelve-week period in the fall, which is the height of the political campaign season. The gang car was fielded three evenings (Thursday–Saturday) per week in two, four-hour shifts. Thus, there are two patrol logs generated each evening. Three of the six logs produced each week were randomly selected for this analysis. In patrol logs, officers record all calls for service assigned to the car in addition to other activities undertaken on a given evening (e.g., routine patrol of parks, and field interrogations). Seventeen logs, which reflected the most active shifts, were then chosen; and recordings of the seventy-three citizens' calls for service assigned to the gang car on those shifts were obtained from the communications division. These seventy-three calls represent 70 percent of all citizen calls assigned to the gang car during this twelve-week period.[4]

The focus of the analysis will be upon the relationship of the call to the subsequent gang categorization. A conversational or interactional analysis (Sacks, Schegloff, and Jefferson 1974) of the calls affords a view of the citizens' own formulations of their problems and how these formulations are constituted and negotiated by operators and citizens as a "gang" problem (see Sasson 1995 for a different use of citizen formulations). Further, they illustrate how police operators encode such problems, a process, that is sensitive to the interactional organization of the call, the political context to which the operator/dispatcher and the police are accountable, and the organization's current solution: namely, the availability of a "gang" car to handle such problems.

The second data set consists of all available records and recordings for one evening's work in the gang car in the same district and includes the transcripts of citizens' calls, dispatchers' assignments of the calls, transcripts of the police response (tape-recorded), the author's field notes from the car, and the corresponding records (e.g., patrol logs) of the police response for that evening.[5] These data allow an examination of how the police assess and respond to the "problem" they have been assigned by the dispatcher, as well as those which problems they initiate on their own (i.e., "on view"), and how these activities are utilized by officers to construct their recordwork (e.g., patrol logs) for the evening. These materials illustrate how the responding officers constitute the activities of persons as a "gang," to use Harold Garfinkel's (1967) term, "for all practical purposes."

The logs for this one evening are also compared with the thirty-four gang car patrol logs in the first data set in order to assess the representativeness of that night's work. The analysis shows that, if anything, the officers responded to my presence with a more conservative use of the gang designation. That is, the logs from the other thirty-four shifts show a significantly greater proportion of gang designations. Therefore, generalizing from that night's work does not overestimate the effect.

In addition to my data set of actual calls for service, I utilize a statistical data set developed by Glenn Pierce (personal communication) that aggregates the department's categorizations of all citizen calls for service to Bigcity emergency 911 during a six-year period (3.2 million calls). This allowed for a comparison of statistics on gangs for the period covered by my research with statistics for prior and subsequent years. The analysis shows that significantly more calls received a gang designation during the election year than calls in the years immediately before or after.

The variety of records available allows for a consideration of whether and how the police interpretation and transformation of an incident into a gang problem is preserved in a documentary form. I argue that police recordkeeping is geared toward external accountability and is only a gloss for "what happened." To the patrol officer, recordwork is secondary in importance to the job of policing the streets. That job consists of managing the continual problematic contingencies created by the ambiguities inherent in social interaction in such a way as to render nonproblematic the meaning of the task at hand (Meehan 1986).

Therefore, the officers' organization and use of the category "gang" is responsive not only to the immediate problems of achieving the police relevance of a citizen's complaint (i.e., within a call for service) but also to the organization's work relevancies (i.e., generating "activity") and the larger political framework to which the police are held accountable (e.g., "solving" a problem in an election year to make the incumbent mayor look good). In this fashion, "solutions" to problems may in fact produce the records that are used to constitute the statistical existence of a problem in the first place. The statistic represents the organizational response under specific conditions of accountability. It does not represent what the police consider to be real gang activity. Research results based upon such records are as much out of step with the "reality" behind the documents as the political action that created them and which they sustain.

The Political Context of the Gang Problem

In May 1979, a mayoral election year in Bigcity, the Corktown police district, along with other police districts throughout the city, initiated a supplemental weekend patrol, as they had for several previous summers, to help control teen behavior on the streets. Corktown is a predominantly white (99.5 percent), Irish, working-class area of Bigcity with approximately twenty thousand residents. It is one square mile in size and contains two housing projects, although most of the residents live in one- and two-family dwellings. The gang car was a supplemental unit to the regularly assigned patrol cars for Corktown. In previous years, these supplemental units had been fielded at the discretion of the district captain, and were called the "drinking" car by the police (taking care of public drinking in the district), not the "gang" car. This supplemental unit was an overtime assignment for district officers who drew double pay for each four-hour shift. Two shifts, back to back (7:45 P.M.–11:45 P.M. and 11:45 P.M.–3:45 A.M.), were assigned each evening from Thursday through Saturday. In 1979, they became "gang" cars for the first time. More significantly, until the summer before the election, this effort had not been a media event.

Statistically, gangs appeared to be a big problem for Corktown[6] as well as for Bigcity as a whole. For example, an aggregate analysis of the 3.2 million calls for police service to Bigcity's 911 emergency number during the years 1977–1982 reveals that gang calls were one of the most prominent categories of problem reported to the police and handled by officers. In 6.4 percent ($N = 206,101$) of these 3.2 million calls for service, it was the 911 *police operators* who initially classified a call as a "gang" call. The gang category was the third most frequent category used by 911 operators, following the categories "investigate" (10.6 percent) and "internal assistance" (8.3 percent), which do not identify any specific type of problem. Thus, gang activities would appear to figure prominently in the police operators' categorization of a reported problem into a police relevant category.[7]

In June, the police chief announced a citywide program to curtail street gangs. The primary component was a citywide gang squad, not controlled by the district captain, that would patrol the various districts throughout the city. At the onset of this citywide program there was considerable media coverage of the gang cars. One Bigcity newspaper reported: "The Bigcity police began what they termed 'an all out war' on teenage gangs across the city last night." Newspapers reported that the police program included a unit of men, dubbed the "G-Squad," who would patrol selected areas of the city. One report also announced that each of the districts would field a car to curb the behavior of "gangs" in the neighborhoods. In addition, a newspaper reported that officers would file Field Interrogation/Observation (FIO) reports with headquarters downtown for youths who are seen in groups, even when they are not causing trouble. The information would be entered into a computerized database, and if a name showed up more than one time the police would send a letter to the parents to alert them that their child was part of a neighborhood gang.

Ten days after the beginning of the citywide gang patrols, Bigcity's mayor and police chief announced that the gang program was a *success*. Citing statistics based upon officers' responses to calls for service, they claimed that throughout the city, and in Corktown, the gang squads were effective. While the unit generated increased statistics documenting gang activities, calls for service regarding "gangs" were reportedly declining as the police announced that the message had gone out to the youth gangs. The mayor announced in a newspaper report: "The added police presence in the neighborhoods is just what is needed to convey to young people we are serious about controlling and eventually eradicating youth gangs in this city. The destruction and disruptiveness youth gangs represent can no longer be tolerated." The police chief, in an interview with one of Corktown's community newspapers, commented:

> When the people of Corktown begin to notice our prompt response, I think you'll find more residents willing to call 911 when local gangs begin to cause problems for neighborhood residents. I'm quite sure that

the Anti-Gang patrol will prove a very successful component of our overall gang prevention effort.

Perhaps the best explanation of the "gang squad" came from some of the officers during the ride-alongs who simply said: "It's an election year, time for the mayor to show something's being done for the neighborhoods." This view was shared by a youth who, when asked what he thought of the use of dogs by the gang squad, was quoted in the newspaper saying: "It's election year, the dogs will be around until the election is over and then you won't see them any more."[8] As predicted, the gang program ended approximately fifteen days after the November election, which the incumbent mayor won.

Monitoring newspaper reports in the year following the election showed that the city had no "gang problem" that year. Over the next two years, the Bigcity police, due to layoffs in the department and city budget problems, announced that the police would no longer respond to calls about groups "bothering the neighborhood" because there were more pressing crime problems and not enough police personnel. This was, in some sense, more consistent with police experience on the street than the original formulation of and response to the "gang" problem. Further, there were no supplemental overtime units fielded during the summer months. Bigcity also closed a number of district stations during this time period and attempted to consolidate its police force. As the next election year approached, however, Bigcity finally managed to overcome the many political problems that they faced in funding additional police. As the summer prior to the election approached, the mayor and police chief unveiled a new neighborhood patrol in each precinct to supplement existing units to help stop the underage drinking and vandalism. The program, they said, was not like the "gang" units during the last election. However, by all the accounts of their activities reported in the newspaper, they sounded extremely similar.

Table 1 provides aggregate data on gang calls before and after the election year, data that support the "election year" interpretation of the gang problem and illustrate how the number of gang calls changed over the course of the six-year period. These data show that, during the election year, the number of gang calls, as classified by the 911 operator, increased by 12.8 percent (4,982 calls) from the previous year. Gang calls represented 9.8 percent of all dispatched calls to the 911 operator during the election year, the highest during the six-year period. After the election year, the total number and percentage of gang calls declined. As expected during the election year, the number of calls categorized by responding officers with a gang designation also increased, although slightly, from the previous year. After the election year, both the number of gang calls and the number confirmed by responding officers progressively declined, reaching its low point some three years later.[9]

Table 1 Operator and Officer Categorization of Gang Calls by Year

Year	911 Calls Dispatched[a]	Categorized Gang by 911 Operator		Confirmed Gang by Officer	
		Number	Percentage	Number	Percentage
2 yrs. before	384,807	34,715	9.0 %	56,976	14.8 %
1 yr. before	427,749	38,901	9.0	52,681	12.3
Election	446,171	43,883	9.8	56,094	12.5
1 yr. after	436,523	38,905	8.9	49,152	11.2
2 yrs. after	393,934	28,914	7.3	37,136	9.4
3 yrs. after	333,955	20,783	6.2	26,096	7.8

[a] This number reflects the total number of 911 calls that resulted in the dispatch of a patrol unit. It excludes internal or administrative calls made to the 911 number.

While the social construction of a gang problem offered obvious benefits to both the police and the mayor, the question remains how such a complex process is managed and what role individual citizens, 911 police operators, dispatchers, and officers played in generating the statistics on which the appearance of the problem depends.

911 Calls Reporting "Gang" Activity

The calls analyzed in this section are from Corktown residents to Bigcity's 911 emergency number.[10] These calls report incidents that operators categorized as "gang incidents." The gang car for the Corktown section of the city was then dispatched to respond to the citizen's call. Moreover, the categorization of these calls as involving "gang" problems was entered on the computer records of calls for service retained by the department. Subsequently, the official department records of these calls became part of the official police statistics on the gang problem in Bigcity and Corktown.

Some Conversational Features of "Gang Calls"

The analysis of actual calls to the police, categorized by the police operator as "gang calls," indicates that what constitutes a gang problem is equivocal in a number of ways. The phenomenon, a gang problem, and how it comes to be seen as a problem, is an issue. Increased attention to gangs as a "problem" (e.g., via media attention) may itself constitute and produce the visibility and problematic character of groups of youths for citizens and police alike. Consequently, any next incident involving young persons can be inspected for its gang relatedness. The use of a categorization device (Sacks 1972) such as "gang" can be said to be in vogue given this newfound relevance and possible remedy (that is, a gang car will be sent). If attention to the gang problem and the availability of an official categorization increases the percentage of calls recorded as gang calls, then a statistical increase in gang problems may be due to the various ways in which police, media, and citizens come to use the term "gang" to refer to some activity, or collection of activities, rather than representing a real increase in what was formerly considered to be gang activity.

For example, in the call below, *playing tag football* under the new lights is formulated by the caller, and accepted by the operator, as a gang-related activity. (Note: **Boldface** print highlights the features of the call discussed in the text. Timed pauses are in parentheses. Double slashes // indicate overlapped talk. PD represents the police operator, CA represents the citizen caller.)[11]

[Call 32: Tape 1]

PD: Bigcity police three eight five
CA: In Corktown
PD: Yes
CA: **In front of ninety eight Bedford Street there's a gang of teenagers playing tag football under these new lights (.5) can you get them out of here please?**
PD: Yes, ma'am

In the following call, no activities of the persons being reported are described by the citizen, and nothing is revealed about the nature of the incident except the label "gang":

[Call 10: Tape 2]

PD: Bigcity Police
CA: Yeah you wanna send a car down to twenty seven Parton Street in Corktown//**for the gang of ki-**
PD: What's the prob-(1.0)
PD: What's the address again sir?

Indeed, no activities are described, and it appears that the use of the term "gang" suffices for a description of the problem. However, the use of the term gang to describe the persons being reported to the police is not a necessary feature of calls that were categorized as "gang" calls, either. One notable observation about the vast majority of citizen reports in the collection of "gang" calls under consideration here is that the term "gang" is rarely used. Yet the calls are designated "gang" calls by the police operator and dispatched to the "gang car" for the district. The category has organizational accountability for the police operator which enhances its use. Indeed, various types of activity (not necessarily involving legal violations) appear in these calls as if they were categorically tied to "gangs" and seem to be usable by both caller and operator as a resource for constituting the "gangness" of the incident.

Such gang-associated activities include drinking, fighting, smoking pot, throwing rocks or beer bottles, banging on doors, being in the hallways, hanging out on corners, "pissing on the steps of the rectory," or any combination of the above. The term "gang," and those activities associated with it, are clearly interchangeable with "kids," "group," and "youths," and these terms were typically found in calls subsequently categorized as "gang" calls. Indeed, descriptions of "rowdy" behavior were, in these calls, presumed by police operators to be categorically tied to any gathering of young people and officially categorized as "gang" behavior.

For example, in the following call, the use of "gang" by the police *operator* indicates that the term is not necessarily tied to particular people or identifiable groups per se but rather to the types of activities *expected* from groups of young people in general:

[Call 16: Tape 2]

PD: Bigcity Police
CA: Yeah, I'd like to report a disturbance on the corner of Shakerhill and Alton Street in Corktown (.5)
PD: Shakerhill and Alton?
CA: That's right
PD: And what's the problem? (.5)
CA: **They're throwing beer bottles and uh//**
PD: **What's this a gang?**
CA: Yeah

The caller's description "They're throwing beer bottles" is formulated by the operator in next turn as "What's this a gang?" This formulation solicits and receives an agreement from the caller. Thus, in this call, it is the activity of "throwing beer bottles" that is treated as "gang" behavior.

In the following call, where the report is about "some boys," it is not immediately clear how the operator arrives at the categorization of the problem as a "gang" problem:

[Call 40: Tape 2]

CA: Hi **I'd like to report some boys** right now there on Masters Street, somebody has to call the cops right?
PD: Alright, what number Masters?
CA: It's right down from the (.5) one twenty nine Bastille Way (.5)
PD: What number are you at now?
CA: One twenty nine (.5)
PD: You're at one twenty nine Bastille Way?
CA: Yes
PD: **And the gang is out there?**
CA: **The gang is out there yeah they gotta go home and go to bed**
PD: All right we'll be down

The caller begins the call by stating what they want to do in the call (report some boys) rather than report what the "boys" are actually doing. After determining a location for the complaint, the operator formulates a description of the problem in the form of a question: "And the gang is out there?" In this utterance, some "boys" have now been constituted by the police operator as a "gang," a categorization the caller agrees with in their next turn. How the "boys" become the "gang" cannot be inferred from any activities reported by caller, as in the previous cases, because no such activities are reported. Nor does the caller offer the category themselves. But *it doesn't really matter.* The operator's candidate categorization, "gang," is "police relevant" and provides for police intervention, whereas exploring the caller's reason for "reporting some boys" would require more time on the call, which has already been occupied with some difficulties in establishing the location. Further exploration might also turn up the police *irrelevance* of "they gotta go home and go to bed." The caller concludes by agreeing with the operator's categorization.

In calls 16 and 40 above, the operator clearly selects the category "gang" and then solicits an agreement for the proposed categorization of the problem. These dispatcher formulations "And the gang is out there?" (call 40) and "What's this a gang?" (call 16) are themselves distinctive interactional practice in calls to the police (see Meehan 1989), and illustrate the negotiated character of these reports which are then produced as *"facts" for all practical purposes* (Garfinkel 1967). The calls make it clear that many different types of activities are classifiable within the calls themselves, as gang related. There are some calls where the categorization of the problem as a "gang" problem is explicitly formulated in the complaint by the caller or operator, that is, where the caller and/or operator utilize the categorization "gang" to formulate the problem. In other calls, the designation of the problem as a "gang problem" is an achievement arrived at by the operator only *over the course of the call.* Sometimes the designation "gang" does not appear in the call at all. But the "gang car" is dispatched, and the call results in a gang statistic nevertheless. Therefore, it is misleading to search for explicit uses of the term "gang" by the operator or caller, simply because all of the calls have resulted in a "gang" statistic. The operator's categorization of the call as an official "gang" statistic obviously does not depend upon such initial displays, but rather, relies on how, for all practical purposes, what is being produced by the caller in the complaint can be heard for its "gang" relevance.

There are several points raised by this analysis of citizens' calls with respect to police records, and the statistics generated from them. First, the fact that each call resulted in a statistic regarding youth gangs cannot be overlooked. Calls such as the "gang playing tag football under the new lights" are a clear case for arguing that taking the "outcome" of the call to represent the problem as reported by the caller creates misinterpretations of police problems regarding gangs. Second, by analyzing calls for service, we can see that problems are often constituted as "gang" problems, not at the beginning of the call, but only over its course. The negotiations between the police operator and caller generate the record and project a particular organizational career for the reported problem. The response by the police patrol, and the records generated therein, constitute further categorizations, negotiations, and interpretations of the incident. How this response contributes to the "facts" about the gang problem is the focus of the remaining sections of this article.

The Police Response: An Evening's Work in the Gang Car

Calls to the 911 number that report "gangs" suggest that a wide variety of activities are labeled as gang activities by callers, operators, and dispatchers. The police officers' role in this labeling process begins when a car is dispatched. The following discussion of the organizational career of incidents is based upon data collected during one evening (2 four-hour shifts) in the Corktown gang car. Although I rode along in the gang car on other evenings, I chose this evening's work for analysis because of the detailed interactional data available for this particular evening, including audio-taped citizens' calls, audiotapes of both the dispatchers and the police response in the car, and my field notes. My goal is to compare the actual police response to the evening's events to both the reported problem in the original citizen's call and with the officer's actual patrol logs that report and document the "official" record of the incident.

In comparing the actual police responses at various levels of the organization to the problem as reported by the citizen, this analysis is not a comparison of facts with social constructions. Rather, I treat all of these as levels of socially constructed activity. The police response is one level of socially constructed activity. The problem as reported in the original citizen's call is another level of socially constructed activity. Finally, the resulting official record is a social construction comprised of a complex combination of the other levels.

This following discussion is divided into five key areas:

1. Keeping the patrol log and its relationship to the documentary reality of the police organization;
2. Citizens' complaints as a source of ambiguity for the responding patrol officers;
3. The most typical police response to citizens' calls (brooming);
4. On-view, or proactive, responses that are *recorded* in the patrol logs;
5. Incidents that are *not* recorded in the patrol logs.

Keeping-the-Patrol-Log

The patrol logs are part of the work relevancies of officers, where maintaining a record of their response is a part of the context of accountability operating within the police organization. That is, officers can be held accountable for what they do and don't do and for how they do it. The hyphenated term, keeping-the-log, is used to indicate that this is not just a task or an instance of an action, but rather a set of practices officers have created that display their orientation to organizational accountability. From the patrol officer's viewpoint, keeping-the-patrol log is, first and foremost, displaying police "activity" *for the record.* As Jonathan Rubenstein (1973 p. 44) observes: "'Activity' is the internal product of police work. It is the statistical measure which the sergeant uses to judge the productivity of his men, the lieutenant uses to assure himself that the sergeant is properly directing his men, the captain to assure his superiors that he is capably administering his district, and the department administrators to assure the public that their tax dollars are not being squandered."

For example, in Corktown, patrol logs were often reviewed by the precinct captain and lieutenants prior to attending community meetings with residents, so that they would have a sense of what had been happening in the district. Or, when citizens complained about a specific problem or the lack of patrol in their neighborhood, the logs would be consulted to determine how often officers had been in a specific area, neighborhood, or address. At roll call, officers would be instructed about those areas or addresses where the "brass" (supervisory police officers above the rank of sergeant) or citizens had requested extra patrols. Such areas would typically receive additional attention throughout the shift, but most important, whether the officers actually patrolled that area or not, those areas or addresses would be reported in the logs as having received extra patrols. Thus, the logs do not necessarily reflect "what happened" but rather a version of "what happened" created by the work demands and relevancies entailed in keeping-the-log and its accountability to organizational expectations (McCleary 1977; Meehan 1986).[12]

The patrol logs consist of a sheet filled out by officers during the course of a shift. These logs figure prominently in the recordwork for the shift, as they are the primary documents that officers produce to account for their time. In patrol logs, officers record how they received an incident (BC = Bigcity central dispatch; OS = on-view); the times of dispatch, arrival, and clearance of the incident; the location of the incident (using street address or common landmark) and sector location (an organizational designation); the nature of the incident; and a disposition code. Figures 1, 2, and 3 below replicate the logs for the two shifts discussed and the accompanying coding instructions for filling them out.[13]

The description of an incident is initially shaped by the dispatcher's description of the problem when a call is dispatched to a car. Although such

Figure 1 Gang Car Patrol Log (Shift 1).
(All hand printed entries made by officers are in italics.)

BIGCITY POLICE   OFFICERS' LOG   STATION: *9*   DATE: *8-12-79*

     Odometer 15825 22 mi.   *7:45 p.m.–11:45 p.m.*

OFFICER'S NAME	BADGE #	PARTNER'S NAME	BADGE #	TOUR	CAR
Sgt. Rossi	*0321*	*Ptlm. Alpen*	*2931*	*B*	*290 Gang Car*

Assigned by	Dispatch Time	Time of Arrival	Time Cleared	Location of Incident	Sector	Nature of Incident	Disp.
BC	*7:45 pm*	*7:45 pm*	*7:45 pm*	*Station*	*C*	*Log on*	*O-N*
BC	*7:59 pm*	*7:59 pm*	*8:10 pm*	*Station garage*	*C*	*Gas 19 gals.*	*C.R.*
	8:10 pm	*8:13 pm*	*8:18 pm*	*Mountain Square*	*C*	*Assist k-9 group*	
BC	*8:18 pm*	*8:21 pm*	*8:33 pm*	*Peters School*	*C*	*Group disturbing*	*7-B*
OS	*9:15 pm*	*9:15 pm*	*9:25 pm*	*Rainey Field*	*C*	*Disbursed group*	*NA*
BC	*9:25 pm*	*9:27 pm*	*9:35 pm*	*1 O'Malley Way*	*B*	*Loud Music*	*12-P*
OS	*9:45 pm*	*9:45 pm*	*10:05 pm*	*Peters School*	*C*	*Kids disturbing neighbors*	*NA*
OS	*10:07 pm*	*10:07 pm*	*10:15 pm*	*Murtry Playground*	*C*	*Area check*	*NEG*
OS	*10:30 pm*	*10:30 pm*	*10:50 pm*	*Davis Playground*	*C*	*Area check*	*NEG*
BC	*10:55 pm*	*10:55 pm*	*11:05 pm*	*1 Barker St.*	*C*	*Disbursed group*	*7-P*
OS	*11:07 pm*	*11:07 pm*	*11:12 pm*	*Wolcott School*	*C*	*Disbursed group*	*NA*
BC	*11:12 pm*	*11:15 pm*	*11:20 pm*	*52 Corsant St.*	*C*	*Group disturbance*	*9-C*
OS	*11:35 pm*	*11:35 pm*	*11:40 pm*	*31 Salk St. area*	*B*	*Area check*	*NEG*
BC			*11:45 pm*	*Station (5 FIOs)*	*C*	*Logoff*	*O-F*

formulations are generally considered "imprecise" characterizations by the responding officers (Manning 1988, p. 21), when reporting the disposition of the call they must confirm or disconfirm the initial characterization of the "nature of the incident" through a disposition code. The disposition code contains two designations: a number that indicates the type of incident and a phonetic designation that indicates the type of police action taken (Figure 3). For example, in Figure 2 the dispatcher reports a "gang" at 74 Alcon Street, and this is entered in the log. After the incident is handled, the officer will radio the dispatcher a disposition code. The disposition code, 7-Paul (or 7-P in the logs) would be read as "gathering causing annoyance (outside) and services were rendered" (i.e., group dispersed). Even though not obviously a "gang" designation, the disposition confirms the original report and the dispatch categorization of the incident as a gang incident stands for the record.

Figure 2 Gang Car Patrol Log (Shift 2).
(All hand printed entries made by officers are in italics.)

BIGCITY POLICE   OFFICERS' LOG   STATION: 9   DATE: *8-12/13-79*

11:45 p.m.–3:45 p.m.

OFFICER'S NAME	BADGE #	PARTNER'S NAME	BADGE #	TOUR	CAR	
Sgt. Rossi	*0321*	*Ptlm. Cramer*	*1345*	*A*	*290 Gang Car*	

Assigned by	Dispatch Time	Time of Arrival	Time Cleared	Location of Incident	Sector	Nature of Incident	Disp.
BC	*11:45 pm*			*Station*		*Log on*	*C-R*
BC	*11:50 pm*	*11:55 pm*	*12:00 am*	*74 Alcon*	*C*	*Gang*	*7-P*
BC	*12:00 am*	*12:05 am*	*12:10 am*	*65 Salk*	*C*	*Gang on roof*	*7-P*
BC	*12:15 am*	*12:17 am*	*12:20 am*	*Manelt & Mountainhill*	*C*	*Gang on roof*	*7-P*
BC	*12:30 am*	*12:35 am*	*12:40 am*	*65 Salk*	*C*	*Gang*	*8-P*
BC	*1:45 am*	*1:50 am*	*1:55 am*	*Mtain & Mountainhill*	*C*	*Gang*	*8-P*
BC	*2:00 am*	*2:10 am*	*2:15 am*	*Kane Crt.*	*C*	*Gang*	*7-P*
BC	*2:30 am*	*2:35 am*	*2:40 am*	*Battlehill & Mountain*	*C*	*Disturbance*	*7-B*
BC	*2:45 am*	*2:50 am*	*2:55 am*	*50 Walters Way*	*C*	*Disturbance*	*7-P*
BC	*3:00 am*	*3:05 am*	*3:10 am*	*127 Redfern St.*	*C*	*Log off*	*O-F*
BC	*3:45 am*			*Station*	*C*		

In the logs for the two shifts discussed here (Figures 1 and 2), thirteen calls for service were handled, four on the first shift and nine on the second shift. The 7-Paul disposition code (gathering causing annoyance and services rendered) was used in six out of the thirteen calls. The 7-Boy code (gathering causing annoyance and no person can be found) was used in three calls; the 8-Paul code (investigate persons and services rendered) was used in two calls. The 9-Charles code (investigate premises and no such address) and 12-Paul code (loud music and services rendered) were each used once. No arrests were made by the officers on these two shifts.

I compared the log sheets for this evening with thirty-four other gang car log sheets. A total of 103 citizens' calls for service were handled for an average of three calls per four-hour shift. So this particular evening was busier in terms of handling citizen calls for service. For the 34 tours, only one arrest was made by the gang car, and three drunks were taken to the station. In spite of the obvious lack of serious problems handled, however, the Adam disposition code, which indicates that an incident was "not a bona fide" police matter was only used once over this three-month period.[14]

Figure 3 Bigcity Log Disposition Codes Used on These Shifts

Procedure Codes:
O-N = unit logging on
O-F = unit logging off
C-R = unit clearing from assignment not requiring code

Reporting Codes for Disposition:

No.	Incident
7	Gathering causing annoyance (outside)
8	Investigation persons (routine)
9	Investigation premises (routine)
12	Noisy Party-Radio, T.V., etc.

Phonetic	Police Action
A-Adam	Not a bona fide incident
B-Boy	No person can be found
C-Charles	No such address
P-Paul	Services rendered

The logs are a type of *pre-structured observation schedule,* and the task of the responding officers is to *fit* the behaviors they encounter (e.g., gathering causing annoyance; disturbance) and their response (e.g., service rendered; peace restored) into one of the available categories. This involves making sense of the scenic unfolding of behaviors they observe, and finding in that process, some feature that is usable in determining a category code for the record (i.e., the patrol logs). In short, the keeping-of-the-log requires making the codes appear to be a sensible and rational procedure by formulating how, in some way, the codes correspond to "what happened" for all practical purposes.

The correspondence of the written log to "what happened" (i.e., what the officers in the car observed, and their interpretation of it, and their actions) is, in an important sense, irrelevant. Formulating the night's work in police relevant terms is much more important. That is, *it is the appearance of orderliness that is necessary* for the log to do its work. For example, Figure 1 shows that the car began the shift at 7:45 P.M. and ended at 11:45 P.M. While this shows that the time the car was in service corresponds to the time it was supposed to be in service (according to the organization schedule), this does not correspond to when the car actually left and returned. In fact, there was about a five to ten minute difference between the actual and recorded times. The reported times on the log correspond to scheduled organizational shift changes and display organizationally ordered time not the time as experienced in the car. If the sequence of events, as the officers experienced it, was entered in the log it would be problematic from both a practical point of view (i.e., not enough space) as well as from an organizational standpoint. Practical problems, such as checking out the portable radios, and remembering a flashlight or ticket book, are part of routine shift changes. Yet, for purposes of keeping the log, noting those routine checks, or the consequences of their occurrence (i.e., forgetting to log on), would not provide a display of an "efficient" organization. By contrast, recording that the shift began and ended on time *is* a display of efficiency, thus making the "organization" appear as though it is working as planned.

The keeping-of-the-log, by its very format and use, exhibits in documentary form, for any next reader, the "rational procedures" for responding to incidents. "Rule following" and "hierarchy" are clear via the proper entries. When dispatched to a location, officers record they went there, announced their arrival to dispatch, and informed them when matters were under control (even if that is not what happened, i.e., the police don't see anyone but record that they do so as to confirm the dispatch code). "Technical skills" and "competency" are evidenced in the learning of and application of special codes that provide an "organization" for the meaning of an incident and the corresponding actions of the officers. By encoding events that are initially understood through commonsense knowledge of "policing the streets" into a technical or analytical format, the officer creates a record of the incident that only has meaning in the context of the practice. It is through the keeping-of-the-log that the "formal organization" is created and sustained. The encoding procedure and the document it produces provide no insight into the discovery procedures (commonsense practices) that officers use in policing the streets. It is that social "organization" of discovery which is the focus of the remaining analysis.

Citizens' Calls as a Source of Ambiguity

Patrol officers often encounter considerable ambiguity in determining the nature of the problem they are dispatched to handle. The citizen's description of the problem, which is encoded into some organizationally actionable, yet cryptic category by the operator (e.g., "gang"), requires officers to interpret what the category "means" in the context of the actual police response. The police task when responding to a call such as the "gangs" or groups disturbing the neighborhood is threefold: (1) if possible, approach the area without being seen and "find" and "see for oneself" the reported problem, (2) determine if the behavior constitutes a problem that requires police action, and (3) take some action. Police consider the second task as the most critical and, as the next two examples illustrate, it entails important interpretive work.

In the first example which occurred at 74 Alcon (Shift 2: 11:50 P.M.), we observe how the citizen's call initially creates considerable ambiguity about *both* the problem and location, due to the lack of specific information provided by the caller. In the call, the citizen requests police presence because of a bottle-throwing incident that occurred the night before by "people" who caused recurring problems in the neighborhood. The operator's attempt to provide an excuse for the lack of police presence is met with a sharp reply by the citizen ("I don't want another bottle through my window").

[Call 7: Tape 1 (11:42 P.M.)]

PD: What's the problem?

CA: Well, we had an incident last night where **someone threw a bottle through our window at twelve o'clock and the police said that they would patrol now at night. Now these people are out on the street again and screaming and just carrying on the same** and I would just appreciate it if—I don't want anyone to come to the house, but if they could please patrol the street as they said they were going to

PD: If they could what?

CA: Patrol Battlehill Street between Prince and Alcon, this goes on every single night

PD: Okay, but this is Friday night ma'am there's a lot of crime in the city and we're short on police everywhere I guess. But I'll put the call in

CA: Well, ya know I don't wanna have another bottle through our window, this happened last night (1 .0)

PD: Okay we'll put the call in. They're on the corner of Prince and Battlehill? [caller's address given earlier in call]

CA: No, right now they're down on Alcon, which is just two streets down **but they're screaming and there's a whole bunch of them together tonight.**

The lack of a specific location is relevant to the dispatch and response of the gang car, as the problem reported is essentially a "bunch of them screaming" (note that there is no mention of youths, a group, or gang). The officers received the assignment over the telephone at the station house, instead of in the car, because they were ten minutes late beginning the shift (which of course is not noted in the logs). Central dispatch had called to inquire about the availability of the district's gang car. The dispatcher's formulation of the problem to the officer over the telephone was "a gang in the area," not "a group of them screaming."

The call presents a twofold task for the police responding to the call: to find *both* the location and the problem. After several minutes of driving around the block, the officers located a group of four to six youths (age fifteen to seventeen), described by the police as "troublemakers." They were hanging out in a doorway leading to some project apartments. Although there was no noticeable legal violation, when they saw the car, they gestured in a taunting manner, as if to say "come and get us," which generated a discussion in the car that illustrates the trivial nature of the officer's prior contacts with this "gang":

[Field tape number one]

Off1: **There's the crew, that's the crew**
Off2: **They're going into Debbie's house**
Off1: Yep
      (10.0) ((still driving))
Off2: My patience is about run out with them
Off1: It doesn't do any good, Bob
Off2: No, it doesn't do any good at all
Off1: Give them a break, you give them another break (2.0) you give them a shake,
      is that what they call it? [referring to kids' term for letting them off this time]
      come back the next day and they shit all over you. That's it. What's the sense
      of it? Then you're back with them again. (4.0) You can't be nice to them.
Off2: Yeah
Off1: **Let me go in there and let me see (inaudible) we'll check around the
      side.**
Off2: No, they're all gone, John, I'm sure.
Off1: They might be upstairs
Off2: They're all gone, they sit in that hallway, they go in and out of the street.
Off1: All right.
      (3.0)
Off1: **Should we give them an adam robert?** ((tell dispatch the car has ar-
      rived at the call))
Off2: **Yeah, did we go out ocean nora?** ((code to dispatch that unit is logged
      on for the tour))
Off1: **David two-ninety (.) give us a 7-Paul** ((disposition code for the call))
Disp: **David two-ninety. 7-Paul. You going out car two-ninety?**
Off1: **Give us ocean nora** ((code for logged on))
Disp: **All right** ((we continue driving slowly turn car around and view the same
      hallway))
Off2: They're all in the hallway there
Off1: Yeah they're in Debbie's there, they go in and out of Debbie's. They just
      want a chase see//they just want a chase.
Off2: Yeah

The disposition of the call 7-Paul indicates *for the record* that there was
a "gathering causing annoyance (outside)" and that a service was rendered.[15] This disposition confirms the dispatcher's original designation of
the call as a gang call. Was the group causing an annoyance that could constitute some legal violation? No. Was the group outside? No. Were they
screaming? No. Was the group a "gang?" No. At the time the group was located, they were in the hallway, and *presumed* to be moving from this semi-
private space to a public space (outside) and to a private space (Debbie's
apartment). What service was rendered? The police showed up. Did they
have verbal contact with the group? No. In fact, the suggestion that contact be made was considered to be of "no use." Yet, for the keeping-of-the-
log, the officers have constituted *this* group as the "gang" and have coded
the relevant police response and disposition.

A second example illustrating the ambiguity of the process is O'Malley Way (Shift 1: 9:25). The caller reported a party of people "sitting on the stairs(.) they have the radio kinda real loud and they're kinda loud themselves they just woke up my kids(.) I was wondering could you do anything about it?" The call was dispatched to the gang car as a "group playing loud music on the steps." On the way to the location, one officer (who regularly walks a beat in that neighborhood) commented, "we *never* get a gang call for this address." Upon arrival, three local residents in their early thirties, who were known to the officer, were sitting on the stairs playing a radio that was audible from our vantage point of twenty-five yards. The following conversation between the officers (Off1, Off2) and myself (AJM) occurred in the car:

[Field tape number one]

Off1: Loud music coming from over there
Off2: Let me go talk to them
Off1: (said to author) That's loud music that's why, I knew, I knew I figured it would be loud music here that's just what it was here because we never get no calls for here
AJM: Right
Off1: Very, very seldom get a call here. I walk through here and never get it— people in front talk—they're adults
AJM: So this is a music call?
Off1: This is just loud music, sure, that's what it is just, that's exactly ((laughing)) what it is. They didn't say ((referring to radio dispatch)), they take—they figured a group or we got the group there but then you've got to evaluate what you're up against when you get here
AJM: Right. Have you had any really tough gang calls this summer though or has it been a lot of this routine stuff?
Off1: That's it, routine stuff, that's all. Loud music and loud music. Hey what are you gonna do, hit them with the city ordinance? They got so many. I've never *yet* really got a call where there's destruction. We do get a lot of stolen cars and they strip them. It's not gangs, it's two or three kids doing it.

At this call, the music was turned down and the entry in the log reflected the officer's assessment above. It read "Loud Music 12-P" (services rendered).[16] The officer's assessment is interesting and reflects the interpretive work entailed in policing. The dispatch to that location for a "group" was incongruous with the officer's knowledge and experience of the location and his assumptions about the behavior of the people who typically occupy that place. Thus, he concluded that he "knew," prior to actual arrival on the scene, that it had to be a loud music call and *not* a group or gang call. He refers to the dispatcher who "figured" a group was responsible (hence, send the gang car), but then notes, "We got the group but then you have to evaluate what you're up against" (i.e., not a gang). Distinctions between types of groups are quite evident; adult groups are treated differently from youth

groups. In fact, adults routinely sat out on their front steps on warm summer evenings in Corktown, playing music and cards and talking with neighbors without being harassed.

Furthermore, when asked about the types of gang calls he had responded to, the officer answered that he has yet to have a call (this summer) where there is "destruction." This provides some insight into how
gang calls were evaluated in Corktown that summer. In the officer's view,
a "real" gang call involves some destruction or serious criminal problem.
Routine music calls and other violations that entail enforcement of city or-
dinances (e.g., with respect to hanging out, drinking, etc.) would seem to
be the appropriate legal designation for most of the problems handled by
the gang car. Nevertheless, many calls that officers do not believe involve
gangs, like this one, receive service as a gang problem and end up in both
the logs and calls database confirmed as gang calls.

Reactive Policing: Brooming the Gang

As noted earlier, over this three-month period, the gang car made only one
arrest and brought three drunks to the station house for protective custody.
While the gang car was generating substantial statistics on gang activities,
the police were in most cases doing nothing more than "brooming," a term
they used to refer to simply moving a group. Usually, a brooming results in
the group moving to another corner. The police consider this a legitimate, if
only a temporary solution, hoping that the next corner chosen by the group
will not house a citizen who will call in a complaint. The problem from the
police standpoint is that standing on the corner is *not* illegal and, while citizens frequently call to complain about it, there is very little the police can
actually do. Yet, if the calls continue they can create problems for the officer (Meehan 1992). Therefore, citizen calls about this "problem" often result
in the dispatch of the gang car. One example from the shift I observed illustrates a typical problem the police have in evaluating "what the citizen has
called about" and then deciding what the police can, or should do about it.

In this call (Mountain and Mountain Hill, Shift 2: 1:45), the caller reported that there was a "noisy gang playing a radio on top of the car which
woke me up." The records at communications show that the caller had
called *three times* within *fourteen minutes*. The officers approached the scene
of the call unobtrusively and upon arrival could *not* "hear" *loud* music.
Three people (about eighteen to twenty years old) were observed sitting on
the hood of their car with a (boombox) radio on the roof. The radio was
playing but not loudly. The officers had the following discussion between
themselves and then spoke to the group:

[Field tape number one]

Off1: Should I broom them or just let them
Off2: I don't know what do you think you wanna do anything?
Off1: They're not doing anything

(3.0)

Off2: They're not doing anything ((we drive the car over to the group))

Off2: Somebody just called I don't know who it was but if we have to—if they call again, we'll have to make you move all right?

Cit: Okay

The officers stopped no more than fifty yards away from this corner to speak to a friend of one of the officers. We were there for five minutes when the dispatcher radioed to the car that the "gang had returned to the corner playing their radio." However, the group had never left the corner and neither had the police. The volume of the radio was not turned up (as the caller had reported in their second call). The officer informed the dispatcher that the matter was handled: the officer backed up the car and told the group that if they just moved somewhere else, this caller would stop calling. They readily complied.

This example highlights a major problem for the police. As long as there are calls about a group, the police have to take some action, even if they can see for themselves that there is no problem. The key here is that the police can exert some control over the group but not over the caller's behavior. Callers often ask the police to solve problems they have no legal jurisdiction over. If the police do not do something, the caller will continue to call, and complaints may find their way to the precinct captain, or worse, city hall and/or the media.

In brooming the group, the police make it clear that they don't hold the group accountable or responsible for the problem. They tell the group that it is the caller's problem. Yet, the log entry for the call (7-P) read as "gathering causing annoyance and services rendered," and the gang car was dispatched. The resulting gang designation is interesting in light of the officer's obvious judgment that the caller, not the group, is the problem. They could have reported the disposition under the "Adam" code: not a bona fide incident. Given the comparison between the caller's report of a gang playing loud music and the police assessment of the situation at the scene, the "Adam" code would seem to have been appropriate in this case. By reporting services rendered and not using the Adam code, the police create a statistical database representing "gang" problems that do not, in their own assessment, exist.

By contrast, even when there were problems (e.g., loud, disturbing behavior) being caused by groups that involve illegal activities (such as drinking and/or smoking pot), the police would still "broom" the group in an effort to displace the problem from the caller. For example, two calls to the Salk Street public housing projects within twenty minutes resulted in "brooming" a group the officers knew were responsible for making noise and drinking. In the first call to 65 Salk (Shift 2: 12:00 A.M.), the caller reported a "noisy gang on the roof drinking with a loud radio." When we arrived, there was a group of five teenagers (ages fifteen to seventeen) in the courtyard area with a radio playing loudly. One officer went up to the roof, the other went over and had the kids shut off the radio. The group was told to keep their radio off because it was bothering people in the apartments. When we returned the second time (65 Salk, Shift 2: 12:35 A.M.) because the caller reported the "gang" was still there playing its radio, the radio had in fact been turned off and the youths were milling about the courtyard. The following discussion occurred between the group and the police:

[Field tape number one]

Off2: Hey, somebody keeps—somebody's calling on you guys what's the story?
Kid1: huh?
Off2: Somebody's calling. Were you making a lot of noise here or what?
Kid1: Nope!
Off2: Why don't you guys move okay so we don't have to come back here again, all right?
Kid2: Yeah
Off2: Go around to the other corner ((kids begin to leave))
Off2: They must be smoking ((dope)), there's no bottles around
Off1: They had some beer earlier I broke some upstairs
Off2: Was there?
Off1: I broke some on the roof—they had some Michelob—Lowenbrau, looked like I'm not sure maybe a six pack.

Proactive Responses and Recorded Log Entries

Accounting for how time is spent on patrol is an age-old problem because a complete accounting for time spent on activities other than dispatched calls is impossible (Rubenstein 1973; Fogelson 1977). When officers spend less time on calls, they report other activity so as to look "busy." But they can never report everything. For example, the on-view activities of officers during the first gang car shift are quite extensively reported in the logs (six OS or "on view" entries), whereas there are no on-view entries for the second, much busier shift. The first shift had four calls, whereas the second shift had nine and therefore no extra time needed to be accounted for.

During the course of a shift, only certain activities are selected for recording in the log, not because they merit police attention but because *recording* their occurrence can fill the spaces of time between calls to show that *initiative is being undertaken by officers.* With the gang car, there are particular on-view entries that are likely to be recorded. There are certain areas that the captain requests the gang car to check throughout the evening. These are areas from which the captain has received citizen complaints; his solution is to designate these places for "patrol." Officers know that the logs are inspected by their supervisors to see that these areas are indeed being checked, especially when the place has achieved a reputation for direct complaints to the captain. Thus, these are "ready-made" on-view entries. The entries for the first shift indicate that these areas were checked, and indeed they were checked. During the second shift, however, even though these areas were checked, no log entries were made because the officers already had enough "call" activity to fill the log and account for their time. When areas are designated to be checked, however, the question "are they doing anything illegal?" is irrelevant. The area has achieved a reputation, and people occupying that place are presumed to be responsible for both the place and the behaviors that occur there.

Three of the area checks for the first shift showed "negative": no one was there. The other three indicate that officers found a "group" and in two cases dispersed them (at Rainey Field and the Walcott school). At Rainey Field, which borders a playground, the car pulled in and was immediately approached by ten young children (approximately eight to ten years old) checking out "who's working" in the police car tonight. One of the officers was well known and quite popular with young children in Corktown, and he was recognized immediately. While this was happening, the other officer noticed that a group of older teenagers were hastily leaving the area and that they had beer bottles. After a minute of talking with these younger children, the officer pulled the car down to the area where these older youths were seen leaving. That was the extent of our contact with the group that was, according to the log, "dispersed."

At the Walcott school, a group of about seven to ten youths was drinking on the steps of the school and playing music on a boom box. As we approached the schoolyard, the regular patrol unit dispersed the group (their car had been parked where we could not see it). These other officers yelled "get the hell out of here," and the kids scattered. One officer then smashed two six-packs of beer and picked up the boom box while the other picked up two other six-packs. On seeing us, one of the officers came over to our car and gave us two six-packs of beer saying they already had too much in their car (we returned directly to the station and placed the beer in the departmental refrigerator). However, if you look at the log entry, it indicates that we dispersed the group at the Walcott school, which of course we did not.

The last on-view incident I discuss occurred during the first shift: the Peter's School entry. There are two points of analytic interest about this on-view incident: (1) it is not really an on-view incident, and (2) it is a follow-up action from an earlier dispatched call. To simplify matters, I will first discuss the earlier call and police response.

In the earlier call, the citizen asked the 911 operator if the police could move a gang of kids out of the play area in the schoolyard: "They're lighting fireworks and putting them in cans and everything else." We were dispatched to the schoolyard for a "group of kids disturbing the neighbors" with no mention made of the fireworks. Upon arrival, we could not see any "disturbance." However, a woman (the one who, it turned out, had made the call) standing on the curb waved to us to come over. She reported that a group of thirteen- to fourteen-year-old "little punks" who had "split the scene" just before the police arrived had a "big fire" burning in the doorway and that they were exploding firecrackers.

The officer then drove the car to the front of the school where there were four girls sitting on the steps. He asked them if they were with the ones who lit the firecrackers, to which they replied, "No." The log entry read 7-Boy (gathering causing annoyance and no person can be found). This means that the officer's log entry verifies that the reported problem of firecrackers occurred and that the person(s) responsible could not be located. Yet there was no attempt to see if there was any evidence of a "big fire" in the alleyway, and the officers had not seen any firecrackers. This example contrasts with the earlier example on Alcon (call seven, tape I) where the problem was formulated as a "gang" of young males on the basis of the officer's prior knowledge of them and their presence within a two-block area of the call. Here, the young females are not similarly perceived. Even though they are at the location of the problem, they do not "fit" the officer's conception of a group or gang and their demeanor is appropriately respectful as opposed to the "taunting" gestures of the males. The treatment of their account by the police is very restrained, and the police do not challenge their claim when they deny being involved with the kids lighting fireworks.

The officer told the citizen that they would keep an eye on the area, to which the citizen delivered a sarcastic but realistic appraisal of the problem: "You'll be here every five minutes" and "You don't have enough gas." Approximately an hour later, we were returning to the schoolyard (at the suggestion of one of the officers) when the dispatcher reported "a gang of kids back in the schoolyard again." The word "again" indicated the dispatcher's awareness that this was a repeat call. Having promised to keep an eye on the situation, being "on-view" at just that moment, and having intended to be there at the time anyway, *the call was entered into the log as an on-view incident* even though it came in as a call from dispatch.

When we arrived at the school, a group of about thirty kids was in the alleyway. The officers went into the alleyway to investigate. As this was happening, two youths approached me, asking questions about who I was and what I was doing. I asked them what had been happening:

[Field tape number one]

Kid1: Nothing much, some girls wrote something about this one girl and then their sisters came down and made them erase it
Kid2: Oh Magoo, that lady's over there talking to the cop
Kid1: The lady next door talking to them now, drop the dime this lady always calls the cops ((referring to lady we spoke to earlier)) we call her a dime dropper she always calls—drops the dime on us calls the cops you know you don't even do nothing, you sit in the pit and she'll call the cops [the pit is the kids' term for the alleyway between the school building and the fence]

The youths did not mention firecrackers or fires. The officers, upon returning to the car, reported that there was a verbal dispute about some writing on the wall, but it was "nothing major." They concluded that the woman who called was upset about having all the kids down in the alley-way. Thus, their assessment essentially corroborated the kids' version as reported to me independently and not the caller's.

The call for this incident, which was the citizen's second call, differs both from what the officers observed and what they entered into their log as an on-view entry. The citizen's second call reported a complaint about kids drinking, although no evidence of this was found at the scene by the officers:

[Call 3: Tape 1]

CA: Yes could you do me a favor put a call into the Corktown Police and **tell them to do their jobs**
PD: What job, ma'am?
CA: **Getting the kids off the corner drinking**
PD: What corner, ma'am? What corner?
CA: It's the Peter's School (gives address) right there in the schoolyard right in front of everything.
     ((police and citizen have interchange to confirm address))
CA: I called earlier// for
PD: Okay we'll send someone over

Citizens will often upgrade the seriousness of the problem they report to police operators in order to increase the probability that the police will respond (Meehan 1989). By reporting "drinking" as the problem, the citizen provides a specific legal violation to mobilize the police rather than what apparently is her "real" problem, which was "kids" in the alleyway. The former requires no justification, whereas the latter may require more elaboration. Further, beginning the call with a complaint about the police (tell them to "do their jobs"), the "job" of controlling drinking (whether it is really the case or not), is more "police relevant" than complaining about kids hanging around. When the police arrive, the complaint from the caller is the "kids." The complaint from the kids is the "lady." The job for the police is to check out the complaint from the caller, which is considered "minor" (i.e., there was a verbal dispute, no fighting). But there is one other matter.

A repeat call, by the same person, may lead to a specific complaint to the precinct captain that the police weren't doing their jobs as promised. *Solution:* Show this incident as one's own initiative. *Procedure:* Log it as on-view and as a minor problem, "group of kids disturbing neighbors." Characterizing the nature of the incident in this manner ("group of kids disturbing neighbors") as opposed to reporting what they did on-view ("dispersed group") suggests that the disturbance may not have been legitimate police business even though the police did indeed disperse the group. Usually, officers would use the log entry "dispersed group" even when they didn't. Therefore, the log can be read by the police or their supervisors as the *neighbor's* problem, not a police matter, and therefore not a problem for which the police should take action. By officially recording it as on-view, the officers can claim they were doing their job as promised, that there was not a problem requiring the notation of a police disposition, as there is with calls for service, and that the "proof" is in the log.

These matters of internal accountability provide the police with good reasons for recording a "gang" problem as on-view, when they actually did not locate any police relevant business. Thus, the generation of a gang statistic shows that they responded to the caller's demands, not that there was a gang in the area.

Unrecorded Proactive Incidents

In this section, I discuss one encounter during the first shift that could have been logged as an on-view incident but was not entered at all. This police mobilization was initiated by a citizen on the street, not a phone call. So it was not assigned by dispatch and did not result in a dispatch statistic. This encounter is selected for analysis due both to its serious nature and to the amount of time spent on the incident (both initially and subsequently in talking to the youths observed), all of which would seem to have warranted an entry into the log. The incident did result in the writing of FIO cards, an informal, internal record that police officers treat more seriously than the official log (Meehan 1986; 1993). But it did not generate a gang statistic.

A citizen informed the officers on patrol that several kids, who were in an alley across the street, might be trying to break into the window of a second floor apartment. We immediately pulled over and found several kids in the alley whom the officers believed had been trying to open the window of an apartment. The kids told the officers they were in the alley "taking a piss," which the officers skeptically characterized as the "taking a piss routine." The officers treated this routine as a cover for, as they put it, "breaking in a house right in their own back yard" (said in a disgusted tone of voice).

This incident was never recorded in the log, although clearly the officers "believed" that the youths were attempting to break into the apartment. As we drove away, one officer began filling out FIO cards on each youth that was in the alley. The first officer to go into the alley said, "One was trying the window," *as if* he had seen it occurring. But he didn't. However, the officers did not arrest. Instead, they chose to question the youths, who were known to them, regarding their activity. I was told by the officers that each youth in this group had a record for breaking and entering. In situations where it appears that an arrest could have been made and wasn't, the "legal elements" for a prosecution to hold up in a court of law may not be present, or the officers have chosen not to create the "legal elements" by lying in their arrest report (see Manning 1997; Meehan 1986). The absence of a call leaves it to the discretion of the police whether or not to log it in. Responses to calls, on the other hand, must be logged in because the police organization is accountable to the caller.

Thus, this incident, which involved considerable time and interaction between police and juveniles, and was far more serious than other calls labeled as gang calls, was preserved "for the record" elsewhere (i.e., on FIO cards) but not entered on the log.[17] Therefore, it did not generate a "gang" statistic, even though the activities of these youths (who, according to the police, each had "records" and were in a group) represent, in the officer's view, the closest approximation to serious criminal activity observed during that evening.

Conclusion

The police are responsive to the political and organizational contexts that selected "gangs" as a problem for the community. Certainly, the people of Corktown, as well as Bigcity, had their share of problems with young people who hang out on corners, make noise, drink, harass neighbors, and engage in some criminal activity. "Gangs" are real and not themselves an artifact of organizational recordkeeping practices. On the other hand, activities by groups that the police considered to be "real gangs" did not constitute a significant proportion of the incidents handled by the gang car that resulted, nonetheless, in official "gang" statistics. Treating these gang statistics as reflecting actual gang activity reifies gangs to the point where a fiction *is* created: "gangs" and their activities are the primary source of trouble for the community that the political organization can "solve." Indeed, it is *this* fiction that the recordkeeping practices can effectively create and manage. In this sense, the popularized conception of the gang problem is a complex artifact; it is the consequence of increasing police attention to the activities of young people in the community and of shifting definitions and perceptions of gangs in the community. As such, the "gang" problem can only be examined through the various interactional and recordkeeping practices that create this version of reality.

In Plantville in 1999, the development of this process continues. The identification of gangs as an important problem facing the city, and specifically using the term "gangs" as a frame for the city's problem with its young people, shapes political discourse and organizational action. One officer observed:

> Hey if you're the mayor of Plantville and you say hey we're gonna get a group of six–eight guys together and we're gonna handle these youth problems, that ain't shit. But you say gangs, everybody looks and goes, "Gangs! What the hell, we got gangs in Plantville. Now we're dedicating six officers to a gang problem? We got a gang problem!" If you say that we're gonna do a youth intervention program, nobody gives a shit. Because it's not politically correct. Politically correct is to say, "We got a gang problem and we got six guys on it." And that's how it is. (Plantville Focus Group, February 4, 1998)

This officer's comments capture the sort of moral panic (McCorkle and Miethe 1998) that can be created by framing troubles with young people as gang problems. Using the term "gang" has an important symbolic meaning and conveys a sense of threat and urgency to the community. The community perceives that the threat posed by gangs requires drastic action of the sort not captured by "youth intervention programs." It is precisely this meaning of "gangs" that is used to justify the creation of gang units. Some have observed that the initial response to claims of gang activity is often denial, in large part due to the negative public relations impact such an admission might generate (Klein 1995, p. 87). However, in both Bigcity and Plantville, the gang issue provided a convenient political opportunity sufficient to overcome such considerations.

The connection between the gang problem, the gang unit, and winning votes is not lost on police officers in Plantville either. One officer commented (while his fellow officers nodded their heads in agreement and chuckled throughout):

> He's [the mayor] a year and a half away from getting reelected. Most likely he's gonna be reelected, but he sure has to score points. He says, "I gotta gang unit, I live on the east side, I gotta gang unit over there and they are taking care of problems." If he said, "Hey we've put six officers for youth intervention," people would look at him like, "What are they crazy, they aren't doing nothing. Youth intervention, what are they gonna do with that?" But you say, "I got a gang squad. Man, that's politically correct." (Plantville Focus Group, February 4, 1998)

As Plantville's newly formed "gang unit" approaches its task of responding to gangs in the community, no doubt there will be a need for constructing a corresponding documentary reality to satisfy the politicians and the department's brass that the "gang" problem not only exists, but that the police have it under control.

One important implication of police recordkeeping practices is that research measuring the extent of the gang problem, while relying upon police estimates of the number of gangs, or on records generated by patrol and specialized gang units, without understanding how such records are generated and what their internal uses are, is problematic. It is critical to examine how these organizational efforts are affected by the political process that uses the "gang problem." The consequences of the gang label can be serious for individuals who find their names in gang databases, as legislators are stiffening penalties for offenses that are deemed "gang related" or committed by "known" gang members (Spergel 1995; Klein 1996). Currently, gang intelligence databases are being generated and shared by criminal justice officials on local, regional, and national levels (Klein 1995; Spergel 1995; U.S.BJA 1997). Malcolm Klein (1995, p. 189) notes that, while such increased information sharing has increased police cohesiveness, it may just be "disseminating, reifying and distorting the general image of street gangs."

In addition, the proliferation of gang databases has the consequence of labeling individuals as gang members who do not meet specified criteria. Klein (1995, p. 193) observes, "We stand, it seems on the threshold of a national gang roster system . . . without anything approaching an evaluation of its utility to enforcement or its endangerment of civil liberties. Even careful assessment of system errors—false positives and negatives—has yet to be undertaken." No matter how strict the definitional criteria for inclusion in these databases are, it is how these criteria are actually applied that is at issue. As one officer from New York commented, "I don't really have any great problem with the definition, how we are going to use it is another story" (Spergel and Bobrowski 1989, p. 51).

The recordkeeping practices of the police easily accommodate and manage the various political and organizational pressures brought to bear upon them. The management of documentary reality is an important competency and resource for any individual who is accountable to a bureaucracy. Social scientists tend to ignore this process and often approach the matter of their use of official statistics and police records with a "caveat emptor" warning to readers that a certain amount of "measurement error" is attributable to organizational processes. But this is not enough. It is not solely an issue of measurement error but rather that organizational features of policing, and other organizations, which can change from year to year, determine the incident count and records from which those statistics are derived. Social science research must focus on those interactional and recordkeeping processes that constitute the careers of organizational statistics rather than treat statistics as standing in a correspondence relationship to the incidents they purport to represent.

Research is needed that focuses on the process through which statistics are generated. This entails a multilevel approach to the social construction of statistics that would examine the various levels of organizational practices and the corresponding member's competencies, which together result in the statistic. Statistics generated by organizational personnel, for their own "good" organizational reasons (Garfinkel 1967), should never be treated as an indicator of events as they would appear to an observer. This means they are not intended as an interpretation of events. They are intended to represent organizational work as rational and orderly. Consequently, they are a direct indicator of the organization's priorities, that is, of its context of accountability and how its members orient to and develop competencies to produce "facts" that are relevant within this context.

Acknowledgments

I would like to thank the anonymous *TSQ* reviewers and Norman Denzin, editor, for their helpful comments. Harold Garfinkel, Doug Maynard, and Peter Manning read this article in various drafts, and I have benefitted from their suggestions and encouragement. I also thank the Department of Sociology and Anthropology Faculty Workshop, organized by David Maines, for their comments and support. Finally, I owe my deepest gratitude to Anne

Warfield Rawls, my staunchest critic, editor, and supporter, whose guidance has been immeasurable and persistence endless despite my shortcomings.

Notes

1. Plantville is a Midwestern city with a population of 170,000. Its police force is comprised of 265 officers. I have been conducting field research in this department for four years (1996–1999), studying how the organization utilizes information technologies. My research includes extensive ride-alongs with patrol officers (two hundred hours), twenty-five formal interviews with all levels of the command staff and specialized units (e.g., detective bureau, internal affairs, community policing unit), focus groups drawing upon officers from different units as well as a specialized community policing unit, and analysis of department records (e.g., calls for service data in computer-aided dispatch). Plantville's emerging construction of its gang problem and response are similar to what I observed in Bigcity and report on in this article. I juxtapose relevant data from Plantville to illustrate the similar underlying political and organizational processes involved in the social construction of a gang problem.

2. Even within a given department, reaching agreement about the criteria used to define a gang in practice can be problematic. This is illustrated by the following exchange among officers in a focus group discussion of various problems (including troubled youths/gangs) that the Plantville police face on the east side, a high crime area:

Gang Unit Officer: Throughout the country there is no set criteria, no set definition of what a gang is. [Referring to officers around the table] He's got a different definition than he does and he does and he does. So you ask all of us and we'll all give different reasons. "He's not a gang banger he's just a troubled kid. But yeah here's a gang banger because you know he looks like he's from LA." There's different reasons for that throughout the department

Patrol Officer 1: I don't view most of them as gangs. If you go by his [the gang unit officer's] criteria, the whole east side is a gang.

Patrol Officer 2: [to gang officer] All you're doing is labeling. (Plantville Focus Group, February 4, 1998)

As this discussion illustrates, the conflict between definition and practice is not easily resolved. The patrol officers disagree with the gang unit officer's criteria for applying the term "gang." Accounting for these differences is beyond the scope of the present article. However, it is important to consider that gang unit officers receive specialized "gang" training at regional seminars and return to their departments armed with new beliefs about gangs, including issues such as the problem of definition, which is nicely articulated in the above exchange. The skepticism of their fellow officers does not deter them. In fact, gang unit officers are told that "denial" is the typical response of the community (and fellow officers) when gangs first make their presence felt in communities. As one ranking officer observed, there is definitely a "true believer quality to the gang squad members" that suggests a sort of conversion process at work in transforming them to the view that "gangs" are an important threat to communities. As Klein (1995) notes, one of the consequences of gang training for law enforcement has been to increase their group cohesion.

3. The use of official agency statistics for doing social science research has been the subject of considerable discussion (Merton 1957; Kitsuse and Cicourel 1963; Skogan 1975; McCleary, Nienstedt, and Erven 1982). Yet there are few studies of the actual practices for producing the records from which those statistics are derived. Specifically, how an interactional event is reduced to some written form, whether that form is an extended report, or as in the case of calls for service, a simple category designation such as "gang," raises important issues. For example, the transformation of some "interactional" fact into a written format presupposes a "correct" correspondence between the two. However, the initial problem posed by such a process is achieving the interactional "facticity" of an event in the first place. Thus, analyzing the interactions which constitute the organizational career of a record from which statistics are derived is essential.

4. Combining these seventy-three calls with the thirteen calls from the two shifts I discuss in the article, a total of eighty-six gang calls were collected. Locating the actual calls on stored tapes was a very tedious, time-consuming process as the calls are not stored by district but by their time of occurrence. A technician assisted me over two full days. I am grateful to command staff who generously aided me in this process.

5. I also spent time in the gang car on four other evenings (eight shifts) and, in terms of type of calls and police response, the evening analyzed in this article was representative of these other gang car shifts I observed. The research project during which these data were collected spanned a two-year period and required considerable time in the field (on average, one to two days a week). I also conducted other ride-alongs and semistructured interviews with patrol officers, youth officer detectives, and command staff officers in the district. These data were gathered as part of a policy-making project on the police handling of juveniles in two urban police departments. As one of three sociologists and two lawyers who worked full time on the project, I was primarily responsible for coordinating research on the police. This included collecting and analyzing police and court records, conducting surveys of the police and citizenry, coordinating ride-alongs for project staff, attending community meetings, and working closely with a police and citizen task force on the development of policies related to the police handling of juveniles.

6. This claim is supported by the following data. All patrol officers' logs from Corktown for a two-month period were examined to see what types of activities and problems officers encountered on patrol. A winter month (December) and a summer month (June) were selected to observe seasonal variation. For this sixty-one-day period, officers' log entries for all three shifts per day totaled 3,079, with June (1,664 entries) a slightly more active month than December (1,415 entries). In June, patrol officers' responses to gangs and groups ranked first, constituting 23 percent of all activities listed in their logs. This was followed by patrol and area checks (15.2 percent) and traffic offenses (10.7 percent). During December, traffic ranked first (20.7 percent), patrol and area checks were second (19.3 percent), and gangs and groups ranked third (14.0 percent) despite the cold weather. In addition, thirty-nine of the sixty patrol officers in the Corktown district also completed a questionnaire that asked them to rate the seriousness and troublesomeness of juvenile-related problems in the district. Police officers rank-ordered street gangs second in terms of seriousness (surpassed only by auto theft) and first in terms of troublesomeness. Clearly, from data gathered from official sources (patrol logs) as well as the questionnaire, street gangs and groups were considered a significant problem in Corktown. A questionnaire similar to the one for patrol officers was distributed to a group of Corktown teenagers. While they reported hanging out in groups on street corners with high frequency, they rated this problem as one of the least serious (ranked 29). Thus, for police, street gangs and groups were a serious and troublesome problem although more as a nuisance than a crime problem, whereas for teenagers they were not.

7. When the gang category was analyzed by looking at how *responding officers* categorize the problem *after* their response, gang calls represented 8.7 percent ($N = 278{,}135$) of all calls, a 2.3 percent difference. When compared with other categories, gang calls still ranked third, preceded only by "services rendered" (29.6 percent) and "investigation" (21.2 percent). *More calls are subsequently recategorized as a gang problem by the responding officers* than are initially dispatched as gang calls. The following list identifies the initially reported problems and the percentage from each category that are recategorized as "gang" problems by responding officers: disturbances (22.1 percent), fights (21.5 percent), public nuisance (12.8 percent), argument (12.1 percent), crime in progress (10.3 percent) and loud party (8.8 percent). If officers use the category to gloss the range of problems they confront on the streets, this expands the use of the term "gang" to cover many problems having nothing to do with gangs. This analysis suggests that the "gang" designation is a label that officers often find useful and at times politically advantageous. Thus, the resulting gang statistics generated by the police in this sort of political and organizational environment report a much higher rate of problems caused by gangs than the police actually assess as gang problems during the encounter.

8. In one letter to the editor of a Bigcity newspaper, a youth complained that the gang units were indiscriminately moving groups of people even when they were doing nothing wrong. Some Corktown residents reported in community meetings that the citywide gang units were just brooming everybody, even though the Corktown gang car passed by and said nothing in many cases. My observations in the field confirmed this view as well. Some Corktown officers complained that they were taking a lot of the heat for the actions of these other officers

who did not "know who the good kids are." In newspaper reports of the effectiveness of the "gang patrols," however, no distinction was made between the activities of the Corktown unit and the citywide unit.

9. These data lend support to the election year interpretation and they also raise some other interesting issues that cannot be fully addressed here. First, it is clear that responding officers were categorizing more calls into gang calls than the police operators or dispatchers over the total six-year period, although the differential between operators' categorizations and officers' categorizations is smaller for each successive year. The first year of data represented in Table 1 was also the first full year after the department employed civilian operators and the computer-aided dispatch system was installed. The convergence of categorization between operator and officer over the six-year period may reflect this adjustment to some degree. Second, although calls classified by the operators as gang problems also increased for the two years prior to the election year, these two years also coincide with the use of "drinking cars" by district captains to control rowdy youth behavior and drinking (noted earlier). Thus, the gang category was in all likelihood a global, catchall category for both operators and officers. However, it did not have the same significance for purposes of public-political discourse until the election year. The dramatic decline in the number of gang calls in the subsequent years illustrates the malleability of the category and the importance of the categorization process.

10. In Bigcity, the 911 emergency number handles between 500,000 and 600,000 calls per year; an average of about 1,600 calls on any given day (in a twenty-four-hour period). The 911 emergency number receives calls from all parts of the city. Thus, there is no special operator for a particular section of the city, such as Corktown. Each call is automatically routed into a queuing system and the call is handled on a "first-come-first-served" basis by the next available operator. The police telephone operators in Bigcity are trained civilians, whereas the dispatchers are sworn officers. All transcription symbols are taken from the transcription system developed by Jefferson (in Schenkein 1978). All references to individuals and places have been changed to preserve the anonymity of speakers.

11. The argument is not citizens use the category "gang" in a naïve or incorrect manner. Rather, the point is that there is a utility to the use of the category. Police operators formulate the caller's problem into a category that reflects organizational utility and priorities. Through this process, callers learn that certain categories are more useful than others in generating a police response.

12. One reviewer requestioned the significance of calling attention to various department log-keeping "practices" given the fact that "everyone including supervisors knows that they are actually estimations." My point is that the relationship between practice and recordwork is not a relationship of correspondence, whether imprecise or otherwise. The log is a very complex, patterned social construction, not an estimation. The police have a vested interest in constructing a record that displays their organizational accountability. Further, when statistics derived from those records are utilized to define a problem without an understanding of and appreciation for this accountability, the claims based upon those "facts" are further distortions. The fact that any competent member of a police organization "knows" this suggests that when they utilize data like these in the public arena to defend police actions or to solicit additional funding for personnel, equipment, and budgets to staff programs like "gang" cars, their uses are politically motivated.

13. From an organizational standpoint, the logs should indicate all calls that officers respond to as well as other activities performed during the shift (e.g., on-view encounters, traffic stops, etc.). Elsewhere, I argue that these types of records have important actuarial uses within the organization, for purposes of accountability, and are therefore subject to considerable manipulation by patrol officers. This is one reason why the logs are often called the "cheat sheets" or "my lies" (Meehan 1986). This article, however, illustrates in detail, just how these logs are managed by officers and their role in keeping the visibility of gangs prominent for the record. I have only reproduced the logs and log codes used for this one evening (the log code sheet is quite extensive, with numerous codes). The logs are not corrected for spelling errors.

14. On the other thirty-four shifts, 7-Paul was the disposition code in 75 percent ($N = 77$) of the calls. This differs from the two shifts I observed where 7-Paul was used for only 46 percent ($N = 6$) of the calls. On the other thirty-four shifts, the 7-Boy code (gathering causing annoyance–no person can be found) was used in only 8 percent ($N = 8$) of all calls, while on my two shifts 7-Boy was used 23 percent ($N = 4$) of the time. Three other codes also showed differences. For the other thirty-four shifts, the 8-Paul code (investigate persons–services ren-

dered) was used in only 2 percent of all calls ($N = 2$) and the 12-Paul (loud music–services rendered) and 9-Charles (investigate persons–no such address) were not used at all. During the two shifts discussed here, these designations appeared four times. This suggests that the presence of a researcher in the car prompted the officers to use their codes more carefully. In all likelihood, my presence in the car made them more conscious of their work (including paperwork) and instead of using 7-P for all sorts of calls, they used other appropriate designations. So we need to consider that what was observed was a "good" recordkeeping performance.

15. In this example, the officers do not report their arrival on the scene to dispatch, which is required of all patrol cars responding to calls. This omission is recognized and discussed by the officers after the work of responding to the call has begun and their course of action has already been decided. When the officer finally does contact dispatch, he provides the disposition (7-Paul), for the call upon which the failure to log on is raised by the dispatcher. The two omissions (i.e., logging on and reporting arrival to the call) have already been a topic in the car *prior* to contacting dispatch. Thus, we can see how both the officers and the dispatcher orient to organizational accountability and actually produce it. But this orientation is of secondary importance to the in situ work of policing the streets.

16. This entry was the *only* use of this code (12-Paul) not only in this evening's log but also in the thirty-four other gang car logs. Indeed, the disposition code here is not 7-Paul, which as will be shown later, is used in the other music calls (examples 3 and 4 in the text). The primary difference between this call and these other music calls is that at the other calls the presence of juveniles, or teenagers, was observed. When adults are observed doing the same thing, the designation is different.

17. FIO records are discussed in a separate article (Meehan 1992). It is important to note here, however, that retaining this type of information on an FIO form indicates the officer's assessment of the situation as "more serious," because FIOs are considered more useful as internal records, particularly for intelligence or surveillance purposes, whereas the patrol logs are viewed more as "administrative tools," to force officers to account for their time spent in the field. Thus, the officer's recordkeeping here is quite consistent with their action of not making this an on-view log entry but preserving the information elsewhere in a more useful form. While the officer writes in their last entry *"Station (5 FIOs)"* at the end of the shift, this is not linked to any particular log entry, because no entry has been made for this incident.

References

Alexander, Jeffrey, Bernhard Geisen, Richard Munch, and Neil Smelser, eds. 1987. *The Micro-Macro Link.* Berkeley: University of California Press.

Best, Joel. 1995. Images of Issues: *Typifying Contemporary Social Problems.* New York: Aldinede Gruyter

Bowditch, Christine. 1993. "Getting Rid of Troublemakers: High School Disciplinary Procedures and the Production of Dropouts." *Social Problems.* 40(4): 493–509.

Chambliss, William J. 1994. "Policing the Ghetto Underclass: The Politics of Law and Law Enforcement." *Social Problems,* 41:177–195.

Collins, Randall. 1981. "The Microfoundations of Macrosociology." *American Journal of Sociology,* 86:984–1014.

———. 1987. "Interaction Ritual Chains, Power and Property: The Micro-Macro Connection as an Empirically Based Theoretical Problem." Pp. 193–206 in *The Micro-Macro Link,* edited by Alexander, Geisen, Munch, and Smelser.

Curry, G. David, Richard A. Ball, and Scott H. Decker. 1996. "Estimating the National Scope of Gang Crime from Law Enforcement Data." Pp. 21–38 in *Gangs in America,* edited by Huff.

Decker, Scott, and Kimberly Kempf-Leonard. 1991. "Constructing Gangs: The Social Definition of Youth Activities." *Criminal Justice Policy Review* 5(4):271–291.

Emerson, Robert. 1991. "Case Processing and Interorganizational Knowledge: Detecting the 'Real Reasons' for Referrals." *Social Problems* 38:198–212.

Fagan, Jeffrey. 1996. "Gangs, Drugs and Neighborhood Change." Pp. 39–74 in *Gangs in America*, edited by Huff.

Fine, Gary Alan. 1991. "On the Macrofoundations of Microsociology: Constraint and the Exterior Reality of Structure." *The Sociological Quarterly* 32:161–177.

Fogelson, Robert. 1977. *Big City Police*. Cambridge, MA: Harvard University Press.

Garfinkel, Harold. 1967. *Studies in Ethnomethodology*. Englewood Cliffs, NJ: Prentice-Hall.

Gill, Virginia, and Douglas Maynard. 1995. "On Labeling in Actual Interaction: Delivering and Receiving Diagnoses of Developmental Disabilities." *Social Problems* 42(1):11–37.

Huff. C. Ronald, ed. 1996. *Gangs in America*. 2nd ed. Thousand Oaks, CA: Sage.

Kitsuse, John, and Aaron Cicourel. 1963. "A Note on the Use of Official Statistics." *Social Problems* 11:131–139.

Klein, Malcolm. 1995. *The American Street Gang*. New York: Oxford University Press.

———. 1996. "Street Gangs and Deterrence Legislation." Pp. 203–321 in *Three Strikes and You're Out: Vengeance as Public Policy*, edited by David Shichor and Dale Sechrist. Thousand Oaks, CA: Sage.

Lundman, Richard. 1980. *Policing: An Introduction*. New York: Holt, Reinhart, and Winston.

Manning, Peter K. 1988. *Symbolic Communication: Signifying Calls and the Police Response*. Cambridge, MA: MIT Press.

———. 1992. "Technological Dramas and the Police: Statement and Counterstatement in Organizational Analysis." *Criminology* 30:327–346.

———. 1997. *Police Work: The Social Organization of Policing*. 2nd ed. Prospect Heights. IL: Westview Press.

Margolin, Leslie. 1992. "Deviance on Record: Techniques for Labeling Child Abusers in Official Documents." *Social Problems* 39:58–70.

Maxfield, Michael, D. Lewis, and Ron Szoc. 1980. "Producing Official Crimes: Verified Crime Reports as Measures of Police Output." *Social Science Quarterly* 61:221–236.

Maxson, Cheryl, and Malcolm Klein. 1996. "Defining Gang Homicide: An Updated Look at Member Versus Motive Approaches." Pp. 3–20 in *Gangs in America*, edited by Huff.

Maynard, Douglas W. 1988. "Language, Interaction and Social Problems." *Social Problems* 35:311–334.

McCleary, Richard. 1977. "How Parole Officers Use Records." *Social Problems* 24:576–589.

McCleary, Richard, Barbara C. Nienstedt, and James M. Erven. 1982. "Uniform Crime Reports as Organizational Outcomes: Three Time Series Experiments." *Social Problems* 29:361–372.

McCorkle, Richard C., and Terance D. Miethe. 1998. "The Political and Organizational Response to Gangs: An Examination of a 'Moral Panic' in Nevada." *Justice Quarterly* 15(1):50–64.

Meehan, Albert J. 1986. "Recordkeeping Practices in the Policing of Juveniles." *Urban Life* 15(1):70–102.

———. 1989. "Assessing the Police Worthiness of a Citizen's Call to the Police: Accountability and the Negotiation of 'Facts.'" Pp. 116–40 in *The Interactional Order: New Directions in the Study of Social Order*, edited by D. Helm, T. Anderson, A. J. Meehan, and A. W. Rawls. New York: Irvington Press.

———. 1992. "'I Don't Prevent Crime, I Prevent Calls': Policing as Negotiated Order." *Symbolic Interaction* 15:455–80.

———. 1993. "Internal Police Records and the Control of Juveniles: Politics and Policing in a Suburban Town." *British Journal of Criminology* 33:504–524.

Merton, Robert. 1957. *Social Theory and Social Structure*. Glencoe, IL: Free Press.

Mills, C. Wright. 1940. "Situated Action and Vocabularies of Motives." *American Journal of Sociology* 5:315–357.

Padilla, Felix. 1992. *The Gang as an American Enterprise*. New Brunswick, NJ: Rutgers University Press.

Rawls, Anne. 1987. "The Interaction Order Sui Generis: Goffman's Contribution to Social Theory." *Sociological Theory* 5(2):136–149.

Reiss, Albert. 1971. *The Police and the Public*. New Haven, CT: Yale University Press.

Rubenstein, Jonathan. 1973. *City Police*. New York: Farrar, Strauss and Giroux.

Sacks, Harvey. 1972. "An Initial Investigation of the Usability of Conversational Data for Doing Sociology." Pp. 31–74 in *Studies in Social Interaction*, edited by David Sudnow. New York: Free Press.

Sacks, Harvey, and Emmanuel Jefferson Schegloff. 1974. "A Simplest Systematics for the Organization of Turn-Taking in Conversation." *Language* 50(4):696–735.

Sanchez-Jankowski, Martin. 1991. *Islands in the Street: Gangs in American Urban Society*. Stanford, CA: Stanford University Press.

Sasson, Theodore. 1995. *Crime Talk: How Citizens Construct a Social Problem*. Hawthorne, NY: Aldine de Gruyter.

Schegloff, Emanuel. 1987. "Between Micro and Macro: Contexts and Other Connections." Pp. 207–34 in *The Micro-Macro Link*, edited by Alexander, Geisen, Munch, and Smelser. University of California Press.

Schenkein, James. 1978. *Studies in the Organization of Conversational Interaction*. New York: Academic Press.

Seidman, Darryl, and Michael Couzens. 1974. "Getting the Crime Rate Down: Political Pressure and Crime Reporting." *Law and Society Review* 8:457–493.

Short, James. 1996. "Preface." Pp. 21–38 in *Gangs in America*, edited by Huff.

———. 1997. *Poverty, Ethnicity and Violent Crime*. Boulder, CO: Westview Press.

Skogan, Wesley. 1975. "Measurement Problems in Official and Survey Crime Rates." *Journal of Criminal Justice* 3:17–32.

Skolnick, Jerome H., Ricky Bluthenthal, and Theodore Correl. 1993. "Gang Organization and Migration." Pp. 193–218 in *Gangs: The Origins and Impact of Contemporary Youth Gangs in the United States*, edited by Scott Cummings and Daniel Monti. Albany, NY: State University of New York Press.

Smith, Dorothy. 1974. "The Social Construction of Documentary Reality." *Sociological Inquiry* 44:257–268.

Spector, Malcolm, and John Kitsuse. 1977. *Constructing Social Problems*. Menlo Park, CA: Cummings Publishing Company.

Spergel, Irving A. 1994. *Gang Suppression and Intervention: Problem and Response. Research Summary*. Washington, DC: Office of Juvenile Justice and Delinquency Prevention.

———. 1995. *The Youth Gang Problem: A Community Approach*. New York: Oxford University Press.

Spergel, Irving A., and Lawrence Bobrowski. 1989. "Law Enforcement Definitional Conference" (Transcript). Rockville, MD: Juvenile Justice Clearinghouse. http://www.ncjrs.org.txtfiles/ d0030.txt

Taylor, Carl. 1990. *Dangerous Society*. East Lansing: Michigan State University Press.

U.S. Bureau of Justice Assistance (U.S.BJA). 1997. *Urban Street Gang Enforcement*. Washington, DC.

U.S. Senate. 1997. *Gangs: A National Crisis. Hearing Before the Committee on the Judiciary*. 105th Cong. Washington, DC: GPO.

Wheeler, Stanton. 1969. *On Record: Files and Dossiers in American Life*. New York: Russell Sage Foundation.

Zatz, M. 1987. "Chicago Youth Gangs and Crime: The Creation of a Moral Panic." *Contemporary Crises* 11:129–158.

30 Trial by Fire: Media Constructions of Corporate Deviance

Gray Cavender
Aogan Mulcahy

In recent years, criminologists have revitalized their interest in corporate crime and deviance. Their research has revealed much about the frequency and seriousness of corporate crime (Clinard and Yeager 1980; Tonry and Reiss 1993). Even so, researchers still face a conundrum: Although the public is more critical of corporate crime and deviance than is often assumed to be the case (Cullen, Maakestad, and Calender 1987), these are still matters of low salience in public discourse. The outrage that characterizes public concern about crime rarely involves any strong condemnation of corporate wrongdoing. Two obvious questions are "Why?" and "What could be done to remedy this?"

One answer to "Why?" is that the public tends not to condemn corporate crime because the media devote little attention to it. Certainly this answer is partially correct. Crime news, a significant portion of news coverage, focuses on crime in the streets, not crime in the suites (Evans and Lundman 1983).

Nevertheless, corporate crime receives more coverage now than in the past, especially if physical harm is involved (Chermak 1994; Evans, Cullen, and Dubeck 1993; Wright, Cullen, and Blankenship 1995). The rise in investigative reporting, advocacy groups that monitor business, and the need of the media to maintain legitimacy may explain the increased coverage of corporations (Tumber 1993). In any case, it is unlikely that the small amount of media attention, in itself, explains the public's indifference to corporate deviance.

According to a second explanation, some crimes are more newsworthy than others. Reporters claim that corporate deviance is less interesting to the public than is street crime. Yet stories are not inherently newsworthy. As reporters construct stories, they rely on news frames, which are selection principles that determine what they report and how they report it (Tuchman 1978).

News frames are tacit theories "about what exists, what happens, and what matters" (Gitlin 1980:6). They are influenced by the routines of news organizations, by previous frames, and by ideology (Tuchman 1978). News frames affect the agenda of public discourse: Which stories are reported and how they are reported influence the problems we consider and the solutions we contemplate. They are a part of what Bennett and Ferrell (1987) call "epistemic socialization," a process that relates what we know to how we know. The news frames used to report events reflect, reinforce, and shape the very categories we use to make sense of the world, and through which we identify matters worthy of policy interventions. Our knowledge about crime is a part of our general belief system, which is informed by the media (Savelsberg 1994:923, 929). Thus the salience of crime of whatever variety—indeed, the very meaning of crime—is influenced by the frame of coverage for crime news.

Responses to the second question—"What could be done to remedy this?"—also center on the media. The media are now part of the process of social control. Television programs such as *America's Most Wanted* mobilize the public to help police. The media also may be relevant to corporate deviance: Scholars advocate the use of publicity and other "shaming" techniques to fight such deviance. The need for a positive advertising image may make the threat of bad publicity an effective sanction for corporations (Braithwaite 1989, 1993; Fisse and Braithwaite 1983).

Although closer regulation of corporate conduct is a laudable goal, its achievement through the threat of negative media coverage is largely unvested. Fisse and Braithwaite's study, though encouraging, is more suggestive than definitive, and recent research does not address the role of the media (Makaii and Braithwaite 1994). A conceptual model of crime coverage is needed, as well as case studies that address media coverage of corporate wrongdoing.

Here we develop a conceptual model of crime news frames, and use it to analyze two cases of newspaper coverage: (1) a regulatory investigation and a dramatic trial involving General Motors (GM) pickup trucks, and (2) a National Broadcasting Company (NBC) television program about the trucks. We examine how the papers covered these events, and address the potential of the coverage to act as a negative sanction. First, however, we discuss the importance of the crime news frame and describe our conceptual model.

The Crime News Frame

News frames inform news stories and journalists' conceptions of newsworthiness (Tuchman 1978). Journalists share working assumptions about what is newsworthy: Stories should be dramatic and sensational, should focus on notable individuals, and should feature conflict, even wrongdoing

(Ericson, Baranek, and Chan 1989:284). Although stories about corporate wrongdoing meet some of these criteria, such matters usually are not considered newsworthy. They are morally ambiguous in terms of crime, criminal, and victim; they unfold slowly; and they do not culminate in a clear resolution (Ericson et al. 1989). Crime news, in contrast, meets these criteria, especially when the events unfold as in a Hollywood movie (Chermak 1994; Surette 1998).

In their coverage of crime, journalists are informed by previous news frames (Tuchman 1978). We suggest that a standard frame for crime news has evolved in the media, and we have developed a conceptual model for that frame. The crime news frame consists of what we identify as its four recurring elements: the attribution of responsibility, the individualization of responsibility, the reaffirmation of moral boundaries, and the promotion of resolution. These elements also correspond to journalists' notions about the newsworthiness of crime stories.

First, crime news attributes responsibility for wrongdoing. Ericson et al. (1991) note that the news dwells on what is wrong, and assigns responsibility for that wrong. A claim that a law has been violated and that someone violated it is at the heart of the crime coverage (pp. 5–8). This emphasis generates stories about deviance and conflict, which make attribution more dramatic and stories more newsworthy. Because of its focus on "whodunit," crime news tends to blur the line between news and dramatic entertainment (Surette 1998:67–68).

Second, crime news attributes responsibility to individuals (Tumber 1993). Individual responsibility is an assumption of our legal system and of most socioeconomic relations in the United States. It is also at the core of most theories of crime and deviance (Ermann and Ludman 1996; Waegel, Ermann, and Horowitz 1981). Indeed, some scholars suggest that social audiences usually prefer to locate blame at the individual level, a penchant that is reinforced in the news media (Vaughan 1996:393). Individualization and personalization are dramatic techniques that make a story more newsworthy, especially if it involves high-status individuals (Ericson et al. 1991:6; Katz 1987:50–54).

Villains are a common theme in crime stories; they personify evil (Chermak 1994:74). Villains are blamed and denounced in coverage that resembles status degradation ceremonies (Garfinkel 1956). Such ceremonies tend to be public—courts are a frequent setting—and totalizing (Garfinkel 1956). The media may act as "deviance-smiths," heaping wrong upon wrong and making villainy a master status (Lofland 1969). The individualization of responsibility may allow organizations to make individuals the scapegoats responsible for organizational acts (Calender, Jurik, and Cohen 1993).

The media tendency to individualize responsibility produces heroes as well as villains. The media portray the police and some victims are heroes, people who occupy the high ground (Ericson et al. 1991). The focus of crime news on villains and heroes resembles crime fiction.

Third, crime news reaffirms moral boundaries by condemning their violation. Durkheim (1964) argues that crime and punishment reaffirm society's moral boundaries. Successful public denunciations restate the values that were violated (Garfinkel 1956:191). Crime news represents this order—society's moral boundaries. It is framed as mythic morality play that expresses the condemnation formerly displayed in public punishments. This condemnation is even more newsworthy when boundary violations threaten collective integrity or the public interest (Katz 1987). Indeed, Ericson et al. (1991:250) believe that a story's newsworthiness has more relation to the boundaries that were violated than to the harm caused by the violation.

Further, crime stories offer lessons about what is normal and what is deviant, and about which forms of deviance are acceptable and which are not. Crime stories also reinforce stereotypes about crime and criminals (Kappeler, Blumberg, and Potter 1996). By privileging the taken-for-granted nature of these categories as well as a preference for social stability, crime news (like crime fiction) states an ideological view (Barak 1995:13; Hall et al. 1978).

Finally, resolution is a part of the crime news frame. Coverage that assigns responsibility to criminals or deviants for violating moral boundaries equates the public interest with restoring order. In this regard, crime news resembles crime fiction (Best and Hutchinson 1996). Crime fiction ends in resolution: Good defeats evil in the denouement, resolving the tension of the plot and producing a sense of justice. Reporters, like fictional detectives, give a moral closure to their narratives (Campbell 1987): Resolution comes through the capture, punishment, or condemnation of the criminal. Resolution adds an ideological dimension to news coverage in that it highlights dominant definitions of order and authority, blames individuals rather than the social structure for social problems, and implies that the system works (Condit and Selzer 1985; Ericson et al. 1991:8–9; see Kappeler et al. 1996).

This standard frame fits stories about street crime more closely than accounts of corporate wrongdoing. Street crime is easily personalized and reduced to individual responsibility and harm. In corporate wrongdoing, however, harm and blame are diffuse and are not perceived as newsworthy. Therefore corporate deviance and regulation are covered less often or are reduced to their simplest dimension: The individual, not the organization, is blamed (Evans and Lundman 1983; Morash and Hale 1987).

The media tend to use the standard frame in the coverage of corporate wrongdoing. In the Ford Pinto case, for example, an analysis of coverage concluded that when Ford was unrepentant, the media blamed Ford, personalizing the harm and adopting a vocabulary of moral deviance (Swigert and Farrell 1980–1981). Even so, Fisse and Braithwaite (1983) believe that his negative publicity caused senior executives to improve safety features on Ford products. Such cases suggest that negative coverage may induce corporate compliance with regulations.

Shame is an important emotion in social relations and in social control (Scheff 1990). Although shame is associated with premodern societies, Braithwaite (1993) maintains that modern societies are susceptible to its capabilities for social control; shame was not "left behind on the farm." Postmodern societies may be even more responsive to shame, given the impact of the media in those societies and their shift toward culture-centered rather than state-centered formats and mechanisms of control (Foucault 1990; Harvey 1989).

Questions remain about the media, shame, and compliance. Corporations are sensitive to negative publicity but try to minimize its impact. They manage their public image through advertising and public relations; they try to control news stories about their activities, and attack their detractors (Braithwaite 1989; Ericson et al. 1989). They may hide wrongdoing behind the corporate veil, or may make individuals the scapegoats (Ermann and Lundmann 1996; Waegel et al. 1981). As a result, the adequacy of the media as a vehicle for shaming still must be explored in terms of corporate compliance.

Here we examine how the media report corporate wrongdoing. We analyze three newspapers—*The New York Times (NYT)*, *The Wall Street Journal (WSJ)*, and *The Washington Post (WP)*—in their coverage of GM pickup trucks and discuss an NBC *Dateline* program about the trucks. We focus on how the four elements of the crime news frame—attribution, individualization, moral boundaries, and resolutions—shaped the coverage of these events. The crime news frame, we suggest, influences the salience of corporate deviance and the potential success of strategies for controlling it. We describe the controversies surrounding the GM trucks, explain our methodology, and then present our analysis.

The Stories

In August 1992 the Center for Auto Safety (CAS), a consumers' group founded by Ralph Nader, requested a National Highway Traffic Safety Administration (NHTSA) investigation of GM pickup trucks made between 1973 and 1987. CAS claimed that the placement of the gas tank made the trucks vulnerable to fire in side-impact crashes, and that GM knew about the defect. GM responded that the trucks met safety standards when manufactured and were safe. Concurrently, in a civil trial in Atlanta, the plaintiffs claimed that their son had died in a wreck because his GM truck had burned. The jury awarded the plaintiffs $4.5 in compensatory damages and $101 million in punitive damages.

In November, NBC's news magazine Dateline presented a program titled "Waiting to Explode," in which auto experts claimed the the GM trucks were dangerous. The program featured a side-impact crash simulation in which a GM truck caught fire.

GM investigated the program and, only four days after the highly publicized Atlanta verdict, announced a lawsuit against NBC, charging that
Dateline had rigged the truck with incendiary devices. As settlement, NBC
paid GM $1 million, and *Dateline* hosts Jane Pauley and Stone Phillips apol-
ogized on the air. The network retained outside lawyers to investigate the
segment, and dismissed NBC News president Michael Gartner and three
Dateline executives.

GM, however, lost an appeal for a new trial and a reduction in damages
in the Atlanta case. When NHTSA requested that GM recall the trucks, GM
refused. In June 1994, GM successfully appealed the verdict; that case remains unresolved.

On October 17, 1994, Federico Peña, Secretary of the Department of
Transportation (DOT), announced the results of a federal investigation: GM
trucks were unsafe. GM had known about the danger but had put "sales
ahead of safety." On November 17 GM, claiming "immediate and unjusti-
fied harm" to its business and reputation, sued Secretary Peña, the DOT,
and the NHTSA. The NHTSA and GM announced a settlement on December 2, four days before scheduled public hearings on a government-
mandated recall. The investigation into the safety of GM pickup trucks
ended, and GM paid $51.4 million toward auto safety programs and
research.

On April 17, 1995, a U.S. federal appeals court overturned a class action
settlement in which GM had agreed to give each truck owner a $1,000
coupon toward the purchase of a new GM truck. The court criticized the
settlement as a "sophisticated marketing program" for GM. This and other
cases against GM are pending.

Methodology

We analyze coverage of the GM/NBC controversies that appeared in the
NYT, WSJ, and *WP.* These influential national daily newspapers share the
status of "newspaper of record." They are used frequently in research on
media coverage of corporate deviance (see Wright et al. 1995).

The data comprise all stories, op-ed columns, and editorials relating to
the GM/NBC controversies which appeared between August 1992 and June
1993. We chose this period for reasons related to research: CAS petitioned
NHTSA to recall the trucks in August 1992; GM refused NHTSA's request
to recall the trucks in June 1993.

We located stories by using the index of each paper. We made broad
searches under categories that covered appropriate substantive areas. For
GM-related stories, we searched categories such as "automobiles,: "road
safety," and "GM." For NBC-related stories, we looked under categories
such as "journalism," "television," and "NBC." This search yielded 97
items: 36 of these appeared in the *NYT,* 39 in the *WSJ,* and 22 in the WP.

Table 1   Number of Items, by Theme and Location in Each Paper

	NYT		WSJ		WP	
Topic	GM	NBC	GM	NBC	GM	NBC
Location						
Front page	3	5	1	3	3	4
Inside page	15	13	21	14	2	13
Subtotal	18	18	22	17	5	17
Total		36		39		22

We recorded quantitative dimensions for each story, including its major focus and its location in the newspaper. As measured by the number of stories and the prominence of their location, the NBC story was somewhat more newsworthy than the GM story (see Table 1). A total of 52 NBC-related stories appeared during our research period, compared with 45 GM stories. Similarly, 12 of 19 front-page stories that appeared in connection with the GM/NBC affair were related to NBC.

Our research is not intended to be a broad sampling or a quantitative analysis of coverage of the GM/NBC stories. Rather, we are comparing two cases of media coverage of corporate deviance. We adopt Orum, Feagin, and Sjoberg's definition of the case study as "an in-depth, multifaceted investigation, using qualitative research methods, of a single social phenomenon" (1991:2). These authors suggest that the case study, or a comparison of several cases, is especially apt for generating theory (1991:13) and for studying the "hows and whys of a problem" (Orum and Feagin 1991:121). The case study approach is appropriate in view of our efforts to develop a conceptual model for the crime news frame and to understand why media coverage of corporate deviance does not produce more public outrage about the phenomenon.

We are not concerned with public attitudes per se; we do not measure the impact of news coverage of these stories on public opinion about GM, NBC, or corporate deviance in general. We are interested in how the newspapers covered the two stories. Following Brown and Chiang (1993), we analyze two different, though interrelated, cause corporate deviance; these are not crimes in a strict sense, but they fall within the parameters of civil, administrative, and regulatory matters (p. 32). Again, a broad definition seems appropriate for case studies that address a new conceptual model. Our analysis should clarify how the media construct the issue of corporate wrongdoing, and whether (as some claim) such coverage might induce corporate compliance.

We present our qualitative analysis in two sections: GM stories and NBC stories. Although the initial NBC stories referred to GM, these references were made largely for background. NBC was the focus of the NBC stories. We begin our analysis with the GM stories, illustrating how the elements of the crime news frame shaped this coverage.

Analysis

The GM Story

At issue in this phase of the coverage were competing claims about the safety of the 1973-1987 GM pickup trucks. The stories that we analyzed employed the standard crime news frame in covering the NHTSA's investigation and the trial in Atlanta. The coverage attributed responsibility for wrongdoing, blamed individuals, depicted the controversy as a violation of moral boundaries, and favored a resolution to the controversy.

ATTRIBUTION OF RESPONSIBILITY The stories in our analysis offered a series of attributions and were rich with denunciations. A few stories blamed the NHTSA, lawyers, and the media, but most focused on GM during this phase of coverage. GM was not merely blamed but was roundly denounced.

The crux of the coverage was the debate about the safety of GM trucks. The stories noted that the NHTSA investigation was based on a CAS claim that GM's design made the trucks unsafe (*NYT,* 11-17-92, A1; *WSJ,* 11-17-92, A3). A story reported the claim that the trucks had "improperly positioned gas tanks that can rupture and burn" (*WP,* 12-8-92, B1); others featured issues of risk and safety (*WSJ,* 9-15-92, A6; *NYT,* 11-17-92, A1). The stories reported incidence claims and calls for action: CAS claimed that the faulty design had resulted in 100 deaths, and demanded that NHTSA investigate and recall the trucks (*WP,* 12-8-92, B1; *WSJ,* 9-15-92, A6).

The coverage reported GM's response. GM said that the trucks met federal standards when manufactured, and "staunchly denied" that they were unsafe (*WSJ,* 11-17-92, A3; *NYT,* 12-9-92, B9). GM criticized as "misleading" the data suggesting that the trucks were unsafe, characterized as "ad hoc" any reconsideration of NHTSA standards, and vowed to fight a recall effort (*NYT,* 11-17-93, A1).

Despite the coverage of GM's response, stories attributed responsibility to GM. Some stories were exercises in deviance-smithing; they expanded GM's responsibility beyond the trucks to include problems with previous products such as the Corvair and the X-Car (*WSJ,* 11-19-92, B1; *NYT,* 12-9-92, B9). GM's gas tank problem was compared to that of the infamous Ford Pinto (*NYT,* 11-17-92, A1). A discussion of the legal implications of a NHTSA investigation kept the focus of responsibility on GM. Although some reporters noted that an investigation did not mean that a recall was likely (*WP,* 2-8-92, B1), others stated that the legal standard of a "reasonable possibility" of a recall had been met (*WSJ,* 12-9-92, A3). The investigation signaled trouble for GM; the coverage addressed aspects of the trouble, including its impact on cases pending against GM (*WSJ,* 11-17-92, A3; *NYT,* 12-9-92, B9). One such case was the Atlanta trial.

Trials are an important venue for attributing responsibility and may serve as degradation ceremonies. The Atlanta trial was a showcase for blaming and denouncing GM. The coverage presented the plaintiff's claim that their son had been killed because his GM truck was unsafe and GM's defense that speed, not a design defect, had caused the death. The coverage, however, tended to focus legal blame on GM.

INDIVIDUALIZATION OF BLAME   Although the focus of responsibility was on the GM corporation, the coverage spotlighted individuals. That approach, by personalizing the coverage and dwelling on notables, made the stories more newsworthy. This was especially true in the Atlanta trial, where heroes and villains were news themes. The coverage depicted former GM safety engineer Robert Elwell as a hero; former GM CEO Robert Stempel figured as the villain.

Stempel's testimony on GM's behalf was newsworthy. As a former CEO he symbolized GM; indeed, one story noted that, to the jurors, Stempel "was GM" (*WSJ*, 2-5-93, A3,4). Stories covered his ouster from the company (*WSJ*, 11-17-92, A3,4) and his refusal to answer questions about why GM did not warn customers about the gas tank (*NYT*, 1-20-93, D4). A story suggested that Stempel faced negative publicity and economic fallout from the case (*NYT*, 2-5-93, A1). His refusal to respond and his personal economic troubles paralleled and personalized the case against GM.

Elwell figured as a hero. The coverage transformed a civil trial into a courtroom thriller with a dramatic, personalized focus. A headline read "Courtroom Battle Pits GM Against Former Engineer" (*NYT*, 1-19-93,D1). Elwell was depicted as a surprise witness who heightened the drama. He offered sensational testimony: GM had known as early as 1980 that the design posed a danger but did not correct it (*NYT*, 1-19-93, D1; 1-20-93, D4). GM cast Elwell as a "disgruntled employee" (*WSJ*, 11-19-92, B1, 10), but the newspapers hailed him as a hero. One story described him as a "white-haired man of 56 years with the stolid manner of an engineer" (*NYT*, 1-19-93, D1). Another described his outrage at GM for withholding results of crash tests (*NYT*, 1-19-93, D1,16).

Posttrial coverage also named heroes. Two stories, for example, reported interviews with a juror. He symbolized the jury as a body of decent citizens who criticized GM for allowing a dangerous situation to continue; he was angry that Stempel had denied the existence of a problem with the trucks (*NYT*, 2-5-93, A1,16; *WSJ*, 2-5-93, A3,4). A story featuring Ralph Nader recalled his denunciation of GM's Corvair (*WSJ*, 11-19-92, B1,10).

MORAL BOUNDARIES   The attribution of responsibility for GM went beyond legal issues. GM was blamed not only for a design defect but also for a moral failure that was related to knowledge of the defect, delay in repairing it, and refusal to inform the public. The newspapers framed their coverage with a series of paired juxtapositions: a consumers' group, the government, and a jury of citizens, all representing the public interest and all aligned against the recalcitrant GM. The pairing suggested that GM had violated the public's collective integrity.

GM's morally questionable behavior made the regulatory investigation more newsworthy. According to one headline, GM had known about the gas tank problems for years but had not changed the design until 1988 (*NYT,* 11-17-92, A1). The story reported that 300 persons (not 100, as claimed initially) had died because of the design and that 6 million of the trucks were still on the road (*NYT,* 11-17-92, A1).

The theme of moral wrongdoing figured in stories about data on GM crash tests. Reports that GM had given the data to NHTSA (*WSJ,* 11-17-92, A3) were followed by stories about discrepancies in the data (*NYT,* 12-19-92, A8). Stories noted GM's admission that the data were misleading (*WSJ,* 12-3-92, C20; *NYT,* 12-20-92, A20). One story reported that a "widely respected" insurance industry group had denounced GM because the data about the design danger were "clear-cut" (*NYT,* 12-5-92, A7).

GM's moral failure engulfed other aspects of its corporate situation as well. Throughout the NHTSA investigation and the Atlanta trial stories detailed the company's economic failures. GM had lost $10 billion over the past two years, and its market share had declined (*WSJ,* 2-5-93, A3). Other, sometimes unrelated stories situated nearby on the page—stories dealing with sluggish auto sales, layoffs, or plant closures at GM—portrayed GM as a company that had failed its employees and its shareholders ethically and financially (*WSJ,* 11-17-92, A3,6; 12-9-92, A3; 12-18-92, A3,4).

Trial stories emphasized GM's moral failure. According to one report, Robert Elwell "drew a chilling portrait of GM as a company that altered documents, conducted secret tests and ordered employees not to put criticism of its vehicles in writing" (*NYT,* 1-19-93, D1). In another story, Elwell "told the jury that the company had intentionally hidden its knowledge of a dangerous safety defect" (*NYT,* 2-5-93, A1,16).

The posttrial stories about the punitive damages award were moralistic. Jurors expressed indignation that GM had delayed repairs and was unrepentant. According to one story, the juror would have mitigated the punitive damages had GM admitted responsibility (*WSJ,* 2-5-93, A3,4). Another reported a juror's hope that the verdict would lead GM to "make it right," to recall the trucks (*NYT,* 2-5-93, A1,16). These moral denunciations were part of a resolution to the GM story.

RESOLUTION Whereas regulatory stories are less newsworthy because they lack resolution, crime news ends in resolution, even if it consists only of denunciations. The Atlanta trial included a resolution: The coverage focused on the verdict and the punitive damages. Stories were filled with denunciations of GM.

The jury's verdict was the resolution of a sensational court case. The verdict was reported not only as a decision that GM was negligent, but also as a determination that GM was responsible "for the death of a Georgia teen-ager" (*WP*, 2-5-93, A1; *NYT*, 2-5-93, A1). It was paired with similar verdicts: The *WSJ* and the *WP* viewed the punitive damages award as "reminiscent" of the Ford Pinto case (*WSJ*, 2-5-93, A3,4; *WP*, 2-5-93, A1,4,5).

The coverage of the large punitive damages award allowed jurors to ex-press outrage toward GM. One juror, who said that Stempel's testimony an-gered the jury, denounced GM for a "wanton and willful disregard of common sense" (*WSJ*, 2-5-93, A3,4). The stories repeatedly noted that the verdict came from a jury, an important indicator of public denunciation (*NYT*, 2-5-93, A1,16; *WSJ*, 2-5-93, A3,4; *WP*, 2-5-93, A1,4,5).

The coverage of the resolution in the Atlanta trial framed a broad in-dictment of GM. Stories contained speculations that the verdict might prompt a costly recall, hurt future GM truck sales, or lower resale values (*WSJ*, 2-5-93, A3; *NYT*, 2-5-93, A11,16; *WP*, 2-5-93, A1,4). They observed that after the verdict, GM stock prices declined and its credit rating was downgraded (*NYT*, 2-5-93, A1; *WSJ*, 2-5-93, A3).

The coverage during the NHTSA investigation and the Atlanta trial blamed GM. Using the vocabulary of moral deviance, stories denounced GM for violations of legal and moral boundaries which transgressed the public interest. The coverage of the trial also blamed Stempel, a notable fig-ure who personalized GM. The vedict served as a resolution to the trial sto-ries. In short, adherence to the elements of the crime news frame made the story newsworthy.

NBC Stories

The newspapers that we analyzed also employed the crime news frame in their coverage of NBC's *Dateline* program. The issues during this phase were NBC's journalistic failures and, by extension, those of all media. Tied to the failure of the media was the claim of an antibusiness climate. Once again, the coverage attributed responsibility, individualized blame, con-demned the violation of moral boundaries, and emphasized resolution.

ATTRIBUTION OF RESPONSIBILITY Initially the *Dateline* coverage re-ferred to the NHTSA investigation and the Atlanta trial (*NYT*, 2-7-93, 30; *WSJ*, 2-8-93, A4; *WP*, 2-7-93, A5). Stories described GM's anger at the Date-line piece, NBC's decision to "stand by it," and NBC's claim that GM was trying to divert attention from the Atlanta verdict (NYT, 2-8-93, D12; *WSJ*, 2-8-93, A4). The coverage changed when Harry Pearce, GM's vice-president and general counsel, claimed at a news conference Dateline had rigged a truck with incendiary devices (*NYT*, 2-9-93, B6; *WP*, 2-9-93, A1,8). The cov-erage blamed NBC.

The attribution of responsibility was straightforward: NBC paid money and apologized to GM. The attribution of responsibility in the stories, how-ever, had several dimensions.

A story noted that *Dateline* producers aired the crash simulation despite objections (*WP*, 2-28-93, A1,22). Stories featured NBC's admission of responsibility: A spokesperson called the simulation "a stupid mistake," and Jane Pauley, in her on-the-air apology, said it was "a bad idea from start to finish" (*WSJ*, 2-10-93, B1; 2-28-93, A1,22; *NYT*, 2-10-93, A1,16). A story blamed NBC for rigging the truck and for doing a bad job of it; it described a video in which firefighters were laughing at the pitful 15-second fire and, by extension, at NBC (*WSJ*, 2-9-93, A3,4).

The attribution of responsibility was a wide-ranging example of deviance-smithing. Stories cited other *NBC News* mistakes such as a report on an environmental disaster which used the wrong footage (*NYT*, 2-27-93, 47). *Dateline* was blamed for NBC's economic troubles. Stories described GM's decision to stop ads on *NBC News*. NBC lost no revenue—GM ads ran on other programs—but stories speculated that the action might hurt the news division's budget (*NYT*, 2-11-93, A1,21; *WP*, 2-11-93, A11). Other stories noted that NBC had failed to air a successful news magazine like *60 Minutes* or *20/20* until *Dateline*. *Dateline* had been a success prior to the GM fiasco (*WSJ*, 2-11-93, A17; *WP*, 2-28-93, A1,22). According to another story, NBC ranked third in network news (*WP*, 2-16-93, A13)

In part, GM caused NBC's problems. GM had planned a public relations campaign to counter adverse publicity from the Atlanta verdict, but that became unnecessary as soon as GM could blame NBC (*WSJ*, 2-8-93, A4; 2-11-93, A1). The coverage of GM was an exercise in "normal-smithing": GM was praised for clever investigative work and for mounting a "powerful offensive" and a "brilliant public relations coup" (*WSJ*, 2-9-93, A3,4; 2-11-93, A1).

INDIVIDUALIZATION   Although NBC as an organization was denounced, the coverage that vindicated GM and blamed NBC focused heavily on individuals such a producers who overrode reporter Michelle Gillen's objections to the crash simulation (*WP*, 2-28-93), A1,2). The stories mainly blamed NBC News president Michael Gartner, a notable figure who personalized and personified the story. One story noted that he lacked credentials in TV journalism (*NYT*, 3-3-93, A1,B11). The story detailed mistakes by Gartner such as removing popular *Today* co-host Jane Pauley. He had offended NBC affiliates and *NBC News* anchor Tom Brokaw (*NYT*, 3-3-93, A1,B11; *WP*, 3-3-93, A1, 12). He was described as "arrogant," "aloof," and an "outsider" (*NYT*, 3-3-93, A1,B11; *WP*, 3-3-93, A1,12; *WSJ*, 3-3-93, A1,12). Commentators said that Gartner was bad for journalism, and demanded his removal (*WSJ*, 2-11-93, A1,7; *WP*, 2-16-93, A13; *NYT*, 3-3-93, A1,B11).

The coverage vilified other individuals as well. Reporters Edward R. Murrow, Bob Woodward, and Carl Bernstein were blamed for leading journalism down the path to the *Dateline* episode (*WP*, 2-22-93, A15; 4-3-93, B1,2). Stories included denunciations about unnecessary lawsuits. Expert witnesses who testified against automakers were denounced as "hired witnesses" and essentially as liars (*WSJ*, 2-10-93, A14; 2-11-93, A1,7; *WP*, 2-28-93, C2).

In contrast, GM notables were depicted as heroes. Harry Pearce was described as building his case with the "relentlessness of the seasoned trial attorney" (*WSJ*, 2-11-93, A1,7). He was praised for his use of videotapes and photographs of the incendiary devices (*WSJ*, 2-9-93, A34). GM's CEO, John 'Jack" Smith, was depicted as the polar opposite of NBC's Gartner: Gartner was aloof, Smith was personable; NBC affiliates disliked Gartner, but even the autoworkers' union liked Smith; Gartner was a failure, while Smith and 'his crew of yuppie revolutionaries" had turned things around at GM (*WSJ*, 2-19-93, A1,7; *NYT* 3-3-93, A1,B11). Such coverage idealized individuals and depicted GM as morally superior to NBC.

MORAL BOUNDARIES The newspapers depicted NBC as a violator of moral boundaries. The moral dimension is similar to that in the first phase; here, however, *moral* also refers to journalistic standards, which are depicted as professional ethics that were violated by NBC. NBC and other news media were pitted against GM and the business community, which, by implication, represented the public interest.

The coverage created a dichotomy between moral and legal boundaries; it evidenced a double standard. Pearce denounced NBC in language that established a legal theme in the coverage (*WP*, 2-9-93, A1,8; 2-10-93, A1,15). Stories praised GM's lawyers but condemned NBC's lawyers as if they had violated moral boundaries. GM's lawyers "worked"; NBC's lawyers "plotted" (*WSJ*, 2-11-93, A1,7). Stories and op-ed columns characterized NBC's response to GM as bearing "the unmistakable fingerprints of lawyers" (*WP*, 2-16-93, A13; 2-22-93, A15). A blistering editorial accused NBC of "abdication to their lawyers" (NYT, 2-17-93, A18).

Pearce and others also used evocative, moralistic language, characterizing the *Dateline* program as a "blatant deception" and as "grossly unfair and irresponsible" (*NYT*, 2-9-93, B6; *WSJ*, 2-8-93, A4). Media and ethics scholars, journalists, pundits, and editorials denounced NBC for abandoning standards of objectivity, for being unethical, for lying (*NYT*, 2-14-93, E3; 2-17-93, A18; *WSJ*, 2-10-93, B1,8; *WP*, 2-10-93, A1,15).

NBC's moral and ethical lapse was embedded in a critique of TV news, which was denounced for sensationalism and for an obsession with ratings that had diluted standards of objectivity. TV reporters and producers blamed tabloid and reality-type programs (*NYT*, 2-14-93, E3; 2-17-93, A18; *WSJ*, 2-10-93, B1,8). Others charged that "advocacy journalism" had eroded objectivity (*WP*, 2-22-93, A15; 4-3-93, B1,2). Some critics bashed the media for bashing business; this coverage detailed wrongful media attacks on business (*NYT*, 2-15-93, D5; *WSJ*, 2-9-93, A16; 2-11-93, B1,7).

The charge of anti-business bias also figured in another condemnation: The media were said to be in league with consumer groups, plaintiffs, attorneys, and expert witnesses (*WSJ*, 2-7-93, A4; 2-9-93, A16; 4-7-93, B1,8).

When NHTSA asked GM to recall the trucks, a headline asked "Is U.S. Recall Request on GM Trucks Driven By Safety or Politics?" (*WSJ*, 4-9-93, A1,7). According to this story, NHTSA had responded to advocacy groups; the writer commented that such a recall would not have occurred in the Bush administration. The media were hurting American business (*NYT*, 2-8-93, D1,2; 2-11-93, C30). (The critics did not mention that NBC and other media were large businesses.)

In contrast, GM was morally vindicated. A story called GM's actions "corporate self-defense" (*NYT*, 2-15-93, D5). Others compared past GM glories. In the early coverage, GM trucks were paired negatively with the X-Car. In the second phase, a story noted that GM had won the X-Car case, described it as "the only recall battle that NHTSA has ever lost," and recalled that Harry Pearce had gained prominence at GM by winning that case (*WSJ*, 4-12-93, A3,25).

RESOLUTION   The coverage highlighted resolution. Some resolutions were specific to the GM/NBC controversy; others were generalized to corporate America.

The resolution was presented in a fictionlike denouement. GM's investigation was presented as a "detective story" in which its "gumshoes" solved the case (*WP*, 2-10-93, A1,15; *WSJ*, 2-9-93, A3,4; 2-11-93, A1,7). Other stories read like a courtroom drama, in which Pearce's press conference had "the air of a courtroom" (*WSJ*, 2-11-93, A3,4). NBC settled; therefore no trial was held, but GM's press conference was a double of the Atlanta trial. This time, however, GM won.

The newspapers detailed the triallike resolution. After *Dateline* hosts Jane Pauley and Stone Phillips apologized, four *NYT* stories (three of which were front-page items) characterized the apology as an "extraordinary public confession" (*NYT*, 2-10-93, A1; 2-11-93, A1; 2-14-93, E3; 3-3-93, A1). GM's triumph was heralded in headlines such as "Pendulum Swings Back for GM: Once Forced Into Red-Faced apology, Carmaker Now Wins One" and "Tale of the Tape: How GM one-Upped and Embarrassed NBC On Staged News Event" (*WP*, 2-12-93, B1; *WSJ*, 2-11-93, A1).

Another form of resolution came with the "normal-smithing" of GM. The company still had economic woes, but the coverage now was upbeat. The *Dateline* fiasco deflated morale at NBC but boosted morale at GM. (*WP*, 2-12-93, B1,4). The ultimate resolution came in stories about profits: GM's profits increased (*WSJ*, 2-11-93, A1). In addition, GM stock increased and stock in GE (NBC's parent company) decreased in value (*NYT*, 2-14-93, III3).

The "economic recovery" stories credited individuals. Jack Smith was praised for his handling of GM's economic woes, and for his remedy, "downsizing" (*WSJ*, 2-19-93, A1,11). Further, GM's victory ended a long-term malaise dating to the company's harassment of Ralph Nader (*WSJ*, 2-11-93, A17; *WP*, 2-12-93, B14).

Resolution entails winners and losers: GM won and NBC lost. In detective fiction parlance, someone at NBC had to "take the fall." Editorials called for Gartner's head (*NYT*, 3-3-93, A1, B11; *WSJ*, 2-11-93, A1,7; 3-2-93, A1,12; *WP*, 2-11-93, A13; 3-3-93, A1,12). After an outside investigation, three Dateline producers also were fired (*NYT*, 3-22-93, 49).

These actions promoted the "normal-smithing" of NBC. By dismissing Gartner and the others, NBC made them the scapegoats: They, not NBC, had violated journalistic standards (*NYT*, 2-12-93, A14; *WSJ*, 2-10-93, B1,8). The external investigators agreed: Despite "administrative and journalistic failures," NBC was "fundamentally honest" (*NYT*, 3-23-93, D23; *WSJ*, 3-23-93, B10). Another story focused on Andrew Lack, Gartner's replacement. He was Gartner's opposite—effervescent, relatively young, and curly-haired; in short, the double of GM's Jack Smith (*WP*, 4-13-93, B2). The stories suggested that with Lack heading the division, NBC News was a happy family.

The coverage blamed and denounced NBC's *Dateline*. Denunciations, which included all TV news, focused on moral violations such as a lack of objectivity and an antibusiness bias. The vilification of high-ranking NBC executives personalized the coverage. GM combated its bad publicity: GM executives were depicted as heroes. The adherence to the elements of the crime news frame made the NBC stories more newsworthy.

Conclusion

At the outset we suggested that the crime news frame might help to explain the low salience of corporate crime and deviance. The media report corporate wrongdoing, but how do they do so, and with what effect? To address these questions, we created a conceptual model of the crime news frame and used it to compare two case studies. We analyzed *NYT*, *WSJ*, and *WP* coverage of allegedly defective GM trucks and an NBC *Dateline* program about the trucks.

The coverage fit the four elements of the crime news frame: attribution and individualization of responsibility, maintenance of moral boundaries, and resolution. The coverage attributed responsibility to GM and NBC, but also vilified individuals for violating moral and legal boundaries. The stories ended in resolution. Wrongdoing was proved or admitted, and wrongdoers were punished by public denunciations, monetary loss, and resignations. The denunciations, stated in a vocabulary of moral deviance (Swigert and Farrell 1980-1981), went beyond the immediate issues and suggested that deviance was a master status trait for GM, NBC, and the executives. Yet just as deviance-smithing may be an aspect of resolution, so, too, is normal-smithing (Lofland 1969): GM and NBC made a comeback in the coverage. Of course, both corporations actively managed their images.

The conventions of crime fiction informed the crime news frame (Best and Hutchison 1996; Campbell 1987). The stories read like "whodunits," featuring courtroom drama with surprise witnesses, lawyers who were noble or not so noble, even private eyes. Such coverage continues to blur the line between news and fiction, and may increase newsworthiness (Campbell 1987).

The crime news frame, like all news frames and like crime fiction, is informed by dominant ideologies (Campbell 1987; Tuchman 1978). The stories that we analyzed expressed ideological preferences, often in terms of boundary violation or maintenance. The condemnation of NBC's journalistic faux pas supported objectivity as a media ideal. The Atlanta verdict and the resignation of NBC executives delivered the message that the system was working. The newspaper aligned their coverage with the public interest, but the coverage offered ideological instructions as to what constituted that interest. The public interest, initially exemplified by the CAS, the NHTSA, and the Atlanta jury, shifted to GM and the business community; in fact, people who led corporations or reporters who investigate them were portrayed as un-American. Finally, because these stories were interrelated, the reporters inevitably compared GM's and NBC's respective culpability. The coverage offered an ideological measure for the comparison: the wisdom of the market. GM's profits and stock increased, while GE's stock and NBC's profits decreased.

As Ericson et al. (1991:6-7) observe, the news media, like the law, offer "disciplinary and normalizing discourses," which are interrelated with each other and with other institutions and discourses. Thus law, morality, and profits and losses are tied together on an ideological bundle by news frames—in this case, by the crime news frame. The media help us to make sense of the world through these interconnected discourses and the categories they create, such as "crime" and "not crime" (Bennett and Ferrell 1987; Savelsberg 1994).

Despite the ideological consistency present in news coverage, we cannot assume that readers passively accept either the presentation or its ideological preferences. The coverage questioned the safety of GM's trucks and the commitment of GM executives to customers' safety. Similarly, the coverage suggested that NBC News (like other TV news services) was so strongly motivated by ratings and profits that its claim to objective reporting were shaky at best. Such "bad news" coverage, which exposes the mistakes of the powerful, may destabilize dominant ideologies (Ericson et al. 1991:19).

We do not know whether the GM/NBC coverage reinforced or destabilized readers' dominant views about law, crime, and the economy. Our analysis demonstrates, however, that the crime news frame, with its echo of crime fiction, may increase the news-worthiness of corporate wrongdoing; yet that frame also may limit the salience of corporate deviance and the ability of the media to control it. News frames favor simple explanations for organizational and structural-level problems; they also facilitate, through denials, scapegoats, and resignations, efforts to wipe the slate clean so that the organization can continue with its good name intact (Vaughan 1996:392; see Cavender et al. 1993:163).

Unfortunately we share Braithwaite's (1989) pessimism about the ability of the media to control such misconduct through negative publicity. There is now more reflection about media reflections than about actual serious harm. After all, the media shamed a corporation that staged a fake truck fire as severely as they shamed a corporation whose real truck fires may have caused people's deaths.

References

Barak, G. 1995. "Media, Society, and Criminology." Pp. 3-45 in *Media, Process, and the Social Construction of Crime: Studies in Newsmaking Criminology*, edited by G. Barak. New York: Garland.

Bennett, S. and J. Ferrell. 1987. "Music Videos and Epistemic Socialization," *Youth and Society* 18:344-62.

Best, J. and M. Hutchinson, 1996. "The Gang Initiation Rite As a Motif in Contemporary Crime Discourse." *Justice Quarterly* 13:383-404.

Braithwaite, J. 1989, *Crime, Shame and Reintegration*. Cambridge, UK: Cambridge University Press.

———. 1993. "Shame and Modernity," *British Journal of Criminology* 33:1-18.

Brown, S. and C. Chiang. 1993. "Defining Corporate Crime: A Critique of Traditional Parameters." Pp. 29-55 in *Understanding Corporate Criminality*, edited by M. Blankenship. New York: Garlane.

Campbell, R. 1987. "Securing the Middle Ground: Reporter Formulas in *60 Minutes.*" *Critical Studies in Mass Communications* 4:325-50.

Cavender, G., N. Jurik, and A. K. Cohen. 1993. "The Baffling Case of the Smoking Gun: The Social Ecology of Political Accounts in the Iran-Contra Affair." *Social Problems* 40:152-66.

Chermak, S. 1994. "Body Count News: How Crime is Presented in the News Media." *Justice Quarterly* 11:561-82.

Clinard, M. and P. Yeager. 1980. *Corporate Crime*. New York: Free Press.

Condit, C. and A. Sezer. 1985. "The Rhetoric of Objectivity in the Newspaper Coverage of a Murder Trial." *Critical Studies in Mass Communication* 2:197-216.

Cullen, F., W. Makkestaad, and G. Cavender. 1987. *Corporate Crime under Attack: The Ford Pinto Case and Beyond*. Cincinnati: Anderson.

Durkheim, E. 1964. *The Division of Labor in Society*. New York: Free Press.

Ericson, R., P. Baranek, and J. Chan. 1989, *Negotiating Control: A Study of News Sources*. Toronto: University of Toronto Press.

———. 1991. *Representing Order: Crime, Law and Justice in the News*. Toronto: University of Toronto Press.

Ermann, D. and R. Lundman. 1966. "Corporate and Governmental Deviance: Origins, Patterns, and Reactions." Pp. 3-44 in *Corporate and Governmental Deviance: Problems of Organizational Behavior in Contemporary Society*, 5th ed., edited by D. Ermann and R. Lundman. New York: Oxford University Press.

Evans, D., F. Cullen, and P. Dubeck. 1993. "Public Perceptions of Corporate Crime." Pp. 85-114 in *Understanding Corporate Criminality*, edited by M. Blankenship. New York: Garland.

Evans, S. and R. Lundman. 1983. "Newspaper Coverage of Corporate Price-Fixing." *Criminology* 21:529-41.

Fisse, B. and J. Braithwaite. 1983. *The Impact of Publicity on Corporate Offenders*. Albany: SUNNY Press.

Foucault, M. 1990. *The History of Sexuality.* Vol. 1: *An Introduction.* New York: Vintage.

Garfinkel, H. 1956. "Conditions of Successful Degradation Ceremonies." *American Journal of Sociology* 61:420–24.

Gitlin, T. 1980. *The Whole World is Watching.* Berkeley: University of California Press.

Hall, S., C. Critcher, T. Jefferson, J. Clarke, and B. Roberts. 1978. *Policing the Crisis: Mugging, the State, and Law and Order.* London: Macmillan.

Harvey, D. 1989. *The Condition of Postmodernity.* Baltimore: John Hopkins University Press.

Kappeler, V., M. Blumberg, and G. Potter. 1996. *The Mythology of Crime and Criminal Justice.* 2nd ed. Prospect Heights, IL: Waveland.

Katz, J. 1987. "What Makes Crimes News?" *Media Culture and Society* 9:47–75.

Lofland, J. 1969. *Deviance and Identity.* Englewood Cliffs, NJ: Prentice-Hall.

Makaii, T. and J. Braithwaite. 1994. "Reintegrative Shaming and Compliance with Regulatory Standards." *Criminology* 32:361–83.

Morash, M. and D. Hale. 1987. "Unusual Crime or Crime As Usual: Images of Corruption at the Interstate Commerce Commission." Pp. 129–49 in *Organized Crime in America: Concepts and Controversies,* edited by T. Bynum. Monsey, NY: Criminal Justice Press.

The New York Times. 1992–3. Selected articles: August 1992-June 1993.

Orum, A., J. Feagin, and G. Sjoberg. 1991. "Introduction: The Nature of the Case Study." Pp. 1–26 in *A Case for the Case Study,* edited by J. Feagin, A. Orum, and G. Sjoberg. Chapel Hill: University of North Carolina Press.

Orum, A. and J. Feagin, 1991. "A Tale of Two Cases." Pp. 121–47 in *A Case for the Case Study,* edited by J. Feagin, A. Orum, and G. Sjoberg. Chapel Hill: University of North Carolina Press.

Savelsberg, J. 1994. "Knowledge, Domination, and Criminal Punishment." *American Journal of Sociology* 99:911–43.

Scheff, T. 1990. *Microsociology,* Chicago: University of Chicago Press,

Surette, R. 1998. *Media, Crime, and Criminal Justice: Images and Realities.* 2nd ed. Pacific Grove, CA: Brooks/Cole.

Swigert, V. and R. Farrell, 1980–1981. "Corporation Homocide: Definitional Processes in the Creation of Deviance," *Law & Society Review* 15:161–82/

Tonry, M. and A. Reiss. 1993. "Organizational Crime." Pp. 1–10 in *Crime and Justice,* Vol. 18, edited by M. Tonry and A. Reiss. Chicago: University of Chicago Press.

Tuchman, G. 1978. *Making News: A Study in the Construction of Reality.* New York: Free Press.

Tumber, H. 1993. "Selling Scandal: Business and the Media." *Media, Culture and Society* 15:345–61.

Vaughan, D. 1996. *The Challenge Launch Decision: Risky Technology, Culture, and Deviance at NASA.* Chicago: University of Chicago Press.

Waegel, W., D. Ermann, and A Horowitz. 1981. "Organizational Responses to Imputations of Deviance." *Sociological Quarterly* 22:43–55.

The Wall Street Journal. 1992–3. Selected Articles: August 1992-June 1993.

The Washington Post. 1992–3. Selected Articles: August 1992-June 1993.

Wright, J., F. Cullen, and M. Blankenship. 1995. "The Social Construction of Corporate Violence: Media Coverage of the Imperial Food Products Fire." *Crime and Delinquency* 41:20–36.

Social-Control Agents, Sanctioning, and the Production of Institutional Careers and Identities

In this section we take a much closer look at how the process of identifying and sanctioning produces institutional careers and identities. We do so by focusing on how individuals are recruited into their institutional careers and on how clients' "bodies or selves" become the embodiment of deviancy and therefore the focus of change. The first selection provides some insight into the sanctioning process and how it actually contributes to institutional careers. One important observation that should be made at this point is that selected moral campaigns may expand to include new agencies as managers or identifiers of deviance. Such is the case of medicalization, discussed earlier, and the point of this article.

In "Criminalizing Women's Behavior," Nora S. Gustavsson and Ann E. MacEachron show how moral campaigns can coopt other agencies into their struggle and create new paths of entry into institutional careers. The drug war in the United states has cost billions of dollars a year for more than a decade, with the bulk of the war on drugs being waged against major suppliers and distributors, and managed for the most part by the criminal justice system. More recently, the drug war has been expanded to include pursuit of individuals who use illegal substances as well as those who supply the drug. And by coopting the medical establishment it is possible to monitor drug use in a vast number of individuals, in this case, childbearing women.

The authors carefully dismantle the notion that potential fetal harm is either the reason for punitive policies against drug-using pregnant women or legitimation for the sexist policies that victimize poor women. It becomes clear that illicit drug use by women is the concern and the focus of management, since fetal harm is caused by many factors that remain unregulated (e.g., the harm to the reproductive process and fetal development that may occur as a result of drug use by fathers). In the end, this type of state intervention results in the "manufacture" and introduction of two sets of misfits: mothers (the fastest growing population in the criminal justice system) and children (taxing an already stressed and often inadequate child welfare agency). Once shunted into an institutional career, the process of detecting, diagnosing, and treating the deviancy—thought to lie within the person—is initiated.

Vincent Lyon-Callo, in "Medicalizing Homelessness: The Production of Self-Blame and Self-Governing within Homeless Shelters," draws on three years of ethnographic research in an emergency homeless shelter and reveals important issues relating to the medicalized treatment of the homeless. One aspect of the medicalization of deviance is that it places the origins of the deviance within the individual, and hence absolves society of any real responsibility. As Lyon-Callo observes "[w]hen homelessness is individualized and medicalized, those concerns remain peripheral to the central work of normalizing perceived shortcomings or deviance within homeless people." The end result of this process is that the individual must accept the diagnosis and then accept the responsibility for his or her deviance.

As noted throughout, agencies' theory of the office remains central, since the diagnostic categories emerge or flow from this guiding ideology. In this specific case, medicalized conceptions—the theory of the office—guide institutional responses. But there is more of interest here. The behavior of social control agents that is designed to resolve the "disease" actually helps to reproduce and to reinforce the dominant images of homelessness within the institution and the larger society, and of homeless people, and contribute to producing particular states among the homeless. These states can be viewed as iatrogenic subjectivities, experiences, self-images, and behavior. If individuals are resistant to treatment, they may be identified or categorized as being troublemakers and then released from the program, or an additional label may be applied—such as "the person is in denial." What is interesting about this particular label is that any resistance to the label is perceived as evidence that the diagnosis is, in fact, correct. And in a very real sense, the individual becomes mired in an "institutional catch-22" situation—he or she becomes locked in.

31   Criminalizing Women's Behavior

Nora S. Gustavsson
Ann E. MacEachron

Introduction

Criminalizing the behavior of drug-using pregnant and parenting women is a policy fraught with contradictions and helps to perpetuate actions that can harm women and their children. The assumptions used to support these punitive policies are based upon suspect evidence and questionable data. We critically examine the evidence as well as the policies and suggest an alternative policy approach to dealing with families in which parental drug use may be an issue.

Incidence of Drug Use

 The seemingly simple task of identifying the number of pregnant women using drugs presents serious challenges. Estimates of drug use vary widely. Some estimates are inferred from estimates of drug use by all women of childbearing age. Other estimates are drawn from incidence studies at hospitals and clinics. Variability among estimates is influenced by the nature, location, and size of the sample; the definition of drugs; and the methods used for drug identification. Moreover, after reviewing these studies it becomes clear that we do not know how many pregnant women are using drugs, what drugs they are using, in what quantities and with what frequency, and during which stages of pregnancy.

The National Institute on Drug Abuse (NIDA) is a commonly cited source of data. The Institute's (1993b) data suggest that illicit drug use has been declining. In 1985 the household survey reported 22.3 million current users of illicit drugs. This dropped to 11.7 million in 1993. Cocaine use dropped during the same period from 4.2 million to 1.3 million. Drug use by adolescents, however, is on the increase, as is the use of heroin. Chronic or hard core drug users represent one fifth of the drug-using population and consume two thirds of the cocaine (Office of National Drug Control Policy 1995).

Estimating the number of women of childbearing age using both licit and illicit drugs can be complex. For example, there are a reported 100 million users of alcohol (NIDA 1989). If 30% of these users are women of childbearing age, then a large number of infants could be at risk for prenatal alcohol exposure.

Studies conducted at hospitals report different incidence rates. A Miami study reported a 12% perinatal cocaine exposure rate (Bandstra et al. 1989). A study at a Detroit public hospital revealed that 27% of delivering women tested positive for one or more drugs, with marijuana the most common (Land and Kushner 1990). A study at Boston City Hospital reported that 18% of mothers had used cocaine and 27% had used marijuana (Zuckerman et al. 1989). Another study at an urban hospital of women using prenatal services reported that 17% of the women had used cocaine (Frank et al. 1988). The Federal government estimates that 100,000 infants are exposed prenatally to cocaine (U.S. General Accounting Office 1990). Another study of 36 hospitals in urban areas found an average incidence rate of illicit drugs of 11% with a range of 0.4 to 27% (Chasnoff 1989). Hospitals that intensively screened for drugs reported a higher incidence rate.

These studies were conducted at public hospitals that serve primarily poor and minority women. A Florida study of 715 pregnant women attempted to address the class and race bias. Women using both public and private obstetrical offices were screened. More than 14% tested positive for one or more drugs. There was little difference in the rates between public and private patients and between white and African-American women. Florida has legislation requiring mandated health workers, educational staff, and many human resources workers to notify the state of pregnant, drug-using women. African-American women in the study were 10 times more likely to be reported to state officials than were white women (Chasnoff et al. 1990).

Using data from a number of sources, Gomby and Shiono (1991) estimate that 2% to 3% of newborns were exposed prenatally to cocaine and 3% to 12% were exposed to marijuana. They also suggest that a large number of pregnant women drank alcohol (73%) during their pregnancies and that 37.6% smoked cigarettes. Based on these percentages, approximately 158,000 infants were prenatally exposed to cocaine, 611,000 to marijuana, 2.6 million to alcohol, and 1.3 million to cigarettes. A few million infants may thus be exposed prenatally to licit and illicit drugs annually. However, the consequences of this exposure have yet to be understood.

Effects of Prenatal Exposure

Consistent with the lack of knowledge about the actual incidence of drug use among pregnant women, there is inconsistent and contradictory evidence about the effects of prenatal drug exposure. The drugs with well established and documented negative consequences for fetal well being are two legal drugs—alcohol and tobacco. The consequences of illicit drug exposure for the fetus are unclear.

The effects of alcohol on the fetus have been studied for decades, especially since Fetal Alcohol Syndrome (FAS) was identified (Jones and Smith 1973). The syndrome is characterized by growth deficiency and central nervous system impairments. Fetal Alcohol Effect (FAE) is a more common condition in which the infant suffers some but not all of the characteristics of FAS. FAE is estimated to occur at 10 times the frequency of FAS (Rosengren 1990), and FAS is estimated to occur at the rate of 1.9 births per thousand (Abel and Sokel 1987). What remains unclear are the mechanisms of interaction, contributions of other factors, how much alcohol is used and how frequently, and during which phase of fetal development its use results in fetal harm.

Low birth weight, sudden infant death syndrome, spontaneous abortion, premature rupture of the membranes, and abnormal placentation are associated with maternal tobacco use (Li and Daling 1991; Office on Smoking and Health 1988; Williams et al. 1991). More recent studies are suggesting a relationship between maternal smoking and increased systolic and diastolic blood pressure in the infants of women who smoked during pregnancy (Beratis et al. 1996). Intrauterine growth retardation, and the incidence of both orofacial clefts and congenital urinary tract anomalies are associated with maternal cigarette smoking (Nordentoft et al. 1996; Shaw et al. 1996; Li et al. 1996). The mechanisms of harm are poorly understood due in part to the large number of chemicals found in cigarette smoke. It seems clear that there are significant risks associated with cigarette smoking (Benowitz 1991).

Unlike alcohol and tobacco, the consequences of illicit drugs such as cocaine have only recently been studied in depth. Early studies reported a number of negative consequences including preterm birth, small head circumference, and genitourinary malformations (Bingol et al. 1987; Cordero and Custard 1990; Chasnoff et al. 1987; McGregor et al. 1987; and Zuckerman et al. 1989). Other studies have reported few differences between cocaine and non-cocaine exposed infants (Woods et al. 1993). There is some evidence to suggest that infants exposed prenatally to cocaine may have more difficulty with habilitation (reduced response to repeated stimuli) and experience more stress behaviors (Eisen et al. 1991).

Studies of maternal marijuana use suggest an association with impaired fetal growth, exaggerated startles, an increase in fine tremors and tremors associated with the Moro reflex (Fried and Makin 1987; and Zuckerman et al. 1989). Long-term consequences have been studied and suggest that few differences exist until age 48 months, when memory and verbal measures were negatively affected in children prenatally exposed to heavy marijuana use. Another study suggests that attentional behaviors of 6-year-olds are also negatively affected (Fried and Watkinson 1990; Fried et al. 1992).

Consequences of opioid exposure include the risk of preterm birth, low birth weight, small head circumference, and a neonatal abstinence syndrome (Wilson 1989). The syndrome is characterized by high pitched crying, exaggerated reflexes, sneezing, restlessness, and diarrhea. Longitudinal studies indicate these children may suffer difficulties with visual-motor-perception skills and poor school performance (Wilson 1989).

Analysis of the Research

Generalizing the results of these studies is problematic. The samples are often small, composed primarily of poor women with an over-representation of minority women, and the studies do not separate out the effects of other variables. Samples with an $n = 1$ have been reported (Telsey et al. 1988). Poor women are likely to face additional challenges to successful reproductive outcomes such as lack of access to early, consistent, and quality prenatal care (Burns et al. 1985). Negative environmental factors such as poor housing and nutrition, living in neighborhoods that experience violence and lack social supports and services, depression, histories of abuse and neglect, as well as involvement with male partners who may be drug involved and violent are not conducive to positive infant and maternal outcomes (Amaro et al. 1990; Regan et al. 1987).

Research designs often have difficulty controlling for the effects of other variables. Polydrug use, particularly the use of tobacco and alcohol, is common (Hutchings 1990). These two legal drugs have clearly established negative consequences for the fetus. If a woman is using marijuana and/or cocaine along with legal drugs, attributing fetal harm to any one drug becomes difficult. An experimental design, for example, in which there is random assignment of pregnant women to a cocaine group or a control group is not ethically or legally feasible.

Caution must be exercised in attributing negative fetal outcomes to drug use. It is estimated that 10% to 15% of congenital malformations are due to environmental agents, 10 to 15% are due to hereditary factors, and the rest are a result of multiple or unknown factors (Hutchings 1985). Prescription medications such as diethystilbestrol (DES), Accutane, lithium, and anticonvulsants are particularly toxic to the fetus.

Reproductive outcomes are influenced by multiple variables. The small, non-representative samples and the inability to control for all variables that can influence reproductive outcomes compromise the conclusions of many of the medical studies. Of particular interest is the political ideology such research represents. Not only is this reproductive research focused exclusively on only one party (the female), but studies that report minimal or no negative consequences of drug use have little visibility in the professional literature.

The exclusion of men from studies on the influence of drugs on the fetus lends credence to the notion that research serves the purposes of power elites who want to police women and control their behavior. The dearth of research on the effects of drugs on male reproduction is striking. There are a few studies that offer preliminary evidence to suggest that chemically abusing men face an elevated risk of infertility and chromosome damage (Close et al. 1990; Shafer et al. 1990). Licit drugs are also reported to adversely impact the morphology of sperm (Office of Technology Assessment 1985). A recent study reported the presence of tobacco residue in semen (Davis et al. 1992).

Tobacco may provide a vehicle for including the contributions of men to fetal and infant health. It has become more commonplace to see reports on the relationship between smoking and health. There was a period in which the medical community and tobacco companies were allies. The medical organizations discounted studies which reported negative consequences of smoking and tobacco companies opposed federal legislation that would regulate physicians, their services, and their fees. Today, respected medical journals publish studies that indicate children are at risk from the adults in their environments who use tobacco and advocate for new laws to protect children from the harm attributable to the use of tobacco products by others (DiFranza and Lew 1996).

In addition to the role of damaged sperm, men contribute to fetal outcomes by their abuse of the mother. This is another understudied area. Estimates on the number of women battered during pregnancy vary from 4% to 8% (Helton 1987). A more recent study at public prenatal clinics, which served primarily poor women, found an exceedingly high rate of physical abuse. Only 17% of the patients had *not* been physically abused during their current pregnancy (McFarlane et al. 1992).

Another disturbing factor in the research on drug-using, pregnant women is the reluctance to acknowledge that much of what has passed for fact is more accurately described as myth. Even the medical establishment is beginning to recognize the role of political ideology in their research. In a recent article a physician suggested that the desire to exert control over women, and identifying black women in particular for criminal prosecution and child protection referrals, meets political goals but ignores the social factors in women's lives such as family dysfunction, untreated addiction, and persistent poverty (Neuspiel 1993).

The medical community has added to the myth of maternal illicit drug use and severe fetal harm by its hesitancy to provide a forum for research that suggests that the association between maternal drug behavior and fetal harm is tangential. Studies that showed a negative association between maternal cocaine use and fetal outcome were significantly more likely to be accepted for presentation by the Society for Pediatric Research than studies showing no association, even though they were more methodologically sound. These studies had a negligible chance for acceptance (Koren et al. 1989).

The difficulty in establishing causal links between drug use and fetal harm is beginning to be reported in the professional literature. Measures of overall competence do not show any difference between cocaine exposed and non-cocaine exposed infants. Some of the difficulties observed in drug exposed infants attenuate with age (Chasnoff et al. 1992; Zuckerman and Frank 1992). There are questions about the later developmental problems experienced by drug exposed children (Day et al. 1994; Fried et al. 1992). However, the contributions of illicit drugs to these problems is not clear. Poverty seems to be a major contributor to the problems experienced by these children (NIDA 1993a).

The unwillingness to evaluate commonly accepted myths about the frequency and extent of fetal harm due to maternal behavior leads inexorably to the conclusion that the attempts to control women in their reproductive role is due to factors other than concern for the well being of infants.

Elevating Fetal Rights

Criminalizing the behavior of pregnant women results, in part, from perceiving the fetus as a person with enforceable rights. This is a new development made possible through advances in medical science. The technology of the 20th century has made it commonplace to monitor and even see the developing fetus. There are a number of serious consequences of making the fetus a person.

The resolution of potential conflicts between the developing fetus and the mother is complicated by viewing the fetus as a person. The state has intervened in the lives of pregnant women in an attempt to protect the fetus. It is important to note that the State is protecting the fetus *against* the mother. An adversarial relationship between mother and fetus is thus established by State intervention. These political intrusions are supported by the medical industry. This raises another set of questions that are beyond the scope of this paper about the omniscience of medical science and the price a woman can pay for failing to do what she is told.

Precedents for State intervention in cases in which the fetus was assumed to be at risk and the mother was assumed to be recalcitrant for not following the advice of medical providers can be found in many jurisdictions. The State has forced blood transfusions on pregnant women, even when the women object on religious grounds. The State argues that the viable fetus must be protected and its welfare takes precedence over the mother's wishes (*in re Jamaica Hospital* 1985).

Forced cesareans are even more invasive medical procedures and courts have been willing to order them against the wishes of the mother. In one especially sad case, the court ordered a cesarean section over the objections of a terminally ill woman (*in re A.C.* 1990). The court decided that because the mother was going to die anyway, her wishes need not be respected. Saving the fetus was deemed more important. The 26-week-old fetus died 3 hours after the surgery. The mother died the next day.

Pregnant women bear an obligation, which can carry the weight of law, to place the needs and welfare of the fetus above their own. No other group of Americans are expected to sacrifice their individual rights to autonomy, privacy, or even health, to enhance the viability of another person, much less a developing fetus. Whether this is an unintended consequence of biology and anatomy is open to debate. It is a gender specific duty. Only women, at least at this time, can sustain a fetus.

The State's interest in fetal well being is highly specific and appears limited to monitoring maternal behavior. Yet the State is reluctant to provide other services that could enhance fetal well being such as accessible and affordable prenatal care, nutrition, housing, and environments free from hazards.

Intrusive medical procedures assumed to benefit the fetus provide the base for extending the interests of the State into maternal behaviors. If the State can force unwanted procedures onto pregnant women, then the next step of proscribing acceptable behaviors follows easily.

Criminalizing Maternal Conduct

There are a number of major assumptions in the policy of criminalizing maternal behaviors in addition to the belief that the fetus is a person. There is the belief that women have an affirmative duty to refrain from activities that medical practitioners say are harmful and if they do not, then prosecution is an appropriate response. One justification for this policy is the belief that fetal outcomes will be improved by criminalizing maternal behavior. Pregnancy has become the basis for determining criminal behavior. A biologically based temporary condition is a sufficient condition for the determination of criminal action.

One example of the criminalization approach occurred in California (*People v. Stewart* 1987). The case involved a woman who gave birth to a severely damaged preterm infant who died a few weeks after birth. Blood tests revealed amphetamines in the baby's blood. The mother was arrested and charged with failing to provide medical care to her fetus under a child support statute. The mother had been told to stop using drugs and not to have intercourse. She allegedly engaged in both of the forbidden activities. The charges were eventually dismissed. But the policy precedent of trying to force pregnant women to behave in acceptable ways by relying on prosecution was established.

Another California case occurred a decade earlier and involved trying to prosecute a woman addicted to heroin for felony endangerment (*Reyes v. Superior Court* 1977). The case was dismissed because the action occurred before the birth of the twins and the statute was intended to cover harm to already born children.

Other states have used existing laws to prosecute women such as those that prohibit manslaughter and the delivery of drugs, especially to a minor.

The state of Illinois charged a woman with both manslaughter and delivering drugs to a minor when her child died shortly after birth and cocaine was found in the infant's urine and the mother's blood (American Bar Association 1989).

Florida convicted a woman for giving birth to two children, both of whom tested positive for drugs, under a statute used to prosecute drug dealers (*Johnson v. State* 1991). She was sentenced to 15 years probation and 200 hours of community service for delivering drugs through the umbilical cord to her children. The conviction was later overturned by the Florida Supreme Court. Yet this case was important because the umbilical cord had been redefined as a piece of drug paraphernalia, a method for the delivery of contraband. There are no other human organs so viewed.

Texas prosecuted a woman for possession of a controlled substance when she gave birth to a stillborn premature infant (*Jackson v. State* 1992). The prosecution argued that because a high level of cocaine was found in the infant's blood, it had to have passed to the infant from the mother. The conviction was later overturned.

In addition to criminal prosecution, pregnant, drug-using women are at an elevated risk for "protective" incarceration. A judge in the District of Columbia sentenced a pregnant cocaine-using woman convicted of forgery to jail to protect her fetus from further illicit drug exposure (McNulty 1990). The benevolent, paternalistic concern of the judge for the health of the fetus might be more commendable if jails provided high quality prenatal care and were, indeed, drug-free environments. Miscarriage rates in jails and prisons are disturbingly high. The miscarriage rate in California's prisons is 33% and in some county jails, this rate is 50 times higher than the State rate (Barry 1985).

Examples from these States demonstrate a disturbing policy response to criminalize the behavior of woman. Although there have been few successful criminal prosecutions, the trend is clearly established that some women will be punished for drug use during pregnancy. Another State system that can be used to hurt women and their children is the child welfare system, and although the motivations of child welfare agencies may be less punitive, the ramifications of child welfare involvement can have dire consequences for families.

The Child Welfare Response

Child maltreatment has become increasingly visible. Legislative initiatives at the State and Federal level designed to address the complexities associated with child abuse are common. The 1980s were marked by significant increases in the number of children reported as abused and neglected. In addition, the number of children entering substitute care began to increase and issues associated with maternal drug use became another rallying point for new legislation and expansion of the child welfare system.

The problems in public child welfare have been subject to extensive study and have resulted in congressional hearings. Large numbers of children drifting through the foster care system, receiving few if any services and without a plan for stability, were not uncommon. The Federal government enacted major child welfare legislation in 1980 that was supposed to reduce the number of children in foster care and help the children find secure living arrangements (Gustavsson and Segal 1994). The legislation appeared to be successful—for a while. By 1986 the number of children in care had dropped to 280,000. However, 3 years later the number had jumped to 360,000, a 27% increase (Subcommittee on Human Resources 1990). By the end of 1993, an estimated 450,000 children were in foster care (U.S. General Accounting Office 1995a).

These increases in the incidence of foster care placement paralleled increases in the number of children reported as abused or neglected. Maternal drug use was identified as the major contributor to these increases. Between 1983 and 1993 reports of child abuse and neglect doubled to 2.3 million, the foster care caseload grew by two-thirds, and in 1991 in four large cities, 62% of preschool-age foster children were at risk of health problems due to prenatal drug exposure compared to just 21% 5 years earlier (U.S. General Accounting Office 1995a). During a 6-year period in the early 1980s, Los Angeles County experienced a 500% increase in the number of children placed in foster care due to parental drug use, and in some California counties, drug-exposed children comprised two-thirds of the foster care population (Select Committee on Children, Youth, and Families 1989). Child welfare agencies began, in the 1980s, to actively assess for drug use in referred families. As many as 80% of the families substantiated for child maltreatment are affected by drug use (Child Welfare League of America 1990).

Minority children fare poorly in the foster care system. In 1990, 40% of the children in foster care were African-American, 11% were Hispanic, and 39% were white (U.S. General Accounting Office 1995b). Not only do minority children enter foster care more frequently, but they stay longer. More than half of the children leaving care in 1987 were white and 26% were African-American (Committee on Ways and Means 1991). Foster care has become a major form of family life for increasing numbers of minority children.

The median age of children entering care has been dropping since the late 1980s, and the number of infants entering care increased by two-thirds between 1983 and 1990 (U.S. General Accounting Office 1995b). This is consistent with the increased recognition afforded poor, pregnant drug-using women. As these woman became identified, their children became subject to State child welfare intervention.

The precedent for considering an infant maltreated and in need of protection due to maternal drug use was clearly established as early as 1980 (in re Baby X). This was a Michigan case in which an infant suffering from a drug withdrawal syndrome was considered neglected and removed from the custody of the parent. Most States have amended their child abuse reporting statutes to include drug use by pregnant women and/or positive toxicology screens of an infant or a mother as a reportable offense (Gustavsson 1991a). This change in policy had both anticipated and unanticipated consequences.

By increasing the number of reportable offenses, child welfare agencies received more referrals. More resources were needed to investigate these referrals and then to provide services to the families. Unfortunately, few child welfare agencies had the resources to help families dealing with drug abuse issues, especially when the mother was drug-involved. Child welfare agencies were now faced with trying to provide services to an increasingly large population for which few resources existed.

Child welfare agencies were forced to develop strategies for helping drug-using women. The traditional drug treatment system had little to offer the child welfare agency. The proprietary sector served primarily white affluent men with health insurance (Wesson and Smith 1985). Public facilities faced a high demand for their services and often had waiting lists. It misses the point to ask a pregnant drug user to wait 6 months for a drug rehabilitation program. To further complicate the delivery of services, slots for pregnant drug users were few.

More than half of the drug treatment facilities in New York City refuse to admit pregnant drug users, and Massachusetts allocated only 15 residential treatment slots, statewide, to pregnant women (U.S. General Accounting Office 1990). Child welfare agencies would have to develop partnerships with the drug treatment sector to offer services to an increasingly large percentage of their caseload.

The priorities of drug treatment centers and child welfare agencies differ. Issues associated with abuse, neglect, and parenting are priorities for child welfare. These are also issues women bring with them to drug-treatment settings. The traditional drug-treatment agency is male oriented. It reflects the paths men take into treatment as well as the needs of men and has not served women, especially pregnant women, well (Center for Substance Abuse Treatment 1993; Kumpfer 1991). Child welfare agencies continue to experiment with gender sensitive programs (Carten 1996).

Mixed Messages and the Drug War

Systems that come into contact with the drug-using pregnant woman, such as health care, criminal justice, child welfare, education, and drug treatment, have failed to serve her well. There are a number of factors that may account for this lack of quality service. A major contributor to the lack of comprehensive services is that we do not know how to view this woman. Is she a criminal, who inflicts harm on her fetus, or is she someone with a problem who needs assistance?

The attempt to use the force of law to compel women to behave in a proscribed fashion is doomed to failure (Hawk 1994). Criminalizing maternal conduct may also have unintended consequences such as discouraging women from seeking health care. Prenatal care is essential if fetal and maternal outcomes are to be improved. Of particular concern is the latent gender, social class, and racial bias in the criminal justice approach.

Criminalizing behavior for only one group of citizens, based solely on their gender and a temporary biological condition, establishes a worrisome precedent. There may be other maternal behaviors which could be harmful to the fetus. Homelessness, not obtaining prenatal care, poor eating habits, failure to follow a physician's orders, working in a setting with hazardous chemicals, being abused, and being poor are also associated with negative fetal outcomes. However, there has not yet been a suggestion to criminalize these behaviors.

Drug behavior is subject to sanction because it is assumed to indicate a character flaw. Drug users are seen as defective people who deliberately engage in harmful behavior. In a recent Arizona case in which a woman was indicted for child abuse because she allegedly gave birth to a heroin-addicted baby, the judge explained that the woman made a choice to engage in sexual conduct and also chose to take heroin (*Reinesto v. Superior Court of the State of Arizona* 1994). The degree of choice that the drug dependent person can exercise, or that women can exercise in both the sexual and drug areas, is unclear. It may soon be argued that women chose to be poor, homeless, or involved with a violent partner.

Women have become the latest casualties in the war on drugs (Gustavsson 1991b). Pregnant drug users are viewed unsympathetically and are easy to want to punish. Saving children who are being deliberately harmed by the actions of the drug-using mothers can serve as a rallying point in the drug war. The lack of gender-sensitive drug treatment has not impeded the development of punitive responses.

The drug war has increased the prison population. The percentage of State prisoners serving a drug sentence tripled from 1980 to 1993 (6% to 22%) and the number of Federal prisoners serving a drug sentence more than doubled from 25% in 1983 to 60% in 1993 (Bureau of Justice Statistics 1995a). There has been a ninefold increase (19,000 to 172,300) in the number of convicted drug offenders (Bureau of Justice Statistics 1995b). Between 1982 and 1991, the number of women arrested for drug offenses increased by 89% (National Institute of Justice 1994). Women constitute the fastest growing population in the criminal justice system.

The political realities of drug importation and use in America should not be ignored. Cocaine and heroin, for example, are derived from plants that are not indigenous to the United States. These products must be imported and questions arise about how so many drugs are able to enter the country and find their way to poor inner city neighborhoods. There have been allegations that suggest a link between the importation of cocaine and the Central Intelligence Agency (Webb 1996). Recent congressional hearings did not find any evidence to support these allegations.

The criminal justice approach to drug use is expensive. For fiscal year 1996, President Clinton requested $14.6 billion for the drug war, a 9.7% increase over the 1995 budget of $13.3 billion (Office of National Drug Control Policy 1995). Almost $3 billion would be used for drug treatment. The rest of the money is allocated for reducing the drug supply. The results of these efforts to reduce the supply of drugs are mixed (U.S. General Accounting Office 1995c). There is also funding for the drug war in Title V of the Violent Crime Control and Law Enforcement Act of 1994. This act created drug courts whose effectiveness is unknown (U.S. General Accounting Office 1995b). The Crime Control Act also allocates funds for more law enforcement officers.

Criminalizing illicit drug use for pregnant women ignores the most serious threats to fetal well being—tobacco and alcohol. With a current prison population of over one million, it may not be practical to incarcerate all pregnant women who smoke. There also is a tobacco lobby that can be counted on to advocate on behalf of women and their fundamental right to smoke.

The more appropriate response to maternal drug use is to place it in an ecological context and see it as one of many factors that can negatively influence both maternal and fetal outcomes. The billions spent in the drug war and for incarceration could do much to bring prenatal care, nutrition programs, counseling, parenting classes, housing assistance, and income support programs to pregnant women. These programs would do more to ensure infant health than maternal prosecution and incarceration strategies.

The cost effectiveness of these supportive strategies are well established. Helping pregnant women, for example, deliver full-term babies is much less costly than caring for a premature infant. (Children's Defense Fund 1989). The fact that there are still many women in America who do not get prenatal care or receive it late in their pregnancy suggests that concern for fetal well being may not be the real reason behind the trend toward criminalization.

References

Abel, E. L., and R. J. Sokel
1987 Incidence of fetal alcohol syndrome and economic impact of FAS related anomalies. *Drug and Alcohol Dependence* 19:51–70.
Amaro, H., L. Fried, and H. Cabral
1990 Violence during pregnancy and substance abuse. *American Journal of Public Health* 80:5.
American Bar Association
1989 Crime and Pregnancy. *American Bar Journal* 14–16.
Bandstra, E., B. Steele, G. Burkette, D. Paltrow, N. Levandowski, and B. Rodriguez
1989 Prevalence of perinatal exposure in an urban multi-ethnic population (Summary). *Program Issues of Pediatric Research* 25(2):247.
Barry, E.
1985 Quality of prenatal care for incarcerated women challenged. *Youth Law News* 6(6):1–4.

Benowitz, N. L.
1991 Nicotine replacement therapy during pregnancy. *Journal of the American Medical Association* 266(22):3174–3177.

Beratis, N. G., D. Panagoulias, and A. Varvarigou
1996 Increased blood pressure in neonates and infants whose mothers smoked during pregnancy. *Journal of Pediatrics* 128(6):806–812.

Bureau of Justice Statistics
1995a *Prisoners in 1994.* Washington, DC: U.S. Department of Justice.

Bureau of Justice Statistics
1995b *Correctional populations in the United States.* Washington, DC: U.S. Department of Justice.

Burns, K., M. Melamed, W. Burns, I. Chasnoff, and R. Hatcher
1985 Chemical dependency and clinical depression in pregnancy. *Journal of Clinical Psychology* 41(6):851–854.

Carten, A. J.
1996 Mothers in recovery: Rebuilding families in the aftermath of addiction. *Social Work* 41:214–223.

Center for Substance Abuse Treatment
1993 *Pregnant, substance-using women.* Rockville, MD: U.S. Department of Health and Human Services.

Chasnoff, I. J.
1989 Drug use and women: Establishing a standard of care. *Annals of New York Academy of Sciences* 562:2008–10.

Chasnoff, I. J., D. Griffith, C. Freier, and J. Murray
1992 Cocaine/polydrug use in pregnancy: Two year followup. *Pediatrics* 89:284–289.

Chasnoff, I. J., H. J. Landress, and M. E. Barrett
1990 The prevalence of illicit drug or alcohol use during pregnancy and the discrepancies in mandatory reporting in Pinellas County, Florida. *New England Journal of Medicine* 322(17):1202–1206.

Child Welfare League of America
1990 *Crack and other addictions: Old realities and new challenges.* Washington, DC: Author.

Children's Defense Fund
1989 *A vision for America's future.* Washington, DC: Children's Defense Fund.

Close, C., P. Roberts, and R. Berger
1990 Cigarettes, alcohol and marijuana are related to pyospermia in infertile men. *Journal of Urology* 144(4):900–903.

Committee on Ways and Means
1991 *Background material and data on programs within the jurisdiction of the Committee on Ways and Means.* Washington, DC: U.S. Government Printing Office.

Cordero, L. and M. Custard
1990 Effects of maternal cocaine abuse on perinatal and infant outcomes. *Ohio Medicine* 86(5):410–412.

Davis, D. L., G. Friedler, R. Mattison, and R. Morris
1992 Male-mediated teratogenesis and other reproductive effects: Biologic and epidemiologic findings and a plea for clinical research. *Reproductive Toxicology* 6:289–292.

Day, N. L., G. A. Richardson, L. Goldschmidt, N. Robles, P. M. Taylor, D. S. Stoffer, M. D. Cornelius, and D. Geva
1994 Effect of prenatal marijuana exposure on the cognitive development of offspring at age three. *Neurotoxicology and Teratology* 16(2):169–175.

DiFranza, J. R., and R. A. Lew
1996 Morbidity and mortality in children associated with the use of tobacco products by other people. *Pediatrics* 97(4):560–568.

Eisen, L. N., T. M. Field, E. S. Bandstra, J. P. Roberts, C. Morrow, S. K. Larson, and B. M. Steele
1991 Perinatal cocaine effects on neonatal stress behavior and performance on the Brazelton scale. *Pediatrics* 88:477–480.

Fried, P. A. and J. E. Makin
1987 Neonatal behavioral correlates of prenatal exposure to marijuana, cigarettes, and alcohol in a low risk population. *Neurotoxicology and Teratology* 9:1–7.

Fried, P. A., B. Watkinson, and R. Gray
1992 A follow-up study of attentional behavior in 6 year old children exposed prenatally to marijuana, cigarettes, and alcohol. *Neurotoxicology and Teratology* 14:299–311.

Gomby, D. S., and P. H. Shiono
1991 Estimating the number of substance-exposed infants. *The Future of Children* 1(1):17–25.

Gustavsson, N. S.
1991a Chemically exposed children: The child welfare response. *Child and Adolescent Social Work Journal* 8(4):297–307.

Gustavsson, N. S.
1991b The war metaphor: A threat to vulnerable populations. *Social Work* 36:277–278.

Gustavsson, N. S.
1992 Drug exposed children and their mothers: Facts, myths, and needs. *Social Work in Health Care* 16(4):87–100.

Gustavsson, N. S. and E. A. Segal
1994 *Critical issues in child welfare.* California: Sage.

Hawk, M. A.
1994 How social policies make matters worse: The case of maternal substance abuse. *Journal of Drug Issues* 24(3):517–526.

Hutchings, D.
1985 Prenatal opioid exposure and the problem of causal inference. In *Current research on the consequences of maternal drug abuse,* ed. T. Pinkert, 6–19. Maryland: National Institute on Drug Abuse.

Hutchings, D.
1990 Issues of risk assessment: Lessons from the use and abuse of drugs during pregnancy. *Neurotoxicology and Teratology* 12(3):183–189.

Jones, K. and D. Smith
1973 Recognition of fetal alcohol syndrome in early infancy. *Lancet* II(7836):999–1001.

Koren, G., H. Shear, K. Graham, and T. Einarson
1989 Bias against the null hypothesis: The reproductive hazards of cocaine. *Lancet* 2(December 16):1440–1442.

Kumpfer, K.
1991 Treatment programs for drug abusing women. *The Future of Children* 1(1):50–60.

Land, D., and R. Kushner
1991 Drug abuse during pregnancy in an inner-city hospital: Prevalence and patterns. *Journal of the American Osteopathic Association* 90(5):421–426.

Li, D. K., and J. R. Daling
1991 Maternal smoking, low birth weight, and ethnicity in relation to sudden infant death syndrome. *American Journal of Epidemiology* 134:958–964.

Li, D. K., Mueller, B. A., Hickok, D. E., Daling, J. R., Fantel, A. G., Checkoway, H., and N. S. Weiss
1996 Maternal smoking during pregnancy and the risk of congenital urinary tract anomalies. *American Journal of Public Health* 86(2):249–253.

McFarlane, J., B. Parker, K. Soeken, and L. Bullock
1992 Assessing for abuse during pregnancy. *Journal of the American Medical Association* 267(23):3176–3178.
McNulty, M.
1990 Pregnancy police: Implications of criminalizing fetal abuse. *Youth Law News* 11(1):33–37.
National Institute of Justice
1994 *Drug-abusing women offenders: Results of a national survey.* Washington, DC: U.S. Department of Justice.
National Institute on Drug Abuse
1993a *Conference Highlights from the 2nd National Conference on Drug Abuse Research and Practice.* Rockville, MD: National Institute on Drug Abuse.
1993b *National household survey on drug abuse.* Rockville, MD: National Institute on Drug Abuse.
Neuspiel, D. R.
1993 Cocaine and the fetus: Mythology of severe risk. *Neurotoxicology and Teratology* 15:305–306.
Nordentoft, M., Lou, H. C., Hansen, D., Nim, J., Pryds, O., Rubin, P., and R. Hemmingsen
1996 Intrauterine growth retardation and premature delivery: The influence of maternal smoking and psychosocial factors. *American Journal of Public Health* 86(3):347–354.
Office of National Drug Control Policy
1995 *National drug control strategy.* Washington, DC: Executive Office of the President.
Office on Smoking and Health
1988 *The health consequences of smoking: Nicotine addiction.* Washington, DC: U.S. Government Printing Office.
Office of Technology Assessment
1985 *Reproductive health hazards in the workplace.* Washington, DC: U.S. Government Printing Office.
Regan, D., S. Ehrlich, and L. Finnegan.
1987 Infants of drug addicts: At risk for child abuse, neglect, and placement in foster care. *Neurotoxicology and Teratology* 9:315–319.
Rosengren, J.
1990 Alcohol: A bigger drug problem? *Minnesota Medicine* 73:33–34.
Select Committee on Children, Youth, and Families
1989 *Born hooked: Confronting the impact of perinatal substance abuse.* Washington, DC: U.S. Government Printing Office.
Shafer, D., V. Dunbar, A. Falek, R. Donahoe, R. Madden, and P. Bokos
1990 Enhanced assays detect increased chromosome damage and sister-chromatid exchanges in heroin addicts. *Mutation Research* 234(5):327–336.
Shaw, G. M., Wasserman, C. R., Lammer, E. J., O'Malley, C. D., Murra, J. C., Bassart, A. M., and M. M. Tolarova
1996 Craniofacial clefts, parental cigarette smoking, and transforming growth factor-alpha gene variants. *American Journal of Human Genetics* 58(3):551–561.
Subcommittee on Human Resources
1990 The impact of crack cocaine on the child welfare system. Hearing held in Washington, DC.
Telsey, A., A. Merrit, and S. Dixon
1988 Cocaine exposure in a term neonate: Necrotizing enterocolitis as a complication. *Clinical Pediatrics* 258(11):547–550.
U.S. General Accounting Office
1990 *Drug exposed infants: A generation at risk.* Washington, DC: U.S. Government Printing Office.

1995a *Child welfare: Complex needs strain capacity to provide services.* Washington, DC: U.S. Government Printing Office.
1995b *Drug courts: Information on a new approach to address drug-related crime.* Washington, DC: U.S. Government Printing Office.
1995c *Drug war: Observations on the U.S. international drug control strategy.* Washington, DC: U.S. Government Printing Office.
Webb, G.
1996 Drug network linked street gangs, contras. *The Arizona Republic,* August 25, A23.
Williams, M. A., R. Mittendorf, E. Leiberman, R. R. Monson, S. C. Schoenbaum, and D. R. Genest
1991 Cigarette smoking during pregnancy in relation to placenta previa. *American Journal of Obstetrics and Gynecology* 165:28–32.
Wilson, G.
1989 Clinical studies of infants and children prenatally exposed to heroin. In *Prenatal abuse of licit and illicit drugs,* ed. D. E. Hutchings, 183–194. New York: New York Academy of Sciences.
Woods, N. S., F. D. Eyler, M. Behnke, and M. Conlon
1993 Cocaine use during pregnancy: Maternal depressive symptoms and infant neurobehavior over the first month. *Infant Behavior Development* 16:83–98.
Zuckerman, B., and D. Frank
1992 Crack kids not broken. *Pediatrics* 89:337–339.
Zuckerman, B., D. Frank, R. Hingson, H. Amaro, S. Levenson, H. Kayne, S. Parker, R. Vinci, K. Aboagye, L. Fried, H. Cabral, R. Timperi, and H. Bauchner
1989 Effect of maternal marijuana and cocaine use on fetal growth. *New England Journal of Medicine* 320(12):762–767.

Cases Cited

In re A.C., 573 A.2d 1235 (D.C. App. 199 0).
In re Baby X, 293 N.W. 2d 736, 739 (Mich. Ct. App. 1980).
In re Jamaica Hospital, 491 N.Y.S. 2d at 900 (N.Y. 1985).
Jackson v. State, 833 S.W. 2d 220, 221 (Tex. 1992)
Johnson v. State, 578 So. 2d 419, 419 (Fla. 1991).
People v. Stewart, No. M508097 (San Diego County Court, February 23, 1987).
Reinesto v. Superior Court of the State of Arizona (ICA-SA 94-0348 1994).
Reyes v. Superior Court 141 Cal. Rptr. 912 (Cal. Ct. App. 1977).

Medicalizing Homelessness: The Production of Self-Blame and Self-Governing within Homeless Shelters

32

Vincent Lyon-Callo

> Sometimes I just can't believe how stupid people here are. They know they're being oppressed, but they won't say anything about it.

Raymond, a homeless African American man in his late forties, spoke those words to me one evening in 1996 as we sat in the living room of an emergency homeless shelter in Northampton, Massachusetts.[1] We had just left another in a long series of shelter meetings where many staff and guests advocated increased staff surveillance of homeless people's individual behaviors as the most reasonable means for responding to increasing local homelessness. They appeared to be suggesting that surveillance was a key tool for uncovering "causes" of homelessness that need to be treated if we hoped to decrease homelessness.

Raymond, a man with a long history of social activism focused on racism and poverty, was one of the few people at the shelter to openly question routine shelter practices. Many guests complained about shelter rules, but Raymond was nearly alone in characterizing the staff counseling and training efforts as misplaced, insofar as they did not work against systemic inequities in the community. Consequently, Raymond spent much time arguing against staff "helping" practices, which he characterized as inhumane for misplacing attention on individual homeless people. At the meeting we had just left, Raymond had been the only person staying at the shelter to argue against a proposal to initiate drug testing of shelter residents and another to begin using "workfare" recipients as "volunteers" within the shelter. He could not understand why he and I were the only people at the meeting voicing opposition to those policies. He read the compliance of other homeless people as the result of their being too stupid or uninformed to know any better.

I told Raymond I shared his sentiment that efforts to resolve homelessness through disciplining homeless people and reforming their perceived deviancy were misplaced. We both interpreted such practices as ignoring increasing structural violence as well as the historical and political-economic context within which homelessness has become a "normal" feature of life in the United States. But I also suggested an alternative interpretation to Raymond. I asserted that it doesn't really help us either understand or work against consent to domination if we simply think of people who disagree with us as lacking the intelligence to see "the truth" about homelessness and inequality. Instead, we need to analyze how particular understandings and practices are constituted and come to make sense to those embracing and enacting them. This article is a part of that effort.

As recent work by Susan Ruddick (1995), David Wagner (1993), and Talmadge Wright (1997) makes clear, homeless people are active social agents who respond to homelessness in a variety of ways. Wright and Wagner document how responses sometimes take the form of open defiance. But I have observed that many people who find themselves homeless often engage in more individualized strategies of coping and accommodating. This article analyzes these strategies and the seeming acquiescence to the systemic conditions of homelessness they represent by ethnographically exploring how homelessness is medicalized through the discourses surrounding it. I accomplish this by examining the everyday practices of staff and guests within one homeless shelter.

Medicalizing Social Inequity

Scholarship has demonstrated clear links between tactical business and governmental decisions and the recent production of homelessness in the United States. The increasing globalization of capital, deindustrialization (Hopper et al. 1985), the growth of temporary labor, altered tax policies, declining union membership, the growth of non-unionized service sector employment, institutionalized racism, gentrification in the name of community development (Marcuse 1989; Williams 1996), and a changing political landscape all have contributed to the production of increased economic inequality and homelessness during the past 20 years. In addition, neither the public nor private housing markets have managed to keep up with the growing demand for affordable housing (Burt 1992). In short, homelessness has become routine during a two-decade period characterized by growing inequality in wealth and income in the United States.

Despite these clear connections, very few practices aimed at resolving homelessness have specifically addressed such conditions. The implementation of emergency shelters was the initial dominant response, as homelessness first became widespread in the 1970s and 1980s. These shelters simply provided a "safe" place to sleep, often a meal, and sometimes a shower and place to store one's belongings.[2] However, large emergency shelters did little to address homelessness and were often unsafe, inhumane, and degrading places that warehoused poor people (Dordick 1997;

Gounis 1992; Liebow 1993). Often shelter rules even made it nearly impossible for a person to maintain employment and still reside at the shelter (Roofless Women's Action Research Mobilization 1996).

As the limitations and abuses of the emergency shelter approach have been documented in recent years, advocates and policy makers have searched for more effective methods of addressing the homelessness crisis. While many cities have opted to criminalize homelessness, federal agencies and some local communities have responded by advocating a "continuum of care" approach. Under this model, communities develop programs and services to treat the myriad symptoms thought to create homelessness, and shelters offer the services understood to be needed to help people obtain (and maintain) housing.[3] The move toward this model is part of a broader effort undertaken by some advocates and policy makers to reframe homelessness as a condition afflicting those victimized by disease and dysfunction rather than the result of bad individual choices. For example, efforts have been made to publicly represent people who find themselves homeless as suffering from the effects of traumatic episodes in their youth or during military service, a poorly functioning foster care system, depression or schizophrenia, the disease of alcoholism and substance abuse, domestic abuse, or similar ailments that restrict their capacity to remain employed and housed. The goal is a more effective and caring response to homelessness.

However, the move toward a disease model often has ambiguous and conflicting impacts (Singer et al. 1992). On the one hand, recent efforts may have facilitated increased services to reform, treat, and retrain individualized homeless people, and such efforts do improve the lives of some individuals who are homeless. On the other hand, however, the "continuum of care" approach also does not fundamentally address questions of access to and distribution of resources in the community. In fact, I argue here that the focus on "disease" within the discourses of "helping" actually obliterates discussion of alternative explanations and thus hinders developments aimed at resolving homelessness through altering class, race, or gender dynamics. When homelessness is individualized and medicalized, those concerns remain peripheral to the central work of normalizing perceived shortcomings or deviancy within homeless people.

Undoubtedly, this outcome is partly the result of a combination of both dominant imaginings and stigmatized perceptions about homeless people (Dear and Gleeson 1991) and the impact that federal funding concerns and religious organizations have on influencing public priorities and sheltering industry practices (Lyon-Callo 1998). Yet these are only small pieces needed to understand the complex puzzle of social processes and social relations that produce widespread homelessness. What is also needed is an understanding of how such understandings and practices have come to be so common. One small part of that larger project involves examining how medicalized and individualized understandings about homeless people as deviant are constituted, reproduced, and reinforced through discourses and practices.

It is hardly surprising that a medicalized conceptual framework guides responses to homelessness at this moment in history. Homelessness is just one social condition among many that have been medicalized in recent years. Conditions and behaviors ranging from sexual decision-making, depression, credit card debt, sexuality, drug use, gambling, weight problems, and teen pregnancy are increasingly portrayed in popular and scientific discourses as the results of pathology or disorders within particular bodies or the bodies of groups of people. One effect of conceptualizing social problems through a lens of diseased bodies is often a neglect of systemic inequality. Consideration of the material and historical conditions that might contribute to the production of problems is silenced or marginalized by a focus on individual traits and habits.

As Vicente Navarro describes it, the medicalization of social problems plays the ideological function of legitimizing existing class relations and serves to "depoliticize what is intrinsically a political problem. Thus, within a medical framework, what requires a collective answer is presented as an individual problem, demanding an individual response" (1986:40). Navarro argues that much of what is thought of as illness is in fact the result of a fundamentally disproportionate distribution of resources. Yet, rather than working collectively to alter class relations and the distribution of health services, many health care and social service efforts focus on treating perceived disorders within individual bodies.

Critical medical anthropologists writing from the perspective of political economy have produced much work related to Navarro's arguments. Paul Farmer et al. (1996) stress the degree to which AIDS research and social policy efforts focus on discovering and treating behaviors. They argue that such practices have the effect of silencing work against the class and gender processes that also contribute to illness. Other scholars have analyzed how racial, class, and gender inequities are often manifested in terms of alcohol abuse, AIDS, poverty, physical illness, mental illness, and homelessness (Morsy 1990; Singer and Baer 1996). Merrill Singer, for example, argues that to understand a "disorder" such as alcohol abuse, one needs to consider the broader historical and material conditions that produce the behavior (Singer et al. 1992).

Similar dynamics apply to homelessness. In her study of the medicalization of homelessness in New York City during the 1980s, Arline Mathieu (1993) discusses how representations of "the homeless" by government officials as mentally ill served to marginalize the political-economic context of homeless people. She details how press releases from the mayor's office in support of a policy of randomly taking homeless people off the streets by force emphasized that the people still living on the streets were homeless due to mental illness. Mathieu argues that as long as homeless people were biomedically represented as deviant, their living on the streets could be "solved" by housing them in shelters and forcing them into treatment programs. Attention to systemic inequities that contribute to producing widespread homelessness was thus deemed unnecessary.

Through my work on homelessness, I have come to agree that systemic inequities contribute to the production of many behaviors that are commonly read as pathological disorders in people without permanent shelter.[4] Reading these behaviors as individual disorders certainly plays a role in silencing work against exploitative social conditions and in limiting our ability as medical anthropologists to work more effectively against the conditions the work documents (Hopper 1988; Singer 1995). However, there is another component that deserves analytical attention. Something much more subtle and insidious than simply mystification takes place when homelessness is medicalized. It is my contention that routine, everyday practices undertaken by shelter staff and guests to resolve "diseases" actually reproduce and reinforce dominant imaginings about homelessness and homeless people and, thus, contribute to producing particular subjectivities, experiences, self-images, and behaviors among homeless people.

To make this argument, I draw upon insights coming out of the critical-interpretive approach in medical anthropology represented by Robert Desjarlais (1997), Margaret Lock and Nancy Scheper-Hughes (1990), and Alan Young (1995), as well as by scholars outside of anthropology writing on the production of medicalized knowledge (Hacking 1986, 1995), governmentality, and the practices of self-making (Rose 1990, 1996). These scholars demonstrate how all knowledge of society, normality, illness, and self is socially produced and determined and that all knowledge about the body, health, and illness is constituted through historically situated cultural negotiations (Scheper-Hughes and Lock 1990). To analyze that process it is imperative to examine the techniques and practices through which people who are without a permanent place of residence are made into subjects to be governed by their selves, social workers, social planners, and medical experts. In this article, therefore, I outline a strategy for considering the ways in which the homeless body (the social body and the body politic regarding homelessness, as well as individualized homeless bodies) is, in part, produced and reproduced by social practices within homeless shelters.[5]

Even prior to being connected with the facility, many of the people who volunteered, worked, or lived at the shelter I observed articulated understandings supporting the dominant conceptual framework in which homelessness is viewed as embodied deviance. This is hardly surprising given the preponderance of public discourses that pathologize poor people as well as dominant stigmatized images of homeless people as deviants. Yet, in analyzing precise practices in the shelter setting, I uncover how the well-intentioned efforts within the shelter actually work to reproduce and reinforce the image of homelessness as a social problem with an origin in individual deviancy. Reformative efforts often focus on "treatments" that fit within constructed views of "normal" and "deviant." These practices produce subjects who come to understand reform of the individualized self as the most "reasonable" and "realistic" ways of resolving homelessness. Through their experiences in the shelters, many homeless people are thus produced (and reproduced) as political subjects who are more likely to engage in self-blame and self-governing than in collective work against structural violence.

Producing Homeless Subjects: An Exploration of Routine Shelter Practices

From 1993 through 1997, I conducted activist ethnographic research at a 20-bed emergency homeless shelter in Northampton, Massachusetts, where I was also employed as a staff member.[6]

This setting was an ideal location for investigating the effects of the "continuum of care" and disease model for at least two reasons. First, Northampton, like much of the northeastern United States, has undergone vast economic changes in the past two decades. Lost manufacturing jobs have been replaced by low-wage, often part-time employment in food services, social services, and retail trade. Recent gentrification and redevelopment of the downtown area has created a bustling urban core but has led to the loss of one-half of the city's single-room-occupancy units. Housing costs are out of reach of many citizens, while waiting lists for housing assistance are closed for years at a time.

Northampton was also an ideal setting for the study because local shelter providers and policy makers strongly embraced the "continuum of care" concept. As a result, staff members at the shelter counseled people on a wide range of issues as well as referring "guests" to outside experts. Likewise, community planners and policy makers developed a broad array of "helping" services in the community. Such services included increased substance abuse treatment programs, enhanced access to mental health services, veteran's services, job training, increased shelter beds, and an assortment of counseling options and workshops within shelters. Consequently, the city and the shelter were both often described by guests as the best place in the entire state to try to resolve one's homelessness.

In this setting, I conducted archival research on economic and housing conditions at the local level, which provided a systemic context within which I could better contemplate local responses to homelessness. I also spent over 6,000 hours ethnographically detailing how homeless people, shelter staff, local advocates, and local policy makers responded to homelessness. I observed and participated in a broad range of shelter activities, including weekly staff meetings, case management efforts, the daily enforcement of shelter rules, statistical record keeping, the development of shelter policies, intake interviews, staff hiring, efforts to locate housing and income, the development of grant applications, and staff training. Data from these activities were supplemented by a series of open-ended interviews with nine staff members, several dozen homeless people, shelter administrators, local advocates, and local policy makers.[7]

I employed an explicitly activist position while conducting this research. By activist ethnographic research I do not mean a simple stance of advocacy for a particular position or understanding. Rather, I engaged in a constantly evolving dialogue with the community members with whom I worked. The goal was not simply to find data to support my views, nor was it my intention to impose my views or visions upon these people, as if I had "the solution" to homelessness.[8] Homelessness is much too complex for any simple social policy change to "solve." By activist research, what I am referring to is an ethnographic method of openly challenging each other's ideas in an effort to think more critically about all of our views and practices. My intention was to facilitate our learning from each other through engaging in debate and dialogue regarding the effects of our routine, well-meaning practices and by asking how to understand homelessness in as comprehensive and complex a fashion as possible. It was my hope that this engagement might stretch the parameters of what was thinkable and doable and, thus, create the possibility for new discourses, new practices, and new subjectivities to emerge.[9]

Through engagement of this sort, I uncovered and challenged an underlying hegemonic hypothesis of deviancy functioning within the local sheltering industry. I found that routine practices focus primary attention on developing techniques for detecting, diagnosing, and treating pathological disorders within individual homeless people.

Detecting and diagnosing disorders begins the moment a homeless person first enters the shelter. The new shelter guest is quickly directed into the staff office for an intake interview. The intake interview serves several functions. On one level, it is simply an opportunity for the staff to compile basic statistical and demographic data while detailing the shelter rules and procedures. A case history, used to guide case management, is also started. Of paramount importance, though, is that the intake interview is the first opportunity for the staff and guest to diagnose the disorder(s) of the self that caused the person to be homeless.

In addition to the required components of the intake, the staff member works to comfort the recently homeless person, who is often quite nervous about being in a shelter. A caring staff member uses this opportunity to develop a sense of rapport with the new guest. Through this more informal discussion and from the homeless person's mannerisms and articulations, the staff member attempts to gather additional data on possible disorders within the person. If, for example, the staff member detects what he or she perceives to be possible mental illness or substance abuse, these observations are noted in the person's case folder and in the staff log. Other staff can thus be made aware of the diagnosis and look for possible supporting symptoms.

Staff gathers this information in a variety of ways. One specific question during the intake asks the recently homeless person to state his or her "reason for homelessness." The intake form includes a number of suggested reasons, each particular to that individual. As most homeless people have already learned a great deal of self-blame prior to entering the shelter, many guests will respond by disclosing a behavioral or training problem as the cause of their homelessness. For example, 39 percent of the people at this shelter during 1995 stated that they were homeless due to "substance abuse." Thus, overcoming that individualized problem became the focus of their subsequent efforts to become housed.

Formal efforts to diagnose possible causes of homelessness continue throughout the person's stay at the shelter. Within one week, a case management meeting is scheduled for the new arrival to meet with staff for a second intake. This setting is more clearly defined as establishing a counseling relationship. Here, the staff and guest meet privately for a prolonged discussion about the "issues" that brought the person to the shelter and the resources available to help with those needs. A more detailed case management intake form asks about the level of education, employment history, medical history, past therapy or counseling experiences, and any background with substance abuse or mental health treatment programs. This information is used to determine what issues the homeless person should "work on" while at the shelter. Detected problems range from mental illness to a need for employment training, but all are understood as situated within the homeless person.

With the initial diagnosis in hand, the shelter staff and homeless person proceed to look for evidence to support, refute, or augment the initial diagnosis. This evidence is gathered through both formal case management meetings and less formal surveillance mechanisms. Surveillance takes place while monitoring the guest's obedience to shelter rules, counseling guests, resolving conflicts, and engaging in informal discussions in the shelter. As Ann, an ex-staff member, summed it up, "Whenever you are at the shelter, you are supposed to be monitoring the guests."

The monitoring is understood as a vital function through which the staff and guests can garner information for diagnosing the disorder needing treatment. For example, when staff monitoring or guest disclosure reveals an infraction of the rules, the offending person is called into the staff office to discuss the incident. A written warning describing the transgression is placed in the guest's case file. More importantly, a conversation follows wherein the staff member uses the violation of shelter policies as evidence of an issue the homeless person needs to resolve if he or she hopes to become housed. This is portrayed as a mechanism by which homeless people can be made to come to grips with the issues (always disorders within their selves) causing their unstable lives and homelessness.

These practices initially seemed like common sense to many staff and guests. Because such sentiments are currently so ubiquitous in the United

States, they make sense as the normal way to resolve homelessness. Thus, neither the majority of guests nor staff tended to question them. In fact, many shelter guests often sought more stringent staff surveillance and urged stronger disciplinary rules in the shelter. They understood surveillance of their selves as a mechanism for "helping."

Through the application of these shelter practices, the homeless person is turned into a case history, someone known via these diagnostic techniques as a set of individual disorders and symptoms. The staff and guest's determination of cause "types" the homeless person as a "kind" of client defined by "signs" of his or her "disorder." This "typing" thus drives subsequent treatment responses.

Once the staff and guests have detected and diagnosed the disorder(s) within a homeless person, they begin treatment. Gloria, a shelter staff member, explained this process: "I think many staff take the sort of disease model approach. Well, you know, if that's your problem, we'll hook you up with meetings, you'll do this, you'll go into this program, and that will cure your problem and fix you."

Within the shelter, biomedical language and practices focusing attention on diagnosing and treating pathologies understood to cause social problems are augmented by pseudo-scientific discourses arguing that the only "reasonable" way to help many people is through programs aimed at self-help. As a result, one of the first steps in developing a case history is to have the guest and staff look for the factors that caused that person to turn out the way he or she did. A defining feature of the diagnosis is that the homeless guest must be a willing collaborator in self-diagnosis. Guests are taught to ask, "How did I come to be this way?" It is this reflexive inquiry about the self that is at the heart of future reform efforts.

The vast majority of routine shelter treatment plans fall under the rubric of self-help and governing of the self. As Barbara Cruikshank concludes in her work on self-esteem programs for poor women, self-help and self-government promise "to deliver a technology of subjectivity that will solve social problems like homelessness and inequality by waging a social revolution, not against capitalism, racism, and gender inequality, but against the order of the self and the way we govern our selves" (1996:231). Let me illustrate this process with a few ethnographic examples.

Jerry, a 24-year-old white man, tried his hardest to work his way out of homelessness through paid employment. He came to the shelter shortly after being honorably discharged from the military and maintained a job at a local branch of a supermarket chain for over nine months. Jerry's strategy of attempting to resolve homelessness through paid employment is far from unique. In 1995, 74 (38 percent) of the 193 people who stayed at the shelter were employed. However, over 90 percent of those employed worked in either food service or in retail trade jobs with unsteady work schedules, low pay, and no health benefits. Those are the jobs available in this community.[10] Consequently, only four of the 193 shelter guests were able to secure an apartment or house in Northampton that year. When rents average approximately $650 per month for a one-bedroom apartment (Watson 1996:16) and there are thousands of people on the waiting list for subsidized housing, it is fairly difficult to afford rent with an income less than $200 per week.

Jerry was one homeless person who understood his low pay as the result of broader political-economic processes. After one particularly frustrating evening of work at the supermarket, Jerry and I had a long conversation about his working conditions. At one point, he argued, "It's just shit. If this was the 1950s, I wouldn't be homeless. My uncle graduated from high school and got a job right away in doing tool and die work. They gave him good pay and benefits and he was able to buy a house. There just aren't good jobs like that anymore. I work just as hard and I'm still stuck in this job and in the shelter."

Feeling powerless to alter the wages paid in the existing jobs in the community, he desperately wanted to go to college as a path toward a better job and more financial stability. However, he couldn't figure out a way to pay for school. He couldn't afford to rent a room in a rooming house, let alone pay for college. Jerry tried to hold down a second food service job, but the two sets of work hours conflicted too often and he was forced to quit the second job. He also persistently searched for better paying jobs in the community, but was unsuccessful in obtaining one.

After Jerry had been in the shelter several months, staff began to worry about how to help him move out. Weekly discussions at staff meetings ensued focusing on how to help Jerry. Some staff began to pressure him to work more closely with them on diagnosing the reasons for his homelessness and his inability to find a higher-paying job. Several staff members suggested that his inability to save enough money to move out of the shelter was a "sign" of deeper problems than simply a low-paying job. When Jerry and I countered that he was working long hours but was just not being paid enough to afford local rents, he was urged to think "realistically" about what he could do to afford a place to live.

When I again suggested that the problem might not be within Jerry but with the wages being paid locally, I was seen as diverting attention from "realistic" solutions. As Karen, a newer staff member, commented, "I agree that those are problems, but I wouldn't know where to start to solve those problems. I feel like all I can do is to do what I can to really help people on a practical level. And people here have real problems with personal issues." It was suggested that Jerry was unable to obtain a higher-paying job because of lingering depression and substance abuse. I then suggested that perhaps these conditions were the result of his current life circumstances. A few staff members thought that made sense, but, again, they had to be practical and work on what they could change. What they could change was Jerry.

Increased staff attention focused on helping Jerry resolve his "issues" of substance abuse and depression. At case management meetings, he was urged to look at past behaviors as possible indicators of disorders. In particular, drunken episodes in high school and the military were portrayed as symptoms of a substance abuse disorder. Even though he had only drunk alcohol two times during the previous two months, it was suggested that staff mandate that Jerry have bi-weekly meetings with a therapist and attend at least three Alcoholics Anonymous meetings each week as conditions for receiving further extended stays at the shelter.

He was encouraged to understand his homelessness as the result of traumatic stress related to his youth, insecurity about his sexuality, depression, and substance abuse. In fact, he was rewarded with extended staff "help" and extra time at the shelter for doing so and threatened with expulsion from the shelter if he did not work to reform his self. Several staff members urged him to quit his job so he could focus more energy on his self. He did not comply with that suggestion, but he did agree to seek therapy, to take antidepressant medication, and to attend self-help programs. Through these efforts, he soon came to articulate his problem as being within his self. What else could he do, but struggle to change his self? Clearly, nothing could be done about the fact that 45 percent of new jobs in the region are projected to pay wages below the federal poverty level for a family of two (Turner 1998). Likewise, nothing could be done about the fact that the supermarket chain Jerry worked for made $73 million in profits in 1995 and paid its CEO a base salary of $1.19 million while paying its workers wages inadequate to afford housing (Spain and Talbott 1996:1351). It was understood that nothing could be done about those circumstances. Therefore, the only reasonable path was to teach Jerry to reform his self.

A second example details a similar subject-making effect. On a June night in 1996, Maria came down the stairs of the shelter and asked if she could speak with me. Maria had entered the shelter approximately two months earlier. Like Raymond, she had a fairly extensive history of social activism around racial inequality in the region. She had also worked for many years in social service jobs. When she entered the shelter, both Maria and the staff believed she would quickly find a job and move out of the shelter. After two months of unsuccessful job searches, some staff began to understand Maria's problems as the result of a disorder within her self. At the same time, her relationship with the father of her children began to become difficult. Several staff counseled Maria and urged "self-empowerment" through focusing on the "issues within her own life." Maria was urged to stop seeking a job and to focus on her "issues."

Our conversation began with Maria stating that she was now willing to address a disorder of the self that a staff member had previously diagnosed. She explained that she was now willing to seek counseling and therapy for her depression. She said, "I'm starting to feel really low. It started at the end of the week, and by Friday and Saturday I didn't want to see anyone."

When I asked her why she now thought she needed therapy, she explained,

> I feel stuck here. I need a job. I've done everything I can think of to get a job. I even applied at Burger King for an assistant manager. I've sent out my resume to a thousand places, but I can't get a job. I'm starting to think that I must be doing something during the interviews to turn these people off. I know sometimes it's discrimination, because I'm someone who speaks my mind and people don't like Puerto Rican women who speak up, but I'm starting to blame myself also. Thinking that there's something wrong with me. . . . I think I'll call this woman I used to talk to on Monday. She was pretty good, except she tried to push the pills on me. A job don't come in no pill. If you got a pill that gets me a job, I'll take it.

Both Maria and Jerry are strong, bright, energetic people. After a few months of working with the shelter staff, however, both were contemplating medication for mental health problems. As Maria stated, "A job don't come in no pill," but neither she nor Jerry were provided with any way of understanding their inability to resolve homelessness that did not involve focusing on treating the individualized self. Within the dominant medicalized conceptual framework, it becomes common sense to understand the coping strategies of people surviving in homeless shelters as symptoms and evidence of mental illness. These people are thus understood as passive victims of biological disorders rather than situated social agents. Rather than providing a collective, social, or political understanding, shelter practices help to reproduce self-blame and self-governing.

People who come to believe that the solution to homelessness lies in treating or reforming the self are unlikely to engage in collective action. Within that discursive framework, collective action makes little sense because it does not involve working on individual issues. However, as Raymond Williams (1977) elucidates, hegemony is never totalizing. Peripheral discourses, although marginalized, do provide possibilities for resisting. Some shelter staff and some people who find themselves homeless, like Raymond, do voice a profound desire to change systemic conditions. Like Maria, they often articulate an analysis linking homelessness to class exploitation and social discrimination. However, these noncompliant staff and homeless people also remain enmeshed within the dominant medicalized discourse. In fact, any resistance to medicalizing discourses and practices is often itself medicalized and diagnosed as misplaced attention and further evidence of pathology. "The medical gaze is then a controlling gaze, through which active (although furtive) forms of protest are transformed into passive acts of 'breakdown'" (Lock and Scheper-Hughes 1990:68). Let me demonstrate this with an example.

After Raymond had several bouts with homelessness, a small majority of staff members voted to not allow him to return to the shelter. At the time, the shelter had a long waiting list, and the decision to bar Raymond was based on the argument that the shelter needed to prioritize those people they could really help. It was argued that it would be a waste of resources to allow him to return because he did not cooperate with prior case management procedures designed to "help" him. As Karen argued, "We can only help people if they are willing to work with us."

I suggested that maybe the staff was projecting a politically dangerous message by prioritizing who was worthy of shelter. Instead, I urged, we should argue that everyone was deserving of a safe place to live and engage in practices to accomplish that goal. Two other staff members, however, disagreed. They reminded us of what had happened a few years earlier when the shelter had let in everyone requesting a bed. They correctly reminded me that, at the time, I had agreed with them that it was an unhealthy and unhelpful effort.

I then stated that perhaps I was not being clear. I was not suggesting more shelters but, rather, that we work to decrease poverty and inequality and lessen the actual demand for shelters. They agreed with the sentiment but argued that they felt the shelter would alienate supporters with such practices and that we needed to be "realistic" and cognizant of the public sentiment that only those willing to help themselves were deserving of housing.

As one staff member, Leopoldina, reminded me, the shelter had just begun to obtain adequate funding from the state. A condition of the funding was that the shelter submit a monthly summary of how many guests staff had referred to treatment programs, job training programs, and similar reformative efforts. Leopoldina pointed out that it was quite telling that nowhere on the monthly form were there questions about efforts to politically organize homeless people, facilitate the development of collaborative efforts to decrease economic inequality in the community, alter the local wage scale, or address issues of housing cost or availability. In her mind, the state agency was sending a clear message about priorities and what practices the shelter staff must engage in if they wished to continue to receive funding. Not wanting to risk losing funding and, thus, the ability to shelter anyone, most staff complied with this message. No one was happy about turning away 20 to 40 people each night, but prioritizing those seeking shelter was understood by some as the most "practical" and "reasonable" response available.

As a result, Raymond's attention to the collective and racialized experience of homelessness was portrayed as an expression of his unwillingness to help himself. In fact, his focus on historical and political-economic conditions was sometimes represented as a symptom of a mental health disorder both by other shelter residents and by several staff. Other staff read Raymond's noncompliance (and perhaps his race) as a sign of drug use, and he was portrayed in staff meetings as a drug dealer and pimp despite the absence of any concrete evidence. In any case, he was punished for not complying with the idea that the proper way to respond to homelessness was through treating individualized deviancy. Other noncompliant guests have had similar experiences.

If a homeless person openly questions shelter helping efforts, he or she is understood as a problem. Staff use a variety of mechanisms to lessen the significance of such critiques. The homeless person is diagnosed as misplacing attention on "political" matters and not focusing on real individual issues. Often, these "political" concerns are understood as symptoms of mental illness and paranoia. Medication has been suggested as a means of "helping" more than a few people who spoke out against what they saw as misplaced shelter practices.

A slightly different set of practices surround a second noncompliant guest. Ariel, a white woman in her late fifties, first came to the shelter in May of 1993. Ariel had maintained a lower-middle-class life, doing light clerical work until the mid-1980s. When she was no longer able to find such work because of her age and computerization, she began to try to support herself through house cleaning. In 1993, she lost her room at a local rooming house when she was no longer able to secure enough work to pay rent. As soon as Ariel entered the shelter, staff members went to work trying to help her. The strategy used was that of uncovering the disorders within Ariel that resulted in her homelessness.

As with most of the hundreds of homeless people I have met, Ariel was full of self-blame and, consequently, was quite angry and upset over her situation when we first met. As she put it, "I didn't know what to do with this anger, so I blamed myself." Ariel's feelings of anguish would be manifested in her sometimes losing her patience with a fellow guest, becoming distraught, crying, and feeling unable to concentrate at times. She was clearly in a great deal of emotional pain. A few times, she was forgetful in the kitchen, and tea kettles were left on the stove unattended.

Ariel's emotions and behaviors were read by most staff as symptomatic of a mental illness. She was characterized as "clinically depressed" or suffering from post-traumatic stress disorder. Further evidence of a mental health disorder was gathered from her frequent suggestions for improving shelter policies and practices. Ariel's seemingly helpful suggestions, for example, that staff save dinners for shelter residents working the second shift, or her offer to wash the window curtains were read as directing attention away from the "cause" of her homelessness and as symptoms of her disorder. Staff members often did not respond to her suggestions because they did not want to "encourage her denial."

During July of 1993, this diagnosis resulted in a group of shelter staff developing a treatment plan for Ariel. The first step was to get her into counseling and on anti-depressant medications. When she resisted, staff devised a second plan to obtain money for Ariel by having her declared mentally disabled so that she would be eligible for social security disability payments. Ariel wanted nothing to do with that form of help. She explained that she was poor, not mentally ill.

Staff at the shelter continued to push the plan on Ariel. She was routinely called into a staff office for counseling sessions. At these sessions, well-meaning staff members would point out to Ariel how she was unable to care for herself. They would explain that they were concerned about her, but she could not stay at the shelter forever if she did not want to "help herself." Ariel told me how, during these meetings, staff members would tell her she was going to freeze to death or lose limbs from frostbite that winter if she did not comply with their helping efforts. When she still refused to comply, Ariel was denied further time at the shelter.

As a result of her resistance to medicalized shelter practices, Ariel was kicked out of the shelter for being difficult. *Being difficult* was defined as not claiming a mental health disability. The hope of the staff was that living on the streets would "break through her denial" once Ariel "hit bottom." Instead, her resistance to the medicalization of her body resulted in physical hardship. She survived outside from August through mid-December, when my constant advocacy, the empty shelter beds, the extreme cold, and the guilt of the Christmas season led staff to allow her to move back into the shelter. But then the efforts to push Ariel toward self-reform began anew.

Ariel described to me how some staff would ask her why she just wouldn't go along and comply. They could not understand how she could "keep living like this." Ariel told me, "The alternative is to commit suicide, and I'm not going to commit suicide. I'm willing to walk around with no place to live because I have no place to live. Because I'm willing to keep on living, that's why. I'm willing to walk around all night or sit up in Stop and Shop [a regional supermarket] because I'm not willing to jump off a bridge. Those are my options."

I asked, "And you think that getting social security payments so you can have a room in a rooming house wouldn't be living, it would be giving up?"

Ariel replied, "Right. I'm not going to lie. I'm going to tell them the truth. They better not declare me mentally disabled. I am not mentally disabled, but I do need money to get a place to live. It's like they're saying, 'We can't change the economy, so we have to change you.'"

Everyone in this situation did the best they could. Clearly, Ariel was resisting, but her resistance remained quite constrained. Let me be clear: I am not simply describing a case by mystification or false consciousness. Not everyone I worked with believes that homelessness is simply the result of deviancy within homeless people. As Stuart Hall notes, hegemony functions such that "ruling ideas may . . . set the limit to what will appear as rational, reasonable, credible, indeed sayable or thinkable" (1988:44). The hegemony of the medicalized discourse of deviancy operating within the homeless sheltering industry produces everyday practices of self-disclosure and self-government as routine habits that are accepted as "common sense."

The combination of a dominant medicalized discourse of deviancy, the belief in the naturalness and inevitability of capitalist exploitation, and widespread feelings of powerlessness to alter systemic conditions produce practices within the narrowly defined parameters of what is "reasonable" and "realistic" to think and do. The actual practices, even of noncompliant homeless people, remain enmeshed within the hegemony of the discourses of deviancy. To paraphrase Michel de Certeau, everyday practices enacted by noncompliant homeless people often allow them to "escape domination without leaving it" (1984:xiii). They are resisting the hegemony of the bio-medical discourse by refusing to comply and collaborate in their oppression, but are not working collectively to escape or alter the systemic oppression that results in widespread inequality and homelessness.

Agents within the sheltering industry develop diagnostic tools, statistical representations, treatments, and reforms to make the homeless person into a new kind of self-blaming and self-governing person. Under these discursive conditions, the staff and guests function as institutional agents whose job it is to govern "the homeless" through a regime of surveillance, discipline, and personal enhancement. In short, a "normal" person is to be made by governing a "deviant" homeless person.

Those advocating governing the self as the solution to homelessness do not pay attention to the extent to which personal life is governed. The self (like poverty, homelessness, inequality, and racism) is not only personal but also the product of power relations, the outcome of strategies and technologies (Cruikshank 1996:248). Self-help, self-fulfillment, and self-reform are technologies that produce certain kinds of selves and marginalize the possibilities of producing alternative subjectivities. When statistical typologies and case histories diagnose disorders within homeless people and, thus, reinforce knowledge about homeless deviants, it becomes only "common sense" that helping efforts focus on treating these disorders of the self. Homeless subjectivities are made up through shelter helping practices such that it makes perfect sense for many people living in shelters to willingly comply with more surveillance and reform of their bodies and selves.

If we are to understand the durability of homelessness despite the well-meaning efforts of the sheltering industry, we must contemplate how *the homeless* and *homelessness,* as categories, are produced and resisted. These categories are products of discursive conditions that give rise to concrete ways of thinking and acting. This article focuses on one particular community and one shelter. Although not representative of all shelters, it does provide a case study by which to examine the ambiguous effects of adapting the "disease" model for responding to homelessness. We need to examine practices designed to validate the categories of *homelessness* and *the homeless* in a range of settings. Through that work, we can begin to uncover how dominant discursive conditions reinforce routine practices that normatively silence or devalue other possible ways of perceiving and being in regard to homelessness.

Notes

Correspondence may be addressed to the author at Department of Anthropology, Western Michigan University, Kalamazoo, MI 49008, e-mail: vincent.lyon-callo@wmich.edu.

1. The names of all homeless people and shelter staff referred to in this article have been changed. Everyone quoted formally agreed to take part in this study.

2. Many shelters were created as charitable institutions by religious organizations. In these shelters, a homeless person also often received a lecture or gospel reading as a condition for a night's stay.

3. As one example, New York City instituted a program in 1998 whereby the city paid shelter operators bonuses for moving homeless families and individuals into permanent housing. This was represented as an incentive to the shelters to develop more effective helping programs (Holloway 1998).

4. This is certainly not meant to suggest that some people do not display symptoms of what are commonly diagnosed as mental illnesses or substance abuse disorders prior to becoming homeless. However, I would argue that even in such cases, homelessness is a result of political and historical conditions. There is no inherent reason why mental illness or substance abuse must lead to homelessness. In fact, in other historical moments and geographic locations, it has not. Nor do all people displaying such behaviors in the United States today become homeless.

5. See Desjarlais 1997 for a related ethnographic study focused on practices within a shelter for people deemed mentally ill.

6. Activist ethnographic research, like advocacy or action research, strives to be accurate and non-biased without claiming to be value-free or neutral. For more detailed arguments on this research methodology, see Schensul and Schensul 1978 and Singer 1990.

7. I did not formally interview two staff members because of their time commitments outside the shelter. All shelter staff and regular volunteers agreed to participate in the study, sign consent forms, and allow me to tape weekly staff meetings.

8. In fact, several staff members and shelter residents frequently urged me to speak up and assert my views within the community, as if I had "the answer." I tried to explain that my goal was to push all of us to think more critically about our assumptions and practices so that we (including myself) could learn from each other.

9. Again, to be clear, I am not arguing that such engagement will lead people to see "the truth" or free them from the false consciousness hidden by ideological conditions. Instead, my hope was that new discursive practices might lead to different social outcomes, which, hopefully, would decrease the violence of structural inequalities and homelessness.

10. As in much of New England, deindustrialization has hit western Massachusetts quite hard. A 15 percent decrease in manufacturing jobs and a 12 percent increase in service sector jobs occurred countywide during the 1980s (Market Street Research 1994:14). This trend continued throughout the 1990s. According to the Northampton Chamber of Commerce, 42 percent of the jobs in Northampton in 1998 were in the service sector.

References

Burt, Martha
1992 Over the Edge: The Growth of Homelessness in the 1980s. Washington, DC: The Urban Institute Press.
Cruikshank, Barbara
1996 Revolutions Within: Self Government and Self Esteem. *In* Foucault and Political Reason: Liberalism, Neo-Liberalism, and Rationalities of Government. Andrew Barry, Thomas Osborne, and Nikolas Rose, eds. Pp. 231–252. Chicago: University of Chicago Press.
Dear, Michael, and Brendan Gleeson
1991 Community Attitudes Toward the Homeless. Urban Geography 12:155–176.
de Certeau, Michael
1984 The Practice of Everyday Life. Steven F. Rendall, trans. Berkeley: University of California Press.
Desjarlais, Robert
1997 Shelter Blues: Sanity and Selfhood among the Homeless. Philadelphia: University of Pennsylvania Press.
Dordick, Gwendolyn
1997 Something Left to Lose: Personal Relations and Survival among New York's Homeless. Philadelphia, PA: Temple University Press.

Farmer, Paul, Margaret Conners, and Janie Simmons, eds.
1996 Women, Poverty and AIDS: Sex, Drugs and Structural Violence. Monroe, ME: Common Courage Press.

Gounis, Kostas
1992 The Manufacture of Dependency: Shelterization Revisited. New England Journal of Public Policy 8(1):685–693.

Hacking, Ian
1986 Making Up People. *In* Reconstructing Individualism: Autonomy, Individualism, and the Self in Western Thought. Thomas Heller, Morton Sosna, and David Wellberry, eds. Pp. 222–236. Stanford, CA: Stanford University Press.
1995 Rewriting the Soul: Multiple Personality Disorder and the Science of Memory. Princeton, NJ: Princeton University Press.

Hall, Stuart
1988 The Toad in the Garden: Thatcherism among the Theorists. *In* Marxism and the Interpretation of Culture. Cary Nelson and Lawrence Grossberg, eds. Pp. 58–74. Urbana: University of Illinois Press.

Holloway, Lynette
1998 Shelter Operators to Get Bonuses for Finding Homes for the Homeless. The New York Times, September 6:B3.

Hopper, Kim
1988 More than Passing Strange: Homelessness and Mental Illness in New York City. American Ethnologist 15:155–167.

Hopper, Kim, Ezra Susser, and Sarah Conover
1985 Economics of Makeshift: Deindustrialization and Homelessness in New York City. Urban Anthropology 14:183–235.

Liebow, Elliot
1993 Tell Them Who I Am: The Lives of Homeless Women. New York: The Free Press.

Lock, Margaret, and Nancy Scheper-Hughes
1990 A Critical-Interpretive Approach in Medical Anthropology: Rituals and Routines of Discipline and Dissent. *In* Medical Anthropology: Contemporary Theory and Methods. Thomas M. Johnson and Carolyn F. Sargent, eds. Pp. 47–72. New York: Praeger Books.

Lyon-Callo, Vincent
1998 Constraining Responses to Homelessness: An Ethnographic Exploration of the Impact of Funding Concerns on Resistance. Human Organization 57:1–8.

Marcuse, Peter
1989 Gentrification, Homelessness, and the Work Process. Housing Studies 4: 211–220.

Market Street Research
1994 Health and Human Service Needs of Hampshire County Residents: Needs Assessment Report. Northampton, MA: Market Street Research, Inc.

Mathieu, Arlme
1993 The Medicalization of Homelessness and the Theater of Repression. Medical Anthropology Quarterly 7:170–184.

Morsy, Soheir
1990 Political Economy in Medical Anthropology. *In* Medical Anthropology: Contemporary Theory and Methods. Thomas M. Johnson and Carolyn F. Sargent, eds. Pp. 26–46. New York: Praeger Books.

Navarro, Vicente
1986 Crisis, Health, and Medicine: A Social Critique. New York: Tavistock.

Roofless Women's Action Research Mobilization
1996 A Hole in My Soul: Experiences of Homeless Women. *In* For Crying Out Loud: Women's Poverty in the United States. Diane Dujon and Ann Withorn, eds. Pp. 41–55. Boston: South End Press.

Rose, Nikolas
1990 Governing the Soul: The Shaping of the Private Self. London: Routledge
1996 The Death of the Social? Re-Figuring the Territories of Government. Economy and Society 25:327–356.
Ruddick, Susan
1995 Young and Homeless in Hollywood: Mapping Social Identities. London: Routledge.
Schensul, Stephen L., and Jean J. Schensul
1978 Advocacy and Applied Anthropology. *In* Social Scientists as Advocates: Views from the Applied Disciplines. George H. Weber and George J. McCall, eds. Pp. 121–165. Beverly Hills, CA: Sage.
Singer, Merrill
1990 Another Perspective on Advocacy. Current Anthropology 31:548–549.
1995 Beyond the Ivory Tower: Critical Praxis in Medical Anthropology. Medical Anthropology Quarterly 9:80–106.
Singer, Merrill, and Hans Baer
1996 Critical Medical Anthropology. Amityville, NY: Baywood.
Singer, Merrill, Freddie Valentin, Hans Baer, and Zhongke Jia
1992 Why Does Juan Garcia Have a Drinking Problem? Medical Anthropology 14(1):77–106.
Spain, James, and Robert Talbott
1996 Hoover's Handbook of American Businesses, 1996. Austin, TX: The Reference Press.
Turner, Maureen
1998 The Division of Labor: Employment Numbers Look Good on Paper, but They Hide Serious Weak Spots in the Market. The Valley Advocate, February 26:20–22.
Wagner, David
1993 Checkerboard Square: Culture and Resistance in a Homeless Community. Boulder, CO: Westview Press.
Watson, Bruce
1996 Tight Rental Market Aggravates Annual Housing Scramble. The Daily Hampshire Gazette, August 28:15–16.
Williams, Brett
1996 There Goes the Neighborhood: Gentrification, Displacement, and Homelessness in Washington, DC. *In* There's No Place Like Home: Anthropological Perspectives on Housing and Homelessness in the United States. Anna Lou Dehavenon, ed. Pp. 145–163. Westport, CT: Bergin and Garvey.
Williams, Raymond
1977 Marxism and Literature, Oxford: Oxford University Press.
Wright, Talmadge
1997 Out of Place: Homeless Mobilizations, Subcities, and Contested Landscapes. Albany: State University of New York Press.
Young, Alan
1995 The Harmony of Illusions: Inventing Post Traumatic Stress Disorder. Princeton, NJ: Princeton University Press.

Managing Institutional Careers and Identities

We have argued previously that the labeling ceremony or institutional processing can be viewed from two major perspectives—the institution's or the actor's. Thus far, the selections have dealt with processing primarily from the institution's perspective and little direct attention has been given to the actor's perceptions and responses. If we are to approach a more complete understanding of the range of effects that various types of bureaucratic processing can produce at selected stages, then we must try to assume the perspective of individuals who become caught up in the deviant-defining process. How, for example, does being identified, selected, and processed, and ultimately accorded the status of social deviant affect one's public and personal identity and one's self-image? Does the organizationally-created deviant accept his or her new status and associated labels, or does the newly-created deviant reject such organizational products and tags? Perhaps the patient will, in a therapeutic setting, accept the "sick role," but out on the ward the patient may reject the role and protest that he or she is not sick. Predicting which type of outcome is likely to occur is problematic.

Erving Goffman's work, "The Moral Career of the Mental Patient," examines contingencies such as these. Goffman is concerned with analyzing the *moral career* of the mental patient, particularly in terms of how patients perceive and respond to their treatment. Of major concern is the impact of the ward experience upon *self*. He points out initially that very few patients come willingly to the hospital. Rather, many arrive as a result of family or police action. (In this sense, the article further substantiates the discussion of the ways in which behavior in private domains may become regulated by some institution.) Goffman argues that the prepatient career can be analyzed in terms of an "extrusory model." In essence, this means that the patient initially has certain relationships and rights; however, he or she is left with very few after admission. Through Goffman's insightful analysis, one understands how the actor's public identity becomes transformed into a "deviant" identity—in this case, that of a mental patient. Important to this process are such phenomena as the "alienative coalition" and the "betrayal funnel." Goffman argues further that "the last step in the prepatient career can involve his realization—justified or not—that he has been deserted by society and turned out of relationships by those closest to him." At this stage the patient may begin to orient himself or herself to the "ward system." Some patients may, for example, accept the "sick role" and develop a set of rationalizations to "explain" their hospitalization. Such strategies enable the patient to regain and sustain a certain semblance of self—a self that has been subjected to a frontal assault from the institution, its personnel, family members and relatives, and,

485

frequently, other patients. With his or her acceptance of this label, the individual begins to take on the identity of the secondary, or career, deviant.

Thomas J. Schmid and Richard S. Jones, in "Suspended Identity: Identity Transformation in a Maximum Security Prison," present an interesting variant of the identity change process. They examine inmates incarcerated in a maximum security prison. Of interest are not only the ways in which inmates may suspend their preprison identities but how inauthentic prison identities may be constructed. They note initially that most inmates have little in common prior to their imprisonment; they also have little knowledge about what prison is like. However, inmates are required to come to grips with the fact of their incarceration. An inmate often finds himself trying to manage a dualistic self, trying to balance his "true" identity (i.e., his preprison identity) with his "false" identity (i.e., his prison identity). The researchers note that this separation of identities "represents two conscious and interdependent identity-preservation tactics, formulated through self-dialogue and refined through tentative interaction with others." Schmid and Jones present an excellent diagram illustrating the major features involved in the identity change process. They conclude by discussing how an inmate's postprison identity may be influenced in various domains.

33 ▶ The Moral Career of the Mental Patient

Erving Goffman

Traditionally the term *career* has been reserved for those who expect to enjoy the rises laid out within a respectable profession. The term is coming to be used, however, in a broadened sense to refer to any social strand of any person's course through life. The perspective of natural history is taken: unique outcomes are neglected in favor of such changes over time as are basic and common to the members of a social category, although occurring independently to each of them. Such a career is not a thing that can be brilliant or disappointing; it can no more be a success than a failure. In this light, I want to consider the mental patient, drawing mainly upon data collected during a year's participant observation of patient social life in a public mental hospital,[1] wherein an attempt was made to take the patient's point of view.

One value of the concept of career is its two-sidedness. One side is linked to internal matters held dearly and closely, such as image of self and felt identity; the other side concerns official position, jural relations, and style of life, and is part of a publicly accessible institutional complex. The concept of career, then, allows one to move back and forth between the personal and the public, between the self and its significant society, without having overly to rely for data upon what the person says he thinks he imagines himself to be.

This paper, then, is an exercise in the institutional approach to the study of self. The main concern will be with the *moral* aspects of career—that is, the regular sequence of changes that career entails in the person's self and in his framework of imagery for judging himself and others.[2]

The category "mental patient" itself will be understood in one strictly sociological sense. In this perspective, the psychiatric view of a person becomes significant only in so far as this view itself alters his social fate—an alteration which seems to become fundamental in our society when, and only when, the person is put through the process of hospitalization.[3] I therefore exclude certain neighboring categories: the undiscovered candidates who would be judged "sick" by psychiatric standards but who never come to be viewed as such by themselves or others, although they may cause everyone a great deal of trouble;[4] the office patient whom a psychiatrist feels he can handle with drugs or shock on the outside; the mental client who engages in psychotherapeutic relationships. And I include anyone, however robust in temperament, who somehow gets caught up in the heavy machinery of mental hospital servicing. In this way the effects of being treated as a mental patient can be kept quite distinct from the effects upon a person's life of traits a clinician would view as psychopathological.[5] Persons who become mental hospital patients vary widely in the kind and degree of illness that a psychiatrist would impute to them, and in the attributes by which laymen would describe them. But once started on the way, they are confronted by some importantly similar circumstances and respond to these in some importantly similar ways. Since these similarities do not come from mental illness, they would seem to occur in spite of it. It is thus a tribute to the power of social forces that the uniform status of mental patient cannot only assure an aggregate of persons a common fate and eventually, because of this, a common character, but that this social reworking can be done upon what is perhaps the most obstinate diversity of human materials that can be brought together by society. Here there lacks only the frequent forming of a protective group-life by ex-patients to illustrate in full the classic cycle of response by which deviant subgroupings are psychodynamically formed in society.

This general sociological perspective is heavily reinforced by one key finding of sociologically oriented students in mental hospital research. As has been repeatedly shown in the study of nonliterate societies, the awesomeness, distastefulness, and barbarity of a foreign culture can decrease in the degree that the student becomes familiar with the point of view to life that is taken by his subjects. Similarly, the student of mental hospitals can discover that the craziness or "sick behavior" claimed for the mental patient is by and large a product of the claimant's social distance from the situation that the patient is in, and is not primarily a product of mental illness. Whatever the refinements of the various patients' psychiatric diagnoses, and whatever the special ways in which social life on the "inside" is unique, the researcher can find that he is participating in a community not significantly different from any other he has studied.[6] Of course, while restricting himself to the off-ward grounds community of paroled patients, he may feel, as some patients do, that life in the locked wards is bizarre; and while on a locked admissions or convalescent ward, he may feel that chronic "back" wards are socially crazy places. But he need only move his sphere of sympathetic participation to the "worst" ward in the hospital, and this too can come into social focus as a place with a livable and continuously meaningful social world. This in no way denies that he will find a minority in any ward or patient group that continues to seem quite beyond the capacity to follow rules of social organization, or that the orderly fulfillment of normative expectations in patient society is partly made possible by strategic measures that have somehow come to be institutionalized in mental hospitals.

The career of the mental patient falls popularly and naturalistically into three main phases: the period prior to entering the hospital, which I shall call the *prepatient phase;* the period in the hospital, the *inpatient phase;* the period after discharge from the hospital, should this occur, namely, the *expatient phase.*[7] This paper will deal only with the first two phases.

The Prepatient Phase

A relatively small group of prepatients come into the mental hospital willingly, because of their own idea of what will be good for them, or because of wholehearted agreement with the relevant members of their family. Presumably these recruits have found themselves acting in a way which is evidence to them that they are losing their minds or losing control of themselves. This view of oneself would seem to be one of the most pervasively threatening things that can happen to the self in our society, especially since it is likely to occur at a time when the person is in any case sufficiently troubled to exhibit the kind of symptom which he himself can see. As Sullivan described it,

> What we discover in the self-system of a person undergoing schizophrenic changes or schizophrenic processes, is then, in its simplest form, an extremely fear-marked puzzlement, consisting of the use of rather generalized and anything but exquisitely refined referential processes in an attempt to cope with what is essentially a failure at being human—a failure at being anything that one could respect as worth being.[8]

Coupled with the person's disintegrative re-evaluation of himself will be the new, almost equally pervasive circumstance of attempting to conceal from others what he takes to be the new fundamental facts about himself, and attempting to discover whether others too have discovered them.[9] Here I want to stress that perception of losing one's mind is based on culturally derived and socially engrained stereotypes as to the significance of symptoms such as hearing voices, losing temporal and spatial orientation, and sensing that one is being followed, and that many of the most spectacular and convincing of these symptoms in some instances psychiatrically signify merely a temporary emotional upset in a stressful situation, however terrifying to the person at the time. Similarly, the anxiety consequent upon this perception of oneself, and the strategies devised to reduce this anxiety, are not a product of abnormal psychology, but would be exhibited by any person socialized into our culture who came to conceive of himself as someone losing his mind. Interestingly, subcultures in American society apparently differ in the amount of ready imagery and encouragement they supply for such self-views, leading to differential rates of *self*-referral; the capacity to take this disintegrative view of oneself without psychiatric prompting seems to be one of the questionable cultural privileges of the upper classes.[10]

For the person who has come to see himself—with whatever justification—as mentally unbalanced, entrance to the mental hospital can sometimes bring relief, perhaps in part because of the sudden transformation in the structure of his basic social situations; instead of being to himself a questionable person trying to maintain a role as a full one, he can become an officially questioned person known to himself to be not so questionable as that. In other cases, hospitalization can make matters worse for the willing patient, confirming by the objective situation what has theretofore been a matter of the private experience of self.

Once the willing prepatient enters the hospital, he may go through the same routine of experiences as do those who enter unwillingly. In any case, it is the latter that I mainly want to consider, since in America at present these are by far the more numerous kind.[11] Their approach to the institution takes one of three classic forms: they come because they have been implored by their family or threatened with the abrogation of family ties unless they go "willingly"; they come by force under police escort; they come under misapprehension purposely induced by others, this last restricted mainly to youthful prepatients.

The prepatient's career may be seen in terms of an extrusory model; he starts out with relationships and rights, and ends up, at the beginning of his hospital stay, with hardly any of either. The moral aspects of this career, then, typically begin with the experience of abandonment, disloyalty, and embitterment. This is the case even though to others it may be obvious that he was in need of treatment, and even though in the hospital he may soon come to agree.

The case histories of most mental patients document offense against some arrangement for face-to-face living—a domestic establishment, a work place, a semipublic organization such as a church or store, a public region such as a street or park. Often there is also a record of some *complainant,* some figure who takes that action against the offender which eventually leads to his hospitalization. This may not be the person who makes the first move, but it is the person who makes what turns out to be the first effective move. Here is the *social* beginning of the patient's career, regardless of where one might locate the psychological beginning of his mental illness.

The kinds of offenses which lead to hospitalization are felt to differ in nature from those which lead to other extrusory consequences—to imprisonment, divorce, loss of job, disownment, regional exile, noninstitutional psychiatric treatment, and so forth. But little seems known about these differentiating factors; and when one studies actual commitments, alternate outcomes frequently appear to have been possible. It seems true, moreover, that for every offense that leads to an effective complaint, there are many psychiatrically similar ones that never do. No action is taken; or action is taken which leads to other extrusory outcomes; or ineffective action is taken, leading to the mere pacifying or putting off of the person who complains. Thus, as Clausen and Yarrow have nicely shown, even offenders who are eventually hospitalized are likely to have had a long series of ineffective actions taken against them.[12]

Separating those offenses which could have been used as grounds for hospitalizing the offender from those that are so used, one finds a vast number of what students of occupation call career contingencies.[13] Some of these contingencies in the mental patient's career have been suggested, if not explored, such as socio-economic status, visibility of the offense, proximity to a mental hospital, amount of treatment facilities available, community regard for the type of treatment given in available hospitals, and so on.[14] For information about other contingencies one must rely on atrocity tales: a psychotic man is tolerated by his wife until she finds herself a boyfriend, or by his adult children until they move from a house to an apartment; an alcoholic is sent to a mental hospital because the jail is full, and a drug addict because he declines to avail himself of psychiatric treatment on the outside; a rebellious adolescent daughter can no longer be managed at home because she now threatens to have an open affair with an unsuitable companion; and so on. Correspondingly there is an equally important set of contingencies causing the person to bypass this fate. And should the person enter the hospital, still another set of contingencies will help determine when he is to obtain a discharge—such as the desire of his family for his return, the availability of a "manageable" job, and so on. The society's official view is that inmates of mental hospitals are there primarily because they are suffering from mental illness. However, in the degree that the "mentally ill" outside hospitals numerically approach or surpass those inside hospitals, one could say that mental patients *distinctively* suffer not from mental illness, but from contingencies.

Career contingencies occur in conjunction with a second feature of the prepatient's career—the *circuit of agents*—and agencies—that participate fatefully in his passage from civilian to patient status.[15] Here is an instance of that increasingly important class of social system whose elements are agents and agencies, which are brought into systemic connection through having to take up and send on the same persons. Some of these agent-roles will be cited now, with the understanding that in any concrete circuit a role may be filled more than once, and a single person may fill more than one of them.

First is the *next-of-relation*—the person whom the prepatient sees as the most available of those upon whom he should be able to most depend in times of trouble; in this instance the last to doubt his sanity and the first to have done everything to save him from the fate which, it transpires, he has been approaching. The patient's next-of-relation is usually his next of kin; the special term is introduced because he need not be. Second is the *complainant*, the person who retrospectively appears to have started the person on his way to the hospital. Third are the *mediators*—the sequence of agents and agencies to which the prepatient is referred and through which he is relayed and processed on his way to the hospital. Here are included police, clergy, general medical practitioners, office psychiatrists, personnel in public clinics, lawyers, social service workers, school teachers, and so on. One of these agents will have the legal mandate to sanction commitment and will exercise it, and so those agents who precede him in the process will be involved in something whose outcome is not yet settled. When the mediators retire from the scene, the prepatient has become an inpatient, and the significant agent has become the hospital administrator.

While the complainant usually takes action in a lay capacity as a citizen, an employer, a neighbor, or a kinsman, mediators tend to be specialists and differ from those they serve in significant ways. They have experience in handling trouble, and some professional distance from what they handle. Except in the case of policemen, and perhaps some clergy, they tend to be more psychiatrically oriented than the lay public, and will see the need for treatment at times when the public does not.[16]

An interesting feature of these roles is the functional effects of their interdigitation. For example, the feelings of the patient will be influenced by whether or not the person who fills the role of complainant also has the role of next-of-relation—an embarrassing combination more prevalent, apparently, in the higher classes than in the lower.[17] Some of these emergent effects will be considered now.[18]

In the prepatient's progress from home to the hospital he may participate as a third person in what he may come to experience as a kind of *alienative coalition*. His next-of-relation presses him into coming to "talk things over" with a medical practitioner, an office psychiatrist, or some other counselor. Disinclination on his part may be met by threatening him with desertion, disownment, or other legal action, or by stressing the joint and explorative nature of the interview. But typically the next-of-relation will have set the interview up, in the sense of selecting the professional, arranging for time, telling the professional something about the case, and so on. This move effectively tends to establish the next-of-relation as the responsible person to whom pertinent findings can be divulged, while effectively establishing the other as the patient. The prepatient often goes to the interview with the understanding that he is going as an equal of someone who is so bound together with him that a third person could not come between them in fundamental matters; this, after all, is one way in which close relationships are defined in our society. Upon arrival at the office the prepatient suddenly finds that he and his next-of-relation have not been accorded the same roles, and apparently that a prior understanding between the professional and the next-of-relation has been put in operation against him. In the extreme but common case the professional first sees the prepatient alone, in the role of examiner and diagnostician, and then sees the next-of-relation alone, in the role of advisor, while carefully avoiding talking things over seriously with them both together.[19] And even in those nonconsultative cases where public officials must forcibly extract a person from a family that wants to tolerate him, the next-of-relation is likely to be induced to "go along" with the official action, so that even here the prepatient may feel that an alienative coalition has been formed against him.

The moral experience of being third man in such a coalition is likely to embitter the prepatient, especially since his troubles have already probably led to some estrangement from his next-of-relation. After he enters the hospital, continued visits by his next-of-relation can give the patient the "insight" that his own best interests were being served. But the initial visits may temporarily strengthen his feeling of abandonment; he is likely to beg his visitor to get him out or at least to get him more privileges and to sympathize with the monstrousness of his plight—to which the visitor ordinarily can respond only by trying to maintain a hopeful note, by not "hearing" the requests, or by assuring the patient that the medical authorities know about these things and are doing what is medically best. The visitor then nonchalantly goes back into a world that the patient has learned is incredibly thick with freedom and privileges, causing the patient to feel that his next-of-relation is merely adding a pious gloss to a clear case of traitorous desertion.

The depth to which the patient may feel betrayed by his next-of-relation seems to be increased by the fact that another witnesses his betrayal—a factor which is apparently significant in many three-party situations. An offended person may well act forbearantly and accommodatively toward an offender when the two are alone, choosing peace ahead of justice. The presence of a witness, however, seems to add something to the implications of the offense. For then it is beyond the power of the offended and offender to forget about, erase, or suppress what has happened; the offense has become a public social fact.[20] When the witness is a mental health commission, as is sometimes the case, the witnessed betrayal can verge on a "degradation ceremony."[21] In such circumstances, the offended patient may feel that some kind of extensive reparative action is required before witnesses, if his honor and social weight are to be restored.

Two other aspects of sensed betrayal should be mentioned. First, those who suggest the possibility of another's entering a mental hospital are not likely to provide a realistic picture of how in fact it may strike him when he arrives. Often he is told that he will get required medical treatment and a rest, and may well be out in a few months or so. In some cases they may thus be concealing what they know, but I think, in general, they will be telling what they see as the truth. For here there is a quite relevant difference between patients and mediating professionals; mediators, more so than the public at large, may conceive of mental hospitals as short-term medical establishments where required rest and attention can be voluntarily obtained, and not as places of coerced exile. When the prepatient finally arrives he is likely to learn quite quickly, quite differently. He then finds that the information given him about life in the hospital has had the effect of his having put up less resistance to entering than he now sees he would have put up had he known the facts. Whatever the intentions of those who participated in his transition from person to patient, he may sense they have in effect "conned" him into his present predicament.

I am suggesting that the prepatient starts out with at least a portion of the rights, liberties, and satisfactions of the civilian and ends up on a psychiatric ward stripped of almost everything. The question here is *how* this stripping is managed. This is the second aspect of betrayal I want to consider.

As the prepatient may see it, the circuit of significant figures can function as a kind of *betrayal funnel*. Passage from person to patient may be effected through a series of linked stages, each managed by a different agent. While each stage tends to bring a sharp decrease in adult free status, each agent may try to maintain the fiction that no further decrease will occur. He may even manage to turn the prepatient over to the next agent while sustaining this note. Further, through words, cues, and gestures, the prepatient is implicitly asked by the current agent to join with him in sustaining a running line of polite small talk that tactfully avoids the administrative facts of the situation, becoming, with each stage, progressively more at odds with these facts. The spouse would rather not have to cry to get the prepatient to visit a psychiatrist; psychiatrists would rather not have a scene when the prepatient learns that he and his spouse are being seen separately and in different ways; the police infrequently bring a prepatient to the hospital in a strait jacket, finding it much easier all around to give him a cigarette, some kindly words, and freedom to relax in the back seat of the patrol car; and finally, the admitting psychiatrist finds he can do his work better in the relative quiet and luxury of the "admission suite" where, as an incidental consequence, the notion can survive that a mental hospital is indeed a comforting place. If the prepatient heeds all of these implied requests and is reasonably decent about the whole thing, he can travel the whole circuit from home to hospital without forcing anyone to look directly at what is happening or to deal with the raw emotion that his situation might well cause him to express. His showing consideration for those who are moving him toward the hospital allows them to show consideration for him, with the joint result that these interactions can be sustained with some of the protective harmony characteristic of ordinary face-to-face dealings. But should the new patient cast his mind back over the sequence of steps leading to hospitalization, he may feel that everyone's *current* comfort was being busily sustained while his long-range welfare was being undermined. This realization may constitute a moral experience that further separates him for the time from the people on the outside.[22]

I would now like to look at the circuit of career agents from the point of view of the agents themselves. Mediators in the person's transition from civil to patient status—as well as his keepers, once he is in the hospital—have an interest in establishing a responsible next-of-relation as the patient's deputy or *guardian;* should there be no obvious candidate for the role, someone may be sought out and pressed into it. Thus while a person is gradually being transformed into a patient, a next-of-relation is gradually being transformed into a guardian. With a guardian on the scene, the whole transition process can be kept tidy. He is likely to be familiar with the prepatient's civil involvements and business, and can tie up loose ends that might otherwise be left to entangle the hospital. Some of the prepatient's abrogated civil rights can be transferred to him, thus helping to sustain the legal fiction that while the prepatient does not actually have his rights he somehow actually has not lost them.

Inpatients commonly sense, at least for a time, that hospitalization is a massive unjust deprivation, and sometimes succeed in convincing a few persons on the outside that this is the case. It often turns out to be useful, then, for those identified with inflicting these deprivations, however justifiably, to be able to point to the cooperation and agreement of someone whose relationship to the patient places him above suspicion, firmly defining him as the person most likely to have the patient's personal interest at heart. If the guardian is satisfied with what is happening to the new inpatient, the world ought to be.[23]

Now it would seem that the greater the legitimate personal stake one party has in another, the better he can take the role of guardian to the other. But the structural arrangements in society which lead to the acknowledged merging of two persons' interests lead to additional consequences. For the person to whom the patient turns for help—for protection against such threats as involuntary commitment—is just the person to whom the mediators and hospital administrators logically turn for authorization. It is understandable, then, that some patients will come to sense, at least for a time, that the closeness of a relationship tells nothing of its trustworthiness.

There are still other functional effects emerging from this complement of roles. If and when the next-of-relation appeals to mediators for help in the trouble he is having with the prepatient, hospitalization may not, in fact, be in his mind. He may not even perceive the prepatient as mentally sick, or, if he does, he may not consistently hold to this view.[24] It is the circuit of mediators, with their greater psychiatric sophistication and their belief in the medical character of mental hospitals, that will often define the situation for the next-of-relation, assuring him that hospitalization is a possible solution and a good one, that it involves no betrayal, but is rather a medical action taken in the best interests of the prepatient. Here the next-of-relation may learn that doing his duty to the prepatient may cause the prepatient to distrust and even hate him for the time. But the fact that this course of action may have had to be pointed out and prescribed by professionals, and be defined by them as a moral duty, relieves the next-of-relation of some of the guilt he may feel.[25] It is a poignant fact that an adult son or daughter may be pressed into the role of mediator, so that the hostility that might otherwise be directed against the spouse is passed on to the child.[26]

Once the prepatient is in the hospital, the same guilt-carrying function may become a significant part of the staff's job in regard to the next-of-relation.[27] These reasons for feeling that he himself has not betrayed the patient, even though the patient may then think so, can later provide the next-of-relation with a defensible line to take when visiting the patient in the hospital and a basis for hoping that the relationship can be re-established after its hospital moratorium. And of course this position, when sensed by the patient, can provide him with excuses for the next-of-relation, when and if he comes to look for them.[28]

Thus while the next-of-relation can perform important functions for the mediators and hospital administrators, they in turn can perform important functions for him. One finds, then, an emergent unintended exchange or reciprocation of functions, these functions themselves being often unintended.

The final point I want to consider about the prepatient's moral career is its peculiarly *retroactive* character. Until a person actually arrives at the hospital there usually seems no way of knowing for sure that he is destined to do so, given the determinative role of career contingencies. And until the point of hospitalization is reached, he or others may not conceive of him as a person who is becoming a mental patient. However, since he will be held against his will in the hospital, his next-of-relation and the hospital staff will be in great need of a rationale for the hardships they are sponsoring. The medical elements of the staff will also need evidence that they are still in the trade they were trained for. These problems are eased, no doubt unintentionally, by the case-history construction that is placed on the patient's past life, this having the effect of demonstrating that all along he had been becoming sick, that he finally became very sick, and that if he had not been hospitalized much worse things would have happened to him—all of which, of course, may be true. Incidentally, if the patient wants to make sense out of his stay in the hospital, and, as already suggested, keep alive the possibility of once again conceiving of his next-of-relation as a decent, well-meaning person, then he too will have reason to believe some of this psychiatric work-up of his past.

Here is a very ticklish point for the sociology of careers. An important aspect of every career is the view the person constructs when he looks backward over his progress; in a sense, however, the whole of the prepatient career derives from this reconstruction. The fact of having had a prepatient career, starting with an effective complaint, becomes an important part of the mental patient's orientation, but this part can begin to be played only after hospitalization proves that what he had been having, but no longer has, is a career as a prepatient.

The Inpatient Phase

The last step in the prepatient's career can involve his realization—justified or not—that he has been deserted by society and turned out of relationships by those closest to him. Interestingly enough, the patient, especially a first admission, may manage to keep himself from coming to the end of this trail, even though in fact he is now in a locked mental hospital ward. On entering the hospital, he may very strongly feel the desire not to be known to anyone as a person who could possibly be reduced to these present circumstances, or as a person who conducted himself in the way he did prior to commitment. Consequently, he may avoid talking to anyone, may stay by himself when possible, and may even be "out of contact" or "manic" so as to avoid ratifying any interaction that presses a politely reciprocal role upon him and opens him up to what he has become in the eyes of others. When the next-of-relation makes an effort to visit, he may be rejected by mutism, or by the patient's refusal to enter the visiting room, these strategies sometimes suggesting that the patient still clings to a remnant of relatedness to those who made up his past, and is protecting this remnant from the final destructiveness of dealing with the new people that they have become.[29]

Usually the patient comes to give up this taxing effort at anonymity, at not-hereness, and begins to present himself for conventional social interaction to the hospital community. Thereafter he withdraws only in special ways—by always using his nickname, by signing his contribution to the patient weekly with his initial only, or by using the innocuous "cover" address tactfully provided by some hospitals; or he withdraws only at special times, when, say, a flock of nursing students makes a passing tour of the ward, or when, paroled to the hospital grounds, he suddenly sees he is about to cross the path of a civilian he happens to know from home. Sometimes this making of oneself available is called "settling down" by the attendants. It marks a new stand openly taken and supported by the patient, and resembles the "coming out" process that occurs in other groupings.[30]

Once the prepatient begins to settle down, the main outlines of his fate tend to follow those of a whole class of segregated establishments—jails, concentration camps, monasteries, work camps, and so on—in which the inmate spends the whole round of life on the grounds, and marches through his regimented day in the immediate company of a group of persons of his own institutional status.[31]

Like the neophyte in many of these "total institutions," the new inpatient finds himself cleanly stripped of many of his accustomed affirmations, satisfactions, and defenses, and is subjected to a rather full set of mortifying experiences: restriction of free movement; communal living; diffuse authority of a whole echelon of people; and so on. Here one begins to learn about the limited extent to which a conception of oneself can be sustained when the usual setting of supports for it are suddenly removed.

While undergoing these humbling moral experiences, the inpatient learns to orient himself in terms of the "ward system."[32] In public mental hospitals this usually consists of a series of graded living arrangements built around wards, administrative units called services, and parole statuses. The "worst" level involves often nothing but wooden benches to sit on, some quite indifferent food, and a small piece of room to sleep in. The "best" level may involve a room of one's own, ground and town privileges, contacts with staff that are relatively undamaging, and what is seen as good food and ample recreational facilities. For disobeying the pervasive house rules, the inmate will receive stringent punishments expressed in terms of loss of privileges; for obedience he will eventually be allowed to reacquire some of the minor satisfactions he took for granted on the outside.

The institutionalization of these radically different levels of living throws light on the implications for self of social settings. And this in turn affirms that the self arises not merely out of its possessor's interactions with significant others, but also out of the arrangements that are evolved in an organization for its members.

There are some settings which the person easily discounts as an expression or extension of him. When a tourist goes slumming, he may take pleasure in the situation not because it is a reflection of him but because it so assuredly is not. There are other settings, such as living rooms, which the person manages on his own and employs to influence in a favorable direction other persons' views of him. And there are still other settings, such as a work place, which express the employee's occupational status, but over which he has no final control, this being exerted, however tactfully, by his employer. Mental hospitals provide an extreme instance of this latter possibility. And this is due not merely to their uniquely degraded living levels, but also to the unique way in which significance for self is made explicit to the patient, piercingly, persistently, and thoroughly. Once lodged on a given ward, the patient is firmly instructed that the restrictions and deprivations he encounters are not due to such things as tradition or economy—and hence dissociable from self—but are intentional parts of his treatment, part of his need at the time, and therefore an expression of the state that his self has fallen to. Having every reason to initiate requests for better conditions, he is told that when the staff feels he is "able to manage" or will be "comfortable with" a higher ward level, then appropriate action will be taken. In short, assignment to a given ward is presented not as a reward or punishment, but as an expression of his general level of social functioning, his status as a person. Given the fact that the worst ward levels provide a round of life that inpatients with organic brain damage can easily manage, and that these quite limited human beings are present to prove it, one can appreciate some of the mirroring effects of the hospital.[33]

The ward system, then, is an extreme instance of how the physical facts of an establishment can be explicitly employed to frame the conception a person takes of himself. In addition, the official psychiatric mandate of mental hospitals gives rise to even more direct, even more blatant, attacks upon the inmate's view of himself. The more "medical" and the more progressive a mental hospital is—the more it attempts to be therapeutic and not merely custodial—the more he may be confronted by high-ranking staff arguing that his past has been a failure, that the cause of this has been within himself, that his attitude to life is wrong, and that if he wants to be a person he will have to change his way of dealing with people and his conceptions of himself. Often the moral value of these verbal assaults will be brought home to him by requiring him to practice taking this psychiatric view of himself in arranged confessional periods, whether in private sessions or group psychotherapy.

Now a general point may be made about the moral career of inpatients which has bearing on many moral careers. Given the stage that any person has reached in a career, one typically finds that he constructs an image of his life course—past, present, and future—which selects, abstracts, and distorts in such a way as to provide him with a view of himself that he can usefully expound in current situations. Quite generally, the person's line concerning self defensively brings him into appropriate alignment with the basic values of his society, and so may be called an *apologia*. If the person can manage to present a view of his current situation which shows the operation of favorable personal qualities in the past and a favorable destiny awaiting him, it may be called a *success story*. If the facts of a person's past and present are extremely dismal, then about the best he can do is to show that he is not responsible for what has become of him, and the term *sad tale* is appropriate. Interestingly enough, the more the person's past forces him out of apparent alignment with central moral values, the more often he seems compelled to tell his sad tale in any company in which he finds himself. Perhaps he partly responds to the need he feels in others of not having their sense of proper life courses affronted. In any case, it is among convicts, "wino's," and prostitutes that one seems to obtain sad tales the most readily.[34] It is the vicissitudes of the mental patient's sad tale that I want to consider now.

In the mental hospital, the setting and the house rules press home to the patient that he is, after all, a mental case who has suffered some kind of social collapse on the outside, having failed in some overall way, and that here he is of little social weight, being hardly capable of acting like a full-fledged person at all. These humiliations are likely to be most keenly felt by middle-class patients, since their previous condition of life little immunizes them against such affronts; but all patients feel some downgrading. Just as any normal member of his outside subculture would do, the patient often responds to this situation by attempting to assert a sad tale proving that he is not "sick," that the "little trouble" he did get into was really somebody else's fault, that his past life course had some honor and rectitude, and that the hospital is therefore unjust in forcing the status of mental patient upon him. This self-respecting tendency is heavily institutionalized within the patient society where opening social contacts typically involve the participants' volunteering information about their current ward location and length of stay so far, but not the reasons for their stay—such interaction being conducted in the manner of small talk on the outside.[35] With greater familiarity, each patient usually volunteers relatively acceptable reasons for his hospitalization, at the same time accepting without open immediate question the lines offered by other patients. Such stories as the following are given and overtly accepted.

> I was going to night school to get a M.A. degree, and holding down a job in addition, and the load got too much for me.

> The others here are sick mentally but I'm suffering from a bad nervous system and that is what is giving me these phobias.

> I got here by mistake because of a diabetes diagnosis, and I'll leave in a couple of days. [The patient had been in seven weeks.]

> I failed as a child, and later with my wife I reached out for dependency.

> My trouble is that I can't work. That's what I'm in for. I had two jobs with a good home and all the money I wanted.[36]

The patient sometimes reinforces these stories by an optimistic definition of his occupational status: A man who managed to obtain an audition as a radio announcer styles himself a radio announcer; another who worked for some months as a copy boy and was then given a job as a reporter on a large trade journal, but fired after three weeks, defines himself as a reporter.

A whole social role in the patient community may be constructed on the basis of these reciprocally sustained fictions. For these face-to-face niceties tend to be qualified by behind-the-back gossip that comes only a degree closer to the "objective" facts. Here, of course, one can see a classic social function of informal networks of equals: they serve as one another's audience for self-supporting tales—tales that are somewhat more solid than pure fantasy and somewhat thinner than the facts.

But the patient's *apologia* is called forth in a unique setting, for few settings could be so destructive of self-stories except, of course, those stories already constructed along psychiatric lines. And this destructiveness rests on more than the official sheet of paper which attests that the patient is of unsound mind, a danger to himself and others—an attestation, incidentally, which seems to cut deeply into the patient's pride, and into the possibility of his having any.

Certainly the degrading conditions of the hospital setting belie many of the self-stories that are presented by patients; and the very fact of being in the mental hospital is evidence against these tales. And of course, there is not always sufficient patient solidarity to prevent patient discrediting patient, just as there is not always a sufficient number of "professionalized" attendants to prevent attendant discrediting patient. As one patient informant repeatedly suggested to a fellow patient:

> If you're so smart, how come you got your ass in here?

The mental hospital setting, however, is more treacherous still. Staff has much to gain through discreditings of the patient's story—whatever the felt reason for such discreditings. If the custodial faction in the hospital is to succeed in managing his daily round without complaint or trouble from him, then it will prove useful to be able to point out to him that the claims about himself upon which he rationalizes his demands are false, that he is not what he is claiming to be, and that in fact he is a failure as a person. If the psychiatric faction is to impress upon him its views about his personal make-up, then they must be able to show in detail how their version of his past and their version of his character hold up much better than his own.[37] If both the custodial and psychiatric factions are to get him to cooperate in the various psychiatric treatments, then it will prove useful to disabuse him of *his* view of their purposes, and cause him to appreciate that they know what they are doing, and are doing what is best for him. In brief, the difficulties caused by a patient are closely tied to his version of what has been happening to him, and if cooperation is to be secured, it helps if this version is discredited. The patient must "insightfully" come to take, or affect to take, the hospital's view of himself.

Notes

1. The study was conducted during 1955–56 under the auspices of the Laboratory of Social-environmental Studies of the National Institute of Mental Health. I am grateful to the Laboratory Chief, John A. Clausen, and to Dr. Winfred Overholser, Superintendent, and the late Dr. Jay Hoffman, then First Assistant Physician of Saint Elizabeth's Hospital, Washington, D.C., for the ideal cooperation they freely provided. A preliminary report is contained in Goffman, "Interpersonal Persuasion," pp. 117–193; in *Group Processes: Transactions of the Third Conference,* edited by Bertram Schaffner: New York, Josiah Macy, Jr. Foundation, 1957. A shorter version of this paper was presented at the Annual Meeting of the American Sociological Society, Washington, D.C., August 1957.

2. Material on moral career can be found in early social anthropological work on ceremonies of status transition, and in classic social psychological descriptions of those spectacular changes in one's view of self that can accompany participation in social movements and sects. Recently new kinds of relevant data have been suggested by psychiatric interest in the problem of "identity" and sociological studies of work careers and "adult socialization."

3. This point has recently been made by Elaine and John Cumming, *Closed Ranks;* Cambridge, Commonwealth Fund, Harvard Univ. Press, 1957; pp. 101–102. "Clinical experience supports the impression that many people define mental illness as 'That condition for which a person is treated in a mental hospital.' . . . Mental illness, it seems, is a condition which afflicts people who must go to a mental institution, but until they do almost anything they do is normal." Leila Deasy has pointed out to me the correspondence here with the situation in white collar crime. Of those who are detected in this activity, only the ones who do not manage to avoid going to prison find themselves accorded the social role of the criminal.

4. Case records in mental hospitals are just now coming to be exploited to show the incredible amount of trouble a person may cause for himself and others before anyone begins to think about him psychiatrically, let alone take psychiatric action against him. See John A. Clausen and Marian Radke Yarrow, "Paths to the Mental Hospital," *J. Social Issues* (1955) 11:25–32; August B. Hollingshead and Fredrick C. Redlich, *Social Class and Mental Illness;* New York, Wiley, 1958: pp. 173–174.

5. An illustration of how this perspective may be taken to all forms of deviancy may be found in Edwin Lemert, *Social Pathology;* New York, McGraw-Hill, 1951; see especially pp. 74–76. A specific application to mental defectives may be found in Stewart E. Perry, "Some Theoretic Problems of Mental Deficiency and Their Action Implications," *Psychiatry* (1954) 17: 45–73; see especially p. 68.

6. Conscientious objectors who voluntarily went to jail sometimes arrived at the same conclusion regarding criminal inmates. See, for example, Alfred Hassler, *Diary of a Self-made Convict;* Chicago, Regnery, 1954; p. 74.

7. This simple picture is complicated by the somewhat special experience of roughly a third of ex-patients—namely, readmission to the hospital, this being the recidivist or "repatient" phase.

8. Harry Stack Sullivan, *Clinical Studies in Psychiatry;* edited by Helen Swick Perry, Mary Ladd Gawel, and Martha Gibbon; New York, Norton, 1956; pp. 184–185.

9. This moral experience can be contrasted with that of a person learning to become a marihuana addict, whose discovery that he can be "high" and still "op" effectively without being detected apparently leads to a new level of use. See Howard S. Becker, "Marihuana Use and Social Control," *Social Problems* (1955) 3:35–44; see especially pp. 40–41.

10. See note 4: Hollingshead and Redlich, p. 187, Table 6, where relative frequency is given of self-referral by social class grouping.

11. The distinction employed here between willing and unwilling patients cuts across the legal one, of voluntary and committed, since some persons who are glad to come to the mental hospital may be legally committed, and of those who come only because of strong familial pressure, some may sign themselves in as voluntary patients.

12. Clausen and Yarrow; see note 4.

13. An explicit application of this notion to the field of mental health may be found in Edwin M. Lemert, "Legal Commitment and Social Control," *Sociology and Social Research* (1946) 30:370–378.

14. For example, Jerome K. Meyers and Leslie Schaffer, "Social Stratification and Psychiatric Practice: A Study of an Outpatient Clinic," *Amer. Sociological Rev.* (1954) 19:307–310, Lemert, see note 5; pp. 402–403. *Patients in Mental Institutions,* 1941; Washington, D.C., Department of Commerce, Bureau of Census, 1941; p. 2.

15. For one circuit of agents and its bearing on career contingencies, see Oswald Hall, "The Stages of a Medical Career," *Amer. J. Sociology* (1948) 53:227–336.

16. See Cumming, note 3; p. 92.

17. Hollingshead and Redlich, note 4; p. 187.

18. For an analysis of some of these circuit implications for the inpatient, see Leila C. Deasy and Olive W. Quinn, "The Wife of the Mental Patient and the Hospital Psychiatrist," *J. Social Issues* (1955) 11:49–60. An interesting illustration of this kind of analysis may also be found in Alan G. Gowman, "Blindness and the Role of Companion," *Social Problems* (1956) 4:68–75. A general statement may be found in Robert Merton, "The Role Set: Problems in Sociological Theory," *British J. Sociology* (1957) 8:106–120.

19. I have one case record of a man who claims he thought *he* was taking his wife to see the psychiatrist, not realizing until too late that his wife had made the arrangements.

20. A paraphrase from Kurt Riezler, "The Social Psychology of Shame," *Amer. J. Sociology* (1943) 48:458.

21. See Harold Garfinkel, "Conditions of Successful Degradation Ceremonies," *Amer. J. Sociology* (1956) 61:420–424.

22. Concentration camp practices provide a good example of the function of the betrayal funnel in inducing cooperation and reducing struggle and fuss, although here the mediators could not be said to be acting in the best interests of the inmates. Police picking up persons from their homes would sometimes joke good-naturedly and offer to wait while coffee was being served. Gas chambers were fitted out like delousing rooms, and victims taking off their clothes were told to note where they were leaving them. The sick, aged, weak, or insane who were selected for extermination were sometimes driven away in Red Cross ambulances to camps referred to by terms such as "observation hospital." See David Boder, *I Did Not Interview the Dead;* Urbana, Univ. of Illinois Press, 1949; p. 81; and Elie A. Cohen, *Human Behavior in the Concentration Camp;* London, Cape, 1954; pp. 32, 37, 107.

23. Interviews collected by the Clausen group at NIMH suggest that when a wife comes to be a guardian, the responsibility may disrupt previous distance from in-laws, leading either to a new supportive coalition with them or to a marked withdrawal from them.

24. For an analysis of these nonpsychiatric kinds of perception, see Marian Radke Yarrow, Charlotte Green Schwartz, Harriet S. Murphy, and Leila Calhoun Deasy, "The Psychological Meaning of Mental Illness in the Family," *J. Social Issues* (1955) 11:12–24; Charlotte Green Schwartz, "Perspectives on Deviance: Wives'; Definitions of their Husbands' Mental Illness," *Psychiatry* (1957) 20:275–291.

25. This guilt-carrying function is found, of course, in other role-complexes. Thus, when a middle-class couple engages in the process of legal separation or divorce, each of their lawyers usually takes the position that his job is to acquaint his client with all of the potential claims and rights, pressing his client into demanding these, in spite of any nicety of feelings about the rights and honorableness of the ex-partner. The client, in all good faith, can then say to self and to the ex-partner that the demands are being made only because the lawyer insists it is best to do so.

26. Recorded in the Clausen data.

27. This point is made by Cumming, see note 3; p. 129.

28. There is an interesting contrast here with the moral career of the tuberculosis patient. I am told by Julius Roth that tuberculosis patients are likely to come to the hospital willingly, agreeing with their next-of-relation about treatment. Later in their hospital career, when they learn how long they yet have to stay and how depriving and irrational some of the hospital rulings are, they may seek to leave, be advised against this by the staff and by relatives, and only then begin to feel betrayed.

29. The inmate's initial strategy of holding himself aloof from ratifying contact may partly account for the relative lack of group-formation among inmates in public mental hospitals, a connection that has been suggested to me by William R. Smith. The desire to avoid personal bonds that would give license to the asking of biographical questions could also be a factor. In mental hospitals, of course, as in prisoner camps, the staff may consciously break up incipient group-formation in order to avoid collective rebellious action and other ward disturbances.

30. A comparable coming out occurs in the homosexual world, when a person finally comes frankly to present himself to a "gay" gathering not as a tourist but as someone who is "available." See Evelyn Hooker, "A Preliminary Examination of Group Behavior of Homosexuals," *J. Psychology* (1956) 42:217–225; especially p. 221. A good fictionalized treatment may be found in James Baldwin's *Giovanni's Room;* New York, Dial, 1956; pp. 41–63. A familiar instance of the coming out process is no doubt to be found among prepubertal children at the moment one of these actors sidles *back* into a room that had been left in an angered huff and injured *amour-propre.* The phrase itself presumably derives from a *rite-de-passage* ceremony once arranged by upper-class mothers for their daughters. Interestingly enough, in large mental hospitals the patient sometimes symbolizes a complete coming out by his first active participation in the hospital wide patient dance.

31. See Goffman, "Characteristics of Total Institutions," pp. 43–84; in *Proceedings of the Symposium of Preventive and Social Psychiatry;* Washington, D.C., Walter Reed Army Institute of Research, 1958.

32. A good description of the ward system may be found in Ivan Belknap, *Human Problems of a State Mental Hospital;* New York, McGraw-Hill, 1956; see especially p. 164.

33. Here is one way in which mental hospitals can be worse than concentration camps and prisons as places in which to "do" time; in the latter, self-insulation from the symbolic implications of the settings may be easier. In fact, self-insulation from hospital settings may be so difficult that patients have to employ devices for this which staff interpret as psychotic symptoms.

34. In regard to convicts, see Anthony Heckstall-Smith, *Eighteen Months;* London, Wingate, 1954; pp. 52–53. For "wino's" see the discussion in Howard G. Bain, "A Sociological Analysis of the Chicago Skid-Row Lifeway;" unpublished M.A. thesis, Dept. of Sociology, pp. 141–146. Bain's neglected thesis is a useful source of material on moral careers.

Apparently one of the occupational hazards of prostitution is that clients and other professional contacts sometimes persist in expressing sympathy by asking for a defensible dramatic explanation for the fall from grace. In having to bother to have a sad tale ready, perhaps the prostitute is more to be pitied than damned. Good examples of prostitute sad tales may be found in Sir Henry Mayhew, "Those that Will Not Work," pp. 210–272; in his *London Labour and the London Poor,* Vol. 4; London, Griffin, Bohn, and Cox, 1862. For a contemporary source, see *Women of the Streets,* edited by C. H. Rolph; London, Zecker, and Warburg, 1955; especially p. 6. "Almost always, however, after a few comments on the police, the girl would begin to explain how it was that she was in the life, usually in terms of self-justification." Lately, of course, the psychological expert has helped out the profession in the construction of wholly remarkable sad tales. See, for example, Harold Greenwald, *Call Girl;* New York, Ballantine, 1958.

35. A similar self-protecting rule has been observed in prisons. Thus, Hassler, see note 6, in describing a conversation with a fellow-prisoner: "He didn't say much about why he was sentenced, and I didn't ask him, that being the accepted behavior in prison" (p. 76). A novelistic

version for the mental hospital may be found in J. Kerkhoff, *How Thin the Veil: A Newspaper-man's Story of His Own Mental Crack-up and Recovery;* New York, Greenberg, 1952; p. 27.

36. From the writer's field notes of informal interaction with patients, transcribed as near verbatim as he was able.

37. The process of examining a person psychiatrically and then altering or reducing his status in consequence is known in hospital and prison parlance as *bugging,* the assumption being that once you come to the attention of the testers you either will automatically be labeled crazy or the process of testing itself will make you crazy. Thus psychiatric staff are sometimes seen not as *discovering* whether you are sick, but as *making* you sick; and "Don't bug me, man," can mean, "Don't pester me to the point where I'll get upset." Sheldon Messinger has suggested to me that this meaning of bugging is related to the other colloquial meaning, of wiring a room with a secret microphone to collect information usable for discrediting the speaker.

Suspended Identity: Identity Transformation in a Maximum Security Prison

34

Thomas J. Schmid
Richard S. Jones

The extent to which people hide behind the masks of impression manage-ment in everyday life is a point of theoretical controversy (Goffman 1959; Gross and Stone 1964; Irwin 1977; Douglas et al. 1980; Douglas and John-son 1977; Messinger et al. 1962; Blumer 1969, 1972). A variety of prob-lematic circumstances can be identified, however, in which individuals find it necessary to accommodate a sudden but encompassing shift in so-cial situations by establishing temporary identities. These circumstances, which can range from meteoric fame (Adler and Adler 1989) to confine-ment in total institutions, place new identity demands on the individual, while seriously challenging his or her prior identity bases.

A prison sentence constitutes a "massive assault" on the identity of those imprisoned (Berger 1963:100–101). This assault is especially severe on first-time inmates, and we might expect radical identity changes to ensue from their imprisonment. At the same time, a prisoner's awareness of the chal-lenge to his identity affords some measure of protection against it. As part of an ethnographic analysis of the prison experiences of first-time, short-term inmates, this article presents an identity transformation model that differs both from the gradual transformation processes that characterize most adult identity changes and from such radical transformation processes as brainwashing or conversion.

Data for the study are derived principally from ten months of partici-pant observation at a maximum security prison for men in the upper mid-west of the United States. One of the authors was an inmate serving a felony sentence for one year and one day, while the other participated in the study as an outside observer. Relying on traditional ethnographic data collection and analysis techniques, this approach offered us general obser-vations of hundreds of prisoners, and extensive fieldnotes that were based on repeated, often daily, contacts with about fifty inmates, as well as on personal relationships established with a smaller number of inmates. We subsequently returned to the prison to conduct focused interviews with

Figure 1 Prison Images and Strategies of New Inmates

Anticipatory Image ⟶ **Anticipatory Survival Strategy**

Ousider's perspective:
violence; uncertainty; fear

Protective resolutions: to avoid unnecessary contacts with inmates; to avoid unnecessary contacts with guards; not to be changed in prison; to disregard questionable information; to avoid all hostilities; to engage in self-defense if hostilities arise

Survival Strategy

Territorial caution;
Selective interaction with inmates;
Impression management with inmates;
Partnership with another inmate;
Redefinition of prison violence as "explained" rather than random events

Mid-Career Image ⟶ **Adaptation Strategy**

Insider's perspective:
boredom

Legal and illegal diversions;
Suppression of thoughts about outside world;
Minimization of outside contacts;
Impression management with inmates and outsiders;
Partnership

Concluding Image ◀ ⟶ **Dissipation of Adaptation Strategy**

Synthetic perspective:
revision of prison image and reformulation of outside image

Continued diversions;
Decreasing impression management;
Decreasing suppression of outside thoughts;
Disassociation with partner;
Formulation of outside plan

other prisoners; using information provided by prison officials, we were able to identify and interview twenty additional first-time inmates who were serving sentences of two years or less. See Schmid and Jones (1987) for further description of this study.

Three interrelated research questions guided our analysis: How do first-time, short-term inmates define the prison world, and how do their definitions change during their prison careers? How do these inmates adapt to the prison world, and how do their adaptation strategies change during their prison careers? How do their self-definitions change during their prison careers? Our analyses of the first two questions are presented in detail elsewhere (Schmid and Jones 1987, 1990); an abbreviated outline of these analyses, to which we will allude throughout this article, is presented in Figure 1. The identity transformation model presented here, based on our analysis of the third question, is outlined in Figure 2.

▶Preprison Identity

Our data suggest that the inmates we studied have little in common before their arrival at prison, except their conventionality. Although convicted of felonies, most do not possess "criminal" identities (cf. Irwin 1970:29–34).

Figure 2 Suspended Identity Dialectic

They begin their sentences with only a vague, incomplete image (Boulding 1961) of what prison is like, but an image that nonetheless stands in contrast to how they view their own social worlds. Their prison image is dominated by the theme of violence: they see prison inmates as violent, hostile, alien human beings, with whom they have nothing in common. They have several specific fears about what will happen to them in prison, including fears of assault, rape, and death. They are also concerned about their identities, fearing that—if they survive prison at all—they are in danger of changing in prison, either through the intentional efforts of rehabilitation personnel or through the unavoidable hardening effects of the prison environment. Acting on this imagery (Blumer 1969)—or, more precisely, on the inconsonance of their self-images with this prison image—they develop an anticipatory survival strategy (see Figure 1) that consists primarily of protective resolutions: a resolve to avoid all hostilities; a resolve to avoid all nonessential contacts with inmates and guards; a resolve to defend themselves in any way possible; and a resolve not to change, or to be changed, in prison.

A felon's image and strategy are formulated through a running self-dialogue, a heightened state of reflexive awareness (Lewis 1979) through which he ruminates about his past behavior and motives, and imaginatively projects himself into the prison world. This self-dialogue begins shortly after his arrest, continues intermittently during his trial or court hearings, and becomes especially intense at the time of his transfer to prison.

> You start taking a review—it's almost like your life is passing before your eyes. You wonder how in the heck you got to this point and, you know, what are—what's your family gonna think about it—your friends, all the talk, and how are you going to deal with that—and the kids, you know, how are they gonna react to it?. . . . All those things run through your head. . . . The total loss of control—the first time in all my life that some other people were controlling my life.
>
> * * *
>
> My first night in the joint was spent mainly on kicking myself in the butt for putting myself in the joint. It was a very emotional evening. I thought a lot about all my friends and family, the good-byes, the things we did the last couple of months, how good they had been to me, sticking by me. I also thought about my fears: Am I going to go crazy? Will I end up fighting for my life? How am I going to survive in here for a year? Will I change? Will things be the same when I get out?

His self-dialogue is also typically the most extensive self-assessment he has ever conducted; thus, at the same time that he is resolving not to change, he is also initiating the kind of introspective analysis that is essential to any identity transformation process.

Self-Insulation

A felon's self-dialogue continues during the initial weeks and months of his sentence, and it remains a solitary activity, each inmate struggling to come to grips with the inconsonance of his established (preprison) identity and his present predicament. Despite the differences in their preprison identities, however, inmates now share a common situation that affects their identities. With few exceptions, their self-dialogues involve feelings of vulnerability, discontinuity, and differentiation from other inmates, emotions that reflect both the degradations and deprivations of institutional life (cf. Goffman 1961; Sykes 1958; and Garfinkel 1956) and their continuing outsiders' perspective on the prison world. These feelings are obviously the result of everything that has happened to the inmates, but they are something else as well: they are the conditions in which every first-time, short-term inmate finds himself. They might even be called the common attributes of the inmates' selves-in-prison, for the irrelevance of their preprison identities within the prison world reduces their self-definitions, temporarily, to the level of pure emotion.[1] These feelings, and a consequent emphasis on the "physical self" (Zurcher 1977:176), also constitute the essential motivation for the inmates' self-insulation strategies.[2]

An inmate cannot remain wholly insulated within the prison world, for a number of reasons. He simply spends too much of his time in the presence of others to avoid all interaction with them. He also recognizes that his prison image is based on incomplete and inadequate information, and that he must interact with others in order to acquire first-hand information about the prison world. His behavior in prison, moreover, is guided not only by his prison image but by a fundamental ambivalence he feels about his situation, resulting from his marginality between the prison and outside social worlds (Schmid and Jones 1987). His ambivalence has several manifestations throughout his prison career, but the most important is his conflicting desires for self-insulation and for human communication.

Managing a Dualistic Self

An inmate is able to express both directions of his ambivalence (and to address his need for more information about the prison) by drawing a distinction between his "true" identity (i.e., his outside, preprison identity) and a "false" identity he creates for the prison world. For most of a new inmate's prison career, his preprison identity remains a "subjective" or "personal" identity while his prison identity serves as his "objective" or "social" basis for interaction in prison (see Weigert 1986; Goffman 1963). This bifurcation of his self (Figure 2) is not a conscious decision made at a single point in time, but it does represent two conscious and interdependent identity-preservation tactics, formulated through self-dialogue and refined through tentative interaction with others.

First, after coming to believe that he cannot "be himself" in prison because he would be too vulnerable, he decides to "suspend" his preprison identity for the duration of his sentence. He retains his resolve not to let prison change him, protecting himself by choosing not to reveal himself (his "true" self) to others. Expressions of a suspension of identity emerged repeatedly and consistently in both the fieldwork and interview phases of our research through such statements as

> I was reserved. . . . I wouldn't be very communicative, you know. I'd try to keep conversation to a minimum. . . . I wasn't interested in getting close to anybody . . . or asking a lot of questions. You know, try to cut the conversation short . . . go my own way back to my cell or go to the library or do something.

* * *

> I didn't want nobody to know too much about me. That was part of the act.

An inmate's decision to suspend his preprison identity emanates directly from his feelings of vulnerability, discontinuity and differentiation from other inmates. These emotions foster something like a "proto-sociological attitude" (Weigert 1986:173; see also Zurcher 1977), in which new inmates find it necessary to step outside their taken-for-granted preprison identities. Rather than viewing these identities and the everyday life experience in which they are grounded as social constructions, however, inmates see the *prison* world as an artificial construction, and judge their "naturally occurring" preprison identities to be out of place within this construction. By attempting to suspend his preprison identity for the time that he spends in prison an inmate believes that he will again "be his old self" after his release.

While he is in confinement, an inmate's decision to suspend his identity leaves him with little or no basis for interaction. His second identity tactic, then, is the creation of an identity that allows him to interact, however cautiously, with others. This tactic consists of his increasingly sophisticated impression management skills (Goffman 1959; Schlenker 1980), which are initially designed simply to hide his vulnerability, but which gradually evolve into an alternative identity felt to be more suitable to the prison world. The character of the presented identity is remarkably similar from inmate to inmate:

> Well, I learned that you can't act like—you can't get the attitude where you are better than they are. Even where you might be better than them, you can't strut around like you are. Basically, you can't stick out. You don't stare at people and things like that. I knew a lot of these things from talking to people and I figured them out by myself. I sat down and figured out just what kind of attitude I'm going to have to take.

* * *

> Most people out here learn to be tough, whether they can back it up or not. If you don't learn to be tough, you will definitely pay for it. This toughness can be demonstrated through a mean look, tough language, or an extremely big build. . . . One important thing is never to let your guard down.

An inmate's prison identity, as an inauthentic presentation of self, is not in itself a form of identity transformation but is rather a form of identity construction. His prison identity is simply who he must pretend to be while he is in prison. It is a false identity created for survival in an artificial world. But this identity nonetheless emerges in the same manner as any other identity: it is learned from others, and it must be presented to, negotiated with, and validated by others. A new inmate arrives at prison with a general image of what prisoners are like, and he begins to flesh out this image from the day of his arrival, warily observing others just as they are observing him. Through watching others, through eavesdropping, through cautious conversation and selective interaction, a new inmate refines his understanding of what maximum security prisoners look like, how they talk, how they move, how they act. Despite his belief that he is different from these other prisoners, he knows that he cannot appear to be too different from them, if he is to hide his vulnerability. His initial image of other prisoners, his early observations, and his concern over how he appears to others thus provide a foundation for the identity he gradually creates through impression management.

Impression management skills, of course, are not exclusive to the prison world; a new inmate, like anyone else, has had experience in the creation of his prison identity. He has undoubtedly even had experience in presenting a "front" to others, and he draws upon his experience in projecting the very attributes—strength, stoicism, aplomb—required by his prison identity. Impression management in prison differs, however, in the totality with which it governs interactions and in the perceived costs of failure: humiliation, assault, or death. For these reasons the entire impression management process becomes a more highly conscious endeavor. When presenting himself before others, a new inmate pays close attention to such minute details of his front as eye contact, posture, and manner of walking:

> I finally got out of orientation. I was going out with the main population, going down to get my meals and things. The main thing is not to stare at a bunch of people, you know. I tried to just look ahead, you know, not stare at people. 'Cause I didn't really know; I just had to learn a little at a time.

* * *

> The way you look seems to be very important. The feeling is you shouldn't smile, that a frown is much more appropriate. The eyes are very important. You should never look away; it is considered a sign of weakness. Either stare straight ahead, look around, or look the person dead in the eyes. The way you walk is important. You shouldn't walk too fast; they might think you were scared and in a hurry to get away.

To create an appropriate embodiment (Weigert 1986; Stone 1962) of their prison identities, some new inmates devote long hours to weightlifting or other body-building exercises, and virtually all of them relinquish their civilian clothes—which might express their preprison identities—in favor of the standard issue clothing that most inmates wear. Whenever a new inmate is open to the view of other inmates, in fact, he is likely to relinquish most overt symbols of his individuality, in favor of a standard issue "prison inmate" appearance.

By acting self-consciously, of course, a new inmate runs the risk of exposing the fact that he *is* acting. But he sees no alternative to playing his part better; he cannot "not act" because that too would expose the vulnerability of his "true" identity. He thus sees every new prison experience, every new territory that he is allowed to explore, as a test of his impression management skills. Every nonconfrontive encounter with another inmate symbolizes his success at these skills, but it is also a social validation of his prison identity. Eventually he comes to see that many, perhaps most, inmates are engaging in the same kind of inauthentic presentations of self (cf. Glaser and Strauss 1964). Their identities are as "false" as his, and their validations of his identity may be equally false. But he realizes that he is powerless to change this state of affairs, and that he must continue to present his prison identity for as long as he remains in prison.

A first-time inmate enters prison as an outsider, and it is from an outsider's perspective that he initially creates his prison identity. In contrast to his suspended preprison identity, his prison identity is a *shared* identity, because it is modeled on his observations of other inmates. Like those of more experienced prisoners, his prison identity is tied directly to the social role of "prison inmate" (cf. Scheff 1970; Solomon 1970); because he is an outsider, however, his prison identity is also severely limited by his narrow understanding of that role. It is based on an outsider's stereotype of who a maximum security inmate is and what he acts like. It is, nonetheless, a *structural* identity (Weigert 1986), created to address his outsider's institutional problems of social isolation and inadequate information about the prison world.

By the middle of his sentence, a new inmate comes to adopt what is essentially an insider's perspective on the prison world. His prison image has evolved to the point where it is dominated by the theme of boredom rather than violence. (The possibility of violence is still acknowledged and feared, but those violent incidents that do occur have been redefined as the consequences of prison norm violations rather than as random predatory acts; see Schmid and Jones 1990.) His survival strategy, although still extant, has been supplemented by such general adaptation techniques as legal and illegal diversionary activities and conscious efforts to suppress his thoughts about the outside world (Figure 1). His impression management tactics have become second nature rather than self-conscious, as he routinely interacts with others in terms of his prison identity.

An inmate's suspension of his preprison identity, of course, is never absolute, and the separation between his suspended identity and his prison identity is never complete. He continues to interact with his visitors at least partially in terms of his preprison identity, and he is likely to have acquired at least one inmate "partner" with whom he interacts in terms of his preprison as well as his prison identity. During times of introspection, however—which take place less frequently but do not disappear—he generally continues to think of himself as being the same person he was before he came to prison. But it is also during these periods of self-dialogue that he begins to have doubts about his ability to revive his suspended identity.

That's what I worry about a lot. Because I didn't want to change. . . . I'm still fighting it, 'cause from what I understood, before, I wasn't that bad—I wasn't even violent. But I have people say stuff to me now, before I used to say "O.k., o.k."—but now it seems like I got to eye them back, you know.

* * *

I don't know, but I may be losing touch with the outside. I am feeling real strange during visits, very uncomfortable. I just can't seem to be myself, although I am not really sure what myself is all about. My mind really seems to be glued to the inside of these walls. I can't even really comprehend the outside. I haven't even been here three months, and I feel like I'm starting to lose it. Maybe I'm just paranoid. But during these visits I really feel like I'm acting. I'm groping for the right words, always trying to keep the conversation going. Maybe I'm just trying to present a picture that will relieve the minds of my visitors, I just don't know.

* * *

I realized that strength is going to be an important factor whether I'm going to turn into a cold person or whether I'm going to keep my humanitarian point of view. I knew it is going to be an internal war. It's going to take a lot of energy to do that. . . . I just keep telling myself that you gotta do it and sometimes you get to the point where you don't care anymore. You just kinda lose it and you get so full of hate, so full of frustration, it gets wound up in your head a lot.

At this point, both the inmate's suspended preprison identity and his created prison identity are part of his "performance consciousness" (Schechner 1985), although they are not given equal value. His preprison identity is grounded primarily in the memory of his biography (Weigert 1986) rather than in self-performance. His concern, during the middle of his sentence, is that he has become so accustomed to dealing with others in terms of his prison identity—that he has been presenting and receiving affirmation of this identity for so long—that it is becoming his "true" identity.[3]

An inmate's fear that he is becoming the character he has been presenting is not unfounded. All of his interactions within the prison world indicate the strong likelihood of a "role-person merger" (Turner 1978). An inmate views his presentation of his prison identity as a necessary expression of his inmate status. Unlike situational identities presented through impression management in the outside world, performance of the inmate role is transsituational and continuous. For a new inmate, prison consists almost exclusively of front regions, in which he must remain in character. As long as he is in the maximum security institution, he remains in at least partial view of the audience for which his prison identity is intended: other prison inmates.[4] Moreover, because the stakes of his performance are so high, there is little room for self-mockery or other forms of role distance (Ungar 1984; Coser 1966) from his prison identity, and there is little possibility that an inmate's performance will be "punctured" (Adler and Adler 1989) by his partner or other prison acquaintances. And because his presentation of his prison identity is continuous, he also receives continuous affirmation of this identity from others—affirmation that becomes more significant in light of the fact that he also remains removed from day-to-day reaffirmation of his preprison identity by his associates in the outside world. The inauthenticity of the process is beside the point: Stone's (1962:93) observation that "one's identity is established when others *place* him as a social object by assigning him the same words of identity that he appropriates for himself or *announces*" remains sound even when both the announcements and the placements are recognized as false.

Standing against these various forms of support for an inmate's prison identity are the inmate's resolve not to be changed in prison, the fact that his sentence is relatively brief (though many new inmates lose sight of this brevity during the middle of their careers) and the limited reaffirmation of his preprison identity that he receives from outsiders and from his partner. These are not insubstantial resources, but nor do they guarantee an inmate's future ability to discard his prison identity and revive the one he has suspended.

Identity Dialectic

When an inmate's concerns about his identity first emerge, there is little that he can do about them. He recognizes that he has no choice but to present his prison identity so, following the insider's perspective he has now adopted, he consciously attempts to suppress his concerns. Eventually, however, he must begin to consider seriously his capacity to revive his suspended identity; his identity concerns, and his belief that he must deal with them, become particularly acute if he is transferred to the minimum security unit of the prison for the final months of his sentence.[5] At the conclusion of his prison career, an inmate shifts back toward an outsider's perspective on the prison world (see Figure 1); this shift involves the dissipation of his maximum security adaptation strategy, further revision of his prison image, reconstruction of an image of the outside world, and the initial development of an outside plan.[6] The inmate's efforts to revive his suspended identity are part of this shift in perspectives.

It is primarily through a renewed self-dialogue that the inmate struggles to revive his suspended identity—a struggle that amounts to a dialectic between his suspended identity and his prison identity. Through self-dialogue he recognizes, and tries to confront, the extent to which these two identities really do differ. He again tries to differentiate himself from maximum security inmates.

> There seems to be a concern with the inmates here to be able to dis-
> tinguish . . . themselves from the other inmates. That is—they feel they
> are above the others. . . . Although they may associate with each other,
> it still seems important to degrade the majority here.

And he does have some success in freeing himself from his prison identity.

> Well, I think I am starting to soften up a little bit. I believe the identity
> I picked up in the prison is starting to leave me now that I have left the
> world of the [maximum security] joint. I find myself becoming more
> and more involved with the happenings of the outside world. I am even
> getting anxious to go out and see the sights, just to get away from this
> place.

But he recognizes that he *has* changed in prison, and that these changes run
deeper than the mask he has been presenting to others. He has not returned
to his "old self" simply because his impression management skills are used
less frequently in minimum security. He raises the question—though he
cannot answer it—of how permanent these changes are. He wonders how
much his family and friends will see him as having changed. As stated by
one of our interview respondents:

> I know I've changed a little bit. I just want to realize how the people I
> know are going to see it, because they [will] be able to see it more than
> I can see it. . . . Sometimes I just want to go somewhere and hide.

He speculates about how much the outside world—especially his own network of outside relationships—has changed in his absence. (It is his life,
not those of his family and friends, that has been suspended during his
prison sentence; he knows that changes have occurred in the outside
world, and he suspects that some of these changes may have been with-
held from him, intentionally or otherwise.) He has questions, if not serious
doubts, about his ability to "make it" on the outside, especially concerning
his relationships with others; he knows, in any case, that he cannot simply
return to the outside world as if nothing has happened. Above all, he repeatedly confronts the question of who he is, and who he will be in the
outside world.

An inmate's struggle with these questions, like his self-dialogue at the
beginning of his prison career, is necessarily a solitary activity. The identity he claims at the time of his release, in contrast to his prison identity,
cannot be learned from other inmates. Also like his earlier periods of self-
dialogue, the questions he considers are not approached in a rational, systematic manner. The process is more one of rumination—of pondering one
question until another replaces it, and then contemplating the new question until it is replaced by still another, or suppressed from his thoughts.
There is, then, no final resolution to any of the inmate's identity questions.
Each inmate confronts these questions in his own way, and each arrives at
his own understanding of who he is, based on this unfinished, unresolved

self-dialogue. In every case, however, an inmate's release identity is a synthesis of his suspended preprison identity and his prison identity.[7]

Postprison Identity

Because each inmate's release identity is the outcome of his own identity dialectic, we cannot provide a profile of the "typical" release identity. But our data do allow us to specify some of the conditions that affect this outcome. Reaffirmations of his preprison identity by outsiders—visits and furloughs during which others interact with him as if he has not changed—provide powerful support for his efforts to revive his suspended identity. These efforts are also promoted by an inmate's recollection of his preprison identity (i.e., his attempts, through self-dialogue, to assess who he was before he came to prison), by his desire to abandon his prison identity, and by his general shift back toward an outsider's perspective. But there are also several factors that favor his prison identity, including his continued use of diversionary activities; his continued periodic efforts to suppress thoughts about the outside world; his continued ability to use prison impression management skills; and his continuing sense of injustice about the treatment he has received. Strained or cautious interactions with outsiders, or unfulfilled furlough expectations, inhibit the revival of his preprison identity. And he faces direct, experiential evidence that he has changed: when a minimum security resident recognizes that he is now completely unaffected by reports of violent incidents in maximum security, he acknowledges that he is no longer the same person that he was when he entered prison. Turner (1978:1) has suggested three criteria for role-person merger: "failure of role compartmentalization, resistance to abandoning a role in the face of advantageous roles, and the acquisition of role-appropriate attitudes"; at the time of their release from prison, the inmates we studied had already accrued some experience with each of these criteria.

Just as we cannot define a typical release identity, we cannot predict these inmates' future, postprison identities, not only because we have restricted our analysis to their prison experiences but because each inmate's future identity is inherently unpredictable. What effect an ex-inmate's prison experience has on his identity depends on how he, in interaction with others, defines this experience. Some of the men we have studied will be returned to prison in the future; others will not. But all will have been changed by their prison experiences. They entered the prison world fearing for their lives; they depart with the knowledge that they have survived. On the one hand, these men are undoubtedly stronger persons by virtue of this accomplishment. On the other hand, the same tactics that enabled them to survive the prison world can be called upon, appropriately or not, in difficult situations in the outside world. To the extent that these men draw upon their prison survival tactics to cope with the hardships of the outside world—to the extent that their prison behavior becomes a meaningful part of their "role repertoire" (Turner 1978) in their everyday lives—their prison identities will have become inseparable from their "true" identities.

The Suspended Identity Model

As identity preservation tactics, an inmate's suspension of his preprison identity and development of a false prison identity are not, and cannot be, entirely successful. At the conclusion of his sentence, no inmate can ever fully revive his suspended identity; he cannot remain the same person he was before he came to prison. But his tactics do not fail entirely either. An inmate's resolve not to change, his decision to suspend his preprison identity, his belief that he will be able to revive this identity, and his subsequent struggle to revive this identity undoubtedly minimize the identity change that would otherwise have taken place. The inmate's tactics, leading up to his suspended identity dialectic, constitute an identity transformation process, summarized in Figure 2, that differs from both the gradual, sequential model of identity transformation and models of radical identity transformation (Strauss 1959). It also shares some characteristics with each of these models.

As in cases of brainwashing and conversion, there is an external change agency involved, the inmate does learn a new perspective (an insider's perspective) for evaluating himself and the world around him, and he does develop new group loyalties while his old loyalties are reduced. But unlike a radical identity transformation, the inmate does not interpret the changes that take place as changes in a *central* identity; the insider's perspective he learns and the new person he becomes in prison are viewed as a false front that he must present to others, but a front that does not affect who he really is. And while suspending his preprison identity necessarily entails a weakening of his outside loyalties, it does not, in most cases, destroy them. Because he never achieves more than a marginal status in the prison world, the inmate's ambivalence prevents him from accepting an insider's perspective too fully, and thus prevents him from fully severing his loyalties to the outside world (Schmid and Jones 1987). He retains a fundamental, if ambivalent, commitment to his outside world throughout his sentence, and he expects to reestablish his outside relationships (just as he expects to revive his suspended identity) when his sentence is over.

Like a religious convert who later loses his faith, an inmate cannot simply return to his old self. The liminal conditions (Turner 1977) of the prison world have removed him, for too long, from his accustomed identity bearings in everyday life. He does change in prison, but his attempts to suspend and subsequently revive his preprison identity maintain a general sense of identity continuity for most of his prison career. As in the gradual identity transformation process delineated by Strauss (1959), he recognizes changes in his identity only at periodic "turning points," especially his mid-career doubts about his ability to revive his suspended identity and his self-dialogue at the end of his sentence. Also like a gradual identity transformation, the extent of his identity change depends on a balance between the situational adjustments he has made in prison and his continuing commitments to the outside world (Becker 1960, 1964). His identity depends, in other words, on the outcome of the dialectic between his prison identity and his suspended preprison identity.

The suspended identity model is one component and a holistic analysis of the experiences of first-time, short-term inmates at a specific maximum security prison. Like any holistic analysis, its usefulness lies primarily in its capacity to explain the particular case under study (Deising 1971). We nonetheless expect similar identity transformation processes to occur under similar circumstances: among individuals who desire to preserve their identities despite finding themselves involved in temporary but encompassing social situations that subject them to new and disparate identity demands and render their prior identities inappropriate. The suspended identity model presented here provides a basis for further exploration of these circumstances.

Acknowledgments

We wish to thank Jim Thomas, Patricia A. Adler and the reviewers of *Symbolic Interaction* for their useful comments and suggestions.

Notes

1. This is a matter of some theoretical interest. Proponents of existential sociology (cf. Douglas and Johnson 1977) view feelings as the very foundation of social action, social structures, and the self. From this theoretical framework, a new inmate would be viewed as someone who has been stripped to that core of primal feelings that constitutes his existential self; the symbolic construction of his former world, including his cognitive definition of himself (learned from the definitions that others hold of him) are exposed as artificial, leaving the individual at least partially free to choose for himself what he wants to be and how he wants to present himself to others. Whether or not we view the feelings of vulnerability, discontinuity, and differentiation as the core of an inmate's self, or even as attributes of his self, we must note that the inmate does not reject his earlier self-image (or other symbolic constructions) as artificial. He continues to hold on to his preprison identity as his "true" self and he continues to view the outside world as the "real" world. It is the prison world that is viewed as artificial. His definitions of the outside world and the prison world do change during his prison career, but he never fully rejects his outsider's perspective.

2. There are four principal components to the survival strategies of the inmates we studied, in the early months of their prison sentences. "Selective interaction" and "territorial caution" are essentially precautionary guidelines that allow inmates to increase their understanding of the prison world while minimizing danger to themselves. "Partnership" is a special friendship bond between two inmates, typically based on common backgrounds and interests (including a shared uncertainty about prison life) and strengthened by the inmates' mutual exploration of a hostile prison world. The fourth component of their strategies, impression management, is discussed in subsequent sections of this article.

3. Clemmer (1958:299) has defined "prisonization" as the "taking on in greater or less degree of the folkways, mores, customs, and general culture of the penitentiary." Yet new inmates begin to "take on" these things almost immediately, as part of the impression they are attempting to present to other inmates. Thus, we would argue instead that prisonization (meaning assimilation to the prison world) begins to occur for these inmates when their prison identities become second nature—when their expressions of prison norms and customs are no

longer based on self-conscious acting. A new inmate's identity concerns, during the middle of his sentence, are essentially a recognition of this assimilation. For other examples of problems associated with double identity, see Warren and Ponse (1977) and Lemert (1967); Adler and Adler (1989) describe self-diminishment problems, as well as self-aggrandizement effects, that accompany even highly valued identity constructions.

4. This finding stands in contrast to other works on total institutions, which suggest that inmates direct their impression management tactics toward the staff. See, for example, Goffman (1961:318) and Heffernan (1972; chapter VI). First-time, short-term inmates certainly interact with guards and other staff in terms of their prison identities, but these personnel are neither the primary source of their fear nor the primary objects of their impression management. Interactions with staff are limited by a concern with how other inmates will define such interactions; in this sense, presentation of a new inmate's prison identity to staff can be viewed as part of the impression he is creating for other inmates.

5. Not all prisoners participate in this unit; inmates must apply for transfer to the unit, and their acceptance depends both on the crimes for which they were sentenced and staff evaluation of their potential for success in the unit. Our analysis focuses on those inmates who are transferred.

6. There are three features of the minimum security unit that facilitate this shift in perspectives: a more open physical and social environment; the fact that the unit lies just outside the prison wall (so that an inmate who is transferred is also physically removed from the maximum security prison); and greater opportunity for direct contact with the outside world, through greater access to telephones, an unrestricted visitor list, unrestricted visiting hours and, eventually, weekend furloughs.

7. This is an important parallel with our analysis of the inmate's changing prison definitions: his concluding prison image is a synthesis of the image he formulates before coming to prison and the image he holds at the middle of his prison career; see Schmid and Jones (1990).

References

Adler, Patricia A. and Peter Adler. 1989. "The Gloried Self: The Aggrandizement and the Constriction of Self." *Social Psychology Quarterly* 52:299–310.

Becker, Howard S. 1960. "Notes on the Concept of Commitment." *American Journal of Sociology* 66:32–40.

———. "Personal Change in Adult Life." 1964. *Sociometry* 27:40–53.

Berger, Peter L. 1963. *Invitation to Sociology: A Humanistic Perspective.* Garden City, NY: Doubleday Anchor Books.

Blumer, Herbert. 1969. *Symbolic Interactionism: Perspective and Method,* Englewood Cliffs, NJ: Prentice Hall.

———. 1972. "Action vs. Interaction: Review of *Relations in Public* by Erving Goffman." *Transaction* 9:50–53.

Boulding, Kenneth. 1961. *The Image.* Ann Arbor: University of Michigan Press.

Clemmer, Donald. 1958. *The Prison Community.* New York: Holt, Rinehart & Winston.

Coser, R. 1966. "Role Distance, Sociological Ambivalence and Traditional Status Systems." *American Journal of Sociology* 72:173–187.

Deising, Paul. 1971. *Patterns of Discovery in the Social Sciences.* Chicago: Aldine-Atherton.

Douglas, Jack D., Patricia A. Adler, Peter Adler, Andrea Fontana, Robert C. Freeman, and Joseph A. Kotarba. 1980. *Introduction to the Sociologies of Everyday Life.* Boston: Allyn and Bacon.

Douglas, Jack D. and John M. Johnson. 1977. *Existential Sociology.* Cambridge: Cambridge University Press.

Garfinkel, Harold. 1956. "Conditions of Successful Degradation Ceremonies." *American Journal of Sociology* 61:420–424.

Glaser, Barney G. and Anselm L. Strauss. 1964. "Awareness Contexts and Social Interaction." *American Sociological Review* 29:269–279.

Goffman, Erving. 1959. *The Presentation of Self in Everyday Life.* Garden City, NY: Doubleday Anchor Books.
———. 1961. *Asylums.* Garden City, NY: Doubleday Anchor Books.
———. 1963. *Stigma: Notes on the Management of Spoiled Identity.* Englewood Cliffs, NJ: Prentice Hall.
Gross, Edward and Gregory P. Stone. 1964. "Embarrassment and the Analysis of Role Requirements." *American Journal of Sociology* 70:1–15.
Heffernan, Esther. 1972. *Making It in Prison: The Square, the Cool and the Life.* New York: Wiley-Interscience.
Irwin, John. 1970. *The Felon.* Englewood Cliffs, NJ: Prentice Hall.
———. 1977. *Scenes.* Beverly Hills: Sage.
Lemert, Edwin. 1967. "Role Enactment, Self, and Identity in the Systematic Check Forger." Pp. 119–134 in *Human Deviance, Social Problems and Social Control.* Englewood Cliffs, NJ: Prentice Hall.
Lewis, David J. 1979. "A Social Behaviorist Interpretation of the Median I." *American Journal of Sociology* 84:261–287.
Messinger, Sheldon E., Harold Sampson, and Robert D. Towne. 1962. "Life as Theater: Some Notes on the Dramaturgic Approach to Social Reality." *Sociometry* 25:98–111.
Schechner, Richard. 1985. *Between Theater and Anthropology.* Philadelphia: University of Pennsylvania Press.
Scheff, Thomas. 1970. "On the Concepts of Identity and Social Relationships" Pp. 193–207 in *Human Nature and Collective Behavior,* edited by T. Shibutani. Englewood Cliffs, NJ: Prentice Hall.
Schlenker, B. 1980. *Impression Management: The Self Concept, Social Identity and Interpersonal Relations.* Belmont, CA: Wadsworth.
Schmid, Thomas and Richard Jones. 1987. "Ambivalent Actions: Prison Adaptation Strategies of New Inmates." American Society of Criminology, annual meetings, Montreal, Quebec.
———. 1990. "Experiential Orientations to the Prison Experience: The Case of First-Time, Short-Term Inmates." Pp. 189–210 in *Perspectives on Social Problems,* edited by Gale Miller and James A. Holstein. Greenwich, CT: JAI Press.
Solomon, David N. 1970. "Role and Self-Conception: Adaptation and Change in Occupations." Pp. 286–300 in *Human Nature and Collective Behavior,* edited by T. Shibutani. Englewood Cliffs, NJ: Prentice Hall.
Stone, Gregory P. 1962. "Appearance and the Self." Pp. 86–118 in *Human Behavior and Social Processes,* edited by Arnold Rose. Boston: Houghton Mifflin.
Strauss, Anselm L. 1959. *Mirrors and Masks: The Search for Identity.* Glencoe: The Free Press.
Sykes, Gresham. 1958. *The Society of Captives: A Study of a Maximum Security Prison.* Princeton: Princeton University Press.
Turner, Ralph H. 1978. "The Role and the Person." *American Journal of Sociology* 84:1–23.
Turner, Victor. 1977. *The Ritual Process: Structure and Anti-Structure.* Ithaca, NY: Cornell University Press.
Ungar, Sheldon. 1984. "Self-Mockery: An Alternative Form of Self-Presentation." *Symbolic Interaction* 7:121–133.
Warren, Carol A. and Barbara Ponse. 1977. "The Existential Self in the Gay World." Pp. 273–289 in *Existential Sociology,* edited by Jack D. Douglas and John M. Johnson. Cambridge: Cambridge University Press.
Weigert, Andrew J. 1986. "The Social Production of Identity: Metatheoretical Foundations." *Sociological Quarterly* 27:165–183.
Zurcher, Louis A. 1977. *The Mutable Self.* Beverly Hills: Sage.

Building Deviant Careers and Identities

In Part IV, we described how institutional careers and identities may be produced. The material in that section examined how various types of institutional typing and processing may affect an actor's personal and public identity, as well as self-image. An equally important concern is the way in which noninstitutional careers evolve. As we noted earlier, such careers or activities generally arise as a result of an actor's own desires and needs; this means that frequently the actor plays an assertive role in moving into a particular type of activity, consciously structuring and presenting a specific image of self to others. Often, as the general introduction indicates, there may be a degree of overlap between institutional and noninstitutional careers. For instance, prostitutes, skid-row alcoholics, homosexuals, and thieves may be arrested and thus pulled into, rather than intentionally entering, an institutional career. Although the distinction between institutional and noninstitutional careers is useful analytically, we must recognize that if an actor is to assume the status of a secondary or career deviant, he or she must become familiar with and act in accord with existing ideology, culture, practices, and traditions. Obtaining a more complete understanding of how a deviant career or identity is actually built, however, requires that we initially examine an occupation's or profession's underlying organizational structures and associated ideologies. Once such elements have been located, characterized, described, and set, we are in a much better position to understand such processes as recruitment and socialization.

"The Social Organization of Deviants," by Joel Best and David F. Luckenbill, provides an excellent framework for understanding the social organizations in which deviants become involved. The authors make an initial distinction between the social organization of *deviants* and the social organization of *deviance*. The former refers to the "patterns of relationships between deviant actors," whereas the latter refers to the "patterns of relationships between the various roles performed in deviant transactions." Best and Luckenbill elect to focus on the social organization of deviants. Deviant organizations, they reason, can vary along certain dimensions, most notably in terms of their sophistication (i.e., complexity, degree of coordination, and purposiveness). For example, with regard to complexity, organizations can have varying divisions of labor, degrees of stratification, and degrees of role specialization. Best and Luckenbill note that, in terms of sophistication, deviants organize in identifiable ways. They discuss five organizational forms: loners, colleagues, peers, mobs, and formal organizations. Each of these forms can be analyzed relative to four variables: whether the deviants associate with each other, whether they engage in deviance together, whether there is an elaborate division of labor, and whether activities extend over time and space. The authors describe various types of each organizational form. They then examine the consequences of organizing as loners, colleagues, peers, mobs, or formal organizations. Best and Luckenbill argue that the degree of sophistication of a deviant organization has consequences for deviants and social-control agents. Five propositions are advanced in support of this argument. The authors' second hypothesis is especially relevant for the next section on entering and learning about deviant cultures. Specifically, they hypothesize that "the more sophisticated the form of deviant organization, the more elaborate the socialization of its members." The underlying assumption here is that "neophyte deviants" not only must learn how to perform deviant acts and attain the appropriate skills and techniques, but they must also develop a *cognitive perspective* (e.g., learn the relevant rationalizations and language). For example, loners do not depend on others for instruction, but pool hustlers do.

Phyllis Coontz, in "Managing the Action: Sports Bookmakers as Entrepreneurs," examines the social organizational and occupational features of bookmaking. Bookmaking shares many common features with other forms of deviance. For example, getting into the business requires contact with others—current or former participants—and learning the skills and attitudes favorable to bookmaking occurs through interaction. To be successful in any deviant career requires a level of individual and organizational sophistication; this is true of bookies, who cannot openly advertise their services but who are dependent on "paying customers." Minimizing risk is essential both with regard to avoiding apprehension by social-control agents and with regard to avoiding economic loss. Possessing and applying specialized skills and knowledge help the bookie continue to operate. Coontz also shows that certain organizational features contribute directly to the length of a bookie's career. She demonstrates that bookmaking is significantly different in a number of ways (e.g., career duration) from many other deviant careers.

Coontz's analysis suggests that in many ways, the social organization of bookmaking shelters bookies from arrest, prosecution, jail or prison time, and the like. There are also several features that serve an insulating function. Initially, there is no material exchange, and taking the bet requires only a verbal agreement between the one placing the bet and the bookmaker. Further, face-to-face interaction is not required, and there are no middlemen—no producers, no suppliers, no vendors. These features minimize the risk of detection and help to solidify and extend the deviant career.

One of the many interesting observations revolves around the relationships that exist between the bookmaker and the client in deviant transactions. Bookies have no legal recourse for clients who do not pay their debts. It is essential, therefore, that the bookie operate honestly and with integrity with each customer. Commitment to conventional values such as these contributes to long-term career paths by reducing competition and insuring faithful clientele and suggests an entrepreneurial approach to deviant careers such as bookmaking.

35 The Social Organization of Deviants

Joel Best
David F. Luckenbill

Ethnographic research on particular social scenes provides data for general, grounded theories (Glaser and Strauss, 1967). For the study of deviance, field studies have supplied the basis for the development of general theories of the social psychology of deviance (Goffman, 1963; Lofland, 1969; Matza, 1969). However, while several reports about specific forms of deviance focus on social organization (Einstader, 1969; McIntosh, 1971; Mileski and Black, 1972; Shover, 1977; Zimmerman and Wieder, 1977), there is no satisfactory general theory of the social organization of deviance.

Sociologists of varying perspectives have debated the nature of social organization among juvenile delinquents, professional criminals, organized criminals and white-collar criminals. Others have developed typologies of deviants that include social organizational features (Clinard and Quinney, 1973; Gibbons, 1965, 1977; Miller, 1978). However, these statements of social organization suffer from several flaws. First, they are often too narrow, focusing on a single type of deviance, such as burglary or more broadly, crime. Second, they usually are content with describing the organizational forms of different types of deviance. They fail to locate such forms along a dimension of organization or examine the consequences of organizational differences for deviants and social control agents. Third, they typically confuse two different bases for analyzing social organization: a general theory must distinguish between the social organization of *deviants* (the patterns of relationships between deviant actors) and the social organization of *deviance* (the patterns of relationships between the various roles performed in deviant transactions).

In this paper, we present a framework for understanding the social organization of deviants.[1] By examining reports of field research, several forms of social organization are identified and located along a dimension of organizational sophistication. Then some propositions are developed regarding the consequences of organizational variation for deviants and social control agents. Finally, some implications for the study of social organization are considered.

Forms of Deviant Organization

The social organization of deviants refers to the structure or patterns of relationships among deviant actors in the context of deviant pursuits. The social organization of deviants varies along a dimension of sophistication. Organizational sophistication involves the elements of complexity, coordination and purposiveness (cf. Cressey, 1972). Organizations vary in the complexity of their division of labor including the size of membership, degree of stratification, and degree of specialization of organizational roles. Organizations also vary in their coordination among roles including the degree to which rules, agreements, and codes regulating relationships are formalized and enforced. Finally, organizations vary in the purposiveness with which they specify, strive toward, and achieve their objectives. Forms of organization which display high levels of complexity, coordination, and purposiveness are more sophisticated than those forms with lower levels.

Research reports suggest that deviants organize in several identifiable ways along the dimension of sophistication. Beginning with the least sophisticated, we will discuss five forms: loners, colleagues, peers, mobs and formal organizations. These organizational forms can be defined in terms of four variables: (1) whether the deviants associate with one another; (2) whether they participate in deviance together; (3) whether their deviance requires an elaborate division of labor; and (4) whether their organization's activities extend over time and space (see Table 1). Loners do not associate with other deviants, participate in shared deviance, have a division of labor, or maintain their deviance over extended time and space. *Colleagues* differ from loners because they associate with fellow deviants. *Peers* not only associate with one another, but also participate in

Table 1 Characteristics of Different Forms of the Social Organization of Deviants

Variable	Type of Organization				
	Loners	Colleagues	Peers	Mobs	Formal Organizations
Mutual association	−	+	+	+	+
Mutual participation	−	−	+	+	+
Division of labor	−	−	−	+	+
Extended organization	−	−	−	−	+

deviance together. In *mobs,* the shared participation requires an elaborate division of labor. Finally, *formal organizations* involve mutual association and participation, an elaborate division of labor, and deviant undertakings extended over time and space.

The descriptions of these forms of organization must be qualified in two ways. First, the forms are presented as ideal types. There is variation among the types of deviants within each form, as well as between one form and another. The intent is to sketch out the typical features of each form, recognizing that particular types of deviants may not share all of the features of their form to the same degree. Organizational sophistication can be viewed as a continuum, with deviants located between, as well as on, the five points. Describing a number of forms along this continuum inevitably understates the complexities of social life. Second, the descriptions of these forms draw largely from field studies of deviance in the contemporary United States, and attempt to locate the deviants studied along the dimension of organizational sophistication. A particular type of deviant can be organized in various ways in different societies and at different times. The references to specific field studies are intended to place familiar pieces of research within this framework; they are not claims that particular types of deviants invariably organize in a given way.

Loners

Some deviants operate as individuals. These loners do not associate with other deviants for purposes of sociability, the performance of deviant activities, or the exchange of supplies and information. Rather, they must supply themselves with whatever knowledge, skill, equipment and ideology their deviance requires. Loners lack deviant associations, so they cannot receive such crucial forms of feedback as moral support or information about their performance, new opportunities, or changes in social control strategies. They often enter deviance as a defensive response to private troubles (Lofland, 1969). Because their entry does not require contact with other deviants, as long as they can socialize themselves, loners frequently come from segments of the population which are less likely to be involved in the more sophisticated forms of deviance; it is not uncommon for loners to be middle-aged, middle-class or female. Because their deviance often is defensive, and because they lack the support of other deviants, loners' careers typically are short-lived. Examples of loners include murderers (Luckenbill, 1977), rapists (Amir, 1971), embezzlers (Cressey, 1953), check forgers (Lemert, 1967:99–134; Klein and Montague, 1977), physician narcotic addicts (Winick, 1961), compulsive criminals (Cressey, 1962), heterosexual transvestites (Buckner, 1970), amateur shoplifters (Cameron, 1964), some gamblers (Lesieur, 1977), and many computer criminals (Parker, 1976).[2]

Colleagues

query 3

Like loners, colleagues perform as individuals. Unlike loners, however, colleagues associate with others involved in the same kind of deviance. Colleagues thus form a simple group which provides important services for members. First, colleagues often socialize newcomers, providing training in deviant skills as well as an ideology which accounts for and justifies their deviance. Association also offers sociability among members with whom one's deviant identity need not be concealed: an actor can take down his or her guard without fear of discovery by agents of social control (Goffman, 1959, 1963). Also, association provides a source of information about ways to obtain deviant equipment, new techniques, new opportunities for engaging in deviance, and strategies for avoiding sanctioning. Colleagues learn and are held to a loose set of norms which direct conduct in both deviant and respectable activities. "Don't inform on a colleague" and "Never cut in on a colleague's score" exemplify such norms. The moral climate established by these expectations increases the stability of colleagues' social scene. At the same time, only some deviant activities and some people are suited for such a loose form of organization. A successful career as a colleague depends ultimately on the individual's performance when operating alone. As a result, newcomers often sample the scene and, when they encounter difficulties, drift away. Only the more successful colleagues maintain extended deviant careers. Some examples of colleagues include most prostitutes (Hirschi, 1962; Bryan, 1965, 1966), pimps (Milner and Milner, 1972), and pool hustlers (Polsky, 1967).

Peers

Like colleagues, peers associate with one another and benefit from services provided by their fellows. Peers are involved in the socialization of novices, considerable sociable interaction, and the maintenance of a loose, unwritten code of conduct to be followed by individuals who wish to remain in the peer group. Unlike colleagues, peers participate in deviant *query 3* acts together; they are involved in deviant transactions at the same time and in the same place. In some cases, such mutual participation is required by the nature of the deviant activity. This is exemplified in the performance of homosexual acts, or in the "task force raids" where a collection of young men engages in simple acts of violence such as gang fighting or rolling drunks (Cressey, 1972). In other cases, mutual participation is required because peers form a network for supplying one another with essential goods and services, as found in the distribution of illicit drugs. In either event, peers interact basically as equals; there is a minimal division of labor and specialized roles are uncommon. Although individuals pass through these social scenes, peer groups often are quite stable, perhaps because peer groups solve structural problems within society for their members. Two common varieties of deviant peers are young people who have not yet entered integrated adult work roles, and those who frequent a deviant marketplace and depend on their contacts with one another for the satisfaction of illicit needs. Examples of peers include hobos (Anderson, 1923), homosexuals (Humphreys, 1970; Mileski and Black, 1972; Warren, 1974), group-oriented gamblers (Lesieur, 1977), swingers (Bartell, 1971), gang delinquents (Shaw, 1930; Matza, 1964; Rosenberg and Silverstein, 1969), motorcycle outlaws (Thompson, 1966), skid row tramps (Wiseman, 1970; Rubington, 1978), and illicit drug users (Blumer, 1967; Carey, 1968; Feldman, 1968; Stoddart, 1974).

Mobs

Mobs are small groups of professional or career deviants organized to pursue specific, profitable goals.[3] Their deviance requires the coordinated actions of members performing specialized roles—a more sophisticated division of labor than that found among peers. Thus, work is divided among confidence artists (the inside man and the outside man), pickpockets (the tool and the stall), or card and dice hustlers (the mechanic and the shootup man; Maurer, 1962, 1964; Prus and Sharper, 1977). Ordinarily, at least one of the roles in the mob is highly skilled, requiring considerable practice and training to perfect. This training (normally via apprenticeship), the need for on-the-job coordination, and the common practice of traveling from city to city as a mob lead to intensive interaction between mobsters. Elaborate technical argots develop, as well as elaborate codes specifying mobsters' obligations to each other.

Mobs have complex links to outsiders. They are organized to accomplish profitable yet safe crimes. McIntosh (1971) describes the historical shift from craft thieving, where mobs develop routine procedures for stealing relatively small sums from individuals, to project thieving, where larger amounts are taken from corporate targets using procedures specifically tailored to the particular crime. In either case, mob operations are planned and staged with an eye toward avoiding arrest. Also, mobs may attempt to neutralize the criminal justice system by bribing social control agents not to make arrests, "fixing" those cases where arrests take place, or making restitution to victims in return for dropped charges. Mobs also have ties to others who purchase stolen goods, provide legal services, and supply information and deviant equipment. Finally, a network of sociable and business contacts ties mobs to one another, enabling strategic information to spread quickly. These arrangements ensure that mobs can operate at a consistently profitable level with minimal interference. Consequently, the careers of individual mobsters, as well as those of specific mobs, seem to be more stable than those of deviants organized in less sophisticated ways.[4] Examples of mobs are the groups of professional criminals specializing in confidence games (Sutherland, 1937; Maurer, 1962), picking pockets (Maurer, 1964), shoplifting (Cameron, 1964), armed robbery (Einstader, 1969; Letkemann, 1973), burglary (Shover, 1977), and card and dice hustling (Prus and Sharper, 1977).

Formal Organizations

Formal organizations of deviants differ from mobs in the scope of their actions.[5] Normally they involve more people, but, more importantly, their actions are coordinated to efficiently handle deviant tasks on a routine basis over considerable time and space. While mobsters work as a group in a series of episodic attacks, formal organizations are characterized by delegated responsibility and by routine and steady levels of productivity. In many ways, formal organizations of deviants share the features which characterize such respectable bureaucracies as military organizations, churches, and business firms. They have a hierarchal division of labor, including both vertical and horizontal differentiation of positions and roles and established channels for vertical and horizontal communication. A deviant formal organization may contain departments for planning, processing goods, public relations and rule enforcement, with positions for strategists, coordinators, accountants, lawyers, enforcers, and dealers in illicit goods. There may be recruitment policies for filling these diversified positions, and entry into the organization may be marked by a ritual ceremony of passage. Formal organizations usually have binding, but normally unwritten, rules and codes for guiding members in organizational action, and these rules are actively enforced.

Formal organizations of deviants can make large profits by operating efficiently. At the same time, they must protect themselves from harm or destruction. As in less sophisticated forms of organization, loyal members are expected to maintain the group's secrets. In addition, deviant formal organizations attempt to locate power in the office, rather than in an individual charismatic leader. Although charismatic leadership obviously plays a part in some deviant formal organizations, the successful organization is able to continue operations when a leader dies or is arrested. Finally, deviant formal organizations typically invest considerable energy in neutralizing the criminal justice system by corrupting both high- and low-level officials. The scope and efficiency of their operations, their organizational flexibility, and their ties to agencies of social control make formal organizations of deviants extremely stable. Examples of such deviant formal organizations include very large urban street gangs (Keiser, 1969; Dawley, 1973), smuggling rings (Green, 1969), and organized crime "families" (Cressey, 1969; Ianni, 1972).

The Significance of the Social Organization of Deviants

The identification and description of these different organizational forms permit a comparative analysis. What are the consequences of organizing as loners, colleagues, peers, mobs, or formal organizations? A comparison suggests that the sophistication of a form of deviant social organization has several consequences for both deviants and social control agents. Five propositions can be advanced.

I. *The more sophisticated the form of deviant organization, the greater its members' capability for complex deviant operations.* Deviant activities, like conventional activities, vary in their complexity. The complexity of a deviant operation refers to the number of elements required to carry it through; the more component parts to an activity, the more complex it is.[6] Compared to simple activities, complex lines of action demand more careful preparation and execution and take longer to complete. The complexity of a deviant activity depends upon two identifiable types of elements. First, there are the *resources* which the actors must be able to draw upon. Some activities require that the deviant utilize special knowledge, skill, equipment, or social status in order to complete the operation successfully, while simple acts can be carried out without such resources. Second, the *organization of the deviant transaction* affects an activity's complexity.[7] Some deviant acts can be accomplished with a single actor, while others require two or more people. The actors in a transaction can share a common role, as in a skid row bottle gang, or the transaction may demand different roles, such as offender and victim or buyer and seller. Furthermore, the degree to which these roles must be coordinated, ranging from the minimal coordination of juvenile vandals to the precision routines performed by mobs of pickpockets, varies among situations. The more people involved, the more roles they perform; and the more coordination between those roles, the more complex the deviant transaction's organization. The more resources and organization involved in a deviant operation, the more complex the operation is.

In general, deviants in more sophisticated forms of organization commit more complex acts.[8] The deviant acts of loners tend to be simple, requiring little in the way of resources or organization. Although colleagues work apart from one another, they generally share certain resources, such as shared areas. The hustlers' pool hall and the prostitutes' red light district contain the elements needed to carry out deviant operations, including victims and clients. Peers may interact in situations where they are the only ones present, performing complementary or comparable roles, as when two people engage in homosexual intercourse or a group of motorcycle outlaws makes a "run." Peers also may undertake activities which involve nonmembers, as when members of a delinquent gang rob a passerby. The activities carried out by mobs involve substantially more coordination among the members' roles. In an armed robbery, for instance, one member may be assigned to take the money, while a second provides "cover" and a third waits for the others in the car, ready to drive away on their return. Finally, the activities of formal organizations tend to be particularly complex, requiring substantial resources and elaborate organization. Major off-track betting operations, with staff members at local, district and regional offices who carry out a variety of clerical and supervisory tasks on a daily basis, represent an exceedingly complex form of deviance.

The relationship between the sophistication of organization and the complexity of deviant activities is not perfect. Loners can engage in acts of considerable complexity, for example. The computer criminal who single-handedly devises a complicated method of breaking into and stealing from computerized records, the embezzler who carries through an elaborate series of illicit financial manipulations, and the physician who juggles drug records in order to maintain his or her addiction to narcotics are engaged in complex offenses requiring substantial resources. However, these offenses cannot be committed by everyone. These loners draw upon resources which they command through their conventional positions, turning them to deviant uses. The computer criminal typically is an experienced programmer, the embezzler must occupy a position of financial trust, and the physician has been trained in the use of drugs. Possessing these resources makes the loner's deviance possible. Thus, the more concentrated the resources necessary for a deviant operation, the less sophisticated the form of organization required. However, when resources are not concentrated, then more sophisticated forms of organization are necessary to undertake more complex deviant operations.

Sophisticated forms of deviant organization have advantages beyond being able to undertake complex operations by pooling resources distributed among their members. Some deviant activities require a minimal level of organization; for example, homosexual intercourse demands the participation of two parties. In many other cases, it may be possible to carry out a deviant line of action using a relatively unsophisticated form of organization, but the task is considerably easier if a sophisticated form of organization can be employed. This is so because more sophisticated forms of deviant organization enjoy several advantages: they are capable of conducting a larger number of deviant operations; the operations can occur with greater frequency and over a broader range of territory; and, as discussed below, the members are better protected from the actions of social control agents. Of course, sophisticated organizations may engage in relatively simple forms of deviance, but the deviant act is often only one component in a larger organizational context. Taking a particular bet in the policy racket is a simple act, but the racket itself, handling thousands of bets, is complex indeed. Similarly, a murder which terminates a barroom dispute between two casual acquaintances is very different from an execution which is ordered and carried out by members of a formal organization, even though the two acts may appear equally simple. In the latter case, the killing may be intended as a means of maintaining discipline by demonstrating the organization's ability to levy sanctions against wayward members.

II. *The more sophisticated the form of deviant organization, the more elaborate the socialization of its members.* Neophyte deviants need to acquire two types of knowledge: (1) they must learn how to perform deviant acts, and how to gain appropriate *skills and techniques;* (2) they must develop a *cognitive perspective,* a distinctive way of making sense of their new, deviant world (cf. Shibutani, 1961:118–127). Such a perspective includes an ideology which accounts for the deviance, the individual's participation in deviance, and the organizational form, as well as a distinctive language for speaking about these and other matters.

As forms of deviant organization increase in sophistication, socialization becomes more elaborate. Loners do not depend upon other deviants for instruction in deviant skills or for a special cognitive perspective; they learn through their participation in conventional social scenes. Murderers, for instance, learn from their involvement in conventional life how to respond in situations of interpersonal conflict, and they employ culturally widespread justifications for killing people (Bohannon, 1960; Wolfgang and Ferracuti, 1967). Embezzlers learn the technique for converting a financial trust in the course of respectable vocational training, adapting justifications such as "borrowing" from conventional business ideology (Cressey, 1953). In contrast, colleagues teach one another a great deal. Although pool hustlers usually know how to shoot pool before they enter hustling, their colleagues provide a rich cognitive perspective, including a sense of "we-ness," some norms of behavior, a system for stratifying the hustling world, and an extensive argot (Polsky, 1967).[9] Peers receive similar training or, in some cases, teach one another through a process of emerging norms (Turner, 1964). Juvenile vandals, for example, can devise new offenses through their mutually constructed interpretation of what is appropriate to a particular situation (Wade, 1967). Sometimes, the knowledge peers acquire has largely symbolic functions that affirm the group's solidarity, as when a club of motorcycle outlaws devises a written constitution governing its members (Reynolds, 1967:134–136). In mobs and formal organizations, the cognitive perspective focuses on more practical matters; their codes of conduct specify the responsibilities members have in their dealings with one another, social control agents and others. Greater emphasis is also placed on the acquisition of specialized skills, with an experienced deviant coaching an apprentice, frequently over an extended period of time.

Two circumstances affect the socialization process in different forms of deviant organization. First, the sophistication of the organization affects the scope and style of the training process. The amount of training tends to increase with the sophistication of the organization. The skills required to perform deviant roles vary, but there is a tendency for more sophisticated forms of organization to incorporate highly skilled roles. Further, the more sophisticated forms of organization often embody cognitive perspectives of such breadth that the deviant must acquire a large body of specialized knowledge. In addition, the socialization process tends to be organized differently in different forms of deviant organization. While loners serve as their own agents of socialization, and colleagues and peers may socialize one another, mobs and formal organizations almost always teach newcomers through apprenticeship to an experienced deviant. Second, the socialization process is affected by the newcomer's motivation for entering deviance. Loners, of course, choose deviance on their own. In the more sophisticated forms, newcomers may ask for admission, but they often are recruited by experienced deviants. While peers may recruit widely, as when a delinquent gang tries to enlist all of the neighborhood boys of a given age, mobs and formal organizations recruit selectively, judging the character and commitment of prospective members and sometimes demanding evidence of skill or prior experience. For loners, entry into deviance frequently is a defensive act, intended to ward off some immediate threat. Peers, on the other hand, often are using deviance to experience stimulation; their deviance has an adventurous quality (Lofland, 1969). In contrast, mobs and formal organizations adopt a more professional approach: deviance is instrumental, a calculated means of acquiring economic profits.[10] These differences in the scope of socialization, the way the process is organized, and the neophyte's motivation account for the relationship between sophistication of organization and the elaborateness of the socialization.

III. *The more sophisticated the form of deviant organization, the more elaborate the services provided its members.* Every social role poses practical problems for its performers. In some cases these problems can be solved by providing the actors with supplies of various sorts. Actors may require certain *equipment* to perform a role. They may also need *information* about their situation in order to coordinate their behavior with the ongoing action and successfully accomplish their part in an operation. One function of deviant social organization is to solve such practical problems by supplying members with needed equipment and information. More sophisticated forms of social organization are capable of providing more of these services.

Deviants differ in their requirements for equipment. Some need little in the way of equipment; a mugger may be able to get by with a piece of pipe. In other cases, deviants make use of specialized items which have few, if any, respectable uses (e.g., heroin or the booster boxes used in shoplifting).[11] Most loners require little equipment. When specialized needs exist, they are met through conventional channels accessible to the deviants, as when a physician narcotic addict obtains illicit drugs from hospital or clinic supplies. Colleagues also supply their own equipment, for the most part, although they may receive some assistance; pool hustlers, for example, provide their own cues, but they may rely on financial backers for funding.

Peers adopt various patterns toward equipment. In some cases, peer groups develop to facilitate the distribution and consumption of deviant goods, such as illicit drugs. In other instances, peers use equipment as a symbol of their deviant status, as when gang members wear special costumes. The equipment used by mobsters is more utilitarian; many of their trades demand specialized tools, for safecracking, shoplifting and so forth. In addition to a craftsman's personal equipment, the mob may require special materials for a specific project. Norms often exist that specify the manner in which these equipment purchases will be financed. In still other instances, some mobsters with expensive pieces of equipment may cooperate with several different mobs who wish to make use of them (such as the "big store" which is centrally located for the use of several confidence mobs). Formal organizations also have extensive equipment requirements. Because their operations extend over considerable time, formal organizations may find it expedient to invest in an elaborate array of fixed equipment. Off-track bookmaking, for example, may involve the purchase or rental of offices, desks, calculators, computer lines, special telephone lines, office supplies and automobiles. Special staff members may have the responsibility for maintaining this equipment (Bell, 1962:134). In addition, some formal organizations are involved in producing or distributing deviant equipment for the consumption of other deviants; drug smuggling offers the best example.

Deviants need information in order to determine their courses of action. To operate efficiently, they need to know about new opportunities for deviant action; to operate safely, they need to know about the movements of social control agents. The more sophisticated forms of organization have definite advantages in acquiring and processing information. Loners, of course, depend upon themselves for information; opportunities or threats outside their notice cannot be taken into account. Colleagues and peers can learn more by virtue of their contacts with the deviant "grapevine," and they may have norms regarding a member's responsibility to share relevant information. In mobs, information is sought in more systematic ways. In the course of their careers, mobsters develop perceptual skills, enabling them to "case" possible targets (Letkemann, 1973). In addition, some mobs rely on outsiders for information; spotters may be paid a commission for pointing out opportunities for theft. A formal organization can rely upon its widely distributed membership for information and its contacts with corrupted social control agents.

The degree to which deviants need special supplies varies with the requirements of their operations, the frequency with which they interact with victims or other nondeviants, and their visibility to social control agents. Supplies other than equipment and information may be required in some instances. However, for most supply problems, sophisticated forms of social organization enjoy a comparative advantage.

IV. *The more sophisticated the form of deviant organization, the greater its members' involvement in deviance.* Complex deviant operations require planning and coordinated action during the deviant act. Socialization and supply also involve interaction among an organization's members. More sophisticated forms of deviant organization, featuring complex operations and elaborate socialization and supply, are therefore more likely to involve intensive social contact with one's fellow deviants. Furthermore, because deviants face sanctions from social control agents and respectable people, their contacts with other deviants are an important source of social support. The differences in the ability of forms and social organization to provide support for their members have important social psychological consequences for deviants' careers and identities.

The dimensions of deviant careers vary from the form of deviant organization. Longer deviant careers tend to occur in more sophisticated forms of organization. For naive loners, deviance can comprise a single episode, a defensive act to ward off an immediate threat. For systematic loners, and many colleagues and peers, involvement in deviance is limited to one period in their life. Prostitutes grow too old to compete in the sexual marketplace, delinquents move into respectable adult work roles, and so forth. Members of mobs and formal organizations are more likely to have extended careers. Where the roles are not too physically demanding, deviance can continue until the individual is ready to retire from the work force (Inciardi, 1977). Deviant careers also vary in the amount of time they demand while the individual is active; some kinds of deviance take up only a small portion of the person's hours, but other deviant roles are equivalent to full-time, conventional jobs. Although the relationship is not perfect, part-time deviance is associated with less sophisticated forms of deviant organization.[12]

Social organization is also related to the relative prominence of the deviant identity in the individual's self-concept. Individuals may view their deviance as tangential to the major themes in their lives, or as a central focus, an identity around which much of one's life is arranged. The latter pattern is more likely to develop in sophisticated forms of deviant organization, for, as Lofland (1969) points out, several factors associated with deviant social organization facilitate the assumption of deviant identity, including frequenting places populated by deviants, obtaining deviant equipment, and receiving instruction in deviant skills and ideology. These factors also would appear to be associated with the maintenance of deviance as a central identity. Loners seem especially adept at isolating their deviance, viewing it as an exception to the generally conventional pattern their lives take. This is particularly true when the deviance was initially undertaken to defend that conventional lifestyle from some threat. Even when an individual is relatively committed to deviance, normal identities can serve as an important resource. In his discussion of the World War II underground, Aubert (1965) notes that normal identities served to protect its members. In the same way, an established normal status shields the deviant from the suspicion of social control agents and, if the members refrain from revealing their conventional identities to one another, against discovery brought about by deviant associates who invade their respectable lives. Such considerations seem to be most important in middle-class peer groups organized around occasional leisure-time participation in a deviant marketplace, such as homosexuality and swinging.[13] Other deviants, particularly members of mobs and formal organizations, may associate with their fellows away from deviant operations, so that both their work and their sociable interaction take place among deviants. This is also true for peer groups that expand into "communities" and offer a wide range of services to members. Active members of urban gay communities can largely restrict their contacts to other homosexuals (Harry and Devall, 1978; Wolf, 1979). In these cases there is little need to perform conventional roles, aside from their obvious uses as concealment, and the deviant identity is likely to be central for the individual.

The degree to which an individual finds a deviant career and a deviant identity satisfying depends, in part, on the form of deviant organization of which he or she is a part. As in any activity, persons continue to engage in deviance only as long as the rewards it offers are greater than the rewards which could be obtained through alternative activities. The relevant rewards vary from one person to the next and from one type of deviance to another; a partial list includes money, physical and emotional satisfaction, valued social contacts, and prestige. Because the relative importance of these rewards varies with the individual, it is impossible to measure the differences in rewards between forms of deviant organization. There is some evidence that monetary profits are generally higher in more sophisticated forms of deviant organization. While an occasional loner can steal a very large sum through an embezzlement or a computer crime, most mobs can earn a reasonably steady income, and rackets run by formal organizations consistently bring in high profits. A more revealing measure of satisfaction is career stability; members of more sophisticated forms of deviant organization are more likely to remain in deviance. Loners' careers are short-lived, even when they are involved in systematic deviance. Lemert's (1967) account of the failure of professional forgers to remain at large suggests that the lack of social support is critical. As noted above, persons frequently drift out of their roles as colleagues and peers when other options become more attractive. The long-term careers of members of mobs and formal organizations suggest that these forms are more likely to satisfy the deviant.[14]

V. *The more sophisticated the form of deviant organization, the more secure its members' deviant operations.* The social organization of deviants affects the interaction between deviants and social control agents. This relationship is complicated because increased sophistication has consequences which would seem to make social control effects both easier and more difficult. On the one hand, the more sophisticated the deviant organization, the greater its public visibility and its chances of being subject to social control actions. Because more sophisticated forms of organization have more complex deviant operations, there are more people involved with the organization as members, victims, customers and bystanders. Therefore, there are more people capable of supplying the authorities with information about the identities, operations, and locations of organizational members. On the other hand, more sophisticated forms of organization are more likely to have codes of conduct requiring their members to be loyal to the organization and to maintain its secrets. Further, more sophisticated forms of organization command resources which can be used to protect the organization and its members from social control agents. While highly sophisticated organizations find it more difficult to conceal the fact that deviance is taking place, they often are more successful at shielding their members from severe sanctions.

Notes

1. A second paper, in preparation, will discuss the social organization of deviance.

2. Following Lemert (1967), loners can be subdivided into naive loners, for whom deviance is an exceptional, one-time experience, and systematic loners, whose deviance forms a repeated pattern. Lemert's analysis of the problems confronting systematic check forgers, who have trouble maintaining a deviant identity with little social support, suggests that systematic loners may have particularly unstable careers.

3. The term "mob," as it is used here, is drawn from the glossary in Sutherland: "A group of thieves who work together; same as 'troupe' and 'outfit'" (1937:239; cf. Maurer, 1962, 1964). A more recent study uses the term "crew" (Prus and Sharper, 1977).

4. Although the mob is able to accomplish its ends more efficiently, the same tasks are sometimes handled by loners. For example, see Maurer (1964:166–168) and Prus and Sharper (1977:22).

5. Our use of the term "formal organization" is not meant to imply that these organizations have all of the characteristics of an established bureaucracy. Rather, "formal" points to the deliberately designed structure of the organization—a usage consistent with Blau and Scott (1962:5).

6. The complexity of a deviant activity must be distinguished from two other types of complexity. First, the definition of organizational sophistication, given above, included the complexity of the division of labor among the deviants in a given organizational form as one criterion of sophistication. Second, the complexity of an activity should not be confused with the complexity of its explanation. A suicide, for example, can be easily accomplished, even though a complex social-psychological analysis may be required to explain the act.

7. This point illustrates the distinction, made earlier, between the social organization of deviance (the pattern of relationships between the roles performed in a deviant transaction) and the social organization of deviants (the pattern of relationships between deviant actors). The former, not the latter, affects an activity's complexity.

8. In most cases, loners do not possess the resources required for more than one type of complex deviance; physicians, for instance, are unable to commit computer thefts. In contrast, members of more sophisticated forms of organization may be able to manage several types of operations, as when a mob's members shift from picking pockets to shoplifting in order to avoid the police, or when an organized crime family is involved in several different rackets simultaneously (Maurer, 1964; Ianni, 1972:87–106).

9. Within a given form of organization, some cognitive perspectives may be more elaborate than others. While pool hustlers have a strong oral tradition, founded on the many hours they share together in pool halls, prostitutes have a relatively limited argot. Maurer (1939) argues that this is due to the restricted contact they have with one another during their work.

10. Here and elsewhere, colleagues represent a partial exception to the pattern. Colleagues resemble members of mobs and formal organizations in that they adopt an instrumental

perspective, view deviance as a career, are socialized through apprenticeship to an experienced deviant, and accept deviance as a central identity. While peers have a more sophisticated form of organization, their mutual participation in deviance is based on their shared involvement in an illicit marketplace or leisure-time activity. In contrast, colleagues usually are committed to deviance as means of earning a living.

Yet, because colleagues share a relatively unsophisticated form of organization, they labor under restrictions greater than those faced by mobs and formal organizations. Socialization is of limited scope; call girls learn about handling money and difficult clients, but little about sexual skills (Bryan, 1965). The code of conduct governing colleagues is less encompassing and less binding than those for more sophisticated forms, and the deviance of colleagues is usually less profitable. The absence of the advantages associated with organizational sophistication leads colleagues, despite their similarities to mobs and formal organizations, into an unstable situation where many individuals drift away from deviance.

11. Sometimes such equipment is defined as illicit, and its possession constitutes a crime.

12. Two reasons can be offered to explain this relationship. If a type of deviance is not profitable enough to support the individual, it may be necessary to take other work, as when a pool hustler moonlights (Polsky, 1967). Also, many loners have only a marginal commitment to deviance and choose to allocate most of their time to their respectable roles. This is particularly easy if the form of deviance requires little time for preparation and commission.

13. Swingers meeting new couples avoid giving names or information which could be used to identify them (Bartell, 1971:92–95); and Humphreys (1970) emphasizes that many tearoom participants are attracted by the setting's assurance of anonymity.

14. During their careers, deviants may shift from one organizational form or one type of offense to another. The habitual felons interviewed by Petersilia et al. (1978) reported that, while many of their offenses as juveniles involved more than one partner (presumably members of a peer group), they preferred to work alone or with a single partner on the crimes they committed as adults. The most common pattern was for juveniles who specialized in burglaries to turn to robbery when they became adults.

References

Amir, Menachem
1971 Patterns in Forcible Rape. Chicago: University of Chicago Press.
Anderson, Nels
1923 The Hobo. Chicago: University of Chicago Press.
Aubert, Vilhelm
1965 The Hidden Society. Totowa, N.J.: Bedminster.
Bartell, Gilbert
1971 Group Sex. New York: New American.
Bell, Daniel
1962 The End of Ideology. Revised edition. New York: Collier.
Blau, Peter M. and W. Richard Scott
1962 Formal Organizations. San Francisco: Chandler.
Blumer, Herbert
1967 The World of Youthful Drug Use. Berkeley: University of California Press.
Bohannon, Paul
1960 African Homicide and Suicide. Princeton: Princeton University Press.
Bryan, James H.
1965 "Apprenticeships in prostitution." Social Problems 12:287–297.
1966 "Occupational ideologies and individual attitudes of call girls." Social Problems 13:441–450.
Buckner, H. Taylor
1970 "The transvestic career path." Psychiatry 33:381–389.
Cameron, Mary Owen
1964 The Booster and the Snitch. New York: Free Press.
Carey, James T.
1968 The College Drug Scene. Englewood Cliffs, N.J.: Prentice Hall.

Clinard, Marshall B. and Richard Quinney
    1973 Criminal Behavior Systems: A Typology. Second edition. New York: Holt, Rinehart and Winston.
Cressey, Donald R.
    1953 Other People's Money. New York: Free Press.
    1962 "Role theory, differential association, and compulsive crimes." Pp. 443–467 in Arnold M. Rose (ed.), Human Behavior and Social Processes. Boston: Houghton Mifflin.
    1969 Theft of the Nation. New York: Harper & Row.
    1972 Criminal Organization. New York: Harper & Row.
Dawley, David
    1973 A Nation of Lords. Garden City, N.Y.: Anchor.
Einstader, Werner J.
    1969 "The social organization of armed robbery." Social Problems 17:64–83.
Feldman, Harvey W.
    1968 "Ideological supports to becoming and remaining a heroin addict." Journal of Health and Social Behavior 9:131–139.
Gibbons, Don C.
    1965 Changing the Lawbreaker. Englewood Cliffs, N.J.: Prentice-Hall.
    1977 Society, Crime, and Criminal Careers. Third edition. Englewood Cliffs, N.J.: Prentice-Hall.
Glaser, Barney G. and Anselm L. Strauss
    1967 The Discovery of Grounded Theory. Chicago: Aldine.
Goffman, Erving
    1959 The Presentation of Self in Everyday Life. Garden City, N.Y.: Anchor.
    1963 Stigma. Englewood Cliffs, N.J.: Prentice-Hall.
Green, Timothy
    1969 The Smugglers. New York: Walker.
Harry, Joseph and William B. Devall
    1978 The Social Organization of Gay Males. New York: Praeger.
Hirschi, Travis
    1962 "The professional prostitute." Berkeley Journal of Sociology 7:33–49.
Humphreys, Laud
    1970 Tearoom Trade. Chicago: Aldine.
Ianni, Francis A. J.
    1972 A Family Business. New York: Sage.
Inciardi, James A.
    1977 "In search of the class cannon." Pp. 55–77 in Robert S. Weppner (ed.), Street Ethnography. Beverly Hills, Calif.: Sage.
Keiser, R. Lincoln
    1969 The Vice Lords. New York: Holt, Rinehart and Winston
Klein, John F. and Arthur Montague
    1977 Check Forgers. Lexington, Mass.: Lexington.
Lemert, Edwin M.
    1967 Human Deviance, Social Problems, and Social Control. Englewood Cliffs, N.J.: Prentice-Hall.
Lesieur, Henry R.
    1977 The Chase. Garden City, N.Y.: Anchor.
Letkemann, Peter
    1973 Crime as Work. Englewood Cliffs, N.J.: Prentice-Hall.
Lofland, John
    1969 Deviance and Identity. Englewood Cliffs, N.J.: Prentice-Hall.
Luckenbill, David F.
    1977 "Criminal homicide as a situated transaction." Social Problems 25:176–186.

Matza, David
    1964 Delinquency and Drift. New York: Wiley.
    1969 Becoming Deviant. Englewood Cliffs, N.J.: Prentice-Hall.
Maurer, David W.
    1939 "Prostitutes and criminal argots." American Journal of Sociology 44:346–350.
    1962 The Big Con. New York: New American.
    1964 Whiz Mob. New Haven, Conn.: College and University Press.
McIntosh, Mary
    1971 "Changes in the organization of thieving." Pp. 98–133 in Stanley Cohen (ed.), Images of Deviance. Baltimore, Maryland: Penguin.
Mileski, Maureen and Donald J. Black
    1972 "The social organization of homosexuality." Urban Life and Culture 1:131–166.
Miller, Gale
    1978 Odd Jobs: The World of Deviant Work. Englewood Cliffs, N.J.: Prentice-Hall.
Milner, Christina and Richard Milner
    1972 Black Players. Boston: Little, Brown.
Parker, Donn B.
    1976 Crime by Computer. New York: Scribner's.
Petersilia, Joan, Peter W. Greenwood and Marvin Lavin
    1978 Criminal Careers of Habitual Felons. Santa Monica, Calif.: Rand.
Polsky, Ned
    1967 Hustlers, Beats, and Others. Chicago: Aldine.
Prus, Robert C. and C. R. D. Sharper
    1977 Road Hustler. Lexington, Mass.: Lexington.
Reynolds, Frank
    1967 Freewheelin' Frank. New York: Grove.
Rosenberg, Bernard and Harry Silverstein
    1969 Varieties of Delinquent Experience. Waltham, Mass.: Blaisdell.
Rubington, Earl
    1978 "Variations in bottle-gang controls." Pp. 383–391 in Earl Rubington and Martin S. Weinberg (eds.), Deviance: The Interactionist Perspective. Third edition. New York: Macmillan.
Shaw, Clifford R.
    1930 The Jack-Roller. Chicago: University of Chicago Press.
Shibutani, Tamotsu
    1961 Society and Personality. Englewood Cliffs, N.J.: Prentice-Hall.
Shover, Neal
    1977 "The social organization of burglary." Social Problems 20:499–514.
Stoddart, Kenneth
    1974 "The facts of life about dope." Urban Life and Culture 3:179–204.
Sutherland, Edwin H.
    1937 The Professional Thief. Chicago: University of Chicago Press.
Thompson, Hunter S.
    1966 Hell's Angels. New York: Ballantine.
Turner, Ralph H.
    1964 "Collective behavior." Pp. 382–425 in Robert E. L. Faris (ed.), Handbook of Modern Sociology. Chicago: Rand McNally.
Wade, Andrew L.
    1967 "Social processes in the act of juvenile vandalism." Pp. 94–109 in Marshall B. Clinard and Richard Quinney (eds.), Criminal Behavior Systems: A Typology. New York: Holt, Rinehart and Winston.

Warren, Carol A. B.
1974 Identity and Community in the Gay World. New York: Wiley.
Winick, Charles
1961 "Physician narcotic addicts." Social Problems 9:174–186.
Wiseman, Jacqueline P.
1970 Stations of the Lost. Englewood Cliffs, N.J.: Prentice-Hall.
Wolf, Deborah G.
1979 The Lesbian Community. Berkeley: University of California Press.
Wolfgang, Marvin E. and Franco Ferracuti
1967 The Subculture of Violence. London: Tavistock.
Zimmerman, Don H. and D. Lawrence Wieder
1977 "You can't help but get stoned." Social Problems 25:198–207.

36

Managing the Action: Sports Bookmakers as Entrepreneurs

Phyllis Coontz

More and more states have moved to legalize various forms of gambling as a viable way to raise substantial revenues. And while some have considered adding sports betting to their menu of games, Nevada continues to be the only state where placing a bet on sports events is legal. This is both puzzling and ironic considering the popularity of gambling and the prominence of sports. Despite the lack of concrete knowledge about illegal sports betting, two justifications for keeping it illegal have dominated the public debate. The first has to do with whether legal sports betting could successfully compete with illegal operations were it to be legalized and the second has to do with a purported link between gambling on sports and organized crime.

This paper focuses on the second line of argument and examines the social, organizational, and occupational features of bookmaking. If bookmakers are conduits for organized crime, as is claimed, there should be evidence of this in the day-to-day activities of bookmaking and in the career trajectories of bookmakers. The analysis is based upon interviews with 47 sports bookmakers working in the Rust Belt region. Drawing upon what sports bookies themselves have to say about their experiences in the business and their career trajectories, there appears to be little merit to the organized crime link argument. The analysis suggests that unlike other types of deviance, the social organization of bookmaking insulates bookies from the more typical consequences associated with frequent and prolonged deviant activity, for example, getting arrested, being prosecuted, serving time in prison, and forced association with other criminals. In fact, the findings suggest that bookies are more like entrepreneurs than criminals. While a single study cannot resolve the normative question about whether sports bookmaking should be criminalized, the findings do show that the social construction of bookmaking and bookmakers found in the public debate and popular culture does not reflect the reality of sports bookmaking.

Introduction

As a cultural phenomenon, gambling in the United States has been an en-during contradiction—while it is widespread it is also heavily regulated. Despite the growth of commercialized gambling since the 1960s, some forms of gambling remain off limits. One of these is sports betting.[1] Betting on sports events is illegal in every state except Nevada. This is somewhat puzzling given the popularity of both gambling and sports.

One of the ironies of this is that while Nevada is the only state that allows sports betting, one of the accoutrements for gambling on sports, i.e., the "line"[2] or "point spread," can be found everywhere. It appears daily in the sports section of most major newspapers; it is a link on numerous sports news websites; it is central to sports commentary about winners, losers, and outcomes on network and cable television; it is packaged as advice that can be purchased through various sports services through 900 telephone numbers; and it is woven into conversations that take place at work, in restaurants, classrooms, dorms, country clubs, bars, and parties every day around the country. It is even available through one of the more than 700 gambling casinos operating on the Internet.

Some have suggested that sports betting might be the number one form of gambling (legal or illegal) in the United States (Scarne 1974; Reuter 1983; Congressional Hearings 1995). Industry analysts (e.g., Moody's and Standard and Poor) report that sports betting is one of the biggest growth areas in commercialized gambling (Moody's Industry Review 1995:L46). For example, by the end of fiscal year 1996, bookmakers in Las Vegas handled $2.5 billion in wagers (O'Brien 1998). And according to the Gaming Control Board of Nevada, the amount wagered on sports events has been increasing every year and more sports events are being added to the menu. For example, sports books in Las Vegas added last year's Women's World Cup soccer final to their array of events. Focusing on only a single event, the Super Bowl, the amount wagered almost doubled from $40 million in 1991 to $70 million in 1997 (personal communication, Research Division, June 1998). While illicit wagers are far more difficult to track, it is estimated that in 1997

---

[1] Congress passed legislation in 1992 that prevents any state from legalizing sports betting well into the future.

[2] The daily line refers to betting odds. It consists of the number of points a favored team is penalized in order to win. Since the majority of sports events do not involve equally matched teams in terms of talent, performance, or record, the superior team would almost always win the contest. Such predictability is not very interesting. Although there is a lack of consensus about the origin of the line, it was not widely used until after World War II. The line makes a game more interesting because it equalizes unevenly matched teams with a handicap. For example in the 1999 Super Bowl, the Denver Broncos were the defending Super Bowl champions and favored to beat Atlanta by 7½ points. Denver was assessed a 7½ point deficit while Atlanta was given a 7½ point advantage to the final score. This meant that Denver had to win by more than 7½ points and Atlanta could lose by less than 7½ points for bettors to win. The final score was 34 to 19 in Denver's favor. Denver won the game and bettors that took Denver won their bets.

alone, over $100 billion was wagered illegally on sports (U.S. News & World Report 1997).

Given the magnitude of legal or illegal sports betting and the popularity of sports, it is difficult to understand why it continues to be outlawed. Of course, sociologists have long recognized that a behavior's legal status has little to do with its popularity, intrinsic harm, or even desirability. Far more important in determining legal status is the way the behavior is socially constructed. In the case of sports betting, we see that one of the dominant social constructions involves bookmakers as unsavory characters with ties to the underworld. For example, supporters of the Professional and Amateur Sports Protection Act of 1992 argued that "[I]nstead of standing for healthy competition through team work and honest preparation, professional sport contests would come to represent the fast buck, the quick fix, and the desire to get something for nothing. Betting would undermine the integrity of team sports and public confidence in them. . . . Fans could not help but wonder if a missed free throw, a dropped fly ball, or a missed extra point was part of a player's scheme to fix the game" (S-474, pg S-7302 Temp. Record). Other advocates of criminalization allege a link between bookmaking and organized crime and argue that it is a major source of its total gambling revenue (Cressey 1969; The President's Commission on Law Enforcement and Administration of Justice 1967; Clark 1971). The criminal construction is also common in our popular culture, particularly in films such as *Wiseguy 1986, Goodfellas 1990,* and *Casino 1995* and novels such as Gay Talese's *Honor Thy Father,* Mario Puzo's *The Godfather,* and most recently Bill Bonanno's *Bound by Honor.*

How closely do the social constructions presented in the public debate and the popular culture mirror reality? The research on bookmaking shows that what is known about sports bookies, their methods of operation, career trajectories, lifestyles, and relationships with each other is limited, fragmented, and largely inferred. Some research on bookmaking generally suggests that instead of being members of a larger criminal syndicate, bookmakers are more likely to operate as a loose confederation of independents that may at times cooperate with one another (Chambliss 1978; Anderson 1979; Reuter and Rubinstein 1982; Reuter 1983; Rosencrance 1987; Sasuly 1982). Despite the lack of empirical evidence about the nature of sports bookmaking, the image of the sports bookie as criminal is pervasive.

This study set out to learn about sports bookmaking from those who do it. The assumption was that if sports bookies are a part of an organized crime syndicate, then there should be some evidence of it in the day-to-day operations of bookmaking. The study examines the social organization of bookmaking and the occupational features of being a sports bookie. This approach is useful because it allows us to move beyond the criminal aspects of sports bookmaking and consider what is actually involved in operating a sports book. That is, what sorts of skills, knowledge, processes, and contexts are needed to get into and manage a sports book.

The analysis draws upon face-to-face interviews with 47 different book-makers operating in Western Pennsylvania. This researcher examines how one becomes a sports bookmaker; how sports bookmakers manage and grow their business; their relationships with bettors, other sports book-makers, law enforcement officials, and family; and finally, how they exit the business. If sports bookmaking is indeed a part of a larger criminal or-ganization then it is reasonable to expect that entry into and departure from the business would be determined by the larger organization; that the day-to-day operations would follow norms and practices dictated and moni-tored by an outside organization; and that the conditions under which bookmakers transact business with bettors would involve criminal ele-ments such as coercion, dishonesty, and bribery.

Background for the Study

Although I have been interested in deviant behavior for more than 20 years, I became interested in sports betting only recently through a friend. It happened during dinner with this friend about six years ago when she excused herself so that she could call her bookie to place a bet on a foot-ball game. I didn't know she gambled on sports, and she certainly did not fit my image of someone who would know a bookie. She was a professional and civic minded and did not resemble my image of someone who associ-ated with bookies. This contradiction between my friend and my beliefs piqued my curiosity and is what led to this research.

When I thought about the source of my beliefs, I realized they came mostly from the literature on organized crime and popular culture. I did a thorough literature review and discovered that there was little empirical knowledge about sports bookmaking. In order to learn what sports book-making was all about I would need to do some field work and find bookies who were willing to talk about bookmaking. Like most fieldwork on illicit activities, one needs a contact to gain access. I explained my growing inter-est to my friend and asked whether she would vouch for me with her bookie. My plan was to place bets with her bookie, develop a relationship with him, and then explore whether he would talk to me about the business. For the next several months I placed bets on different football games for an entire season. Eventually, I shared my research interest with my bookie and he agreed to be interviewed. The first interview took place in my home. Si-multaneously, I began talking more openly and frequently with friends, ac-quaintances, and colleagues about betting on sports events and discovered that many of the people I came into contact with—both socially and profes-sionally—bet on sporting events. These interactions led to contacts with other bookies, many of whom agreed to be interviewed. Over the course of a two-year period I interviewed a total of 47 bookies at least once and had follow-up interviews with 11 of them. All of the interviews were tape recorded, transcribed, and analyzed using NUD*IST (a computer based text analysis program). The findings presented here reflect major aspects of the organizational and occupations dimensions of the bookmaking business.

With the exception of the interviews with my bookie, all other interviews took place in locations selected by the bookmakers. Typically we met in restaurants, private clubs, and bars. The interview format focused on the process by which sports bookmakers got involved in the business; their strategies for building and maintaining their business; the duration of their involvement in the business; their relationships with other bookmakers; experiences with outside pressure (from law enforcement, other bookmakers, or professional criminals); the size of their business; the volume of the action; their families and friends; and their perceptions of the business, themselves, and its legal status. I begin the analysis with a general profile of the bookies that participated in this study.

Demographic and General Information about Sports Bookies

All bookmakers were male and ranged in age from 22–72 years old. The mean age for this group was 46. When asked about female bookmakers, I was told that none operated in this region, although some had heard about female sports bookies working elsewhere. All of my informants were originally from the region. All but two of my informants were currently married or living with someone, and all but five had children. Five had gotten divorced as a result of their bookmaking activities, and four remarried. Ninety-one percent ($n = 43$) were currently employed or self-employed in a legitimate job and five reported relying solely on earnings from bookmaking at different times. Four of my informants did not finish high school, 34 completed high school, and 7 completed college. Of those who completed college, one had a graduate degree and another was studying for an MBA.

On average these men had been involved in bookmaking for 17 years, ranging from a low of 2 years to a high of 45 years. None would reveal the amount of income earned from their bookmaking activities explaining their actual income was contingent on a number of factors such as the amount of a bet, the kind of bet made, the number of winners and losers, and whether losers paid their losses. However, all of the bookies in this study reported making money from bookmaking.[3] Most experienced occasional "off" periods meaning they paid out more than they brought in. And one informant revealed he lost $96,000 the first year he went into business.

[3] The informant with the legal island sports book (available through the Internet and 900 access) confided that he made "so much money it would make you crazy." Another informant was under a federal indictment for income tax evasion on an estimated $12 million allegedly made over a nine-month period.

Like other illegal markets, sports betting is a cash business—all transactions are conducted with cash. Payouts were usually made midweek (typically Wednesdays) while collections were made the first part of the week (typically Mondays) and took place at designated locations, which were typically public. If a customer was unable to pay their losses in full, terms were established without an interest penalty. Although there are numerous kinds of wagers that can be made, the four most common were: straight bets,[4] over and under bets,[5] teasers,[6] and parlays.[7] The amount wagered varied by customer, but the average wager was $50.00 per game. All of these bookies established a minimum and maximum amount they would accept with the majority not willing to accept wagers over $5,000. Five, however, accepted bets for $10,000 and occasionally more. The majority accepted wagers only on the day of the game (and usually approximately 30 minutes before the start of a game), but some would accept bets when the line first came out.

The Mechanics of Sports Bookmaking

The "line" which is the basis for taking bets serves two general purposes: (1) to encourage the gambling public to gamble on both opponents playing a game and (2) to balance the amount of money wagered equally between both teams so that amount is equally divided between both teams. According to "Roxy" Roxborough, the guru of the Las Vegas Line, "the fundamental concept of bookmaking is to force people to gamble . . . at odds favorable to the house. The line is used to encourage gambling by equalizing the contest" (Cook 1992). Sports bookies could care less about who wins or loses a game; they are interested in the final score and whether they have more losers than winners for any given game. The point spread then is the bookie's management tool for balancing the betting action on individual games.

The following illustrates how the point spread works. The Super Bowl is the final championship game between the two Conferences in the National Football League (NFL). Although each Conference has a champion,

---

[4] A straight bet is based on the point spread. If the game is between the Denver Broncos and New York Jets and 12 points favor Denver, and the bettor took Denver to win, then Denver would need to win by a score of at least 12 points. The New York Jets on the other hand would receive 12 points and they could lose by a total of 7 points, but a bettor would still win the bet if they took the Jets because there was still 5 points leeway.

[5] For over and under bets, the bettor is gambling on whether the teams will score above the total for the game or below the total. In the Denver Bronco/New York Jet example, suppose the total was 55 points—the bettor would either gamble that the total score would be above 55 or below 55 depending on the direction the bet was made.

[6] In teasers, the bettor is given 5 points to add to the team the gamble is on and 7 points on the over and under point spread. In the Denver Bronco/New York Jet example, if the bettor were taking a teaser on Denver, in the over and under bets and Denver is favored by 12, then they would be given 5 points to subtract from the 12 points in the point spread and 7 points to add or subtract from the total score of 55—either a total of 62 or 48 depending on the direction.

[7] Parlays involve making wagers on multiple (2 or 3) teams at a time. The odds are better, but to win, all teams included in the parlay must win.

one is usually perceived to be stronger than the other (this is based on a combination of record, performance, and hype). In Super Bowl XXX (for the 1995–96 season) the Dallas Cowboys (the National Football Conference [NFC] champions) and the Pittsburgh Steelers (the American Football Conference [AFC] champions) played for the championship. At the time, the NFC and Dallas Cowboys were perceived to be superior to the AFC and Pittsburgh Steelers. Based on this alone, the outcome of the game was seen as a foregone conclusion—Dallas would win.

If you know the outcome of a game before it starts, it will not be very interesting. Because so many matchups are between unequal teams, the line equalizes the contest by giving the underdog an advantage. When the line came out for Super Bowl XXX it was set at 14 points, favoring Dallas. Translated, a 14-point spread meant that the Cowboys would need to win by more than two touchdowns. The question raised by such a high point spread for the bettor, and the question the bookie hopes the bettor will ask, is whether the Cowboys can beat the Steelers by more than 14 points.[8] The line alters what is otherwise a foregone conclusion and entices bettors to put money on the underdog.

Getting into the Business

As argued earlier, if sports bookmaking is controlled by outside interests, then getting into the business should be determined by those associated with these interests. At a minimum, if the external control allegation has merit, there should be accounts of being recruited, coerced, pressured, or getting permission to get started from bookies. None of the bookies reported external pressure—all entered the business voluntarily and most viewed their entry as an opportunity to make money. The oldest bookie in the study, Artie, started out as a numbers runner for another bookmaker when he was only 8 years old. In fact, he told me that during his early years (which he characterized as "hard times") he was the sole support for his family (including his parents and siblings). Artie was the only bookie I interviewed who progressed from numbers to sports bookmaking. He worked in the numbers business for over 30 years and then moved into sports bookmaking when he was in his early 40s.

> I ran numbers and made a pretty nice income for a kid. If you hustled $400–$500 worth, you could make a nice piece of change. I took care of my family—I literally paid the bills. I learned from one of the smartest guys in the area. He's dead now, but he was smart, very wise— he was a cousin of my mother's. He liked me, and he took me under his wing. I used to hang around him and one day he asked me if I

[8] If the difference in the score is exactly 14 points, the game is a "push" which means there are no winners and no losers.

wanted to do something for him. He sent me out to pick up the day's business—in a paper bag. I brought it back and he put me to work. He trusted me even though I was just a kid, he had confidence in me. You can't imagine how good I felt 'cause I looked up to him, he had something and everybody, they admired him too. He trusted me—this skinny kid. My mother didn't like it, but at the time, I was the only one working and bringing any money in. I made enough to pay the rent, food, and utilities. Times were hard back then.

Before setting up their own bookmaking operations, betting on sports had been an integral part of every bookie's everyday experiences. Joe, who is in his 50s and operated a legitimate sports book in the Caribbean, grew up around bookies and bettors. He entered the business as a young man while working in the steel mills and began his involvement as a favor to a coworker.

I was helping a guy I worked with out. A lotta guys bet with him and he couldn't handle it one weekend cause he was sick. We were buddies, he trusted me and asked me to help him out. I took all the action that weekend even though I didn't know what I was doin'. After spending that weekend on the phone I told my buddy I wanted to work with him and I did. The rest is history as they say. After a while I went on my own, I worked every day which is tough when you're workin too, especially during basketball and baseball season. You're takin action all day and all night long. You gotta time everything. You're on the phone all day and sometimes all night. How many games are played in a day during March Madness? You could have a couple dozen games in one day. My first wife really hated it cause I couldn't leave, we didn't go out—I worked all week and I was on the phone all weekend till the games were over. And if I had a bad day, if I got upset—I was an animal. One time I got so upset, I threw a chair through the TV. That was a long time ago, I'm still embarrassed by it. My kids hated it, too. Like now, they'd never get involved with it cause they saw what it did to me—my wife left me 'cause of it—it's your whole life. Things are different now though. The business in the islands, it's legitimate, it's totally different. I have time to enjoy all my hard work—I'm making so much money down there it'd make you crazy. I'm paying taxes, everything's legitimate. My second wife and I can travel, we can go wherever we want and do whatever we want. I could never make this kind of money at anything else. And the way I look at it, I've earned it 'cause I worked hard for over 30 years.

Steve, a student studying for his MBA at an area university at the time I interviewed him, said he was motivated by what he saw was a way to make money. Steve explains:

There was a guy in the dorm and everyone bet with him. I started watching him and saw the potential for making money and thought to myself, 'hey I can do that.' So, one Saturday I started, just like that, with just a few guys I knew. At first I used the local line in the newspaper and I'd talk to other guys to see what they were gettin. I only deal with students around here, so it's not too complicated. I mean, at first I kept track of everything in my head, but as I took on more customers I had to write things down—I couldn't keep them straight. I was doin pretty well and after a couple of months I had over 70 regulars. Then I got a couple of friends of mine involved, 'cause I needed the help—I give 'em a few bucks to help me out. You know, I'm not doin this forever, but for right now it pays the bills—I'm paying for school. I really don't want to have any debt when I graduate.

There was no evidence of coercion, pressure, or an apprenticeship to get into the business. The two main routes through which bookies got into the business were through their personal relationships and perceived economic opportunities. In all cases, entry was voluntary and situational.

Managing and Building the Business

Since bookies can never be certain of the number of bets that will be made on a given game or the amount wagered, being successful involves more than simply taking the action. While several factors affect success, five appear to be common among all bookies: knowledge of sports, building a credible customer base, volatility in the market, productivity of the bookmaker, and avoiding arrest. Roger, a young former bookie who now operates a legitimate sports betting advice service, explains how knowledge of sports plays an integral role in bookmaking and succeeding in the business.

I read everything that's printed about the games and players. I did that when I was in the business and I'm doing it right now. Every morning I'm on the Internet reading what the sports writers have to say, looking at statistics, checkin' the weather conditions, going over last year's statistics, everything. I study; study so I can handicap each game. Half my day is spent digesting information. We offer 1 or 2 picks each week—and my track record is pretty good on this, mostly winners. I miss it now and then, but when you put all the facts and figures together with what the sports experts are saying, then you're more likely to come up with winners. Even though I'm on the other side of the business now, the same rules apply. Rule number one is that you've got to pay attention to the details. When I was takin bets, the only way you could make money was if your people picked losers. They're always looking at the Internet, the paper, and checkin with friends. So if you're gonna make money, you gotta have a solid line—one that's based on the facts and figures of the game. I handicapped all my games, see some guys get their lines from the books in Vegas, but not me, I did it myself. I always prided myself on offering a precise line especially on close games—you know, ½ point difference or maybe a 1 point difference on a close game can make a huge difference. And ½ point is appealing to a lot of bettors. You gotta be firm about your line too. Once you set it, it's the same for everybody. I like to think of myself as an expert on these games—you know, Jimmy the Greek. I've studied them all my life—ask me anything and I can tell you. Bettors are emotional, so they don't think about that ½ point difference—they're gonna go with their hearts. If the bookie's gonna make money, you gotta get 'em to go with their favorites and you do that by a solid line. You don't have to be perfect all the time, 50% of the time will do.

The illegal status of bookmaking limits what bookmakers can do to attract customers. They cannot advertise or make cold calls from the phonebook or random digit dialing, yet a successful bookmaking business requires a customer base. How do bookies build a customer base? Jimmy, a 22-year veteran, claims that the customers are just there waiting for bookies because of the popularity of sports.

Who doesn't like sports? Everybody loves sports—and betting on them is part of the entertainment. Ever been to a Steelers game? Look around right before a game. You see all these guys on the horn talking to guys like me. Betting makes a game interesting. Every guy I ever knew from my neighborhood and school bet on games. My Dad even bet—on boxing matches. My brother bet. Since I got into the business, I never had any trouble findin' customers. Listen, they're just there waiting to give you their business. Some of my customers I've known since school, some of 'em I work with, some I've met here or there. I've even had guys give me customers. You know my brother brought customers to me. My sister's husband bets with me. My biggest problem is keeping it manageable and making sure I got good people. I don't want too many customers, you know I work and that complicates things a little. Fifty, sixty's about all I can handle at a time. It seems like if I lose one, then I pick up another one or two.

In addition to building a customer base, bookmakers assume the financial risks in their business. Like any for-profit business, the focus is on the bottom line which means bookies must be attuned to the market, especially patterns and changes in betting action. Volatility of the market affects success and while the line enables the bookie to balance the action between opposing teams, it is insufficient by itself for ensuring a profit. Knowing this, bookies take other steps to minimize potential risks from dramatic swings in the action. According to Carl, who has been in the business for 18 years, limiting your customer base and setting a maximum limit on wagers are two such steps.

If you're gonna hold everything yourself, you've got to have a minimum of 40 players. Right now I got about 100 people. You've gotta have a strong limit, say $500 and not take any more on a game from any one person because if you get 20 of those people giving you a $500 bet, you've got $10,000 you could lose.

An instrumental factor that affects success is knowing how closely specific customers fit the average customer profile. For example, bookies know that bettors tend to wager on multiple games. Multiple game bettors always work to the bookie's advantage and Tony, who has been in the business for 25 years, explains why:

> As you research this, you'll find out that the more games people play, the more chance the bookie has to make money. They gotta pick about 66% to break even. They don't realize it 'cause everybody thinks if they pick 50% they're even, but they're not, they're losing money cause you gotta pay the juice.[9] For the customer to come out ahead, they gotta pick about 66% of the time. There's only one way to make money betting and that's to bet one game. Of course, most people bet a lot of games and they bet their hearts—which is good for the bookie.

Like many small businesses, bookmaking requires a high degree of commitment from the bookie. I frequently heard this level of commitment described in terms of bookmaking being a bookie's life. Bookmaking has a higher priority than other activities. To sustain a business for any length of time, bookies must set aside their other interests and be on call for their customers. Depending on the sports season this could range from every day to every weekend of that season. The bookie must learn to manage his time and balance his bookmaking responsibilities against other responsibilities. Sam describes the various ways that bookmaking consumes the bookie's life.

> You can work year round or you can work a couple seasons. See there's a sport for every season. I work year round. Football's not so bad, but basketball, baseball, and hockey'll kill you—every single day, six and seven days a week. If you're gonna work year round, you basically have no life outside of this. It's not over just 'cause the phones stop ringin' either. You gotta keep track of everything and I don't know many guys who can just turn out the light after the phones stop. I have my set times see, so half hour before a game starts I'm taking action. I get all my 7 and 8:00 games startin at 6:30. Now Sunday football, I've got my 1:00 games and I start around 12:40, my 4:00 games I start around 3:40, and my 9:00 game I start at 8:45. You've gotta little free time in between, but then you're watchin the game to see whether you're makin money. Some games don't end till after midnight. Then I gotta get up and go to work. My wife complains, less now than she used to. I guess she's used to it now. I think the extra money helps. She likes to go out, so I get someone to take over for a day or night. I got a couple of guys who'll do that, you know, answer the phone for me. We always go away in the summer, but I don't relax, 'cause I'm worrying about things. I'm checking every day when I'm away. It's just part of you, it's there all the time.

With the exception of online sports books (who accept credit cards), bookmaking is strictly a cash business. Thus, having customers who are

[9] The "juice" refers to the fee the customer pays the bookie when he loses a bet.

willing to pay their losses is essential for profitability. In lieu of a credit report, the bookie depends on informal means of scrutinizing customers. Typically customers are acquired in two ways: either by referral from other customers (which happened in my case) or directly by knowing the customer. What happens when a customer refuses to pay the bookie? Although proponents of criminalization argue that bookies resort to corruption and extortion to collect gambling debts, none of the bookies I talked to engaged in these practices. Instead, they avoid potential losses by screening their customer. Ray, who has been in the business for 35 years, describes how this process works:

> You see, it's not illegal to place a bet, but you can't take bets—that's why you always gotta watch yourself; most guys know that. You gotta know who you're dealing with. I don't take on anybody I don't know. I check, check, check. Say some guy calls me and wants me to take his action. If I don't know him, I won't do it 'cause I don't need the aggravation. I had to learn this though. There was a guy—oh this was about 15 years ago—who bet with a bunch of different guys. Back then what I thought was important was the numbers. I didn't know the guy so well, but I took his bets anyway. He ran up quite a number with me—he owed me about $10,000. I'd call him and he'd tell me he'd have something for me next week. Well, he never gave me a thing—this happened over and over again. Then one night I see the guy out, and he's buying drinks for everybody, playing the big shot. The guy owes me $10,000 and he's buying people drinks. I was mad. I went up to him and said, 'hey where's my money?' The guy was a jerk; he stammered around and told me that if I didn't leave him alone he'd call the feds. He owes me and he's gonna call the feds. I don't want the feds bothering me, I'm not interested in goin' to prison and I don't want anybody checking up on what I'm doing. I knew right then I'd never see any of it and that the guy was a jerk. So what I did was put the word out that he wasn't paying up, that he wasn't good for his bets. You gotta understand, this is a disease for someone like this guy—he just has to bet and there's nothin worse you can do to somebody who likes to bet than to cut him off. When the word is out, nobody will take their action. The only way someone would take his action is if he put money up first.

As discussed earlier, the line is used to balance the action between two teams. There are times however when the betting public is not enticed by fluctuations in the line. When there is more money wagered on one team than another, the bookie could end up having to pay out more than he takes in—a situation he wants to avoid. A degree of bettor psychology is relevant in such cases. Bookies know that sentimentality motivates many bettors. Sentimentality is the tendency to bet on the hometown team—or as one bookie described it, to "bet with your heart." For example, in the recent NBA championship game between the Indiana Pacers and the Los Angeles Lakers, the majority of bettors in the L.A. area bet on the Lakers while the majority of bettors from the Midwest bet on the Pacers. Sentimentality also can explain regional variations in betting patterns, and bookies must always be aware of potential regional differences in betting patterns, and adjust accordingly. When it is impossible to balance the action, bookies can hedge their losses by selling their action to other bookmakers. This practice is called "laying off." Every bookmaker in this study had connections with a layoff bookmaker. Sam, a 17-year veteran, discusses the way sentimentality works:

> What you wanna do is get equal amounts of money on both sides. This is a Steeler town so when the line first came out at 14 then 13½ for the Super Bowl (1995), all the money was on Pittsburgh. I lowered it to 12, but still everyone was takin' Pittsburgh. Even at 12—nobody was taking Dallas. Even though I thought Dallas would win, I was worried. You know, Super Bowl is big, big, big. I was holding a lotta money. I checked around to see what was happening and after thinkin about it, I figured I'd better get rid of it, that's called a layoff, and if I hadn't gotten rid of it, I'd a been ruined.

Layoff bookmakers charge a fee for taking unwanted action. This can be thought of in terms of 'juice.' The existence of layoff operations is essential precisely because of the sentimentality factor. If movement in the line does not affect the direction of incoming wagers on a Pittsburgh/Dallas game, then the Pittsburgh layoff bookie could layoff with a Dallas bookie. Six of the bookies in this study took layoff action from other bookies and would sometimes layoff their layoff action with larger operators. It is important to distinguish the relationships bookies have with layoff bookies from organized crime associations. Bookies choose whether to layoff their action and they have choices of who to lay it off with. Instead of reflecting organized crime connections, these relationships more closely resemble what Reuter (1983:42) calls networks. Occasionally, bookies in these networks combined their bookmaking business with social activities, but this appears to be infrequent.

Although the typical bettor is the bookie's bread and butter, there are always exceptions to typicality and in bookmaking the exception is the wiseguy. The wiseguy almost always beats the bookie. Since bookies lose money to wiseguys they must know who the wiseguy bettors are and limit the action they will accept from them. Eddy, a 52-year-old who has been in the business since high school, differentiates the wiseguy from the typical bettor.

> The wiseguy is someone who follows the games—they really do. They know who they wanta bet before the line comes out of Las Vegas—oh, that's the outlaw line that comes out on Sunday night. They'll bet the game with you Sunday night. They know who they want to bet. They take a chance on the line going up or down. They're sharp, but remember this is their livelihood, that's what they do, they don't do anything else. The way it works is that when the game plays, the line might

be at 16 and they're locked in at 10. Being locked in they have an option, they can keep the bet at 10 or take the 16 backup with somebody else and hope it falls in between, take the game, and make twice the money. They always bet with a couple of people and they study the games. I did that myself one Saturday a couple of weeks ago, it was the playoff games. I took 17 basketball games. I bet a couple of hundred per game. I was trying to catch it in the middle. I made $17,000 that afternoon. A lot of bookies have quit basketball because you can get destroyed with basketball. If you get a wiseguy who's hot, he'll beat you to death. Those guys just don't bet $100, they want to bet your limit—whatever it is, $500, $1,000, $5,000 whatever, and if they're hot, they'll win 9 out of 10 games.

In addition to developing a reliable client base and learning how to avoid losses, sports bookies can affect their profits by the number of hours they work and the sports they will accept. If they choose to, bookies can work year round or limit their business to particular seasons. Harry, who operated one of the larger businesses, took action on all sports events and explains the relation of this to being successful.

I got into this for the money; I figured that the more I worked, the more money I'd make. And I'm good at this. But I've had to put in hundreds of thousands of hours at this thing and that's year round. I mean I take every kind of game there is. I take horses, baseball, boxing, football, the baskets, hockey, jai lai, you name it. If there's some esoteric thing going on, I'll take it too. You should see my house, I got TVs everywhere. I got one of those dishes so I can watch what's going on all over the world and I got a computer to keep up with the scores and see what other people are doin'. If you wanta make money you've got to put the hours in and you have to know what's going on. See it's not the bookie that puts the fix in, but gamblers. You see they're lookin for the big win. But like anything else, if you wanna make money you gotta have a work ethic and you gotta know what's going on. I'll buy whatever I need that gives me an edge.

One of the biggest risks from any form of illicit activity is arrest, but unlike other forms of deviant behavior bookies are not afraid of getting arrested. In fact, none of the bookies in this study had been arrested for their bookmaking activities. Tony explains why:

The cops don't care about guys like me. I don't cause any trouble. I don't drink or do drugs and I don't know of any guys who do, 'cause for one thing you gotta be alert in this business and drinking and drugs will mess up your thought processes. So what kind of a danger am I? What I'm doing is providing a service, that's all, like any other service type of business. That doesn't mean I'm out there advertising what I'm doin', no way. I just don't do anything that's gonna draw attention to me. My customers are happy. So I'm clean, my people are happy, and everything's okay. The idea that we go out and break people's legs is something you see on TV. What sense does that make? I mean, if I broke some guy's legs, I'd get arrested. Just doin this, nobody's gonna arrest me.

Retiring from Bookmaking

Like getting into the business, retirement is a personal and voluntary decision. While not all of the bookies talked about retirement, those who did identified three factors that influenced their decision to leave the business: the desire to spend more time with family, having achieved their economic goals, and retirement from their legitimate job. Pete, who has been in the business approximately 15 years plans to retire within the next year because he wants to spend more time with his family. Pete discusses how the business interferes with spending time with his family and the preparation involved in leaving the business.

> I don't need to do this any more. Financially, things are different now, my wife is working a little and I'm working a lot of hours, I've got seniority. I'm thinking in about a year this thing will come to an end. I mean I don't have the time anymore. I'm coaching my kids, spending a lotta time with them. With the money I've made, I've put it into my house. We couldn't afford the house we're in without this. When I look back on the years, they've been good to me. I made some money where I could buy some things—my house, I got Debbie a new car, and for my kids I've been putting money away for their tuition for school. You know I don't want them going to public school. With my kids, when I'm doing this, they're with me. And to be honest with you, I don't want them growing up with this thing all the time. Everyone in my family, even my wife's family, knows what I do. The way things are now, when there's a family thing, I'm tied up with this—I can't go 'cause I'm answering the phone all the time. I've talked about leaving with George, he doesn't have the responsibilities I have with my family and all, so he can just step right in 'cause the business is running smoothly. He wants to take it over, it's a good deal for him—I've got good customers, I know them, there's no trouble, and things are real good now.

Unlike Pete, Joe's retirement plan does not involve a successor; instead he shifted his business to the Caribbean where he owns a legitimate sports book. Joe views the earnings from his legitimate enterprise as his retirement cushion. In the following excerpt, Joe discusses how his legitimate operation will provide a comfortable lifestyle without the worry that accompanies an illegal operation.

> The island operation is easy. You can advertise. We do, we have a full page advertisement in Las Vegas, in fact, even in some of the local papers we've got ads with a sports book number. You can call, set up an account. You can use a credit card, wire money, or send us a certified

check. Somebody puts money into their account, we give them 10% interest on their money, sometimes 15% depending on the amount they have and the type of bets they make. If somebody puts a considerable amount of money in there, we give 'em 15% right off the bat. If the person is a bettor, you have the money in an account, you know you're getting paid, and that's a big part of the business, getting paid. So we give 'em those extra bucks back to use. It works, it works great. Your regular bettors, guys that have the money and want to bet have no problem puttin' the money up front. It's a beautiful way to do business. So, I'm looking at this as my retirement plan. 'Cause, I'm out of everything here and I don't work any work. I've got eight people employed around the clock there and the action comes in 24 hours a day and a woman who manages the operation for me. She's real good. The business grows each week. Even though I worked all my life, I'm not depending on Social Security to live on—I never trusted the government, I gotta look out for myself. So by the time I'm 65, I'll have enough money saved up from this business to continue to enjoy my life. Like I told you before, me and my wife like to travel, so this way, we can do whatever we want. You know, I'm not a flamboyant guy, I drive a modest car and we live in a nice house, but nothing outrageous. People know me, I belong to the club here, me and my wife come up here a couple times a week, have dinner, watch a game here and there. I'm just beginning to enjoy all that time I've put into this thing 'cause I'll tell you I've worked hard in this business, all those hours. For years, I couldn't leave the house 'cause I was on the phone all day and all night. But now, I can relax now.

Frank, who is 60, is planning to retire from his legitimate job and quit bookmaking at the same time within a year.

I plan to retire in a year and I've been savin' the money I've made so I can enjoy myself. I got this house in Florida, so as soon as I retire I'm gone. I don't have anybody to worry about, my wife left me 30 years ago, no kids, so it's just me. I saved up a little nest egg so I can go here or there. If I wanta go to Atlantic City or out to Vegas every now and then for a week or so, I'll go. You know, I like to play blackjack. Right now, I'm only working with about 45 people anyway, so when I leave they can find somebody else. Some of my people already work with a couple of bookies, so I'm not worrying, they're set up.

Although Pete, Joe, and Frank give different reasons for leaving the business, their accounts show that retirement is their choice. Pete wants to spend more time with his family and has designated a successor; Joe has worked hard and wants to enjoy his life more fully and is depending on the income from his Caribbean operation; and Frank is planning to retire from bookmaking when he retires from his legitimate job and expects his customers to find another bookie. In all three cases, the decision to retire was voluntary. The different paths to retirement further indicate that not only is the decision to retire voluntary, but also the way that one retires is a choice.

Ties to Organized Crime

I asked about the alleged link to organized crime and found no support in bookies' accounts. Joe offers an interesting counterperspective suggesting that the allegation is a government ploy to control competition from bookies.

> The idea that the Mafia is pullin the strings on guys like me is a myth. We keep sports honest, believe me. If you're looking for the crooked angle, then government's the real criminal 'cause they really don't want competition from independents like me. So they keep betting illegal. The truth is that the independents do a better job than the government. Look, our payout is higher, we don't use gimmicks—think about all the gimmicks for the lottery—we don't have the overhead, and we don't cheat. Remember that Nick Perry incident?[10] Bookies have integrity. You gotta have integrity, 'cause if I cheated I'd be outta business. And remember this, we're not on every corner or in every retail store either, pushing people to gamble. But the government can't do it right 'cause they're greedy and most people know that. Just look at the OTB (Off Track Betting). How could you lose money with horses? Think about it. When the government's involved there are too many hands in the till. Guys like me make the government look bad 'cause we know what we're doin' and they don't want us out there. So they gotta make it seem like we're a bunch of thugs fixin' games and workin' players. The only games I ever heard about being fixed are the ones you read about in the paper. I'm not saying that it never happens, but when it does, bookies aren't doing the fixin. It's usually gamblers.

According to Sasuly (1982), all of the major sporting associations (i.e., the NCAA, NBA, NFL, and Thoroughbred Tracks of America) maintain contact with illegal bookmakers as a way of monitoring irregularities. Bookies can be thought of as barometers of irregularities for the world of sports.

Since there have been numerous reports of athletes shaving points, I asked whether bookies had firsthand knowledge of professional athletes betting on games. None of the bookies I talked to knew of any instances where athletes placed bets on or against teams they played for. However, bookies did acknowledge having customers who were professional athletes and who wagered on sports events. Roger describes his experiences with a professional athlete who bets with him.

> I knew players who gambled. I took bets from _____. He didn't call me every week, but once in a while he'd bet on this game or that game. Sometimes he'd win and sometimes he'd lose. If you're askin' whether he'd bet his own game, the answer is no. In fact, he wouldn't bet on any games while he was playing. You know, he had to keep it low key because he could be kicked out of the pros if anyone ever found out. So we kept it quiet. We'd meet at _____, you know a lot of

---

[10] Nick Perry was the television announcer for the Pennsylvania Daily Lottery drawing who was convicted of fixing the live drawing on April 24, 1980.

guys worked out there, you could be sorta invisible there, and you know no one noticed, so we'd square up in the locker room. Players gamble. Believe me, all the players know what the line is on their own game and every other game. But me, personally, I've never known a player who bet his own game. I have known guys who are no longer in the pros who bet on their team. The way I look at it is, it's just part of sports.

When unusual or irregular betting patterns emerge, bookies stop taking bets on the game. This practice is referred to as "taking it off the board." It would not be in the bookie's best interests to try to rig or fix games since it is the bookie that stands to lose. Moreover, rigged games would disrupt the logic of bookmaking and the inherent parity in sports betting.

Discussion and Conclusions

Contrary to the image found in the public debate and popular culture, namely that bookies are slick operators looking for the "fast buck, the quick fix, or the desire to get something for nothing"[11] and have ties to organized crime, this analysis shows that bookmakers work hard, are dedicated, possess skill and specialized knowledge, and operate with integrity. Bookies put in long hours and make many sacrifices in other parts of their life in order to build a successful business.

Despite the maxim that "you can't beat the bookie," bookies need paying customers and since they cannot recruit or solicit their customers openly, they must devise ways that weed out the poor risks. Bookies must also be attuned to betting patterns and know when to raise or lower the line in order to balance the action. When it is not possible to balance the action, bookies need to know when to layoff with another bookmaker to avoid heavy losses. Finally, successful bookies operate with honesty and integrity. The relationship between the bookie and his customer is based on trust, and bookies know that if they cheat their customers they will lose them.

While the findings show that bookies are fully aware that what they are doing is illegal (Ray captures this by saying "You see, it's not illegal to place a bet, but you can't take bets—that's why you always gotta watch yourself"), they do not define themselves or other bookies as deviant or criminal. Instead they perceive themselves as providing a service to a niche market. What accounts for this nondeviant identity? One possible explanation has to do with the way bookmaking is socially organized. To the lay observer deviance appears to lack order, but sociologists know that like the social world of which it is a part, deviance is highly organized. The social organization of all forms of deviance is a microcosm of

[11] From the Professional Amateur Sports Protection Act of 1992.

society—there are distinct roles, norms of interaction, relationships, and distinct settings and contexts for its occurrence. Best and Luckenbill (1994) argue that the social organization of deviance is an endless source of knowledge because it is where the relationship between the individual and the larger society is mediated (5).

Like many service transactions, the product in the transaction (i.e., the bet) is nonmaterial—it consists of a verbal agreement about the outcome of a sports event. But unlike most illegal service transactions, the bet does not require face-to-face interaction. This fact sets bookmaking apart from other types of deviant transactions. Bookies and customers communicate by phone which means that the transaction can take place anywhere—at work, at home, in a car, in a restaurant, or even while walking down the street. This distances the bookie and the bettor from typical deviant or sub-cultural settings such as back alleys, street corners, or designated areas like redlight districts. The deviant transaction is integrated into the rhythms of everyday actions within the context of normal everyday settings.

In addition to occurring outside a criminal milieu, the structure of the transaction is unlike other illegal transactions because it is nonhierarchical. No middlemen are involved. While it is true that most bookies get their line from oddsmakers (usually working out of Las Vegas), the line never-theless is in the public domain; you can find it anywhere. Consequently, nothing in the transaction requires the involvement of suppliers, vendors, or front men. Because the transaction is between the bookie and the bet-tor, bookies have autonomy, discretion, control, and independence over their business.

There are three major phases of the bookmaking process: establishing the terms for betting, taking bets, and settling accounts. Within each of these processes, the bookies maintain independence, autonomy, discretion, and control. The conditions and terms for the transaction are determined by the bookie. This involves making decisions about what the line will be, the maximum and minimum amount to be accepted, the types of bets that will be accepted (a straight bet, over/under bet, parlay, etc.), and whether to extend credit to customers. Bookies know that if their terms are not com-petitive with other bookies, they could lose customers. Taking the bet con-summates the transaction. Bettors tell the bookie who they want to wager on, the amount of the bet, and the type of bet they want to make. Bookies repeat this information back to the customer so that there is no misunder-standing about the wager and both wait for the outcome. Settling accounts involves the transfer of money either from losing bettors to bookies or from bookies to winning bettors and is the only phase that involves face-to-face interaction. Since bookmaking is illegal, bookies have no legal right to col-lect monies owed them nor can bettors demand monies owed to them. In-stead of being coercive, settling accounts is based on trust between the bookie and bettor. In every aspect of the bookmaking process we see that bookies are the innovators, decision makers, and risk-takers. They initiate their involvement in bookmaking and see it as an opportunity to provide a service to a growing market; they hone their skills, gather the resources, and manage the process of building their own business.

There is further evidence that bookies differ from other types of deviants when we examine their career trajectories. On average, the bookies in this study were involved in bookmaking for 17 years, which can only be thought of in terms of a lengthy career. Throughout this period, the majority held full-time legitimate jobs, were committed to their families, planned for the future of their families, set economic goals, were involved in community activities, and generally were committed to conventional values. It also is worth noting that only one of the bookies in this study had ever been arrested. Yet in the literature on deviant careers, it is argued that prolonged deviant involvement requires rejecting conventional values (Stebbins 1971:63).

Best and Luckenbill (1994:235–237) argue that the social organization of deviance affects the duration of deviant careers in at least four ways. First, most deviant careers are dependent on the support of other deviants; the more contacts they have with other deviants, the longer the career. Second, career deviants have connections to other deviant organizations because of the resources such organizations offer. Third, since illegal activities are characterized by unregulated competition, career deviants must minimize competition, and this is usually done through negotiating with other deviants and by sharing or dividing the territory or resources. The final way career length is affected is through contacts with social control agents—the more contacts the higher the risk and the shorter the career. The analysis shows that bookmakers' careers are distinct from other deviant careers in the following ways. First, while bookies may associate with other bookies, this occurs only occasionally. Most importantly, their bookmaking business does not depend on these associations or on other deviants. In short, bookies are independent of other deviants. Second, since bookies assume all of the risks (financial and otherwise) involved in the bookmaking enterprise, they do not need to divide or share their customers nor do they have ties to other deviant organizations. Third, the most effective device against competition is the bookie's honesty and integrity. Finally, bookies are buffered from contact with social control agents because the enterprise has such low criminal visibility. Gambling on sports is integrated into the rhythms of everyday life, particularly male culture, and the bookie is a feature of that culture.

This leads to the question of whether it is time that the organized crime, corruption, and sports betting link be put to rest. The findings presented here provide a compelling argument for doing so. Although there is evidence showing organized crime's involvement in bookmaking, the findings presented here show bookies to be small entrepreneurs who operate independently. They see themselves as providing a service that is in great demand. It could be argued that major media that promote sports events increase the demand for this service. The line is readily available to the public and is very much a part of the hype that accompanies sports events. The line increases public interest in sporting events and betting on events ensures that millions of fans will watch them. Given the ubiquity of these accoutrements of gambling on sports, it is not surprising that sports betting is widespread and that our anti-gambling policies against it have little impact.

Although the sample for this study is small, confined to a single geographical area, and was selected by word of mouth, the accounts show remarkable consistency. It is possible that the bookies I interviewed represent an unusual group of bookies. Since there is no way of knowing just how large the population of bookies is, it is difficult to assess the representativeness of this study's sample. More research is needed, particularly research done in other geographical areas. Nevertheless, the findings presented here show that while bookmaking is illegal, sports betting is widespread, and that bookmakers are more like small business entrepreneurs than petty criminals.

References

Anderson, Annelies. 1979. *The Business of Organized Crime.* Stanford, CA: Hoover Institute.

Best, Joel, and David Luckenbill. 1994. *Organizing Deviance.* Englewood Cliffs, NJ: Prentice Hall.

Bonanno, Bill. 1999. *Bound by Honour.* NY: St. Martin's Press.

Chambliss, William. 1978. *On the Take.* Bloomington, IN: University of Indiana Press.

Clark, Ramsey. 1971. *Crime in America.* New York: Simon and Schuster.

Congressional Hearings for H.R. 497, National Gambling Impact and Policy Commission Act, September, 1995.

Cook, James. "If Roxborough Says the Spread is 7 it's 7." *Forbes,* September 14, 1992, pp. 350–363.

Cressey, Donald. 1969. *Theft of the Nation.* New York: Harper & Row.

DeFina, B., J. P. Reidy (Producers), and M. Scorsese (Director). (1995). *Casino* [Film]. (Available from Universal Pictures).

DeFina, B., B. Pustin, and I. Winkler (Producers), and M. Scorsese (Director). (1990). *Goodfellas* [Film]. (Available from Warner Bros).

Holcomb, R., and P. D. Marshall (Directors). (1987). *Wiseguy* [Film]. (Available from Cannell Films).

McGraw, Dan. "The National Bet." *U.S. News & World Report,* April 7, 1997, pp. 50–55.

Moody's Industry Review. Gaming. April 6, 1995.

National Amateur and Professional Sports Protection Act, S. 474, 1992.

Nevada Gaming Commission and State Gaming Control Board, personal communication with Research Division, June 1998.

O'Brien, Timothy. 1998. *Bad Bet.* New York: Times Business.

President's Commission on Law Enforcement and the Administration of Justice. 1967. *Task Force Report: Organized Crime.* Washington, DC: U.S. Government Printing Office.

Puzo, Mario. 1969. *The Godfather.* New York: Putnum.

Reuter, Peter. 1983. *Disorganized Crime: Illegal Markets and the Mafia.* Cambridge, MA: MIT Press.

Reuter, Peter, and Jonathan Rubinstein. 1982. *Illegal Gambling in New York*. Washington, DC: National Institute of Justice.

Rosencrance, John. 1987. "Bookmaking: A Case Where Honesty is the Best Policy." *Sociology and Social Research* 72(1):7–11.

Sasuly, Richard. 1982. *Bookies and Bettors: Two Hundred Years of Gambling*. New York: Holt Rinehart and Winston.

Scarne, John. 1974. *Scarne's New Complete Guide to Gambling*. New York: Simon and Schuster.

Shapiro, Joseph, Penny Loeb, Kenan Pollack, Timothy Ito, and Gary Cohen. "America's Gambling Fever." *U.S. News & World Report*, January 15, 1996, pp. 52–60.

Stebbins, Robert. 1971. *Commitment to Deviance*. Westport, CT: Greenwood.

Talese, Gay. 1971. *Honor Thy Father*. New York: World Publishing.

The statements by Best and Luckenbill indicate that deviant organizations can be characterized in terms of their relative degree of sophistication. Best and Luckenbill also emphasize that a person can gain initial entry to organizations through various channels. Once individuals gain entry, however, they must, if they elect to stay, learn the existing culture and traditions. A similar requirement exists with respect to the institutional deviant. Failure to meet expectations may result in such penalties as ostracism or exclusion from the group. (The general social-psychological processes involved in learning deviant cultures were highlighted in our discussion of the cultural transmission model in Part II.) The selections in this section deal primarily with entry routes and offer specific illustrations of how actors become socialized into deviant or semideviant careers.

In "Drifting into Dealing: Becoming a Cocaine Seller," Sheigla Murphy, Dan Waldorf, and Craig Reinarman outline the various modes and levels of entry into the world of cocaine sales. Their observations are based on interviews with eighty ex-cocaine sellers. All had sold cocaine for at least a year; however, none had done so for a period of six months prior to the interviews. Actual entry into the world of cocaine sales is, according to the researchers, a fluid process, with most sellers drifting into their dealing career. The authors go on to describe five basic ways that people begin to sell cocaine. The first mode of entry is the *go-between*, in which a person who initially buys for his or her friends begins to envision the profits that may result from selling. The second avenue is the *stash dealer*, in which a user sells small amounts to support his or her own cocaine needs. The *connoisseur*, the third mode of entry, includes those who seek to buy high-quality drugs through wholesale purchases, and the fourth entry route entails the *apprenticeship*, a trainee-style of connection. In this situation, the novice takes over all aspects of an established dealer's business after learning the ropes. The fifth and final entry route described involves what is termed the *product line expansion*. Here dealers start selling other drugs (e.g., marijuana) and then move into cocaine sales when a supply becomes available. Of importance, too, is the authors' analysis of how a seller may exhibit a subtle transformation of his or her identity. Once situated in the role of the dealer, selling often becomes viewed as a job or career. Significant, too, is the observation that the "dealer identity" did not seem to replace former "legitimate" identities but was, instead, added to a subject's other conventional identities. Thus, sellers would, depending upon the situation, emphasize different aspects of their identities. The researchers end by describing some of the values and expectations that characterize the business relationships existing between sellers and customers.

Constance Chapple, in "Self-Control, Peer Relations, and Delinquency," raises important questions related to entry routes into deviance. Chapple is interested in the roles of peers and of self-control on deviant behavior, specifically the process by which youth select into deviant peer groups. Gottfredson's and Hirschi's general theory of crime, with its focus on self-control, constitutes the foundation of the hypotheses. The general theory of crime leads to certain predictions concerning the entry process. First, children lacking self-control are more likely to be rejected by peers, in part because of personal qualities such as self-interest and impulsivity. Second, children lacking self-control choose similar others, often delinquent peer groups. Chapple is interested in the relationship between self-control, peer relationships, and delinquency suggesting that self-control influences delinquency directly through risk-taking behaviors and indirectly by virtue of peer relationships—predictions consistent with the general theory. Using longitudinal data, she finds that peers matter more than Gottfredson and Hirschi might have predicted. Chapple's findings suggest that relationships with peers exert a significant effect on delinquency apart from self-control. Clearly questions remain about the process through which self-control shapes peer relationships and how peer relationships influence delinquency.

37

Drifting into Dealing: Becoming a Cocaine Seller

Sheigla Murphy
Dan Waldorf
Craig Reinarman

Introduction

No American who watched television news in the 1980s could have avoided images of violent drug dealers who brandished bullets while driving BMW's before being hauled off in handcuffs. This new stereotype of a drug dealer has become a staple of popular culture, the very embodiment of evil. He works for the still more vile villains of the "Colombian cartel," who make billions on the suffering of millions. Such men are portrayed as driven by greed and utterly indifferent to the pain from which they profit.

We have no doubt that some such characters exist. Nor do we doubt that there may be a new viciousness among some of the crack cocaine dealers who have emerged in ghettos and barrios already savaged by rising social problems and failing social programs. We have grave doubts, however, that such characterizations tell us anything about cocaine sellers more generally. If our interviews are any guide, beneath every big-time dealer who may approximate the stereotype there are hundreds of smaller sellers who do not.

This paper describes such sellers, not so much as a way of debunking a new devil but rather as a way of illuminating how deviant careers develop and how the identities of the individuals who move into this work are transformed. Along with the many routine normative strictures against drug use in our culture, there has been a mobilization in recent years for a "war on drugs" which targets cocaine dealers in particular. Many armaments in the arsenal of social control from propaganda to prisons have been employed in efforts to dissuade people from using/selling such substances. In such a context it is curious that ostensibly ordinary people not only continue to use illicit drugs but also take the significant additional step of becoming drug sellers. To explore how this happens, we offer an analysis of eighty depth interviews with former cocaine sellers. We sought to learn something about how it is that otherwise conventional people—some legally employed, many well educated—end up engaging in a sustained pattern of behavior that their neighbors might think of as very deviant indeed.

Deviant Careers and Drift

Our reading of this data was informed by two classic theoretical works in the deviance literature. First, in *Outsiders*, Howard Becker observed that, "The career lines characteristic of an occupation take their shape from the problems peculiar to that occupation. These, in turn, are a function of the occupation's position vis-a-vis other groups in society" (1963:102). He illustrated the point with the dance musician, caught between the jazz artist's desire to maintain creative control and a structure of opportunities for earning a living that demanded the subordination of this desire to mainstream musical tastes. Musicians' careers were largely a function of how they managed this problem. When the need to make a living predominated, the basis of their self conceptions shifted from art to craft.

Of course, Becker applied the same proposition to more deviant occupations. In the next section, we describe five discrete modes of becoming a cocaine seller which center on "the problems peculiar to" the world of illicit drug use and which entail a similar shift in self conception. For example, when a drug such as cocaine is criminalized, its cost is often greatly increased while its availability and quality are somewhat limited. Users are thus faced with the problems of avoiding detection, reducing costs, and improving availability and quality. By becoming involved in sales, users solve many of these problems and may also find that they can make some money in the bargain. As we will show, the type of entree and the level at which it occurs are functions of the individual's relationship to networks of other users and suppliers. At the point where one has moved from being a person who *has* a good connection for cocaine to a person who *is* a good connection for cocaine, a subtle shift in self conception and identity occurs.

Becker's model of deviant careers entails four basic steps, three of which our cocaine sellers took. First, the deviant must somehow avoid the impact of conventional commitments that keep most people away from intentional non-conformity. Our cocaine sellers passed this stage by ingesting illegal substances with enough regularity that the practice became normalized in their social world. Second, deviant motives and interests must develop. These are usually learned in the process of the deviant activity and from interaction with other deviants. Here too our cocaine sellers had learned the pleasures of cocaine by using it, and typically were moved toward involvement in distribution to solve one or more problems entailed in such use. Once involved, they discovered additional motivations which we will describe in detail below.

Becker's third step in the development of deviant careers entails public labeling. The person is caught, the rule is enforced, and his or her public identity is transformed. The new master status of "deviant," Becker argues, can be self fulfilling when it shapes others' perceptions of the person and limits his or her possibilities for resuming conventional roles and activities. Few of our respondents had been publicly labeled deviant, but they did describe a gradual change in identity that may be likened to self-labeling. This typically occurred when they deepened their deviance by dealing on top of using cocaine. This shift in self conception for our subjects was more closely linked to Becker's fourth step—movement into an organized deviant group in which people with a common fate and similar problems form subcultures. There they learn more about solving problems and ideologies which provide rationales for continuing the behavior, thus further weakening the hold of conventional norms and institutions and solidifying deviant identities. In the case of our subjects, becoming sellers further immersed them into deviant groups and practices to the point where many came to face the problems of, and to see themselves as, "dealers."

The fact that these processes of deeper immersion into deviant worlds and shifts in self conception were typically gradual and subtle brought us to a second set of theoretical reference points in the work of David Matza (1964; 1969).[1] In his research on delinquency, Matza discovered that most so-called delinquents were not self-consciously committed to deviant values or lifestyles, but on the contrary continued to hold conventional beliefs. Most of the time they were law abiding, but because the situation of "youth" left them free from various restraints, they often *drifted* in and out of deviance. Matza found that even when caught being delinquent, young people tended to justify or rationalize their acts through "techniques of neutralization" (Sykes and Matza, 1957) rooted in conventional codes of morality. Although we focus on *entering* selling careers, we found that Matza's concept of drift (1964) provided us with a useful sensibility for making sense of our respondents' accounts. The modes of entree they described were as fluid and non-committal as the drift into and out of delinquency that he described.

None of the career paths recounted by our subjects bear much resemblance to stereotypes of "drug dealers."[2] For decades the predominant image of the illicit drug dealer was an older male reprobate sporting a long, shabby overcoat within which he had secreted a cornucopia of dangerous consciousness-altering substances. This proverbial "pusher" worked school yards, targeting innocent children who would soon be chemically enslaved repeat customers. The newer villains have been depicted as equally vile but more violent. Old or new, the ideal-typical "drug dealer" is motivated by perverse greed and/or his own addiction, and has crossed a clearly marked moral boundary, severing most ties to the conventional world.

The cocaine sellers we interviewed, on the other hand, had more varied and complex motives for selling cocaine. Moreover at least within their subcultures, the moral boundaries were both rather blurry and as often wandered along as actually crossed. Their life histories reminded us of Matza's later but related discussion of the *overlap* between deviance and conventionality:

> Overlap refers to . . . the marginal rather than gross differentiation between deviant and conventional folk and the considerable though variable interpenetration of deviant and conventional culture. Both themes sensitize us to the regular exchange, traffic, and flow—of persons as well as styles and precepts—that occur among deviant and conventional worlds. (1969:68)

Our subjects were already seasoned users of illicit drugs. For years their drug use coexisted comfortably with their conventional roles and activities; having a deviant dimension to their identities appeared to cause them little strain. In fact, because their use of illicit drugs had gone on for so long, was so common in their social worlds, and had not significantly affected their otherwise normal lives, they hardly considered it deviant at all.

Thus, when they began to sell cocaine as well as use it, they did not consider it a major leap down an unknown road but rather a series of short steps down a familiar path. It was not as if ministers had become mobsters; no sharp break in values, motives, world views, or identities was required. Indeed, few woke up one morning and made a conscious decision to become sellers. They did not break sharply with the conventional world and actively choose a deviant career path; most simply drifted into dealing by virtue of their strategies for solving the problems entailed in using a criminalized substance, and only then developed additional deviant motives centering on money.

To judge from our respondents, then, dealers are not from a different gene pool. Since the substances they enjoy are illegal, most regular users of such drugs become involved in some aspect of distribution. There is also a growing body of research on cocaine selling and distribution that has replaced the simplistic stereotype of the pusher with complex empirical evidence about underground economies and deviant careers (e.g., Langer, 1977; Waldorf et al., 1977, 1991; Adler, 1985; Plasket and Quillen, 1985; Morales, 1986a, 1986b; Sanchez and Johnson, 1987; Sanabria, 1988; and Williams, 1989). Several features of underground economies or black markets in drugs contribute to widespread user participation in distribution. For example, some users who could obtain cocaine had other user-friends who wanted it. Moreover, the idea of keeping such traffic among friends offered both sociability and safety. For others, cocaine's high cost inspired many users to become involved in purchasing larger amounts to take advantage of volume discounts. They then sold part of their supply to friends in order to reduce the cost of personal use. The limited supply of cocaine in the late seventies and early eighties made for a sellers' market, providing possibilities for profits along with steady supplies. For most of our subjects, it was not so much that they learned they could make money and thus decided to become dealers but rather, being involved in distribution anyway, they learned they could make money from it. As Becker's model suggests, deviant motives are learned in the course of deviant activities; motivation follows behavior, not the other way around.

After summarizing our sampling and interviewing procedures, we describe in more detail (1) the various modes and levels of entree into cocaine sales; (2) some of the practices, rights and responsibilities entailed in dealing; and (3) the subtle transformation of identity that occurred when people who consider themselves rather conventional moved into careers considered rather deviant.

Sample and Methods

The sample consists of 80 ex-sellers who sold cocaine in the San Francisco Bay Area. We interviewed them in 1987 and 1988. Most had stopped selling before crack sales peaked in this area. Only five of the eighty had sold crack or rock. Of these five, two had sold on the street and two had sold in "rock party houses"[3] as early as 1978. It is important to note, therefore, that the sellers we describe are very likely to be different from street crack dealers in terms of the product type, selling styles, visibility, and thus the risks of arrest and attendant violence.

The modes and levels of entree we describe should not be considered exhaustive. They are likely to vary by region, subculture, and level of dealing. For example, our sample and locus differed from those of Adler (1985), who studied one community of *professional* cocaine dealers at the *highest levels* of the distribution system. Her ethnographic account is rich in insights about the lifestyles and career contingencies of such high-level dealers and smugglers. These subjects decided to enter into importing and/or dealing and to move up the ranks in this deviant occupation in order to obtain wealth and to live the sorts of lives that such wealth made possible. Adler's dealers were torn, however, between the lures of fast money and the good life and the stress and paranoia inherent in the scene. Thus, she reported "oscillations" wherein her dealers moved in and out of the business, usually to be lured back in by the possibility of high profits. Our dealers tended to have different motivations, career trajectories, and occupational exigencies. Most were lower in the hierarchy and non-professional (some maintained "straight" jobs); few set out to achieve success in an explicitly deviant career, to amass wealth, or to live as "high rollers." Moreover, our study was cross-sectional rather than longitudinal, so our focus was on how a wide variety of cocaine sellers entered careers rather than on the full career trajectories of a network of smugglers and sellers.

To be eligible for the study our respondents had to have sold cocaine steadily for at least a year and to have stopped selling for at least 6

Levels of Sales	Number of Interviews
Smugglers	2
Kilograms/pounds	13
Parts of kilos and pounds	6
Ounce dealers	18
Part-ounce dealers	13
Gram dealers	12
Part-gram dealers	11
Crack dealers	5
Total	80

months. We designed the study to include only *former* sellers so that respondents would feel free to describe all their activities in detail without fear that their accounts could somehow be utilized by law enforcement authorities.

They spoke of six different levels or types of sellers: smugglers, big dealers, dealers, sellers (unspecified), bar dealers, and street dealers. The social organization of cocaine sales probably varies in other areas. We located and interviewed ex-sellers from the full range of these dealer-identified sales levels, but we have added two categories in order to provide a more detailed typology. Our eight levels of sales were defined according to the units sold rather than the units bought. So, for example, if a seller bought quarters or eighths of ounces and regularly sold grams, we categorized him or her as a gram dealer rather than a part-ounce dealer.

Unlike most other studies of dealing and the now infamous street crack dealers, the majority of our respondents sold cocaine hydrochloride (powder) in private places. There are a number of styles of selling drugs—selling out of homes, selling out of rock houses and shooting galleries, selling out of party houses, selling out of rented "safe houses" and apartments, delivery services (using telephone answering, answering machines, voice mail and telephone beepers), car meets,[4] selling in bars, selling in parks, and selling in the street. Within each type there are various styles. For example, in some African-American communities in San Francisco a number of sellers set up business on a street and respond to customers who come by on foot and in automobiles. Very often a number of sellers will approach a car that slows down or stops to solicit customers; drugs and money are exchanged then and there. Such sales activities are obvious to the most casual observers; even television camera crews often capture such transactions for the nightly news. On certain streets in the Mission District, a Latino community in San Francisco, street drug sales are less blatant. Buyers usually walk up to sellers who stand on the street among numerous other people who are neither buyer nor sellers. There, specific transactions rarely take place on the street itself; the participants generally retreat to a variety of shops and restaurants. Buyers seldom use cars for transactions and sellers tend not to approach a car to solicit customers.

Despite the ubiquity of street sales in media accounts and the preponderance of street sellers in arrest records, we set out to sample the more hidden and more numerous sellers who operate in private. Most users of cocaine hydrochloride are working- or middle-class. They generally avoid street sellers both because they want to avoid being observed and because they believe that most street sellers sell inferior quality drugs (Waldorf et al., 1991). Further, we found that people engaged in such illegal and furtive transactions tend to prefer dealing with people like themselves, people they know.

We located our respondents by means of chain referral sampling techniques (Biernacki and Waldorf, 1981; Watters and Biernacki, 1989). This is a method commonly used by sociologists and ethnographers to locate hard-to-find groups and has been used extensively in qualitative research on drug use (Lindesmith, 1947; Becker, 1953; Feldman, 1968; Preble and Casey, 1969; Rosenbaum, 1981; Biernacki, 1986). We initiated the first of our location chains in 1974–1975 in the course of a short-term ethnography of cocaine use and sales among a small friendship network (Waldorf et al., 1977). Other chains were developed during a second study of cocaine cessation conducted during 1986–1987 (Reinarman et al., 1988; Macdonald et al., 1988; Murphy et al., 1989; Waldorf et al., 1991). Another three chains were developed during the present study. We located the majority of our respondents via referral chains developed by former sellers among their previous customers and suppliers. Initial interviewees referred us to other potential respondents whom we had not previously known. In this way we were able to direct our chains into groups of ex-sellers from a variety of backgrounds.

We employed two interview instruments: an open-ended, exploratory interview guide designed to maximize discovery of new and unique types of data, and a more structured survey designed to gather basic quantifiable data on all respondents. The open-ended interviews were tape-recorded, transcribed, and content-analyzed. These interviews usually took from 2 to 4 hours to complete, but when necessary we conducted longer and/or follow-up interviews (e.g., one woman was interviewed for 10 hours over three sessions). The data analyzed for this paper was drawn primarily from the tape-recorded depth interviews.

There is no way to ascertain if this (or any similar) sample is representative of all cocaine sellers. Because the parameters of the population are unknowable, random samples on which systematic generalizations might be based cannot be drawn. We do know that, unlike other studies of drug sellers, we placed less emphasis on street sellers and included dealers at all levels. We also attempted to get a better gender and ethnic mix than studies based on captive samples from jails or treatment programs. Roughly one in three (32.5%) of our dealers are female and two of five (41.2%) are persons of color.

Table 1   Demographics (*N* = 80)

	Number	Percent[a]
Age: Range = 18–60 years		
Mean = 37.1		
Median = 35.4		
Sex:		
Male	54	67.5
Female	26	32.5
Ethnicity:		
African-American	28	35.0
White	44	58.8
Latino(a)	4	5.0
Asian	1	1.2
Education:		
Less than high school grad	11	13.8
High school graduate	18	22.5
Some college	31	38.8
B.A. or B.S. degree	12	15.0
Some graduate	3	3.8
Graduate degree	5	6.3

[a]Percentages may not equal 100% due to rounding.

Our respondents ranged in age from 18 to 60, with a mean age of 37.1 years. Their education level was generally high, presumably an indication of the relatively large numbers of middle-class people in the sample.

Dealers

Dealers are people who are "fronted" (given drugs on consignment to be paid for upon sale) and/or who buy quantities of drugs for sale. Further, in order to be considered a dealer by users or other sellers a person must: (1) have one or more reliable connections (suppliers); (2) make regular co-caine purchases in amounts greater than a single gram (usually an eighth of an ounce or greater) to be sold in smaller units; (3) maintain some consistent supplies for sale; and (4) have a network of customers who make purchases on a regular basis. Although the stereotype of a dealer holds that illicit drug sales are a full-time occupation, many dealers, including members of our sample, operate part-time and supplement income from a legal job.

As we noted in the introduction, the rather average, ordinary character of the respondents who fit this definition was striking. In general, without prior knowledge or direct observation of drug sales, one would be unable to distinguish our respondents from other, non-dealer citizens. When telling their career histories, many of our respondents invoked very conventional, middle-class American values to explain their involvement in dealing (e.g., having children to support, mortgages or rent to pay in a high-cost urban area, difficulty finding jobs which paid enough to support a family). Similarly, their profits from drug sales were used in "normal" ways—to buy children's clothes, to make house or car payments, to remodel a room. Moreover, like Matza's delinquents, most of our respondents were quite law-abiding, with the obvious exception of their use and sales of an illicit substance.

When they were not dealing, our respondents engaged in activities that can only be described as mainstream American. For example, one of our dealers, a single mother of two, found herself with a number of friends who used cocaine and a good connection. She needed extra income to pay her mortgage and to support her children, so she sold small amounts of cocaine within her friendship network. Yet while she sold cocaine, she worked at a full-time job, led a Girl Scout troop, volunteered as a teacher of cardio-pulmonary resuscitation (CPR) classes for young people, and went to Jazzercize classes. Although she may have been a bit more civic-minded than many others, her case served to remind us that cocaine sellers do not come from another planet.

Modes of Entree into Dealing

Once they began selling cocaine, many of our respondents moved back and forth between levels in the distribution hierarchy. Some people dealt for short periods of time and then quit, only to return several months later at another level of sales.[5] The same person may act as a broker on one deal, sell a quarter gram at a profit to a friend on another, and then pick up an ounce from an associate and pass it on to another dealer in return for some marijuana in a third transaction. In a few instances each of these roles were played by the same person within the same twenty-four hour period.

But whether or not a dealer/respondent moved back and forth in this way, s/he usually began selling in one of five distinct ways. All five of these modes of entree pre-suppose an existing demand for cocaine from people known to the potential dealers. A person selling any line of products needs two things, a group of customers and a product these customers are interested in purchasing. Cocaine sellers are no different. In addition to being able and willing to pay, however, cocaine customers must also be trustworthy because these transactions are illegal.

The first mode of entree, *the go-between,* is fairly straightforward. The potential seller has a good cocaine connection and a group of friends who place orders for cocaine with him/her. If the go-between's friends use cocaine regularly enough and do not develop their own connections, then a period of months or even years might go by when the go-between begins to spend more and more time and energy purchasing for them. Such sellers generally do not make formal decisions to begin dealing; rather, opportunities regularly present themselves and go-betweens gradually take advantage of them. For example, one 30-year-old African-American who became a gram dealer offered this simple account of his passage from go-between to seller:

> Basically, I first started because friends pressured me to get the good coke I could get. I wasn't even making any money off of it. They'd come to me and I'd call up my friend who had gotten pretty big selling a lot of coke. (Case # E-5)

This went on for six months before he began to charge his friends money for it. Then his connection started fronting him eighths of ounces at a time, and he gradually became an official dealer, regularly selling drugs for a profit. Others who began in this way often took only commissions-in-kind (a free snort) for some months before beginning to charge customers a cash mark-up.

Another African-American male began selling powdered cocaine to snorters in 1978 and by the mid-eighties had begun selling rock cocaine (crack) to smokers. He described his move from go-between to dealer as follows:

> Around the time I started indulging [in cocaine] myself, people would come up and say, "God, do you know where I can get some myself?" I would just say, "Sure, just give me your money," I would come back and either indulge with them or just give it to them depending on my mood. I think that's how I originally set up my clientele. I just had a certain group of people who would come to me because they felt that I knew the type of people who could get them a real quality product.
>
> And pretty soon I just got tired of, you know, being taken out of situations or being imposed upon. . . . I said that it would be a lot easier to just do it myself. And one time in particular, and I didn't consider myself a dealer or anything, but I had a situation one night where 5 different people called me to try to get cocaine . . . not from me but it was like, "Do you know where I can get some good cocaine from?" (Case # E-11)

Not all go-betweens-cum-dealers start out so altruistically. Some astute businessmen and women spot the profit potential early on and immediately realize a profit, either in-kind (a share of the drugs purchased) or by tacking on a surcharge to the purchase price. The following respondent, a 39-year-old African-American male, described this more profit-motivated move from go-between to formal seller:

> Well, the first time that I started it was like I knew where to get good stuff . . . and I had friends that didn't know where to get good stuff. And I knew where to get them really good stuff and so I would always

put a couple of dollars on it, you know, if I got it for $20 I would sell it to them for $25 or $30 or whatever.

It got to be where more and more people were coming to me and I was going to my man more and I would be there 5 or 6 times a day, you know. So he would tell me, "Here, why don't you take this, you know, and bring me x-amount of dollars for it." So that's how it really started. I got fronted and I was doing all the business instead of going to his house all the time, because he had other people that were coming to his house and he didn't want the traffic. (Case # E-13)

The second mode of entree is the *stash dealer,* or a person who becomes involved in distribution and/or sales simply to support or subsidize personal use. The name is taken from the term "stash," meaning a personal supply of marijuana (see Fields, 1985, on stash dealers in the marijuana trade). This 41-year-old white woman who sold along with her husband described her start as a stash dealer this way:

Q: So what was your motivation for the sales?
A: To help pay for my use, because the stuff wasn't cheap and I had the means and the money at the time in order to purchase it, where our friends didn't have that amount of money without having to sell something. . . . Yeah, friendship, it wasn't anything to make money off of, I mean we made a few dollars. . . . (Case # E-7)

The respondents who entered the dealing world as stash dealers typically started out small (selling quarter and half grams) and taking their profits in product. However, this motivation contributed to the undoing of some stash dealers in that it led to greater use, which led to the need for greater selling, and so on. Unless they then developed a high-volume business that allowed them to escalate their cocaine use and still make profits, the reinforcing nature of cocaine tempted many of them to use more product than was good for business.

Many stash dealers were forced out of business fairly early on in their careers because they spent so much money on their own use they were financially unable to "re-cop" (buy new supplies). Stash dealers often want to keep only a small number of customers in order to minimize both the "hassle" of late-night phone calls and the risk of police detection, and they do not need many customers since they only want to sell enough to earn free cocaine. Problems arise, however, when their small group of customers do not buy the product promptly. The longer stash dealers had cocaine in their possession, the more opportunities they had for their own use (i.e., for profits to "go up your nose"). One stash dealer had an axiom about avoiding this: "It ain't good to get high on your own supply" (Case # E-57). The predicament of using rather than selling their product often afflicts high-level "weight dealers" as well, but they are better able to manage for longer periods of time due to larger volumes and profit margins.

The third mode of entry into cocaine selling had to do with users' desire for high-quality, unadulterated cocaine. We call this type the *connoisseur.* Ironically, the motivation for moving toward dealing in this way is often health-related. People who described this mode of entree described their concerns, as users, about the possible dangers of ingesting the various adulterants or "cuts" commonly used by dealers to increase profits. User folklore holds that the larger the quantity purchased, the purer the product. This has been substantiated by laboratory analysis of the quality of small amounts of street drugs (typically lower) as opposed to larger police seizures (typically higher).

The connoisseur type of entry, then, begins with the purchase of larger quantities of cocaine than they intend to use in order to maximize purity. Then they give portions of the cocaine to close friends at a good price. If the members of the network start to use more cocaine, the connoisseurs begin to make bigger purchases with greater regularity. At some point they begin to feel that all this takes effort and that it makes sense to buy large quantities not only to get purer cocaine but to make some money for their efforts. The following 51-year-old, white business executive illustrated the connoisseur route as follows:

> I think the first reason I started to sell was not to make money or even to pay for my coke, because I could afford it. It was to get good coke and not to be snorting a lot of impurities and junk that people were putting into it by cutting it so much. So I really think that I started to sell it or to get it wholesale so that I would get the good stuff. And I guess my first. . . . what I did with it in the beginning, because I couldn't use all that I had to buy to get good stuff, I sold it to some of my friends for them to sell it, retail it. (Case # E-16)

Connoisseurs, who begin by selling unneeded quantities, often found they unlearned certain attitudes when they moved from being volume buyers looking for quality toward becoming dealers looking for profit. It was often a subtle shift, but once their primary motivation gradually changed from buying-for-purity to buying-to-sell they found themselves beginning to think and act like dealers. The shift usually occurred when connoisseurs realized that the friends with whom they had shared were in fact customers who were eager for their high quality cocaine and who often made demands on their time (e.g., friends seeking supplies not merely for themselves, but for other friends a step or two removed from the original connoisseur). Some connoisseurs also became aware of the amount of money that could be made by becoming business-like about what had been formerly friendly favors. At such points in the process they began to buy-to-sell, for a profit, as well as for the purpose of obtaining high-quality cocaine for personal use. This often meant that, rather than buying sporadically, they had to make more regular buys; for a successful businessperson must have supplies when customers want to buy or they will seek another supplier.

The fourth mode of entree into cocaine selling is an *apprenticeship*. Like the other types, apprentices typically were users who already had loosened conventional normative strictures and learned deviant motives by interacting with other users and with dealers; and they, too, drifted into dealing. However, in contrast to the first three types, apprentices moved toward dealing less to solve problems inherent in using a criminalized substance than to solve the problems of the master dealer. Apprenticeships begin in a personal relationship where, for example, the potential seller is the lover or intimate of a dealer. This mode was most often the route of entry for women, although one young man we interviewed learned to deal from his father. Couples often start out with the man doing the dealing—picking up the product, handling the money, weighing and packaging, etc. The woman gradually finds herself acting as an unofficial assistant—taking telephone messages, sometimes giving people prepackaged cocaine and collecting money. Apprentices frequently benefit from being involved with the experienced dealer in that they enjoy both supplies of high-quality cocaine and indirect financial rewards of dealing.

Some of our apprentices moved into official roles or deepened their involvement when the experienced dealer began to use too much cocaine to function effectively as a seller. In some such cases the abuse of the product led to an end of the relationship. Some apprentices then left dealing altogether while others began dealing on their own. One 32-year-old African-American woman lived with a pound dealer in Los Angeles in 1982. Both were freebasers (cocaine smokers) who sold to other basers. She described her evolution from apprentice to dealer this way:

> I was helping him with like weighing stuff and packaging it and I sort of got to know some of the people that were buying because his own use kept going up. He was getting more out of it, so I just fell into taking care of it partly because I like having the money and it also gave me more control over the situation, too, for awhile, you know, until we both got too out of it. (Case # E-54)

The fifth mode of entree into cocaine selling entailed the *expansion of an existing product line*. A number of the sellers we interviewed started out as marijuana salespersons and learned many aspects of the dealers' craft before they ever moved to cocaine. Unlike in the other modes, in this one an existing marijuana seller already had developed selling skills and established a network of active customers for illicit drugs. Expansion of product line (in business jargon, horizontal integration) was the route of entry for many of the multiple-ounce and kilo cocaine dealers we interviewed. The combination of the availability of cocaine through their marijuana connection and their marijuana customers' interest in purchasing cocaine, led many marijuana sellers to add cocaine to their product line.

Others who entered dealing this way also found that expanding from marijuana to cocaine solved some problems inherent in marijuana dealing. For example, cocaine is far less bulky and odoriferous than marijuana and thus did not present the risky and costly shipping and storage problems of multiple pounds of marijuana. Those who entered cocaine selling via this product line expansion route also recognized, of course, that there was the potential for higher profits with cocaine. They seemed to suggest that as long as they were already taking the risk, why shouldn't they maximize the reward? Some such dealers discontinued marijuana sales altogether and others merely added cocaine to their line. One white, 47-year-old mother of three grown children described how she came to expand her product line:

Q: How did you folks [she and her husband] get started dealing?
A: The opportunity just fell into our lap. We were already dealing weed and one of our customers got this great coke connection and started us onto dealing his product. We were selling him marijuana and he was selling us cocaine.
Q: So you had a network of weed buyers, right? So you could sell to those . . . ?
A: There was a shift in the market. Yeah, because weed was becoming harder [to find] and more expensive and a bulkier product. The economics of doing a smaller, less bulkier product and more financially rewarding product like cocaine had a certain financial appeal to the merchant mentality. (Case # E-1)

Conscious Decision to Sell

As noted earlier, the majority of our sample were middle class wholesalers who, in the various ways just described, drifted into dealing careers. The few street sellers we interviewed did not drift into sales in the same way. We are obliged to note again that the five modes of entry into cocaine selling we have identified should not be taken as exhaustive. We have every reason to believe that for groups and settings other than those we have studied there are other types of entree and career trajectories. The five cases of street sellers we did examine suggest that entree into street-level sales was more of a conscious decision of a poor person who decided to enter an underground economy, not an effort to solve a user's problems. Our interviews with street sellers suggest that they choose to participate in an illicit profit-generating activity largely because licit economic opportunities were scarce or nonexistent. Unlike our other types, such sellers sold to strangers as well as friends, and their place of business was more likely to be the street corner rather than homes, bars, or nightclubs. For example, one 30-year-old Native American ex-prostitute described how she became a street crack dealer this way:

I had seen in the past friends that were selling and stuff and I needed extra money so I just one day told one of my friends, you know, if he could help me, you know, show me more or less how it goes. So I just went by what I seen. So I just started selling it. (Case # E-AC 1)

A few higher-level dealers also made conscious decisions to sell (see Adler, 1985), particularly when faced with limited opportunity structures. Cocaine selling, as an occupation, offers the promise of lavish lifestyles otherwise unattainable to most ghetto youth and other impoverished groups. Dealing also provides an alternative to the low-paying, dead-end jobs typically available to those with little education and few skills. A 55-year-old African-American man who made his way up from grams to ounce sales described his motivation succinctly: "The chance presented itself to avoid the 9 to 5" (Case # E-22).

Street sellers and even some higher-level dealers are often already participating in quasi-criminal lifestyles; drug sales are simply added to their repertoire of illicit activities. The perceived opportunity to earn enormous profits, live "the good life," and set your own work schedule are powerful enticements to sell. From the perspective of people with few life chances, dealing cocaine may be seen as their only real chance to achieve the "American Dream" (i.e., financial security and disposable income). Most of our sample were not ghetto dwellers and/or economically disadvantaged. But for those who were, there were different motivations and conscious decisions regarding beginning sales. Popular press descriptions of cocaine sellers predominantly portray just such street sellers. Although street sellers are the most visible, our data suggest that they represent what might be called the tip of the cocaine dealing iceberg.

Levels of Entry

The levels at which a potential dealer's friends/connections were selling helped determine the level at which the new dealer entered the business. If the novitiate was moving in social scenes where "big dealers" are found, then s/he is likely to begin by selling grams and parts of grams. When supplies were not fronted, new dealers' personal finances, i.e., available capital, also influenced how much they could buy at one time.

Sellers move up and down the cocaine sales ladder as well as in and out of the occupation (see Adler, 1985). Some of our sellers were content to remain part-ounce dealers selling between a quarter and a half an ounce a week. Other sellers were more ambitious and eventually sought to become bigger dealers in order to increase profits. One interviewee reported that her unusually well organized suppliers had sales quotas, price fixing, and minimum purchase expectations which pushed her toward expansion. The levels of sales and selling styles of the new dealer's suppliers, then, interacted with personal ambitions to influence eventual sales careers.

Another important aspect of beginning to sell cocaine is whether the connection is willing to "front" the cocaine (risk a consignment arrangement) rather than requiring the beginner to pay in full. Having to pay "up front" for one's inventory sometimes slowed sales by tying up capital, or even deterred some potential dealers from entering the business. Fronted cocaine allowed people with limited resources to enter the occupation. Decisions to front or not to front were based primarily on the connection's evaluation of the new seller's ability to "move" the product. This was seen as a function of the potential volume of business the beginning seller could generate among his/her networks of friends and/or customers. The connection/fronter also evaluates the trustworthiness of the potential dealer, as well as their own capability of absorbing the loss should the deal "go bad" and the frontee be unable to pay. The judgment of the fronter is crucial, for a mistake can be very costly and there is no legal recourse.

Learning to Deal

In the go-between, stash and connoisseur modes of entree, novices gradually learn the tricks of the trade by observing the selling styles of active dealers, and ultimately by doing. Weighing, packaging, and pricing the product are basic techniques. A scale, preferably a triple-beam type . . . accurate to the tenth of a gram, is a necessary tool. In the last ten years answering machines, beepers, and even cellular phones have become important tools as well. Learning how to manage customers and to establish selling routines and rules of procedure are all essential skills that successful dealers must master.

The dealers who enter sales through the apprenticeship and product line expansion modes have the advantage of their own or their partner/seller's experience. Active marijuana sellers already have a network of customers, scales, familiarity with metric measures, and, most important, a connection to help them move into a new product line. Apprentices have lived with and/or observed the selling styles of their dealer/mentors and have access to their equipment, connections and customers. Both apprentices and marijuana dealers who have expanded into cocaine also know how to "maintain a low profile" and avoid any kind of attention that might culminate in arrest. In this way they were able to reduce or manage the paranoia that often inheres in drug dealing circles.

Many sellers learn by making mistakes, often expensive mistakes. These include: using too much cocaine themselves, fronting drugs to people who do not pay for them, and adding too much "cut" (usually an inactive adulterant such as vitamin B) to their product so they develop a reputation for selling inferior cocaine and sometimes have difficulty selling the diluted product. One 32-year-old African-American male made one such error in judgment by fronting to too many people who did not "come through." It ended up costing him $15,000:

> It was because of my own recklessness that I allowed myself to get into that position. There was a period where I had a lot of weight that I just took it and just shipped it out to people I shouldn't have shipped it out

to. . . . I did this with 10 people and a lot of them were women to be exact. I had a lot of women coming over to my house and I just gave them an ounce apiece one time. . . . So when maybe 6 of those people didn't come through . . . there was a severe cramp in my cash flow. This made me go to one of the family members to get the money to re-cop. (Case # E-11)

Business Sense/People Sense

Many people have a connection, the money to make the initial buy, a reputation for being reliable, and a group of friends interested in buying drugs, but still lack the business sense to be a successful dealer. Just because a person drifts into dealing does not mean that he or she will prosper and stay in dealing. We found a variety of ways in which people initially became dealers, few of which hinged on profits. But what determined whether they continued dealing was their business sense. Thus even though a profit orientation had little to do with becoming a dealer, the ability to consistently realize profits had a major influence over who remained a dealer. In this sense, cocaine selling was like any other capitalist endeavor.

According to our respondents, one's ability to be a competent dealer depended on being able to separate business from pleasure. Success or failure at making this separation over time determined whether a profit was realized. Certain business practices were adopted by prosperous dealers to assist them in making this important distinction. For example, prepackaging both improves quality control and helps keep inventory straight; establishing rules for customers concerning when they can purchase and at what prices reduces the level of hassle; limiting the amount of fronting can reduce gross sales volume, but it also reduces financial risk and minimizes the amount of debt collection work; and limiting their own personal use keeps profits from disappearing up one's nose or in one's pipe.

Being a keen judge of character was seen as another important component of being a skilled dealer. Having the "people skills" to judge whether a person could be trusted to return with the money for fronted supplies, to convince people to pay debts that the dealer had no legal mechanisms for collecting, and to engender the trust of a connection when considerable amounts of money were at stake, are just a few of the sophisticated interpersonal skills required of a competent dealer.

Adler also discusses the importance of a "good personal reputation" among upper level dealers and smugglers:

> One of the first requirements for success, whether in drug trafficking, business enterprise broadly, or any life undertaking, is the establishment of a good personal reputation. To make it in the drug world, dealers and smugglers had to generate trust and likability. (1985:100)

Adler's general point applies to our respondents as well, although the experiences of some of our middle and lower level dealers suggested a slight amendment: A likable person with a good reputation could sell a less than high quality product, but an unlikable person, even one with a bad reputation, could still do a considerable amount of business if s/he had an excellent product. One 47-year-old white woman described her "difficult" husband/partner, "powder keg Paul":

> He would be so difficult, you couldn't believe it. Somebody [this difficult] better have a super primo product to make all this worthwhile. . . . He's the kind of guy you don't mind buying from because you know you'll get a good product, but he's the kind of guy you never want to sell to . . . he was that difficult. (Case # E-1)

High quality cocaine, in other words, is always at a premium in this subculture, so even without good people skills a dealer or connection with "good product" was tolerated.

From User to Dealer: The Transformation of Identity

In each of our respondents' deviant careers there occurred what Becker referred to as a change in self conception. Among our respondents, this took the form of a subtle shift in identity from a person who *has* a good connection for cocaine to a person who *is* a good connection for cocaine. There is a corresponding change in the meaning of, and the motives for, selling. The relationship between the seller and the customer undergoes a related transformation, from "picking up something for a friend" to conducting a commercial transaction. In essence, dealing becomes a business quite like most others, and the dealer gradually takes on the professional identity of a business person. Everett Hughes, writing on the sociology of work, urged social scientists to remember that when we look at work,

> We need to rid ourselves of any concepts which keep us from seeing that the essential problems of men at work are the same whether they do their work in the laboratories of some famous institution or in the messiest vat of a pickle factory. (1951:313)

When they had fully entered the dealer role, our respondents came to see selling cocaine as a job—work, just like other kinds of work save for its illegality. For most, selling cocaine did not mean throwing out conventional values and norms. In fact, many of our respondents actively maintained their conventional identities (see Broadhead, 1983). Such identities included those of parents, legally employed workers, neighbors, church-goers and softball players, to list just a few. Dealer identities tended not to replace former, "legitimate" identities but were added to a person's repertoire of more conventional identities.

Like everyone else in modern life, sellers emphasized one or another dimension of their identities as appropriate to the situation. In his study of heroin addicts Biernacki notes that, "The arrangement of identities must continuously be managed in such a way as to stress some identities at certain points in particular social worlds and situations, and at the same time to de-emphasize others" (1986:23). Our sellers, too, had to become adept at articulating the proper identity at the proper time. By day, one woman dealer was a concerned mother at her daughter's kindergarten field trip, and that same evening she was an astute judge of cocaine quality when picking up an ounce from her connection. At least for our interviewees, selling cocaine rarely entailed entirely terminating other social roles and obligations.

Yet, at some point in all of our sellers' careers, they found themselves transformed from someone who has a good connection to someone who is a good connection, and they gradually came to accept the identity of dealer as a part of their selves. Customers began to treat them like a salesperson, expecting them to be available to take calls and do business and even for services such as special off-hour pick-ups and deliveries or reduced rates for volume purchases. When dealers found themselves faced with such demands, they typically began to feel *entitled* to receive profits from selling. They came to be seen as dealers by others, and in part for this reason, came to see themselves as dealers. As Becker's (1963) model suggests, selling *behavior* usually preceded not only motivation but also changes in attitude and identity. As one 38-year-old white woman put it,

> I took over the business and paid all my husband's debts and started to make some money. One day I realized I was a coke dealer. . . . It was scary, but the money was good. (Case # E-75)

Acceptance of the dealer identity brings with it some expectations and values shared by dealers and customers alike. Customers have the expectation that the dealer will have a consistent supply of cocaine for sale. Customers also expect that the dealer will report in a fairly accurate manner the quality of his/her present batch of drugs within the confines of the *caveat emptor* philosophy that informs virtually all commercial activities in market societies. Buyers do not expect sellers to denigrate their product, but they do not expect the dealer to claim that their product is "excellent" if it is merely "good." Customers assume the dealer will make a profit, but dealers should not be "too greedy." A greedy dealer is one who makes what is estimated by the buyer to be excessive profits. Such estimations of excessiveness vary widely among customers and between sellers and buyers. But the fact that virtually all respondents spoke of some unwritten code of fairness suggests that there is, in E. P. Thompson's (1971) phrase, a "moral economy" of drug dealing that constrains the drive for profit maximization even within an illicit market.[6]

For their part, dealers expect that customers will act in a fashion that will minimize their chances of being arrested by being circumspect about revealing their dealer status. One simply did not, for example, bring to a dealer's house friends whom the dealer had not met. Dealers want customers to appreciate the risks undertaken to provide them with cocaine. And dealers come to feel that such risks deserve profits. After all, the seller is the one who takes the greatest risks; s/he could conceivably receive a stiff jail sentence for a sales conviction. While drifting into dealing and selling mostly to friends and acquaintances mitigated the risks of arrest and reduced their paranoia, such risks remained omnipresent.

In fact, the growing realization of such risks—and the rationalization it provided for dealing on a for-profit basis—was an integral part of becoming a cocaine seller. As our 38-year-old white woman dealer put it, "When it's all said and done, I'm the one behind bars, and I had better have made some money while I was selling or why in the hell take the risk?" (Case # E-75)

Acknowledgment

The research reported herein was funded by a grant from the National Institute of Justice (#7-0363-9-CA-IJ), Bernard A. Gropper, Ph.D., Program Manager, Drugs, Alcohol and Crime Programs, Center for Crime Control Research. The views expressed herein are those of the authors alone. The authors are grateful to the anonymous reviewers of *Qualitative Sociology* for helpful comments.

Address correspondence to Sheigla Murphy, Institute for Scientific Analysis, 2235 Lombard Street, San Francisco, CA, 94123.

Notes

1. Adler also refers briefly to Matza's formulations within her discussion of becoming a dealer (pp. 127–128, 1985).

2. It must be noted at the outset that the predominately white, working and middle-class cocaine sellers we interviewed are very likely to differ from inner-city crack dealers depicted in the media. While there is now good reason to believe that both the profits and the violence reported to be endemic in the crack trade have been exaggerated (e.g., Reuter, 1990, and Goldstein et al., 1989, respectively), our data are drawn from a different population, selling a different form of the drug, who were typically drawn to selling for different reasons. Thus the exigencies they faced and their responses to them are also likely to differ from those of inner-city crack sellers.

3. Rock party houses are distinct from "rock houses" or "crack houses." In the former, sellers invite only selected customers to their homes to smoke rock and "party." Unlike crack houses, where crack is sold to all comers, outsiders are never invited to rock party houses, and the arrangement is social and informal. Proprietors of both types, however, charge participants for the cocaine.

4. Car meets are transactions that take place in cars. Arrangements are made over the telephone in advance and both buyer and seller arrange to meet at parking lots, usually at busy shopping centers, and exchange drugs and money. Each arrives in his or her own car and leaves separately.

5. These movements back and forth among different levels of involvement in dealing were different from the "shifts and oscillations" found among the cocaine dealers studied by Adler (1985:133–141). She studied a circle of high-level dealers over an extended period of field work and found that the stresses and strains of dealing at the top of the pyramid often led her participants to attempt to get out of the business. While many of our interviewees felt similar

pressures later in their careers and subsequently quit, our focus here is on becoming a cocaine seller.

6. In addition to lore about "righteous" and "rip off" dealers, there were present other norms that suggested the existence of such an unwritten code or moral economy, e.g., refusing to sell to children or to adults who "couldn't handle it" (i.e., had physical, familial, or work-related problems because of cocaine use).

References

Adler, P. (1985). *Wheeling and Dealing: An Ethnography of an Upper-Level Drug Dealing Community.* New York: Columbia University Press.

Becker, H. S. (1953). "Becoming a marijuana user." *American Journal of Sociology* 59:235–242.

Becker, H. S. (1963). *Outsiders.* New York: Free Press.

Becker, H. S. (1986). *Pathways from Heroin Addiction.* Philadelphia: Temple University Press.

Biernacki, P., and Waldorf, D. (1981). "Snowball sampling: problems and techniques of chain referral sampling." *Sociological Methods and Research* 10:141–163.

Broadhead, R. (1983). *The Private Lives and Professional Identity of Medical Students.* New Brunswick, NJ: Transaction Books.

Feldman, H. W. (1968). "Ideological supports to becoming and remaining a heroin addict." *Journal of Health and Social Behavior* 9:131–139.

Fields, A. (1985). "Weedslingers: a study of young black marijuana dealers." *Urban Life* 13:247–270.

Goldstein, P., Brownstein, H., Ryan, P., and Belucci, P. (1989). "Crack and homicide in New York City, 1988." *Contemporary Drug Problems* 16:651–687.

Grinspoon, L., and Bakalar, J. (1976). *Cocaine: A Drug and Its Social Evolution.* New York: Basic Books.

Hughes, E. (1951). "Work and the self." In John Rohrer and Muzafer Sherif (eds.), *Social Work at the Crossroads.* New York: Harper and Brothers, 313–323.

Langer, J. (1977). "Drug entrepreneurs and dealing culture." *Social Problems* 24:377–386.

Lindesmith, A. (1947). *Addiction and Opiates.* Chicago: Aldine Press.

Macdonald, P., Waldorf, D., Reinarman, C., and Murphy, S. (1988). "Heavy cocaine use and sexual behavior." *Journal of Drug Issues* 18:437–455.

Matza, D. (1964). *Delinquency and Drift.* New York: Wiley.

Matza, D. (1969). *Becoming Deviant.* Englewood Cliffs, NJ: Prentice Hall.

Morales, E. (1986a). "Coca culture: the white gold of Peru." *Graduate School Magazine of City University of New York* 1:4–11.

Morales, E. (1986b). "Coca and cocaine economy and social change in the Andes in Peru." *Economic Development and Social Change* 35:143–161.

Morales, E. (1988). *Cocaine: The White Gold Rush in Peru.* Tucson, AZ: University of Arizona Press.

Murphy, S., Reinarman, C., and Waldorf, D. (1989). "An eleven year follow-up of a network of cocaine users." *British Journal of the Addictions* 84:427–436.

Plasket, B., and Quillen, E. (1985). *The White Stuff.* New York: Dell Publishing Company.

Preble, E., and Casey, J. H., Jr. (1969). "Taking care of business: the heroin user's life on the streets." *The International Journal of the Addictions* 4:1–24.

Reinarman, C., Waldorf, D., and Murphy, S. (1988). "Scapegoating and social control in the construction of a public problem: empirical and critical findings on cocaine and work." *Research in Law, Deviance and Social Control* 9:37–62.

Reuter, P. (1990). *Money from Crime: The Economics of Drug Dealing.* Santa Monica, CA: Rand Corporation.

Rosenbaum, M. (1981). *Women on Heroin.* New Brunswick, NJ: Rutgers University Press.

Sanabria, H. (1988). *Coca, Migration and Socio-Economic Change in a Bolivian Highland Peasant Community.* Ph.D. thesis, University of Wisconsin.

Sanchez, J., and Johnson, B. (1987). "Women and the drug crime connection: crime rates among drug abusing women at Riker's Island." *Journal of Psychoactive Drugs* 19:205–215.

Sykes, G., and Matza, D. (1957). "Techniques of neutralization." *American Sociological Review* 22:664–670.

Thompson, E. P. (1971). "The moral economy of the English crowd in the eighteenth century." *Past and Present* 50:76–136.

Waldorf, D., Reinarman, C., Murphy, S., and Joyce, B. (1977). *Doing Coke: An Ethnography of Cocaine Snorters and Sellers.* Washington, DC: Drug Abuse Council.

Waldorf, D., Reinarman, C., and Murphy, S. (1991). *Cocaine Changes.* Philadelphia: Temple University Press.

Watters, J. K., and Biernacki, P. (1989). "Targeted sampling: options for the study of hidden populations." *Social Problems* 36:416–430.

Williams, T. (1989). *The Cocaine Kids.* New York: Addison-Wesley.

38 Self-Control, Peer Relations, and Delinquency

Constance L. Chapple

Introduction

The role of peers in the etiology of delinquency has been a well-researched topic, but less is known about the process by which adolescents select into deviant peer groups. Gottfredson and Hirschi (1990) maintain that both delinquency and association with deviant peers are tied to an absence of self-control, arguing that "people with low self-control tend to have unstable marriages, friendships and job profiles" (1990, p. 90) and that ". . . adventuresome and reckless children who have difficulty making and keeping friends tend to end up in the company of one another, creating groups made up of individuals who tend to lack self-control" (1990, p. 158). Empirical research has confirmed that low self-control is associated with poorer friendship and personal bonds in adults (Evans, Cullen, Burton, Dunaway, & Benson, 1997), and low self-control is a predictor of association with deviant peers in young adulthood (Baron, 2003; Wright, Caspi, Moffitt, & Silva, 1999). Equally important questions remain regarding how self-control affects early adolescent friendships, peer selection, and adolescent delinquency.

Developmental researchers, similar to Gottfredson and Hirschi (1990, p. 158), suggest that children with low self-control are more likely to be rejected by their peers (Olson, 1989; Olson & Hoza, 1993) and that rejected children are also more likely to be delinquent (Conduct Problems Prevention Research Group, 1992; DeMuth, 2004; Ferguson & Horwood, 1999; Giordano, 1995). Accordingly, children with low self-control are likely to be rejected by their peers and are more likely to select into similar, delinquent peer groups, yet these propositions have not been tested in adolescence. Late childhood and early adolescence are critical times of maturation, identity formation, and for some youths, involvement in delinquency. It is during this time that peer selection plays a particularly important role in the etiology of delinquency.

588

The effect of peers on delinquency, although a key component of social control theory, has not been emphasized in self-control theory. Such a position is understandable, given Gottfredson and Hirschi's focus on self-control as a stable, individual-level characteristic; peers typically exert more transitory influences according to their general theory (1990, p. 159). While not a primary focus of the general theory of crime, the relationship between self-control, peer relations, and delinquency clearly falls within the realm of the authors' suggestions. This research adds to a growing list of research on the peers-delinquency relationship beyond deviant norm acquisition, imitation and reinforcement (Haynie, 2001; Osgood, Wilson, Bachman, O'Malley, & Johnston, 1996; Warr, 2002). To expand the research on self-control, peer relations, and delinquency, I ask three questions: Does self-control predict peer rejection? Do people lacking in self-control select into deviant peer groups? As self-control is hypothesized to affect peer relations and delinquency, do peer relations mediate the effect of self-control on delinquency?

Literature Review

There has been a great deal of research on the etiological impact of peers on delinquency (Akers, 1998; Cloward & Ohlin, 1960; Matsueda & Anderson, 1998; Thornberry, Lizotte, Krohn, Farnworth, & Jang, 1994; Warr, 2002), yet there is less research on selection into delinquent peer groups and the relationship between self-control and peer rejection in adolescence. According to one criminological theory, delinquency, the quality of peer relations and selection into deviant peer groups are all caused by an absence of self-control (Gottfredson & Hirschi, 1990, p.158). In 1990, Gottfredson and Hirschi introduced their general theory of crime, in which they argued that most crime and delinquency are due to a single underlying characteristic, low self-control. According to their theory, we are deterred from acts of crime and deviance by our internal constraint of self-control, which they define as "the differential tendency of people to avoid criminal acts whatever the circumstances in which they find themselves" (1990, p. 87).

Gottfredson and Hirschi suggest that people lacking self-control are impulsive, shortsighted, lacking in diligence and tenacity, and unconcerned with the pain and suffering they create for others (1990, p. 90). The family is primarily responsible for instilling, or failing to instill, self-control in its members (1990, p. 95). In the absence of pro-social teaching from parents, the child is unlikely to develop self-control and will involve themself in a variety of criminal and "analogous" acts such as smoking, drinking, and risky sexual behavior (1990, p. 90). Some argue that the concept of self-control is not new (Jensen, 1973) and is akin to "inner containment" (Jensen, 1973) or "reflected appraisals" (Matsueada, 1992), concepts with well-established ties to peer relations and delinquency (Akers, 1998). The influence of Gottfredson and

Hirschi's measures of self-control on peer relations and adolescent delinquency has not been well documented, however.

Research in the area of self-control, peer relations and delinquency has utilized either adult samples or cross-sectional data, making it difficult to disentangle the causal relationships between self-control, peer relations, and adolescent delinquency. Baron (2003) found that low self-control was associated with having deviant peers for young adults, and Gibson and Wright (2001) found that occupational delinquency was most likely among young adults with low self-control who also associated with deviant peers. Both studies, however utilized cross-sectional data from young adults, thus making casual inferences about adolescent relations difficult to determine. Wright et al. (1999) investigated the relationship between low self-control and association with deviant peers longitudinally, finding that childhood low self-control predicted association with deviant peers in young adults. What is unknown is the extent to which low self-control affects peer relations and peer selection in early adolescence. Prior research has established a relationship between low self-control and association with deviant peers, but Gottfredson and Hirschi (1990) also suggest that self-control has profound effects on the nature and quality of personal relationships.

According to Gottfredson and Hirschi, the characteristics of low self-control "impede educational and occupational achievement, destroy interpersonal relations and undermine physical and economic well-being" (1990, p. 96). Although researchers have found that adults lacking in self-control have unstable personal relationships and attenuated personal bonds (Evans et al., 1997), the effect of self-control on the quality of adolescent peer relations has not been examined. Gottfredson and Hirschi assert that, ". . . self-control is a major factor in determining membership in adolescent peer groups and in determining the quality of relations among members of such groups" (1990, p. 157) and that ". . . adventuresome and reckless children who have difficulty making and keeping friends tend to end up in the company of one another, creating groups made up of individuals who tend to lack self-control" (1990, p. 158). Recent research on the delinquency of "loners" (DeMuth, 2004) has found that children with few friends were more likely to associate with delinquent peers than children with many friends. Self-control and its effect on the quality of peer relationships in adolescence may provide one important insight into how and why juveniles select into deviant peer groups.

It is critical to examine the relationship between self-control, peer relations, and delinquency during early adolescence, when the peer effect on delinquency is particularly strong (Giordano, 1995; Sampson & Laub, 1993; Warr, 2002, p. 23). While embedded in a deviant peer network (Haynie, 2001), youths' delinquency increases due to increased criminal opportunities (Osgood et al., 1996), because delinquency becomes easier or more attractive in a group (McCarthy, Hagan, & Cohen, 1998; Reiss & Farrington, 1991; Sarnecki, 2001) or because the peer group models, imitates, or reinforces deviant behavior (Akers, 1998). Research indicates that peers' deviant behavior strongly influences others' deviant behavior in a reflexive process (Matsueda & Anderson, 1998) and that the effect of deviant behavior on others' delinquency is stronger than the effect of deviant values on delinquency (Thornberry et al., 1994; Warr & Stafford, 1991). Regardless of what occurs while in the deviant peer group, the equally important question remains of how individuals enter deviant peer groups.

When examining the effect of peer relations on delinquency, the question of self-selection vs. acquisition arises. Some researchers suggest that "birds of a feather flock together" (Glueck & Glueck, 1950; Hirschi, 1969), emphasizing the importance of self-selection on the peers-delinquency relationship. In accordance with this "flocking" hypothesis, Kandel's research suggests that prior delinquent behavior influences selection into delinquent peer groups (Kandel, 1978). Kandel's work is echoed in Matsueda and Anderson's findings that the relationship between delinquent peer selection and delinquency is reflexive, and that the effect of delinquency on the selection of delinquent peers is stronger than the effect of delinquent peers on delinquency (1998, p. 299). The finding that youths select into delinquent peer groups because of similar delinquent behavior is particularly in keeping with the idea that most delinquent peer groups are transitory (Esbensen & Huizinga, 1993; Sarnecki, 2001; Warr, 1996) and have higher conflict levels than less delinquent peer groups (Giordano, Cernkovich, & Pugh, 1986). According to Gottfredson and Hirschi, delinquency, homophily of behavior, and self-selection into deviant peer groups are due to one characteristic: low self-control.

Developmental research suggests that anti-social and impulsive behavior impacts peer rejection and peer selection in childhood (Bolger & Patterson, 2001; Garnier & Stein, 2002; Olson, 1989; Olson & Hoza, 1993). Children who exhibited low self-control or impulsivity were more likely to be rejected by their peers in late childhood and early adolescence (Olson, 1989; Olson & Hoza, 1993). Peer rejection was also associated with delinquency and general antisocial behavior (DeMuth, 2004; Dodge et al., 2003; Fergusson & Horwood, 1999; Giordano, 1995; Olson & Hoza, 1993), substance use (Windle, 1994), and violence (Miller-Johnson, Coie, Maumery-Gremaud, Lochman, & Terry, 1999). However, it is unclear from prior research whether impulsive children were rejected by conventional or deviant peers and what is the casual sequencing between peer rejection and association with deviant peers. It does not appear from the literature that a simple linear process can be determined in which peer rejection leads to shunning by conventional peers and association with deviant peers by default. It is equally likely that youths with low self-control are rejected by the deviant peers with whom they are associating, which is exactly what Gottfredson and Hirschi would predict as they describe deviant and unstable personal relations between people with low self-control.

The relationship between self-control, peer rejection, association with deviant peers, and delinquency in adolescence appears clear from Gottfredson and Hirschi's theoretical predictions. First, if children with low self-control are self-interested and impulsive, and have difficulty maintaining friendships as Gottfredson and Hirschi suggest, they are more likely to be rejected by their peers (either conventional or delinquent). Second, whether rejected or not, children with low self-control are suggested to select into similar, delinquent peer groups. The effect of peers on delinquency is particularly pronounced in adolescence, but the effect of self-control on peer relations emerges in childhood. Therefore, it is critical to analyze the relationship between self-control, peer relations and delinquency longitudinally during late childhood and adolescence. According to my suggestions, self-control influences delinquency directly through generalized risk-taking, and indirectly, through its effects on peer relations. With this model in mind, I describe the data and analyses used in the study.

Methods

Sample

Data for this study were taken from the Children of the National Longitudinal Survey of Youth (NLSY-Child and Young Adult data). The original National Longitudinal Survey of Youth (NLSY79) is a nationally representative longitudinal sample of youths aged 14–21 in 1979. The NLSY79 contains "extensive information about the employment, education, training, and family experiences of the respondents" (Center for Human Resource Research, 2000, p. 1). Beginning in 1982, the female respondents of the NLSY79 were surveyed about "pregnancy, postnatal fertility, and child care experiences" (Center for Human Resource Research, 2000, p. 1). Since 1986, separate assessments of the children born to the women of the NLSY79 have been conducted. In 1994, children aged 15 and older were no longer assessed with their mothers, but instead completed personal interviews that focused on a variety of attitudes and behaviors[1].

The NLSY79-Child and Young Adult sample "approximately represent[s] a cross-section of children born to a nationally representative sample of women who were between the ages of 31 and 38 on January 1, 1998" (Center for Human Resource Research, 2000, p. 3).[2] For the analyses, I used mother and child assessments taken from three waves of data when the youths were aged 10–11 in 1994, 12–13 in 1996, and 14–15 in 1998.[3] Self-control was measured in 1994, while age, race, sex, and family's poverty status were measured in 1998. The mediator variables, peer rejection, and association with deviant peers were measured in 1996, and the delinquency was measured in 1998. The original sample contains 669 respondents, but 56 respondents were eliminated from the analysis because of missing data on the delinquency variables. Because siblings are included in the original sample, I randomly selected one respondent out of each sibling pair for inclusion in the sample, bringing the final sample size to 589 respondents.

Table 1 Descriptive information for the sample (N = 589)

	M	SD
Race (0 = White; 1 = non-White)	.582	.493
Sex (0 = male; 1 = female)	.538	.499
Age in 1998 (14–15)	14.7	.472
Family's poverty status 1998 (0–2)	.128	.303
Self-Control (10–27)	22.5	3.40
Peer rejection (2–6)	2.42	.749
Association with deviant peers (1–3)	1.26	.463
Delinquency (0–10)	1.02	1.71

Missing data problems often plague longitudinal research and can cause estimation problems if those with missing data are systematically different from respondents with complete data (Brame & Paternoster, 2003; Brame & Piquero, 2003). According to a means test of missing data on the variables included in my models, those who are missing data on any item were more likely to be non-white; no other significant differences were found. The only variables with missing data were peer rejection, association with deviant peers, self-control, and family poverty status.[4] For the imputation of missing data, mean allocation methods were used for the self-control scale (missing data for one item in the scale was estimated with the scale average of the remaining eight items), and for the remaining variables with missing data (peer rejection, association with deviant peers and family poverty status), missing data were imputed using full information maximum likelihood estimation in AMOS (Arbuckle & Wothke, 1999). I used structural equation models analyzed in AMOS (Arbuckle & Wothke, 1999) to investigate the simultaneous direct and indirect effects of self-control, peer rejection, and association with deviant peers on delinquency. Descriptive information for the sample is presented in Table 1.

Measures

Independent variables

In the analyses, I assessed the effect of self-control on peer relations and delinquency net of sex, age, race, and poverty status. Each of these variables has been shown in past research to be associated with self-control, peer rejection, association with deviant peers, or delinquency. The measures of self-control were taken from the 1994 NLSY-Child assessment (when the children were aged 10 or 11). The mothers of the children in the sample assessed their children on a series of measures of problem behavior and/or self-control. This is the third use of parental reports of children's self-control in the literature testing the general theory of crime using the NLSY79 and NLSY-Child data (see also Hope & Chapple, 2005; Turner & Piquero, 2002).[5] Parents' reports of children's self-control should be conservative estimates of children's actual low self-control; parents may underestimate the extent to which their children are "problematic" or may not be aware of most or all of their children's problem behavior.[6] The general "Behavioral Problems Index" (BPI) from which I took the self-control items has been validated and used extensively in the developmental literature (Center for Human Resource Research, 2000). Descriptions of the items comprising the self-control scale are presented in the Appendix.

The 11 items from the BPI that measured self-control were entered into a principle components factor analysis with varimax rotation. One factor emerged. The nine items that had factor loading scores higher than .50 (Tabachnick & Fidell, 1997, p. 677) comprised the self-control scale and measured impulsivity, insensitivity to others, and incorrigibility. Parents were asked "How true the following are of your child?" and the items were scored so that 1 = often true, 2 = sometimes true, and 3 = not true. The additive self-control scale was coded so that high values indicated high self-control. The alpha reliability of this scale was .82. The mean for self-control was 22.5, with a range of 10–27, indicating that the sample had relatively high levels of self-control.

In terms of the demographic profile of the sample, 58 percent of the sample is non-white, and 54 percent of the sample is female. Race is coded so that 0 = white and 1 = non-white, and sex is coded so that 0 = male and 1 = female. The respondents were 14–15 years old in 1998. Poverty status is a maternal self-report of the family's poverty status in 1998. Responses range from 0 (never lived in poverty), to 1 (lived in poverty but not in 1998) to 2 (lived in poverty in 1998). The mean for poverty status was .128, indicating that few respondents had lived in poverty in 1998.

Dependant variables

Because of the conventions of structural equation modeling analysis in AMOS, mediating variables (peer rejection and association with deviant peers) as well as dependent variables (delinquency) are considered endogenous variables. The proposed mediator variables, peer rejection and association with deviant peers, were measured in 1996 when the youths were 12–13 years old, and the outcome variable, delinquency, was measured in 1998 when the youths were aged 14–15.

Factor analysis with varimax rotation was used to construct the peer rejection variable and the delinquency scale. All variables with factor-loading scores higher than .50 were retained for reliability analysis. Peer rejection was measured by a two-item composite variable in which the mothers of the respondents were asked whether their child, "has trouble getting along with other children" and "is not liked by other children." Responses were assessed on a 3-point scale in which 1 = often true, 2 = sometimes true, and 3 = not true. The variables were reverse-coded so that high scores indicated greater peer rejection. Peer rejections has an alpha of .68, a range of 2–6, and a mean of 2.42, suggesting that few youths experienced significant peer rejection. Approximately 74 percent of youths in the sample experienced no peer rejection, while approximately 13 percent experienced moderate to high levels (scores of four or higher). Similar measures of peer rejection using maternal reports have appeared in other research (Fergusson & Horwood, 1999).

Association with deviant peers was measured by one item in which the mothers were asked how true it was that "[their child] hangs around with kids who get into trouble." Responses were reverse-coded so that 1 = not true, 2 = sometimes true, and 3 = often true. High values indicate a greater association with deviant peers. Association with deviant peers has a mean of 1.26, with 76.1 percent of parents indicating that this is "not true" of their child, 21.6 percent indicating that this is "sometimes true" of their child, and 2.3 percent indicating that this is "often true" of their child. The bivariate correlation between peer rejection and deviant peers is .30 (p < .001), suggesting that children whose mothers feel are rejected by their peers are more likely to hang around with kids who get into trouble.

Thirteen items measuring violence and property crime were entered into a principle-components factor analysis with varimax rotation. Ten items had factor-loading scores above .50 and loaded on one factor. The 10-item delinquency scale comprised the following items:

> How often in the last year have you: stolen from a store, damaged others' property, stolen something less than $50, stolen something greater than $50, used force to get something you wanted, hit or threatened to hit someone, attacked to seriously hurt someone, broken into a building, held or sold stolen goods and hurt someone bad enough to need a doctor?

Responses were coded so that 0 = no and 1 = yes, and added together to create a summary delinquency scale. The reliability of the delinquency scale was .80. Scores ranged from 0 to 10 and had a mean of 1.02, indicating little involvement in delinquency for the majority of the sample. Perhaps not surprising given the youthfulness of the sample, approximately 59 percent had never engaged in any of the delinquent acts, while 15 percent had engaged in three or more delinquent acts. All of the endogenous variable were positively skewed and were logged before entering them into the analysis (Tabachnick & Fidell, 1997, p.85).

Results

Because I am interested in whether self-control predicts peer rejection and whether self-control predicts association with deviant peers, I created two models. I also assessed whether peer relations mediate the effect of self-control on delinquency in both models. I used multiple-least squares analysis in AMOS (Arbuckle & Wothke, 1999) to analyze the effects of self-control

Figure 1 Self-control, peer relations, and delinquency.

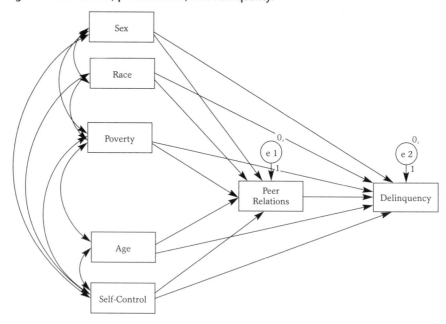

on delinquency via peer rejection and association with deviant peers. The same initial theoretical model (see Figure 1) was specified for each analysis. The model was adjusted so that only the significant paths and correlations were retained. The results of the analyses are listed in Figures 2 and 3 and are summarized in Table 2.

I present the results of the AMOS analysis of self-control on peer rejection and delinquency in Figure 2. I also summarize all of the significant ($p < .05$ or higher) paths for both models in Table 2. The model specified was a good fit to the data ($p = .395$; RMSEA = .000; $\chi^2 / df = .928$; NFI = 998).[7] According to the model presented in Figure 2, peer rejection was significantly predicted by self-control ($ß = -.33$) indicating that, as in past research, children with low self-control at age 10–11 were more likely to be rejected by their peers in early adolescence. Self-control alone explained approximately 11 percent of the "variance" in peer rejection, as indicated by the squared multiple correlation.

Delinquency was significantly predicted by peer rejection ($ß = .14$), moderately predicted by low self-control ($ß = -.09$, $p = .06$), and significantly associated with living in poverty ($ß = .09$). Although the direct effect of self-control on delinquency was significant at only the $p < .10$ level, removal of this path resulted in a lower p-value and a higher AIC, both indicators of a worse-fitting model. In an analysis not presented here, the direct effect of self-control on delinquency without the peer variables included in the model was significant at the $p < .01$ level ($ß = -.13$). Because self-control was not a significant predictor of delinquency at the

Figure 2   Self-control, peer rejection, and delinquency. *p* = .395; RMSEA = .000; χ^2 = 1.857; χ^2 / *df* = .928; NFI = .998. †Self-control is significant at the *p* = .68 level.

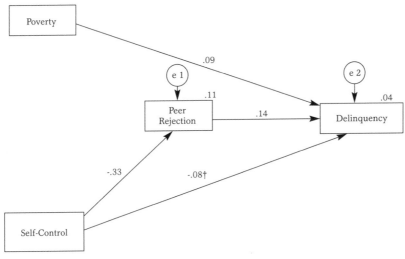

p < .05 level with peer rejection in the model, peer rejection mediates the effect of self-control on delinquency (Baron & Kenny, 1986).

I present the results of the AMOS analysis of the effects of self-control on association with deviant peers and delinquency in Figure 3. The model fits the data well (*p* = .162; χ^2 / *df* = 1.82; RMSEA = .037; NFI = .998).

Figure 3   Self-control, peer deviance, and delinquency. *p* = .162; RMSEA = .037; χ^2 = 3.636; χ^2 / *df* = 1.818; NFI = .998. †Poverty status is significant at the *p* = .60 level.

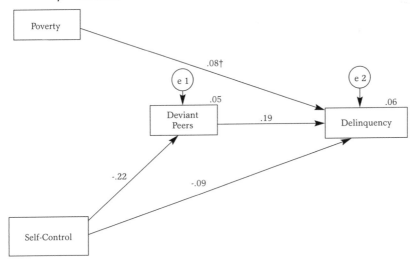

Table 2   Standardized regression coefficients of significant paths for the delinquency models

	Peer rejection	Deviant peers	Delinquency (peer rejection)	Delinquency (deviant peers)
Sex	—	—	—	—
Poverty status in 1998	—	—	.09*	.08†
Race	—	—	—	—
Age	—	—	—	—
Peer rejection	—	—	.14**	—
Association with deviant peers	—	—	—	.19***
Self-control	-.33***	-.22***	-.08†	-.09*
Squared multiple correlation	.11	.05	.04	.06

***$p < .001$; **$p < .01$; *$p < .05$; †$p < .10$.

According to this model, association with deviant peers was predicted by self-control ($ß = -.22$), suggesting that those youth with less self-control at age 10–11 were more likely to associate with deviant peers at age 12–13. The squared multiple correlation for association with deviant peers was only .05, suggesting that self-control explained only 5 percent of the "variance" in association with deviant peers. Delinquency, in turn, was significantly predicted by both low self-control ($ß = -.09$) and association with deviant peers ($ß = .19$). As in the previous model for peer rejection, although poverty status was not significant at the $p < .05$ level ($ß = .08; p = .07$), removal of this direct path reduced the fit of the model. Although self-control was a significant predictor of association with deviant peers, the direct effect of self-control on delinquency declines in significance from $p < .01$ to $p < .05$. Therefore, the relationship between self-control and delinquency in this model is partially mediated by association with deviant peers (Barton & Kenny, 1986).

According to the results presented in Figures 2 and 3, self-control was a significant predictor of both peer rejection and association with deviant peers, and the effect of self-control on delinquency was mediated by peer rejection and partially mediated by association with deviant peers. Association with deviant peers and peer rejection were also significantly associated with delinquency net of self-control.

Conclusion and Discussion

The general theory of crime has received a tremendous amount of attention in the last 14 years. Researchers have assessed the stability of self-control, the versatility of low self-control offenders, the scope of the theory, and the dimensionality of self-control, but less attention has been paid to how self-control affects interpersonal relationships in adolescence. Gottfredson and Hirschi (1990) clearly suggest that children with low self-control encounter and create serious difficulties in making and maintaining friendships in childhood and adolescence. As such, youths exhibiting low self-control are likely to find themselves in the company of other "birds" with low self-control. My tests of these ideas centered around three research questions: Does self-control predict peer rejection and association with deviant peers, and do peer relations mediate the effect of self-control on delinquency?

The answer to all of the questions is "yes". Self-control was a strong predictor of peer rejection in early adolescence. It alone accounted for 11 percent of the variance in peer rejection. Self-control was also a significant predictor of association with deviant peers, suggesting that youths with low self-control select into delinquent peer groups. Association with deviant peers, in turn, partially mediated part of the effect of self-control on delinquency, although self-control remained a significant predictor of delinquency net of deviant peers. However, peer rejection completely mediated the effect of self-control on delinquency, a finding that would surprise the authors of the general theory. Gottfredson and Hirschi would suggest quite the opposite, that the effect of peers on delinquency would be mediated by self-control.

My results suggest that peer relations exert a significant effect on delinquency, net of self-control, a finding that is contrary to the predictions of Gottfredson and Hirschi. According to the findings presented earlier, low self-control causes peer rejection, association with deviant peers and delinquency. It has been suggested by other research that peer rejection is tied to association with deviant peers (DeMuth, 2004) and is a predictor of delinquency (Dodge et al., 2003; Fergusson & Horwood, 1999; Giordano, 1995; Olson & Hoza, 1993). It is also possible that low self-control causes delinquency, which causes peer rejection and association with deviant peers. However, the finding that peer rejection mediates the effect of self-control both confirms Gottfredson and Hirschi's suggestion that low self-control causes disrupted personal relationships and also is in contrary to their suggestion that self-control should remain a significant predictor of delinquency. I believe that the strong effect of peer rejection on delinquency is testament to the importance of peer relations early in adolescence, and perhaps with replication with older youth, self-control would remain a significant predictor as the peer effect wanes.

These data indicate that both peer rejection and association with deviant peers are predicted by low self-control. I do not know from these data whether the rejecting peers are deviant or conventional peers. It seems likely, given the positive correlation between peer rejection and association with deviant peers in the same wave of data, that youths with low self-control are likely to be rejected by their *deviant* peers. As much as the peer effect on delinquency is normally considered a process of social learning, this finding would question this proposition. Social learning theory would predict that delinquent youth embrace other delinquents rather than rejecting each other. Peer rejection by deviant peers may instead point to the possibility that delinquent peer groups are conflictive (Cernkovich et al., 1987) or are acutely afraid of ridicule (Warr, 2002, p. 47), two processes that may undermine the strength of deviant peer groups. However, until a more longitudinal analysis is conducted to disentangle the time at which youths first engage in delinquency, first associate with delinquent peers, and first are rejected by their peers, I can only assume that at least some of the youths who were rejected were rejected by deviant peers, while they continue to hang out with these deviant peers. At this point, a resolution of this dilemma is outside the scope of these analyses and would require reciprocal effects models and additional waves of data to analyze. It would also require information on the deviance of rejecting peers, which is not available in this data. However, a proper assessment of the sequencing of these events remains critical to the etiology of delinquency and lies at the heart of debates between learning and control theories.

Researchers interested in situational and opportunity explanations of crime may also be interested in the findings presented here. Debate continues regarding the relationship between self-control, criminal opportunity and crime (Grasmick, Tittle, Bursick, & Arneklev, 1993; LaGrange & Silverman, 1999; Longshore, 1998; Longshore & Turner, 1998) This research suggests that it is equally important to examine the effect of self-control on peer relations as an additional situational influence on delinquency. The delinquent peer group may provide increased opportunities for crime or exert situational pushes towards delinquency net of the self-control of the members comprising these groups. Although Gottfredson and Hirschi suggest that peers exert transitory influences on delinquency net of self-control (1990, p. 159), the findings presented earlier challenge this suggestion. According to the results presented earlier, peer rejection and association with deviant peers at age 12–13 have significant influences on delinquency at age 14–15, even when we account for self-control.

This research has several strengths, as well as several limitations. The quality of the longitudinal data, which are drawn from a sample of children across the country with an over-sample of children born to young mothers, is a major strength. Longitudinal data allow for a causal analysis of self-control, peer relations, and delinquency, which is a particular strength of this research. Many previous tests of the general theory of crime have utilized cross-sectional data or have tested these propositions only in adulthood. Because my findings indicate that childhood self-control significantly predicts peer rejection and association with deviant peers in early adolescence, this research provides one important insight into the mechanisms underlying selection into deviant peer groups. Finally, although researchers have found that low self-control is tied to poor personal realtionships in adulthood, I tested this proposition among adolescents, a group whose delinquent activity is well known and whose peer relations are particularly important.

This research also has three notable limitations regarding the measurement of self-control, peer rejection, and association with deviant peers. I used mother reports of children's self-control, peer rejection, and a single-item report of adolescent's association with deviant peers. These were the only reliable measures available in the data set, but they were, at best, conservative estimates of peer rejection, association with deviant peers, and low self-control. Mothers are unlikely to know the extent of their children's risk-taking and impulsive behavior, the extent to which their child is rejected by other children, and how often they associate with deviant peers. The underestimation of low self-control, peer rejection, and association with deviant peers is primarily a problem of effect size which is likely to attenuate the associations between self-control, peer rejection, deviant peers, and delinquency. However, a different validity problem is also possible as the measures of self-control, peer rejection and assocation with deviant peers, are mothers' interpretations of their children's behavior. It is possible that mothers are inaccurate reporters or, worse, unfairly labeling their children's behavior as problematic or their friendships as troubled. Although other research indicates that mothers are accurate reporters of adolescent's behavior (Whitbeck, Hoyt, & Ackley, 1997), maternal reports of children's self-control and peer relationships need to be validated with adolescent self-reports.

I have examined an important, yet overlooked, dimension of the general theory of crime, peer relations. Much as Gottfredson and Hirschi suggest, those lacking in self-control have trouble making and keeping friends, and find themselves in the company of criminally inclined peers. However, other important questions remain regarding the sequencing of events through which self-control influences peer relations, and peer relations influence delinquency. Peer attachment and peer conflict were not examined in this research and are outside the scope of these data to answer. Both are fruitful areas of inquiry because the general theory of crime would suggest that those with low self-control would be present in less committed and more conflictive peer groups. It also would be important to disentangle the effect of peer rejection on the composition of peer networks. Not all youths who are rejected by their peers have low self-control, and not all rejected youths join deviant peer groups. This question has important ramifications for the debate surrounding the self-selection vs. acquisition effect of delinquent peer groups on delinquency. The findings presented earlier suggest that the confluence of low self-control, peer relations, and delinquency remains an important area of inquiry.

Notes

1. In actuality, a proportion of 14-year-old youth who are close to their 15th birthday are interviewed as young adults each survey year. In the sample I selected, approximately 30 percent of 14-year-olds were interviewed as young adults and therefore had missing data on the child assessments of self-control and peer relations. It was for this reason that I chose to include only the 14-year-olds as young adults, thus reducing my overall sample size but increasing the proportion of respondents with complete data at all three waves.

2. The youngest women of the original NLSY79 sample are now 40 years old. When these women complete their childbearing, the child and young adult sub-samples will be a nationally representative sample of children born to women who were born between 1960 and 1965.

3. Unfortunately, due to interview decisions by CHHR, every year a proportion of 14-year-olds who are close to their 15th birthday receive the young adult interview rather than the child interview and therefore have missing data on the child questions. The items measuring peer rejection and peer deviance are only available in the child data (they are maternal self-reports which end with the child data), thus necessitating a difficult decision. If child data are used, as they must be to measure the peer relation variables and include data from 14-year-olds, then approximately 30 percent of the peer relations variables have missing data because they were being interviewed not as children but as young adults. Because these data are systematically missing (in which older 14-year-olds are not interviewed as children), missing data imputation is not an option. Instead, I included the 14-year-old respondents only as young adults in my sample, thus decreasing my sample size by only including 14–15-year-olds in 1998, 12–13-year-olds in 1996 (i.e., not including any 14-year-olds in the child data measures) and 10–11-year-olds in 1994. Although I lose cases in this smaller sample with a restricted age range, the problem of missing data is considerably reduced.

4. In an analysis of missing data per item, delinquency, age, race, and sex all have complete data; 8 percent of respondents have missing data on self-control, 10 percent are missing data on peer rejection, 10 percent are missing data on peer deviance, and 18 percent are missing data on the family's poverty status in 1998.

5. Michael Gottfredson (personal communication, October 2002) suggested that parental reports of their children's behavior should be reliable measures of self-control. He commented that, if anything, this measurement strategy underestimates the extent of low self-control in the sample, thus attenuating the effects of self-control on peer relations and delinquency.

6. Parental reports of children's behavior have a history in criminology, beginning with the Glueck data in 1950 and continuing with Sampson and Laub's re-assessment of the Glueck data (1993). Additionally, Whitbeck et al. (1997) find that parents' and adolescents' assessment of home environment and parenting behavior for homeless and runaways, although not identical, were similar and in the same direction.

7. According to Arbuckle and Worthke (1999), for good-fitting models, the p-value should be nonsignificant, RMSEA should be less that .05, and NFI should be close to 1.00.

References

Akers, R. L. 1998. *Social learning and social structure: A general theory of crime and deviance.* Boston: Northeastern University Press.

Arbuckle, J. L., and Wothke, W. 1999. *Amos 4.0 user's guide.* Chicago: SmallWaters Corporation.

Baron, R. M., and Kenny, D. A. 1986. The moderator-mediator variable distinction in social psychological research: Conceptual, strategic and statistical considerations. *Journal of Personality and Social Psychology,* 56, 1173–1182.

Baron, S. W. 2003. Self-control, social consequences, and criminal behavior: Street youth and the general theory of crime. *Journal of Research in Crime and Delinquency,* 40, 403–425.

Bolger, K. E., and Patterson, C. J. 2001. Developmental pathways from child maltreatment to peer rejection. *Child Development,* 72, 549–568.

Brame, R., and Paternoster, R. 2003. Missing data problems in criminological research: Two case studies. *Journal of Quantitative Criminology,* 19, 55–78.

Brame, R., and Piquero, A. R. 2003. Selective attrition and the age-crime relationship. *Journal of Quantitative Criminology,* 19, 107–127.

Center for Human Resource Research, 2000. *1998 child & young adult data: User's guide.* Columbus: The Ohio State University.

Cloward, R. A. and Ohlin, L. E. 1960. *Delinquent boys: The culture of the gang.* New York: The Free Press.

Conduct Problems Prevention Research Group. 1992. A developmental and clinical model for the prevention of conduct disorders: The FAST track program. *Development and Psychopathology,* 4, 509–527.

DeMuth, S. 2004. Understanding the delinquency and social relationships of loners. *Youth & Society,* 35, 366–392.

Dodge, K. A., Lansford, J. E., Salzer Burks, V., Bates, J. E., Pettit, G. S., Fontaine, R., and Price, J. M. 2003. Peer rejection and social information-processing factors in the development of aggressive behavior problems in children. *Child Development,* 74, 374–393.

Esbensen, F. A., and Huizinga, D. 1993. Gangs, drugs and delinquency in a survey of urban youth. *Criminology,* 31, 565–590.

Evans, T. D., Cullen, F. T., Burton, V. S. Jr., Dunaway, R. G., and Benson, M. L. 1997. The social consequences of self-control: Testing the general theory of crime. *Criminology,* 35, 475–501.

Fergusson, D. M., and Horwood, L. J. 1999. Prospective childhood predictors of deviant peer affiliations in adolescence. *Journal of Child Psychology and Psychiatry,* 40, 581–592.

Garnier, H. E., and Stein, J. A. 2000. An 18-year model of family and peer effects on adolescent drug use and delinquency. *Journal of Youth and Adolescence,* 31, 45–56.

Gibson, C., and Wright, J. 2001. Low self-control and coworker delinquency: A research note. *Journal of Criminal Justice,* 29, 483–492.

Giordano, P. C. 1995. The wider circle of friends in adolescence. *American Journal of Sociology,* 101, 661–697.

Giordano, P. C., Cernkovich, S. A., and Pugh, M. D. 1986. Friendships and delinquency. *American Journal of Sociology,* 19, 1170–1202.

Glueck, S., and Glueck, E. 1950. *Unraveling juvenile delinquency.* New York: The Commonwealth Fund.

Gottfredson, M. R., and Hirschi, T. 1990. *A general theory of crime.* Stanford: Stanford University Press.

Grasmick, H. G., Tittle, C. R., Bursik, R. J., and Arneklev, B. J. 1993. Testing the core empirical implications of Gottfredson and Hirschi's general theory of crime. *Journal of Research in Crime and Delinquency,* 30, 5–29.

Haynie, D. L. 2001. Delinquent peers revisited: Does network structure matter? *American Journal of Sociology,* 106, 1013–1058.

Hirschi, T. 1969. *Causes of delinquency.* Berkley: University of California Press.

Hope, T. L., and Chapple, C. L. (2005). Maternal characteristics, parenting and adolescent sexual behavior: The role of self-control. *Deviant Behavior.*

Jensen, G. F. 1973. Inner containment and delinquency. *Journal of Criminal Law and Criminology,* 64, 464–470.

Kandel, D. B. 1978. Homophily, selection and socialization in adolescent friendships. *American Journal of Sociology,* 84, 427–436.

LaGrange, T. C., and Silverman, R. A. 1999. Low self-control and opportunity: Testing the general theory of crime as an explanation for gender differences in delinquency. *Criminology,* 37, 41–69.

Longhore, D. 1998. Self-control and criminal opportunity: A prospective test of the general theory of crime. *Social Problems,* 45, 102–113.

Longhore, D., and Turner, S. 1998. Self-control and criminal opportunity: Cross-sectional test of the general theory of crime. *Criminal Justice and Behavior,* 25, 81–99.

Matsueda, R. L. 1992. Reflected appraisals, parental labeling and delinquency: Specifying a symbolic interactionist theory. *American Journal of Sociology,* 47, 489–504.

Matsueda, R. L., and Anderson, K. 1998. The dynamics of delinquent peers and delinquent behavior. *Criminology,* 36, 269–308.

McCarthy, B., Hagan, J., and Cohen, L. E. 1998. Uncertainty, cooperation and crime: Understanding the decision to co-offend. *Social Forces,* 77, 155–184.

Miller-Johnson, S., Coie, J. D., Maumery-Germaud, A., Lockman, J. and Terry, R. 1999. Relationship between childhood peer rejection and aggression and adolescent delinquency severity and type among African American youth. *Journal of Emotional & Behavioral Disorders,* 7, 137–147.

Olson, S. L. 1989. Assessment of impulsivity in preschoolers: Cross-measure convergences, longitudinal stability and relevance to social competence. *Journal of Clinical Child Psychology*, 18, 176–183.

Olson, S. L., and Hoza, B. 1993. Preschool developmental antecedents of conduct problems in children beginning in school. *Journal of Clinical Child Psychology*, 22, 60–67.

Osgood, W. D., Wilson, J. K., Bachman, J., O'Malley, P., and Johnston, L. 1996. Routine activities and deviant behavior. *American Sociological Review*, 63, 635–655.

Reiss, A. J., and Farrington, D. P. 1991. Advancing knowledge about co-offending: Results from a prospective longitudinal survey of London males. *Journal of Criminal Law and Criminology*, 82, 360–395.

Sampson, R. J., and Laub, J. H. 1993. *Crime in the making: Pathways and turning points through life.* Cambridge, MA: Harvard University Press.

Sarnecki, J. 2001. *Delinquent networks: Youth co-offending in Stockholm.* Cambridge, UK: Cambridge University Press.

Tabachnick, B. J. and Fidell, L. S. 1997. *Using multivariate statistics.* New York: Harper-Collins College.

Thornberry, T. P., Lizotte, A. J., Krohn, M. D., Farworth, M., and Jang, S. J. 1994. Delinquent peers, beliefs and delinquent behavior: A longitudinal test of interactional theory. *Criminology*, 32, 47–983.

Turner, M. G., and Piquero, A. R. 2002. The stability of self-control. *Journal of Criminal Justice*, 30, 457–471.

Warr, M. 1996. Organization and instigation in delinquent groups. *Criminology*, 34, 11–37.

Warr, M. 2002. *Companions in crime: The social aspects of criminal conduct.* Cambridge, UK: Cambridge University Press.

Warr, M., and Stafford, M. C. 1991. The influence of delinquent peers: What they think or what they do? *Criminology*, 29, 851–866.

Whitbeck, L. B., Hoyt, D. R., and Ackley, K. A. 1997. Families of homeless and runaway adolescents: A comparison of parent/caretaker and adolescent perspectives on parenting, family violence and adolescent conduct. *Child Abuse & Neglect*, 21, 517–528.

Windle, M. 1994. A study of friendship characteristics and problem behaviors among middle adolescents. *Child Development*, 65, 1764–1777.

Wright, B. R. E., Caspi, A., Moffitt, T. E., and Silva, P. A. 1999. Low self-control, social bonds, and crime: Social causation, selection or both? *Criminology*, 37, 479–514.

Appendix Items Comprising the Self-Control Scale

Description of items in the self-control scale

How often are these statements true about your child . . . ?

Child bullies or is cruel to others

Child is not sorry after misbehaving

Child is impulsive, acts without thinking

Child is restless or over-active

Child is stubborn, sullen or irritable

Child has a very strong temper

Child cheats of tells lies

Child argues too much

Child has difficulty concentrating

$\alpha = .82$

Deviant Careers and Identities: Some Additional Forms and Shapes— Peers, Gangs, and Organizations

As the preceding descriptions reveal, deviant or semideviant occupations vary in terms of their sophistication and corresponding organizational structure; the house prostitute, given the particular nature of the profession, is subjected to a more elaborate and intense degree of socialization than is the call girl. This means that deviance and the deviant career can exhibit a variety of patterns, each with its own recruiting offices, entry routes, career lines, socialization mechanisms, and career shifts. Deviant pursuits can also exhibit (in accord with Best and Luckenbill's concern over the social organization of deviance) a range of mutually beneficial relationships; this is especially evident in the next two selections.

The current era of globalization has created a context in which corporate deviance is likely to increase in the foreseeable future according to Verghese Chirayath, Kenneth Eslinger, and Ernest DeZolt. The authors present their argument as supported by data in their article, "Differential Association, Multiple Normative Standards, and the Increasing Incidence of Corporate Deviance in an Era of Globalization." In some cases entry into deviant careers may be a result of tasks that are required through employment. Organizations may become deviant by embracing goals or means that are deviant from societal norms or laws. The era of globalization has produced a condition of rampant competition in a more or less unregulated global economy. As a result of varied national regulations, multiple normative standards may exist within a corporation. Shifts from one standard to another may seem reasonable in the pursuit of profits, and may become a part of deviant corporate culture. It should be remembered, however, that organizations do not have "mind" or intent apart from the people who act on behalf of the organization. Differential association shapes the development of coalitions based on personal interests. Dominant coalitions emerge and are willing to commit organizational resources to altered organizational goals or to embrace means that are deviant or perhaps criminal.

Andrew Szasz, in "Corporations, Organized Crime, and the Disposal of Hazardous Waste: An Examination of the Making of a Criminogenic Regulatory Structure," offers another interesting account of the types of relationships that can exist among legitimate and illegitimate enterprises or entrepreneurs. He focuses on the disposal of toxic waste, particularly the way in which organized crime became involved in its disposal. Szasz argues that corporate generators of hazardous waste products helped to create a regulatory structure that was accessible and attractive to organized crime. Szasz begins by describing how attempts were made to regulate the disposal of hazardous

605

waste—efforts that resulted in the creation of the federal Resource Conservation and Recovery Act (RCRA). RCRA established procedures for the safe disposal of hazardous substances and authorized states to register the corporate generators of the waste. RCRA also mandated the licensing of hauling and disposal firms. Given organized crime's traditionally heavy involvement in garbage hauling and landfilling, extension of their influence to the illegal disposal of hazardous wastes was relatively straightforward. For example, when RCRA mandated the licensing of firms, mob-connected haulers acquired state permits and called themselves hazardous waste haulers. Organized crime also controlled some final disposal sites; hence, it was easy to have the manifest signed and then state that the waste had been disposed of properly. Other organized crime figures seized control of phony disposal sites and treatment facilities. Szasz continues by describing those political and social-structural factors that enabled organized crime to "'colonize' the hazardous waste disposal industry." Specifically, lax implementation and incompetent enforcement of the provisions of RCRA allowed organized crime to gain a strong foothold in the hazardous waste business. Interim licenses were granted and the manifest system was monitored loosely. Szasz also points to the role of generators of waste. For example, corporate generators lobbied for narrow definitions of hazardous waste as well as less stringent rules for disposal.

Differential Association, Multiple Normative Standards, and the Increasing Incidence of Corporate Deviance in an Era of Globalization

Verghese Chirayath
Kenneth Eslinger
Ernest De Zolt

> . . . *multinational corporations operate in countries where bribery, sexual harassment, racial discrimination, and a lack of concern for the environment are neither illegal nor unethical or unusual. The company must decide whether to adhere to constant ethical principles or to adjust to the local rules to maximize profits.*
>
> (*Marshall B. Clinard and Peter C. Yeager with collaboration of Ruth Blackburn Clinard, 1980*)

Introduction

Starting with the theoretical assumptions of its authors (see below), and a discussion of the antecedents of corporate deviance, this paper reviews the role of law as it applies to decisions that are favorable to corporate wrongdoing. Using secondary data from the *U.S. Department of Justice*, this paper suggests that changes in the global economy, toward increased oligopolization, lend themselves to additional opportunities for corporate deviance.

Theoretical Assumptions

The theoretical assumptions herein are co-founded on the sociological tradition of the Frankfurt School and on the research in organizational behavior. They inform both the narrative of this paper and its conclusions.

- Individuals change institutions and institutions change society. However, the individuals acting on their own behalf are incidental to corporate deviance and corporate crime. Only individuals in the role of corporate "actors" can be said to engage in corporate misconduct.

- The literature on organizational environments has demonstrated that organizational survival is inevitably linked to how organizations cope with multiple, even competing, normative standards that simultaneously operate under the same corporate umbrella. Corporate actors initiate decisions through differential association and dominant coalitions in the pursuit of profit and sharehold interests.
- The transnational encouragement of the hyper-mobility of capital, the unending search for cheap foreign labor, and the immobility of domestic labor, leads to the misuse and abuse of power by the corporate state. Globalization leads to oligopolization and expansionism rather than genuine economic development.
- Corporate decisions are made as an extension of private interests for the accumulation and mobility of capital required for increased productivity. To the extent that corporate decisions are private, they are in opposition to the interests of the public at large.
- Corporate criminal behavior is learned, as is conventional corporate behavior, through formal channels of corporate socialization and through selective association with competitors. This learning includes not only the techniques of committing crime but the values associated with their rationalization.
- The commission of corporate crime occurs through the internalization of criminal corporate goals or through the use of deviant means in accomplishing conventional corporate goals.

Classical Economics and the Antecedents of Corporate Deviance

The discussion and study of corporate business ethics have come into vogue in the corporation, the university, the popular press, and in deliberations in the board rooms of corporations. This trend occurs at a time when changes in the global economy make the rights of ordinary men and women more difficult to respect. This problem of rights is especially problematic for individuals who belong to a workforce outside of the United States. A situation often develops where corporate ethics are given lip service, as seen in corporate codes of conduct regarding workplace safety issues, inside trading of securities, environmental despoliation and labor force reductions. Wages as an issue are often decisive, and can become the driving force of downsizing, mergers and acquisitions, often under the umbrella of performance as measured in actual or potential profits. This occurs in an era when the core interests of capitalist societies have converged to create insatiable opportunities for profiteering in virtually all areas of advanced technological applications (Boatright, 2000, pp. 73–99).

The classical economics of Adam Smith is relevant to the analysis of corporate legal and ethical infractions. In the first one hundred years following the publication of *The Wealth of Nations* (1776), Smith's ideas served as a useful framework for understanding, even guiding the growth of entrepreneurial capitalism. The form which nineteenth century capitalism took owed much to the insights and interpretations to Smith and other thinkers of classical economics such as Thomas Malthus (1792) and David Ricardo (1820).

In the *Wealth of Nations*, Adam Smith provided an analysis of free-market mechanisms, which he believed showed the greatest promise for economic growth among European nations. His approach emphasized aggregate economic growth, and did not evince great concern for the future of individuals, much less the poverty of those left behind by competitive economic growth. As classical economics developed, this practice continued as a working assumption, though not always so stated. As Thomas Malthus and David Ricardo continued the tradition, and as it joined with classical liberalism in political philosophy, the workings of the market place were elevated to near super-natural status in parceling rewards, and by extension, economic justice. As John Kenneth Galbraith (1998) states in *The Affluent Society*, the market was understood to work with "ferocious inequality" by the thinkers who developed classical economics.

Ideas from classical economics on private initiative, governmental regulation, tax policy, pursuit of self-interest, and the invisible hand in the "market place" have become part of the cultural mythology of corporate capitalism. The basic principles that Adam Smith embodied in his book explain that a natural order exists whereby the enlightened selfishness of all men adds up to the maximum good of society, since there is a "divine hand" which guides each man in pursuing his own gain to contribute to the social welfare, it must follow that government is superfluous except to preserve order and perform routine functions. The best government is the government which governs least, the best economic policy is that which arises from the spontaneous and unhindered actions of individuals.

Adam Smith's system of thought took shape as an intense reaction against the elaborate structure of controls which the surviving feudal and mercantilistic institutions were still imposing on individuals. The private pursuit of material gain by self-interested rational individuals became a cornerstone of Adam Smith's principles of economics. These principles became in simplified and often distorted summaries the guiding principles and daily justifications for business activities. Over two centuries later these principles still find expression in a liberal rhetoric of capitalism often carrying connotations of a self-balancing market system regulated most effectively by competitive process. Ignored in this liberal rhetoric is the organizational structure of the modern corporation with its rationalized operations and hierarchically driven personnel actions. Also missing are the new marketplace conditions in many industries of oligopolistic and even monopolistic competition, price leadership, market timing, and careful collusion regarding mutually beneficial market arrangements.

The justification of avarice and profligacy inherent in economic liberalism have contributed to anomic criminal actions on the part of white collar felons and corporate organizations. When we add the administrative environment of modern corporate life to the insights of modern criminology on the behavior of corporate deviants, we have the beginnings of a theoretical schematic structure.

As in the time when Adam Smith wrote, the last decades of the twentieth century have ushered an era of unprecedented wealth accumulation. In industry after industry the pattern of paring down the giants that eventually control larger portions of the market is manifested. The computer, electrical, automotive, pharmaceutical and steel industries are illustrative of this dominant trend. Furthermore, with the weakening of domestic labor movements, the formula for the creation of wealth has come to include massive layoffs, forced overtime with reduced benefits, off-shore production, and the creation of niche markets for the production of innovative products in the service sector of the economy, even as manufacturing has declined in our post-industrial economy.

In time, and in response to unscrupulous practices of the great robber barons and the scathing writings of the so-called early twentieth century Muckrakers, government intervention in the form of a series of laws were passed. Labor Laws sought protection of worker rights including the right to strike and to engage in collective bargaining. The range of government regulatory agencies such as the Federal Trade Commission, Food and Drug Administration, Environmental Protection Agency, Office of Safety and Health Administration, United States Department of Agriculture, and the Securities and Exchange Commission were established with the conviction that without the guidelines of these agencies, no amount of self-regulation, however well-intentioned, would result in adequate protection of the workplace and worker rights.

One of the great ironies connected to the writings of Adam Smith is that he believed that the economic maxims that he so carefully developed and advocated would lessen inequality in the emerging Western economies. This would occur through general increments in wealth in these economies and the augmentation of numerous personal fortunes among entrepreneurs in farming, the trades, distribution, service industries and through local retail activity. Today we hear Adam Smith fondly quoted in a liberal rhetoric that is useful in justifying centralization of property. How convenient is it to ignore the fact that mergers and acquisitions are a classic symptom of oligopoly and the ascendence of rational modes of managing financial blocs. A less celebrated aspect of the modern economy, with its drift toward monopoly practice in major sectors is that the original promise of free-market capitalism, to diminish inequality, is belied through ever increasing centralization of holdings, a reduced middle-class, and a widening gap between rich and poor.

The writings of C. Wright Mills in sociology disengage from economic liberalism with a forceful analysis of the social organization of economic production. Utilizing the insights of German sociologists such as Max Weber (1947) and Karl Mannheim (1936), C. Wright Mills demonstrated the role of corporation as a modern engine of power, often linked to the state, in such classic works as *White Collar* (1951) and *The Power Elite* (1956). A theme developed early in both books asserts that the new start on the North American continent with republican government and an absence of aristrocracy has meant that the predominant economic class has been the business class, originally as small farmer or planter, from the beginning of this nation. A combination of laws favoring business and the accumulation of private property along with the rich resources of the new nation created a climate which facilitated expansionist development and the growth and ascendance of a wealthy class of corporate investors.

Law as a Precursor to Social and Economic Change

In the absence of American aristocracy, and true to its class-system, the American corporation, through its corporate actors, enjoys distinct legal advantages over ordinary citizens and the public interest. Historically, the states of Michigan and New Jersey are illustrative (Ermann and Lundman, 1982).

This corporate class, and their corporate agents, wield enormous contemporary influence on American and global societies through their sponsors and the tradition of sponsorship that dates back to an earlier class of industrialists. While, as previously noted, corporate interests and economic expansion occur with simultaneous regularity, it was not until the direct application of legal advantage through classical economics that a growing incidence of corporate deviance excelled. In particular, the creation of the distinction between *natural* and *juristic* persons was an artifact that insulated corporate advantage from non-corporate interests.

Just as the changing nature of twentieth century American law compliments corporate capitalism (Securities and Stock Exchange statutes and the Law of the Seas are illustrative here), the changing structure of law in Britain was tailored to the expression and expansion of primitive mercantile capitalism in the seventeenth and eighteenth centuries. While the law is theoretically impartial to all citizens and is entrusted to arbitrate conflicts, it does so within the interests of their corporate class and at the expense of ordinary citizens. The historical development of law in this regard goes back to the middle ages in Germany. Questions arose whether the ownership of churches was in the hands of the landowner, the priest, or the patron saints for which the church had been named. To whom did the rights belong?

Similarly, in a seminal case in sixteenth century England, Edward the IV, then a nine-year old boy, sold property to the Duchy of Lancaster. The question arose of his legal authority to do so as a minor. The king's counsel argued successfully that as king, Edward possessed two bodies, one physical (e.g., natural) and the other juristic. Legal deference to the juristic body gave rise to the legitimacy of Edward's claim of the "corporation sole" (Coleman, 1974, pp. 13–47).

Another example of the law-in-action and its relation to the social forces of change is that of the transfer of land holdings. According to fourteenth century English law, land transfers, unlike personal property, could not occur upon death through a will and testament. Land must be passed to the first-born son, with large inheritance taxes going to the lord. To avoid paying the lord inheritance taxes, *inter vivos trusts* were developed. Landowners transferred their land to a set of trustees who held it during their lifetimes. Upon their deaths, landowners were simply replaced in the order of the "trustee set" without their land being taxed; the land holdings belong to a surrogate, that is, a juristic legal entity and not a sole person. As was true for the mercantile capitalists of fourteenth century England, trusts are used today by corporations to amass enormous amounts of economic power (Coleman, 1974).

It is from the initial action of churches, kings and trusts that the distinction between *physical* and *juristic* persons enabled corporate actors to insulate themselves through the advancement of the "corporation sole." From this legacy, modern corporations receive a competitive legal advantage over other players. The law provides for the perpetuation of the status quo even as it appears to promote social change. While the law provides guidance with the adjudication of conflicts, it is unwilling to address underlying contradictions that permeate American society as a result of the non-competitive advantage enjoyed by corporate entities for centuries.

Organizational Framework and Corporate Deviance

While this paper focuses on corporate conduct and misconduct, the literature that supports this thesis is found in the works dealing with the larger framework of organizations that subsumes organizational deviance in both corporate and governmental settings (cf. Aldrich, 1999; Buckley, 1967; Hall, 2002; Ott, 1989; Scott, 1998; Weber, 1947). Simply stated, corporate acts are those actions that occur in corporations when the corporate entity is the prime actor or beneficiary of the act, despite the presence of individuals that act on behalf of the company, and carry out corporate acts.

Ermann and Lundman (1982) state that corporate acts may be produced by the complexity of positions within large corporations, or by corporate elites who may establish corporate norms that govern their corporate acts, or by coalitions near the top of organizations that may either initiate behavior, or implement corporate acts as part of a larger strategy. The social organization within which corporate acts occur, according to Peter Blau (1962), "refers to the ways in which human conduct becomes socially organized, that is, to the observed regularities in the behavior of people that are due to the social conditions in which they find themselves rather than to their physiological or psychological characteristics as individuals." Blau goes on to differentiate organization on the basis of his well-known *cui bono*, or "prime beneficiary" criteria. While it is analytically desirable to make distinctions between corporate and individual acts in practice, the acts may not neatly fit their pattern.

The sociology of organizations provides the basis for studies of the role of multiple normative standards in corporate misconduct. Sociological literature on organizations provides a wealth of perspectives from which one might examine organizational conduct and misconduct. One of the most well-known perspectives comes from the German sociologist, Max Weber (1947), whose classic essay on bureaucracy outlines, in ideal circumstances, the strategy of bureaucratic adherence to hierarchy, authority, loyalty, written records, and rules in gaining competitive advantage over non-bureaucratic organizations. Central to Weber's conceptualization of organizations was his notion of rationalism, which he defined as "the methodological attainment of a definitely given and practical end by means of an increasingly precise calculation of adequate means." For Weber, the increased rationalization of social organization, accompanied by legal-rational authority, was a central explanation of the advance of industrial societies.

To be sure, Weber has had his critics. Natural systems, open systems, and chaos theories have each taken issue with Weber's analysis of bureaucratic organizations and rational action. The work by James Thompson (1967), entitled: *Organizations in Action*, attempts to reconcile natural systems, open systems, and chaos into one theoretical perspective. Thompson's interest in integrating all three theoretical perspectives in the study of organizations surrounds his analysis of "dominant coalitions."

Dominant coalitions center on the implications of decision-making in organizations. Thompson introduces the idea of dominant coalitions as a framework by which either individuals or groups are positioned in ways to commit organizational resources depending on their "computational strategy," and the completeness or incompleteness of the existing knowledge about the decision that is to be made. Thompson specifies that a "pervasive constraint on the dominant coalition occurs when the object worked on is itself dynamic, for here some of the pertinent variables are not unilaterally under control of the organization" (Thompson, 1967).

The literature on organizational behavior provides perspectives that are especially useful in the analysis of corporate misconduct. Specifically, the literature on goal succession and goal displacement suggest ways in which what were once regarded as acceptable goals may be subverted by an emergent dominant coalition in the pursuit of personal gain. In order to maintain their appeal and influence, organizational goals have to be re-examined from time to time, and interpreted in view of the latest changes, notably in their organizational environments and internal structure. Here the classic work of David Sills (1957), with the March of Dimes, suggests that once organizational success in achieving goals has been established, the organization may seek new goals rather than disband.

Internal constraints pertaining to goal succession notwithstanding, external governmental constraints are frequently mandatory as in the case of regulatory laws that come from regulatory agencies. While corporate goals are ideally structured for the pursuit of profits, governmental regulations, in the form of myriad documents, are frequently perceived as hampering this pursuit.

If individuals shape institutions and institutions shape society it is also true that organizations represent the backbone of institutional structures. While organizations direct individual efforts toward the fulfillment of organizational goals, individual personalities do not always succumb to organizational efforts. Individuals may instead direct their efforts with others which may differ from those of organizations. "Organizations become deviant in two ways. One way is the adoption of organizational goals that are deviant from societal norms or laws. The other way is the organizationally approved use of means that deviate from societal norms or laws to achieve societally legitimate organizational goals" (Sherman, 1987).

The attraction of adopting organizational goals that are deviant from societal norms is often a function of organizational culture. Writings in this area (c.f. Ott, 1989; Martin, 2002) suggest that organizational culture has a pervasive influence in the conduct of corporations, both within their operating units as well as with their external environments. Beliefs and commitments of particular organizations give them a "distinctive character structure" that may well include some combination of deviant organization goals with deviant means in pursuit of such goals. Formal organizational goals are "displaced" by informal goals that may chart techniques of organizational survival and growth when the original, formal goals, have ceased to operate. Different factions in an organization coalesce around similar interests. Patterns of "differential association", lead to the emergence of dominant coalitions.

Sherman (1987) notes that organizations become deviant by adopting either deviant goals or means. "The more difficult it is to achieve legitimate goals through legitimate means, the more likely it may be that organizations adopt illegitimate means in order to achieve their goals." In order for organizational goals to remain functional and effective their manifest functions must be reinforced through daily transactions. Latent functions in organizations and institutions remain hidden. And so it is in organizations that have emerging dominant coalitions. These coalitions may remain dormant for a while. Eventually, should they seek official recognition and an increasingly larger proportion of the organization's resources, they will have to disband their hidden status for one that is formal, "real", and public. Dominant coalitions remain a process, and not an entity. The competition and struggles to maintain dominance are continuous, not unlike territorial males in animal ecology.

In sum, the literature on organizational behavior, as it relates to corporate deviance, suggests that when corporations find themselves in rampant competition (a characteristic feature of multinationals in an era of globalization), and when available institutional means seem woefully inadequate in the pursuit of profits, the temptation to alter corporate goals, or the available means to accomplish them become paramount. Through patterns of "differential association" (Sutherland, 1983) dominant coalitions emerge. These coalitions commit organizational resources and even new means to pursue existing goals that may initially shade into deviant acts and eventually become criminal. Corporate crime is rarely politically defined in leading newspapers and magazines. Instead, these crimes are treated as a variation of regular business transactions. Recently, Microsoft has also run afoul of antitrust regulations even as it promotes its latest software that its competitors view as a continuation of regulatory violations.

Data Summary

The data used in this paper were compiled by the Bureau of Justice Statistics for the purpose of presenting reports on overall trends in white collar crime. The data in Table I are on cases of corporate crime filed in district court by offense and years from 1984–1985 and 1998–1999. While data in Table I do not comprise an exhaustive test, they lend support to our hypothesis of existence growth of corporate deviance and crime in a generally unregulated global economy.

In the year 1984–1985, acts of corporate deviance and white collar crime were defined under fraud, "other regulatory" tax, and bribery categories. Given the limited scope of these original definitions, it is not surprising that cases of corporate deviance and white collar criminality, in the words of Edwin Sutherland (1949), "may not be derived at all from the available data." Sutherland's caveat suggests some mechanism for projecting the actual incidence of white collar crime based on cases that have been litigated. This strategy continues to be employed by the Immigration and Naturalization Service in estimating "illegal aliens" in the

United States based on actual arrests. In 1993–1994, more comprehensive categories for fraudulent and regulatory noncompliance in antitrust, food and drug, and transportation were added. While these expanded data categories lend themselves to more complete analysis of the nature and frequency of corporate deviance and white collar criminality they may not be compared to previous data.

Data Analysis

An analysis of Table I suggest patterns of significant decline in cases that were prosecuted in fraud, antitrust food and drug, transportation, regulatory, taxes and bribery. In 1984, corporate criminality cases totaled 5977. In subsequent years of 1994–1995, criminal prosecutions increased to 12,338 cases. Prosecutions have declined to 10,814 cases in 1998–1999. Is this five-year decline in corporate deviance and criminality a result of an assault on government regulation in the U.S., or a general decline in patterns of corporate deviance and corporate crime? We conclude that oligopolization of most industries provides additional opportunities for corporate crime. As far back as 1969, studies by the Staff of the Cabinet Committee on Price Stability concluded that corporations having assets of one billion dollars or more (N = 78, or 0.04% of all U.S. corporations) comprised 43% of all manufacturing assets, and 49% of all manufacturing profits. By comparison corporations with assets of under ten million dollars (N = 185,000, or 98.7% of all U.S. corporations) comprised 14% of all manufacturing assets and 12% of all manufacturing profits. Given the rise of globalized oligopolies fewer corporations account for increased levels of corporate criminality. Sharp declines in prosecuted cases, from 12,999 in 1993–1994 to 10,661 cases in 1998–1999, lend support to this claim. As far back as 1980, *Forbes* reported that the twenty largest U.S. multinational corporations had substantial foreign revenues. The largest, Exxon, had in excess of 70% of its revenues from foreign sources. With increasing globalization at General Motors, 39% of its employees were foreign. According to the International Labor Organization website, "most of the largest American and European companies in terms of resources are also the largest in terms of foreign assets".

Two alternative explanations are presented in contrast to the one above, the first of which may be regarded as an assault on United States regulatory agencies resulting in decreased prosecutions even as budgets and personnel in these agencies have been decimated. Alternatively, decreasing incidence of prosecuted cases may be a function of federal court dockets rather than of ineffective regulation.

Table 1 Cases of corporate crime field in U.S. District Court by offense and year

Year	Fraud #	Fraud %	Antitrust #	Antitrust %	Food/Drug #	Food/Drug %	Transport #	Transport %	Regulatory #	Regulatory %	Taxes #	Taxes %	Bribery #	Bribery %	Total
(84–85)															
Prosecuted	3552/	59.4	*/	*	*/	*	*/	*	835/	14.0	1590/	26.6	*/	*	5,977
Declined	3407/	81.9	*/	*	*/	*	*/	*	347/	8.3	402/	9.7	*/	*	4,156
(93–94)															
Prosecuted	9414/	82.3	34/	0.3	98/	0.9	83/	0.7	569/	5.0	927/	8.1	320/	2.8	11,445
Declined	11062/	85.1	28/	0.2	63/	0.5	152/	1.2	867/	6.7	502/	3.9	325/	2.5	12,999
(94–95)															
Prosecuted	10424/	84.5	27/	0.2	106/	0.9	120/	1.0	584/	4.7	881/	7.1	196/	1.6	12,338
Declined	11575/	85.5	16/	0.1	63/	0.5	206/	1.5	927/	6.8	419/	3.1	328/	2.4	13,534
(95–96)															
Prosecuted	10111/	84.3	34/	0.3	68/	0.6	141/	1.2	609/	5.1	862/	7.2	168/	1.4	11,993
Declined	10356/	84.2	24/	0.2	117/	1.0	179/	1.5	907/	7.4	509/	4.1	212/	1.7	12,304
(96–97)															
Prosecuted	9462/	83.6	19/	0.2	108/	1.0	128/	1.1	532/	4.7	897/	7.9	168/	1.5	11,314
Declined	8818/	83.9	19/	0.2	85/	0.8	204/	1.9	731/	7.0	415/	3.9	241/	2.3	10,513
(97–98)															
Prosecuted	8936/	83.7	45/	0.4	61/	0.6	103/	1.0	680/	6.4	661/	6.2	191/	1.8	10,677
Declined	7859/	83.5	9/	0.1	72/	0.8	167/	1.8	823/	8.7	339/	3.6	140/	1.5	9,409
(98–99)															
Prosecuted	8811/	81.5	21/	0.2	89/	0.8	52/	0.5	958/	9.0	737/	6.8	146/	1.4	10,814
Declined	8481/	79.6	9/	0.1	92/	0.9	47/	0.4	1413/	13.3	421/	3.9	198/	1.9	10,661

* Lack of recorded data by specific offense type for 1984–1985.
** Data source is the US Department of Justice/Bureau of Justice Statistics.

Conclusion

The research reported in this paper provides evidence of linear trend toward greater corporation wrongdoings and this trend is increasingly seen as a world-wide trend. From the white-collar crime of the early and middle twentieth century, documented by Sutherland and others, we see a shift toward political machinations and environmental crime on a global basis, often articulated within the nexus of favorable competitive and labor conditions for Western multinational corporations.

The organizational context of the large corporation has been our point of departure in analysis of these data. Given unprecedented opportunities for the accumulation of wealth as represented in multinational oligopolies, and the competitive advantage that has been gained through technology, this era of globalization represents what Immanuel Wallerstein has aptly termed the World System Economy, with the United States at its core. Regulatory agencies which came into being in response to an earlier era of laissez-faire capitalism have been rebuffed as multinational corporations have sought refuge in off-shore manufacturing operations. The new global economy may well usher in an era of technological neo-colonialism under the guise of "new" free-market capitalism.

In sum, we conclude that:

- The accumulation of wealth lends itself to greater corporate avarice, corporate deviance, and corporate crime.
- The disregard of government regulatory agencies suggests that in an era of globalization more and more corporations will seek the "freedom" of offshore production rather than being subjected to the "punitive" climate of current U.S. government regulation. The hyper mobility of capital and the relative lack of labor mobility facilitates this trend.
- The general pattern of decline in the prosecution of cases especially in the area of taxes, bribery, food and drug, antitrust, and transport suggests the need for increased vigilance in these areas. Self-regulation has proven ineffective.
- The oligopolization of the world economy lends itself to greater opportunities for criminal wrongdoing and resistance to outside control.
- Organizational goals and the means to achieve them are often turned around and revised in the pursuit of profits to include deviant goals and deviant means.
- Dissatisfaction with corporate policies lead to the formation of dominant coalitions that challenge and succeed in replacing decision-making bodies with a more conservative leadership that

more aggressively pursues their corporate agenda. This self-interested action, on behalf of their corporate moiety, leads to greater political machinations and "deal-making" in regard to favorable environmental regulations and labor contracts with sizeable concessions.

References

Aldrich, Howard. 1979. *Organizations and Environment* (Prentice Hall, Englewood Cliffs, NJ).

Aldrich, Howard. 1979. *Organizations Evolving* (Sage Publications, London).

Blau, Peter. 1962. *Formal Organizations* (Chandler Publishing Company, San Francisco, CA).

Boatright, John. 1999. *Ethics and the Conduct of Business* (Prentice Hall, Englewood Cliffs, NJ).

Buckley, Walter. 1967. *Sociology and Modern Systems Theory* (Prentice Hall, Englewood, NJ).

Clinard, Marshall B. and Peter C. Yeager. 1980. *Corporate Crime* (The Free Press, Glencoe, IL).

Coleman, James S. 1974. 'Power and the Structure of Society', in M. David Ermann and Richard D. Lundman (eds.), *Corporate and Governmental Deviance*, 2nd Edition (Oxford University Press, NY) pp. 36–52.

Ermann, M. David and Richard D. Lundman. 1982. *Corporate and Governmental Deviance* (Oxford University Press, NY).

Galbraith, John Kenneth. 1998. *The Affluent Society* (New American Library, NY).

Hall, Richard H. 2002. *Organizations: Structures, Process, and Outcomes* (Prentice Hall, Upper Saddle River, NJ).

International Labor Organization, Multinational Corporations. http://www.itcilo.it/english/actrav/telearn/global/ilo/multinat/multinat.htm.

Kuhn, Thomas. 1962. *The Structure of Scientific Revolutions* (Chicago University Press, Chicago, IL).

Mannheim, Karl. 1936. *Ideology and Utopia*, (Harcourt, NY).

Martin, Joanne. 2002. *Organizational Culture: Mapping the Terrain* (Sage Publications, Thousand Oaks, CA).

Mills, C. Wright. 1951. *White Collar* (Oxford Univeristy Press, NY).

Mills, C. Wright. 2000. (1956). *The Power Elite* (Oxford University Press, NY).

Ott, J. Steven. 1989. *The Organizational Culture Perspective* (Brooks/Cole Publishing Company, Pacific Grove, CA).

Ricardo, David. 1951. (1820). 'The Works and Correspondence of David Ricardo', in Piero Sraffa (ed.) (Cambridge University Press, Cambridge, England).

Scott, W. Richard. 1998. *Organizations: Rational, Natural, and Open Systems* (Prentice Hall, Upper Saddle River, NJ).

Sherman, Lawrence W. 1987. 'Deviant Organizations', in M. David Ermann and Richard D. Lundman (eds.), *Corporate and Governmental Deviance*, 3rd edition (Oxford University Press, NY), pp. 52–62

Sills, David L. 1957. *The Volunteers* (The Free Press, Glencoe, IL).

Smith, Adam. 1937 (1776). *The Wealth of Nations* (The Modern Library, NY).

Sutherland, Edwin. 1983. *White Collar Crime: The Uncut Version* (Yale University Press, New Haven, CT).

Thompson, Victor A. 1967. *Modern Organizations* (Knop, NY).

Wallerstein, Immanuel. 1984. *The Politics of the World Economy: The State, the Movements and the Civilizations* (Cambridge University Press, NY).

Weber, Max. 1946. 'Essays in Sociology', in H. H. Gerth and C. Wright Mills (eds.), *Translation and Eds* (Oxford University Press, NY).

Weber, Max. 1947. *Max Weber: The Theory of Social and Economic Organization* (Oxford University Press, NY).

Corporations, Organized Crime, and the Disposal of Hazardous Waste: An Examination of the Making of a Criminogenic Regulatory Structure

Andrew Szasz

The generation of hazardous waste is a necessary side effect of modern industrial production. Factories must cope daily with large accumulations of unrecyclable chemical byproducts generated by normal production techniques. The processing or disposal of these byproducts is a significant cost of production, a cost that, like all other costs of production, the prudent owner or manager minimizes.

Until recently, industrial hazardous waste was not legally distinguished from municipal garbage and other solid wastes. It was disposed of with ordinary garbage, at very low cost to the generator, mostly in coastal waters or in landfills unfit to adequately contain it. However, concern grew during the 1970s that improper disposal of hazardous waste was creating an environmental and public health burden of unknown but potentially massive scale. This concern finally moved some states and eventually the federal government to begin to legislate new regulations. The centerpiece of this regulatory effort was the federal Resource Conservation and Recovery Act (RCRA) of 1976. On paper, RCRA mandated comprehensive mechanisms to guarantee the safe disposal of hazardous waste. It established standards and procedures for classifying substances as hazardous. It authorized the states to register corporate generators of hazardous waste and license hauling and disposal firms. It mandated the creation of a manifest system that would document the movement of hazardous waste "from cradle to grave," from the generator, through the hands of the transporter, to the shipment's final destination at a licensed disposal site.

By legally distinguishing hazardous waste from other wastes and by directing that such wastes be treated differently than municipal solid waste, the new regulations dramatically increased, almost overnight, the demand for hazardous waste hauling and disposal services. Unhappily, recent state and federal investigations have documented both that illegal waste disposal is widespread (U.S. General Accounting Office, 1985; U.S. House of Representatives, 1980) and that organized crime elements traditionally active

in garbage hauling and landfilling have entered this burgeoning and potentially profitable new market (Block and Scarpitti, 1985; U.S. House of
Representatives, 1980, 1981a). Although the exact extent of organized
crime involvement in hazardous waste hauling and disposal is uncertain,[1]
the fact of that involvement is beyond question. A situation exists, then, in
which corporations, some at the heart of the American economy, discharge
their regulatory obligations under RCRA by entering into direct contractual
relationships with firms dominated by organized crime. The goal in this
paper is to analyze in detail the complex nature of this relationship between
corporate generators of hazardous waste and elements of organized crime
that are active in industrial waste disposal. This goal will be approached
by analyzing the formation and implementation of RCRA legislation.

The subject of this paper speaks to two distinct criminological litera-
tures: works that examine the relationship between legitimate and illicit
enterprise and works that examine crimogenic market structures. Recent
scholarship has challenged the commonsense distinction between legitimate business and organized crime. Schelling (1967), Smith and Alba
(1979), Smith (1980), and Albanese (1982) all argue that the most fundamental aspect of organized crime is that it is a form of entrepreneurial
activity and that its ethnic or conspiratorial nature is of secondary importance. Recent scholarship also challenges the equally widely held belief
that the relationship between the underworld and legitimate business consists solely of the former exploiting the latter through extortion, racketeering, and so on (Drucker, 1981). At minimum, it is argued that the
relationship is one of mutually beneficial interdependence (Martens and
Miller-Longfellow, 1982). This is clearly supported by excellent case studies of labor racketeering (Block and Chambliss, 1981), organized crime on
the waterfront (Block, 1982), and arson (Brady, 1983). Chambliss (1978:
181–182) argues the even stronger view that organized crime can exist only
because the structure of the legitimate economy and its accompanying political organization make its emergence possible and even inevitable. In a
similar vein, Smith (1980) and Smith and Alba (1979) challenge the very
distinction between business and organized crime and begin to dissolve
that distinction in the common dynamic of a market economy. The study
of organized crime participation in hazardous waste disposal presents an
opportunity to once again examine this relationship between legitimate and
illegitimate entrepreneurship.

The story of RCRA may also have links to the concept of crimogenic
market processes. Farberman's (1975) and Leonard and Weber's (1977)
studies of auto retailing and Denzin's (1977) study of the liquor industry
showed that the normal operating logic of an industry may force some
sectors of that industry into illegal activity in order to survive, much less
thrive, in doing their part of the business. Needleman and Needleman
(1979) subsequently expanded the concept by describing a second type
of criminogenesis in which the criminal activity is not forced. It is, in-

stead, an unwelcome drain on business, but it is unavoidable because the conditions that make it possible are necessary to the overall functioning of that industry and could not be altered without fundamentally affecting how business is conducted in that industry. Needleman and Needleman discussed securities fraud as an example of what they call a "crime-facilitative," as opposed to a "crime-coercive" market sector. The fact that RCRA not only cannot prevent illegal hazardous waste dumping but has also attracted organized crime participation in illegal hazardous waste activity suggests that the concept of criminogenesis may be fruitfully extended to regulatory processes as well.

In the first sections of this paper, some background is presented on hazardous waste as a social issue and the nature and extent of organized crime involvement in hazardous waste hauling and disposal is summarized. At the core of the paper, the conditions that made this involvement possible are analyzed. It is shown that the most common explanations—lax implementation and enforcement by state and local officials—are incomplete. Analysis of the formation of RCRA legislation shows that corporate generators of hazardous waste were instrumental in securing a regulatory structure that would prove highly attractive to and well suited for organized crime participation. In other words, generators are deeply implicated in the creation of conditions that have made their relationship to organized crime possible. This finding is used to critique two explanations of this relationship suggested during Congressional hearings, generator "ignorance" and generator "powerlessness." It is then argued that the relationship has two other important aspects: generators did not consciously desire or intend this outcome, but they nonetheless benefited from it once it occurred. The paper concludes with a discussion of the relevance of the findings to the two areas of criminological research mentioned above.

The Issue Background: Hazardous Waste Facts

The Environmental Protection Agency (EPA) defines waste products as "hazardous" if they are flammable, explosive, corrosive, or toxic. Major industries central to the modern national economy, such as the petroleum, chemical, electronic, and pharmaceutical industries, generate copious amounts of hazardous waste. Although there is still great uncertainty about the exact effect of industrial hazardous waste on public health (Greenberg and Anderson, 1984:84–105), improper management may result in explosions, fires, pollution of water resources, and other uncontrolled releases that put surrounding communities at risk and may result in physical harm ranging from skin irritation to increased incidence of cancer, lung disease, birth defects, and other serious illnesses.

How much hazardous waste has accumulated? How much is currently generated? Neither question can be answered confidently at this time. The generation and disposal of hazardous waste was completely unregulated until the late 1970s. In the absence of regulation, there was no systematic data-gathering effort. Consequently, there is great uncertainty about the magnitude and composition of hazardous waste accumulated up to the passage of the RCRA. Estimates have risen regularly as more sites are located and assessed. The EPA's most recent estimate is that there are 25,000 sites nationally that contain some hazardous waste. Of these, about 2,500 are priority sites judged by the EPA to be imminently hazardous to public health. More recent research by the General Accounting Office (GAO) and the Office of Technology Assessment (OTA) suggests that there may be 378,000 total sites nationally, perhaps 10,000 of them requiring priority attention (Shabecoff, 1985).

In theory, at least, the availability of data should have improved greatly following passage of the RCRA. Generators of hazardous waste were now required to create written documentation—the manifest—of the amount and content of every shipment of hazardous waste signed over to outside haulers and disposers. This documentation would be forwarded to state agencies following final disposition of each waste shipment. However, the actual quality of the data produced was compromised by several factors. First, there was little agreement over what substances should be defined as hazardous. Congressional and EPA testimony (U.S. Environmental Protection Agency, 1976, 1979; U.S. House of Representatives, 1975, 1976; U.S. Senate, 1974, 1979) shows that industrial spokesmen argued that too many substances had been unjustifiably included, while environmentalists argued that some materials had been improperly excluded. Second, firms generating less than one metric ton (2,200 lbs.) of hazardous waste per month are exempt from RCRA regulation (U.S. House of Representatives, 1983:56, 60). There are over four million privately owned industrial sites in the nation. The "small generator" exemption leaves all but a few tens of thousands of these sites out of RCRA's registration and manifest system. Third, some firms that generate significant amounts of hazardous waste have either failed to cooperate with EPA requests for data (Williams and Matheny, 1984:436–437) or have failed to identify themselves to the EPA as regulable generators (U.S. General Accounting Office, 1985:14–20). Fourth, even those firms that appear to comply with reporting requirements may not be reporting accurately the types and quantities of hazardous waste they generate (U.S. GAO, 1985:20–23). Consequently, knowledge of the amount and content of current hazardous waste generation is still imprecise. Estimates, like estimates of historical accumulation, have been rising. In 1974, the EPA was estimating hazardous waste generation at 10 million metric tons per year (U.S. Senate, 1974:70). In 1980, the EPA estimate had risen to 40 million metric tons. In 1983, new research led the EPA to nearly quadruple its estimate to 150 million metric tons (Block and Scarpitti, 1985:46), while the OTA was estimating 250 million metric tons per year (U.S. House of Representatives, 1983:1).[2]

Where does hazardous waste end up? In response to EPA inquiries in 1981, 16% of generating firms reported treating their wastes completely on site and another 22% reported treating part of their wastes on site. The remaining 62% contracted with other parties to handle all of their wastes (Block and Scarpitti, 1985:48–49). Where do transported wastes actually end up? The exemptions and noncooperation cited above leave an unknown fraction of total hazardous waste movement out of the paperwork of the manifest system (U.S. GAO, 1985:3–4, 14–24). The manifests that are filed are poorly monitored and vulnerable to undetected falsification (Greenberg and Anderson, 1984:242; U.S. GAO, 1985:25–31; U.S. House of Representatives, 1980:140, 1981b:124). Consequently, this question also cannot be answered with great certainty. On the basis of admittedly poor and incomplete data, the OTA estimates that no more than 10% to 20% of all hazardous waste is rendered harmless by incineration or by chemical or biological treatment. There are few facilities that can treat wastes in these ways and the price of treatment is much higher than the price of other means of disposal (U.S. House of Representatives, 1983:2, 5–6). The remaining 80% to 90% is either landfilled or disposed of illegally. Only a small proportion of hazardous waste goes into landfills that have the siting studies, proper containment practices, and continuous monitoring to be fully licensed by the EPA, since there are only about 200 such landfills in the nation (Block and Scarpitti, 1985:49; U.S. House of Representatives, 1981b:187). Even these top landfills are only required by the EPA to keep wastes contained for 30 years (U.S. House of Representatives, 1983:2).[3] Most hazardous waste goes to landfills that have only interim license to operate, landfills that are of much poorer quality and are likely to pollute the surrounding land and water within a few years.

Illegal hazardous waste dumping is even more likely to have adverse short-term environmental and public health consequences. The full extent of illegal hazardous waste disposal is not known. State officials interviewed by the GAO agreed that illegal disposal was occurring, but had no firm information on the scope of this activity (U.S. GAO, 1985:10). One study done for the EPA surveyed hazardous waste generators in 41 cities and estimated that one in seven generators had illegally disposed of some of their wastes during the two years preceding the study (U.S. GAO, 1985:10). A wide array of illegal disposal practices have been documented. Waste shipments may end up commingled with ordinary garbage. A 20 cubic yard "dumpster" full of dry garbage can be made to absorb up to sixty 55 gallon drums of liquid hazardous waste (U.S. House of Representatives, 1980:63) and then be deposited in unlicensed municipal landfills never designed to contain hazardous waste. Liquid hazardous waste may be released along a roadway. An 8,000 gallon truck can be emptied in 8 minutes (U.S. House of Representatives, 1980:101). Shipments may simply be stockpiled at sites awaiting alleged transfer that never happens or at disposal facilities that have no real disposal capability (U.S. House of Representatives, 1980:10).

Wastes may be drained into local city sewer systems, rivers, and oceans, or dumped in out-of-the-way rural spots (U.S. House of Representatives, 1980:93). Flammable hazardous waste may be commingled with fuel oil and sold as pure heating oil (U.S. House of Representatives, 1980:63–64) or sprayed on unsuspecting communities' roads for dust control (U.S. House of Representatives, 1980:151).

Organized Crime Participation in the Hazardous Waste Disposal Industry

Congressman Albert Gore: "At what point did companies picking up garbage begin to get into the toxic waste disposal business?"

Harold Kaufman: "To my knowledge, it's when the manifest system came out is when they found out the profit motive" (U.S. House of Representatives, 1980:8).

New Jersey Attorney General John J. Degnan pointed out to a Congressional audience that organized crime activity accounts for only a fraction of the illegal dumping taking place in the United States (U.S. House of Representatives, 1980:87). Nonetheless, organized crime was ideally suited to develop the methodology of illegal hazardous waste practices to the fullest. In those parts of the nation where garbage hauling and landfilling was historically controlled by organized crime, their movement into the newly created hazardous waste market was an obvious extension of current activity. In New Jersey, for example, organized crime had controlled the garbage industry through ownership of garbage hauling firms, through ownership of or control of landfills, and through labor racketeering (U.S. House of Representatives, 1981:1–45). The new regulations governing hazardous waste would have had to have been carefully written and tenaciously enforced were organized crime to be kept from applying this highly developed infrastructure to the new market. In fact, as will be shown below, the opposite happened and organized crime easily entered both the hauling and the disposal phases of the hazardous waste handling industry.

Hauling. Organized crime had dominated traditional garbage hauling in states like New York and New Jersey for decades. Once associates of organized crime owned a number of hauling firms in any geographical area, they established an organizational infrastructure that governed their relationships and ensured high profits. Threats and violence persuaded other firms to join that infrastructure and abide by its rules or to sell and get out. The keystone of this infrastructure was the concept of "property rights" or "respect." Municipal solid waste hauling contracts were illegally apportioned among haulers. Having a property right meant that a hauler held rights to continue picking up the contract at sites he currently serviced without competition from others. Other firms would submit artificially high bids or would not bid at all when a contract came up for renewal, thereby assuring that the contractor kept his traditional site. This system of *de facto* territorial monopolies permitted noncompetitive pricing and made the lowly business of garbage hauling a very lucrative activity. Property rights were recognized and enforced by organized crime authorities. Conflicts were adjudicated in meetings of the Municipal Contractors Association. Decisions of the MCA were enforced by threats and, if necessary, violence (U.S. House of Representatives, 1981a:1–42).[4] As is shown below, when the RCRA mandated the licensing of firms deemed fit to transport hazardous waste, mob-connected garbage haulers found it easy to acquire state permits and declare themselves to be hazardous waste haulers. Quite naturally, they brought their traditional forms of social organization with them. Individual haulers holding established property rights assumed that they would transfer those property rights to a new type of waste (U.S. House of Representatives, 1980:22). They also met as a group to set up a Trade Waste Association modeled after the Municipal Contractors Association to apportion and enforce property rights in the new market (U.S. House of Representatives, 1980:9–10, 1981a:1–12, 212).

Disposal.   The manifest system requires that someone will be willing to sign off on the manifest and declare that a waste shipment has been properly disposed of. This means, as Congressman Florio (Democrat, New Jersey) pointed out (U.S. House of Representatives, 1980:30), that mob control over hauling is not enough: organized crime figures had to have ownership of, or at least influence over, final disposal sites. This requirement did not prove to be a serious stumbling block, however. Many landfills were already owned wholly or in part by organized crime figures, a legacy of past mob involvement in the garbage business. These sites readily accepted dubious shipments of hazardous waste thinly disguised as ordinary municipal waste (U.S. House of Representatives 1981a:228, 1981b). Landfill owners not directly associated with organized crime could be bribed to sign manifests for shipments never received or to accept hazardous waste that was manifested elsewhere (U.S. House of Representatives, 1980:70, 90). In addition, known organized crime figures started or seized control of a network of phony disposal and "treatment" facilities such as Chemical Control Corporation, Elizabeth, New Jersey; Modern Transportation, Kearny, New Jersey; and Duane Marine, Perth Amboy, New Jersey.[5] Licensed by the state, these outfits could legally receive hazardous waste and sign off on the manifest. They would then either stockpile it on site (where it would stay until it exploded, burned, or otherwise came to the attention of authorities) or dump it along roadways, down municipal sewers, into the ocean, or elsewhere (Block and Scarpitti, 1985:145, 158, 298; U.S. House of Representatives, 1980:25). In the extreme, actual ownership of or access to disposal sites was unnecessary for those willing to file totally fanciful manifests. Congressman Gore cited one case in which several major corporations signed over their wastes to an out-of-state facility that subsequently was shown to simply not exist (U.S. House of Representatives, 1980:70, 135).[6]

Enabling Causes: The Making of a Vulnerable Regulatory Structure

In retrospect, it is hardly surprising that, given the opportunity, organized crime would enter the newly created market for hazardous waste handling. It was an extension of their current business activity. They had the equipment and organization. They had both the know-how and the will to corrupt the manifest system. It was an attractive prospect. Both the potential size of the market and the potential profits were enormous. Even if they charged only a fraction of the true price of legitimate disposal, that price would be much higher than the price they charged to move the same stuff when it was legally just garbage, but their operating expenses would stay the same (if they commingled hazardous waste with ordinary garbage) or decrease (if they simply dumped). Why organized crime would want to enter into a relationship with corporate generators when the opportunity presented itself needs no subtle unraveling. The more complex task is to determine what political and social-structural conditions made it possible for them to "colonize" the hazardous waste disposal industry.

Lax Implementation, Incompetent and/or Corrupt Enforcement

Explanations of organized crime presence in hazardous waste handling focused on lax implementation and improper enforcement. Congressional hearings produced dramatic evidence that, at least in New Jersey, the state where organized crime intrusion into hazardous waste is most thoroughly documented, the major provisions of the RCRA were poorly implemented and enforced. Interim hauling and disposal licenses were freely granted. The manifest system was not sufficiently monitored.

Interim Licensing. Congress had mandated an extended transition period during which both transporters and disposal firms would operate under temporary permits until an adequate national hazardous waste industry developed. Generators lobbied quite heavily on this point (U.S. EPA, 1976:238, 1979:153, 307; Gansberg, 1979) and Congress had to agree to this provision because the shortage of adequate hazardous waste facilities was so severe. American industry would have choked in its own accumulating wastes had it not been permitted to continue to use less-than-adequate means of disposal. A reasonable concession to economic realities, implementation of interim licensing was poorly managed. House of Representatives testimony shows that New Jersey issued hauling permits to any applicant who paid a nominal $50 fee (U.S. House of Representatives, 1980:14–15). Existing landfills and even totally bogus firms with no real disposal facilities found it equally easy to get interim disposal permits (U.S. House of Representatives, 1980:10).

> Harold Kaufman (key FBI informant on mob involvement in hazardous waste disposal, testifying about his old firm, Duane Marine): The State licensed us. We were the first ones licensed . . . .
>   Gore: And this was a chemical waste disposal facility, is that right?
> Kaufman: Well, that is what it was called. It never disposed of anything, but you can call it that.

Manifest Oversight.   Once a license was obtained, lax supervision of the manifest system made illegal and unsafe disposal of hazardous waste a relatively straightforward, low-risk activity (U.S. House of Representatives, 1980:140).

> Gore: What enforcement efforts are you making to prevent the abuse of the manifest system?
> Edwin Stier (New Jersey Division of Criminal Justice): The only way the manifest system is going to be properly, effectively enforced is through the proper analysis of the information that comes from the manifest. . . . Anyone who assumes that a manifest system which looks good on paper can control the flow and disposition of toxic waste without the kind of support both technical and manpower support that is necessary to make it effective, I think, is deluding himself. [However] . . . we aren't looking specifically for manifest case violations. We aren't pulling every manifest in that is filed with the department of environmental protection and looking for falsification of manifests specifically because we don't have the time, the resources, or the specific lead information to do that.

Congressional testimony revealed that until 1980 New Jersey did not have a single person assigned to monitor the manifests being filed in Trenton (U.S. House of Representatives, 1981b:124). A recent study by the General Accounting Office (U.S. GAO, 1985:25–31) found that the manifest system does not detect illegal disposal, in part because of inadequate monitoring.

Congressional hearings also produced evidence suggesting that the relevant New Jersey agencies—the Interagency Hazardous Waste Strike Force, the Division of Criminal Justice, and the Division of Environmental Protection—were incapable of producing effective enforcement even when tipped off to specific instances of hazardous waste dumping (U.S. House of Representatives, 1980:144–146, 1981b:110–124). Block and Scarpitti (1985) present many other examples that appear to show corruption or, at best, ineptitude on the part of state officials responsible for investigation and prosecution of illegal hazardous waste practices.

Lax implementation and enforcement undoubtedly played a big role in facilitating organized crime entry into the hazardous waste disposal industry. There are, however, more fundamental conditioning factors that logically and temporally preceded these causes. RCRA is a regulatory structure ripe with potential for subversion. Why did Congress create a regulatory structure so vulnerable to lax enforcement? A review of RCRA's legislative history shows quite clearly that corporate generators moved decisively to shape the emerging federal intervention to their liking. They determinedly fought for and achieved a regulatory form that would demand of them the least real change and a form that would minimize their liability for potential violations of the new regulations.

Generators' Strategic Intervention in the Legislative Debate over the Form of Policy

Compared to the regulatory mechanism written into the final language of the RCRA, some potential alternative forms that were proposed and then rejected would have proved much less hospitable to noncompliance in general and to the entry of organized crime in particular. The federal government could have mandated specific treatment and disposal practices, or directed generators to treat all of their wastes themselves, or legislated that generators retain full responsibility for their wastes even if they assign them to other parties for shipping and disposal. Generators, led by representatives of major oil and chemical corporations, explicitly and vigorously opposed any such language. They hammered away with striking unanimity at two fundamental points: that the government should in no way interfere in firms' production decisions, and that generators should not be held responsible for the ultimate fate of their hazardous wastes.

Generators repeatedly warned Congress neither to appropriate to itself the power to intervene in production processes nor to require generators to follow specific waste treatment practices. They stressed, instead, that regulatory controls are more properly imposed at the stage of final disposition. Here are some representative statements:

> We believe that the disposal of wastes ought to be regulated instead of regulating the nature and use of the product or the type of manufacturing process used (E.I. DuPont de Nemours and Co., U.S. Senate, 1974:454).

> Authority to control production, composition, and distribution of products . . . would be devastating to free enterprise commerce (Dow Chemical, U.S. Senate, 1974:1,478).

> [Stauffer Chemical opposes generator permits which] would place controls on raw materials, manufacturing processes, products and distribution (Stauffer, U.S. Senate, 1974:1,745).

> . . . legislation should not impede the natural interaction of raw materials, market and other forces that ultimately control the nature, quality,

price, and success of products developed in our free enterprise system (Union Carbide, U.S. Senate, 1974:1,748).

No specific requirements or prohibitions should be set governing the recovery, reuse or disposal of industrial wastes. . . . Generators should be free to increase or decrease waste production rates, terminate waste production, treat their own wastes, and negotiate treatment or disposal service contracts in a free and competitive market (American Petroleum Institute, U.S. EPA, 1976:1,406, 1,410).

. . . the generator should be free to decide whether to treat or dispose of wastes (Manufacturing Chemists Association, U.S. EPA, 1976:565).

. . . economic incentive alone should determine the degree of waste recycle and recovery. . . . We are opposed to regulations specifying the kind and amount of processing and recycle of wastes [by the generator]. [The] greatest emphasis should be placed on establishing standards which assure that the ultimate disposal method is satisfactory (DuPont, U.S. EPA, 1976:72–73).[7]

Generator unanimity was equally impressive on the second issue of responsibility. They were willing to have limited responsibility, to label their wastes, and make sure they contracted only with firms approved by state authorities, but they vehemently opposed the idea that generators should bear legal responsibility for their wastes from cradle to grave. They argued that responsibility should pass to the party in physical possession of the hazardous waste. Under such a system, they further pointed out, only the hauler and disposer need to be licensed and the government should not license generators. Here are some representative statements:

We agree that the generator has some responsibility in the area, . . . [i.e.] make some determination that the disposer is competent and has the proper permits for disposal. . . . However, the waste hauler and disposer have responsibility to assure, respectively, that the wastes are delivered for disposal at the proper location and are properly disposed. Irresponsible action is invited if the person holding the waste has no responsibility for it (DuPont, U.S. EPA, 1976:73–74).

[The generator should] confirm the competence and reliability of transporters, treaters and processors to whom the waste may be transferred. . . . Each transporter, treater and disposer should be responsible for his individual activities while the waste is in his possession (Monsanto, U.S. EPA, 1976:410–411).

MCA recommends that the responsibility for the waste should be associated with physical possession of the waste, so that the generator should not be held liable for negligence of the transporter and the disposer of the waste. (Manufacturing Chemists Association, U.S. EPA, 1976:565).

> We feel that permits should only be required of the disposal site oper-
> ator (B.F. Goodrich, U.S. Senate, 1974:1,441).

> . . . permits for both generation and disposal of hazardous waste is dou-
> bly redundant. . . . A permit system for generators of wastes is un-
> needed and would tend to stagnate technology at the level prevailing
> at the time the permit was issued (Dow Chemical, U.S. Senate,
> 1974:1,478–1,479).

> . . . we consider permits for the generation of hazardous wastes to be
> unneeded, and could result in unnecessary restriction of manufactur-
> ing operations (Union Carbide, U.S. Senate, 1974:464).[8]

The generators also lobbied for the other provisions to their liking—a narrow definition of what substances should be regulated as hazardous, flexible time frames for implementation, and less stringent rules for on-site disposal[9]—but the two points above were the heart of their legislative intervention. In the end, they didn't get everything they wanted. The government would make generators register with the EPA. On-site, generator self-disposal would be subject to the same rules that governed off-site disposal firms. However, the overall forms of RCRA passed by Congress embodied both of their major demands.

The Legacy of Generator Inattention and Inaction

The generators also contributed indirectly to the shaping of RCRA legislation through their historical lack of attention to proper hazardous waste disposal. The EPA estimated in 1974 that ocean dumping and improper landfilling cost about 5% of the price of environmentally adequate disposal and it reported that

> Given this permissive legislative climate, generators of waste are under
> little or no pressure to expend resources for adequate management of
> their hazardous wastes. (U.S. Senate, 1974:71)

Lack of generator demand for adequate disposal facilities discouraged the inflow of investment capital, and an adequate waste disposal industry had failed to develop by the time RCRA legislation was being debated. Had legislators ignored this situation and required an immediate shift to proper disposal, a production crisis could have been triggered as wastes accumulated and firms found few legal outlets for them. Industrial spokesmen predicted dire consequences. In a representative statement, a Union Carbide spokesman warned legislators:

> Those wastes which are non-incinerable and have no commercial value
> must be disposed of. To deny opportunity for disposal would effectively
> eliminate much of the chemical process industry. Disposal in or on the

land or disposal in the oceans are the only viable alternatives available. (U.S. Senate, 1974:461)

Neither individual officeholders nor whole governments stay in office long if they pass legislation which, even for the best and most popular of reasons, brings to a halt industrial sectors central to the national economy. Congressmen had to be realistic and mandate years of transition during which hazardous waste would be hauled and disposed by operators having only interim licenses. This reasonable concession to the reality of the situation, a legacy of generator inattention, created a loophole through which many less-than-qualified parties could legally participate as providers in the hazardous waste market.[10]

Notes

I wish to gratefully acknowledge that this paper has benefited from comments by Frank Henry, Judith Gerson, Wendy Strimling, Vern Baxter, John Campbell, Carroll Estes, members of the Pew Writing Seminar, and several anonymous reviewers.

1. The extent of involvement is unclear for two reasons:

First, investigation has focused on the New York, Connecticut, and New Jersey region. This is a strategic site for investigation because so much hazardous waste is produced in the Tri-State area (for example, New Jersey ranks number one in the nation in annual hazardous waste generation) and because mob involvement in garbage in this region has been thoroughly documented. But, for the same reasons, this region may not be typical of the rest of the nation. Recent investigatory reporting concerning environmental pollution and political corruption in Louisiana (Getschow and Petzinger, 1984; Petzinger and Getschow, 1984a, 1984b; Snyder, 1985a, 1985b, 1985c, 1985d, 1985e, 1985f) shows that waste disposal is a corrupt business there as well, but that corruption grows out of the specific history of oil industry domination of that state's economy and its politics and appears to be quite different from patterns of corruption in the Northeast. This suggests that the post-RCRA relationship between corporate generators and waste disposers may be heavily influenced by variations in regional history predating RCRA.

Second, on a more theoretical level, the boundary between organized crime and legitimate business is, at points, somewhat ambiguous. Take, for example, SCA, the nation's third largest hazardous waste company. SCA undertook a vigorous acquisition program in New Jersey and quickly bought up about 20 garbage hauling and landfill companies. Some of these were formerly owned by organized crime figures. SCA is a corporation whose stock is traded on the New York Stock Exchange and its corporate board boasts outside directors associated with IBM, Houghton-Mifflin Co., MIT, and the Boston Co. (U.S. House of Representatives, 1980, 1981a), but Congressional testimony indicates that when SCA bought mob-owned firms, it hired the former owners as managers and appears to have allowed them free hand to run their business as they had before acquisition.

2. Methods of estimation are discussed in depth by Greenberg and Anderson (1984).

3. It is generally admitted that even the best landfill is only temporary and inadequate: "No landfill can be made safe from all substances"—Albert Gore (U.S. House of Representatives, 1983:2). George J. Tyler, Assistant Commissioner of the New Jersey Department of Environmental Protection, speaking about the Lone Pine landfill in Freehold, New Jersey (U.S. House of Representatives, 1981b:188): "The landfill is leaking into the water, but so does every landfill in the country." The landfill at Wilsonville, Illinois, owned and operated by SCA (see Note 1), is, according to Dr. Raymond D. Harbison, a toxicologist, EPA consultant, and professor of pharmacology at Vanderbilt University, "the most scientific landfill in this country" (U.S. House of Representatives, 1981a:267). Geological and soil permeability feasibility tests were conducted before construction was begun. Trenches were carefully dug. Arriving waste is sampled and tested, then buried in either nonleaking 55 gallon drums or double-walled paper bags. Monitoring wells surround the site. Yet subsequent studies show that the soil is more

porous than originally thought and water is seeping in at rates greater than predicted. Furthermore, the landfill is built over an abandoned coal mine and feasibility tests underestimated the likelihood of "subsidence," land sinkage that may compromise the site's ability to keep substances safely contained. If this is the best site in the nation, the Office of Technology Assessment is right to worry that current efforts to clean up the worst abandoned sites under the Superfund program only transfer the problem to other places and future times (Shabecoff, 1985:31).

4. Of parenthetical interest here is the methodological similarity between organized crime's property rights system in garbage and price-fixing by Westinghouse, General Electric, and other firms in the famous heavy electrical equipment price fixing scandal of 1961 (Geis, 1977).

5. Modern Transportation, a firm that would ultimately receive half the manifested hazardous waste originating in northern New Jersey, was incorporated in 1972 by Richard Miele, co-owner with known organized crime figures of numerous garbage-related firms and landfills (Block and Scarpitti, 1985:297). Chemical Control Corporation was taken over by Johnny Albert, one of the organizers of the New Jersey Trade Waste Association (Block and Scarpitti, 1985:256–260; U.S. House of Representatives, 1980:10). Duane Marine was so enmeshed in organized crime networks and activities that its former employee, Harold Kaufman, became the central federal informant on these activities.

6. Albert Gore in the case of Capital Recovery: "The subcommittee's investigation has uncovered evidence that since August, 1976, major industrial companies, such as Koppers, Inc., in one case Exxon, Union Chemical Company in the state of New Jersey certified that over 270,000 gallons of chemical waste were delivered to an out-of-state facility in Wilmington, Delaware, named Capital Recovery. From all the available evidence, Capital Recovery is nothing more than a paper corporation. It has no offices or any site in Wilmington. There is no phone listing, no city or State real estate tax or business tax information; no annual report has been filed . . . " (U.S. House of Representatives, 1980:135–136).

7. Other companies and associations making the same argument during these hearings included Monsanto, Exxon, B.F. Goodrich, Alcoa, the Texas Chemical Council, and the Western Oil and Gas Association.

8. The same point was also raised by Stauffer Chemicals, Marathon Oil, American Cyanamid, Berylco, Shell, Alcoa, the Texas Chemical Council, the Western Oil and Gas Association, the American Petroleum Institute, and the New Jersey Manufacturers Association.

9. The issue of flexible time frames was raised by the National Association of Manufacturers (U.S. House of Representatives, 1976:190) and Exxon (U.S. EPA, 1976:940). Arguing for a restricted definition of what is regulable hazardous waste were DuPont (U.S. EPA, 1976:69), the American Iron and Steel Institute (U.S. EPA, 1976:100), American Cyanamid (U.S. EPA, 1976:1,550), B.F. Goodrich (U.S. Senate, 1974:1,440), Stauffer (U.S. Senate, 1974:1,746). Monsanto (U.S. EPA, 1976:406–407), and Dow (U.S. EPA, 1976:956), argued for fewer restrictions for on-site disposal.

10. It should be noted that generators intervened not only in policy formation but also engaged in ongoing efforts to weaken regulatory impact during implementation. They appeared at EPA implementation hearings to emphasize that the criteria for declaring substances hazardous were still too broad, that proposed disposal requirements were too stringent, that interim standards were burdensome and inflexible, and that recordkeeping and reporting requirements were onerous. Especially active in this period were trade associations such as the Manufacturing Chemists Association, the Synthetic Organic Chemists Manufacturing Association, the American Petroleum Institute, and the National Paint and Coatings Association, as well as large individual corporations such as Dow and DuPont (U.S. EPA, 1976:79; U.S. Senate, 1979). EPA officials complained privately that "the millions of pages of testimony filed by representatives of industry on virtually each clause of every implementation proposal" created "a major obstacle" to timely implementation of RCRA (Shabecoff, 1979:1).

References

Albanese, Jay S.
  1982 What Lockheed and La Cosa Nostra have in common: The effect of ideology on criminal justice policy. Crime and Delinquency 28:211–232.
Barnett, Harold C.
  1981 Corporate capitalism, corporate crime. Crime and Delinquency 27:4–23.

Block, Alan A.
  1982 "On the Waterfront" revisited: The criminology of waterfront organized crime. Contemporary Crisis 6:373–396.
Block, Alan A. and William J. Chambliss
  1981 Organizing Crime. New York: Elsevier.
Block, Alan A. and Frank R. Scarpitti
  1985 Poisoning for Profit: The Mafia and Toxic Waste in America. New York: William Morrow.
Brady, James
  1983 Arson, urban economy and organized crime: The case of Boston. Social Problems 31:1–27.
Chambliss, William J.
  1978 On the Take: From Petty Crooks to Presidents. Bloomington: Indiana University Press.
Clinard, Marshall B., Peter C. Yeager, Jeanne M. Brissette, David Petrashek, and Elizabeth Harries
  1979 Illegal Corporate Behavior. Washington, DC: U.S. Government Printing Office.
Clinard, Marshall B. and Peter C. Yeager
  1980 Corporate Crime. New York: The Free Press.
Crenson, Matthew A.
  1971 The Un-Politics of Air Pollution: A Study of Non-Decisionmaking in the Cities. Baltimore: Johns Hopkins University Press.
Denzin, Norman K.
  1977 Notes on the crimogenic hypothesis: A case study of the American liquor industry. American Sociological Review 42:905–920.
Drucker, Peter P.
  1981 What is business ethics? The Public Interest 63:18–36.
Etzioni, Amitai
  1985 Shady corporate practices. New York Times. November 15.
Farberman, Harvey A.
  1975 A crimogenic market structure: The automobile industry. Sociological Quarterly 16:438–457.
Gansberg, Martin
  1979 New Jersey Journal. New York Times. January 21.
Geis, Gilbert
  1977 The heavy electrical equipment antitrust cases of 1961. In Gilbert Geis and Robert F. Meier (eds.), White-Collar Crime: Offenses in Business, Politics, and the Professions (rev. ed.). New York: Free Press.
Getschow, George and Thomas Petzinger, Jr.
  1984 Oil's legacy: Louisiana marshlands, laced with oil canals, are rapidly vanishing. The Wall Street Journal. October 24.
Governor's Commission on Science and Technology for the State of New Jersey.
  1983 Report of the Governor's Commission on Science and Technology.
Greenberg, Michael R. and Richard F. Anderson
  1984 Hazardous Waste Sites: The Credibility Gap. Piscataway, NJ: Center for Urban Policy Research.
Leonard, William N. and Marvin G. Weber
  1977 Automakers and dealers: A study of crimogenic market forces. In Gilbert Geis and Robert F. Meier (eds.), White-Collar Crime: Offenses in Business, Politics, and the Professions (rev. ed.). New York: Free Press.
Martens, Frederick T. and Colleen Miller-Longfellow
  1982 Shadows of substance: Organized crime reconsidered. Federal Probation 46:3–9.

Marx, Karl
  1967 Capital: A Critique of Political Economy, Vol. 1. New York: International Publishers.
Needleman, Martin L. and Carolyn Needleman
  1979 Organizational crime: Two models of crimogenesis. Sociological Quarterly 20:517–528.
Petzinger, Thomas, Jr. and George Getschow
  1984a Oil's legacy: In Louisiana, big oil is cozy with officials and benefit is mutual. The Wall Street Journal. October 22.
  1984b Oil's legacy: In Louisiana, pollution and cancer are rife in the petroleum area. The Wall Street Journal. October 23.
Shabecoff, Philip
  1979 House unit attacks lags on toxic waste. New York Times. October 14.
  1985 Toxic waste threat termed far greater than U.S. estimates. New York Times. March 10.
Schelling, Thomas C.
  1967 Economics and criminal enterprise. The Public Interest 7:61–78.
Smith, Dwight C., Jr.
  1980 Paragons, pariahs, and pirates: A spectrum-based theory of enterprise. Crime and Delinquency 26:358–386.
Smith Dwight C., Jr., and Richard D. Alba
  1979 Organized crime and American life. Society 3:32–38.
Snyder, David
  1985a Toxic scars crisscross Louisiana. The New Orleans Times-Picayune. September 8.
  1985b Early action was met with disbelief. The New Orleans Times-Picayune. September 8.
  1985c Wastes choke scenic bayous of St. Charles. The New Orleans Times-Picayune. September 10.
  1985d Chemical specter fills Cajun paradise with sense of fear. The New Orleans Times-Picayune. September 11.
  1985e He won't be stopped, landfill operator warns. The New Orleans Times-Picayune. September 11.
  1985f 10-year struggle to shut down waste site stymied by state. The New Orleans Times-Picayune. September 12.
Szasz, Andrew
  1982 The dynamics of social regulation: A study of the formation and evolution of the Occupational Safety and Health Administration. Unpublished doctoral dissertation. Madison: University of Wisconsin.
  1984 Industrial resistance to occupational safety and health legislation: 1971–1981. Social Problems 32:103–116.
U.S. Environmental Protection Agency
  1976 Hazardous Waste Management: Public Meetings. December 2–11.
  1979 Public Hearings on the Proposed Regulations Implementing Sections 3001 to 3004 of the Resource Conservation and Recovery Act. February 22–23.
U.S. General Accounting Office
  1985 Illegal Disposal of Hazardous Waste: Difficult to Detect or Deter. Comptroller General's Report to the Subcommittee on Investigations and Oversight, Committee on Public Works and Transportation, House of Representatives.
U.S. House of Representatives
  1975 Waste Control Act of 1975. Hearings held by the Subcommittee on Transportation and Commerce, Committee on Interstate and Foreign Commerce. April 8–11, 14–17.

1976 Resource Conservation and Recovery Act of 1976. Hearings held by the Subcommittee on Transportation and Commerce, Committee on Interstate and Foreign Commerce. June 29–30.
1980 Organized Crime and Hazardous Waste Disposal. Hearings held by Subcommittee on Oversight and Investigations, Committee on Interstate and Foreign Commerce. December 16.
1981a Organized Crime Links to the Waste Disposal Industry. Hearings held by Subcommittee on Oversight and Investigations, Committee on Energy and Commerce. May 28.
1981b Hazardous Waste Matters: A Case Study of Landfill Sites. Hearings held by Subcommittee on Oversight and Investigations, Committee on Energy and Commerce, June 9.
1982 Hazardous Waste Enforcement. Hearings held by Subcommittee on Oversight and Investigations, Committee on Energy and Commerce. December.
1983 Hazardous Waste Disposal. Hearings held by Subcommittee on Oversight and Investigations. Committee on Science and Technology. March 30 and May 4.
U.S. Senate
1974 The Need for a National Materials Policy. Hearings held by the Subcommittee on Environmental Pollution, Committee on Public Works. June 11–13, July 9–11, 15–18.
1979 Oversight of RCRA Implementation. Hearings held by the Subcommittee on Environmental Pollution and Resource Protection, Committee on Environmental and Public Works. March 28–29.
Williams, Bruce A. and Albert R. Matheny
1984 Testing theories of social regulation: Hazardous waste regulation in the American states. Journal of Politics 46:428–458.

Managing Deviant Careers and Identities

As explained by Johann le Roux and Cheryl Sylvia Smith, in "Is the Street Child Phenomenon Synonymous with Deviant Behavior," street children evoke strong feelings from those who wish to help and those who wish to get rid of them. While the individual biographies among street children vary, once homeless, each of these youth is confronted with his or her marginal social position. This is a group with few safety nets, precisely because they are alienated from society and seen as "social junk." The authors show that because of the negative attitudes toward street children, as well as the frequent contact with social-control agents, by virtue of their behavior being defined as deviant, it is very difficult to maintain a healthy self-concept.

Because of a lack of resources, the experience of living on the street may also require involvement in other forms of deviance. Engaging in additional forms of deviance serves not only to further antagonize an already impatient community but also to provide rationale for punitive attitudes and actions against them. A significant concern is whether the harsh reality of the streets and the process of labeling pushes these children more deeply into a path of primary and secondary deviance. One of the few buffers against developing a negative self-perception may be the support they receive from other street children. However, one significant barrier to energized programs designed to intervene and help these children is "probably due to street children's marginality to society." Street children carry stigma and are discredited.

Finding oneself in a stigmatized group changes everything. Amir Marvasti addresses the experience of Middle Eastern Americans in a post-9/11 world. In his article "Being Middle Eastern American: Identity Negotiation in the Context of the War on Terror," Marvasti uses personal experience to set the context and describe the problem of stigmatization. The lives of Middle Eastern Americans have been changed for the worse. They experience more stereotyping more frequently, and are asked to explain their intentions, politics, beliefs, and mundane daily routines. Marvasti explores the ways in which Middle Eastern Americans respond to these disruptions and calls to account for their identity. The question is how do individuals "establish a situationally practical and useful Middle Eastern self" when called to account for their ethnic identity? Marvasti focuses on "the interpretive practices individuals use to establish or dispute stigma or stigmatized identities." The author identifies several "accounting strategies" used by Middle Eastern Americans in their attempts to salvage spoiled identities in disrupted interactions: humorous, educational, defiant, cowering, and passing. Marvasti makes the important point that people are not simply recipients of stigma who must then manage; rather, people often actively combat stigma and identity challenges.

Is the Street Child Phenomenon Synonymous with Deviant Behavior?

Johann le Roux
Cheryl Sylvia Smith

Introduction

Street children are subjected to physical assault, sexual abuse, harassment from the public, intimidation by gang members and criminals, and arrest by the police (Richter, 1988b). This victimization frequently repeats what has occurred in the home. Though often victims themselves, street children, according to Swart (1988c), are regarded as irresponsible and lawless and a serious financial burden to society.

Richter (cited in the *Natal Mercury,* June 15, 1988) has stated that the phenomenon of street children has become an emotional issue, evoking strong feelings among those committed to helping them, as well as those determined to get rid of them (see also Swart-Kruger and Donald, 1994; Donald and Swart-Kruger, 1994; Jayes, 1985). Further, Richter (1991a, 1991b) has noted that these children live on the periphery of society, and as a result they are often misunderstood.

Characterizing Street Children

The term street children can be applied to a large number of youths, all of whom spend a great deal of time away from home, but do not necessarily share other characteristics (Agnelli, 1986). Definitions vary, but they generally have three main elements in common: (1) these children live or spend a significant amount of time on the street; (2) the street is the children's source of livelihood; and (3) they are inadequately cared for, protected, or supervised by responsible adults. Richter (1988c, 1991b) has pointed out that the characteristics of runaways, or homeless youths, in First World countries differ from those of working Third World street children. These differences will be considered in the context of South Africa.

A survey of the literature on street children reveals that three groups are frequently identified: children with continuous family contacts, who work on the street, usually go to school, and go home to their families at the end of the day; children with occasional family contacts, who work on the street, do not go to school, and seldom go home to their families; and children without family contacts, who consider the street their home, and it is there that they seek shelter, food, and a sense of belonging among peers. Lusk (1992) has emphasized the psychological characteristics of four groups of street children: poor, working children who return to their families at night and usually attend school—they are not likely to exhibit delinquent behavior; independent street workers, whose family ties are in the process of breaking down—their school attendance is erratic and they exhibit increasing delinquency; children who live and work with their families on the street—poverty is the overwhelming reason for their presence; and children who have broken off all contact with their families—they live full time on the streets and are the "real" street children. Aptekar (1994) divides the process into stages, beginning with the child spending a small amount of time away from home, and progressing to the total adoption of the street lifestyle and culture (compare Baizerman, 1988; Visano, 1990).

Richter (1988a), Konanc (1989), Cosgrove (1990), and Aptekar (1995a) have stated that street children can be defined according to their relationships with family. Children *of* the street have left home permanently and usually have little or no contact with their families. Children *on* the street, who constitute the largest group, return home from time to time, usually contributing to the financial support of their families (Ennew, cited in Richter, 1988c; compare Aptekar, 1994).

Thus, street children encompass various categories. In addition, this term is commonly used in Africa, while in Europe, the Americas, and Australia, the terms homeless children, runaways, throwaways, and pushouts are more common.

The United Nations has developed its own definition of street children: "any girl or boy . . . for whom the street in the widest sense of the word, including unoccupied dwellings, wasteland, and so on, has become his or her habitual abode and/or source of livelihood, and who is inadequately protected, supervised, or directed by responsible adults" (Inter-NGO, cited in Swart-Kruger and Donald, 1994, p. 108). Cockburn (1991), noting that most differences in definitions are largely semantic, has defined street children as "those who have abandoned their homes, schools and immediate communities, before they are sixteen years of age, and have drifted into a nomadic street life" (p. 12). Richter (1988a) would add, "or those who have been abandoned by their families." Keen (1989) has proposed the following definition: "A street child is regarded as one who has run away from home and is living on the streets apart from any adult supervision or care" (p. 11). Cosgrove (1990) has emphasized the degree of family involvement and the amount of deviant behavior: a street child is "any individual under the age of eighteen whose behavior is predominantly at variance with community norms, and whose primary support for his/her developmental needs is not a family or family substitute" (p. 192). A recent report by the Human Sciences Research Council (HSRC) of South Africa (cited in Schurink and Mathye, 1993) has put forward the following definition: "A street child is any girl or boy who is under the age of eighteen and who has left his/her home environment part time or permanently (because of problems at home and/or in school, or to try to alleviate those problems) and who spends most of his/her time unsupervised on the street as part of a subculture of children who live an unprotected communal life and who depend on themselves and each other, and not on an adult, for the provision of physical and emotional needs, such as food, clothing, nurturance, direction and socialization" (p. 5).

According to Aptekar (1995a), it has been a common practice to refer to street children as a more or less unified group. However, the uniqueness of each street child should be acknowledged: "The term street children and youth embraces a diverse group of young people dislocated, to various degrees, from family, school and community, who tend to congregate in inner-city areas. Their reasons for being on the street vary, as do their probable educational and adjustment outcomes" (Richter and Swart-Kruger, 1995, p. 31).

It has also been suggested that children who have adjusted to street life are not easily convinced that there is a better alternative (Agnelli, 1986). Samper, cited in Aptekar (1995a), has gone so far as to refer to these children as a "plague."

Aptekar (1995a) has argued that, in most cases, street children are lumped together with working children who return to their families at the end of the day to live a normal but impoverished family life. This serves to make the problem of homelessness seem much greater than it actually is. In fact, the great majority—well over three-quarters and as many as ninety percent in various developing countries—live at home but work on the streets to earn money for their families (Aptekar, 1994).

Geddes (1993), however, has stated that although few street children are actually homeless or orphans, they are functionally homeless. Their parents are incapable of caring for them due to such problems as substance abuse and poverty (similar findings have been reported by Ennew, 1986, 1994; Lusk, 1992; Myers, 1989; Ojanuga, 1990; Patel, 1990; UNICEF, 1986).

A useful typology developed by UNICEF (cited in Aptekar, 1994) has classified street children in relation to their development. It reflects the belief that the experience of children who work on the street is considerably different from children who must look to a peer group or gang for the fulfillment of primary needs, such as protection, sustenance, and nurture. Aptekar (1994) has noted that some researchers classify street children by the different types of experiences they have, including the quality of their play and work and their relations with peers and authority figures. In addition, age and gender are important factors.

There is also the popular misconception that equates street children with gangs (compare Scharf et al., 1986; Swart, 1988a). Unfortunately, both the police and the public are predisposed to characterize street children in this way.

Visano (1990) has claimed that street children are defined mainly by two dimensions: the amount of time spent on the streets and the absence of contact with responsible adults. However, this ignores the individual differences among them, such as coping style.

Deviance

Highly charged reactions to street children make it difficult to remain objective. Thus, the children's ability to survive under the most trying circumstances may be understated, or their problems minimized, making them appear as modern-day Huckleberry Finns. According to Aptekar et al. (1995), "it is so difficult to know to what degree the children are honest, to what degree one's perception of them is accurate, and how what is written about them will be perceived by readers" (pp. 2–3).

Adults' negative interpretations of the lifestyle and hostile, condemnatory responses to street children would seem to make it almost impossible for them to retain healthy self-esteem (Richer, 1989a; compare Scharf et al., 1986; Swart, 1988b). Wilson and Arnold (1986) have stated that "their silent scream and inner rage surface as they cut loose and take to the streets. There are few safety nets for them, because they are alienated from our society and because we regard them as 'deviants' and 'social junk'" (p. 7). Further, "they feel exploited by almost everyone: the media, the pushers, the sex purchasers, the sociologists, and the do-gooders" (p. 6).

South African street children are generally thought of as sly, manipulative, deceitful troublemakers. According to Richter (1991b), "like all stereotypes, these cameos contain a little bit of truth, often enough to reinforce and maintain the stereotype" (p. 6). In addition, these negative appraisals are predominantly all-embracing, and no concessions are made that bad behavior may be temporary or situational (Richter, 1989b).

According to Goliath (1989), "street children are a burden on society. These children often become the adult layabouts and criminals of the future" (p. 5). The literature, on the whole, reveals that by society's standards, street children deviate from social, moral, and legal norms. Swart (1988c) has stated that although some people condone the behavior of street children as that which is to be expected under the circumstances, it is generally "considered deviant in terms of childhood and community norms" (p. 8). Further, Swart-Kruger and Donald (1994) have stated that "it is not surprising . . . that lying and deceit are fundamental tools of survival in an adult world which has aligned itself against them" (p. 120).

Hansson (1991), citing Posel (1990), has claimed that since 1976, when many black children left their homes to take up the political struggle against apartheid, the media have depicted them as being symbols of "anarchy, barbarism, criminality and spiraling violence" (p. 8). According to Hansson, this explains why most programs have been aimed at reinstating adult control and resocializing such children by getting them off the streets and back into some form of schooling. Similarly, Richter (1988c) has pointed out that "one of the chief difficulties in trying to help street children is to find ways of bringing them back into so-called normal society. . . . Their socialization into this lifestyle has been prematurely and, often, traumatically ended" (p. 3).

Richter (1988a) has noted that the longer the children spend on the streets, the more likely it is that they will enter into criminal activities. It would appear that street children engage in criminal activities mainly to ensure their own survival. According to Agnelli (1986), "street children as such are not delinquent, but only immediate candidates for delinquency if their needs are not met" (p. 112).

Society's negative opinion of these children, the low expectations of them, and the closing of legitimate avenues of opportunity may push them into delinquency, resulting in a self-fulfilling prophecy. According to Swart (1988a), a few street children, feeling humiliated and frustrated, have even threatened adults with violence for making their lives unbearable. Paton (1990) has noted that "a child is more often delinquent because he has been deprived of . . . the fundamental needs of security, affection and outlets for his creative and emotional impulses. The change in him is remarkable when these deep needs are satisfied" (p. 99).

In general, street children are perceived by the public as being "deviant" (Swart, 1988b; Mangwana, 1992; Konanc, 1989). Haralambos and Holborn (1992) define deviance as "those activities which bring disapproval from members of society" (pp. 580–581). Richter's (1988a) findings indicate that about one fifth of street children may be involved in antisocial activities, with some having acquired a set of attitudes and beliefs congruent with criminality. Further, "the high visibility of criminal or delinquent activities, even among a small group of street children, tends to antagonize the communities in which they occur, and they provide the authorities with a rationale for adopting a punitive attitude towards all street children" (Richter, 1988a, p. 13).

Agnelli (1986) has stated that the outcome of having to adjust, often alone, in a hostile environment is involvement in delinquent activities. Cemane (1990) has taken a more categorical stance: "street children have no incentive to conform to social sanctions that inhibit antisocial behavior, and will seize any opportunity to engage in deviant behavior" (p. 2).

The brutality of street life and negative interactions with authorities may set into motion a process of primary and secondary deviance, with terrible consequences. Involvement in petty crime, or even proximity to such crime, has frequently made street children victims of violence. Dewees and Klees (1995), citing research from Childhope, have stated that, between 1988 and 1990, an estimated 4,611 Brazilian children and adolescents were murdered by renegade police and vigilante groups.

It is possible that the labeling of street children as deviant pushes them more deeply into antisocial behavior. They may even come to accept society's perceptions of them. This labeling serves to further isolate them from society, intensifying their victimization (Alexander, 1987; O'Connor, 1989; Olson et al., 1980; Aptekar, 1988). Kennedy (1987) has stated that being labeled homeless carries many connotations: dirty, lazy, alcoholic, delinquent, and drug addicted. Perceptions beget attitudes, which, regarding street children, are negative—they are troublesome, they are undeserving. "So we provide *separate* services for them in *separate* hostels or houses, and what services there are, are provided not by the statutory bodies but by underfunded voluntary agencies. This in turn reinforces society's attitudes towards these children, that they don't deserve any better" (Kennedy, 1987, p. 19).

Commenting on street children in the Americas, Connolly (1990) has stated that, on the whole, these children are regarded as either delinquent or deviant. The fact that children who have spent a considerable amount of time on the streets frequently run away from both government and private programs is used as evidence to support the common belief that they are uneducable and incorrigible (see also Balanon, 1989; Konanc, 1989; Hickson and Gaydon, 1989). According to Richter (1989b), UNICEF has identified the inhibition of self-confidence and self-esteem, brought about by society's negative perception of street children and their work, as a significant element in their exploitation (compare Keen, 1990; Richter, 1988a).

Labeling theory views the determination of deviance as a dynamic process. Who is to be considered deviant comes about in the interplay between the powerless and the powerful (Thio, 1988). That the majority expect street children to be criminals as adults (Swart, 1988d) therefore has important repercussions.

Haskell and Yablonsky (1987) have stated that "a youth is defined as a juvenile delinquent when that status is conferred upon him by a court" (p. 7). Thus, when arrested, street children are often incarcerated with adult offenders, who instruct them in the tricks of the trade. This may lead to the entrenchment of a criminal career (Swart, 1988a; compare Olson et al., 1980; Nye, 1980; Gullotta, 1979; Young et al., 1983).

Conclusions

Increasing numbers of children live on the streets (Cemane, 1990; Richter, 1991a; Peacock, 1994). Once there, the attitudes and perceptions of society become that catalyst for the mainly negative self-perceptions that street children have of themselves (Konanc, 1989). The support of other street children, however, may act as a significant emotional buffer (Donald and Swart-Kruger, 1994).

According to Richter (1991a), "children are most especially harmed on the streets by the harsh physical conditions, by violence and harassment, by labor exploitation, by absorption into criminal networks, and by denial of their right to receive an education that will equip them to achieve a better life" (p. 8). Interventions have ranged from government programs to projects by volunteers. These efforts, until recently, have been minimal, probably due to street children's marginality to society (Cockburn, 1991).

Richter, citing Agnelli (1986), has claimed that the presence of street children is an indictment of the way society construes its priorities. These children, who endure significant hardship but hope one day to rejoin the community as productive members, are ignored by a society that systematically excludes them (Richter, 1989a).

References

Agnelli, S. (1986). *Street children: A growing urban tragedy.* London: Weidenfeld & Nicolson.

Alexander, M. (1987). *Street children: Towards global awareness and action. A study of resources available to homeless children in Guatemala, C.A.* Unpublished honors dissertation, Newcomb College, Tulane University.

Aptekar, L. (1988). *The street children of Cali.* Durham, NC: Duke University Press.

———. (1994). Street children in the developing world: A review of their condition. *Cross-Cultural Research, 28*(3), 195–224.

———. (1995a). *Educating the public about the coping strategies of street children.* Paper presented at the Tenth National Congress of the South African Association for Child and Adolescent Psychiatry (Children of Africa: Risk, Resilience, Challenge and Change), Durban.

———. (1995b). *Street children: A cross-cultural perspective.* Paper presented at the HSRC Conference (Street Children: From Resolutions to Action), Pretoria.

Aptekar, L., Cathey, P. J., Ciano, L., & Giardino, G. (1995). Street children in Nairobi, Kenya. *African Urban Quarterly, 10,* 1–26.

Baizerman, M. (1988). Street kids: Notes for designing a program for the youth of and on the streets. *The Child Care Worker, 6*(11), 13–15.

Balanon, L. G. (1989). Street children: Strategies for action. *Child Welfare, 68*(2), 159–166.

Cemane, K. B. (1990). The street-child phenomenon. *Social Work Practice, 1*(90), 2–5.

Cockburn, A. (1991). Street children: An overview of the extent, causes, characteristics and dynamics of the problem. *The Child Care Worker, 9*(1), 12–13.

———. (1995). *Looking after street children: A model indigenous to South Africa.* Paper presented at the Tenth Biennial Conference of the National Association of Child Care Workers, Cape Town.

Connolly, M. (1990). Adrift in the city: A comparative study of street children in Bogota, Colombia, and Guatemala City. In B. Boxhill (Ed.), *Homeless children: The watchers and the waiters* (pp. 129–149). New York: Haworth Press.

Cosgrove, J. (1990). Towards a working definition of street children, *International Social Work, 33,* 185–192.

Dewees, A., & Klees, S. J. (1995). Social movements and the transformation of national policy: Street and working children in Brazil. *Comparative Education Review, 39*(1), 76–100.

Donald, D., & Swart-Kruger, J. (1994). The South African street child: Developmental implications. *South African Journal of Psychology, 24*(24), 169–174.

Ennew, J. (1986). Children of the streets. *New Internationalist, 164,* 10–11.

———. (1994). Parentless friends: A cross-cultural examination of networks among street children and street youth. In F. Nesman & K. Hurrelman (Eds.), *Social networks and social support in childhood and adolescence.* London: De Gruyter.

Geddes, F. (1993). *The drugging patterns and attitudes towards substance abuse in a group of Johannesburg street children.* Unpublished master's thesis, University of the Witwatersrand, Johannesburg.

Goliath, D. (1989). The problem that grows and grows. *Prisma, 4,* 4–5.

Gullotta, T. (1979). Leaving home: Family relationships of the runaway child. *Social Casework, 60*(2), 111–114.

Hansson, D. (1991). *We the invisible: A feminist analysis of the conception of "street children" in South Africa.* Cape Town: Institute of Criminology, University of Cape Town.

Haralambos, M., & Holborn, M. (1992). *Sociology: Themes and perspectives* (3rd ed.). London: Harper Collins.

Haskell, M. R., & Yablonsky, L. (1987). *Juvenile delinquency.* Chicago: Rand McNally College Publishing.

Hickson, J., & Gaydon, V. (1989). Counselling in South Africa: The challenge of apartheid. *Journal of Multicultural Counselling and Development, 17*(2), 85–94.

Jayes, C. S. (1985). *Some characteristics of a group of coloured runaway boys aged 8–16 years and factors that these boys and their mothers perceived as contributing to their runaway behavior.* Unpublished master's thesis, University of Cape Town.

Keen, J. (1989). *A window on the world: A study into the values, interests, perceptions and aspirations of female street children.* Research project, University of Cape Town.

Keen, J. (1990). Dealing with street children. *The Child Care Worker, 8*(11), 8–9.

Kennedy, S. (Ed.). (1987). *Streetwise: Homelessness among the young in Ireland and abroad.* Glendale Press.

Konanc, E. (1989). Street children and children working in the street: Preliminary results of a field study in Turkey. *The Child Care Worker, 7*(11), 13–15.

Lusk, M. (1992). Street children of Rio de Janeiro. *International Social Work, 35,* 293–305.

Mangwana, T. (1992). Working with street children: Hints for child care workers. *The Child Care Worker, 10*(5), 14–15.

Maphatane, M., & Schurink, W. (1993). Legislation and welfare policy regarding street children. In W. Schurink (Ed.), *Street children.* Pretoria: HSRC.

Myers, W. (1989). Urban working children: A comparison of four surveys from South Africa. *International Labor, 128,* 321–335.

Natal Mercury. (1988, June 15). Durban. Page 3.

Nye, F. I. (1980). A theoretical perspective on running away. *Journal of Family Issues, 1*(2), 14–19.

O'Connor, I. (1989). *Our homeless children: Their experiences.* Report to the National Inquiry into Homeless Children by the Human Rights and Equal Opportunity Commission. Sydney: The Printing Place.

Ojanuga, D. (1990). Kaduma beggar children: A study of child abuse and neglect in northern Nigeria. *Child Welfare, 69,* 371–380.

Olson, L., Liebow, E., Mannino, F. V., & Shore, M. F. (1980). Runaway children twelve years later: A follow-up. *Journal of Family Issues, 1*(2), 176–185.

Patel, S. (1990). Street children, hotel boys and children of pavement dwellers and construction workers in Bombay: How they meet their daily needs. *Environment and Urbanization, 2,* 9–26.

Paton, A. (1990). *Diepkloof: Reflections on Diepkloof Reformatory.* Cape Town: David Philip.

Peacock, R. (1994). Street children. *Africa Insight, 24*(2), 138–143.

Richter, L. (1988a). Street children: The nature and scope of the problem in Southern Africa. *The Child Care Worker, 6*(7), 11–14.

——. (1988b). *A psychological study of street children in Johannesburg: An investigation requested by "Street-Wise," Johannesburg* (Report 89–01). Pretoria: Unisa.

——. (1988c). *Thinking on your feet in the street: Discussion to determine the educational potential of a group of "street children" in Johannesburg.* Address delivered at the Open Day of the Unit for Cognitive Development. Pretoria: Vista University.

——. (1989a). *South African street children: Comparisons with Anglo-American runaways.* Pretoria: Unisa.

——. (1989b). *Descriptions of self, family and society given by street children in Johannesburg.* Paper presented at the Seventh National Congress of the South African Association for Child and Adolescent Psychiatry and Allied Disciplines, Cape Town.

——. (1991a). Street children in South Africa: General theoretical introduction—Society, family and childhood. *The Child Care Worker, 9*(8), 7–9.

——. (1991b). Street children in South Africa: Street children in rich and poor countries. *The Child Care Worker, 9*(9), 5–7.

Richter, L., & Swart-Kruger, J. (1995). AIDS risk among street children and youth: Implications for intervention. *South African Journal of Psychology, 25*(1), 31–38.

Scharf, W., Powell, M., & Thomas, E. (1986). Strollers: Street children of Cape Town. In S. Burman & P. Reynolds (Eds.), *Growing up in a divided society: The context of childhood in South Africa.* Johannesburg: Ravan Press.

Schurink, W., & Mathye, M. (1993). Orientation. In W. Schurink (Ed.), *Street children.* Pretoria: HSRC.

Swart, J. (1986). My professional life on the streets. In N. J. Pines (Ed.), *Street children: Four perspectives.* The Institute for the Study of Man in Africa (ISMA Paper No. 40). Johannesburg: University of the Witwatersrand.

——. (1987). Street children: Refugees, drop-outs or survivors? *The Child Care Worker, 5*(10), 6–8.

——. (1988a). "Street-wise": Opening the way to self-actualization for the street child. *Africa Insight, 18*(1), 33–41.

——. (1988b). Community perceptions of street children in Hillbrow. *The Child Care Worker, 6*(6), 11–13.

——. (1988c). *Community and self-perceptions of the black South African street child.* Paper presented at the International Workshop on the Ethnography of Childhood, Cambridge University, Cambridge.

——. (1988d). *An anthropological study of street children in Hillbrow, Johannesburg, with special reference to their moral values.* Master's thesis, University of South Africa, Pretoria.

Swart-Kruger, J., & Donald, D. (1994). Children of the South African streets. In A. Dawes & D. Donald (Eds.), *Childhood and adversity: Psychological perspectives from South African research.* Cape Town: David Philip.

Thio, A. (1988). *Deviant behavior* (3rd ed.). New York: Harper & Row.

UNICEF. (1986). *Children in especially difficult circumstances: Exploitation of working and street children.* New York: United Nations Children Fund.

Visano, L. (1990). The socialization of street children: The development and transformation of identities. *Sociological Studies of Child Development, 3,* 139–161.

Wilson, P., & Arnold, J. (1986). *Street kids: Australia's alienated young.* Victoria: Collins Dove.

Young, R. L., Godfrey, W., & Adams, G. R. (1983). Runaways: A review of negative consequences. *Family Relations, 32,* 16–24.

Being Middle Eastern American: Identity Negotiation in the Context of the War on Terror

42

Amir Marvasti

About a year after September 11, 2001, I was in a shopping mall in a north-eastern city. For the last thirty minutes, I had been acutely aware of a security guard who had been following me around the mall. I was not completely surprised to see him follow me into the restroom. I was, however, taken aback when he moved closer to me near the urinal and looked over my shoulder as I was urinating. I was not sure what to say or do. I thought, "Is he worried that I am going to contaminate the city's water supply with my toxic urine?" I felt violated but did not want to cause a scene. So I started singing, "Chances are, 'cause I wear a silly grin the moment you come into view . . ." I had learned the lyrics from a Taco Bell toy that played the song when you squeezed it. I did not really know the rest of the song, but it did not matter, crowing in English seemed to have done the job. The security guard backed off and left me alone for the rest of my time at the mall.

As this story from my own life shows, September 11th and the ensuing period that has been named "the War on Terror" have significantly changed the daily lives of Middle Eastern Americans. For members of this ethnic group, it was indeed "the day that changed everything." In the days following September 11th, anything seemed possible, even mass detentions on a scale similar to what Japanese Americans were subjected to after Pearl Harbor. Such fears were so real that on the night of September 11th, I actually packed some of my belongings and essential documents in a small suitcase in preparation for mass detentions. I was, after all, born in Iran and physically resembled the terrorists, whose images were relentlessly displayed in all the mass media.

The extreme measures I feared did not materialize in the aftermath of the terrorist attacks; however, our lives have, in many ways, changed for the worse. In particular, Middle Eastern Americans experience more stereotyping more frequently than before. We are asked to explain our intentions, politics, and personal beliefs, even in the course of the mundane routines of everyday life, such as shopping at a mall. Although prejudice and discrimination against this ethnic group existed for decades before September 11th, the recent intensity and regularity of these demands are unprecedented. As one of my respondents put it, it happened before, "but not with this magnitude, and not with the accusatory tone. . . . Before it was just out of curiosity, and it was incidental, but this is an even more demanding tone of 'Who are you? And why did your people do this?'"

In this article, I investigate how Middle Eastern Americans respond to these disruptions of their daily routines. My original intention was to use interview data as well as my personal experiences as an Iranian immigrant to show how Middle Eastern Americans manage the stigma of their "spoiled identities" (Goffman 1963), especially in the aftermath of September 11th. While working on the first draft, I told my Iranian friend Ahmad,[1] with whom I was having lunch, that I was working on a paper titled "Stigma Management Strategies of Middle Eastern Americans." He nodded with his head down as he swallowed his food. After a short pause, he asked: "Why 'stigma'? What is the stigma?"

I was a little surprised that he failed to see the obvious. I explained, "After September 11th, people from the Middle East, especially Muslims, are treated with suspicion and subjected to ethnic profiling. That's why we are stigmatized."

He replied in a matter-of-fact tone. "Not always. Sitting here with you, talking in this school cafeteria, I don't feel stigmatized."

I began to wonder if this was a case of what Marx would call "false consciousness." I tried harder to convince him of the gravity of the situation of Middle Eastern Americans in a post-9/11 world. Ahmad did not disagree with the entire argument, he just refused to see himself as someone with a chronic stigma, or a permanent and enduring negative identity.

My friend convinced me that in some situations the stigma of being Middle Eastern goes unnoticed or is altogether nonexistent for all practical purposes. How do we then empirically study stigma or even know if it actually exists? One way to answer this question is to explore differences or similarities between audience and self-perceptions. In other words, we can compare Ahmad's self-image with his audience's perceptions of him and then go on to make certain conclusions about the relation between the two perspectives. For example, we may find that many people do in fact have negative perceptions of Ahmad, but he is fortunate to enjoy a high self-esteem that shields him from any emotional damage. This line of thinking could tell us a good deal about the mental state of both sides, but it offers less insight into everyday practice, or what people actually do when they interact with one another.

Self or audience perception are not fixed; they change in the course of practice. Similarly, the meaning of "stigma" varies situationally. A friend in graduate school jokingly referred to me as "the swarthy Iranian" (I did not find that funny). My same brown complexion apparently evoked a different audience response when a waitress at a Denny's told me, "You have such a nice tan!" (To which I smugly replied, "I was born with it.")

How do I really feel about having a brown complexion? Well, it depends on how it is used. I cannot really discuss it without referring to specific interactions and the social context that made my skin tone relevant. In the same vein, the empirical reality of being Middle Eastern is not just a mental property of the self or audience, but is enacted under the concrete conditions of everyday life. Audience or self perceptions about stigma become experientially meaningful and accessible when articulated in a specific setting and for a particular purpose.

Thus, to appreciate the complexity of Ahmad's experiences as a Middle Eastern American, it seemed that I needed to attend to situational variations surrounding how individuals define, enact, and cope with stigma in everyday encounters. This article first offers brief discussions of how I conceptualized stigma and everyday practice for the purpose of this study, and then presents my analysis of how Middle Eastern Americans manage their identities in the aftermath of September 11th.

Stigma and the Management of Spoiled Identity

Numerous studies have highlighted how stigmatized individuals employ various resistance and management strategies in response to negative labels (Cahill and Eggleston 1994; Davis 1961; Evans, Forsyth, and Foreman 2003; Feagin and McKinney 2003; Fothergill 2003; Herman 1993; Karp 1992; Riessman 2000; Roschelle and Kaufman 2004; Snow and Anderson 1987). This body of research treats normal–deviant interactions as an ongoing drama in which the stigmatized try to create positive identities. As they reveal, individuals use various techniques, such as humor and selective disclosure, to either avoid being stigmatized or soften the impact of the stigma on their "spoiled identity."

Much of the scholarship cited above is inspired by Goffman's seminal work *Stigma* (1963), in which he states:

> [When a stranger] is present before us, evidence can arise of his possessing an attribute that makes him different from others. . . . He is thus reduced in our minds from a whole and usual person to a tainted, discounted one. Such an attribute is a stigma. (Pp. 2–3)

For Goffman, stigma is a variable social construct and not a fixed characteristic of the person. Stigma is bound by social roles and expectations and derives its meaning from particular social contexts. An ascribed status or attribute, such as one's race or ethnicity, is not inherently stigmatizing, but becomes so under a specific set of social rules and social conditions. For example, a number of studies have suggested that recent demographic and sociopolitical trends in North America may gradually lower the rank of whiteness from a preferred racial status to a social stigma (Killian 1985; Kusow 2004; Storrs 1999).

Furthermore, as Link and Phelan's work (2001) notes, stigma is a multi-faceted concept. Accordingly, studies of stigma can be classified on the basis of which aspect of the stigmatization process they emphasize. In this article, I am most interested in the "obtrusiveness" of stigma (Goffman 1963:129) and its "disruption" of daily routines (Harvey 2001). Specifically, I focus on encounters that become "incidents" or "scenes" (Goffman 1959:210–12). In such situations, as the norms of "audience tact" and "disattention" are suspended, the stigmatized individuals find themselves caught in the interactional spotlight, forced to explain themselves to others. From the perspective of the stigmatized, these disruptions are especially significant for their "moral careers"—or how they judge themselves and others over time (Goffman 1962:128). As one respondent put it, in such moments "the thin veneer of civility" is stripped away and negative labels are openly applied and contested.

We can view these instances of identity dispute as occasions for eliciting and producing "accounts." I borrow this term from Lyman and Scott (1989) to refer to encounters in which a person is called to "explain unanticipated or untoward behavior—whether that behavior is his or her own or that of others, and whether the approximate cause of the statement arises from the actor himself or someone else" (p. 112). Thus, we give accounts when confronting an unusual situation or individual. In their discussion of stigma, Evans, Forsyth, and Foreman (2003) note that "understanding the way individuals use accounts to construct positive self-identities, in the face of occupying a stigmatized . . . position, is indeed important turf for social science" (p. 373).

This article examines stigma-related accounts as performances that involve both the substance of everyday experience (i.e., *what* is being contested or questioned and under *what* conditions) and the social construction of reality (i.e., *how* it is presented). This view of stigma is consistent with the symbolic interactionist premise that objects are not inherently meaningful; rather, individuals assign meanings in general, and identities in particular, through interaction. Stigma is realized in the reflexive interplay between social conditions and self-presentation. The meaning and practical significance of stigma is interactionally achieved in everyday encounters. To better highlight this reflexive approach to accounts and stigma, the next section discusses interpretive practice as an analytic framework that attends to both the substance of stigma and its dramaturgical management.

Interpretive Practice and Accounting

"Interpretive practice," as developed by Gubrium and Holstein (2000), provides a view of lived experience that is faithful to both individual agency and structural conditions. On the one hand, its emphasis on artful practice echoes the interactionist dictum of "if [people] define situations as real, they are real in their consequences" (Thomas and Thomas 1928:572). That is to say, reality is socially constructed through symbolic interaction. On the other hand, an interpretive practice approach has affinities with the Marxist notion that people "make their own history, but they do not make it just as they please; they do not make it under circumstances chosen by themselves, but under circumstances directly encountered, given, and transmitted from the past" (McLellan 2000:329). Approaching social interaction as interpretive practice implies that actors are neither completely passive nor autonomous. Instead, interpretive practice focuses on social life as it is empirically manifested in the interplay between artful construction and concrete circumstance. Indeed, Gubrium and Holstein caution against placing too much emphasis on either the conditions or artfulness of everyday practice. In their words, "Being the two sides of interpretive practice, conditions and artfulness are reflexively intertwined so that the reification of one in service to the analysis of the other is virtually impossible" (1997:121).

Following this approach, stigmatizing encounters involve both concrete realities and fluid practices in which actors use language to settle identity disputes. In this sense, stigma becomes a locally circumscribed achievement. Applying these insights to Middle Eastern Americans' encounters with those who question their identities, specific cultural resources (i.e., racist stereotypes and fear of terrorism perpetuated by the media) provide the social context for inquiries about Middle Eastern people. However, the outcomes of these encounters are never predetermined; each is an occasion for negotiating the practical meaning of Middle Eastern American identity. Each is replete with its own nuances and artful practices.

Social Context and History

Accounts are conditioned by structural factors. As Lyman and Scott point out (1989), there are patterned differences between those actors who request accounts and those who have to account for themselves. In their words,

> The point with respect to accounts is their right to be requested, their establishment of social identity, and their efficacy to change in accordance with the changing status of the group involved. . . . Situations of account confusion are especially acute when a group in transition from one status position to another is undergoing a collective identity crisis. Racial groups provide numerous examples. Before the 1920s some Japanese in America insisted on their identity as "free white persons" in order to circumvent naturalization and franchise barriers, but found few others would accept this definition of their racial status. (P. 151)

In many ways, the case of Middle Eastern Americans is similar to that of Japanese Americans in the first half of the twentieth century. Political turmoil in the Middle East and terrorism have created an identity crisis for those with ancestral ties to that part of the world. The negative stereotypes of Middle Eastern Americans ("Arabs" in particular) predate the September 11th tragedies. For example,

An ABC News poll, conducted during the Persian Gulf crisis in February 1991, found 43% of Americans had a high opinion of Arabs while 41% said they had a low opinion. In that poll, majorities of Americans said the following terms applied to Arabs: "religious" (81%), "terrorists" (81%), "violent" (58%) and "religious fanatics" (56%). (Jones 2001:1)

In fact, negative opinions toward Middle Eastern Americans date back at least to the hostage crisis of 1972 in which Palestinian militants took eleven Israeli athletes hostage during the Olympic Games in Munich. The German authorities' attempt to rescue the hostages ended in a massacre that claimed the lives of all eleven hostages and five of the eight terrorists. Shortly after this event, the Federal Bureau of Investigation launched one of its first national campaigns to interview and deport Arab Americans (Marvasti and McKinney 2004:56). Later, the Iranian hostage crisis in 1979, the first Gulf War in 1991, and the 1993 bombing of the World Trade Center all reinforced negative stereotypes of Middle Eastern Americans. Each conflict was followed by a wave of hate crimes and discrimination. Mosques were vandalized, and people were fired from jobs and assaulted on the streets (Feagin and Feagin 2003:327–30; Marvasti and McKinney 2004:53–60; Schaefer 2006:299–302; U.S. Congress 1986).

These backlashes were relatively isolated and episodic until September 11, 2001, when systematic discrimination against Middle Eastern Americans received considerable public support. A *Newsweek* poll conducted shortly after the terrorist attacks, on September 14–15, 2001, indicated that "32% of Americans think Arabs living in this country should be put under special surveillance as Japanese Americans were" (Jones 2001:3–4). Similarly, in June 2002 a Gallup survey of 1,360 American adults showed that "of the five immigrant groups tested [Arabs, Hispanics, Asians, Africans, and Europeans], the public is least accepting of Arab immigrants, as 54% say there are too many entering the United States" (Jones 2002:3).

Since September 11, 2001, accountability has become an everyday reality for Middle Eastern Americans in light of official policies that systematically demand that they explain their every action. Former Attorney General John Ashcroft articulated this state of heightened awareness quite clearly in public addresses by suggesting that if suspected terrorists as much as spit on the sidewalk, they would be arrested (Gorman 2002). The term "suspected terrorists" has become so broadly defined as to include thousands of Middle Eastern men who have been interviewed, arrested, or deported for minor immigration violations.

Interestingly, under U.S. immigration laws, Middle Eastern Americans (officially defined as those with ancestral ties to a region stretching from Turkey to North Africa) are classified as "white." Indeed, most affirmative action forms specifically instruct people of Middle Eastern descent to identify themselves as "white." However, the phrase "Middle Eastern–looking," almost always used in connection with a terrorist threat, has come to connote the same meaning as the words "black suspect." Their official classification as "white" seems to have no practical relevance in everyday life as Middle Eastern Americans are singled out for antiterrorism measures.

In the post-9/11 era, "Middle Eastern–looking" people, men in particular, have been verbally harassed, physically attacked, and sometimes killed, regardless of their actual nationality or association with Islam or the Middle East. In Mesa, Arizona, an Indian Sikh was shot and killed for being dark-skinned, bearded, and wearing a turban (Delves 2001). The man responsible for this crime also fired shots at a Lebanese gas station worker and an Afghan family. In addition to the rash of indiscriminate violence, in several incidents across the country "Middle Eastern–looking" men were removed from flights after completing all security checks and being seated (Brown 2001). The reason offered in most cases was as vague as the crew not feeling safe flying with them.

Furthermore, the current terror warning system, which is intended to alert the public about potential terrorist attacks, acts as an accounting catalyst. As the level of terror is "elevated," for example, from yellow to orange, public fears and suspicions are equally increased, and subsequently more Middle Eastern people are forced into the position of account-givers. At the same time, terror warnings call on ordinary citizens to be "alert" and report anything "suspicious"—in a sense, deputizing them as semiofficial account-takers. In essence, the terror alert system encourages the suspension of tact and disattention, especially to the detriment of "Middle Eastern–looking" people. To borrow from Goffman (1963), Middle Eastern Americans are suffering "ill-fame" perpetuated by the mass media. In his words, their "public image . . . seems to be constituted from a small selection of facts which . . . are inflated into dramatic news-worthy appearance, and then used as a full picture [of their identity]" (p. 71). Under these circumstances, aspects of one's life that would ordinarily be considered private are routinely subjected to public and official scrutiny in everyday encounters.

However, the outcomes of such encounters are not uniform or predetermined. As Goffman states (1963), and Gubrium and Holstein develop in relation to interpretive practice (2000), stigma is not the property of a person, but of relationships that always unfold through symbolic interaction. Building on these insights, the stigma of being Middle Eastern American is not external to interactions but is constructed or rejected *through* interaction, accounts, and self-presentational strategies.

Methods and Data

From May 2002 to May 2004, my wife (a white woman from the southern United States) and I conducted twenty in-depth interviews with twelve male and eight female respondents, whose age ranged from eighteen to fifty-five years. All were either enrolled in college or had earned a four-year degree (at minimum), and lived in three different states (Florida, Pennsylvania, and Virginia). Eighteen were naturalized citizens and two were long-time immigrants who had lived and worked in the United States for over ten years and planned to become citizens. In our interviews, we asked respondents how they managed being Middle Eastern, particularly when facing discrimination. We began our interviews with demographic questions about age, country of origin, and education. We then followed with questions about whether respondents had experienced any form of ethnic discrimination at work, in school, or in their communities because of their religion, names, accents, appearance, or style of dress. We used probes like "What did you do then?" to encourage respondents to elaborate on their narratives.

Interviews lasted approximately one hour and were taped and subsequently transcribed after obtaining informed consent from the participants. We conducted seventeen interviews face-to-face and three over the phone, and recorded the latter using a speakerphone. The face-to-face interviews took place at the respondents' homes, places of work, or in my campus office. In order to recruit participants, we used snowball sampling, which is considered especially useful when dealing with a sensitive topic that can best be understood from an insider's perspective (Biernacki and Waldorf 1981). Respondents were my relatives, friends, and professional colleagues, who in turn referred me to other potential research participants. Three interviews are not included in my sample of twenty because the respondents did not self-identify as Middle Eastern. These three included an African American man married to an Iranian woman, a white woman married to an Iranian man, and an Indian man who mentioned after the interview that he had been harassed for "looking Middle Eastern" even though he does not consider himself Middle Eastern.

The twenty remaining respondents (Pakistanis, Iranians, Egyptians, a Turk, and a Lebanese) self-identified as Middle Eastern American. This method of self-identification is the norm for most studies of ethnicity and race. Even the U.S. census, an ostensibly objective population count, is based on self-identification. In other words, when answering ancestral background questions in the U.S. census, respondents are free to choose from a number of categories (e.g., "Arab or Arabic," "Middle Eastern," and "North African"). In fact, according to a census report, from 1990 to 2000 the number of people who self-identified as "Middle Eastern" quadrupled (Cruz and Brittingham 2003).

At the same time, it seems that official designations, which as mentioned earlier classify Middle Eastern people as white, are removed from everyday experience and reflective of colonial divisions of the world. Such geopolitical constructs are founded on exaggerated distinctions between "Western self" and the "Arab/Muslim Other." From this perspective, terms like "the Near East," "the Middle East," or "the Far East" respectively represent presumed degrees of similarity between the "orient" and the "occident" (see Edward

Said 1978). The categories of "Muslim American" and "Arab American" are equally problematic because most American Arabs are in fact Christians (AAI 2003). Furthermore, Muslim Iranians and Turks, who are often considered to be Middle Eastern, respectively speak Farsi and Turkish, and thus cannot be labeled "Arab American." Therefore, asking our respondents if their self-identity as Middle Eastern is methodologically sound and theoretically consistent with the phenomenological emphasis of the present analysis.[2]

The interview data was supplemented with autoethnographic data from my experience as an Iranian immigrant who has lived in the United States since 1983. For the purpose of this study, autoethnography refers to an orientation that allows the researcher to use her or his experiences as data in the form of a cultural insider's personal narratives (Ellis and Bochner 2000; Hayano 1979; Ronai 1992). Admittedly, having an insider status does not invariably work to the researcher's advantage. For example, Kusow's research with Somali immigrants in Canada (2003) shows that his insider status raised questions about the researcher's objectivity and aroused suspicion among respondents. In the present case, working with family and friends meant that I had pre-established rapport with my respondents. Rather than concealing my personal background information, I actively used my ethnicity and personal experiences to foster existing relationships with my interviewees and empathize with their troubles.

My data collection took the form of "active interviewing" (Holstein and Gubrium 1995), a process in which both the participants and the researcher contribute to meaning-making. My own experiences frequently entered the discussion as I tried to use my insider status to solicit data and put my respondents at ease. For example, on several occasions I followed a respondent's story with, "You know, that happened to me once." Conversely, sometimes my respondents involved me in their stories by saying, "I'm sure you know what that's like." As work by Mauthner and Doucet (2003) and Lincoln and Denzin (1994) suggests, the subjective stance of autoethnography allows me to locate myself in the data, analysis, and writing of this research. My presence in the text reveals to the readers my epistemological and emotional investment in the topic. In short, I am in the text because I am personally affected by the stigma of being Middle Eastern.

I represent my own and my respondents' accounting for stigma in narrative form to highlight the contextual and existential quality of these experiences. Because the stories I analyze here are reconstructions of normal–deviant encounters, they are subject to retrospective distortions. Having said that, retrospective accounts of accounts have been the primary source of data in many studies of stigma management. Encounter narratives are the norm in the sociology of stigma for both practical and theoretical reasons. Practically, it is difficult to position oneself as a researcher to observe stigma management firsthand. Researchers would have to shadow the stigmatized through their daily routines to isolate specific stigma-related encounters. Theoretically, a person defines stigmatization experiences largely in retrospect. It is after reflecting on an encounter that a person might say, "I am/was stigmatized" or "I resist/resisted stigma in this way." Additionally, similarities between my respondents' accounts suggest that their narratives are not random fictions but reflections of a patterned experience.

Middle Eastern individuals presented or accounted for their selves in disrupted social encounters or "incidents" (Goffman 1959:212). Accounting practices took mainly five forms: humorous accounting, educational accounting, defiant accounting, cowering, and passing. Analyzing these accounting strategies enables us to vividly grasp the interplay between artful self-presentations and obdurate social conditions. Each constitutes a different interpretive practice individuals use to establish a situationally practical and useful Middle Eastern self.

Humorous Accounting

When questioned about their ethnic identity, respondents sometimes use humor as a way of shifting attention away from the stereotypes that threaten their identities. In this way, they use humor as a diversion technique (Taub, McLorg, and Fanflik 2004). Consider, for example, how Ali accounted for his Middle Eastern–sounding name.

AM: Do you get any reactions about your name? Like people asking you what kind of name is that?

Ali: Sometimes they do; sometimes they don't. Sometimes, if they haven't met me or if they are sending me correspondence, they think it's a lady's name and a lot of correspondence comes in Ms. Ali [last name]. They think I'm either Alison or something like that. Nowadays, when my name comes up [in face-to-face contacts with clients], I use my sense of humor. For example, when they can't spell my name or ask questions about it, I say, "I'm the brother of Muhammad Ali, the boxer."

Ali's deliberate use of associations with the famed boxer places his name in a cultural context his account-takers are familiar with. In this type of accounting, individuals use humor to establish a common ground or "facilitating normalized roletaking" (Davis 1961:128).

Another respondent, whose first name, Ladan (the name of a flower in Persian), brings up unwelcome and troubling associations with the notorious terrorist Osama Bin Laden, tells this story about how she used humor with an inquisitive customer.

AM: With the name Ladan, do you run into any problems?

Ladan: Where I work [at a department store] we all wear nametags, with the name Ladan very clearly spelled out L A D A N. And this old couple, they approached me and I was very friendly with them—I usually chitchat with my customers. And he started asking me all these questions like, "You're so pretty, where're you from?"

[I respond,] "I'm from Iran." [He says,] "What?" [I repeat,] "I'm from Iran." So he asks, "What's your name?" And I say, "Ladan." So he bent down to read my nametag and he just looked at me with a funny face and asked, "Are you related to Bin Laden?"

AM: Was he joking?

Ladan: No, he was not. But I did joke back to him and I said, "Yes, he's my cousin and actually he's coming over for dinner tonight." [She chuckles.]

AM: So, when this sort of thing happens, you use humor to deal with it?

Ladan: Yeah, I do, because otherwise, if I don't turn it into a joke or a laughing mood, I get upset. I get really, really offended.

AM: So what was this guy's reaction? Did he laugh with you?

Ladan: When this guy realized my name is Ladan and I'm from Iran, he changed his attitude. He became reserved and he even went one step backward. When I noticed he was uncomfortable, I completed the transaction with his wife and let them leave as soon as they wanted.

In this case, Ladan's use of humor does not necessarily result in the proverbial "happy ending," or a clearly discernible resolution. The customer turned away and ended the interaction. Whether Ladan remained stigmatized by this encounter or whether the customer walked away feeling that he successfully applied the stigma is unknown, perhaps even for the participants involved in the interaction. What is clearer is that Ladan's account allowed her to highlight the ludicrousness of the account-taker's assumptions and his right to solicit an account. Here, the way of speaking shapes the substance of the identity. Ladan is not giving a specific and accurate account of who she "really" is, but is using humor to construct an encounter-specific account that implicitly questions the account-taker's right to ask her questions about her identity.

I also use humor to account for my name. The following encounter took place on election day (November 14, 2002) at a voting precinct in a small town in Pennsylvania where I went to cast my vote in the midterm elections. The encounter begins with the examination of my photo identification.

Election Supervisor: Okay . . . this is a hard one! [squinting at my driver's license] You're ready? [alerting her coworker] It says Amar. . . . It's A . . .

I wait, silent and motionless, as the three old women probe my ID. I fear that any sudden movement might send people running out of the building screaming for help. "Speak!" I scream in my head. The words finally roll out of my mouth:

AM: You know, my dad gave me a long name, hoping that it would guarantee my success in life. [They laugh.]

Election Supervisor: Well, you must be a doctor because you sure sign your name like one.

AM: [I cannot resist] Actually, I am a doctor . . . So maybe my dad had the right idea after all.

In this case, I use humor as a method of introduction, a way of constructing an identity for the occasion that gives more weight to *how* one speaks rather than *what* one speaks. It was not clear to me what they thought about me, but I sensed that they were still puzzled—I had to account for who I am. The immediate substance of my identity was not in question—they had my photo identification in front of them and most likely could tell from my swarthy appearance that I was not a native Pennsylvanian. Instead, humorous accounting allowed me to shape the broad contours of my identity for the occasion. Namely, I was able to communicate that I come from a "normal" family that aspires to the universal notion of "success in life," that I am aware that there are concerns about my identity, and am capable of responding to them in a sensible way.

In humorous accounting, the substance of the account is incidental and is deliberately trivialized. The account-giver acknowledges the demands of the encounter while simultaneously undermining the legitimacy and the urgency of the request for an account. How the account-giver handles the substance of the matter shapes the identity in question.

Educational Accounting

Sometimes accounting takes on a deliberate pedagogical form. In such cases, the account-giver assumes the role of an educator, informing and instructing the account-taker about relevant topics. This strategy of "normalization" (Goffman 1963) combats stigma by correcting stereotypes. Unlike humorous accounting, educational accounting centers on the informational substance of the account.

In response to suspicions and antagonism from his neighbors, a Pakistani Muslim, Hassan, conducted a sort of door-to-door educational accounting:

> After September 11th, I walked the street the whole week and talked to every single one of my neighbors. . . . And one of my neighbors—his brother was in Tower Two and he got out, and his mother was there and she was *furious* with Muslims and me. And we were there for three hours, my wife, my kids, her [the neighbor], her son and her other son that came out of the World Trade Center—he had come down by the time the buildings came down. And I was like, "Look, that's not Islam. That's not who Muslims are. Ask your son, what type of person am I? What type of person is my wife? Do I oppress my wife? Do I beat my wife? Have you ever heard me say anything extreme before?" . . . They all know I don't drink, they all know that I pray five times a day, they all know I fast during the month of Ramadan. At the end of Ramadan, we have a big party and invite everyone over to help celebrate the end of fast. This year, they'll all probably fast one day with me so they can feel what it's like.

Hassan's approach is proactive; it addresses potential questions before they are explicitly asked. In some ways, this form of educational accounting is similar to what Hewitt and Stokes (1975:1–3) call "disclaimers" or a "prospective construction of meaning" that individuals use in an attempt to avoid being categorized in an undesirable way. In this example, Hassan tries to transform the relationship between him, as an account-giver, and the account-takers who suspect him of being an "evildoer." Unlike humorous accounting, where account-givers deliberately trivialize cultural stereotypes, educational accounting explicitly and diligently addresses them in order to debunk them.

Account-givers have to give considerable attention to deciding which inquiries are worthy of an educational account. For example, an Iranian respondent, Mitra, indicates that she filters inquiries about her culture and identity before answering them:

> If they ask about the government or the senate over there [Iran], I don't know anything about it. I know who the president is, but they ask me about the senate or the name of the senator over there, I don't know. Since I don't know I'm not going to get involved. I'll say I don't know or I'm not interested. If they say, "Oh, you are from *that* country!" or "You are from the Middle East and you are a terrorist," those kinds of comments I'm not going to get into. I'll just say, "*No*, I'm not." But if they ask me about the culture I'll tell them, "Alright," and inform them about it—as much as I know.

Although inclined to assume the role of an educator, Mitra is unwilling or unprepared to respond to every question. Part of her educational accounting strategy involves evaluating the degree of her expertise on the subject and the tone of the questions. As she says, if the account-taker begins with accusations, such as "you are a terrorist," the only reasonable reply might be to deny the accusation and end the interaction.

Educational accounting was a common strategy for Middle Eastern Muslim women in my sample, especially those who wear the *hijab*.[3] Many of them were approached by strangers who asked questions such as "Isn't it hot under there?" "Does that come in many colors?" "Why do you wear that?" "Are you going to make *them* [referring to the ten- and twelve-year-old girls who were standing in a grocery store line with their mother] wear it too?" These women were literally stopped on the street by strangers who asked questions about the *hijab*, sometimes so directly as to constitute rudeness. My respondents reported that whenever time and circumstances allowed, they provide accounts of their religious practices and beliefs. Some of these answers include "I wear it because it is my culture," "I wear it so that you won't stare at my body when you are talking to me," or a more flippant response such as, "It's cooler under my scarf than you think."

Similarly, as a Middle Eastern sociology professor, I am often asked by my students to explain a wide range of topics about the region and Islam, from customs and culture to the mindset of terrorists. Like Mitra, I evaluate each question before providing an account. For example, a student in an undergraduate criminology seminar began every session with a trivial question about Iran, such as "Do they have trees over there?" At first, I provided a detailed educational account whenever asked to do so, even for seemingly inane items. Given the limited time I had to cover the assigned readings, later in the semester it became necessary to remind the students that I was not paid to educate them about the Middle East. The topic of the course was crime, specifically, the criminogenic aspects of American culture. In place of my personal instructions, I recommended a trip to the library for references on the Middle East and Iran. In this case, educational accounting became unfeasible because it diverted attention from the task at hand.

Defiant Accounting

When prompted to provide an account, Middle Eastern Americans sometimes express righteous indignation. I call this defiant accounting. Similar to humorous accounting, the account-giver exerts agency by challenging the other's right and the rationale to request it. However, whereas humorous accounting entails indirect and fairly conciliatory objections to stigma, in defiant accounting the stigmatized make explicit demands for counter explanations from the "normals." For example, consider how Alham, a young Iranian woman, describes her experiences with a coworker.

> She [the coworker] would tell me, "I don't know which country you come from but in America we do it like this or that." I let it go because I was older than her and we had to work together. . . . But one day I pulled her aside and I told her, "For your information where I come from has a much older culture. And what I know, you can't even imagine. So why don't you go get some more education. And if you mention this thing again—'my country is *this*, your country is *that*'—, I'm going to take it to management and they're going to fire you or they're going to fire me." And that was it.

Alham does not provide an account to repair the interaction or to restore it to a state of equilibrium. On the contrary, she explicitly seeks to challenge the conventional format of the encounter. Instead of aiming for consensus, defiant accounting foregrounds conflicting viewpoints and signals the account-giver's objection to the entire affair. The interaction is explicitly focused on the fairness of the exchange between the account-giver and the account-taker.

Account-givers are especially likely to use defiant strategies when they find the request for an account unfair. Specifically, ethnic minorities who are subjected to profiling may become defiant in response to the practice. For example, when I learned that, unlike myself, my white colleagues were not asked to show ID cards upon entering the campus gym, I felt justified in becoming defiant. In one instance, while pulling out my ID card from my wallet, I asked the woman at the front counter why my white faculty friend, who had just walked in ahead of me, was not asked to present an

ID. She explained that she had not noticed the other person entering or she would have asked him to do the same.

This encounter highlights the unpredictability of defiant accounting for both parties involved in the interaction. At its core, this strategy counters an account request with another: they ask for my ID and I ask why I should be the only one subjected to this rule. In turn, the other side presents its account and so on. This chain of accounts and counter-accounts could result in a formal dispute. Though it is possible that in some cases, when confronted, the account-takers simply back down and cease their efforts, it is just as likely that they intensify their demands, especially when they are backed by policies or other public mandates.

Defiant accounting is a risky approach that can either shield the account-giver from a potentially humiliating process or generate additional requests and demands. In some cases, defiant accounting can become a type of mass resistance, as with African Americans and the passive resistance component of the civil rights movement of the 1960s.

Cowering

Stigma, particularly when endured for a long period, can cause a person to engage in what Goffman (1963:17) calls "defensive cowering": the stigmatized simply go along with the stereotypical demands of the setting in order to avoid greater harm. With cowering, artful practice and agency take a backseat to external conditions. In encounters of this type, the stigmatized person is virtually powerless in the face of rigid demands of the setting.

Since September 11th, I have been very conscious of this fact when flying. Although I am certain that I have been singled out for security checks, I fear that objecting and confronting these practices would lead to additional hardships (i.e., a direct confrontation with law enforcement agents in which they have the greater authority and likelihood to win). For example, while traveling domestically, my thirteen-year-old daughter (whose mother is white American but has my Middle Eastern-sounding last name) and I were sent to a separate security line for a "random" screening. From my daughter's perspective this was "a good thing" because it meant going to a shorter line, but for me being searched was both humiliating and threatening. The following is an account of this incident.

> *I approach the security gate with my daughter. She goes through. From several feet away, I see them searching her backpack and running a wand over her body as she stands there, still with her arms raised. I am next. I empty my pockets and put the contents on the conveyer belt. A security officer waves me through the gate. The damn thing beeps.*

Security Officer One: Whoa! Back up! [I slowly walk back and await further instructions.]
Security Officer One: Walk through again. [The machine beeps again.]

Security Officer One:	Undo your belt and turn over the buckle. [She runs the wand over my belt and my waist.]
Security Officer Two:	There's a wallet on the conveyer belt. [My wallet was on the other side of the gate on the belt. They had not run it through the x-ray machine because it was not placed in a plastic pan.]
AM:	That's my wallet. [Fearing someone might take my wallet, I walk back through the gate to retrieve it.]
Security Officer Two:	Jesus Christ! You can't do that!
AM:	I meant to get my wallet.
Security Officer Two:	Why did you leave it on the belt?
AM:	I thought I was supposed to put it there.
Security Officer One:	Why didn't you put in a plastic pan?

I raise my shoulders to indicate my confusion. They stare at me, stare at each other, shake their heads and sigh. I am then told sit on a metal chair, take off my shoes, and raise my feet.

Security Officer Three:	Now stand up. [He runs the wand between my legs and down the front of my torso.] Turn around. [He scans my back.] Okay, put on your shoes.
AM:	Can I get my wallet now?
Security Officer Four:	No, we have to search it. [She pulls out the content of the wallet, searches every pocket, and hands it back to me.]
AM:	Can I go now?
Security Office Four:	[Apparently looking for someone to give her approval] Go ahead.

I rejoin my daughter. She smiles at me and we move on.

During this incident, I assumed any kind of "talking back" would draw further unwanted attention and possibly result in hours of interrogation—and a missed flight. I later asked an airline representative at the ticket counter why my daughter and I were so frequently selected for "random" screenings. She responded that we were in fact profiled by a computer program and, for reasons of national security, the airline could not tell us what specific criteria were used for singling us out. After hearing this, I replied, "Thank you for taking the time to speak with me. I am not trying to be difficult, but I think the system is flawed . . . but I am happy to help with whatever it takes to make everyone feel safe. Thanks again."

In another incident, shortly after September 11th, my wife and I were browsing in a video store in Florida. A little boy (maybe about five years old) who was walking in front of us with his parents began frantically tugging at his mother's shirttail with his eyes firmly fixed on me. When his mother finally looked down at him and asked, "What?" the boy said, "Mommy . . . I thought they were all in jail!" The boy's parents looked at me and pulled their child away. I tried very hard to smile, but my wife was outraged and wanted to confront the parents. I advised against it, fearing that a full-blown confrontation would only highlight and give credibility to the stereotype expressed by the boy.

Similarly, when a man driving by in his truck yelled at me "Ragheads go home!" I had no opportunity to account or choose an accounting strategy. The incident was too shocking, too threatening, and too quick for me to rationally decide on an accounting strategy. I just cowered and tried to make sure the driver did not have the chance to run over me.

My interviewees spoke of similar incidents when they were dumbfounded by the sheer incivility of the attack. For example, a Pakistani man recalled being thrown out of an elevator on a college campus by a student who stated he did not want to be in the same space "with people like him." Several female respondents reported being verbally harassed or physically attacked. One was pelted with spitballs when she was in high school, another reported that her friend's scarf was pulled off by a teenage boy at a grocery store, and another was repeatedly yelled at—"Go home!"—by people in passing cars as she walked to her office on campus.

What these incidents have in common is that they severely limit the agency of the stigmatized; in most cases, the best possible performance is cowering, which is more about "saving body," or one's physical safety, than "saving face" (Goffman 1959, 1963). In the biographies of the stigmatized, such overt acts of discrimination, however isolated, have great significance as "turning points" or "epiphanies" (Denzin 1989) that define the self as deviant and powerless in relation to normal others.

Passing

The goal of passing (Goffman 1963) is information control and the concealment of stigmatizing attributes from "normals." As an accounting strategy, passing means eliminating the need for an account (see Lyman and Scott 1989:126–27). How individuals present their identity can potentially eliminate the need for accounting altogether. My respondents accomplished passing by manipulating their appearance. The stereotypical image of a Middle Eastern person roughly translates into someone with dark hair, large facial features, swarthy skin, non-European foreign accent, facial hair on men, and veils and scarves on women. Faced with these stereotypes, some respondents consciously altered their looks to avoid any outside marker that might associate them with these stereotypes. Self-presentation (Goffman 1959), especially attention to clothes and grooming, is an equally important consideration for successful passing. For example, wearing jeans and being clean-shaven draws less attention and leads to fewer occasions for accounting.

Some Middle Eastern Americans try to pass by trading their own ethnic identity for a less controversial one. The simplest way to do this is to move to an ethnically diverse region. The respondents who live in South Florida stated that one reason they did not experience negative episodes of ethnic accounting is because they are perceived as Hispanic. For example, an Iranian woman was asked what kind of Spanish she was speaking when she was having a conversation with her teenage daughter in Farsi at the mall. Another Iranian man tried to pass as Italian by placing an Italian flag vanity license plate on his car. As a general rule, my respondents displayed Western or patriotic symbols (e.g., an American flag) at work, in front of their homes, or on their cars to avoid ethnic accounting. After September 11th, my neighbor gave me an American flag to place outside my apartment. As he put it, "This is for your own safety." In a sense, patriotic symbols are accounting statements in their own right and act as "disidentifiers" (Goffman 1963:93) that help separate "loyal Americans" from suspected terrorists.

Another strategy for passing is to give an ambiguous account in response to ethnic identity questions. For example, asked about his country of origin, an Egyptian man stated that he was Coptic (a pre-Islamic Egyptian culture). He noted that uninformed account-takers typically find it too embarrassing to ask follow-up questions, pretend to know what "Coptic" means, and drop the subject altogether. Iranians create this kind of ambiguity by stating that they are Persians (the designation of ancient Iran). Another way to circumvent accounts is to name one's city of birth instead of country of birth. I once told a college classmate that I was from Tehran. To my astonishment, he asked, "Is that near Paris?"

Changing one's name is another way to pass. Some respondents change their Muslim names (e.g., Akbar) to typical American names (e.g., Michael). When asked why he changed his name, Ahmad explained that he was tired of people slamming down the phone when he made inquiries about jobs. Some change from widely known ethnic-sounding names to lesser known ones as in the change from Hossein to Sina.

Passing strategies pose their own risks for the stigmatized. In particular, the media have constructed passing among Middle Eastern Americans as an extension of the "evil terrorist plot." After September 11th, it was widely reported that the hijackers were specifically instructed to wear jeans and shave their faces to pass as native born ethnics. Therefore, rather than being viewed as a sign of cultural assimilation, Middle Eastern Americans' conspicuous attempts at passing can be cast as a diabolical plan to form a "sleeper cell" or to disguise "the wolves among us." Theses days, when I go to an airport, I am very conscious of how much passing would be considered legitimate. Trying to conceal too much information about oneself can arouse suspicion. In fact, I sometimes wear my gold medallion with its Allah (Arabic for "God") inscription conspicuously on the outside of my shirt to indicate that I am not attempting to "misrepresent" myself or deceive anyone.

Conclusions: Interpretive Practice and Stigma Management

The interpretive practice model used in this study combines the interactionist concepts of accounts and stigma management with the structural emphasis on concrete social conditions. This analysis focuses on accounting as an interpretive process for establishing situationally specific ethnic identities. Rather than treating stigma as an objective reality, I examine the interpretive practices individuals use to establish or dispute stigma and stigmatized identities.

I reject a more objective conceptualization of stigma in part because, as noted by Riessman (2000), such an approach exaggerates the influence of the dominant culture. Instead of considering the myriad ways would-be targets challenge or altogether dismiss stigma, the objective view takes for granted the reality of stigma and proceeds to analyze its management, concealment, or consequences for the stigmatized. As a result, Goffman's original stipulation on the situationally variable and interactionally embedded nature of stigma is lost. Lost also is the understanding that, at least according to Goffman (1963), stigma is a tentative reality project. As he states, "The normal and the stigmatized are not persons but rather perspectives. These are generated in social situations during mixed contacts" (p. 138). Therefore, stigma, the stigmatized, and stigmatizers become meaningful within specific social interactions. The assumption that stigmas are obdurate qualities of particular groups of people might contradict empirical evidence, or the actors' own experiences.

The case of Middle Eastern Americans' spoiled identities suggests that two sets of empirical observations have to be incorporated into the analysis. On the one hand, there is the reality of the so-called War on Terror and pervasive fear of terrorism, both of which have made Middle Eastern Americans "legitimate" targets of scrutiny in everyday life. Similarly, the political turmoil in the Middle East directly affects their lives in the United States, so much so that there is almost a direct correspondence between the volatility of the region and the instability of Middle Eastern identities in the United States. Every terrorist attack, every hostage taking, and every virulent speech issued from the Middle East triggers a corresponding wave of public scrutiny in the United States. These are the conditions, but how do we get at everyday practices? How do Middle Eastern Americans cope in real life situations? Answering these questions requires wearing a different analytic hat, so to speak.

One way my respondents and I cope with these conditions is by being adaptable and fluid with our self presentations. We do not enter daily interaction as members of a stigmatized group. Many of us are devout Muslims who practice our religion proudly despite stereotypes and the negative press. To suggest that we are narrowly defined by the stigma of being Middle Eastern is an empirically unfounded claim. It is equally problematic to imply that the majority of Americans are engaged in a mass stigmatization campaign. On a general level, my analysis is informed by the idea that ethnic difference is variable and interactionally achieved (Garfinkel 1967), and suggests that Middle Eastern Americans use a range of interpretive practices to define their ethnic-national identities in the context of everyday life during the War on the Terror.

My respondents and I experience being forced into positions where we have to account for our ethnic identities. What triggers these accounting encounters (e.g., genuine interest, fear, or malice) is of secondary relevance. As C. Wright Mills (1939) suggests, the motives for these encounters are themselves situated and discerned in the course, and in the language, of the interaction. In these encounters, account-givers and account-takers monitor each other at every turn and respond accordingly. I have labeled this type of interaction *accounting encounters*, and have underlined some of the self-presentation strategies Middle Eastern Americans use as they account for their identity (humorous, educational, and defiant accounting, cowering, and passing). Similar questions could be developed about account-takers and the strategies they use to ask for accounts (e.g., how they respond to humor or confrontation in their identity inquiries).

Although the categories discussed here overlap in some ways (e.g., humor can be educational), they do represent distinct modes of responding to identity challenges. Each represents certain possibilities and limitations for the stigmatized. Specifically, humor can normalize deviant–normal relations and relieve social tension, but at the same time humor can have a "minstrelization" effect (Carling 1962, cited in Goffman 1963:110). In particular, self-deprecatory humor can cast the stigmatized in the role of someone who lacks self-respect and is not to be taken seriously. Furthermore, transforming discriminatory encounters into humorous ones could create the impression that the stigmatized have not been severely harmed by a stereotype, thereby implying that those who cannot laugh at such abuses are overreacting.

Educational accounting can be effective in correcting misconceptions and changing public opinion. Unlike humor, educational accounting grants stereotyping and discrimination the solemnity they deserve. It treats both the account-giver and -taker as rational actors who can enter a mutually beneficial dialogue. The drawback is that it burdens the stigmatized with a constant state of preparedness, requiring them to explain themselves in an articulate and diplomatic way. Educational accounting takes time away from job-related tasks or leisure. With rare exceptions, when professional duties and the accounting demands coincide (such as this article, for example), the work of answering for one's ethnic background and religion could become a considerable chore. At the same time, educational accounting casts the stigmatized in the role of "cultural ambassador" (Jacobs 1999), for which they may not be prepared. Even the most learned account-givers have a relatively limited knowledge of the endless cultural topics that come up in the course of ethnic identity accounting.

Some stigma management strategies actually "further spoil one's identity" (Roshchelle and Kaufman 2004:26). This can certainly be the case with defiant accounting, which has the advantage of providing a sort of immediate psychological relief for the stigmatized, a sense of finally being heard. However, as discussed earlier, defiant accounting poses serious risks for

Middle Eastern Americans, who are already suspected of being militant and fanatical. Thus, such a reaction may reinforce the very stereotypes they are trying to overcome. Additionally, militancy can increase one's "differentness." In Goffman's words, "the individual may find that his very efforts can politicize his own life, rendering it even more different from the normal life initially denied him" (1963:114). The extreme alternative to defiant accounting is cowering, which entails resigning oneself to the limitations of the spoiled self and abandoning any attempt at having an active role or voice in the interaction.

Finally, passing aids the stigmatized by concealing potentially damaging information. For example, after my daughter was called an "Iraqi terrorist" on the school bus, I asked how anyone found out about her being Middle Eastern. She explained that facing her schoolmates' insistence on knowing where she was "really" from, she finally told them she was "half Iranian." Apparently, her classmates did not know or care that there are significant differences between Iranians and Iraqis. After this incident, I instructed my daughter to tell her friends she is an "American." In this way, I hoped to help her disidentify with the stigma of "Iraqi terrorist." This incident highlights how passing creates "ambivalence" or "oscillation of identity," making one able neither to "embrace his group nor let it go" (Goffman 1963:106–8). In the case of Middle Eastern Americans, passing as "an average American" means making forced choices between attachments to one's native culture, on the one hand, and the conveniences of not being different, on the other.

What these accounting strategies share is that they are all attempts at salvaging spoiled identities in disrupted routine interactions. My respondents indicated that they measure the quality of their lives by the number of disruptions they face (i.e., a good day means not receiving unwanted attention). It is true that most people experience some type of "incident" or "scene" in their daily lives, but it is also true that most find "their predicament . . . much less charged and more easily set to rights" (Davis 1961:132).

In addition to its economic effects, stigma also forces its targets to become excessively and constantly conscious about themselves, others, and social interactions in general (Goffman 1967). A poignant example of this heightened state of consciousness is illustrated in my encounter with another shopper at a Wal-Mart store in Florida.

> We were both waiting in a checkout line. The woman, who was momentarily distracted by a tabloid cover, looked up at me abruptly and asked, "Where did you come from?" I hesitated for a second, wondering if I should try to pass as "an average Floridian," but ethnic pride took a hold of me. So I stuck out my chest and blurted, "I am Iranian." She responded with a perplexed look, "I mean, how'd you get in front of me in this line?" I did not know what to say after that. I just kept my head down, paid for my items, and left the store. I did not look back out of embarrassment.

Although laughable, such encounters could have the unfortunate effect of further alienating and weakening the account-givers' bonds with "normal" society. Ultimately, no accounting strategy is a suitable substitute for social interaction unencumbered by stereotypes and the acts of discrimination they engender.

At a different level, this article also hints at the onerous emotional labor (Hochschild 1983) unwilling account-givers have to perform in order to cope with stigma. I believe that examining stigma as interpretive practice has clear political implications. As Gubrium and Holstein put it, interpretive practice "presents the recognition that we could enact alternate possibilities or alternative directions. . . . If we make visible the constructive fluidity and malleability of social forms, we also reveal a potential for change" (2000:503). Like most studies of deviance and stigma, my work is intended to humanize myself and my respondents, but beyond that, I hope for social change. By voicing my own and my respondents' perspectives, I want to inspire my readers to initiate new interpretive practices. Ultimately, this article is a purposeful account in its own right that aims to change negative perceptions and hurtful practices.

Acknowledgments

I am grateful to Simon Gottschalk, the anonymous reviewers, Jaber Gubrium, James Holstein, and Karyn McKinney for their comments on earlier drafts of this article. I am especially thankful to respondents who shared their lives with me.

Notes

1. Most names have been fictionalized to protect the identity of the respondents. Where it is necessary to use an actual first name, every effort has been made to disguise other personal identifying information about a respondent.

2. Theoretically, Israeli Americans could be included in the broader ethnic grouping of Middle Easterners. In particular, Sephardic Jews have much in common with their Arab neighbors and friends. However, in the context of the War on Terror, non-Jewish Middle Easterners are the primary targets of public scrutiny. At the same time, the modern anti-Semitism inflicted on Jews has different origins and is qualitatively different from what Arabs and other Middle Easterners experience. Thus, although the two groups are culturally similar, for the purpose of this article, they are experientially different in everyday life. It should be noted that Sephardic Israelis are sometimes mistaken for "Arab terrorists." The same can also be said about Hispanics who "look Middle Eastern." An analysis of these various groups' public self-presentations would shed considerable light on how the War on Terror has helped or hindered inter-ethnic relations.

3. *Hijab* is the Islamic word for modesty in dress that applies to both men and women. In the case of many Muslim women living in the United States, this means wearing a scarf that covers the hair and the neck, as well as wearing loose-fitting garments so that the outlines of the body are not exaggerated.

References

Arab American Institute (AAI). 2003. "Arab American Demographics." Retrieved July 30, 2003, from www.aaiusa.org/demographics.htm.

Biernacki, Patrick and Dan Waldorf. 1981. "Snowball Sampling: Problems and Techniques of Chain Referral Sampling." *Sociological Methods & Research* 10:141–63.

Brown, Anthony. 2001. "Nervous Pilots Order Off 'Arab' Passengers." *The Observer*, September 23, p. 2.

Cahill, Spencer and Robin Eggleston. 1994. "Managing Emotions in Public: The Case of Wheelchair Users." *Social Psychology Quarterly* 57:300–12.

Carling, Finn. 1962. *And Yet We Are Human*. London: Chatto & Windus.

Cruz, Patricia G. and Angela Brittingham. 2003. *The Arab Population 2000*. Washington, DC: U.S. Census Bureau.

Davis, Fred. 1961. "Deviance Disavowal: The Management of Strained Interaction by the Visibly Handicapped." *Social Problems* 9:121–32.

Delves, Philip. 2001. "New Prejudices Emerge in an Embittered City: New York's Arab Community Is Living in Fear of Attack," *The Daily Telegraph*, September 20, p. 7.

Denzin, Norman. 1989. *Interpretive Biography*. Newbury Park, CA: Sage.

Ellis, Carolyn and Arthur P. Bochner. 2000. "Autoethnography, Personal Narrative, Reflexivity: Researcher as Subject." Pp. 733–68 in *Handbook of Qualitative Research*, 2nd ed., edited by N. Denzin and Y. S. Lincoln. Thousand Oaks, CA: Sage.

Evans, Rhonda D., Craig J. Forsyth, and Rachel A. Foreman. 2003. "Psychic Accounts: Self-Legitimation and the Management of a Spoiled Identity." *Sociological Forum* 23:359–75.

Feagin, Joe and Clairece Feagin. 2003. *Racial and Ethnic Relations*, 7th ed. Upper Saddle River, NJ: Prentice Hall.

Feagin, Joe and Karyn McKinney. 2003. *The Many Costs of Racism*. Lanham, MD: Rowman and Littlefield.

Fothergill, Alice. 2003. "The Stigma of Charity: Gender, Class, and Disaster Assistance." *Sociological Quarterly* 44:659–80.

Garfinkel, Harold. 1967. *Studies in Ethnomethodology*. Englewood Cliffs, NJ: Prentice Hall.

Goffman, Erving. 1959. *The Presentation of Self in Everyday Life*. Garden City, NY: Doubleday Anchor Books.

———. 1962. *Asylums: Essays on the Social Situation of Mental Patients and Other Inmates*. Garden City, NY: Doubleday Anchor Books.

———. 1963. *Stigma: Notes on the Management of Spoiled Identity*. Englewood Cliffs, NJ: Prentice Hall.

Gorman, Siobhan. 2002. "National Security: The Ashcroft Doctrine." *National Journal* 34:3712–19.

Gubrium, Jaber and James Holstein. 1997. *The New Language of Qualitative Method*. Thousand Oaks, CA: Sage.

———. 2000. "Analyzing Interpretive Practice." Pp. 487–508 in *Handbook of Qualitative Research*, 2nd ed., edited by N. Denzin and Y. S. Lincoln. Thousand Oaks, CA: Sage.

Harvey, Richard D. 2001. "Individual Differences in the Phenomenological Impact of Social Stigma." *The Journal of Social Psychology* 14:174–89.

Hayano, David M. 1979. "Auto-ethnography: Paradigms, Problems, and Prospects." *Human Organizations*, 38:113–20.

Herman, Nancy J. 1993. "Return to Sender: Reintegrative Stigma-Management Strategies of Ex-Psychiatric Patients." *Journal of Contemporary Ethnography* 22:295–330.

Hewitt, John P. and Randall Stokes. 1975. "Disclaimers." *American Sociological Review* 40:1–11.

Hochschild, Arlie. 1983. *The Managed Heart: Commercialization of Human Feeling*. Berkeley: University of California Press.

Holstein, James A. and Jaber Gubrium. 1995. *The Active Interview*. Thousand Oaks, CA: Sage.

Jacobs, Bruce A. 1999. *Race Manners: Navigating the Minefield between Black and White Americans*. New York: Arcade.

Jones, Jeffrey M. 2001. "Americans Felt Uneasy toward Arabs Even before September 11th," *The Gallup Organization* (www.gallup.com).

———. 2002. "Effects of September 11th on Immigration Attitudes Fading but Still Evident," *The Gallup Organization* (www.gallup.com).

Karp, David A. 1992. "Illness Ambiguity and the Search for Meaning: A Case Study of a Self-Help Group for Affective Disorders." *Journal of Contemporary Ethnography* 21:130–70.

Killian, Lewis M. 1985. "The Stigma of Race: Who Now Bears the Mark of Cain?" *Symbolic Interaction* 8:1–14.

Kusow, Abdi M. 2003. "Beyond Indigenous Authenticity: Reflections on the Insider/Outsider Debate in Immigration Research." *Symbolic Interaction* 26:591–99.

———. 2004. "Contesting Stigma: On Goffman's Assumptions of Normative Order." *Symbolic Interaction* 27:179–97.

Lincoln, Yvonna S. and Norman K. Denzin. 1994. "The Fifth Moment." Pp. 575–86 in *Handbook of Qualitative Research*, edited by N. Denzin and Y. S. Lincoln. Thousand Oaks, CA: Sage.

Link, Bruce and Jo Phelan. 2001. "Conceptualizing Stigma." *Annual Review of Sociology* 27:363–85.

Lyman, Stanford and Marvin Scott. 1989. *A Sociology of the Absurd*. Dix Hills, NY: General Hall.

Marvasti, Amir and Karyn McKinney. 2004. *Middle Eastern Lives in America*. New York: Rowman and Littlefield.

Mauthner, Natasha and Andrea Doucet. 2003. "Reflexive Accounts and Accounts of Reflexivity in Qualitative Data Analysis." *Sociology* 37:413–31.

McLellan, David. 2000. *Karl Marx: Selected Writings*. New York: Oxford University Press.

Mills, C. Wright. 1939. "Situated Actions and Vocabularies of Motive." *American Sociological Review* 5:904–13.

Riessman, Catherine K. 2000. "Stigma and Everyday Resistance Practices: Childless Women in South India." *Gender & Society* 14:111–35.

Ronai, Carol R. 1992. "The Reflexive Self through Narrative." Pp. 102–24 in *Investigating Subjectivity*, edited by C. Ellis and M. Flaherty. Newbury Park, CA: Sage.

Roschelle, Anne R. and Peter Kaufman. 2004. "Fitting In and Fighting Back: Stigma Strategies among Homeless Kids." *Symbolic Interaction* 27:23–46.

Said, Edward. 1978. *Orientalism*. New York: Vintage.

Schaefer, Richard T. 2006. *Racial and Ethnic Groups*, 10th ed. Upper Saddle River, NJ: Prentice Hall.

Snow, David and Leon Anderson. 1987. "Identity Work among the Homeless: The Verbal Construction and Avowal of Personal Identities." *American Journal of Sociology* 92:1336–71.

Storrs, Debbie. 1999. "Whiteness as Stigma: Essentialist Identity Work by Mixed Race Women." *Symbolic Interaction* 22:187–212.

Taub, Diane E., Penelope A. McLorg, and Patricia L. Fanflik. 2004. "Stigma Management Strategies among Women with Physical Disabilities: Contrasting Approaches of Downplaying or Claiming Disability Status." *Deviant Behavior* 25:169–90.

Thomas, William I. and Dorothy S. Thomas. 1928. *The Child in America: Behavior Problems and Programs*. New York: Knopf.

U.S. Congress. House of Representatives. Subcommittee on Criminal Justice of the House Judiciary Committee. July 16, 1986. *Ethnically Motivated Violence against Arab Americans*. 99th Cong., 2nd sess. Serial no. 135. Washington, DC: U.S. Government Printing Office.

VI

Changing Deviance

Parts IV and V offered materials that demonstrate how, both voluntarily and involuntarily, a person's public identity becomes transformed into a "deviant" identity. Central to this process, at least in terms of bureaucratic processing, is the "status denunciation ceremony," in which a collective effort is made to place an institutional tag upon a person. This status-conferring process was especially evident in those articles dealing with the involuntary processing of clients. The articles also helped to underscore the fact that the institutional deviant has relatively little to say about his or her processing. It has been emphasized, too, that the identity-transformation process is generally rather routine.

How the organizationally labeled deviant actually perceives and responds to institutional processing is often difficult to judge. As we have seen, some will accept the label, while others will either reject or ignore it. The individual's response is critical in the alteration of a deviant career and identity—that is, in moving from a deviant to a nondeviant status, with the deviant label being removed during the process of change. For example, if an individual rejects an institutional label, he or she can expect to encounter various types of difficulties. The plight of McMurphy (discussed in the general introduction) offers an illustration of this. Not only did he reject the "sick role," but his resistance, when viewed from the institution's perspective, was taken as a sign that he needed help. In this instance, the prognosis for change—again from the institution's viewpoint (i.e., its theory of the office and associated diagnostic stereotypes)—was extremely poor. A patient may, however, accept the label and act according to institutional expectations. Such patients thus become willing parties in the transformation process.

Even if individuals decide to conform to social norms, they will most certainly encounter numerous structural and individual barriers—

barriers that often reduce the probability that they will elect to change their behavior. The ex-deviant, as we have noted in the general introduction, frequently experiences difficulty finding housing and employment, primarily because others, in general, continue to react to the person as a deviant. Institutional processing is very systematic and efficient in tagging individuals as deviants. The reverse process, however, is anything but systematic and efficient. Specifically, there are few, if any, institutional mechanisms that can be used to systematically remove deviant labels (and the associated stigma) from individuals. Thus, deviants are often left to fend for themselves. Obviously, giving ex-cons a bit of money and a suit of clothes, without helping them to deal with potential structural barriers (e.g., having to indicate they are ex-cons on job applications) and individual problems (e.g., feelings of low self-esteem), is not going to do much by way of "rehabilitating" them. A viable model of change or "rehabilitation" must incorporate a concern for both individual and structural factors. Even this, however, is not enough.

Clearly, if the underlying images, conceptions, and categories of deviance are altered (as discussed in Part I), then the picture of deviance and the deviant must undergo some corresponding changes. Analytically, it is useful to think in terms of the transformation of deviant categories, as well as the transformation of actors and structures. As an example, certain crimes may become decriminalized, and acts that were formerly perceived as deviant may become acceptable. The selections in this part explore possibilities such as these.

PART VI

Transforming Deviance: Conceptions, Actors, and Organizations

SECTION 1

A central theme in Part I was the idea that the reactions of social observers provide acts with meanings—that is, indicate whether the acts are deviant or nondeviant. In "Reform the Law: Decriminalization," Samuel Walker provides a provocative analysis of how removing selected types of behavior from the statutes may affect the picture of crime and deviance. He begins by drawing most heavily upon the classic work by Morris and Hawkins, *The Honest Politician's Guide to Crime Control*, and notes that these authors propose to decriminalize acts in seven areas: (1) drunkenness, (2) narcotics and drug abuse, (3) gambling, (4) disorderly conduct and vagrancy, (5) abortion, (6) sexual behavior, and (7) juvenile delinquency. The rationale for decriminalizing these domains is predicated primarily upon three arguments: Many of the existing laws, in their applications, are "criminogenic" (i.e., produce more crime); they overburden the justice system; and they violate individual rights. Walker's working proposition, which centers on a major concern of his, is that "with the possible exception of heroin policy, decriminalization is simply irrelevant to the control of robbery and burglary." Hence, he is concerned mainly with what he views as being serious crime. In an effort to establish, as well as substantiate, the irrelevance of a link between most victimless crimes and the serious crimes of robbery and burglary, the author offers a balanced and insightful examination of the arguments and evidence associated with each of the areas listed by Morris and Hawkins. For example, in terms of the proposal to decriminalize most sexual activities (e.g., adultery, fornication, cohabitation, prostitution, and the like), he contends that many good arguments—some of which he reviews briefly—have been advanced for doing so. Walker does caution us, however, that decriminalization in a selected area may not reduce the ancillary crime connected with it. Customers may still be mugged or robbed before, during, or after their sexual encounter with a prostitute.

As we have suggested, noninstitutional deviants (e.g., drug addicts and prostitutes) and institutional deviants (e.g., mental patients and delinquents) who elect to change their deviant behavior can expect to encounter a range of structural and individual roadblocks—roadblocks that may ultimately produce a relapse or further deviance.

J. David Brown, in "The Professional Ex-: An Alternative for Exiting the Deviant Career," offers an interesting twist on the processes involved in exiting from deviant careers. He notes that most material on exiting focuses on an actor's abandonment of deviant behavior, identity, and ideologies. Brown, however, contends that the exiting process does not have to entail the total abandonment of a deviant career and identity. Rather, the professionalization of a deviant identity might be more in order for selected types of occupations. In a sense, the contours of a deviant status can be expanded, redefined, and professionalized. And in a sense, a niche can be carved out for the institutionally perceived ex-deviant. Brown illustrates how this process works by using data obtained from interviews with some 35 professional "ex-s" who work in a variety of institutions that provide care for people with drug, drinking, and eating problems. He observes four main stages in the exiting and resocialization process: (1) the emulation of one's therapist, (2) the call to a counseling career, (3) status-set realignment, and (4) credentialization. For example, not only do many of the ex-s come to embrace the counseling profession but, through a process of resocialization and identity transformation, they create a counseling-related identity for themselves. Brown concludes by noting that many organizations are using ex-s in their social control efforts. He cites as examples the prison counselors who counsel delinquents, and the gang counselors who counsel present gang members.

As is evident throughout this book, it is the social actor—usually a person who is relatively powerless—who becomes selected out and processed as a deviant by some type of people-processing or people-changing institution. As we have already argued, it is the actor who must alter behavior. Placing the burden for change exclusively upon the individual, however, means that the decision makers and their organizations escape scrutiny. Yet there is solid evidence of the need for such examinations, and Shichor's examination of the privatization of prisons within a corporate context and Meehan's analysis of gang statistics (Part IV) help to substantiate such a requirement. Such research also offers an important caveat about trying to effect any significant policy changes: If an institution's underlying organizational structure (i.e., its theory of the office, diagnostic stereotypes, career lines, and staff socializing procedures) remains unaltered, then selected categories of clients can expect to be typed and treated in a routinized, stereotypical, and uncaring fashion; this is often a fact of bureaucratic life. And, predictably, when the homeless in Lyon-Callo's study (Part IV) became caught up in a working ideology presuming individual pathology, not only were they forced to accept their perfunctory care and the associated and enduring stigmatization, but failure to do so (i.e., go along with the "program") could produce serious consequences: They could be dropped from the program. Their problems, according to the prevailing ideology, were individual in nature and not systemic, structural, or societal. This ingrained, bureaucratic tendency to operate on the basis of, or to promote, an individual-clinical-medical model of change, whereby the burden for change is placed directly upon the client, is not unique to only a selected few institutions but, rather, generally characterizes most people-processing and people-changing organizations. And probably one of the best, graphic, and most alarming illustrations of this can be found in the educational classifying, sorting, and processing of low-income, minority, and other generally disadvantaged students (Kelly, Part IV). Not only are such students, when compared with their counterparts, often viewed as lacking any significant educational ability, but such a presumption (i.e., the presumption of differential ability) virtually guarantees that a preponderance of the failures, dropouts, and deviants manufactured by our educational systems will be, necessarily, concentrated among these categories of students. Again, it is not that the educational system has failed the individual but, rather, it is the individual who has failed the system. Again, too, the educational system and its decision makers escape scrutiny. This often-overlooked need for dissecting and examining underlying organizational structures and embedded ideologies applies not only to such formal bureaucratic entities as educational systems but to other less formal groupings and organizations as well. Hence, if the values, normative configurations, and associated ideologies of deviant enterprises, activities, and organizations remain intact, recruits, once effectively socialized, will exhibit attitudes and behaviors commensurate with these elements (Part V). Logically, then, if any significant or desired change in outcomes is to occur, it must come initially from an overhaul or redefinition of those values, norms, and ideologies that are inculcated within a social actor. The same type of scenario applies aptly to those formal social control agents who are given the task of policing deviant categories and processing those who are perceived as violating the categories. As an example, if the prevailing content of the diagnostic stereotypes was such that *all* police officers were inculcated with the presumption that the likelihood of committing a crime is equally distributed across racial and ethnic lines and if, further, *all* officers acted in accordance with such a working ideology, then the phenomena of racial and/or ethnic profiling should either be eliminated or else substantially reduced. And in more general terms, such an operating or official institutional perspective should reduce the probability that a range of extra legal factors (e.g., one's race, ethnicity, gender, looks, and the like) will be used as the primary or sole basis upon which to select out actors to play the role of the social deviant.

Jim Leitzel, in the final selection, "Race and Policing," offers additional commentary on points such as these, especially those problems associated with trying to effect changes in organizational ideologies and practices. He notes that preventing crime from occurring is a significant concern for those who police deviant categories and for citizens. Actually preventing crime, however, requires being able to identify those individual characteristics that would enable one to reliably predict future criminal activity. And while criminal profiling has been useful, on an individual basis, in identifying perpetrators of particular crimes, the use of such profiles in *proactive* policing is fraught with significant problems, since race is frequently included as a major component of any profile that may be applied. Leitzel not only points out that using race as the basis for traffic stops is associated with a range of rather predictable negative consequences and criticisms, but he also poses a solution: Do not allow the use of race in policing. For Leitzel, "the operational rule of thumb for police officers who are considering stopping or searching a black person (or potentially a Latino or another minority) should be: would I stop or search this person if he or she was white?"

Quite clearly, then, whether race is invoked as a basis for a stop or search falls squarely on the shoulders of the officer, and even though official policy may advise against such use, the officer may still do it. To counteract this, we would contend that an effective officer monitoring or tracking system must be established and maintained, not only for all police agencies but for social control agencies in general; this will allow for an empirical and ongoing analysis of just how a social control agency's official perspective or working ideology is actually translated into action by its agents. The need for gathering the relevant data is long overdue.

43 ▶ Reform the Law: Decriminalization

Samuel Walker

The "first principle" advanced by Norval Morris and Gordon Hawkins in the 1970 book, *The Honest Politician's Guide to Crime Control,* involved removing a broad range of crimes from the statutes. Decriminalization of certain types of behavior has long been a major item on the liberal crime control agenda. In his book *Crime and Punishment: A Radical Solution,* Aryeh Neier, then Executive Director of the ACLU, offered decriminalization as his most substantive crime reduction proposal.[1]

For liberals the problem is what Morris and Hawkins call the "overreach" of the criminal law. It covers too wide a range of human behavior. Too much of it expresses the moralistic concerns of particular groups who are offended by the behavior of others. Morris and Hawkins urge us to "strip off the moralistic excrescences on our criminal justice system so that it may concentrate on the essential." They propose decriminalization in seven general areas:

1. **Drunkenness.** Public drunkenness shall cease to be a criminal offense.
2. **Narcotics and drug abuse.** Neither the acquisition, purchase, possession, nor the use of any drug will be a criminal offense. The sale of some drugs other than by a licensed chemist (druggist) and on prescription will be criminally proscribed; proof of possession of excessive quantities may be evidence of a sale or of intent to sell.
3. **Gambling.** No form of gambling will be prohibited in the criminal law; certain fraudulent and cheating gambling practices will remain criminal.
4. **Disorderly conduct and vagrancy.** Disorderly conduct and vagrancy laws will be replaced by laws precisely stipulating the conduct proscribed and defining the circumstances in which the police should intervene.

5. **Abortion.** Abortion performed by a qualified medical practitioner in a registered hospital shall cease to be a criminal offense.

6. **Sexual behavior.** Sexual activities between consenting adults in private will not be subject to the criminal law. [In the following areas,] adultery, fornication, illicit cohabitation, statutory rape and carnal knowledge, bigamy, incest, sodomy, bestiality, homosexuality, prostitution, pornography, and obscenity . . . the role of the criminal law is excessive.

7. **Juvenile delinquency.** The juvenile court should retain jurisdiction only over conduct by children which would be criminal were they adult.

The Rationale

The rationale for decriminalization consists of three arguments. First, and of primary concern to us here, many of these laws are criminogenic. They produce crime through at least three different means: labeling, secondary deviance, and the creation of a crime tariff. According to labeling theory, the criminal process itself encourages criminal careers. Any contact with the system—arrest, prosecution, conviction, or incarceration—imposes a "criminal label" on the individual. The person internalizes the label and proceeds to act out the role, committing additional and more serious crimes. Decriminalization advocates argue that the laws covering essentially harmless behavior launch people onto criminal careers. Abolish those laws and these people will never become entangled in the criminal justice system to begin with. As a result, crime will be reduced.[2] The laws also create what is known as "secondary deviance." A person becomes addicted to heroin and then, because the drug is illegal and expensive, must turn to crime to support the habit. If addiction were handled as a medical problem, with appropriate treatment or maintenance programs, addicts would not have to rob and steal. Thus we would reduce much of the drug-related crime. Criminologists also refer to the "crime tariff" problem in this regard. Making a product illegal only drives up the price. Not only does this effect raise the amount of money the person needs to obtain illegally, but it encourages the development of criminal syndicates seeking to control the market. Thus, many decriminalization advocates charge that our gambling statutes are responsible for sustaining organized crime.

Overly broad criminal statutes undermine respect for the law. Prohibition is the classic example. The law made criminals out of millions of people who simply wanted a recreational drink. Today, it is argued that many young people lost respect for the law and the legal system by the illegal status of marijuana, a relatively harmless recreational drug.

In addition to actively generating more crime, the laws in question overburden the criminal justice system. Morris and Hawkins, along with many others, maintain that the police waste far too much time dealing with vagrancy, disorderly conduct, and public intoxication when they should be concentrating on serious crimes against people and property. Moreover, insofar as the gambling statutes sustain organized crime, they are also responsible for the most serious patterns of corruption in the criminal justice system.

The final decriminalization argument is that the laws violate individual rights. Much of the behavior covered by criminal statutes is a private matter: one's sexual preference or the decision to have an abortion, for example. As long as the behavior harms no one, it should not be criminalized. Most of the items on the Morris and Hawkins list are referred to as "victimless crimes."

There is room for debate on many of these issues. To what extent gambling should be legalized is an important social policy question, involving many considerations. Abortion is perhaps the most politically controversial moral issue in the United States today. Whether or not the drug addict is a "victim" is arguable. The debate between the libertarians, who wish to restrict the scope of the criminal law in order to enhance individual liberty, and the legal moralists, who argue that the law can and should reflect fundamental moral principles, has been going on for over a hundred years and will likely continue.

Here we are concerned with the control of serious crime. On the question of decriminalization, our position is:

> PROPOSITION 26: With the possible exception of heroin policy, decriminalization is simply irrelevant to the control of robbery and burglary.

Placing decriminalization at the center of a crime control policy, as Morris and Hawkins and Neier do, evades the issue. There are no easy answers to the problem of serious crime. Conservatives and liberals respond to this dilemma in different ways. Conservatives focus on serious crime but tend to propose unworkable solutions. Liberals tend to shift the subject and talk about social reforms that are not directly related to serious crime at all.

The one possible exception to the general irrelevance of decriminalization involves heroin policy. The connection between heroin addiction and crime is clear, although experts disagree about the nature and extent of that connection. Nonetheless, as we shall see, there is no consensus on the effective solution to the heroin problem. Decriminalization is only one possible alternative, and its efficacy is not clearly established.

Victimless Crimes and Serious Crime

To establish the irrelevance of the connection between most of the victimless crimes and the serious crimes of robbery and burglary we should examine each of the items on Morris and Hawkin's list.

Public drunkenness, disorderly conduct, and vagrancy are public nuisances rather than predatory crimes. They harm no one, even though they may offend the sensibilities of many people. Traditionally, these three crimes have consumed the bulk of police time and energy.[3] In the nineteenth century as many as 80 percent of all arrests were in these three categories, and they still make up the largest single group of arrests. In 1981, they accounted for 18.5 percent of all arrests, or as many as all eight of the Index crimes and three times as many as robbery and burglary.

The public nuisance arrests are indeed a burden on the police, the lower courts, and city jails. There are many good reasons for decriminalizing all three offense categories. From our standpoint, the question is whether or not this step would help reduce serious crime, as it potentially could in two different ways.

The most direct effect would take the form of more efficient police work. In theory, police would be freed from about 20 percent of their arrest work load and would be able to concentrate on the more serious crimes against people and property. There are two reasons why this shift in police priorities would not significantly reduce serious crime. In our discussion of the conservative proposal to add more cops and/or improve detective work, we found that there are some basic limits to the crime control capacity of the police. Decriminalization is simply the liberal means to the same end of making more cops available for serious crime. For all the same reasons, it will not achieve the intended results. In poorly managed departments the savings in officer time will not be effectively used. In well-managed departments, as we have already learned, more patrol and more detectives will not lower the crime rate.

To a great extent, the decriminalization of public nuisances has been occurring gradually over the past fifteen years as a result of two factors. First, courts and legislatures have decriminalized some of the offenses in question. In *Easter v. District of Columbia*, a U.S. District Court ruled that chronic alcoholism was a condition and not a crime. Meanwhile, a number of states have repealed their public intoxication statutes and some cities have replaced arrest with referral to detoxification programs. These steps reflect a growing consensus that criminalization is not the appropriate response to social and medical problems. The arguments of the decriminalization advocates, in other words, have found some acceptance.[4]

On a de facto basis, the police have shifted their priorities away from public nuisance offenses. The percentage of all arrests in the categories of public intoxication, disorderly conduct, and vagrancy fell from 39.7 percent in 1969 to 18.5 percent in 1981. It is unlikely that the number of drunks and unemployed vagrants has declined in those years. If anything, their numbers have probably increased. Instead, the police have simply shifted their priorities to devote more time to serious crime. The redirection effort was probably not the result of a formal policy directive from the chief. Rather, individual patrol officers, perhaps in consultation with their sergeants, made a common-sense judgment about what was important.[5]

Not everyone, however, supports this reordering of police priorities. George L. Kelling and James Q. Wilson argue that the police should devote more attention to the little nuisance problems that define the quality of life on the neighborhood level. Police should be more aggressive in keeping drunks off the street (or at least out of the neighborhood), for example, as a way of maintaining a sense of public safety among law-abiding residents. The police neglect of the small, "quality of life" issues, according to Kelling and Wilson, contributes to neighborhood deterioration.[6]

The second way in which decriminalization of nuisance offenses might reduce serious crime is by negating the labeling effect. The theory is generally applied to juvenile delinquents—and even then its validity remains a matter of debate. The people who are arrested for public intoxication and vagrancy are not the kind who graduate to predatory crime. For the most part they are the chronic alcoholics and the chronically unemployed. Often in helpless condition, they are commonly the victims of crime. Police frequently arrest them, in fact, in order to provide them some protection from either the elements or potential muggers. Being arrested does not encourage them to become predatory criminals. They are not the young, healthy, and aggressive males who become career criminals. Decriminalization of public intoxication, disorderly conduct, and vagrancy may well be sound social policy; but it is not a solution to the problem of serious crime.[7]

Much has happened since Morris and Hawkins recommended the decriminalization of abortion in 1970. Three years later the Supreme Court did just that in *Roe v. Wade*. One can debate the morality of abortion and the wisdom of the *Roe* decision as social policy. But it is hard to establish the connection between the old policy of criminal abortion and serious crime. There is nothing to suggest that a person is transformed into a robber or burglar because abortions are illegal. By the same token, the argument of many Right to Life advocates that abortion undermines the moral fabric of the nation, and thereby contributes to crime, is without foundation. Abortion is a supremely important social policy question, but it has no bearing on serious crime.

Much the same can be said for the proposal to decriminalize various sexual activities between consenting adults. The statutes are still filled with laws criminalizing adultery, fornication, cohabitation, statutory rape, homosexuality, and prostitution. Whether or not these activities are acceptable is a significant moral question. Good arguments can be advanced for removing them from their criminal status and, for the most part, police have accommodated themselves to changing moral standards by simply not enforcing them. Decriminalization, however, will not in any way reduce the level of predatory crime. The one possible exception is prostitution. A certain amount of ancillary crime accompanies this activity. Customers are occasionally mugged and robbed before or after their transactions with prostitutes. But those instances represent only a minor part of the total robbery picture.

A good case can be made that gambling sustains organized crime in America. Most experts on the subject agree that criminal syndicates generate not only a majority of revenues but their steadiest and most secure revenues from gambling. Our social policy of making many forms of gambling illegal creates a potentially lucrative area of enterprise for anyone willing to assume the risks of providing the necessary goods and services. The pernicious effects of criminal syndicates on our society are well known. Organized crime money is the major corruptive force in the criminal justice system and a significant corrupter in politics. Criminal syndicates also invest their money in legitimate businesses and, using their accustomed methods, pervert the free enterprise system. Organized crime does generate some violent crime, but these murders and assaults are directed against other members of the criminal syndicates. To be sure, some threats and actual violence are directed against nonmembers—for example, owners of legitimate businesses that the syndicates are attempting to take over. But this category represents at most a tiny fraction of the violent crimes in this country. Decriminalization of gambling may or may not be a wise social policy. It may or may not strike at the roots of organized crime, as many people believe. But it will not reduce the incidence of robbery and burglary.

The Heroin Problem

The one area in which decriminalization might help reduce crime involves heroin. There is no question that heroin is a terrible problem in our society and that a lot of predatory crime is committed by heroin addicts. Decriminalization is one possible remedy for these related problems, but it is not a self-evident solution. There is considerable disagreement over three central points: the number of heroin addicts, the amount of crime committed by addicts, and whether methadone maintenance or some other form of treatment effectively reduces addiction and crime.

The drug problem, unfortunately, has attracted more than its share of crusaders and quacks. Much of the information put out by drug crusaders is grossly wrong. Sorting our way through the misinformation is a difficult task by itself.

The first question concerns the number of heroin addicts in the United States. Official estimates range from 200,000 to 900,000, with about half of them in New York City alone. Use of the term "addict" is part of the problem. Not everyone who uses heroin is physically addicted. Antidrug propagandists created the myth that even the smallest use results in addiction. But there are large numbers of "weekend chippers" who use heroin occasionally as just another recreational drug. There are also many regular users who are not truly addicted. Even among addicts, there are great differences in the intensity of the addiction and the amount of heroin needed. As we shall see, these differences are important in estimating the amount of crime committed by heroin addicts. For the sake of the argument, let us accept the lower estimates and assume that there are between 200,000 and 300,000 regular users of heroin, including addicts, in the country and that 40 percent to 50 percent of them are in New York City.[8]

The second question is the amount of crime that is the direct result of heroin addiction. Or, to put it another way, how much crime could be eliminated by an effective heroin control policy (leaving the exact policy open for the moment)? On this issue we must sort our way through some truly fantastic estimates. The Rand Corporation estimated in 1969 that heroin addicts were responsible for $2 billion to $5 billion worth of crime in New York City. Frightening estimates of this sort are routine in the drug control business. They bear little relationship to reality, however.

In the pages of *The Public Interest*, Max Singer performed a devastating critique of the Rand heroin/crime estimates. If there were 100,000 addicts in New York City who needed $30 a day to maintain their habit, they would have to raise $1.1 billion over the course of a year (100,000 × $30 × 365). But criminals must sell their stolen goods to fences, who give them at most 25 percent of actual value (Singer may have been overly generous; some goods yield only 10 percent of their value from fences). Thus, the total value of stolen property would be in the neighborhood of $4 to $5 billion in New York City alone. By looking at the figures for particular crimes, Singer found that amount to be utterly absurd. Retail sales in New York City totaled $15 billion annually, and if addicts were responsible for half of the estimated 2 percent inventory loss they would realize only $150 million during the year. Likewise, 500,000 burglaries at an average loss of $200 would yield the addicts another $100 million. In 1969, however, there were only 196,397 reported burglaries in New York City (or about 400,000 total burglaries, if we assume that only half were reported). The same absurdity applies to robbery. At an average take of $100 (high by most recent estimates), 800,000 robberies would yield the addicts $80 million. Unfortunately there were only 61,209 reported robberies, or an estimated 120,000 actual robberies in New York City in 1969. Singer concludes that addicts are responsible for, at most, only one-tenth the amount of crime attributed to them by the Rand report.[9]

How could the Rand report and most of the other drug experts be so wrong? Easy. You begin with a high estimate of heroin users and assume that all users are addicts. Then you multiply the result by a relatively high estimate of the price of satisfying an intense level of addiction each day. This calculation ignores some well-known facts about heroin usage. Not all users are addicts. Neither regular users nor addicts have the same daily need. Some addicts can meet their needs through lawfully gained income. The cases of the addicted physicians and musicians are well known. Some blue-collar and now even white-collar workers can continue to work while addicted. Many addicts meet their financial needs through prostitution, pimping, and drug dealing. Only some heroin addicts, then, must turn to predatory crime to feed their habits. They are indeed responsible for a lot of crime, but it is much less than most of the sensational estimates would have us believe.

A realistic estimate of the amount of crime committed by heroin addicts must take into account the fluctuating intensity of addiction. During a "run" or a period of heavy addiction, an addict/criminal may rob or steal six times as much as during a period of less intense addiction.[10] Estimates based on interviews with addicts who report their needs during peak periods will inevitably result in gross exaggerations of the total heroin/crime picture. In short, there is no such thing as the "average" heroin addict (even forgetting, for the moment, about the nonaddicted users) and, as we discussed in relation to the problem of estimating average offense rates for career criminals, no meaningful "average" amount of crime committed by addicts.

The question of whether heroin causes predatory street crime has been hotly debated. The drug crusaders traditionally paint a picture of the addict driven to crime by the need to supply his or her habit. In this scenario, heroin causes crime. Criminologists tend to take a different view. Research has indicated that among addicts/criminals, the first arrest preceded the first use of heroin by about a year and a half. Crime and heroin use are seen as two parts of a deviant lifestyle, without a strong causal relationship working in either direction. Many factors lead people into this deviant lifestyle, but criminologists have yet to isolate any one of them as taking priority over the others. From our perspective this lack of established causality signifies that the effective control of heroin (by whatever means) would not in and of itself keep substantially more people from entering lives of crime.[11]

We now turn to the question of decriminalization as a method of controlling heroin-related crime. It is only one of several alternatives available. Law enforcement strategies may be divided into two classes: "supply reduction" and "demand reduction."[12] The former attempts to reduce the amount of heroin available on the streets, either by interdicting importation or by cracking down on major dealers. Decades of law enforcement effort have proven this approach to be a will-of-the-wisp. The potential sources of supply are simply too numerous and there are too many people willing to take the risks of becoming importers and major dealers. A number of supply reduction campaigns may actually have backfired. Supply reduction, of course, raises the price of the commodity in question and thus may only force current addicts to increase their criminal activity to meet the higher price. Or it may cause drug users to turn to other drugs to meet their recreational or physical needs.

Nor does demand reduction appear to be any more promising. The most notable effort in this regard is the 1973 New York drug law. . . . Despite its Draconian penalties, the law did not reduce the level of drug usage in New York City. Deterring people from wanting heroin is not a realistic goal.[13]

These lines of reasoning bring us to decriminalization. Many thoughtful observers have argued, quite persuasively, that the criminalization of heroin use has done incalculable damage to our society and our criminal justice system. Criminal penalties have brought suffering to addicts, sustained criminal syndicates, corrupted the criminal justice system, and brought the law and law enforcement into disrepute by exposing their helplessness. As a policy, decriminalization does not mean a total legalization of and disregard for heroin. Advocates of decriminalization acknowledge that the drug is a terribly destructive commodity that requires control. Decriminalization usually means removing criminal penalties for its *use* but not for its sale and distribution. Thus, the individual addict would not face criminal penalties. Heroin trafficking, however, would remain a crime. At the same time, most decriminalization proposals call for some form of treatment or maintenance for the addict. Methadone is the most popular form of maintenance, although some experts propose maintaining addicts through medically prescribed heroin.

The story of methadone maintenance is another example of a familiar syndrome in the treatment literature: a new treatment is announced, its proponents claim amazing success rates amid great publicity, independent evaluations reveal that the successes are greatly exaggerated, and a powerful backlash sets in. In the case of methadone maintenance, Vincent Dole, Marie Nyswander, and Alan Warner claimed, in the pages of the December 1968 issue of the *Journal of the American Medical Association,* a 90 percent success rate in treating heroin addicts. After four years of treatment through methadone maintenance, 88 percent of their 750 addicts with criminal records remained arrest-free. By comparison, 91 percent of the group had had some jail experience before entering treatment. Only 5.6 percent of the group were arrested and convicted while in methadone treatment. Dole, Nyswander, and Warner professed to have saved New York City over $1 million per day in prevented crime. A year later, Dr. Francis Gearing, of Columbia University School of Public Health, asserted that after three years of methadone maintenance his group of heroin addicts had an arrest rate lower than that of the general population.[14]

The backlash was not long in coming. A reevaluation of the Dole, Nyswander, and Warner data showed that while 94 percent of the addicts had not been arrested in the year following treatment, only 80 percent had not been arrested the year before treatment—a drop of but 14 percent. Further studies indicated that many methadone programs were not careful to ensure enrollment of true addicts rather than occasional heroin users. Some provided methadone but no other treatment services. Levels of dosage varied widely. Not all programs monitored the behavior of their clients carefully to ensure that they were not selling their methadone. As is the case with so many evaluations in other forms of correctional treatment, evaluators failed to use adequate controls, and the resulting findings are not reliable. Arnold Trebach concludes that there are "no definitive answers in the 'scientific' studies." The backlash reached its apogee with Edward Jay Epstein's 1974 article, "Methadone: the Forlorn Hope." Appearing in *The Public Interest* in the same year that the magazine published Martinson's "What Works?" article, Epstein's article denounced methadone as a complete failure. Not only was there no evidence of its success but, in many respects, it was as damaging as heroin itself.[15]

The truth is that methadone maintenance is partially but not completely successful. John Kaplan estimates that it achieves permanent success with about 40 percent of the addicts who receive treatment. That may not seem like a terribly high success rate, but, Kaplan argues, it is "about as well as we can do." Methadone maintenance is "the most cost-effective treatment we have today" for this destructive drug that has resisted every form of control and treatment. With respect to crime, it appears that methadone maintenance reduces but does not eliminate criminal activity. In one California experiment, income from criminal activity dropped from $3,900 to $400 a year for one group of former addicts, and from $7,200 to $1,700 for another group. Another study by Dr. Paul Cushman found that arrest rates for addicts fluctuated from 3.1 per 100 person/years before addiction to 35.1 per 100 during addiction (confirming other data indicating that addicts do indeed commit large numbers of crimes). During methadone maintenance, arrest rates dropped from 5.9 per 100 and then rose to 9.0 per 100 after the clients were discharged from the program. We can view this "success" from different perspectives. Discharged clients were committing about three times as much crime after treatment as before addiction, but less than during their addiction period.[16]

As John Kaplan suggests, heroin is indeed "the hardest drug." It is the hardest not just in terms of its addictive powers but also because it has resisted all our attempts to control it. He suggests that decriminalization is the wisest approach to this terrible problem. But he has no illusions about its being a total cure. Decriminalization, with methadone maintenance and accompanying treatment, might make some difference. But it will neither completely reduce addiction nor eliminate heroin-related crime.

Notes

1. Norval Morris and Gordon Hawkins, *The Honest Politician's Guide to Crime Control* (Chicago: University of Chicago Press, 1970), chap. 1; Aryeh Neier, *Crime and Punishment: A Radical Solution* (New York: Stein and Day, 1976).

2. Edwin M. Schur, *Crimes without Victims* (Englewood Cliffs, NJ: Prentice Hall, 1965).

3. Raymond T. Nimmer, *Two Million Unnecessary Arrests* (Chicago: American Bar Foundation, 1971).

4. Nimmer, *Two Million Unnecessary Arrests.*

5. David E. Aaronson, C. Thomas Dienes, and Michael C. Mushneno, *Public Policy and Police Discretion* (New York: Clark Boardman, 1984).

6. George L. Kelling and James Q. Wilson, "Broken Windows: The Police and Neighborhood Safety," *Atlantic Monthly* 249 (March 1982), reprinted in James Q. Wilson, *Thinking about Crime,* rev. ed. (New York: Basic Books, 1983), chap. 5.

7. Nimmer, *Two Million Unnecessary Arrests,* chap. 2.

8. John Kaplan, *The Hardest Drug: Heroin and Public Policy* (Chicago: University of Chicago Press, 1983).

9. Max Singer, "The Vitality of Mythical Numbers," *The Public Interest* 23 (Spring 1971):3–9.

10. Kaplan, *The Hardest Drug,* pp. 55–57.

11. Kaplan, *The Hardest Drug,* p. 55.

12. Mark H. Moore, "Controlling Criminogenic Commodities: Drugs, Guns, and Alcohol," in James Q. Wilson, ed., *Crime and Public Policy* (San Francisco: ICS Press, 1983), pp. 125–144.

13. U.S. Department of Justice, *The Nation's Toughest Drug Law: Evaluating the New York Experience* (Washington, DC: U.S. Government Printing Office, 1978).

14. Arnold Trebach, *The Heroin Solution* (New Haven, CT: Yale University Press, 1982), pp. 259–260.

15. Edward Jay Epstein, "Methadone: The Forlorn Hope," *The Public Interest* 36 (Summer 1974).

16. Kaplan, *The Hardest Drug,* p. 222; Trebach, *The Heroin Solution,* p. 261.

The Professional Ex-: An Alternative for Exiting the Deviant Career

44

J. David Brown

This study explores the careers of professional ex-s, persons who have exited their deviant careers by replacing them with occupations in professional counseling. During their transformation, professional ex-s utilize vestiges of their deviant identity to legitimate their past deviance and generate new careers as counselors.

Recent surveys document that approximately 72% of the professional counselors working in the over 10,000 U.S. substance abuse treatment centers are former substance abusers (NAADAC 1986; Sobell and Sobell 1987). This attests to the significance of the professional ex- phenomenon. Though not all ex-deviants become professional ex-s, such data clearly suggest that the majority of substance abuse counselors are professional ex-s.[1]

Since the inception of the notion of deviant career by Goffman (1961) and Becker (1963), research has identified, differentiated, and explicated the characteristics of specific deviant career stages (e.g., Adler and Adler 1983; Luckenbill and Best 1981; Meisenhelder 1977; Miller 1986; Shover 1983). The literature devoted to exiting deviance primarily addresses the process whereby individuals abandon their deviant behaviors, ideologies, and identities and replace them with more conventional lifestyles and identities (Irwin 1970; Lofland 1969; Meisenhelder 1977; Shover 1983). While some studies emphasize the role of authorities or associations of ex-deviants in this change (e.g., Livingston 1974; Lofland 1969; Volkman and Cressey 1963), others suggest that exiting deviance is a natural process contingent upon age-related, structural, and social psychological variables (Frazier 1976; Inciardi 1975; Irwin 1970; Meisenhelder 1977; Petersilia 1980; Shover 1983).

Although exiting deviance has been variously conceptualized, to date no one has considered that it might include adoption of a legitimate career premised upon an identity that embraces one's deviant history. Professional ex-s exemplify this mode of exiting deviance.

Ebaugh's (1988) model of role exit provides an initial framework for examining this alternative mode of exiting the deviant career. Her model suggests that former roles are never abandoned but, instead, carry over into new roles. I elaborate her position and contend that one's deviant identity is not an obstacle that must be abandoned prior to exiting or adopting a more conventional lifestyle. To the contrary, one's lingering deviant identity facilitates rather than inhibits the exiting process.

How I gathered data pertinent to exiting, my relationship to these data, and how my personal experiences with exiting deviance organize this article, follow. I then present a four stage model that outlines the basic contours of the professional ex- phenomenon. Finally I suggest how the professional ex- phenomenon represents an alternative interpretation of exiting deviance that generalizes to other forms of deviance.

Methods

Data for this research consists of introspective and qualitative material.

Introspective Data

My introspections distill 20 years of experience with substance abuse/alcoholism, social control agents/agencies, and professional counselor training. I spent 13 years becoming a deviant drinker and entered substance abuse treatment in 1979. For 5 years (1981–1986), I was a primary therapist and family interventionist for a local private residential treatment facility.

"Systematic sociological introspection" (Ellis 1987, 1990), "autoethnography" (Hayano 1979), and "opportunistic research" (Reimer 1977) accessed the introspective data. Each group status—abuser, patient, therapist—indicates the "complete membership role" (Adler and Adler 1987) that combines unique circumstances with personal expertise to enhance research. The four stage model of exiting described later is, in part, informed by reexamination of the written artifacts of my therapeutic/recovery experiences (e.g., alco-biography, moral inventory, daily inventory journal) and professional counselor training (e.g., term paper, internship journal).

Qualitative Data

Qualitative data were collected over a six month period of intensive interviews with 35 counselor ex-s employed in a variety of community, state, and private institutions that treat individuals with drug, alcohol, and/or eating disorder problems.[2]

These professional ex-s worked in diverse occupations prior to becoming substance abuse counselors. A partial list includes employment as accountants, managers, salespersons, nurses, educators, and business owners. Although they claimed to enter the counseling profession within two years of discharge from therapy, their decision to become counselors usually came within one year. On the average they had been counselors for four and one half years. Except one professional ex- who previously counseled learning disabled children, all claimed they had not seriously considered a counseling career before entering therapy.

The Exit Process

Ebaugh (1988) contends that the experience of being an "ex" of one kind or another is common to most people in modern society. Emphasizing the sociological and psychological continuity of the ex- phenomenon she states, "[I]t implies that interaction is based not only on current role definitions but, more important, past identities that somehow linger on and define how people see and present themselves in their present identities" (p. xiii). Ebaugh defines the role exit as the "process of disengagement from a role that is central to one's self-identity and the reestablishment of an identity in a new role that takes into account one's ex-role" (p. 1).

Becoming a professional ex- is the outcome of a four stage process through which ex-s capitalize on the experience and vestiges of their deviant career in order to establish a new identity and role in a respectable organization. This process comprises emulation of one's therapist, the call to a counseling career, status-set realignment, and credentialization.

Stage One: Emulation of One's Therapist

The emotional and symbolic identification of these ex-s with their therapists during treatment, combined with the deep personal meanings they imputed to these relationships, was a compelling factor in their decisions to become counselors. Denzin (1987, pp. 61–62) identifies the therapeutic relationship's significance thus: "Through a process of identification and surrender (which may be altruistic), the alcoholic may merge her ego and her self in the experiences and the identity of the counselor. The group leader . . . is the group ego ideal, for he or she is a successful recovering alcoholic. . . . An emotional bond is thus formed with the group counselor. . . . "

Professional ex-s not only developed this emotional bond but additionally aspired to have the emotions and meanings once projected toward their therapists ascribed to them. An eating disorders counselor discussed her relationship with her therapist and her desire to be viewed in a similar way with these words:

> My counselor taught me the ability to care about myself and other people. Before I met her I was literally insane. She was the one who showed me that I wasn't crazy. Now, I want to be the person who says, "No, you're not crazy!" I am the one, now, who is helping them to get free from the ignorance that has shrouded eating disorders.

Counselors enacted a powerfully charismatic role in professional ex-s' therapeutic transformation. Their "laying on of verbal hands" provided initial comfort and relief from the ravaging symptoms of disease. They came to represent what ex-s must do both spiritually and professionally for themselves. Substance abuse therapy symbolized the "sacred" quest for divine grace rather than the mere pursuit of mundane, worldly, or "profane" outcomes like abstinence or modification of substance use/abuse behaviors; counselors embodied the sacred outcome.

Professional ex-s claimed that their therapists were the most significant change agent in their transformation. "I am here today because there was one very influential counselor in my life who helped me to get sober. I owe it all to God and to him," one alcoholism counselor expressed. A heroin addiction counselor stated, "The best thing that ever happened in my life was meeting Sally [her counselor]. She literally saved my life. If it wasn't for her I'd still probably be out there shootin' up or else be in prison or dead."

Subjects' recognition and identification of a leader's charismatic authority, as Weber (1968) notes, is decisive in validating that charisma and developing absolute trust and devotion. The special virtues and powers professional ex-s perceived in their counselors subsequently shaped their loyalty and devotion to the career.

Within the therapeutic relationship, professional ex-s perform a priestly function through which a cultural tradition passes from one generation to the next. While knowledge and wisdom pass downward (from professional ex- to patient), careers build upward (from patient to professional ex-). As the bearers of the cultural legacy of therapy, professional ex-s teach patients definitions of the situation they learned as patients. Indeed, part of the professional ex- mystique resides in once having been a patient (Bissell 1982). In this regard,

> My counselor established her legitimacy with me the moment she disclosed the fact that she, too, was an alcoholic. She wasn't just telling me what to do, she was living her own advice. By the example she set, I felt hopeful that I could recover. As I reflect upon those experiences I cannot think of one patient ever asking me about where I received my professional training. At the same time, I cannot begin to count the numerous times that my patients have asked me if I was "recovering."

Similar to religious converts' salvation through a profoundly redemptive religious experience, professional ex-s' deep career commitment derives from a transforming therapeutic resocialization. As the previous examples suggest, salvation not only relates to a changed universe of discourse; it is also identified "with one's personal therapist."[3]

At this stage, professional ex-s trust in and devote themselves to their counselors' proselytizations as a promissory note for the future. The promise is redemption and salvation from the ever-present potential for self-destruction or relapse that looms in their mental horizon. An eating disorders counselor shared her insights in this way:

> I wouldn't have gotten so involved in eating disorders counseling if I had felt certain that my eating disorder was taken care of. I see myself in constant recovery. If I was so self assured that I would never have the problem again there would probably be less of an emphasis on being involved in the field but I have found that helping others, as I was once helped, really helps me.

The substance abuse treatment center transforms from a mere "clinic" occupied by secularly credentialed professionals into a moral community of single believers. As Durkheim (1915) suggests, however, beliefs require rites and practices in order to sustain adherents' mental and emotional states.

Stage Two: The Call to a Counseling Career

At this juncture, professional ex-s begin to turn the moral corner on their deviance. Behaviors previously declared morally reprehensible are increasingly understood within a new universe of discourse as symptoms of a much larger disease complex. This recognition represents one preliminary step toward grace. In order to emulate their therapist, however, professional ex-s realize they must dedicate themselves to an identity and lifestyle that ensure their own symptoms' permanent remission. One alcoholism counselor illustrated this point by stating:

> I can't have my life, my health, my family, my job, my friends, or anything, unless I take daily necessary steps to ensure my continued recovery. My program of recovery has to come first. Before I can go out there and help my patients I need to always make sure that my own house is in order.

As this suggests, a new world-view premised upon accepting the contingencies of one's illness while maintaining a constant vigilance over potentially recurring symptoms replaces deviant moral and social meanings. Professional ex-s' recognition of the need for constant vigilance is internalized as their moral mission from which their spiritual duty (a counseling career) follows as a natural next step.

Although professional ex-s no longer engage in substance abuse behaviors, they do not totally abandon deviant beliefs or identity. "Lest we become complacent and forget from whence we came," as one alcoholism counselor indicated the significance of remembering and embracing the past.

Professional ex-s' identification with their deviant past undergirds their professional, experiential, and moral differentiation from other professional colleagues. A heroin addiction counselor recounted how he still identified himself as an addict and deviant:

> My perspective and my affinity to my clients, particularly the harder core criminals, is far better than the professor and other doctors that I

> deal with here in my job. We're different and we really don't see things the same way at all. Our acceptance and understanding of these people's diseases, if you will, is much different. They haven't experienced it. They don't know these people at all. It takes more than knowing about something to be effective. I've been there and, in many respects, I will always be there.

In this way, other counselors' medical, psychiatric, or therapeutic skills are construed as part of the ordinary mundane world. As the quotation indicates, professional ex-s intentionally use their experiential past and therapeutic transformations to legitimate their entrance into and authority in counseling careers.

Professional ex-s embrace their deviant history and identity as an invaluable, therapeutic resource and feel compelled to continually reaffirm its validity in an institutional environment. Certainly, participating in "12 Step Programs"[4] without becoming counselors could help others, but professional ex-s' call requires greater immersion than they provide. An alcoholism counselor reflected upon this need thus:

> For me, it was no longer sufficient to only participate "anonymously" in A.A. I wanted to surround myself with other spiritual and professional pilgrims devoted to receiving and imparting wisdom.

Towards patients, professional ex-s project a saintly aura and exemplify an "ideal recovery." Internalization of self-images previously ascribed to their therapist and now reaffirmed through an emotional and moral commitment to the counseling profession facilitate this ideation. Invariably, professional ex-s' counseling careers are in institutions professing treatment ideologies identical to what they were taught as patients. Becoming a professional ex- symbolizes a value elevated to a directing goal, whose pursuit predisposes them to interpret all ensuing experience in terms of relevance to it.

Stage Three: Status-Set Realignment

Professional ex-s' deep personal identification with their therapist provides an ego ideal to be emulated with regard to both recovery and career. They immerse themselves in what literally constitutes a "professional recovery career" that provides an institutional location to reciprocate their counselors' gift, immerse themselves in a new universe of discourse, and effectively lead novitiates to salvation. "I wouldn't be here today if it wasn't for all of the help I received in therapy. This is my way of paying some of those people back by helping those still in need," one alcoholism counselor related this.

Professional ex-s' identities assume a "master status" (Hughes 1945) that differs in one fundamental respect from others' experiencing therapeutic resocialization. Specifically, their transformed identities not only become the "most salient" in their "role identity hierarchy" (Stryker and Serpe 1982), but affect all other roles in their "status-sets" (Merton 1938). One alcoholism counselor reflected upon it this way:

> Maintaining a continued program of recovery is the most important thing in my life. Everything else is secondary. I've stopped socializing with my old friends who drink and have developed new recovering friends. I interact differently with my family. I used to work a lot of overtime but I told my old boss that overtime jeopardized my program. I finally began to realize that the job just didn't have anything to do with what I was really about. I felt alienated. Although I had been thinking about becoming a counselor ever since I went through treatment, I finally decided to pursue it.

Role alignment is facilitated by an alternative identity that redefines obligations associated with other, less significant, role identities. In the previous example, the strains of expectations associated with a former occupation fostered a role alignment consistent with a new self-image. This phenomenon closely resembles what Snow and Machalek (1983, p. 276) refer to as "embracement of a master role" that "is not merely a mask that is taken off or put on according to the situation. . . . Rather, it is central to nearly all situations. . . . " An eating disorders counselor stated the need to align her career with her self-image, "I hid in my former profession, interacting little with people. As a counselor, I am personally maturing and taking responsibility rather than letting a company take care of me. I have a sense of purpose in this job that I never had before."

Financial remuneration is not a major consideration in the decision to become a professional ex-. The pure type of call, Weber (1968, p. 52) notes, "disdains and repudiates economic exploitation of the gifts of grace as a source of income. . . . " Most professional ex-s earned more money in their previous jobs. For instance, one heroin addiction counselor stated:

> When I first got out of treatment, my wife and I started an accounting business. In our first year we cleared nearly sixty thousand dollars. The money was great and the business showed promise but something was missing. I missed being around other addicts and I knew I wanted to do more with my life along the lines of helping out people like me.

An additional factor contributing to professional ex-s' abandonment of their previous occupation is their recognition that a counseling career could resolve lingering self-doubts about their ability to remain abstinent. In this respect becoming a professional ex- allows "staying current" with their own recovery needs while continually reaffirming the severity of their illness. An eating disorders counselor explained:

> I'm constantly in the process of repeating insights that I've had to my patients. I hear myself saying, to them, what I need to believe for myself. Being a therapist helps me to keep current with my own recovery. I feel that I am much less vulnerable to my disease in this environment. It's a

> way that I can keep myself honest. Always being around others with sim-
> ilar issues prevents me from ignoring my own addiction clues.

This example illustrates professional ex-s' use of their profession to secure self-compliance during times of self-doubt. While parroting the virtues
of the program facilitates recognition that they, too, suffer from a disease,
the professional ex- role, unlike their previous occupations, enables them
to continue therapy indirectly.

Finally, the status the broader community ascribes to the professional
ex- role encourages professional ex-s' abandonment of previous roles. Association with an institutional environment and an occupational role gives
the professional ex- a new sense of place in the surrounding community,
within which form new self-concepts and self-esteem, both in the immediate situation and in a broader temporal framework.

The internal validation of professional ex-s' new identity resides in their
ability to successfully anticipate the behaviors and actions of relevant others. Additionally, they secure validation by other members of the professional ex- community in a manner atypical for other recovering individuals.
Affirmation by this reference community symbolizes validation by one's
personal therapist and the therapeutic institution, as a heroin addiction
counselor succinctly stated:

> Becoming a counselor was a way to demonstrate my loyalty and devo-
> tion to helping others and myself. My successes in recovery, including
> being a counselor, would be seen by patients and those who helped me
> get sober. It was a return to treatment, for sure, but the major differ-
> ence was that this time I returned victorious rather than defeated.

External validation, on the other hand, comes when others outside the
therapeutic community accord legitimacy to the professional ex- role. In
this regard, a heroin addiction counselor said:

> I remember talking to this guy while I was standing in line for a movie.
> He asked me what I did for a living and I told him that I was a drug
> abuse counselor. He started asking me all these questions about the
> drug problem and what I thought the answers were. When we finally
> got up to the door of the theater he patted me on the back and said,
> "You're doing a wonderful job. Keep up the good work. I really admire
> you for what you're trying to do." It really felt good to have a stranger
> praise me.

Professional ex-s' counseling role informs the performance of all other
roles, compelling them to abandon previous work they increasingly view
as mundane and polluting. The next section demonstrates how this master
role organizes the meanings associated with their professional counselor
training.

Stage Four: Credentialization

One characteristic typically distinguishing the professions from other occupations is specialized knowledge acquired at institutions of higher learning (Larson 1977; Parsons 1959; Ritzer and Walczak 1986, 1988). Although
mastering esoteric knowledge and professional responsibilities in a therapeutic relationship serve as gatekeepers for entering the counseling profession, the moral and emotional essence of being a professional ex-
involves much more.

Professional ex-s see themselves as their patients' champions. "Knowing
what it's like" and the subsequent education and skills acquired in training
legitimate claims to the "entitlements of their stigma" (Gusfield 1982), including professional status. Their monopoly of an abstruse body of knowledge and skill is realized through their emotionally lived history of shame
and guilt as well as the hope and redemption secured through therapeutic
transformation. Professional ex-s associate higher learning with their experiential history of deviance and the emotional context of therapy. Higher
learning symbolizes rediscovery of a moral sense of worth and sacredness
rather than credential acquisition. This distinction was clarified by an alcoholism counselor:

> Anymore, you need to have a degree before anybody will hire you. I
> entered counseling with a bachelors but I eventually received my MSW
> about two years ago. I think the greatest benefit in having the formal
> training is that I have been able to more effectively utilize my personal
> alcoholism experiences with my patients. I feel that I have a gift to offer
> my patients which doesn't come from the classroom. It comes from
> being an alcoholic myself.

These entitlements allow professional ex-s to capitalize on their deviant
identity in two ways: the existential and phenomenological dimensions of
their lived experience of "having made their way from the darkness into
the light" provide their experiential and professional *legitimacy* among patients, the community, and other professionals, as well as occupational *income*. "Where else could I go and put bulimic and alcoholic on my resume
and get hired?" one counselor put it.

Professional ex-s generally eschew meta-perspective interpretations of
the system in which they work. They desire a counseling method congruent with their fundamental universe of discourse and seek, primarily, to
perpetuate this system (Peele 1989; Room 1972, 1976). The words of one
educator at a local counselor training institute are germane:

> These people [professional ex-s] . . . are very fragile when they get here.
> Usually, they have only been in recovery for about a year. Anyone who
> challenges what they learned in therapy, or in their program of recov-
> ery [i.e., A.A., Narcotics Anonymous, Overeaters Anonymous] . . . is
> viewed as a threat. Although we try to change some of that while

they're here with us, I still see my role here as one of an extended therapist rather than an educator.

Information challenging their beliefs about how they, and their patients,
should enact the rites associated with recovery is condemned (Davies 1963;
Pattison 1987; Roizen 1977). They view intellectual challenges to the disease
concept as attacks on their personal program of recovery. In a Durkheimian
sense, such challenges "profane" that which they hold "sacred."

Within the walls of these monasteries, professional ex-s emulate their
predecessors as one generation of healers passes on to the next an age old
message of salvation. Although each new generation presents the path to
enlightenment in somewhat different, contemporary terms, it is already
well lit for those "becoming a professional ex-."

Discussion

Focusing on their lived experiences and accounts, this study sketches the
central contours of professional ex-s' distinctive exit process. More generally, it also endeavors to contribute to the existing literature on deviant
careers.

An identity that embraces their deviant history and identity undergirds
the professional ex-s' careers. This existing mode is the outcome of a four
stage process enabling professional ex-s to capitalize on their deviant history. They do not "put it all behind them" in exchange for conventional
lifestyles, values, beliefs, and identities. Rather, they use vestiges of their
deviant biography as an explicit occupational strategy.

My research augments Ebaugh's (1988) outline of principles underlying
role exit in three ways. First, her discussion suggests that people are unaware of these guiding principles. While this holds for many, professional
ex-s' intentional rather than unintentional embracement of their deviant
identity is the step by which they adopt a new role in the counseling profession. Second, Ebaugh states that significant others' negative reactions inhibit or interrupt exit. Among professional ex-s, however, such reactions
are a crucial precursor to their exit mode. Finally, Ebaugh sees role exit as
a voluntary, individually initiated process, enhanced by "seeking alternatives" through which to explore other roles. Professional ex-s, by contrast,
are compelled into therapy. They do not look for this particular role.
Rather, their alternatives are prescribed through their resocialization into a
new identity.

Organizations in American society increasingly utilize professional ex-s
in their social control efforts. For example, the state of Colorado uses prisoners to counsel delinquent youth. A preliminary, two year, follow-up
study suggests that these prisoner-counselors show only 13% recidivism
(Shiller 1988) and a substantial number want to return to college or enter
careers as guidance counselors, probation officers, youth educators, or law

enforcement consultants. Similarly, a local effort directed toward curbing gang violence, the Open Door Youth Gang Program, was developed by a professional ex- and uses former gang members as counselors, educators, and community relations personnel.

Further examination of the modes through which charismatic, albeit licensed and certified, groups generate professional ex- statuses is warranted. Although the examples just described differ from the professional ex-s examined earlier in this research in terms of therapeutic or "medicalized" resocialization, their similarities are even more striking. Central to them all is that a redemptive community provides a reference group whose moral and social standards are internalized. Professional ex- statuses are generated as individuals intentionally integrate and embrace rather than abandon their deviant biographies as a specific occupational strategy.

Notes

1. Most individuals in substance abuse therapy do not become professional ex-s. Rather, they traverse a variety of paths not articulated here including (1) dropping out of treatment, (2) completing treatment but returning to substance use and/or abuse, and (3) remaining abstinent after treatment but feeling no compulsion to enter the counseling profession. Future research will explore the differences among persons by mode of exit. Here, however, analysis and description focus exclusively on individuals committed to the professional ex- role.

2. I conducted most interviews at the subject's work environment, face-to-face. One interview was with a focus group of 10 professional ex-s (Morgan 1988). Two interviews were in my office, one at my home, and one at a subject's home. I interviewed each individual one time for approximately one hour. Interviews were semi-structured, with open-end questions designed to elicit responses related to feelings, thoughts, perceptions, reflections, and meaning concerning subjects' past deviance, factors facilitating their exit from deviance, and their counseling career.

3. I contend that significantly more professional ex-s pursue their careers due to therapeutic resocialization than to achieving sobriety/recovery exclusively through the 12 Step Program (e.g., A.A.). It is too early, however, to preclude that some may enter substance abuse counseling careers lacking any personal therapy. My experiences and my interviews with other professional ex-s suggest that very few professional ex-s enter the profession directly through their contacts with the 12 Step Program. The program's moral precepts—that "sobriety is a gift from God" that must be "given freely to others in order to assure that one may keep the gift"—would appear to discourage rather than encourage substance abuse counseling careers. Further, professional ex-s are commonly disparaged in A.A. circles as "two hatters" (cf. Denzin 1987). They are, therefore, not a positive reference group for individuals recovering exclusively through the 12 Step Program. Sober 12 Step members are more inclined to emulate their "sponsors" than pursue careers with no experiential referents or direct relevance to their recovery. Further data collection and analysis will examine these differences. Extant data, however, strongly indicate that therapeutic resocialization and a professional role model provide the crucial link between deviant and substance abuse counseling careers.

4. "12 Step Program" refers to a variety of self-help groups (e.g., A.A., Narcotics Anonymous, Overeaters Anonymous) patterning their recovery model upon the original 12 Steps and 12 Traditions of A.A.

References

Adler, Patricia, and Peter Adler. 1983. "Shifts and Oscillations in Deviant Careers: The Case of Upper-Level Drug Dealers and Smugglers." *Social Problems* 31: 195–207.

———. 1987. *Membership Roles in Field Research.* Newbury Park, CA: Sage.

Becker, Howard. 1963. *Outsiders: Studies in the Sociology of Deviance*. New York: Free Press.

Best, Joel, and David F. Luckenbill. 1982. *Organizing Deviance*. Englewood Cliffs, NJ: Prentice Hall.

Bissell, LeClair. 1982. "Recovered Alcoholism Counselors." Pp. 810–817 in *Encyclopedic Handbook of Alcoholism*, edited by E. Mansell Pattison and Edward Kaufman. New York: Gardner.

Davies, D. L. 1963. "Normal Drinking in Recovered Alcoholic Addicts" (comments by various correspondents). *Quarterly Journal of Studies on Alcohol* 24:109–121, 321–332.

Denzin, Norman. 1987. *The Recovering Alcoholic*. Beverly Hills: Sage.

Durkheim, Emile. 1915. *The Elementary Forms of the Religious Life*. New York: Free Press.

Ebaugh, Helen Rose Fuchs. 1988. *Becoming an Ex: The Process of Role Exit*. Chicago: University of Chicago Press.

Ellis, Carolyn. 1987. "Systematic Sociological Introspection and the Study of Emotions." Paper presented to the annual meeting of the American Sociological Association, Chicago.

———. 1990. "Sociological Introspection and Emotional Experience." *Symbolic Interaction* 13(2).

Frazier, Charles. 1976. *Theoretical Approaches to Deviance*. Columbus: Charles Merrill.

Glassner, Barry, Margret Ksander, Bruce Berg, and Bruce D. Johnson. 1983. "A Note on the Deterrent Effect of Juvenile vs. Adult Jurisdiction." *Social Problems* 31:219–221.

Goffman, Erving. 1961. *Asylums*. Garden City, NY: Anchor.

Gusfield, Joseph. 1982. "Deviance in the Welfare State: The Alcoholism Profession and the Entitlements of Stigma." *Research in Social Problems and Public Policy* 2:1–20.

Hayano, David. 1979. "Auto-Ethnography: Paradigms, Problems and Prospects." *Human Organization* 38:99–104.

Hughes, Everett. 1945. "Dilemmas and Contradictions of Status." *American Journal of Sociology* L:353–359.

Inciardi, James. 1975. *Careers in Crime*. Chicago: Rand McNally.

Irwin, John. 1970. *The Felon*. Englewood Cliffs: Prentice Hall.

Larson, Magali. 1977. *The Rise of Professionalism*. Berkeley: University of California Press.

Livingston, Jay. 1974. *Compulsive Gamblers*. New York: Harper and Row.

Lofland, John. 1969. *Deviance and Identity*. Englewood Cliffs: Prentice Hall.

Luckenbill, David F., and Joel Best. 1981. "Careers in Deviance and Respectability: The Analogy's Limitations." *Social Problems* 29:197–206.

Meisenhelder, Thomas. 1977. "An Exploratory Study of Exiting from Criminal Careers." *Criminology* 15:319–334.

Merton, Robert. 1938. *Social Theory and Social Structure*. Glencoe: Free Press.

Miller, Gale. 1986. "Conflict in Deviant Occupations." Pp. 373–401 in *Working: Conflict and Change*, 3rd ed., edited by George Ritzer and David Walczak. Englewood Cliffs: Prentice Hall.

Morgan, David L. 1988. *Focus Groups as Qualitative Research*. Beverly Hills: Sage.

NAADAC. 1986. *Development of Model Professional Standards for Counselor Credentialing*. National Association of Alcoholism and Drug Abuse Counselors. Dubuque: Kendall/Hunt.

Parsons, Talcott. 1959. "Some Problems Confronting Sociology as a Profession." *American Sociological Review* 24:547–559.

Pattison, E. Mansell. 1987. "Whither Goals in the Treatment of Alcoholism." *Drugs and Society* 2/3:153–171.

Peele, Stanton. 1989. *The Diseasing of America: Addiction Treatment Out of Control.* Toronto: Lexington.

Petersilia, Joan. 1980. "Criminal Career Research: A Review of Recent Evidence." Pp. 321–379 in *Crime and Justice: An Annual Review of Research,* vol. 2, edited by Norval Morris and Michael Tonry. Chicago: University of Chicago Press.

Reimer, Jeffrey. 1977. "Varieties of Opportunistic Research." *Urban Life* 5:467–477.

Ritzer, George, and David Walczak. 1986. *Working: Conflict and Change.* 3rd ed. Englewood Cliffs: Prentice Hall.

———. 1988. "Rationalization and the Deprofessionalization of Physicians." *Social Forces* 67:1–22.

Roizen, Ron. 1977. "Comment on the Rand Report." *Quarterly Journal of Studies on Alcohol* 38:170–178.

Room, Robin. 1972. "Drinking and Disease: Comment on the Alcohologist's Addiction." *Quarterly Journal of Studies on Alcohol* 33:1049–1059.

———. 1976. "Drunkenness and the Law: Comment on the Uniform Alcoholism Intoxication Treatment Act." *Quarterly Journal of Studies on Alcohol* 37:113–144.

Shiller, Gene. 1988. "A Preliminary Report on SHAPE-UP." Paper presented to the Colorado District Attorneys Council, Denver.

Shover, Neil. 1983. "The Later Stages of Ordinary Property Offenders' Careers." *Social Problems* 31:208–218.

Snow, David, and Richard Machalek. 1983. "The Convert as a Social Type." Pp. 259–289 in *Sociological Theory 1983,* edited by Randall Collins. San Francisco: Jossey-Bass.

Sobell, Mark B., and Linda C. Sobell. 1987. "Conceptual Issues Regarding Goals in the Treatment of Alcohol Problems." *Drugs and Alcohol* 2/3:1–37.

Stryker, Sheldon, and Richard Serpe. 1982. "Commitment, Identity Salience, and Role Behavior: Theory and Research Example." Pp. 199–218 in *Personality, Roles, and Social Behavior,* edited by William Ickes and Eric S. Knowles. New York: Springer-Verlag.

Volkman, Rita, and Donald Cressey. 1963. "Differential Association and the Rehabilitation of Drug Addicts." *American Journal of Sociology* 69:129–142.

Weber, Max. 1968. *On Charisma and Institution Building.* Edited by S. N. Eisenstadt. Chicago: University of Chicago Press.

45

Race and Policing

Jim Leitzel

Police in the United States seem to be doing something right: serious crime has been plummeting, declining by more than 20 percent since 1991. The reduction in the number of murders has been even more spectacular, dropping by more than 36 percent between 1993 and 1999: the murder rate in 1999 was lower than in every year since 1966. Simultaneously, many public areas have become decidedly more hospitable. Aggressive "quality-of-life" policing, such as that employed in New York City to clean up the subway or rid the city of "squeegeemen," may be partly responsible for both the drop in the crime rate and improvements in public spaces.

These successes, however, are tarnished by ongoing controversy concerning the role of race in policing. Race has been an element in some high-profile incidents, such as the February 1999 killing of unarmed African immigrant Amadou Diallo by four white New York City police officers, or the 1997 police torture of Haitian immigrant Abner Louima. But the racial disparities in policing appear to go well beyond isolated cases of abuse. Generally speaking, black people, particularly young black males, tend to have much worse experiences with the police than do white Americans. These experiences range from the annoying—frequent traffic stops for minor or imagined violations—to the fatal, as in the Diallo case. To some extent, racial disparities in citizen-police interactions are deliberate, as criminal "profiles" compiled by the police formally or informally employ race as one factor in identifying potential miscreants. In practice, race appears often to be a decisive element in whether a stop is initiated, or in how an encounter is handled.

Given the success evidenced by falling crime rates, it might be thought that the way forward in crime control is to continue with present policing strategies, while redoubling efforts to eliminate the abuses of racist and brutal police. Surely there is wide consensus that such bad cops should be rooted out and prosecuted for their misdeeds. But it is the use of racial profiling, not its abuse, that is the more fundamental problem: even if all abuses associated with race-based policing could somehow be eliminated, racial profiling would remain a bad idea. Race-based policing is counter-productive: it leads to more crime, not less.

Is There Race-Based Policing in the U.S.?

Perhaps the characterization of racial disparities in policing as a problem is itself misguided. Perhaps there are no actual racial disproportions in police-citizen encounters; or, if disparities do exist, they are a necessary evil, the price that has to be paid for a well-policed society.

Do disparities exist? With respect to traffic regulations, for instance, are blacks and other minorities stopped more frequently, for a given level of violations of the law? Statistics on race, age, sex, and other information from traffic stops are not routinely collected. But information that is avail-able suggests wide racial disparities. The Maryland State Police, in settling a lawsuit, agreed to collect racial information on traffic stops. On Interstate 95, 70 percent of the drivers who were stopped by the state police between January 1995 and December 1997 were African Americans, though African Americans comprised only some 17.5 percent of the drivers (and of the speeding drivers). Videotapes of stops for drug interdiction in Volusia County, Florida, also on I-95, indicated that blacks comprised 5 percent of the drivers, but 70 percent of those who were stopped. Other statistics sug-gest that the war on drugs is waged primarily against the non-white seg-ment of the population. According to a report written by David Harris for the American Civil Liberties Union (ACLU), "Today, blacks constitute 13 percent of the country's drug users; 37 percent of those arrested on drug charges; 55 percent of those convicted; and 74 percent of all drug offend-ers sentenced to prison."

Racial disparities in policing exist; indeed, it would be surprising if they did not exist, since race is used as one of the indicators in criminal profil-ing. Are such disparities understandable, the result of scrupulous policing? While young black males are treated with more suspicion by the police it might be argued that this is natural, because young black males cause a dis-proportionate amount of trouble. When attempting to prevent or solve street crime, police shouldn't devote much time to tailing elderly women (except perhaps as potential victims of crime)—young males are the likely perpetrators. Conscientious, unbiased policing would seem to require that police focus their suspicions on the most probable threats. By this reckon-ing, young black males should have more frequent and maybe even less pleasant police encounters than does the rest of the population.

As a seeming bolster to the notion that race-based policing is essential, an appeal might be made to the behavior of private citizens, as opposed to the police. When walking alone down the street at night, suddenly you no-tice some individuals walking toward you. If you perceive them as a threat, you may want to quickly take evasive action, such as crossing the street or returning to some more populated area. But you only have a few seconds in which to make this decision. The only basis that you have for choosing your route is the small amount of information that you can visually gather, and your prior beliefs about likely and unlikely perpetrators. In a quick glance, you can only learn a few basic facts: the number of individuals, perhaps their size, their sex, and roughly, their age, their manner of dress, and their general comportment. If the strangers are two elderly women, you continue on your way, rightly confident that you are not about to become a crime victim. If they are two young adult males, you might implement your evasion plan. You might be even more likely to take evasive action if it is two black males. You would not be alone in such a reaction: Rev. Jesse Jackson notably mentioned back in 1993 his own pain at subconsciously associating blackness with potential criminality in street encounters.

Private behavior, in making judgments about potential criminality, discriminates on the basis of sex, age, race, and other factors. It seems unavoidable that when better information is not available—and in a chance meeting in the street, only a few characteristics will be observable—group reputations, even if mistaken, play a dominant role in determining private actions. And group reputations can quite easily be mistaken. Few of us actually know how much more likely it is that we will be victimized by a black man than a white man, if indeed it is more likely—most crime involves victims and perpetrators of the same race. Nor would knowledge of crime statistics necessarily resolve the issue. If the police focus their crime-fighting resources on young black men, they will end up arresting such suspects more often than others, even if there is no sex- or race-based differential in the actual amount of crime. Group reputations for criminality might then yield the appearance of validity, even when they are actually mistaken.

Nevertheless, young men on average are widely believed to be more inclined to predatory violence than elderly women, and without better information, many people will respond to this perception. Such private actions based on group reputation by people who are not racist cannot simply be condemned as inappropriate. In the words of Harvard Law professor Randall Kennedy (whose overall approach to race-based policing is closely paralleled here), those who legally employ race as a signal of potential criminality, "like everyone, are caught up in a large tragedy that will require more than individual good will and bravery to resolve."

Should good cops, then, behave as good private citizens often do? Perhaps surprisingly, the answer is: no. Police should, in general, not use race as a basis for deciding whom to watch, or, after a crime has been committed, whom to question or arrest on grounds of suspicion. This conclusion is not driven by some philosophical perspective that places a higher weight on racial equality than on crime control. Just the opposite: it derives solely from a concern with crime. As in many other policy arenas, the best long-term approach to crime control appears counterproductive in the short-run.

Costs of Race-Based Policing

Effective crime control in a democracy requires voluntary cooperation between the police and the citizenry. Voluntary cooperation requires trust. Race-based policing undermines trust. Reduced trust means lessened deterrence of crime, as minorities become unwilling to report crime—a not insignificant concern, given that approximately one-half of serious crime in the United States is not reported to the police. Further, hostility between minorities and the police creates an unwillingness to testify at trials, and, when serving on juries, an unwillingness to convict defendants. This lack of cooperation, brought on by racial disparities in policing, reduces criminal deterrence.

Beyond lowering deterrence, race-based policing also provides positive inducements to disobey the law. When all young black males are thought to be and treated as criminals, a law-abiding black male cannot easily overcome this perception through his own virtuous behavior. Being thought a scoundrel in any event, the reward to virtue falls. The perception of criminality that is inherent in race-based policing prevents well-behaving minority youths from distinguishing themselves from those who are criminals, reducing the incentive to be law-abiding.

The problem is not bad or racist cops in an otherwise workable system. Rather, the problem is the hostility and distrust created among police and minority citizens. This pool of hostility between a group of citizens and the police is not the work of a single cop—especially a single good cop—or based on the activities of a single day. Rather, the pool of hostility is created by long-term, numerous interactions between the police and the citizenry. The activities of any single cop over a short period are essentially irrelevant in determining the size of the hostility "pool": they are literally a drop in the ocean. So when a conscientious police officer is doing his (or her) job, he ignores the effect that his actions have on the sea of hostility, because his actions make no noticeable difference. But the sea of hostility is in fact made up of unpleasant police-citizen encounters in the aggregate, despite the fact that any individual encounter, short of an obviously abusive encounter, is of little or no consequence.

Conscientious policing as described above may not only lead to a general mistrust of the police within a minority community, it also can hold rather severe adverse consequences for specific individuals. Police officers who use race and other noisy indicators unrelated to behavior in profiling potential criminals might "rationally" ignore the fact that the same indicators that lead them to make a stop will also lead other officers to do so, too.

Thus their stop is often far from an isolated event for the individual in question, but just one in a continuing series of stops, as the famous "San Diego walker" case [*Kolender v. Lawson* 461 U.S. 352 (1983)] demonstrated. Further, police actions to some extent serve as guides for the behavior of citizens. When private citizens see or learn about racial profiling by police, their own attitudes toward and treatment of minorities are likely to be influenced.

Race-based practices also harm police, even beyond the mistrust that such practices engender. While race-based policing makes it hard for law-abiding young minority males to distinguish themselves from lawbreakers, it simultaneously leads to a parallel stereotyping of police. Race-based policing generates an unfair perception that many or most police officers are best insensitive to the concerns of minorities or, at worst, racists. So good and honest cops also pay a price from the countenancing of race-based policing, as they become perceived as rough equivalents to those few police whose motivations and acts actually are racist.

Race-based policing presents a familiar scenario, where rational individual behavior does not serve the social good. National defense, the paradigmatic "public good," provides an analogy. Whether or not a particular individual pays his or her taxes has essentially no influence upon the amount of government military spending. Nevertheless, the amount spent on national defense depends on the aggregate amount of taxes paid. If tax payments were voluntary, we would expect too little defense to be supplied: people would recognize that their individual contribution would essentially not matter for the amount of defense provided to them, so they might as well not contribute. Unconstrained individual incentives do not serve society's interests with respect to public goods. Taxes, therefore, are not voluntary. Similarly, citizen hostility towards the police is a "public bad," and individual police officers, acting rationally, will create or "supply" too much of it in the aggregate. Unconstrained individual incentives do not serve society's interests with respect to public bads, either.

▶An Imperfect Solution

The remedy to the distorted individual incentives that characterize race-based policing is the same as with taxes: we must not allow the use of race in policing to be voluntary. A stringent ban on race-based policing must be adopted. The operational rule of thumb for police officers who are considering stopping or searching a black person (or potentially a Latino or another minority) should be: would I stop or search this person if he or she was white? If the answer is no, then the black person should not be stopped or searched, either, even if, for instance, the neighborhood is predominately white and blacks stopped in the area have been associated with crime in the past. Police "profiles" of drug couriers or other classes of criminals should not include race, even (as is currently done) as one of a panoply of characteristics.

If a description of a suspect is available, race should then be taken into account in attempting to apprehend the suspect. Even here, however, police must be careful to prevent using a description that includes race to cast too wide a net, or as a pretext for a stop unrelated to the crime for which the description was secured.

Important questions remain about how to enforce a ban on race-based policing, and enforcement surely will be imperfect. But the current federal standard, which allows the police to use race not in isolation, but as one of several factors that determine their profiling of potential criminals, is likewise hard to enforce. In fact, evasion of the current standard cannot be prevented, as it is a simple matter to fabricate other, non-race-based factors to accompany race as rationales for police stops or searches. Perhaps the ban on race-based policing will also be easily evaded. But over time, if good police sincerely adopt it, the rule can alter the behavior of all officers, and reduce the pool of hostility towards the police that now exists among many black Americans.

Because using racial indicators of potential criminality appears to be a rational approach for individual police officers (as for private citizens), a conscientious police officer who currently engages in race-based policing is likely to believe that he or she is doing the right thing, something socially desirable. Adoption of formal rules prohibiting race-based policing will at least make it clear that society does not share that judgment. Race-based activity by police, then, can no longer serve as an open source of pride in a job well done, and this too can reduce the extent of race-based policing over time, even if the prohibition is hard to enforce.

Not all disparities in police-citizen encounters will be eliminated when race-based policing is no longer countenanced: policing high crime areas might require more stops than in other neighborhoods, for instance, and minorities are more likely to live in such neighborhoods. But minorities will also be the beneficiaries of this increased scrutiny, which will be more acceptable when it is not part of an explicit or implicit race-based policing strategy.

Outlawing race-based policing may require other changes. Possibly it might mean an increase in the number of police officers that are required to guard some neighborhoods. It may also mean stopping more citizens in the aggregate, encompassing a broader range than those who are habitually stopped today. (Professor Randall Kennedy discussed these alternatives more fully in his presentation to the National Institute of Justice.) This latter measure would spread more widely the costs imposed by policing, and should not be viewed as necessarily a bad thing. It is easy to support certain laws and police practices if you are unlikely to be burdened by them. But will support for the many searches that take place in the name of the war on drugs, for instance, survive a broadening of the citizenry that is subject to such searches? A rule prohibiting race-based policing will not only serve the long-run goal of controlling crime, but will also help to protect, for all citizens, constitutionally guaranteed rights against illegal search and seizure. One area in which a prohibition on race-based policing might require supplementary measures is in traffic patrolling. The complexity of traffic laws guarantees available pretexts for race-based stops, and as a result, differential traffic stops occasioned by race-based policing currently appear to be widespread. But as traffic stops are more formal than street-to-street encounters (and typically constrained to take place within a short distance of the patrol car), they can be more closely monitored. Videotaping stops (which already occurs in some jurisdictions), and the collection of statistics on the race of stopped drivers (which is now done by law in some states by executive order for federal law enforcers, and voluntarily by other police departments), offer means to ensure that strictures against race-based policing are not ignored.

The formal repudiation of race-based policing can be complemented with a strategy to enforce strict limits on the actions that the state can take in the absence of more compelling evidence of wrongdoing than noisy signals like gender, race, and age. In the drug search example, for instance, the searches can be limited to be of only a few minutes duration, and restrictions can be placed on the extent of their intrusiveness. Whether race-based policing is countenanced or not, there must be strict ceilings to what actions the state can take in the absence of information more incriminating than "suspicion" or group reputation. Otherwise, outrages such as the U.S. internment of Japanese-Americans during World War II, or the mundane, daily outrages that some members of targeted groups are subjected to by police, will continue to be repeated.

In the long run, there is no tradeoff between crime control and race-neutral policing: more of one does not mean less of the other. Indeed, just the opposite. But the immediate rejection of race-based policing will not immediately reduce distrust between police and minority communities. The distrust has been fostered over many years, and it will take sustained changes in police policy and behavior to reduce the sea of hostility. The time to make the change to race-neutral policing, then, is when crime is relatively low. What the police have been doing right has helped to bring about the low crime rates that we currently enjoy. We should take advantage of these low crime rates to change, now, what the police, generally in good faith, have been doing wrong.

Suggested Further Readings

Cole, David. *No Equal Justice: Race and Class in the American Criminal Justice System.* New York: The New Press, 1999

Davis, Marcia. "Traffic Violation: Racial Profiling Is a Reality for Black Drivers." *Emerge,* pp. 42–48, June 1999.

Harris, David. "Driving While Black: Racial Profiling on our Nation's Highways." American Civil Liberties Union Special Report, June 1999, available at www.aclu.org/profiling/report/index.html.

Kennedy, Randall. *Race, Crime, and the Law.* New York: Random House, 1997.

———. "Race, the Police, and 'Reasonable Suspicion.'" Presentation to the National Institute of Justice, February 3, 1998. Perspectives on Crime and Justice: 1997–1998 Lecture Series, available at *www.ojp.usdoj.gov/nij/pubs-sum/172851.htm.*

Merida, Kevin. "Capital Scene: Decriminalizing 'Driving While Black.'" *Emerge,* p. 26, December/January 1999.

Acknowledgments

1. Jack P. Gibbs, "Conceptions of Deviant Behavior: The Old and the New," *Pacific Sociological Review*, Spring 1996, pp. 9–11. Reprinted by permission of JAI Press.

2. Alex Heckert and Druann Maria Heckert, "Using an Integrated Typology of Deviance to Analyze Ten Common Norms of the US Middle Class" from *The Sociological Quarterly*, vol. 45, no. 2, Spring 2004, pp. 209–228. Copyright © 2004 by the Midwest Sociological Association. Reprinted by permission.

3. Howard S. Becker, "Moral Entrepreneurs: The Creation and Enforcement of Deviant Categories," reprinted by permission of The Free Press, a Division of Simon & Schuster, Inc. From *Outsiders*, by Howard S. Becker. Copyright © 1963 by The Free Press.

4. Justin L. Tuggle and Malcolm D. Holmes, "Blowing Smoke: Status Politics and the Shasta County Smoking Ban," reprinted from *Deviant Behavior*, vol. 18, 1997, pp. 77–93. Copyright 1997 from *Deviant Behavior* by Tuggle and Holmes. Reproduced by permission of Taylor & Francis, Inc., http://www.routledge-ny.com.

5. Stephen Spitzer, "The Production of Deviance in Capitalist Society," reprinted from *Social Problems*, vol. 22, no. 5, June 1975, pp. 641–646. Copyright © 1975 by The Society for the Study of Social Problems. Reprinted by permission of the University of California Press Journals.

6. Peter Conrad, "The Discovery of Hyperkinesis: Notes on the Medicalisation of Deviant Behavior," Copyright © 1975 by The Society for the Study of Social Problems. Reprinted from *Social Problems* vol. 23, no. 1, October 1975, pp.12–21, by permission of the University of California Press Journals.

7. Emile Durkheim, "The Normal and the Pathological," reprinted by permission of The Free Press, a Division of Simon & Schuster, Inc. from THE RULES OF SOCIOLOGICAL METHOD by Emile Durkheim, translated by Sarah A. Solovay and John H. Mueller. Edited by George E.G. Catlin. Copyright © 1938 by George E.G. Catlin; copyright renewed 1966 by Sarah A. Solovay, John H. Mueller, George E.G. Catlin.

8. Kai T. Erikson, "On the Sociology of Deviance," reprinted with the permission of Simon & Schuster from the Macmillan College Division title of *Wayward Puritans*, by Kai T. Erikson. Copyright © 1966 by Macmillan Publishing Company.

9. Thorsten Sellin, "The Conflict of Conduct Norms," reprinted from *Culture Conflict and Crime*, a report of the Subcommittee on Delinquency of the Committee on Personality and Culture, *Social Science Research Council Bulletin 41* (New York, 1938).

10. Jeffrey H. Reiman, "A Radical Perspective on Crime." Reprinted by permission of Pearson Education.

11. Rudolph Alexander, Jr., and Jacquelyn Gyamerah, Journal of Black Studies (28:1) pp. 97–111, Copyright © 1997 Reprinted by Permission of Sage Publications, Inc.

12. Gresham M. Sykes and David Matza, "Techniques of Neutralization: A Theory of Delinquency," reprinted from *American Sociological Review*, vol. 22, 1957, pp. 666–670.

13. Donald McCabe, "Influence of Situational Ethics on Cheating Among College Students," from *Sociological Inquiry*, vol. 82, no. 3, 1992, pp. 365–374. Copyright © 1992 by *Sociological Inquiry*. Reprinted by permission of Blackwell Publishers.

14. Robert K. Merton, "Social Structure and Anomie," reprinted from *American Sociological Review*, vol, 3, 1938, pp. 672–682.

15. John M. Hagedorn, "Homeboys, Dope Fiends, Legits, and New Jacks," reprinted by permission of The American Society of Criminology from *Criminology*, vol. 32, no. 2, May 1994, pp. 197–219. Copyright © 1963 by The Free Press; copyright renewed 1991 by Howard S. Becker.

16. Barbara J. Costello, Bradley J. Anderson, and Michael D. Stein, "Heavy Episodic Drinking Among Adolescents: A Test of Hypotheses Derived from Control Theory" from *Journal of Alcohol and Drug Education,* vol. 50, pp. 35–55. Copyright © 2006. Reprinted by permission.

17. Neal Shover and David Honaker, "The Socially Bounded Decision Making of Persistent Property Owners," reprinted from *Howard Journal*, vol. 31, 1992, pp. 276–293.

18. Howard S. Becker, "Career Deviance," reprinted by permission of The Free Press, a Division of Simon & Schuster. From *Outsiders*, by Howard S. Becker. Copyright © 1963 by The Free Press.

19. Frank Tannenbaum, "Definition and Dramatization of Evil," reprinted from *Crime and Community*, pp. 17–22. Copyright © 1938 by Columbia University Press. Reprinted by permission of Columbia University Press.

20. Klaus Boehnke and Dagmar Bergs-Winkels, "Juvenile Delinquency Under Condtitions of Rapid Social Change" from *Sociological Forum*, vol. 17, no. 1, pp. 57–79. Copyright © 2002. Reprinted by permission.

21. Erving Goffman, "Information Control and Personal Identity: The Discredited and the Discreditable," from *Stigma: Notes on the Management of Spoiled Identity* by Erving Goffman. Copyright © 1963 by Prentice Hall. Copyright © renewed 1991 by Simon and Schuster. Reprinted with the permission of Simon & Schuster Adult Publishing Group. All rights reserved.

22. Bruce G. Link and Jo C. Phelan, "Conceptualizing Stigma," *Annual Review of Sociology*, Vol. 27, pp. 363–385. Copyright © 2001 by Annual Reviews www.annualreviews.org. Reprinted with permission.

23. Jim Snyder, Lew Bank, and Bert Burraston, "The Consequences of Antisocial Behavior in Older Male Siblings for Younger Brothers and Sisters," *Journal of*

Family Psychology, Vol 19, No. 4, pp. 643–653. Copyright © 2005. Reprinted by permission of The American Psychological Association.

24. Rhonda D. Evans, "Examining the Informal Sanctioning of Deviance in a Chat Room Culture," reprinted from *Deviant Behavior,* vol. 22, 2001, pp. 195–210. Copyright © 2001 from *Deviant Behavior* by Rhonda D. Evans. Reproduced by permission of Taylor & Francis, Inc., http://www.routledge-ny.com.

25. Delos H. Kelly, "Bureaucratic Slots and Client Processing," from *Creating School Failure, Youth Crime, and Deviance,* by Delos H. Kelly, Los Angeles: Trident Shop, 1982. Copyright © by Delos Kelly.

26. David Shicor, "The Corporate Context of Private Prisons," reprinted from *Crime, Law and Social Change,* vol. 20, 1993, pp. 113–138. Reprinted with kind permission from Kluwer Academic Publishers.

27. Christine Horne, "The Enforcement of Norms: Group Cohesion and Meta-Norms" *Social Psychology Quarterly,* Vol. 64, No. 3, September 2001, pp. 253–266. Copyright © 2001. Reprinted by permission of the American Sociological Association.

28. Troy Duster, "The Epistemological Challenge of the Early Attack on 'Rate Construction,'" reprinted from *Social Problems,* vol. 48, no. 1, pp. 134–136. Copyright © 2001 by The Society for the Study of Social Problems. Reprinted by permission of the University of California Press Journals.

29. Albert J. Mehan, "The Organizational Career of Gang Statistics: The Politics of Policing Gangs," reprinted from *The Sociological Quarterly,* vol. 41, no. 3, Summer 2000, pp. 337–370. Copyright © 2000 by The Midwest Sociological Society. Reprinted by permission of the University of California Press Journals.

30. Gary Cavender and Aogan Mulcahy, "Trial by Fire: Media Constructions of Corporate Deviance," *Justice Quarterly,* vol. 15, no. 4, pp. 697–717. Copyright © 1998. Reprinted by permission.

31. Nora S. Gustavson and Ann E. MacEachron, "Criminalizing Women's Behavior," reprinted from *Journal of Drug Issues,* vol. 27, no. 3, 1997, pp. 673–687. Copyright © 1997 by the *Journal of Drug Issues*s. Reprinted by permission of the *Journal of Drug Issues.*

32. Vincent Lyon-Callo, "Medicalizing Homelessness: The Production of Self-Blame and Self-Governing within Homeless Shelters," reprinted from *Medical Anthropology Quarterly,* vol. 14, no. 3, 2000, pp. 328–345. Copyright © 2000 by American Anthropological Association. Not for sale or further reproduction.

33. Erving Goffman, "The Moral Career of the Mental Patient," reprinted from *Psychiatry,* vol. 22, 1959, pp. 123–142. Copyright © 1963. Reprinted with kind permission of Kluwer Academic Publishers.

34. Thomas J. Schmid and Richard S. Jones, "Suspended Identity: Identity Transformation in a Maximum Security Prison," reprinted from *Symbolic Interaction,* vol. 14, no. 4, Winter 1991, pp. 415–432. Copyright © 1991 by JAI Press. Reprinted by permission of University of California Press.

35. Joel Best and David F. Luckenbill, Social Problems (28:1) Copyright © 1980 by the Society for the Study of Social Problems. Reprinted by Permission of the University of California Press.

36. Phyllis Coontz, "Managing the Action: Sports Bookmakers as Entrepreneurs," reprinted from *Deviant Behavior,* vol. 22., 2001, pp. 239–266. Copyright © 2001 from *Deviant Behavior* by Phyllis Coontz. Reproduced by permission of Taylor & Francis, Inc., http://www.routledge-ny.com.

Index

N
Narcotics/drug abuse,
    decriminalization of, 678
Natural crime, concept of, 16
NBC news stories of corporate
    deviance, 440–444
  attribution of responsibility,
    440–441
  individualization of blame,
    441–442
  moral boundaries, 442–443
  resolution, 443–444
Negative deviance, 12–13, 21–22
  classification of, 28
  and middle-class deviance,
    27–28
"Negro courts," 111
Neutralization, 129, 177
  appeal to higher loyalties,
    126–127
  condemnation of the
    condemners, 125
  denial of injury, 124
  denial of responsibility,
    123–124
  denial of the victim, 124–125
  self-admitted cheaters, 131
  techniques of, 122–127
New jacks, 137, 157, 164–165
News stories, corporate
    deviance, 434–435
Noninstitutional careers, 6–8,
    522–563
  effects of, 7–8
  involvement in, 8
Norms, enforcement of, 101,
    367–385
  argument, 369–370
  beginning each trial, 373–374
  discussion, 381–382
  ending each trial, 376
  experimental results, 377–380
  fungibility of sanctioning
    benefits, 369
  homogeneity, 368

increasing profits from
    exchange, 371–372
  information, 369
  insider sanctioners, 369
  maintaining relationships,
    370–371
  operationalization of variables,
    376–377
  repeated interactions, 368
  rewarding decision, 376
  sanctioning, 368
    effects of rewards on,
      372–373
  sanctioning decision, 374–375
  scope conditions, 368–369
  subjects/procedures, 373
  theoretical argument, 368–373
  theoretical background,
    369–370
Norms, in the U.S., 25–26
Not In My Back Yard (NIMBY)
    phenomenon, 280

O
Older brother deviant peer
    association construct,
    293–295
Older male sibling, antisocial
    behaviors in, 288–308
  analysis strategy, 296–297
  discussion, 303–305
  hanging out with older brother
    construct, 295
  ineffective parenting
    construct, 293
  instruments/constructs,
    292–296
  measurement model and
    construct intercorrelations,
    297
  measurements of constructs,
    294
  older brother deviant peer
    association construct,
    293–295

size/level of threat presented
by, 70
state controls, extensiveness/
intensity of, 70
utility of, 71
Professional criminal,
development of, 202–203
Psychiatrists, influence on
criminal law, 44–45
Public settings, for deviance,
5–6
Punishment
and child's stubbornness, 201
as retribution, 205

R
Race and policing, 702–709
Race-based policing in the U.S.,
703–705
costs of, 705–706
imperfect solution, 706–708
and trust, 705
Rape, 112, 115, 331
Rapid social change
and juvenile delinquency,
236–237
discussion, 249–251
indicators of, 239–240
instruments, 241–244
levels of analysis, 240–241
results of data analyses,
244–249
samples, 241
as precursor of deviant school
behavior, 238
Rate busting, 21, 23, 28–31,
36–37
and middle-class deviance,
28–31
Rate construction, early attack
on, 386
epistemological challenge of,
388–391
Rate killer, 37
Rate production process, 4

Records, institutional, 338–340
Rehabilitation, 8–9
Reiman, Jeffrey H., 103–104
Reinarman, Craig, 564–565,
566–587
Reputation, 201–202
Resource Conservation and
Recovery Act (RCRA),
621–624
generators' strategic
intervention in form of
policy, 630–632
interim licensing, 628–629
manifest oversight, 629–630
Responsibility, denial of,
123–124, 132
Revenge, murder for, 106
Ritalin, 77–80
Rule creators, 13, 43–46
prototype for, 43
Rule enforcers, 13, 46–50
discretion of, 48, 48–49
Rules of Sociological Method, The
(Durkheim), 20

S
Sanctioning, 368
Schmid, Thomas J., 486,
505–520
Self-control, peer relations and
delinquency, 565,
588–604
dependent variables, 594–595
discussion, 598–601
independent variables,
593–594
literature review, 589–592
measures, 593–595
methods, 592–593
multiple-least squares analysis,
595–598
sample, 592–593
Self-control theory, 182–186, 190
and heavy episodic drinking
among adolescents, 184–186